CRIME AND CRIMINAL JUSTICE

SAGE was founded in 1965 by Sara Miller McCune to support the dissemination of usable knowledge by publishing innovative and high-quality research and teaching content. Today, we publish over 900 journals, including those of more than 400 learned societies, more than 800 new books per year, and a growing range of library products including archives, data, case studies, reports, and video. SAGE remains majority-owned by our founder, and after Sara's lifetime will become owned by a charitable trust that secures our continued independence.

Los Angeles | London | New Delhi | Singapore | Washington DC | Melbourne

CRIME AND CRIMINAL JUSTICE

CONCEPTS AND CONTROVERSIES

STACY L. MALLICOAT
CALIFORNIA STATE UNIVERSITY, FULLERTON

Los Angeles | London | New Delhi
Singapore | Washington DC | Melbourne

FOR INFORMATION:

SAGE Publications, Inc.
2455 Teller Road
Thousand Oaks, California 91320
E-mail: order@sagepub.com

SAGE Publications Ltd.
1 Oliver's Yard
55 City Road
London EC1Y 1SP
United Kingdom

SAGE Publications India Pvt. Ltd.
B 1/I 1 Mohan Cooperative Industrial Area
Mathura Road, New Delhi 110 044
India

SAGE Publications Asia-Pacific Pte. Ltd.
3 Church Street
#10-04 Samsung Hub
Singapore 049483

Printed in Canada

Library of Congress Cataloging-in-Publication Data

Names: Mallicoat, Stacy L., author.

Title: Crime and criminal justice: concepts and controversies / Stacy L. Mallicoat, California State University, Fullerton.

Description: First Edition. | Thousand Oaks: SAGE Publications, Inc., 2016. | Includes bibliographical references and index.

Identifiers: LCCN 2016013529 | ISBN 9781483318738 (pbk. : alk. paper)

Subjects: LCSH: Crime. | Law enforcement. | Criminal justice, Administration of.

Classification: LCC HV6025 .M3145 2016 | DDC 364—dc23
LC record available at https://lccn.loc.gov/2016013529

Acquisitions Editor: Jerry Westby
Developmental Editor: Jessica Miller
eLearning Editor: Nicole Mangona
Editorial Assistant: Laura Kirkhuff
Production Editor: Jane Haenel
Copy Editor: Jared Leighton
Typesetter: C&M Digitals (P) Ltd.
Proofreader: Scott Oney
Indexer: Karen Wiley
Designer: Janet Kiesel
Marketing Manager: Amy Lammers

This book is printed on acid-free paper.

16 17 18 19 20 10 9 8 7 6 5 4 3 2 1

BRIEF CONTENTS

DETAILED CONTENTS

PART II: POLICING   149

© iStockphoto.com/Klaus Larsen

Chapter 7: Policing Organizations and Practices 150

© iStockphoto.com/wellesenterprises

Chapter 10: Punishment and Sentencing 232

PART IV: CORRECTIONS   257

© iStockphoto.com/fhogue

Chapter 11: Prisons and Jails 258

PART V: SPECIAL TOPICS IN CRIMINAL JUSTICE   321

© iStockphoto.com/compassandcamera

PREFACE

This text is a unique approach to studying the concepts and controversies of the criminal justice system. Like many introductory texts, this book covers the major structures, agencies, and functions of the criminal justice system. In each chapter, you will learn about the different features and functions of our criminal justice system. You'll also learn about examples of high-profile cases and how the criminal justice system has responded to these crimes. The book also provides an in-depth look at the role of victims and policy in our criminal justice system, two topics that are often either absent or covered in a limited fashion in most texts. In addition, this book provides a unique look at some of the emerging issues in criminal justice for the 21st century, such as homeland security, transnational crime, and the use of drones. Finally, you'll learn about some of the cutting-edge issues and debates that face the criminal justice system.

ORGANIZATION OF THE BOOK

This book is divided into 14 chapters, with each chapter dealing with a different subject related to the criminal justice system. Each chapter begins with an issue or topic about the themes that are discussed in the chapter. Each chapter summarizes some of the basic terms and concepts related to the subject area.

Each chapter also provides the following features:

Spotlights. Each chapter presents either case studies or special topic discussions on the issues presented in the chapter. These spotlights provide you with the opportunity to learn about an issue in depth or to investigate a real-world event in light of the terms and concepts presented in the text.

Around the World. Each chapter presents an international example of how criminal justice systems function around the world.

Careers in Criminal Justice. Each chapter provides an example of a criminal justice career that you may choose to pursue.

Current Controversies. Within each chapter, you'll be presented with two current controversies that the criminal justice system faces. Within each of these debates, you'll be presented with the pros and cons of each topic, followed by critical thinking questions to help you think more deeply about these key issues.

Chapter Contents

Chapter 1: Crime and Criminal Justice provides an introduction to the issues of crime and justice. In this chapter, you will learn about the criminal justice system and the different models that help describe its functions. You'll also learn about the role of the media and how information about crime is shared with the public. The chapter concludes with two Current Controversy debates. The first, by Kareem L. Jordan, questions whether justice is served by our criminal justice system. The second, by Robert Schug, asks whether mental illness causes crime.

Chapter 2: Concepts of Law and Justice investigates the concepts of law and justice within our criminal justice system. In this chapter, you will learn about the development of law and how it relates to the criminal justice system. The chapter begins with a discussion on the different sources of law in the United States. The chapter then focuses on the different types of law and their relationship to the criminal justice system. You'll also learn about the different legal defenses that are used in the criminal courts to explain or justify criminal behaviors. The chapter concludes with two Current Controversy debates. The first, by Clayon Mosher and Scott Akins, looks at the debate over legalizing marijuana. The second, by Craig Hemmens, questions whether the Miranda warning should be abolished.

Chapter 3: Defining and Measuring Crime looks at the types of crime that our criminal justice system manages. This chapter begins with a review of the different types of crime and how we classify these offenses. The chapter then turns to a discussion of how crime is measured in society. You'll learn about the different official sources of crime data, such as the Uniform Crime Reports, the National Incident-Based Reporting System, and the National Crime Victimization Survey, as well as self-reported studies of crime. You'll also learn about international databases of crime that can be used to understand the presence of crime around the world. The chapter concludes with two Current Controversy debates. The first, by Henry N. Pontell, Gilbert Geis, Adam Ghazi-Tehrani, and Bryan Burton, looks at whether white-collar crime is considered harmful to society. The second, by Phillip Kopp, asks whether burglary should be considered a violent crime.

Chapter 4: Explanations of Criminal Behavior investigates the different theoretical explanations for criminal behavior. This chapter begins with a discussion about the classical theories of crime. The chapter then looks at biological and psychological explanations of crime, in which theorists historically looked at factors such as biology and genetics to help understand criminal behavior. This chapter also looks at how external social factors, such as poverty, family, and peers, can help to explain crime. The chapter then moves to a review of some of the contemporary theories of crime, such as life course theory and feminist criminology. The chapter concludes with two Current Controversy debates: The first, by Kenethia McIntosh-Fuller, questions whether race and class can impact criminal behavior, and the second, by Jill L. Rosenbaum, investigates whether female offenders should be treated differently by the criminal justice system.

Chapter 5: Victims and the Criminal Justice System highlights the issues that victims of crime face in dealing with the criminal justice system. This chapter looks at the role of victims in the criminal justice system. The chapter begins with a discussion of the history of the victims' rights movement. The chapter then turns to a review of the theories that help to explain criminal victimization. This follows with a discussion of the types of victims, as well as the extent of victimization, both within the United States and worldwide. The chapter concludes with two Current Controversy debates: The first, by Amy I. Cass, explores whether universities are best suited to respond to rape and sexual assault among college students, while the second, by Kimberly J. Cook, investigates how a restorative justice model might help in the healing process for victims.

Chapter 6: Criminal Justice Policy focuses on how policy can shape and is shaped by the criminal justice system. The chapter begins with a discussion on the need and function of criminal justice policies. The chapter then looks at how policies are developed and the role of politics in this process. The chapter concludes with two Current Controversy debates related to criminal justice policies. The first, by David Bierie and Sarah Craun, looks at whether sex offender registries are an effective tool for keeping the public safe. The second, by Shelly Arsneault, questions whether street-level bureaucracy is a good practice in criminal justice.

Chapter 7: Policing Organizations and Practices presents the different types of police organizations and practices. This chapter begins with a look at the historical roots of policing. The chapter presents the different types of police organizations. The chapter then turns to a review of the various styles of policing, such as order maintenance, community policing, and problem-oriented policing. The chapter concludes with two Current Controversy debates: The first, by Christine Gardiner, investigates whether intelligence-led policing can reduce crime while the second, by Alesha Durfee, asks whether mandatory arrest policies help victims of domestic violence.

Chapter 8: Issues in Policing highlights some of the issues that the police face both as individual officers and as an organization at large. The chapter begins with a discussion of the legal issues in policing and the rules that impact how police officers do their job. The chapter turns to a discussion of ethical challenges, corruption, racial profiling, and the use of force and how these issues can have an effect on the public's perception of the police. The chapter then looks at the nature of police legitimacy and how these types of issues can serve as a threat. The chapter concludes with two Current Controversy debates: The first, by Bill Sousa, investigates how body cameras should be utilized in the line of duty while the second, by Lorenzo M. Boyd, asks whether police discretion is helpful or harmful to our criminal justice system.

Chapter 9: Courts and Crime discusses the role of courts in our criminal justice system. In this chapter, you will learn about the structure of the American courts system and its relationship to the criminal justice system. The chapter begins with a discussion about how courts are organized. The chapter then looks at the different participants in the courtroom and their roles. After that, the chapter moves to a discussion of the stages of a criminal court case. The chapter concludes with two Current Controversy debates related to the criminal courts system. The first, by Julius (Jay) Wachtel, asks whether physical evidence should be required in serious criminal cases. The second, by G. Max Dery, asks whether we should limit the use of plea bargains in criminal cases.

Chapter 10: Punishment and Sentencing introduces you to the different types of sentencing practices that are used in the criminal justice system. The chapter begins with a discussion about the various philosophies that guide sentencing practices. The chapter then looks at the different types of sentences. The chapter concludes with two Current Controversy debates related to the criminal courts system. The first, by Kimberly Dodson, asks whether habitual sentencing laws deter offenders. The second, by Scott Vollum, looks at whether there is a risk of executing an innocent individual.

Chapter 11: Prisons and Jails highlights the various programs and practices that make up the field of community corrections. In this chapter, you will learn about each of these programs and how they balance the safety and security of the community with the needs of the offender. You'll also learn about the process of reentry after prison and the role of parole. The chapter concludes with two Current Controversy debates. The first, by Brett Garland, investigates whether we should use supermax facilities to control violent offenders. The second, by Jason Williams, looks at whether prisons should be segregated.

Chapter 12: Community Corrections focuses on the role of correctional institutions, such as prisons and jails. In this chapter, you will learn about the structure of prisons and jails in the United States. The chapter begins with a historical review of how prisons and jails developed. The chapter then looks at the current state of jails and the different types of populations that these facilities serve. The chapter then turns to a review of the prisons and highlights how issues such as security levels impact the design and organization of a facility. You'll then learn about life behind bars and how issues such as violence, programming, and health care can impact the quality of life of inmates. You'll also learn about the legal rights of prisoners and how landmark Supreme Court cases have impacted the prison environment. Finally, you'll hear about the role of correctional officers in the prison. The chapter concludes with two Current Controversy debates. The first, by Krista Gehring, looks at whether risk assessment tools can accurately identify the needs of offenders. The second, by Christine Scott-Hayward, looks at whether parole is an effective correctional strategy.

Chapter 13: Juvenile Justice shows how the juvenile justice system functions as a separate but similar counterpart to the criminal justice system. The chapter begins with a discussion of the history of the juvenile justice system. The chapter then turns to a review of the structure of the juvenile court and highlights some of the differences between the juvenile and criminal courts. You'll learn about how legal challenges in juvenile justice have changed the way in which youthful offenders are treated by these courts and how due process in juvenile cases has evolved. You'll also be exposed to some of the issues that face these young offenders in the juvenile justice system today. The chapter concludes with two Current Controversy debates. The first, by Alicia Pantoja, Sanna King, and Anthony Peguero, asks whether zero-tolerance policies have made schools safer. The second, by Schannae Lucas, addresses whether the juvenile court should be abolished.

Chapter 14: Emerging Issues for the 21st Century concludes the text with an investigation of the emerging issues that are facing the criminal justice system in the 21st century. This chapter introduces some of these issues and discusses the challenges that criminal justice agencies will face as they navigate their way through these issues. The chapter begins with a discussion of terrorism. The chapter then turns to look at homeland security. You'll also learn about some of the privacy threats that exist with the use of drones. Finally, the chapter turns to a discussion of border control. The chapter concludes with two Current Controversy debates. The first, by Gus Martin, asks whether enemy combatants should be denied due process rights. The second, by Zahra Shekarkhar, asks whether immigration impacts crime.

Through this text, I hope that you get a strong foundation in the organization and issues of our criminal justice system. For those students who are majors in criminal justice, this text supplies the foundation to build your future coursework on. For students who have enrolled in an introductory course to satisfy a basic requirement or who are taking the course out of their general interest in crime, the information in this text will provide you with a new lens to look at how crime and our criminal justice system work together as a function of society.

DIGITAL RESOURCES

SAGE edge offers a robust online environment featuring an impressive array of tools and resources for review, study, and further exploration, keeping both instructors and students on the cutting edge of teaching and learning. SAGE edge content is open access and available on demand. Learning and teaching has never been easier!

edge.sagepub.com/mallicoatccj

Instructor Resources

SAGE edge for Instructors supports teaching by making it easy to integrate quality content and create a rich learning environment for students.

- **Test banks** provide a diverse range of pre-written options as well as the opportunity to edit any question and/or insert personalized questions to effectively assess students' progress and understanding.

- Editable, chapter-specific PowerPoint® slides offer complete flexibility for creating a multimedia presentation for the course.

- **Lecture notes** summarize key concepts by chapter to ease preparation for lectures and class discussions.

- **Discussion questions** help launch classroom interaction by prompting students to engage with the material and by reinforcing important content.

- **Tables and figures** from the printed book are available in an easily downloadable format for use in papers, handouts, and presentations.

- EXCLUSIVE! Access to full-text **SAGE journal articles** that have been carefully selected to support and expand on the concepts presented in each chapter.

- **Learning objectives** reinforce the most important material.

- **Multimedia resources** include timely and relevant video, audio, and web links to further explore topics and highlight responses to critical thinking questions.

- **Current Controversy videos** provide a visual example of how criminal justice issues play out in the real world.

- **Career videos** feature various professions and deliver further guidance into the criminal justice field.

Student Resources

SAGE edge for Students provides a personalized approach to help students accomplish their coursework goals in an easy-to-use learning environment.

- A customized online **action plan** includes tips and feedback on progress through the course and materials, which allows students to individualize their learning experience.

- Mobile-friendly **eFlashcards** strengthen understanding of key terms and concepts.

- Mobile-friendly **practice quizzes** allow for independent assessment by students of their mastery of course material.

- **Learning objectives** reinforce the most important material.

- **Multimedia resources** include timely and relevant video, audio, and web links to further explore topics and highlight responses to critical thinking questions.

- EXCLUSIVE! Access to full-text **SAGE journal articles** that have been carefully selected to support and expand on the concepts presented in each chapter.

- **Current Controversy videos** provide a visual example of how criminal justice issues play out in the real world.

- **Career videos** feature various professions and deliver further guidance into the criminal justice field.

ACKNOWLEDGMENTS

Thank you to Jerry Westby, Jessica Miller, and the amazing support staff at SAGE Publishing. Your support has been instrumental in bringing this book to life. Throughout my career, I have been blessed with amazing colleagues and mentors, many of whom contributed to this book. Your words have breathed life into this book, and I thank you for joining me in this experience. Thank you to my colleagues in the Division of Politics, Administration and Justice for their support and regular supply of Diet Coke and chocolate to get me through the day. To my aca-family—especially Denise Paquette Boots, Hank Fradella, Jill Rosenbaum, Lorenzo Boyd, and Anthony Peguero—I am so appreciative of your love and support as I've traveled on my journey. Finally, I am deeply appreciative to my family and friends who have provided me with the space to create and expand the understanding of what is possible in and for their endless encouragement of my adventures. This book has truly been a labor of love, sweat, and tears and one that would not have been possible without the support and sacrifices of my husband and boys.

A huge thank you as well to the many reviewers who provided suggestions throughout the development of this book:

Stephanie Albertson, *Indiana University Southeast*

Andi Bannister, *Wichita State University*

Kevin Barnas Erie, *Community College, South Campus*

Lauren Barrow, *Chestnut Hill College*

Butch Beach, *Point University*

Ursula Ann Becker, *Georgia Military College*

Michael Bisciglia, *Southeastern Louisiana University*

Nicholas J. Blasco, *The University of South Carolina*

Jennifer Bourgeois, *Lone Star College, CyFair*

Bruce Carroll, *Georgia Gwinnett College*

Darian Carter, *Anne Arundel Community College*

Darla Darno, *East Stroudsburg University*

Jacquelynn Doyon-Martin, *Grand Valley State University*

Katie Ely, *Lock Haven University*

Diane Evett, *Pensacola State College*

Jodie Fairbank, *Husson University*

Brian Fedorek, *Southern Oregon University*

Chivon Fitch, *Indiana University of Pennsylvania*

Laura Fletcher, *College of Southern Nevada*

BC Franson, *Southwest Minnesota State University*

Danny Hayes, *Peru State College*

Shawn Ingalls, *University of Pittsburgh at Johnstown*

Janice Iwama, *Northeastern University*

Casper Johnson, *Valencia College*

Keith Johnson, *Mansfield University*

Jason Jolicoeur, *Washburn University*

Kimberly A. Kampe, *University of Central Florida*

Bobbi Kassel, *Utah Valley University*

William E. Kelly, *Auburn University*

Jim Kerns, *Boise State University*

Kenneth Leon, *George Washington University*

Catherine D. Marcum, *Appalachian State University*

Philip McCormack, *Fitchburg State University*

Naghme Morlock, *Gonzaga University*

Shawn Morrow, *Angelo State University*

Brian Murphy, *Valencia College*

Charles Myers, *Aims Community College*

Mai Naito, *University of West Georgia*

Whitney Nickels, *Northwest Mississippi Community College*

Michael O'Connor, *Upper Iowa University*

Stacy Parker, *Muskingum University*

Rebecca Pfeffer, *University of Houston, Downtown*

Forrest Rodgers, *Salem State University*

John Schafer, *Western Illinois University*

Rachel Schmidt, *Suffolk County Community College*

Margaret Schmuhl, *John Jay College*

Sarah Scott, *Texas A&M University–Corpus Christi*

Renita Seabrook, *University of Baltimore*

Zahra Shekarkhar, *Fayetteville State University*

Diane Sjuts, *Metropolitan Community College*

Sherry Lynn Skaggs, *University of Central Arkansas*

John Sloan, *Piedmont Technical College*

Edward Smith, *Plattsburgh State University*

Elicka Peterson Sparks, *Appalachian State University*

James M. Stewart, *Calhoun Community College*

Jeanne Subjack, *Southern Utah University*

Daniel Swanson, *Southern Utah University*

Sema Taheri, *Northeastern University*

John Tahiliani, *Worcester State University*

N. Prabha Unnithan, *Colorado State University*

Sheryl L. Van Horne, *Arcadia University*

Theodore D. Wallman, *University of North Florida*

Robert E. Wardle III, *Youngstown State University*

Janese Weathers, *University of Maryland Eastern Shore*

Jennifer Wiley, *Sampson Community College*

Bill Williams *Phoenix College*

Donna Wilson, *Prince George's Community College*

Tracey Woodard, *University of North Florida*

ABOUT THE AUTHOR

Stacy L. Mallicoat is a professor of criminal justice and chair of the Division of Politics, Administration and Justice at California State University, Fullerton, where she teaches both face-to-face and online courses. She earned her BA in legal studies and sociology from Pacific Lutheran University and her PhD from the University of Colorado, Boulder, in sociology. She is the author of several books, including *Women and Crime: A Text/Reader*, *Women and Crime: The Essentials*, and *Criminal Justice Policy*. Her work also appears in a number of peer-reviewed journals and edited volumes. She is an active member of the American Society of Criminology, the ASC's Division on Women and Crime, and the Academy of Criminal Justice Sciences.

FOUNDATIONS OF CRIMINAL JUSTICE

©iStockphoto.com/Tomml

PART

I

CRIME AND CRIMINAL JUSTICE

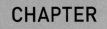

LEARNING OBJECTIVES

- Identify the major stages of the criminal justice system

- Explain the importance of discretion and ethics in the criminal justice system

- Describe the different tiers of the wedding cake model

- Compare and contrast the crime control model with the due process model

- Assess how media can impact the criminal justice system

Sabrina Buie was 11 years old when her body was found in Red Springs, North Carolina, on September 24, 1983. She had been raped and choked to death by her underwear. Her murder shattered the peaceful town. "It was a serious impact on families . . . at that time . . . our families wanted us, when it turned dark, they wanted us in. It put the town on lockdown."[1] Two days later, the police obtained confessions from two half-brothers, Henry Lee McCollum, age 19, and Leon Brown, age 15. A year later, the two were tried, convicted, and sentenced to death.

In many cases, the story would end there. Since their conviction, the brothers have maintained their innocence and have recanted their confession hundreds of times. Why would McCollum and Brown confess to a crime that they didn't commit? Evidence throughout the appellate process notes that the brothers are developmentally disabled and have IQ scores that render them the intellectual equivalent of 9-year-olds. Their confessions were obtained after a five-hour interrogation in which the police fed them details about the crime that were known only to police. McCollum stated that he "just made up a story and gave it to them so they would let me go home." The confession was the only piece of evidence in their trial. Even though new trials were ordered for both men on appeal, both were convicted a second time. McCollum was

Applause erupts around Henry Lee McCollum as the convictions of McCollum and his codefendant are overturned. New DNA evidence proved they were innocent of the 1983 rape and murder of Sabrina Buie. How have advances in technology influenced the criminal justice system?

resentenced to death, and Brown was given a sentence of life in prison.[2] Even though another man (Roscoe Artis) was convicted of a similar crime that occurred just weeks after Sabrina's death, the criminal justice system still believed that McCollum and Brown were guilty of this crime. Yet despite the similarities between these two cases, authorities never looked at Artis as a potential suspect in Sabrina's murder.[3]

Three decades later, this case has a different outcome. After a four-year effort by the Innocence Inquiry Commission, McCollum and Brown were able to test evidence from the scene of the crime. Luckily, police had preserved this evidence, which consisted of a cigarette butt that was found near Sabrina's body. The DNA on the cigarette matched that of Roscoe Artis, who was already serving a life sentence for murder. In September 2014, McCollum and Brown, now 50 and 46 years old, were released from prison.

WEB LINK
North Carolina Innocence
Commission

This text is designed to provide an overview of our criminal justice system. In each chapter, you will learn about different features and functions of our criminal justice system. You'll also learn about different high-profile cases and how the criminal justice system has responded to these crimes, as well as some examples of how criminal justice issues are handled in a global context. As a student of criminal justice, you'll also learn about some of the different careers that you might pursue within this field. Finally, you'll explore some of the cutting-edge issues and debates that face the criminal justice system.

In this chapter, you will learn about the criminal justice system and the different models that help describe its functions. You'll also learn about the role of the media and how information about **crime** is shared with the public. The chapter concludes with two explorations of Current Controversies that debate the pros and cons of key issues in criminal justice. The first, by Kareem L. Jordan, questions whether justice is served by our criminal justice system. The second, by Robert Schug, asks whether mental illness causes crime.

Crime
An act that is against the law
and causes a punishment.

Police
Police are tasked with
investigating crime and
apprehending offenders.

Courts
The courts are responsible
for determining whether an
offender should be charged
with a crime and also manage
the process to determine
whether the offender should
be held criminally responsible
for the crime.

Corrections
The corrections system
carries out the punishment
as ordered by the court.

STAGES OF THE CRIMINAL JUSTICE SYSTEM

There are three major components of the criminal justice system: police, courts, and corrections. Each of these systems functions both in relationship to the others and as a separate entity. In terms of the criminal justice system, the **police** are tasked with investigating crime and apprehending offenders. The **courts** are responsible for determining whether an offender should be charged with a crime and managing the process to determine whether he or she should be held criminally responsible. The courts are also responsible for handing down a punishment in cases where the court determines that the offender is guilty of a crime. It is then up to the **corrections** system to carry out the punishment as ordered by the court. Throughout this text, you'll be exposed to each of these groups and learn about their key functions and processes.

With so many different players, how do each of these components work together to form our criminal justice system? While the police, courts, and our correctional systems all have different roles and responsibilities, each group makes decisions that ultimately impact the other groups. Figure 1.1 highlights how a case moves through the different stages of the criminal justice system.

Policing

Police officers are generally the first point of contact in the system, and they learn about crime in a variety of ways. They might be called to the scene of a crime to take a statement from a victim or witness or preserve and collect evidence in a case. If an offender is identified, the police may arrest the offender. In cases in which the perpetrator is unknown, the police investigate the crime in an attempt to identify a suspect.

The Courts

Once this information is collected and processed, it is forwarded on to the courts. Here, a district attorney (also called a prosecutor) will review the information and determine what charges, if any, will be filed against an offender, also known as the **defendant**. In order to proceed with a case, the prosecutor must prove that she or he has probable cause that the accused committed the crime. If someone has been arrested and is currently in custody, courts will begin the proceedings on whether the offender is eligible for release or must stay in custody. The offender will also plead guilty or not guilty at an arraignment. If the offender enters a guilty plea, the judge will issue a sentence. If the offender pleads not guilty, then the case will proceed. The prosecutor may choose to take the case to trial or may decide to offer a plea bargain, which generally allows the offender to enter a guilty plea for a lesser charge and reduced sentence. While it is the responsibility of the district attorney to carry out the legal proceedings of the case, it is the job of the defense counsel to ensure that the rights of the accused are upheld and to defend the client throughout the criminal justice process.

The judge is an impartial moderator of the court process. The judge resolves disputes between the prosecution and the defense. In some cases, the judge may also be responsible for making a decision on whether the defendant is guilty or not guilty. In other cases, a jury determines the outcome. A jury is made up of a group of citizens who are charged with reviewing the evidence presented in court and then making a decision about the defendant's guilt. In certain cases (like capital punishment cases), a jury is also responsible for determining the sentence for the guilty offender. However, in the majority of criminal cases, it is up to the judge to make this decision during a sentencing hearing.

> Discretion refers to the freedom to make decisions. It is perhaps the most powerful tool of the criminal justice system.

Corrections

If an offender is sentenced to a period of incarceration, he or she will serve that sentence in either a jail or prison. In other cases, an offender may be sentenced to community-based supervision, such as probation. This allows the offender to remain in the community rather than being sent to a facility.[4]

DISCRETION AND ETHICS IN THE CRIMINAL JUSTICE SYSTEM

The decision-making power of criminal justice agents is called **discretion**. Discretion refers to the freedom to make decisions. It is perhaps the most powerful tool of the criminal justice system. Laws and policies can help guide the discretion of individuals in the criminal justice system, such as the police, prosecutors, and the courts.

Related to this issue is the question of **ethics**. Ethics in criminal justice refers to the understanding of what constitutes good or bad behavior. As agents of criminal

Defendant
Someone who has criminal charges filed against her or him.

Discretion
The power to make decisions by criminal justice officials.

Ethics
The understanding of what constitutes good or bad behavior.

Figure 1.1   The Criminal Justice Process

What is the sequence of events in the criminal justice system?

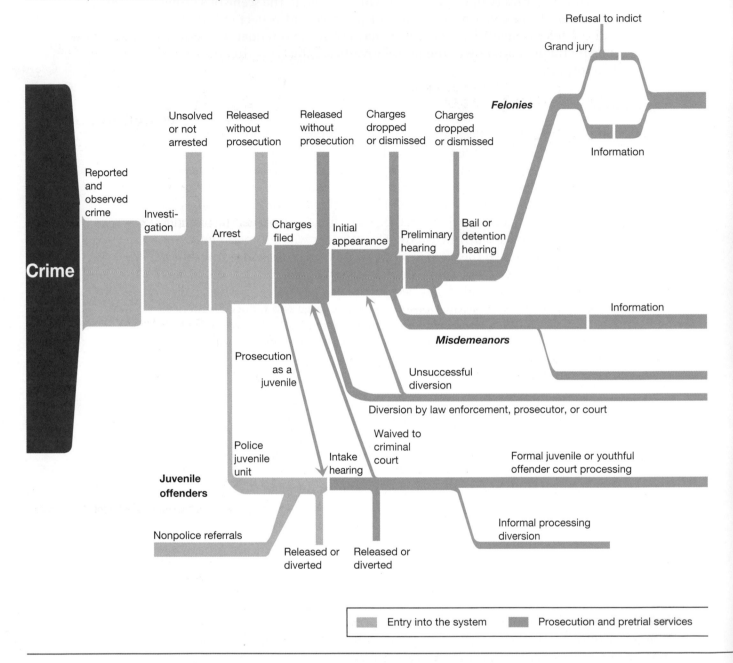

Refusal to indict

Grand jury

Felonies

Unsolved or not arrested

Released without prosecution

Released without prosecution

Charges dropped or dismissed

Charges dropped or dismissed

Information

Reported and observed crime

Investigation

Arrest

Charges filed

Initial appearance

Preliminary hearing

Bail or detention hearing

Crime

Information

Misdemeanors

Prosecution as a juvenile

Unsuccessful diversion

Diversion by law enforcement, prosecutor, or court

Waived to criminal court

Formal juvenile or youthful offender court processing

Police juvenile unit

Intake hearing

Juvenile offenders

Nonpolice referrals

Informal processing diversion

Released or diverted

Released or diverted

| Entry into the system | Prosecution and pretrial services |

Source: Bureau of Justice Statistics. Criminal Justice System Flow Chart. Retrieved at http://www.bjs.gov/content/largechart.cfm

VIDEO
Exonerated North Carolina Men Freed

justice exercise their discretion, they may face ethical challenges about which course of action is the most appropriate. Ethics can help guide the decision-making process. In some cases, ethical violations occur. Consider the case that you were introduced to at the beginning of this chapter. Henry Lee McCollum and Leon Brown were given details about a crime that were known only by the police in order to encourage confessions to a crime that they didn't commit. Was this ethical behavior on the part of the police? Throughout this text, you'll learn about how the police, courts, and correctional systems are faced with ethical challenges.

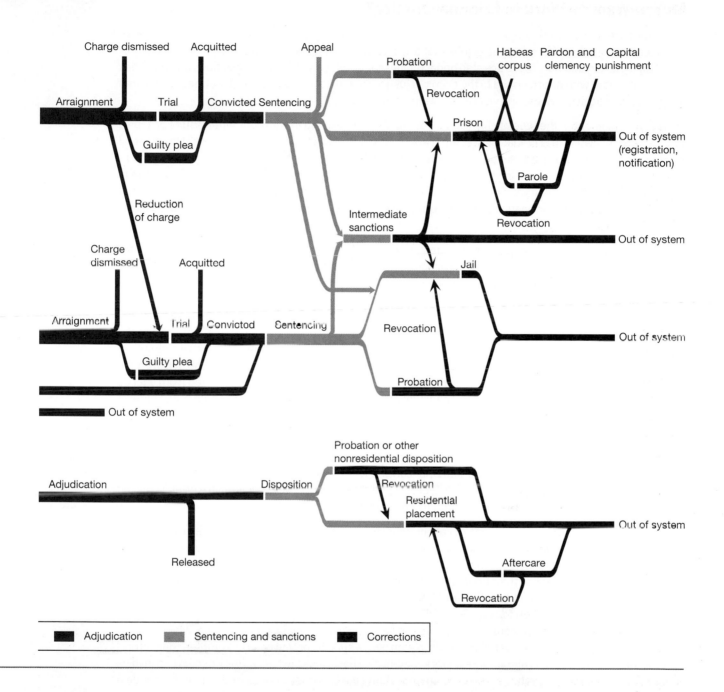

Charge dismissed   Acquitted   Appeal   Probation   Habeas   Pardon and   Capital
                                                                                      corpus   clemency punishment

Arraignment   Trial   Convicted Sentencing   Revocation
                                                                          Prison
            Guilty plea   Out of system
                                                                                                     (registration,
                                                                                          Parole   notification)
         Reduction
         of charge   Intermediate
                                        sanctions   Revocation
      Charge   Out of system
      dismissed   Acquitted
                                                                    Jail
   Arraignment   Trial   Convicted   Sentencing
                                                        Revocation
            Guilty plea   Out of system
                                         Probation

   Out of system

                                  Probation or other
                                  nonresidential disposition

Adjudication   Disposition   Revocation
                                                        Residential
                                                        placement
                                                                                                   Out of system

      Released   Aftercare

                                                       Revocation

   ■ Adjudication   ■ Sentencing and sanctions   ■ Corrections

Another example of the use of discretion by our criminal justice system can be observed by investigating how different types of offenders are treated by the system. For example, there is a large body of research highlighting the mistreatment of individuals at every stage of the criminal justice system based on their race or gender. In other cases, you'll note that certain groups receive preferential treatment. In some cases, we blame increases in crime on certain groups of individuals, such as immigrants or the mentally ill. Yet many of these populations require increased attention by the criminal justice system as a result of their unique needs for services and rehabilitation. You'll be exposed to some of these findings throughout this text as well as within some of the Current Controversy debates.

WEB LINK
Federal Bureau of
Investigation (FBI) Careers

CAREERS IN CRIMINAL JUSTICE

So You Want to Work in Criminal Justice?

There are many different opportunities to work in the criminal justice system. Throughout this text, you'll learn about the different types of jobs that are available throughout the police, courts, and correctional agencies. In addition, there are also opportunities for employment with organizations and agencies that are affiliated with or are linked to the criminal justice system, such as offender treatment programs and facilities, social services, and victim assistance programs.

As you think about the type of career that you might be interested in, consider what issues or topics you are most drawn to in criminal justice. What are the requirements to work in these fields? Do you need a bachelor's degree or a graduate degree? Is there specialized training that is involved? Will being fluent in multiple languages help you in your career? You will also want to consider how your personality fits in with your career choice. Are you someone who likes to work as part of a team, or do you prefer work that is more independent? Your answers to these questions will help you determine what your future career might look like.

Many jobs within criminal justice agencies are government-related. This means that postings for these positions can be quite competitive and involve several steps as part of the application process. Jobs are typically advertised online with each agency. For example, if you are interested in working for a local police agency, you would want to seek out information about the hiring department for that specific city or county. Meanwhile, jobs with the federal government (such as the Department of Homeland Security) are often posted on the USAJobs website for all federal agencies. If you are thinking about a job in the federal government, make sure you consider different types of agencies, as many agencies employ similar types of positions. For example, maybe you're set on being a special agent for the Federal Bureau of Investigation (FBI). These jobs are often very competitive, and only a few people are selected from a large pool of applicants. But there are several opportunities for these types of positions within other federal agencies, such as the U.S. Fish and Wildlife Service or the Office of Criminal Investigations for the U.S. Food and Drug Administration.

Some criminal justice occupations require a number of different security screenings as part of the application process. Many jobs require that applicants undergo a background investigation, and applicants may also be required to complete a polygraph examination. Finally, applicants are often required to complete a physical fitness test and submit to a drug test.

In order to get a sense of the types of career opportunities that are available, you may want to consider an internship with a criminal justice agency. Internships are a great way to get applied experience with an agency in the criminal justice field. Depending on the requirements of your educational program, an internship may be part of the curriculum, or you may be able to receive academic credit for your work with an agency. You should talk with a faculty member or adviser from your program to determine whether this is an option for you. Depending on the placement, internships may be paid or unpaid work. Alternatively, you might consider volunteering with an agency. Unlike an internship, which usually requires that a specific number of hours be completed over a specific period of time, volunteer opportunities can vary dramatically. While volunteer work may involve basic tasks (whereas internships can involve more professional tasks), volunteers serve an important role for organizations and can also provide a window into the different types of careers that are available within the organization.

THE WEDDING CAKE MODEL OF JUSTICE

Wedding cake model
Model that demonstrates how cases are treated differently by the criminal justice process.

While Figure 1.1 earlier in this chapter demonstrates how a case can move through the criminal justice system, not all cases are handled in the same way. Some cases may be handled more informally because they are minor offenses. In other instances, some offenders may receive preferential treatment as a result of their status in society. The **wedding cake model** (Figure 1.2) helps us understand how cases can be treated differently by the criminal justice process. Consider that a wedding cake is generally made up of several different tiers, with the largest tier appearing at the bottom of the cake and tiers of decreasing size as one moves up to the top layer of the cake, which is the smallest.

Figure 1.2   The Wedding Cake Model of Justice

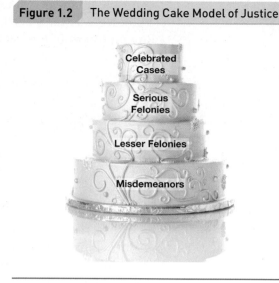

Source: © iStockphoto.com/azshooter

If we apply this analogy to the criminal justice system, the bottom layer of the cake represents the largest number of cases that are handled by the criminal justice system. **Misdemeanors** are the least serious types of crimes that are typically handled by the criminal justice system. However, these types of cases also make up the majority of those in the criminal justice system. Given the nature of these offenses, the majority of these cases are not resolved by a trial, and the offenders in these cases are offered plea bargains with reduced sentences or other lower level punishments. Generally speaking, the maximum punishment for a misdemeanor crime is less than one year in jail. In comparison, punishment for a **felony** crime can range from more than one year in prison to life without the possibility of parole or, in some cases, the death penalty. The severity of the punishment is linked to the severity of the crime.

The second tier is smaller and composed of lower level felony cases. These cases are typically nonviolent in nature, and the offenders in these cases are generally lower level offenders. Like misdemeanors, many of these cases are handled with plea agreements and generally do not involve significant incarceration sentences. The next tier is filled with upper-level felony cases, which tend to be violent in nature and involve offenders with significant criminal histories. Unlike the cases in the lower levels, these cases are more likely to proceed to a trial if the offender pleads not guilty. If the offender is found guilty, she or he will likely face time in prison.

Finally, the top layer of the cake represents the high-profile cases. These cases tend to be covered by the media and often involve the potential for significant penalties, such as life in prison or the death penalty. However, there are other cases that are also found in this category that involve well-known offenders, such as celebrities. For example, the singer CeeLo Green pled not guilty to furnishing a controlled substance in a Los Angeles courtroom in October 2013. While he was also accused of sexually assaulting the victim, charges were not filed because prosecutors determined that they did not have enough evidence to substantiate the charge.[5] Another example of a high-profile celebrity case was Oscar Pistorius. Pistorius rose to fame as a double-amputee sprinter from South Africa who competed in the London Olympics in 2012. On Valentine's Day 2013, Pistorius shot and killed his girlfriend, Reeva Steenkamp, in what defense counsel described as a horrible accident. Pistorius believed that an intruder had entered their home, so he fired several shots into their bathroom. Pistorius was found guilty of the charge of

Misdemeanors
Lower level crimes that are punished by less than one year in jail. Punishments can also involve community-based sanctions, such as probation.

Felony
Serious crimes that can be punished by more than one year in prison.

Family members of Reeva Steenkamp listen in court as a guilty verdict against South African Olympic athlete Oscar Pistorius is announced. Pistorius was found guilty of culpable homicide in the death Steenkamp, who was his girlfriend. Which layer in the wedding cake model would this case represent?

VIDEO
Oscar Pistorius Found
Guilty of Murder

culpable homicide, which is similar to the American definition of negligent homicide. He was sentenced to five years in prison but was released after only serving one-sixth of his sentence. However, his release was blocked. In addition, South African law allows for prosecutors to appeal a verdict. His appeal was denied, and he is currently awaiting sentencing.[6]

MODELS OF CRIMINAL JUSTICE

Within our criminal justice system, there are two competing ideologies: the crime control model and the due process model (Table 1.1).[7]

The Crime Control Model

The **crime control model** believes that the most important function of the criminal justice system is to suppress and control criminal behavior as a function of public order in society. This philosophy is often aligned with a more conservative perspective. The crime control model focuses on a criminal justice system that processes criminals in an efficient, consistent manner. Justice under the crime control model resembles an "assembly line." Under the crime control model, the plea bargain is an essential tool, as it allows the wheels of justice to continue to move. Trials are viewed as taking up excessive time in the system and can slow down the efficiency of the "factory." Here, the focus is on swift and severe punishments for offenders. For example, supporters of a crime control model would argue that the identification and detention of enemy combatants following the 9/11 terror attacks was a good policy in fighting against future terrorist threats. Any risk of violating individual liberties was considered secondary to the need to protect and ensure the safety of the community.

Crime control model
Model of criminal justice that advocates for the suppression and control of criminal behavior as a function of public order in society.

Due process model
Model of criminal justice that believes that the protection of individual rights and freedoms is the most important function of the system.

The Due Process Model

In contrast, the **due process model** believes that the protection of individual rights and freedoms is of utmost importance. The due process model embodies more of a liberal perspective compared with the crime control model. One could argue

Table 1.1	Crime Control Model Versus Due Process				
Model	Main Goal	Values	Punishment	Example	Concerns With This Model
Crime Control	Suppress and control criminal behavior as a function of public order in society	A criminal justice system that processes criminals in an efficient and consistent manner	Should be swift and severe; it is important that offenders are punished for their crimes	Criminal justice as an assembly line	Infringes on the rights of individuals
Due Process	Protects the rights and freedoms of individuals	A criminal justice system that represents a fair and equitable treatment of all cases and all offenders during each stage of the process	Should be fair and just; it is better for the guilty to go free than to risk incarcerating the innocent	Criminal justice as an obstacle course	Ignores crime victims and gives criminals too much leeway to escape justice

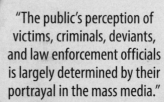

Under the crime control model, criminal justice is seen as an assembly line where efficiency and productivity are valued. The due process model views criminal justice as an obstacle course made up of legal challenges to protect individual rights. Which approach makes more sense to you?

under the due process model that it is better for the guilty to go free than to risk incarcerating or executing the innocent. In contrast to his identification of the crime control model as an "assembly line," Packer suggested that the due process model resembles an "obstacle course," consisting of a variety of legal challenges that must be satisfied throughout the criminal justice process in order to hold someone accountable for a criminal action (and therefore, be punished for said action). The due process model emphasizes the formalized legal practices of the criminal justice process and requires that each stage of the criminal justice system represent a fair and equitable treatment of all cases and all offenders. Drawing from the 9/11 example used earlier, supporters of the due process model would argue that individuals identified as enemy combatants were denied their due process rights and were therefore detained by the U.S. government illegally following the 9/11 terror attacks. Under the due process model, it is not acceptable to engage in such practices just to suppress the risk for potential harm. While liberals would argue that the crime control model infringes on the rights of individuals, conservatives fear that the due process model ignores crime victims and gives criminals too much leeway to escape "justice."

THE INFLUENCE OF THE MEDIA ON THE CRIMINAL JUSTICE SYSTEM

The majority of Americans have limited direct experience with the criminal justice system. As a result, what most people know about crime comes not from personal interactions but perhaps from the experiences of others known to them (peers and family members) or within the general community.

The mass media also has significant power in shaping individuals' perceptions of crime and justice.[8] The scope of the media is extensive, as it includes "mechanisms for public presentations of entertainment, propaganda, and nonfiction information."[9] More important than the levels of media consumption is how the information is interpreted.[10] For the majority of Americans, the images generated by the media regarding crime and criminal justice are often internalized as "facts" about the world we live in.[11]

"The public's perception of victims, criminals, deviants, and law enforcement officials is largely determined by their portrayal in the mass media."[12] However, the content and prevalence of stories relating to crime

AUDIO
Due Process and the Trial of Terrorism Suspects

> "The public's perception of victims, criminals, deviants, and law enforcement officials is largely determined by their portrayal in the mass media."

AROUND THE WORLD

Crime, Law, and Justice From a Global Perspective

The issues of crime, law, and justice vary dramatically around the world. While many other countries have similar functions, practices, and policies compared with the American criminal justice system, there are many countries whose perceptions of crime and punishment are very different. For example, in countries such as Pakistan and Turkey, honor killings have been carried out in cases of adultery—or even perceived infidelity. Harsh punishment can even be handed down for acts that many Western cultures would consider to be normal, everyday occurrences, such as requesting a love song on the radio or strolling through the park. However, not only are such acts rarely reported, but even when they are brought to the attention of legal authorities, the perpetrators are rarely identified, and as a result, such crimes often go unpunished.[a] Yet other crimes are often punished more severely than they would be in the American legal system. In March 2016, Otto Frederick Warmbier, a student from the University of Virginia, was sentenced to 15 years of hard labor in North Korea after he was arrested for committing a hostile act against the state. His crime? Warmbier confessed to tearing down a poster of a political slogan at the hotel where he was staying as part of a student tour group. There have been other incidents in recent years where Americans were detained for similar acts of defiance. As a result, the State Department has strongly recommended that Americans do not travel to North Korea due to their inconsistencies in the identification and punishment of criminal law violations.[b]

CRITICAL THINKING QUESTIONS

1. How are issues of culture reflected in the development of crime, law, and justice in a global society?

2. Research a case in which an American was punished for a crime in a foreign country. How was this person treated in a foreign legal system? Would he or she be treated in a similar fashion if the crime happened in the United States?

Throughout this text, you'll learn about various examples of crime, law, and justice from countries around the world. As you read about these examples, consider how they relate to the American criminal justice system. Are there features that you can identify as similar to the practices that we use here? How are things different? Are there ways in which these systems could benefit from our experiences here in the United States? Or are there features in other countries that we should consider adopting as part of our system?

presents a distorted view of the realities of the criminal justice system. The popular expression "If it bleeds, it leads" represents the prevalent position of crime stories for media outlets. While stories about violent crime make up almost one third of all news time, that does not reflect the reality of crime in society.[13] These exaggerations have a direct relationship to public understanding of crime. Adding to this equation are findings that individuals tend to retain the content of these stories, affirming any negative notions regarding crime, criminals, and criminal justice.[14]

The CSI Effect

AUDIO
Is the "CSI Effect" Influencing Courtrooms?

In addition to the portrayal of crime within the news, stories of crime, criminals, and criminal justice have been a major staple of television entertainment programming. These images, too, present a distorted view of the reality of crime, as they generally present crimes as graphic, random, and violent incidents. Entertainment television about crime has covered a variety of topics, including policing, courtroom portrayals, forensic investigations, and corrections. For example, the number of different installments of the *Law & Order* series covers all aspects of the criminal justice system, from offenders to police and investigators to the court process and its actors. These crime dramas have such an impact on individuals that criminologists have begun to study the *CSI effect*, which references the popular crime drama *CSI: Crime Scene Investigation*, in which crimes are solved in a single episode using sophisticated techniques of crime analysis that aren't readily available or utilized in a typical criminal case. The CSI effect can have a significant impact on real issues of criminal justice. For example, juries may believe that DNA evidence is readily available and required in every case in order to secure a conviction.

Reality TV

Crime is also present in reality TV programming. From *COPS* to *Forensic Files*, viewers are afforded the opportunity to see the criminal justice system in action. In addition, networks such as A&E, the Discovery Channel, truTV, and the History Channel have made documentaries about crime and justice a major component of their programming. Even airing real-life criminal justice cases on networks such as Court TV (now truTV) can have an effect on the public. Often it is the atypical, high-profile cases, such as the trials of O. J. Simpson, Casey Anthony, and George Zimmerman, that garner the greatest attention. This fascination with crimes of violence has created a demand for multiple avenues for information about issues of crime and justice. Live streaming of these proceedings on cable television and online, as well as online updates via social media, provides an all-access pass to the courtroom action. Such attention also creates "wanna-be" experts out of ordinary citizens. Like many other high-profile cases, these themes were displayed in the case of Jodi Arias.

The Media and Perception of Crime Rates

While there is documentation that the saturation of crime stories on the news impacts viewers' opinions of crime, how does crime as "entertainment" influence fears about crime and victimization? Crimes of murder and violence in general are overemphasized in television entertainment.[15] For example, the victimization of women is often portrayed by "movie of the week" outlets such as Lifetime TV that showcase story lines of women being sexually assaulted, stalked, or otherwise injured by a stranger.

Unfortunately, these popular-culture references paint a false picture of the realities of crime, as most women are not maltreated by strangers (as portrayed in these story lines) but are victimized by people known to them.[16] While the enjoyment of reality-based crime programming is related to punitive attitudes on crime, such an effect is not found for viewers of fictional crime dramas.[17] However, viewers of nonfiction television shows (such as *The First 48*) can experience increased fear of crime.[18]

Influencing Public Policy

While the public's concern about crime may be very real, it can also be inflamed by inaccurate data on crime rates or a misunderstanding about the community supervision of offenders and recidivism rates. Indeed, a fear of crime, coupled with the public's perception about rising crime rates, contributes to a lack of faith by citizens in the efficacy of the criminal justice

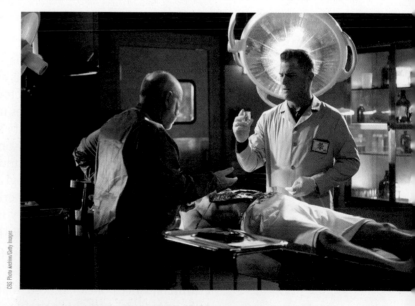

Dramatic and reality-based television programming about crime and criminal justice is designed to entertain the public, not educate. Such programming can lead to an inaccurate understanding of the criminal justice system. What are some inaccuracies you can spot in your favorite crime drama?

Violence. Murder. Lies. And a woman behind it all. The case of Jodi Arias had everything it needed to be a television movie. Yet this was no fictionalized story line. Over the course of her four-month trial, every moment was broadcast on cable television. In addition, there was no shortage of "legal experts" waiting to give their opinion on the events of the day, the evidence presented, or the demeanor of the defendant.

Arias was charged and ultimately convicted for the murder of her boyfriend, Travis Alexander. This was no simple murder but rather an act of extreme aggression as Alexander was found in his shower, where he had been stabbed 27 times, had his throat slit, and was shot in the head. But it wasn't just the excessive nature of the crime that drew the attention of the media. Arias was the perfect candidate to fuel the media fire. The frenzy began when Arias changed her story about the crime several times. At first, she denied any involvement in his murder. Later, she alleged that she and Alexander had been attacked by two masked intruders who murdered Travis but allowed her to live. During the trial, her story was amended once again to one of self-defense. Arias asserted that Travis Alexander had frequently abused her throughout their relationship, and she killed him during one of these attacks. However, she claimed that she did not remember the specific events of his death and that she had blocked out these events due to her emotional trauma.[a]

One of the particularly sensationalized parts of the trial involved Arias's own testimony, which lasted 18 days. Under Arizona law, members of the jury are allowed to submit questions to the accused should she or he choose to take the stand to offer a defense. "Some of the questions seemed to serve no other purpose but to mock Arias and illustrate the jurors' annoyance with her claims."[b] While she was convicted of first-degree murder, the same jurors were unable to reach an agreement on the sentence, resulting in a hung jury. During a second sentencing hearing, the jury was unable to reach a unanimous verdict on a death sentence. As a result, she was sentenced to life without the possibility of parole.[c]

CRITICAL THINKING QUESTIONS

1. Why do you think this case was so sensationalized in the media?

2. What impact does the media representation of this case have on other cases before the courts?

system.[19] Watching television news programs also contributes to this because the increased viewing of local news is associated with punitive beliefs in the punishment of offenders.[20] Together, these factors can influence a rise in the public dialogue about crime, which can lead to changes in criminal justice policies. Agents of criminal justice can respond to a community's fear of crime by increasing police patrols while district attorneys pursue tough-on-crime stances in their prosecution of criminal cases. Politicians respond to community concerns about violent crime by creating and implementing tough-on-crime legislation, such as habitual sentencing laws like "three strikes," and targeting perceived crimes of danger, as the "war on drugs" attempts to do. Unfortunately, "public policy is influenced more by media misinformation and sensationalized high profile cases than by careful or thoughtful analysis."[21]

The use of the public's fear of crime as momentum for generating policies to control crime can be a dangerous incentive. Chapter 5 of this text highlights the development of criminal justice policies. Indeed, many of our criminal justice policies have been named after crime victims or high-profile events that helped inspire or influence the development and passage of such legislation. Given that much of the public's fear of crime is not generated from their personal experiences, it is important to remain aware of the role of the media in generating fear (and therefore, crime control policies; see Figure 1.3).

Figure 1.3   Public Perception of Crime Rate at Odds With Reality

Of the Americans surveyed in 2014, 63% said that crime was on the rise, even though the rate of violent crime has declined over the last 20 years.

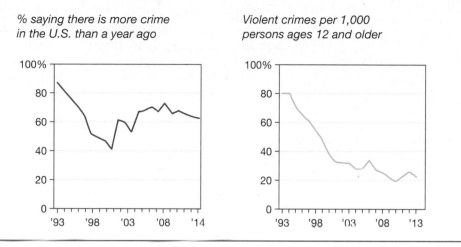

% saying there is more crime in the U.S. than a year ago

Violent crimes per 1,000 persons ages 12 and older

Source: PEW Research Center

"Even if information coming through the media causes fear, first amendment protections for freedom of the press have to be respected and many follow the credo that the public has a right to know regardless of the outcome."[22]

CONCLUSION

The criminal justice system contains powerful tools to combat crimes, such as laws, discretion, and ethics. Each of these tools is used at different stages to move cases through the system. However, there are often competing interests that impact this process and how agents of the system respond to cases. Throughout this text, you'll learn about the functions of each stage of the system as well as the challenges that arise. As you read the Current Controversy debates at the end of this chapter, consider how the tools used by the criminal justice system both help and harm society. How do we balance the diverse needs of society with our criminal justice system? With competing interests throughout society, how do we know if justice is served?

CURRENT CONTROVERSY 1.1

PRO   **CON**

CURRENT
CONTROVERSY
VIDEO
Where Do You Stand?
Cast Your Vote!

Is Justice Served by Our Criminal Justice System?

—Kareem L. Jordan—

INTRODUCTION

There is not an easy way to define justice. There is some debate on whether "justice" means a fair process, regardless of the outcome, or a fair outcome, regardless of the process. In other words, is justice based on the *means* or the *ends*? Historically, the American criminal justice system has defined justice in terms of process, with the hope that the correct outcome will be achieved. In fact, some would suggest that the criminal justice system's process is thought to be so fair that it is better to let many of those criminally guilty go free than to punish one innocent person. Stated differently, the criminal justice process should be fair and set such a high threshold for conviction that the outcomes should be presumed "just" because the process was "just."

If we look at this issue through the lens of policing, we would argue that one of the primary responsibilities of the police is to enforce the laws established by lawmakers.[23] Police officers have the legal authority to deprive people of their physical freedom (e.g., temporarily detain and/or arrest) if appropriate circumstances exist. They also have the legal authority to use force (even deadly force) in certain situations. How do we determine whether justice is served in these cases? Is justice about whether the law is followed? What if the law itself or its application is viewed as unjust?

 Justice Is Served by Our Criminal Justice System

Police represent the first stage in serving justice. Crimes are reported to the police, who, in turn, respond to identify and apprehend a suspect. A just policing system means that the police exercise their responsibilities based on objective factors, without regard to discriminatory practices.[24] For example, police officers should only arrest when they have, at a minimum, probable cause for believing that a crime was committed. This ensures that the police have a minimum legal standard to meet in order to make an arrest. Such a standard ensures that all cases are handled in a similar fashion, which promotes a just and fair system.

The court plays an integral role in the criminal justice system. After an arrest takes place, the court is the venue where certain important decisions and actions occur: bail decision, the trial, and sentencing, if convicted. During the court process, the prosecutors and judges are presumed to want justice, though again, it is not always clear that every key actor in the system agrees on the definition.[25] Judges are actors in the court process who interpret the law in such a way to provide impartiality in outcomes. The decisions of judges are to be based on the law and legally relevant factors (e.g., offense charged, prior record of defendant, conviction offense, etc.). In order to minimize potential biases in court, judges are typically required to use written statutory guidelines to help guide in their decision-making. These sentencing guidelines ensure that each case of a similar nature is decided in a similar fashion. Such a process is a key characteristic of a just system.

The American correctional system is considered the last phase of the criminal justice system.[26] There is debate on whether the purpose of the correctional system is to rehabilitate or punish. Most of those under correctional supervision will return to the community at some point.[27] In some cases, the correctional system helps prepare offenders for (re)integration into the community (i.e., rehabilitation). In other cases, the sentence is designed to punish the offender. The correctional system is unique because it must be responsive to the orders of the criminal court. If defendants are convicted in the court system and sentenced to confinement, the correctional system must confine those offenders in either a local or state correctional facility. Or if convicted offenders are sentenced to community supervision, the correctional system must supervise those offenders in the community to ensure they are adhering to the conditions set by the court. Depending on how you define the role of our correctional system, both options can be considered ways in which justice is served.

Under the crime control model, justice is served by cases moving through the system in a consistent, efficient, and fair manner. The majority of cases in our system are managed in this fashion. As a result, we can say that justice is served by our criminal justice system.

 Justice Is Not Served by Our Criminal Justice System

We have examples throughout each stage of the criminal justice system wherein justice is not served.

Consider how injustices occur in policing. While research generally indicates that those objective factors influence the decision to arrest and use force, empirical studies also find that extralegal factors influence these very important acts by police officers.[28] For instance, Blacks are more likely to be arrested, be given a speeding ticket rather than a warning,[29] and be victims of police use of force.[30] In cases of discriminatory applications of the law, would we suggest that the quest for justice has failed? We also have examples of injustices occurring within our court system. In practice, legally relevant factors are the biggest predictors of court outcomes. Most research does find that the seriousness of the offense and prior record are the factors that largely influence judicial decision-making. Other factors, though, are also significant in this process. Empirical research generally indicates that race, gender, and age influence particular outcomes.[31] Blacks are less likely to be released on bail[32] and are sentenced more harshly than Whites.[33] Hispanics are also shown to have some harsher sanctions within the court process.[34] While males are generally sentenced more harshly than women (due to men committing more serious offenses), research does indicate that females are sometimes given more punitive sentences than males, especially when they commit offenses that are generally viewed as counter to the "traditional" and historical roles of females.[35] Stated differently, females are often treated more leniently than males in court outcomes because of the patriarchal view of females being weak and needing protection. However, when females step outside of those "traditional behaviors," they are given harsher outcomes than males as a form of punishment for not being consistent with the established gender roles. In addition, age has been shown to influence court decisions. The impact of age on court decisions varies, though, based on the age of the offenders. Although race, gender, and age have independent effects on court decisions, the combination of the three has been shown to produce a very substantial impact. Young Black males are often treated more harshly than most groups, which can be observed when examining court outcomes.[36] One rationale provided is that this group is perceived to be more dangerous and threatening.[37] Although crime statistics debunk the myth of the "dangerous" Black male, it still appears to enter the decision-making process within the criminal court process. In these cases, does it appear that justice is always a fair and equitable process?

As a result of these processes, the correctional population can reflect many of the problems that exist within the criminal justice system. Many jails and prisons are overcrowded, which results in more uncomfortable and tighter living conditions, decreased services and programming, and increased costs to address the needs (food, health care, etc.) of those confined.[38] Some have challenged whether these conditions are a violation of the 8th Amendment protection against cruel and unusual punishment. In addition, the racial/ethnic makeup of those confined is indicative of a broken criminal justice system, given the disproportionately higher numbers of minority inmates who fill our nation's correctional institutions.[39]

SUMMARY

The ideals of the criminal justice system allow for justice to be served. After all, the law provides for certain due process rights for every individual who is accused of a crime. But does the reality differ from the ideal? Certainly, we can say that the criminal justice system is not overrun with systematic discrimination, which would occur across all stages of the criminal justice system, in every jurisdiction, and at all times. At the same time, it is reasonable to conclude that pure justice is an elusive concept and that discrimination does occur.[40] So where does that leave us? Do we have the best system that is possible? Or are there opportunities for reform at a fundamental level?

DISCUSSION QUESTIONS

1. Do you believe that the criminal justice system is fair and just? Or are some groups more likely than others to have a negative experience?

2. What does it mean for justice to be served? How might this change depending on the perspective of the community? The criminal justice system? The victim?

Does Mental Illness Cause Crime?

—Robert Schug—

INTRODUCTION

Adam Peter Lanza (Sandy Hook Elementary School shooting, December 2012), James Eagan Holmes (Aurora, Colorado, movie theater shooting, summer 2012), Jared Loughner (Tucson, Arizona, parking lot shooting), Seung Hoi Cho (Virginia Tech shooting spree, April 2007)—we are repeatedly reminded via a seemingly never-ending stream of news media stories and images that individuals with mental illness commit extreme and even bizarre acts of crime and violence, which often may seem to defy rationality. Killers acting at the command of voices in their heads or under the belief that Satan is guiding their hands both suggest and continually underscore what appears to be a close association between mental illness and crime. Though the association may seem rather clear (at least to the average media consumer and even to a growing number of scientists and researchers), the question arises: Does mental illness cause crime?

Clearly, the question of whether or not mental illness causes crime is both timely and important. Socially, it is a phenomenon that appears to be gaining more public attention. Research continues to demonstrate a relationship between different forms of mental illness and criminal and violent behavior.[41] However, the concepts of mental illness and crime are both complex, as is the relationship between the two. For example, *mental illness* as a term is often misused or poorly understood. In reality, mental illness is an umbrella term that may represent a number of different types of conditions. Individuals may have as few as one or two symptoms, which do not rise to the level of *clinical significance*, or several symptoms that meet the criteria of one or more full-blown clinical diagnoses. Similarly, *crime* is an umbrella term, encompassing a spectrum of behaviors and acts that are against the law. But other behaviors—aggressive, antisocial, and violent behaviors—are also worthy of study in their relationship with mental illness and often the focus of research in this area. When looking at the relationship between mental illness and crime, we need to be specific about what we mean by crime. For example, the relationship of mental illness to petty theft may be very different from its relationship to murder.

Even with an understanding of the concepts of mental illness and crime separately, appreciating the relationship between the two can be challenging. To that end, three general relationships have been suggested based on the *role* of mental illness symptoms in crime and violence: (1) Mental illness causes crime and violence; (2) mental illness contributes to (but does not directly cause) crime and violence; and (3) crime and violence occur in spite of mental illness. This section looks at the relationship between the first perspective, compared with the second and third arguments.

 PRO **Mental Illness Causes Crime and Violence**

Scholars argue that mental illness may play a role in causal factors leading to crime and violence—specifically in the area of *motivation* for offending.[42] While this is a tremendous oversimplification (and remembering that as a cause, the onset of the illness must occur *before* the onset of the offense behavior), anecdotal clinical evidence has indicated support for the notion that symptoms of mental illness can become the *motivation* for criminal and violent behavior. Psychotic symptoms (which represent a subjective break from reality for the individual), which may characterize disorders on the schizophrenia spectrum or some types of mood disorders, may serve as motivations for acts of violence. Auditory hallucinations (e.g., hearing voices which are not actually there), for example, may instruct an individual to kill another. Delusional beliefs (strong, unconventional beliefs maintained despite evidence to the contrary) may also provide motivation for criminal offending. For example, an individual may commit sexual assaults against children based on religious delusions. One paroled sexual offender assaulted his own daughters because he thought the Bible instructed him to teach his daughters about sex. In this case, the delusion could be seen as the motivator or cause of the crime.

 CON **Mental Illness Does Not Cause Crime and Violence**

Mental illness contributes to (but does not directly cause) crime and violence. In this viewpoint, symptoms of mental illness do not directly cause crime and violence, but contribute to impairments in behavioral "safeguards" which may have—under normal circumstances—prevented the criminal and violent acts from occurring. Put another way, they *facilitate* crime, insomuch as the symptoms do not *cause* the criminal behavior but rather do nothing to help the individual *not* commit the criminal behavior. Such *facilitative impairments* would include symptoms such as impulsivity, paranoia, and decreased judgment. Also in this role, mental illness symptoms could serve to exacerbate situational factors or preexisting (yet unrealized) tendencies toward crime and violence. Examples of the latter might be racist views or having a "bad temper," whereas examples of the former might include homelessness. One hypothesis related to this role might be that the type of mental illness or symptom may not, in and of itself, contribute to a specific relationship with crime and violence (e.g., schizophrenia more or less so than depression). Rather, life may simply be more challenging when one suffers from a mental disorder—of any kind—and it is the additive effects of these challenges that contribute to criminal and violent behavior.

Crime and violence occur in spite of mental illness. In this viewpoint, mental illness in essence plays *no* role in the occurrence of crime and violence—the two are independent and unrelated to each other. Here, the contributions of traditional and contemporary criminology, which you'll learn about in Chapter 4, provide better explanations for the crime committed by the individual with mental illness. It is noteworthy that these theories can apply to individuals with full-blown mental illnesses (a point often overlooked given the unusual and even bizarre nature of the presentation of some of these illnesses), but they can also explain crime and violence occurring before the onset of mental disorder (i.e., an individual who was criminal and/or violent before the illness developed—a nuanced phenomenon not always addressed in studies of mental illness and crime).

Finally, often lost in the argument is an understanding that individuals with mental illness may commit crimes or become violent for exactly the same reasons that people *without* mental illness do. For example, individuals with mental illness may experience economic hardship (i.e., they need money), get into an argument with a family member or loved one (i.e., they got angry), or simply choose to commit crime (i.e., for no reason other than they thought they could get away with it). Individuals with even the most severe forms of mental illness may have periods of lucidity and clarity and can be capable of planning and organizing even elaborate criminal behaviors. They may even experience periodic symptom remission—in fact, when adhering to prescribed medication regimens, these individuals may even function at relatively normative levels. Criminal, violent, and antisocial behavior occurring during these periods thus cannot be directly attributed to the effects and influences of mental illness.

Often homeless individuals also suffer from mental illness. How do you think this affects the relationship between crime and mental illness?

SUMMARY

Does mental illness cause crime? The problem with this question is partly the question itself, which fails to capture the complexity of mental illness and crime separately and their relationship (causal or not) together. A more appropriate question is, Does mental illness play a role in crime? And if so, what role? The answer to this better phrased question is maybe a large role, maybe a small role, or maybe no role at all. Ultimately, continued research is needed in this very important area of study, and focusing efforts on understanding the underpinnings of crime and violence in mental illness helps identify treatments and approaches which may help individuals with mental illness who become criminal and violent and reduce stigma associated with those who are not.

DISCUSSION QUESTIONS

1. Why is it important to understand the relationship between mental illness and crime? What are the implications?

2. Who (individuals, organizations, etc.) stands to benefit from a responsible understanding of the relationship between mental illness and crime? Who stands to benefit when this relationship is not understood?

KEY TERMS

Review key terms with eFlashcards | ⑤SAGE edge™ • edge.sagepub.com/mallicoatccj

Corrections 4

Courts 4

Crime 4

Crime control model 10

Defendant 5

Discretion 5

Due process model 10

Ethics 5

Felony 9

Misdemeanors 9

Police 4

Wedding cake model 8

DISCUSSION QUESTIONS

Test your mastery of chapter content • Take the Practice Quiz | ⑤SAGE edge™ • edge.sagepub.com/mallicoatccj

1. What are the three main components of the criminal justice system?

2. How might discretion be used in a positive manner? A negative manner?

3. How does the wedding cake model illustrate how cases are processed by the criminal justice system?

4. What are the differences between the crime control model and the due process model?

5. How does the media influence the public's fear of crime?

6. How does the media influence public policy related to criminal justice?

LEARNING ACTIVITY

1. Pick a television show about criminal justice. As you watch this show, highlight areas that you think might lead the general public to make incorrect assumptions about the criminal justice system.

SUGGESTED WEBSITES

- **U.S. Department of Justice:** https://www.justice.gov
- **National Institute of Justice:** http://www.nij.gov
- *Crime, Media, Culture:* http://cmc.sagepub.com

2

CONCEPTS OF LAW AND JUSTICE

LEARNING OBJECTIVES

- Compare how criminal law differs from civil law

- Identify the historical influences of modern American criminal law

- Describe the four different sources of law

- Discuss the burden of proof required in a criminal case

- Define the four components of a criminal act

- Explain the different types of criminal defenses

On July 20, 2012, during a midnight showing of the film *The Dark Knight Rises*, James Holmes entered a Century 16 movie theater in Aurora, Colorado. Dressed in tactical clothing, Holmes set off tear gas grenades and opened fire into the theater audience. At the end of his rampage, 12 people were dead, and 70 others were injured. He was apprehended outside of the movie theater.[1]

In addition to filing 24 counts of first-degree murder, 116 counts of attempted first-degree murder, and one count of illegal possession of explosives,[2] the district attorney stated that they would seek the death penalty in the case. At the time, Colorado had only three people residing on death row, and the last execution was carried out in 1997.[3] Holmes's attorneys indicated that they would be pursuing an insanity defense. The state sent out juror summonses to 9,000 candidates, and 12 jurors and 12 alternates were selected. The trial began on April 27, 2015.[4] After more than 11 weeks of testimony, the trial concluded, and jury deliberations began. It took 12 hours for the jury to find Holmes guilty of all crimes. While the court-appointed forensic scientist testified that Holmes suffered (and continues to suffer) from significant mental illness, he understood that his actions were wrong at the time of the crime.[5] This finding made it such that an insanity defense was unsuccessful, and the jury found Holmes guilty.

James Holmes appears in a Colorado courtroom with his attorney shortly after his arrest. Holmes was convicted of a mass shooting in an Aurora, Colorado, theater during a screening of *The Dark Knight Rises*. Why was his insanity defense unsuccessful?

The same jury was then faced with the task of determining whether James Holmes should be sentenced to death for his crimes or if he should be sentenced to life without the possibility of parole. They heard stories about Holmes's childhood and evidence about his history of delusions and mental illness. They heard stories about the victims and the lives that were lost or irrevocably damaged as a result of Holmes's actions.[6] In the end, the jury could not reach a unanimous verdict on the death penalty. He received 12 sentences of life without the possibility of parole—one for each victim—and an additional 3,318 years for the nonlethal crimes.[7]

VIDEO
Jury Reaches a Verdict in James Holmes's Murder Trial

In this chapter, you will learn about the development of law and how it relates to the criminal justice system. The chapter begins with a discussion on the different sources of law in the United States. The chapter then focuses on the different types of law and their relationship to the criminal justice system. You'll also learn about the different legal defenses that are used in the criminal courts to explain or justify criminal behaviors. The chapter concludes with two Current Controversy debates. The first, by Clayon Mosher and Scott Akins, looks at the debate over legalizing marijuana. The second, by Craig Hemmens, questions whether the Miranda warning should be abolished.

TYPES OF LAW

Civil Cases

In the United States, we have two separate court systems to respond to our two primary areas of law: civil law and criminal law. **Civil law** governs disputes between individuals or private parties (which can include corporations) and generally involves violations of private acts, such as contracts, property disputes, and family law. In these cases, the person who initiates the case is referred to as the **plaintiff**, and the person who is responding to the case is the defendant. The burden to prove the case is placed on the plaintiff. Under civil law, the plaintiff must provide evidence to prove her or his case by the **preponderance of the evidence**. This means that if the evidence presented is more likely to prove that the law was violated, then the plaintiff wins the case. Under civil law, the form of punishment is financial.

One of the most famous civil court cases was *Liebeck v. McDonald's Restaurants* (1994), otherwise referred to as the McDonald's hot-coffee case. Ms. Liebeck ordered a cup of coffee from the drive-thru at a local McDonald's. While sitting in the passenger's seat, she placed the cup between her knees to steady the coffee while she removed the lid to add cream to the beverage. She subsequently spilled the contents of the cup over her groin and legs and suffered third-degree burns as a result of the high temperature of the beverage. Her burns were so extensive that she required several skin grafts and was partially disabled for two years as a result of her injuries. Ms. Liebeck sought assistance from McDonald's to cover her medical expenses as a result of her injuries. Despite several requests for a settlement, McDonald's refused. She filed a suit with the civil court of New Mexico (where she resided), and her lawyers alleged that by serving the coffee at such a high temperature, McDonald's was guilty of gross negligence. The jury in the case agreed with Ms. Liebeck and awarded

Civil law
Law that governs disputes between individuals or private parties and generally involves the violation of private acts.

Plaintiff
A person who brings a suit in a civil case.

Preponderance of the evidence
The burden of proof in a civil case. Refers to when the totality of the evidence exceeds a 50% likelihood that the law was violated.

her $160,000 in damages for her pain and suffering. The jury also awarded punitive damages in the case of $2.7 million.[8]

Criminal Cases

In contrast to civil law, criminal law cases are brought by the government against a defendant for violating a specific law. In a criminal law case, the burden of proof is **beyond a reasonable doubt.** Figure 2.1 demonstrates how this burden of proof is different from other forms of proof that are used throughout our justice system. This means that in order to convict a defendant of a crime, the court must find that there is little doubt according to the reasonable or typical individual that he or she committed the crime. Depending on the type of crime that the defendant is convicted of, he or she may receive probation, spend time in jail or prison, or be executed as punishment for the crime. You'll learn more about the different types of punishment in Chapter 10.

SAGE JOURNAL ARTICLE
Justifying the Proof
Structure of Criminal Trials

Federal Criminal Laws

Federal criminal laws are enacted by the legislative branch of the federal government. Federal law related to criminal justice includes the regulation of issues such as firearms, drugs, money laundering, fraud, and a variety of other criminal activities. Federal law also governs activities within federal government buildings, in national parks, and on tribal land. In addition, federal law violations can also be triggered when crimes occur across state lines.

State Criminal Laws

States also have the power to make law prohibiting behaviors under the 10th Amendment. Unlike federal criminal law, which applies to all 50 states as well as the District of Columbia and U.S. territories, state law is limited to the specific geographic jurisdiction of that state. While criminal laws may have similar characteristics across the nation, there are also differences in the types of behaviors that are defined as

Beyond a reasonable doubt
In order to convict a defendant of a crime, the court must find that there is little doubt according to the reasonable-person standard.

Figure 2.1 Burden of Proof

As the level of proof needed rises, there are fewer cases that can meet the requirements. It is fairly easy to have reasonable suspicion but much more difficult to prove something beyond a reasonable doubt.

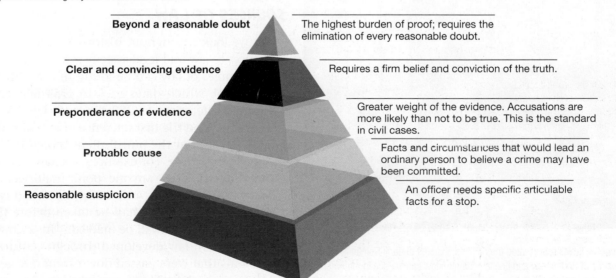

Beyond a reasonable doubt — The highest burden of proof; requires the elimination of every reasonable doubt.

Clear and convincing evidence — Requires a firm belief and conviction of the truth.

Preponderance of evidence — Greater weight of the evidence. Accusations are more likely than not to be true. This is the standard in civil cases.

Probable cause — Facts and circumstances that would lead an ordinary person to believe a crime may have been committed.

Reasonable suspicion — An officer needs specific articulable facts for a stop.

criminal from state to state, as well as the types of punishments that violators are subjected to. For example, states such as Washington and Colorado have legalized the recreational use of marijuana while the majority of states continue to criminalize the behavior. Alabama's criminal law defines the personal possession of marijuana as a misdemeanor, but subsequent possessions can be charged as felonies. Meanwhile, several other states have decriminalized simple possession or limited its enforcement to a civil violation. Even in states that have decriminalized marijuana possession, several have created specific laws about the amount that one is permitted to possess. While Mississippi state law allows for someone to possess up to 30 grams of marijuana in a first offense, Maryland's law on the decriminalization of marijuana only allows for the possession of 10 grams or less. You'll learn more about the debate in the Current Controversy 2.1 section at the end of this chapter.

Lex talionis
Latin term that refers to the theory that punishment should fit the crime. The concept derives from ancient law and is referenced in biblical texts as *eye for an eye*.

Municipal Criminal Laws

Municipalities can have their own body of law. In terms of jurisdiction, these laws are generally the most limited, as they are only applied to a specific city or county. Municipal criminal law is limited to cases involving infractions and misdemeanors. An infraction is a violation that is punishable by a fine but does not carry a potential jail sentence. Unlike misdemeanors and felonies, cases involving infractions do not involve jury trials, nor is the accused provided an attorney if she or he cannot afford one (though defendants are permitted to hire an attorney if they wish). The most common type of infraction is a traffic violation, but infractions can also include jaywalking and disturbing the peace. Infractions are also unique in that they follow the burden of proof similar to a civil case—preponderance of the evidence. Cases that involve misdemeanor crimes at the municipal level are handled just like misdemeanors under state and federal law, and these cases are managed by the same due process protections.

SOURCES OF LAW

If we look throughout history, we see several references to law and legal systems. One of the earliest examples of law can be found in the code of Hammurabi, which dates back to 1754 BCE and contained references to 282 different laws. It is here that we find the first reference of **lex talionis**, which argued that the punishment should fit the nature of the crime. For example, the law against slander stated that "if anyone 'point the finger' at a sister of a god or the wife of any one, and can not prove it, this man shall be taken before the judges and his brow shall be marked."[9] In contrast, ancient Roman law developed through centuries of customs that were passed down from one generation to another. These customs later became

The Twelve Tables represented the codified customs of early Roman law. What influences of Roman law and English common law can we see in the American legal system today?

codified in 449 BCE as the Twelve Tables and stood as the foundation of the Roman law. As the Roman empire expanded, so did its legal system. During the third century BCE, we see the emergence of the first legal scholars. These trained jurists were tasked with interpreting the law, much like the U.S. Supreme Court does today. Indeed, Roman law significantly influenced much of Western law, including the English common-law system.[10] English common law emerged during the Middle Ages. Henry II (1154–1189 CE) established a system whereby judges were sent out to resolve disputes throughout the country. One of the key features that emerged under the common-law system was the doctrine of **stare decisis** (which means "to stand by things settled" in Latin). This refers to a system of **precedent** whereby future legal decisions are required to take into consideration previous rulings. This means that a court should issue a ruling that aligns with not only its own previous decisions but also the rulings of higher level courts. This system is still in use today.

> "The right of the people to be secure in their persons, houses, papers, and effects, against unreasonable searches and seizures, shall not be violated . . ."
> —4th Amendment, U.S. Constitution

Both Roman law and English common law heavily influenced the American legal system. Today, we can find laws among four primary sources: constitutional law, statutory law, administrative law, and case law.

SAGE JOURNAL ARTICLE
Understanding Original Intent and Stare Decisis

Constitutional Law

A constitution serves to establish and govern the government.[11] The U.S. Constitution stands as the highest law of our country and embodies the principles from which all other legal rules and processes are derived. It was written in 1787 in Philadelphia and was ratified by nine states on June 21, 1788. The first 10 amendments compose the Bill of Rights, and several of these amendments relate directly to criminal law. Table 2.1 highlights the **constitutional law** protections that the Bill of Rights provides. The U.S. Constitution is binding on all U.S. states, the District of Columbia, and U.S. territories.

In addition to the U.S. Constitution, each state has its own constitution that serves as a binding document for all laws at the state level. However, these laws bind only that specific state. This means that state laws must abide by the rules set forth in not only their state's constitution but the U.S. Constitution as well. If a law is challenged, it is up to either the state supreme court or the U.S. Supreme Court to determine whether the law violates the constitution. As you will see throughout this book, many of our policies and practices of criminal law have been established through the constitutional review process.

Stare decisis
Latin for "to stand by things settled." Refers to the system of precedent.

Precedent
Refers to the legal standard whereby future decisions are required to take into consideration previous rulings.

Constitutional law
Laws derived from the U.S. Constitution and state constitutions.

Table 2.1	Constitutional Rights That Relate to Criminal Law
Amendment	**Protection**
1st Amendment	Protects freedom of religion, freedom of speech, and freedom of the press, as well as the right to assembly
2nd Amendment	Protects the right to bear arms
4th Amendment	Protects against unreasonable searches and seizures
5th Amendment	Protects against double jeopardy and self-incrimination. Provides due process protection in criminal cases.
6th Amendment	Provides for the right to a speedy trial by an impartial jury of one's peers in the jurisdiction where the crime occurred. Provides the right to be informed of the nature of the charges, to confront witnesses against oneself, and present witnesses in one's defense. Provides the right to an attorney.
8th Amendment	Protects against excessive bail and cruel and unusual punishments
14th Amendment	Extends due process protections to the states

Statutory Law

Federal Statutory Law

Statutory law refers to laws that are established by governments. Federal law is created by members of Congress, who first introduce a bill in either the House or the Senate (wherever their seat is held). These bills are then debated by a committee (and in some cases, a subcommittee, which comprises a small number of congressional members). Once the bill is approved by committee, it is returned to the House or the Senate for general debate. At this stage, members can reject the bill, propose amendments to the bill, or pass the bill. The bill is then sent to the president, who either signs the bill and allows it to become a law or vetoes the bill. However, Congress can override the presidential veto with a two-thirds vote by each of its chambers.[12]

State Statutory Law

At the state level, statutory law is proposed by a member of the state legislature and is debated in a fashion similar to the federal process. Once a majority of the members of the state legislature approve the measure, it is sent to the state's governor for approval. State law exists in partnership with federal law. In cases where there is a conflict between state and federal law, it is up to the federal court system to resolve these disputes. Since each state has its own set of laws for its jurisdiction, you may often find differing and contradictory approaches to issues.

In addition to legislators, citizens of several states can create laws as a result of direct democracy. Twenty-four states allow for laws to be adopted via a ballot initiative process. Under a direct initiative, signatures are gathered by registered voters to place an initiative on the election ballot. If the measure passes by a majority vote, then the initiative is enacted into law. This method of direct democracy is particularly popular in California, which has used this practice to enact a number of state laws, including several related to criminal justice. For example, Proposition 83 (otherwise known as Jessica's Law) was passed by a vote of 70.5% of Californian voters in 2006 and was designed to increase the punishment for individuals who are convicted of sex crimes against adults and children. The law also increased the postincarceration restrictions on convicted sex offenders through residency requirements and requiring offenders to wear GPS tracking devices. The law was challenged on the grounds that the residency requirements, which prohibited convicted sex offenders from living within 2,000 feet of a school or park, were too strict. Since many offenders were forced to live on the streets (which could be viewed as a violation of their parole), the court held that these provisions were a violation of the liberty and privacy interests of the individuals. The court also held that restricting the residency of convicted offenders did little to protect the community. In their decision, the California Supreme Court determined that while such restrictions could be upheld in certain types of cases (like those involving victims under the age of 14), a blanket restriction was unconstitutional.[13]

Administrative Law

Administrative law refers to the body of law that governs the creation and function of state and federal government agencies. Administrative law focuses on the powers that are granted to these agencies, the types of rules that they make, and how these agencies are linked to other areas of the government as well as the general public. Administrative law spans across virtually every topic, including intelligence, security, banking, finance, food, education, and communications—if there is a governmental

Statutory law
Laws that are established by governments.

Administrative law
Body of law that governs the creation and function of state and federal government agencies.

SPOTLIGHT

Concealed Weapons on College Campuses

The issue of allowing concealed weapons on college campuses has been the subject of significant debate in recent years. While some states have passed laws permitting the practice, others have moved in the opposite direction to oppose it. While all 50 states have laws that allow citizens to carry concealed weapons in certain circumstances, only 19 states permit individuals to carry a concealed weapon on a college campus. An additional 23 states allow individual campuses to determine their own policies on the practice.[a] In June 2015, Texas governor Greg Abbott signed Senate Bill 11, which permits individuals with a concealed-handgun license to legally carry on college campuses. The sponsor of the bill, Allen Fletcher, argued that since Texas law already permits individuals with a concealed weapons permit to carry in public, it is likely that many students already carry in class unbeknownst to university faculty and staff.[b] Like other states, Texas state colleges and universities must create policies for their individual campuses that must determine where concealed weapons can be carried. While the law does provide the creation of gun-free zones, it is unclear as to how these zones can be defined.[c]

Local police arrive on scene at Seattle Pacific University on June 5, 2014, after Aaron Ybarra opened fire in the university library, killing one student and injuring two others. Should concealed weapons be allowed on college campuses?

Texas already allows teachers in public elementary and secondary schools to carry a concealed weapon in the classroom if they have permission from their school district superintendent.[d] Meanwhile, other universities are purchasing bulletproof whiteboards for professors to help protect in the case of an active shooter.[e] In contrast, California governor Jerry Brown signed a bill in October 2015 banning concealed guns from all California schools, including universities.[f] In addition, states such as Michigan and Montana have vetoed bills that would permit the expansion of concealed-weapon carry laws on college campuses.[g]

CRITICAL THINKING QUESTIONS

1. Do you think that allowing concealed weapons on college campuses will increase or decrease student safety?

2. What are the laws for concealed-weapons carry for your state? What do these laws mean for the schools in your community?

agency involved in its regulation, then administrative law is at the center of this discussion. The primary source for administrative law is the Federal Administrative Procedure Act (APA). The APA has four primary purposes: (1) to mandate that government agencies inform the public of the nature, procedures, and rules of their organization; (2) to provide a process whereby the public can participate in making such rules; (3) to establish and implement a uniform process by which rules are made and violations are adjudicated; and (4) to define the scope of judicial review.[14] Current administrative law is published daily in the *Federal Register* and is reorganized on an annual basis into the *Code of Federal Regulations*.

VIDEO
Students Allowed to Carry
Handguns on Campus

Administrative law is often involved in criminal justice matters. For example, the Department of Agriculture was one of the first agencies involved in the investigation of Michael Vick. While Vick was ultimately convicted of federal crimes related to his involvement in dog-fighting events, it was administrative law that granted the Department of Agriculture the necessary jurisdiction to initiate the investigation in conjunction with the Department of Justice. Vick was ultimately sentenced to 23 months in prison. While his conviction did not prohibit him from being reinstated by the NFL, the case did result in new federal laws, such as the Animal Fighting Prohibition Enforcement Act of 2007. This new law amended the Animal Welfare Act and increased the penalties in cases of animal-fighting ventures.[15] In addition, dog fighting is now a felony in all 50 states.[16]

Case Law

Unlike statutory law, which is typically created by legislatures (and in some cases, the initiative process), **case law** is created as a result of legal decisions by courts. These new interpretations of the law are called precedent. You learned earlier in this chapter that the origins of precedent lie in English common law, which served as a significant influence on the American judicial system. Case law involves a judge (or panel of judges) who provide a written explanation of their decision in a court case. These explanations are called **opinions**. Opinions are generally written in appellate cases, so they focus on issues of law rather than the facts of the case. These opinions lay out the reasoning used by the justices to make their decision. These written opinions often build upon—or in some cases even overturn—previous decisions. Case law is directly linked to statutory law. Most legal challenges that create case law arise out of a conflict of statutory law. Generally speaking, in order to challenge statutory law, there needs to be an allegation that the law or its application is in violation of the governing constitution (such as a state constitution or the U.S. Constitution).

An example of case law is the recent U.S. Supreme Court decision in *Rodriguez v. United States*. Dennys Rodriguez was stopped by the Nebraska Highway Patrol for driving on the shoulder of the highway. The stop was legal, as such conduct is prohibited by state law. The officer requested and received the license of Mr. Rodriguez and his passenger and subsequently issued a traffic citation for the conduct. The officer then asked if Mr. Rodriguez would consent to a perimeter search of his vehicle by his K-9 dog, who was in the patrol car. When Mr. Rodriquez denied the request, the officer detained him until a second officer arrived. Upon the arrival of the backup officer, the K-9 dog performed a perimeter search of the vehicle and detected an illegal substance. A subsequent content search of the vehicle found methamphetamine. The length of time between the issuing of the traffic citation and the alert by the dog was seven to eight minutes. While Mr. Rodriguez's attorney argued that the evidence from the traffic stop should not be admissible, the objection was overruled by the trial court. He was subsequently convicted on federal drug charges. Mr. Rodriguez appealed his conviction. The case ultimately appeared before the justices of the U.S. Supreme Court (*Rodriguez v. United States*, 2015) who agreed with Mr. Rodriguez. In their opinion, the Court stated that the extension of a traffic stop in order to conduct a dog sniff is a violation of the 4th Amendment's protection against illegal search and seizure.[17]

CRIMINAL LAW

Each crime is defined under various different bodies of law—municipal law, state law, federal law, and even international law. In order to define an act as a crime, there must be a law that identifies this behavior as wrong. Laws are designed to represent the interests of the citizens. Laws about crime generally fall into one of two categories: mala in se and mala prohibita. Crimes that are **mala in se** are acts that are considered

Case law
Law that is created as a result of legal decisions by the court.

Opinions
A written decision of the court. Focuses on issues of law that can be used as precedent in future cases.

Mala in se
Latin for crimes that are considered to be inherently wrong and therefore illegal.

AROUND THE WORLD

International Law

Each government has its own body of law to govern its citizens. International law focuses on regulations between nations. International law covers a number of different topics, including human rights, international crime, refugee and migration issues, and conditions of war. International law also provides guidance on global issues, such as the environment, international waters, trade, and communications.

The United Nations is the primary body tasked with supporting issues of international law. Founded in 1945, it is made up of 193 member states. According to the governing charter, the UN promotes discussion among the member nations to help address the needs of various countries and help

The UN Security Council is tasked with maintaining international peace and security. Here, members meet in January 2016 to discuss the current security concerns in the Republic of Mali, which is located in West Africa. The region has been battling a civil war since 2012. How does international law differ from other forms of law?

solve problems that exist between countries. In addition, the UN provides support for issues that impact the global community as a whole.[a] To date, more than 500 treaties have been deposited with the UN. One example of such a treaty is the International Convention for the Suppression of the Financing of Terrorism. Passed in 1999, the treaty aims to criminalize the financial support of terrorist entities and acts. It has been ratified by 187 states, making it one of the most successful antiterrorism treaties.[b]

The International Court of Justice (ICJ) is the judicial entity within the United Nations that is used to resolve disputes between states and violations of international law. The court can also provide advisory opinions on issues of law and policy. In addition to the ICJ, there are several UN tribunals that are established by the UN Security Council and used to resolve specific disputes.[c] For example, the Special Court for Sierra Leone was established in 2002 to address significant war crimes that occurred during the country's civil war between 1991 and 2002.[d] However, the legal authority of these courts and tribunals is often limited as they are often established to address specific issues. In 1998, the international community adopted the Rome Statute, which provided the legal basis to establish a permanent international court system. The International Criminal Court is involved in prosecuting cases of war crimes, genocide, and crimes against humanity. Since its creation, it has been involved in 23 cases stemming from nine international events.[e]

While the other forms of law discussed in this chapter reflect the various sources of law that can be found in many different jurisdictions, international law is unique in that it represents the needs and interests of the international community as a whole.

CRITICAL THINKING QUESTIONS

1. What are the challenges of maintaining a system of international law?

2. How does international law influence the legal decision-making of the United States?

---

to be inherently illegal. Murder is an example of a crime that is mala in se. In comparison, acts that are **mala prohibita** are only crimes because they have been defined under the law as illegal. Examples of crimes that are mala prohibita are drug use, prostitution, and gambling.[18]

Mala prohibita
Latin for crimes that are illegal only because they have been defined as such under the law.

Components of a Criminal Act

Under criminal law, there are four components of a criminal act (Figure 2.2). The first is **actus reus**. Actus reus is Latin and means "evil act." In order for a crime to exist, there must be an act that is defined by society as bad or wrong. The second component is **mens rea**. While the actus reus is the act, mens rea is the "evil thought" that accompanies the crime. Another way to think about mens rea is **intent**. In order for something to be considered a crime, there must be an evil act (or actus reus) and the bad intention to cause harm (or mens rea). When mens rea joins with actus reus, this is called **concurrence**. In a criminal case, both mens rea and actus reus must be proven beyond a reasonable doubt in order to convict someone of the crime. However, some crimes are defined as **strict liability** crimes. This means that mens rea does not need to be proven in order for an individual to be guilty of the criminal act. For example, someone who drives drunk and ends up killing someone likely did not intend to harm anyone when he or she got into the car to drive. Yet we define this as a crime. In many cases, there will also be attendant circumstances to a crime. **Attendant circumstances** refer to what happens within the context of the act that makes it a crime. It is the relationship between mens rea and actus reus. For example, in the crime of rape, the act of sexual intercourse is not, in and of itself, a crime. However, in order for sex to be a lawful behavior, you must have consent from the parties involved in the act. Failure to obtain consent is an example of an attendant circumstance and is what defines the act as a crime. Finally, there is the **result**, or the harm, that is experienced as a result of the act and the intent joining together.

Substantive Criminal Law

Defining what makes something a crime is a part of **substantive criminal law**. Substantive criminal law is another way to describe statutory law, as it refers to what acts we define as criminal. For example, substantive criminal law in many states defines the possession of marijuana as an illegal act. You'll learn more about the criminalization of this act in the debate at the end of this chapter. Substantive criminal law also defines the potential punishment for someone who is convicted of a crime. For example, Title 21 of the United States Code, otherwise known as the Controlled Substance Act, states that it is against the law to intentionally purchase more than 9 grams of certain controlled substances over a 30-day period that are typically used in the creation of methamphetamine. The law further states that violators are subject to a punishment of a minimum fine of $1,000 as well as an imprisonment sentence of no more than one year. If, however, the individual has a prior conviction for a drug-related charge, the sentence increases to a $2,500 fine and the potential for up

WEB LINK
International Court of Justice (ICJ)

Actus reus
Latin for "evil act." One of the four required components of a criminal act.

Mens rea
One of the four required components of a criminal act. Latin for the "evil thought." Refers to the intent of an offender.

Intent
Refers to the conscious decision to engage in a criminal act.

Concurrence
When the mens rea and actus reus join together in a crime.

Strict liability
Select cases where acts are crimes even if the individual lacked the mens rea or intent to commit a crime.

Attendant circumstances
The relationship between mens rea and actus reus. Refers to what happens within the context of the act that makes it a crime.

Result
Component of a crime that refers to the harm that is experienced as a result of the mens rea and actus reus joining together.

Substantive criminal law
Defines what makes behavior a criminal act under the law.

Figure 2.2   Components of a Criminal Act

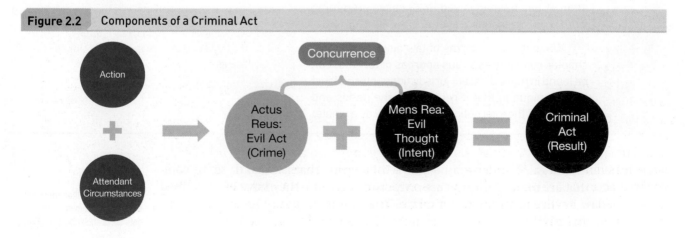

to two years in prison. The potential sentence increases for those offenders with two or more prior convictions.[19]

Procedural Criminal Law

While substantive criminal law tells us what is a crime and how such crimes should be punished, **procedural criminal law** provides the structure by which such cases should move through the system. In Chapter 1, you were introduced to the criminal process and learned about how a case moves through the criminal justice system. It is procedural criminal law that provides the rules and regulations for how a case will proceed. It dictates the roles and responsibilities for each of the courtroom participants. It also provides guidance on how to ensure that a defendant's constitutional rights are protected. For example, procedural criminal law provides the time line by which the accused must receive a probable-cause hearing or how to waive her or his right to a speedy trial. Procedural criminal law also requires that police officers inform someone of his or her constitutional right to remain silent if placed under arrest for a crime. The Miranda warning also informs the accused of his or her right to an attorney and that one will be provided if he or she is indigent. Informing suspects of their rights and ensuring that they are upheld is an important feature of procedural criminal law. You'll learn more about these practices in the debate at the end of this chapter.

AUDIO
A Genocide Conviction
For Radovan Karadzic

The Federal Rules of Criminal Procedure guide the federal criminal court system. They also provide the procedures that investigators must follow when building their case. This includes the rules for questioning a suspect as well as how searches are conducted. Each state also has its own code of procedural law. For example, Colorado procedural criminal law is one of 22 separate volumes. While many of the laws governing the criminal courts are contained within the Colorado Rules of Criminal Procedure, there are other volumes that impact the criminal courts as well, such as the Colorado Rules of Evidence, which contain laws on issues such as the use of expert testimony, hearsay, and witnesses.

Procedural criminal law
Provides the legal structure and rules by which cases should move through the system.

Defense
A strategy to justify, explain, or excuse criminal behavior.

Innocence
Refers to a case where evidence excludes someone from having committed the crime.

CRIMINAL DEFENSES

When someone is accused of a crime, it is up to the prosecutor to prove that the defendant is guilty. In order to prevent a guilty verdict, offenders or their legal counsel will present their own evidence to refute or challenge the facts of the prosecution's case. This is called a **defense**. In this section, you'll learn about several common types of criminal defenses. You'll also learn about insanity defenses, which are far less common in real life compared with their representation on television series.

Innocence

Under the American criminal justice system, defendants are presumed to be "innocent until proven guilty," or so goes the reference in popular culture. It is important to note that very few defendants are determined to be innocent by the courts. Trial courts determine whether someone is guilty or not guilty. Declaring someone not guilty is not the same as finding someone innocent. Indeed, someone who is found not guilty by the criminal courts may have committed the crime, but it was not possible for the court to prove this beyond a reasonable doubt. **Innocence** refers to a case where evidence such as DNA excludes someone from having committed the crime. The challenge, as noted above, is that this information often comes to light after someone has been wrongfully

> **"**
> Trial courts determine whether someone is guilty or not guilty. Declaring someone not guilty is not the same as finding someone innocent.

Kirk Bloodsworth was wrongfully convicted of the rape and murder of a 9-year-old girl. He was sentenced to death. In 1993, he was the first person exonerated by DNA and was released from prison after serving 9 years for a crime that he did not commit. What steps can be taken to reduce the number of wrongful convictions?

convicted. However, it is very difficult to identify these cases. In many cases, people are placed on trial even though they allege that they didn't commit the crime, and we do have cases in which offenders are found not guilty. Alas, some of these cases still result in a conviction, and among those cases are innocent individuals who are sent to jail or even sentenced to death.

Research indicates that there are several causes of wrongful conviction. Eyewitness misidentification is the most common cause of wrongful conviction. People remember things in error or think that they see things that couldn't have occurred. But such evidence can be very persuasive to a jury, and as a result, convictions can be handed down on the grounds of testimony by a single eyewitness. Anthony Porter was convicted, in 1983, of a double murder in Chicago, Illinois. His conviction hinged on the testimony of William Taylor. Taylor first stated that he did not see who shot the victims, Marilyn Green and Jerry Hillard. When he arrived at the station, he told police that he did see Porter run by after the shots were fired. Taylor's story subsequently changed again after 17 hours of interrogation by Chicago police, at which point he said that he saw Porter shoot Green and Hillard. In 1998, Taylor recanted his testimony, stating that he was pressured to identify Porter as the shooter. Porter was released in February 1999 after serving more than 17 years on Illinois's death row.[20]

In addition to flawed eyewitness testimony, some of the other causes of wrongful conviction include errors in science, prosecutorial misconduct, and even false confessions. Why would someone confess to a crime that he or she did not commit? In some cases, a defendant may be pressured or coerced to confess to the crime by unethical criminal justice officials. In other cases, a mental defect may lead an individual to confess to a crime. For example, Earl Washington was 22 years old when he was convicted of raping and murdering Rebecca Lynn Williams in Virginia. Washington's IQ was measured at 69, which meant that he was in the lower 5% of the population in terms of intelligence and had the cognitive understanding of an elementary school child. The characteristics of Washington's disability were such that he deferred to authority figures (such as the police) in order to gain their approval. This allowed Washington to be manipulated into giving a false confession based on the crime details provided to the police. In fact, Washington regularly misidentified the details of the crime and had to be taken to the scene of the crime on multiple occasions before he could accurately describe it in his statement. Washington was ultimately exonerated by DNA and released in 2000.[21]

Necessity, Duress, and Entrapment

In some cases, defendants will admit that they broke the law but that their actions were justifiable. Cases of **necessity** suggest that the individual had to break the law in order to prevent a more significant harm from occurring. In these cases, the original violation is considered moot. Consider a case where, in walking by an abandoned building, an individual hears someone scream. The building is locked, and "Do Not Trespass" signs are displayed prominently. However, the individual ignores these signs and breaks a window to gain illegal entry into the building where he or she finds a

Necessity
Refers to cases in which an individual had to break the law in order to prevent a more significant harm from occurring.

CAREERS IN CRIMINAL JUSTICE

So You Want to Be a Defense Attorney?

When someone is accused of either a misdemeanor or a felony crime, the U.S. Constitution guarantees the right to an attorney under the 6th Amendment. In their interpretation of the Constitution, the U.S. Supreme Court has held that if a defendant cannot afford an attorney, the state or federal government is required to provide one. This right was first upheld in the case *Powell v. Alabama* (1932).[a] In *Powell*, the Court reversed the convictions of nine young Black men who had been convicted and sentenced to death for the rape of two White women on a train traveling through Scottsboro, Alabama. Their ruling stated that the right to an attorney is necessary in order to ensure that a defendant receives a fair trial. While the ruling initially applied only to death-eligible cases, the right to an attorney for the indigent was extended to all felony cases in *Gideon v. Wainwright* (1963).[b] You'll learn more about these cases in Chapter 9.

The job of a defense attorney is to ensure that the defendant's rights are upheld and to defend him or her in a criminal case. Defense attorneys can be either retained privately by the defendant or employed by the government as a public defender. As a defense attorney, it is your job to ensure that your client's rights are upheld at every stage of the criminal justice system—from arrest, to the trial, and beyond.

Those who are interested in working as defense counsel attend law school following their undergraduate studies. During law school, students who are interested in careers in this field might intern with a local public defender's office or private office. They must pass the bar exam in the state that they wish to practice law in.

young woman being assaulted. The second offender runs away, and the young woman is spared additional harm. In this case, the courts would view the case of trespass and destruction of property as necessary and justified in order to prevent the assault of the woman. In comparison, someone who engages in a criminal act under **duress** is forced to violate the law out of fear for her or his own safety. In order for duress to be seen as a viable justification, the threat must be serious (generally involving serious bodily injury to oneself or loved ones). In addition, the threat must be immediate, meaning that there is no option to escape.

Entrapment is different from duress and necessity in that it involves the actions of government officials. Entrapment occurs when an individual is deceived by an official (such as a police officer) into engaging in an illegal act. While the police are allowed to use techniques to gain information on a suspect, it is against the law to encourage or persuade someone to break the law in order to make an arrest. The involvement of the defendant must be of his or her own free will and not the result of any pressure or promises made by law enforcement.

Self-Defense

In some cases, individuals may engage in criminal acts in **self-defense**, meaning they feared for their own safety. Cases of self-defense require that the use of force is justified based on the nature of the intrusion. For example, many states have provisions for castle law (otherwise known as "make my day" laws), which allows citizens to protect their homes (and in some cases, their property and workplace). These allow individuals to defend themselves with force, including, in some cases, deadly force, if they feel that their home or the individuals inside the home are under attack. One of the most liberal rules is found in Texas, which allows for the use of lethal force in cases

CAREER VIDEO
Defense Attorney

AUDIO
Make My Day Laws
and Self-Defense

Duress
A defense strategy that describes people who are forced to violate the law out of fear for their own safety or the safety of others around them.

Entrapment
A defense strategy that describes when an individual is deceived by a government official to engage in an act that is against the law.

Self-defense
A defense strategy that allows for the use of force to defend oneself against an attacker.

where an intruder has either unlawfully entered or attempted to enter one's home for any purpose. Other states restrict the use of force to cases in which a person believes that he or she is in physical danger.

Intoxication

> While being under the influence of drugs and/or alcohol is often used as a justification for offending, it is rarely a successful defense strategy.

While being under the influence of drugs and/or alcohol is often used as a justification for offending, it is rarely a successful defense strategy. Under this strategy, defendants argue that they were unable to appreciate the wrongfulness of their actions due to their intoxicated state. The **intoxication** defense hinges on the argument that a person who is under the influence lacks the mens rea to commit a criminal act. Alas, most state laws do not require the prosecution to prove *specific intent*—meaning that the individual intentionally caused the act and intended for that act to lead to a specific result. Rather, most crimes require only *general intent*, which states that the defendant intended to engage in the criminal act, regardless of the outcome of the crime. While involuntary intoxication (meaning that the person did not consent to intoxication) is more likely to be presented as a reasonable defense strategy, success in even these cases is rare.

Insanity

While the depiction of insanity as a criminal defense is present in a number of films and television episodes, the use of it as a defense strategy is rare in the real world. The concept of **insanity** means that an individual is not held responsible for her or his criminal actions as a result of a mental condition. One of the most famous insanity trials in the 20th century was of John Hinckley. Hinckley became infatuated with Jodi Foster when she first appeared as a child prostitute in the film *Taxi Driver*. Hinckley's obsession with Foster continued while she was a student at Yale, but he failed to gain her attention after numerous letters and phone calls. In 1981, Hinckley attempted to assassinate President Ronald Reagan in an effort to impress Foster. He was found not guilty by reason of insanity (NGI) for his crimes and was committed to St. Elizabeths Hospital in Washington, D.C., for treatment. Today, he is allowed extended overnight visits outside of the hospital with his family, though he remains in the custody of the facility. In 2015, Hinckley petitioned the court to allow him to live outside of the facility full-time. Prosecutors continue to oppose this request as they believe that Hinckley remains a potential threat, even though he has been stable for more than 15 years.[22]

The concept of not guilty by reason of insanity has been a feature of law throughout history. The argument was that someone who is insane lacks the mens rea to understand his or her actions and to punish that person would not deter the rest of society.[23] Throughout the 20th century, the American criminal justice system has developed several different standards to determine whether a defendant is insane.

The M'Naghten Rule

The first standard is the M'Naghten rule, which is the foundation for most state definitions of insanity. The **M'Naghten rule** comes from the acquittal of Daniel M'Naghten by the British courts in 1843 for the murder of Edward Drummond. M'Naghten suffered from delusions. The court held that this condition made it such that the defendant was unable to understand the difference between right and wrong. Following the trial, M'Naghten was sent to a local asylum for two decades, until his death. Today, a court that finds a defendant insane under the M'Naghten rule must

Intoxication
A criminal defense that uses being under the influence of drugs or alcohol as a justification for offending.

Insanity
An individual is not held responsible for his or her criminal actions as a result of his or her mental state.

M'Naghten rule
One of the standards of insanity. Refers to situations when the defendant is unable to understand the difference between right and wrong at the time of the crime.

answer two questions: (1) Did the defendant know what he or she was doing at the time of the crime? And (2) did the defendant understand that these actions were wrong? If the answer to both of these questions is no, the defendant is found not guilty by reason of insanity.

The Irresistible Impulse Test

While the M'Naghten rule is still used by many jurisdictions, several states have adopted alternative measures. The **irresistible impulse test** expands the M'Naughten rule to include the issue of control—even though offenders may know that their actions are wrong, are they unable to stop themselves from engaging in the act? The **American Law Institute (ALI) standard** (also referred to as the **model penal code test**) combines the features of the M'Naghten rule and the irresistible impulse test to establish that defendants can be found criminally insane if, as a result of a mental disease or defect, they are unable to understand the difference between right and wrong or to control their behavior.[24] Texas is one state that uses the model penal code as its definition of insanity. Andrea Yates, for example, was initially found guilty for drowning her five children in 2001 in Texas. Her conviction was overturned on appeal as a result of false and misleading evidence that was used against her. She was retried in 2006 and was found not guilty by reason of insanity.

Andrea Yates appears before a Texas court after admitting to drowning her five children in a bathtub at the family home. Her life sentence was overturned on appeal, and she was sent to a mental hospital instead of prison.

VIDEO
Insanity Defense in Sometimes Horrific Crimes Can Lead to Early Release

Guilty but Mentally Ill

Finally there is the distinction of **guilty but mentally ill** (GBMI). This standard was developed to provide an alternative to the NGI verdicts. However, some scholars have questioned whether the GBMI distinction does more harm than good. In particular, does the GBMI classification result in a longer punishment than a traditional guilty plea would give?[25] Unlike NGI cases, GBMI defendants are still sentenced to prison. To date, there have been several high-profile cases involving a ruling of guilty by mentally ill. In 1997, John E. du Pont, an heir to the du Pont fortune, was found guilty but mentally ill for the death of Dave Schultz, who trained and supported several Olympic athletes on du Pont's estate in Pennsylvania.[26] The film *Foxcatcher* (2014), starring Steve Carell, Channing Tatum, and Mark Ruffalo, is based on the story of du Pont and Mark and Dave Schultz.[27]

CONCLUSION

The sources of criminal law guide our systems not only on what acts constitute crimes but also on how the criminal justice system should respond to these violations. From the roots of lex talionis to stare decisis, modern criminal law has been influenced by historical legal traditions. It is important to remember that not only is the law derived from a variety of different sources—which can influence how a crime is defined and processed—but the role of jurisdiction determines which court is charged with responding to the violation. While many of the features of our criminal law have remained constant throughout history, it is also important to remember that it is always growing and changing in response to society's issues and challenges.

Irresistible impulse test
One of the tests of the insanity defense. Expands the M'Naghten rule with the issue of control. Describes the condition that even though an offender may know that an action is wrong, she or he is unable to refrain from engaging in the criminal act.

Model penal code test
Combines the features of the M'Naghten rule and the irresistible impulse test to establish that a defendant can be found criminally insane if, as a result of a mental disease or defect, he or she is unable to understand the difference between right and wrong or to control his or her behavior. Also known as the **American Law Institute standard**.

Guilty but mentally ill
Legal ruling that allows courts to hold an offender guilty for a crime but acknowledges the issues of mental illness as a cause of the criminal behavior.

CURRENT CONTROVERSY 2.1

PRO CON

Should Marijuana Be Legalized?

—Clayton Mosher and Scott Akins—

INTRODUCTION

Marijuana is the most widely used illegal drug in the world. Although the estimates vary widely, globally, between 125 and 203 million people use marijuana,[28] and in the United States, close to half of all residents are estimated to have used marijuana at least once in their lifetime. Between 1980 and 2014, several million people were arrested for marijuana offenses in the United States, the overwhelming majority for simple possession of the substance. For example, in 2011, there were approximately 1.5 million drug arrests in the United States (constituting the highest single category of all arrests). Comparing these data with the 2014 Uniform Crime Reports data, we note that there have not been any changes to the number of drug abuse violations. In contrast, there were 534,704 arrests for all violent crimes combined in 2011 and 498,666 in 2014.[29] Of the approximately 750,000 marijuana arrests in 2011, close to 90% were for possession of the substance. There is also a tremendous racial disparity in marijuana arrests; even though Blacks and Whites are estimated to use marijuana at roughly equivalent rates, Blacks are almost 4 times more likely to be arrested for marijuana offenses than Whites.[30]

 CON   Marijuana Should Not Be Legalized

Under the Controlled Substances Act, passed as part of the Comprehensive Drug Abuse Prevention and Control Act of 1970 (and still in effect today), marijuana is classified as a Schedule I drug (along with heroin, MDMA [ecstasy], and PCP, among other substances). A Schedule I substance is defined as a drug that has "a high potential for abuse, no medical use in the United States, and a lack of accepted safety for use under medical supervision."[31]

Most states created legislation prohibiting marijuana use over the 1900–1930 period, and in 1937, marijuana was effectively banned at the federal level with the passage of the Marijuana Tax Act. This was largely in response to the efforts of Harry Anslinger and the Federal Bureau of Narcotics (FBN, essentially the precursor to the current Drug Enforcement Administration), who engaged in a concerted campaign to demonize marijuana to justify federal legislation banning the substance. Some may recall the movie *Reefer Madness* (produced with the influence of the FBN), in which the FBN emphasized several themes to demonize the substance: the notion that marijuana led to violence and involvement in aberrant sexual behaviors, that its primary users were members of minority groups, that its use led to an array of adverse psychological effects, and that use of the drug was spreading to young people.

Led by federal government agencies such as the Office of National Drug Control Policy (ONDCP) and the National Institute on Drug Abuse (NIDA), in response to the liberalization of marijuana policies, there has been an effort to increase the enforcement of marijuana drug laws. A 2012 ONDCP publication, *What Americans Need to Know About Marijuana*, emphasizes the theory that marijuana is a "gateway" to the use of harder drugs, such as heroin and cocaine, and that the THC (the primary psychoactive ingredient) in marijuana available to consumers today is considerably higher than in the past. NIDA has also expressed concern that the legalization of marijuana will be associated with increases in youth use of the substance. In recent years, there have also been dozens of studies focused on other adverse effects associated with the use of marijuana, many of which have been widely publicized in the media. Some studies have also suggested that marijuana use among youth leads to decreased IQ, brain abnormalities, and mental diseases, such as schizophrenia. Finally, the Food and Drug Administration (FDA) requires that in order for drugs to be shown as safe and effective, they must undergo clinical trials to provide scientific data on their efficacy in treatment. To date, no such trials have been approved by the FDA.[32]

The legalization of marijuana brings additional concerns, such as possible increases in *drugged driving*. Drugged driving could result in slow reaction time, weaving between lanes, and lack of attention to road conditions. According to the 2013–2014 National Roadside Survey, the number of drivers who test positive for THC has increased significantly in recent years, with 12.6% of drivers on weekend nights testing positive. Some have also claimed that marijuana consumption leads to traffic fatalities, using as evidence the fact that in recent years, a higher proportion of those involved in traffic fatalities are found to have marijuana in their system.

Despite its legalization in several states, it is important to reiterate that marijuana remains a Schedule I drug under the Controlled Substances Act, and as such, it is possible that federal government agencies will attempt to thwart the current and future legalization measures at the state level. Given the conflict between federal and state laws, as well as the concerns for public safety, marijuana should remain an illegal substance.

 PRO Marijuana Should Be Legalized

Marijuana's classification as a Schedule I drug is curious, given that the substance has been used for medicinal purposes for possibly thousands of years, and more than 100 articles on its therapeutic uses were published in medical journals between 1840 and 1900. Cannabis was recognized as a medicine in the United States until 1942 and, in some states, could be purchased at pharmacies. As the use of marijuana spread to middle-class youth in the 1960s and 1970s, 11 states removed criminal penalties for those found in possession of the drug. Beginning in 1996 with the state of California, several states enacted legislation allowing for marijuana use for medicinal purposes. As of 2016, 23 states and the District of Columbia allow for the use of marijuana for medicinal purposes, and in recent years, some states (e.g., California, Oregon, Colorado, and Washington) have included marijuana legalization measures on voters' ballots. In the latter two states, the ballot measures passed with approximately 55% of the vote, and recreational use of marijuana became legal for those age 21 and over as of 2016 (Figure 2.3).

Several public opinion polls over the last few years, including polls by the Pew Research Center, Gallup, and the *New York Times*, indicate that the majority of Americans support marijuana legalization, and it is likely that several other states will consider marijuana legalization soon. These marijuana legalization measures are primarily driven by the fact that the baby boomers who consumed marijuana in their youth do not share previous generations' fear of the substance and by state governments, which are seeking alternative sources of revenue (by taxing marijuana production and sales) in light of economic crises.

While some research has suggested that the legalization of marijuana may lead to increased harm in society, critics of these studies have pointed out that there are problems with respect to determining causal order—for example, does cannabis use increase the risk of schizophrenia, or are those with schizophrenia predisposed to using cannabis? Indeed, the research on marijuana use and traffic fatalities suffers from the same condition. The science with respect to this issue by no means definitively proves that increases in marijuana use will lead to more traffic fatalities and collisions.

In recent years, many jurisdictions have been faced with the legalization or decriminalization of marijuana. Here, residents participate in a protest against the criminalization of marijuana. What effect does public opinion have on the legalization debate?

Figure 2.3 Marijuana Laws in 50 States as of 2015

How does the state you live in regulate marijuana use?

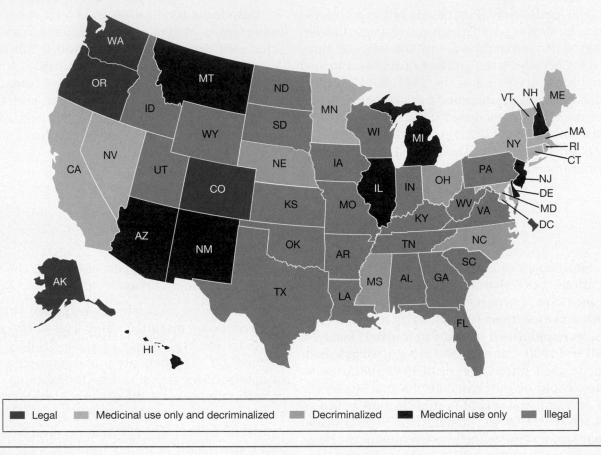

| ■ Legal | ■ Medicinal use only and decriminalized | ■ Decriminalized | ■ Medicinal use only | ■ Illegal |

Source: Pew Research Center

Even in cases of marijuana use and traffic fatalities, it is not clear that the marijuana use caused the collision that led to the fatality. And in some cases, marijuana legalization has not led to increased risk of harm. In fact, a study of trends in traffic fatalities in the state of Colorado following marijuana legalization found that these were at "near historic lows," and a study of the impact of medical marijuana laws on traffic fatalities in states with such laws similarly found decreases in fatalities. The authors of the latter study claimed that the decrease in traffic fatalities was largely due to the fact that the legalization of medical marijuana was associated with reduced alcohol consumption, especially among adults.

Finally, legalization of marijuana does not necessarily mean that use of the substance will increase. Here we can look at how the use of marijuana shifted with the legalization of medical marijuana. A study of states that allow medical marijuana use found no significant increase in adolescent marijuana use within two to three years following the passage of medical marijuana laws. While there have been substantial increases in treatment admissions for marijuana for both adults and youth, it is important to note that the overwhelming majority of these admissions were mandated by the criminal or juvenile justice systems. Does this mean that the substance is more dangerous, or are we simply shifting our response to these cases?

In a December 2012 interview with Barbara Walters, in reference to the legalization measures in Colorado and Washington, President Obama stated, "We've got bigger fish to fry. It would not make sense for us to see a top priority as going after recreational users in states that have determined it's legal."[33] It is likely that several other states will consider marijuana legalization in the coming years. If additional states legalize the use of recreational marijuana (as is likely to happen), will the federal government intervene? It remains to be seen how authorities will respond to these changes in law at the state level.

DISCUSSION QUESTIONS

1. What purposes are served by maintaining marijuana as an illegal substance?

2. If marijuana is legalized by states, what types of laws should be put in place to regulate its use?

3. What lessons can we learn from the legalization and decriminalization of marijuana around the United States and abroad?

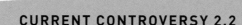

CURRENT CONTROVERSY 2.2

PRO CON

Should Miranda Warnings Be Abolished?
—Craig Hemmens—

CURRENT
CONTROVERSY
VIDEO
Where Do You Stand?
Cast Your Vote!

INTRODUCTION

The 5th Amendment provides that persons shall not be compelled to incriminate themselves. While self-incrimination cannot be compelled, it is permitted. A significant number of cases are solved through obtaining incriminating statements from the suspect. The standard for admissibility of a confession was, until the decision in *Miranda v. Arizona*, voluntariness. Precisely what constituted a voluntary statement was determined on a case-by-case basis by the Supreme Court. The Court determined that police use of physical force, mental coercion, and extended interrogation in isolation all rendered confession involuntary. But what about confessions obtained voluntarily? Was there any limit on these? In *Miranda v. Arizona*, the Court held that evidence obtained by the police during a custodial interrogation of a suspect could not be used at trial unless the suspect first was informed of both his privilege against self-incrimination (the so-called "right to remain silent") and his right to counsel. Miranda is probably one of the most controversial criminal procedure decisions ever handed down by the Supreme Court, in large part because police feared it would lead to a dramatic reduction in confessions.

In *Miranda*, the Supreme Court did not merely hold that police must inform suspects of their rights; the Court set forth exactly what the police should say—suspects must be told the following: (1) They have a right to remain silent, (2) anything they say can be used against them in court, (3) they have a right to have an attorney present during questioning, and (4) if they cannot afford an attorney, one will be appointed for them prior to any questioning.

The Miranda warnings are required when there is a *custodial interrogation*. Custody has been defined as when the suspect has been either arrested or subject to the functional equivalent of arrest, which the Court has defined as a situation in which a reasonable person in the suspect's position would conclude that he or she is not free to leave. Interrogation occurs when the police are asking questions, the answers to which may incriminate, or when the police, through their actions, create the functional equivalent of an interrogation. The police create the functional equivalent of an interrogation when they engage in activity they know is likely to evoke an incriminating response from the suspect. If there is not both custody and interrogation, Miranda warnings are not required.

As a result of Supreme Court decisions, the police must read arrested persons the Miranda Warning. The police will also ask accused persons whether they understand their rights and, having these rights in mind, do they wish to talk to the police. Are Miranda warnings required for every arrest?

© Can Stock Photo Inc./lisafx

Chapter 2 • Concepts of Law and Justice   41

The Supreme Court has decided more than 50 cases involving the Miranda warnings.[34] Most of these decisions have restricted the reach of *Miranda*. Additionally, the rights mentioned in the Miranda warnings may be waived by the suspect so long as the written waiver is "voluntary, knowing, and intelligent," meaning that the suspect is fully informed and understands the possible consequences of waiving his or her rights and does so free of any coercion.

Miranda v. Arizona has had a huge impact on police practices and the investigation of criminal activity. Supporters of the Miranda decision hailed it as properly protective of individual rights, whereas critics accused the Court of being soft on crime and coddling criminals.

 PRO   **Miranda Warnings Should Be Abolished**

Opponents of the Miranda warnings set forth several reasons why the warnings should be abolished. These include the following:

1. Informing suspects of their right to remain silent will lead to some or many suspects not speaking with the police and therefore not incriminating themselves. This will make police work much more difficult, as many cases are solved only because the police are able to obtain a confession.

   Con: This argument would seem strong from a "common sense" perspective, as one would expect people not to speak if doing so could hurt their position. But history indicates this is not the case—suspects confess at rates similar to those before Miranda and have done so for more than 50 years. It appears criminals are not always rational or smart.

2. Fewer confessions will lead to fewer convictions, which will lead to some wrongdoers going unpunished and reduce public safety.

   Con: As with the first point, time has proven this incorrect—requiring police to issue the Miranda warnings has not reduced the number of confessions and thus not reduced the number of convictions.

3. The existence of the warnings sends the symbolic message that the rights of criminals are more important than public safety and erodes public confidence in courts. The public, often ill informed about criminal justice procedures, tends to have a low opinion of the courts in general.

   Con: On the other hand, there is much to be said for the rule of law and requiring the government to "play fair" when dealing with citizens, including those who commit crimes.

4. While there may have, at one time, been a need to impose rules on the police, police today are much better educated, better trained, and more professional. Restrictive bright-line rules intended to constrain out-of-control police officers are no longer needed.

   Con: It is no doubt true that police are much improved in all aspects than they were prior to the *Miranda* decision. It is unclear whether eliminating the Miranda warnings would result in police efforts to avoid following the Constitution, but it is not unreasonable to assume police will generally do whatever they can, within the rules, to get a conviction. Allowing the police to avoid the Miranda warnings will no doubt result in the police doing just that.

5. The Supreme Court misinterpreted the 5th Amendment, which does not ban self-incrimination, just compelled self-incrimination—and this refers to physical or psychological torture, not asking questions of a suspect. Nothing in the 5th Amendment (or any other provision of the Bill of Rights) says a suspect has to be told of her or his rights.

   Con: This argument has a strong legal foundation, but it is unclear whether the public would understand the distinction.

Miranda Warnings Should Not Be Abolished

Supporters of the Miranda warnings set forth several reasons why the warnings should continue to be required. These include the following:

1. Informing suspects of their right to remain silent has not reduced the number of confessions and thus has not hampered the use of confessions to solve cases.

   Con: This is accurate, but the counterargument is that it is silly to help criminals by telling them they have the right to stay quiet; obviously, some criminals do take advantage of this opportunity and make it harder for the police to obtain incriminating evidence.

2. Without the Miranda warnings, police could, if they chose, engage in a number of coercive activities in an attempt to elicit incriminating information. While these practices are less likely today, given the increase in police professionalism and standards, there is no reason to risk a return to the bad old days.

Con: This argument assumes the police will do whatever they can to obtain convictions, even if doing so means infringing on the rights of suspects. It seems reasonable to assume this is less likely to, in fact, occur, given the greater degree of police education, training, and professionalism.

3. Requiring the warnings is an important symbolic message that the criminal justice system is built upon the rule of law and that the state, with its awesome power and resources, will not use an individual's weakness against him or her. It increases public confidence that the court and the state "play fair." This is a strong argument, based on the assumption that the rule of law is more important than the outcome in a particular case.

   Con: There are many, however, who disagree. They feel that justice in an individual case should always be the paramount objective of society and that bright-line rules make it difficult to achieve justice in particular cases.

SUMMARY

The *Miranda* decision remains a controversial criminal justice–related decision issued by the Supreme Court. Its detractors have long argued that its focus on the rights of a suspect mistakenly downplays the impact on society that provision of the warnings has. One would think that telling suspects they do not have to talk to the police would result in fewer confessions and make it more difficult to convict wrongdoers. The evidence indicates otherwise, however. Suspects, for whatever reason, often incriminate themselves even after they have been warned. While the Supreme Court has settled the debate over whether the Miranda warnings are required by the Constitution or are just a rule of evidence, does this decision make sense legally? Police departments have proven adept at finding (legal) ways to work around the limits imposed by the warnings, and the Supreme Court has frequently endorsed those actions, repeatedly narrowing the reach of *Miranda*. Given these contradictions, are Miranda warnings here to stay?

DISCUSSION QUESTIONS

1. Why did the Supreme Court feel the need to require the police to issue Miranda warnings? Do the reasons for requiring the warnings that existed in the 1960s still exist today?

2. How does requiring the police to issue the Miranda warnings affect public perception of the criminal justice system?

3. How does requiring the police to issue the Miranda warnings protect society? How does it weaken public safety?

KEY TERMS

Actus reus 32	Guilty but mentally ill 37	Necessity 34
Administrative law 28	Innocence 33	Opinions 30
American Law Institute standard 37	Insanity 36	Plaintiff 24
Attendant circumstances 32	Intent 32	Precedent 27
Beyond a reasonable doubt 25	Intoxication 36	Preponderance of the evidence 24
Case law 30	Irresistible impulse test 37	Procedural criminal law 33
Civil law 24	Lex talionis 26	Result 32
Concurrence 32	M'Naghten rule 36	Self-Defense 35
Constitutional law 27	Mala in se 30	Stare decisis 27
Defense 33	Mala prohibita 31	Statutory law 28
Duress 35	Mens rea 32	Strict liability 32
Entrapment 35	Model penal code test 37	Substantive criminal law 32

DISCUSSION QUESTIONS

1. What are the key differences between civil and criminal cases?

2. How do statutory law, case law, and constitutional law all work together?

3. What are the components of a criminal act?

4. How is substantive law related to procedural law?

5. What is the difference between being declared innocent and being declared not guilty?

6. Why is it so difficult to find someone not guilty by reason of insanity?

LEARNING ACTIVITIES

1. Review the criminal code in your state. Identify a particular crime, and determine the four components of the criminal act under the law.

2. Identify a U.S. Supreme Court decision related to a criminal justice issue from the most recent term. How did the court reach its decision?

What implications does this decision have for the system?

3. Select an article from the newspaper about a crime. What are the *actus reus*, *mens rea*, attendant circumstances, and result of this crime? Is this crime *mala in se* or *mala prohibita*?

SUGGESTED WEBSITES

- **U.S. Supreme Court:** http://www.supremecourt.gov
- **U.S. Constitution:** https://www.congress.gov/constitution-annotated
- **U.S. Code Title 18, Crimes and Criminal Procedure:** https://www.law.cornell.edu/uscode/text/18/part-I

STUDENT STUDY SITE

3

DEFINING AND MEASURING CRIME

LEARNING OBJECTIVES

- Identify the six different categories of crime

- Compare the differences between the Uniform Crime Reports, the National Incident-Based Reporting System, and the National Crime Victimization Survey

- Explain how crime rates are used to understand the prevalence of crime in society

- Assess how self-report studies of crime provide a different perspective on offending

In 2012, the city of Chicago registered 500 homicides, leading some to characterize the city as the murder capital of the country.[1] Certainly, there was a kernel of truth to this characterization.[2] Chicago had the highest murder count nationwide that year. This means that there were more murders in Chicago compared with other cities, such as New York City or Los Angeles. However, crime data can be deceiving. Chicago actually had fewer homicides in 2013—88 fewer deaths. In 2015, the murder rate for the city was the lowest since 1965.[3] Cities such as Detroit, Michigan; New Orleans, Louisiana; and Jackson, Mississippi, all had higher rates of homicide than Chicago when you take into account the populations of these cities. With more than 2.7 million residents, it is reasonable to assume that there will be a greater number of crimes compared with many other cities in the United States.[4]

What has led to the changes in Chicago's crime rate? Police have cited an increased police presence on the streets, targeted enforcement of gang activity, and an increase in community youth programs. Meanwhile, others have suggested that recent years are not reflective of the overall trend in the city and nationwide—that violent crime has decreased since the early 1990s.[5] Still others cite concerns about the way in which crimes are classified, which may provide inaccurate perceptions about whether crime is really decreasing.[6] Given the different voices on this issue, what should Chicago residents believe about crime and violence in their city?

What effect do you think an increased police presence may have had on the crime rate in Chicago?

VIDEO
Chicago's 2016 Killings

In Chapter 2, you learned that a crime is an act that goes against the law. In this sense, crimes can be harmful to either an individual or the community at large. In many cases, there are punishments associated with these violations. This chapter begins with a review of the different types of crime and how we classify these offenses. The chapter then turns to a discussion of how crime is measured in society. You'll learn about the different official sources of crime data, such as the Uniform Crime Reports, the National Incident-Based Reporting System, and the National Crime Victimization Survey, as well as self-reported studies of crime. You'll also learn about international databases of crime that can be used to understand the presence of crime around the world. The chapter concludes with two Current Controversy debates. The first, by Henry N. Pontell, Gilbert Geis, Adam Ghazi-Tehrani, and Bryan Burton, looks at whether white-collar crime is considered harmful to society. The second, by Phillip Kopp, asks whether burglary should be considered a violent crime.

DEFINING CRIME

Even though we look at crime as a general category, there are several different categories of crime. Each of these categories contains several different types of crimes. In this book, crimes are organized into six categories: violent offenses, property offenses, status offenses, victimless crimes, white-collar offenses, and crimes against the government.

Violent Offenses

Violent offenses generally involve a criminal action against another person. When people tend to talk about crime, it is violent offenses that are typically the first that come to mind. Certainly, violent crime plays a major role in both fictionalized and true-crime portrayals and is responsible for much of the public's fear of crime and victimization. Despite the high degree of attention that is given to violent crime, these acts are much less common than other forms of crime. Murder is a great example of this phenomenon.

> Even though the crime of murder invokes high levels of fear among the public, it is the least common type of crime.

Murder

Murder involves the killing of one human being by another. Even though the crime of murder invokes high levels of fear among the public, it is the least common type of crime. Murder also carries with it the most serious penalty; depending on the laws of the region where the crime was committed and the circumstances of the crime, an offender may be put to death as punishment. Within the crime of murder, there are several different degrees or classifications, in terms of severity and responsibility, to help distinguish different acts from each other. While the laws vary from state to state, murder can generally be classified into four subcategories:

- First-degree murder—generally includes acts that are premeditated, committed with malice, or committed during the commission of a felony.

- Second-degree murder—includes acts that are not premeditated or planned and do not involve torture.

- Voluntary manslaughter—involves acts in which the offender intended to take someone's life, but there are mitigating circumstances that might excuse or minimize the actions of the offender. For example, crimes of passion are generally considered voluntary manslaughter.

Violent offenses
Crimes that typically involve acts against another person.

Murder
A crime that involves the killing of one human being by another.

- Involuntary manslaughter—involves acts in which there was no intent to take someone's life, but the loss of life occurred due to negligence. For example, someone who drives while under the influence of alcohol and causes an accident that results in the death of another has committed involuntary manslaughter.

Sexual Assault

Another set of crimes that falls within the category of violent crime is **rape and sexual assault**. These acts involve sexual activity without consent. In many jurisdictions, the definition of rape involves unwanted penile–vaginal sexual contact or penetration, whereas sexual assault is considered a general term for all other forms of unwanted

Contrary to what is seen on popular crime dramas, murder occurs less often than other types of crimes. Why do you think this difference exists, and how might it affect the public's perception of crime?

sexual contact, including genital fondling, forced oral copulation, sodomy, and penetration by a foreign object, among others. Many states also have laws prohibiting sexual contact with someone who is unable to consent due to intoxication or disability. Offenders who are in a position of trust (such as a teacher or clergy member) or who engage in multiple acts of sexual assault may be prosecuted under specific laws that allow for enhanced penalties. Finally, laws may also be distinguished by the age of the victim, as in the cases of child rape or molestation. However, not all sexually based offenses are considered violent crimes. Unlike other forms of violent sexual assault, **statutory rape** generally involves someone who is legally unable to consent to sexual activity due to her or his age. Statutory rape is considered a strict liability crime. As you learned in Chapter 2, a strict liability crime does not require someone to have mens rea in order for an act to be against the law. Some would consider the crime of statutory rape a victimless crime, as individuals in these cases often do not define themselves as victims. Rather, they see themselves as willing participants in sexual activity. It is purely the legal distinction of who can and cannot consent that makes these acts crimes. For example, the age of sexual consent in California is 18, and anyone under 18 who engages in intercourse is in violation of the state's statutory rape law. So two 17-year-olds who engage in intercourse would be breaking the law.

Assault

Perhaps the most common form of violent crime is assault. **Assault** involves the physical harm (or the threat of physical harm) of a victim. Cases of assault are generally divided into two categories. Cases of *simple assault* generally do not involve the use of a weapon and minor, if any, injuries, whereas cases of *aggravated assault* may involve serious injury to the victim or the use of a weapon. For example, a bar fight between two individuals is often considered a simple assault. However, if one of the individuals pulls out a knife and stabs the other person during the fight, this would be considered an aggravated assault.

Robbery

The last type of violent crime is robbery. **Robbery** involves taking personal property from someone through the use of force or fear. In some cases, a weapon might be used to facilitate a robbery. Robbery is often confused with the crime of burglary. While both involve the taking of personal property, the crime of robbery involves

AUDIO
Steubenville
Teen Rape Case

Rape and sexual assault
A crime that involves sexual activity without consent.

Statutory rape
A crime that involves sexual activity with someone who is legally unable to consent to sexual activity due to her or his age.

Assault
A crime that involves the physical harm (or threat) to a victim.

Robbery
A crime that involves taking personal property from someone through the use of force or fear.

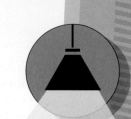

SPOTLIGHT

The Steubenville High School Rape Case

Steubenville, Ohio, is a small town located along the Ohio River. According to the 2012 census, the town had only 18,429 residents, 79% of whom are White.[a] Sporting events at the local high school are popular community events, and Steubenville High School stands as one of the best football programs among high schools in the country and has won three state championships.

In August 2012, Steubenville was thrust into the national spotlight after a 16-year-old girl was sexually assaulted by several of her peers. What made this case particularly noteworthy is that her assault was videotaped, and her assailants posted the video on social-media sites, such as YouTube and Twitter. In the photos and videos, two Steubenville High football team members, Trent Mays and Ma'lik Richmond (both 16 at the time of the offense), are shown carrying the victim by her hands and feet, as she was so intoxicated that she was unable to walk. Video also documents the accused penetrating the victim's vagina with their fingers and flashing her breasts to the camera.[b] While under many state laws this would be considered sexual assault, Ohio's state law includes digital penetration under its definition of rape.[c]

Many blamed the victim (who was so intoxicated that she did not know she had been violated until she saw the photos and videos online) and called her a "train whore." Even one of the football coaches joined in on the blaming, stating, "What else are you going to tell your parents when you come home drunk like that and after a night like that? She had to make up something. Now people are trying to blow up our football program because of it."[d] During the trial, the defense counsel introduced testimony that tried to paint the victim as culpable in her own attack by calling two former friends who testified that the victim not only had a history of drinking in excess but also told contradictory stories about the events of the evening.[e]

The judge found that the victim was so intoxicated that she lacked the cognitive ability to consent to sexual activity.[f] Both Mays and Richmond were found guilty in juvenile court and sentenced to one year in the state juvenile correctional facility. Mays received an additional one-year sentence for the crime of distributing nude images of a minor.[g] In her report of the verdict, CNN reporter Poppy Harlow critiqued the court's decision, stating that it had been "incredibly difficult [to watch] as these two young men—who had such promising futures, star football players, very good students—literally watched as they believed their life fell apart."[h] On January 7, 2014, Richmond was released from custody after serving nine months of his sentence. Even though he was sentenced in the juvenile court, he is required to register as a sex offender for the next 20 years.[i] Mays remains incarcerated.

In addition to charging the assailants, officials have questioned whether bystanders and others involved in the event should be charged with a crime. What about those who were not in attendance but shared photos and videos of the assault? What is their responsibility? These are people whose social-media commentary included statements such as "The song of the night is Rape Me by Nirvana" and "Some people just deserve to be peed on."[j] While none of these individuals have been charged with any crimes, the case does not end with Mays

Trent Mays and Ma'lik Richmond appear in juvenile court in Steubenville, Ohio. Mays and Richmond were adjudicated delinquent of rape in a case that highlighted the use of social media and victimization. Should others who were involved have been held accountable for these crimes?

and Richmond, as several school personnel have been indicted by a grand jury on charges related to the rape case. William Rhinaman, who served as the school's information technology director, and Superintendent Michael McVey have been indicted on charges that include tampering with evidence, obstruction of justice, obstructing official business, and perjury. Matthew Belardine, a volunteer football coach, was charged with allowing underage drinking and contributing to the delinquency of a child. In addition, two teenage girls received 6 months probation for threating the victim with bodily harm on Facebook and Twitter.[k]

CRITICAL THINKING QUESTIONS

1. How should these criminal acts be defined under the UCR, NIBRS, and NCVS? Do you believe that our data sources accurately capture these crimes?

2. How has social media altered the way in which we identify and apprehend offenders of crimes? How has it changed the way we think about victims of crime?

a face-to-face confrontation, whereas someone can be burglarized without being present. Crimes such as carjacking or purse snatching are examples of robbery.

Property Offenses

Property crimes are the most common criminal offense and involve the taking or damage of physical goods. Within this classification, there are several types of crimes. In the previous section, you learned a bit about burglary, which is considered a property crime. **Burglary** occurs when someone enters a building or other physical space (residence, business, or car) with the intent of taking property without permission. Note that the crime of burglary does not require that anything be taken, and it is the act of entering without permission that constitutes the crime. You'll learn more about the crime of burglary in Current Controversy 3.2 at the end of this chapter. The most common property crime is larceny-theft. **Larceny-theft** involves the taking of property without the use of force. Larceny-theft includes shoplifting and motor vehicle theft and can also be combined with acts of burglary in cases where property is taken during the course of unlawfully entering a building. Finally, acts such as vandalism and arson are also considered property crimes. **Vandalism** involves the destruction or damage of a physical structure or building. For example, smashing storefront windows during a riot is considered an act of vandalism. In comparison, the crime of **arson**

Property crimes
Crimes that involve the taking of or damage to physical goods.

Burglary
A crime that occurs when someone enters a building or other physical space with the intent of taking property without permission.

Larceny-theft
A crime that involves the taking of property without the use of force.

Vandalism
A crime that involves the destruction or damage of a physical structure or building.

Arson
A crime that involves the destruction of a physical structure or item by fire.

Of the two crimes depicted above, which would be considered robbery, and why?

involves the destruction of a physical structure or item (such as a home, business, or automobile) by fire.

Status Offenses

Status offenses are acts that are considered illegal for only certain groups of offenders. Status offenses are most commonly committed by juveniles, and certain acts are defined as illegal only because of the offender's age. Examples of status offenses include truancy (skipping school), underage consumption of alcohol, and running away from home. Historically, juveniles could be institutionalized for engaging in these illegal acts. Today, these acts can lead to intervention by the juvenile court. You'll learn more about these offenses and the response by the juvenile justice system in Chapter 12.

Victimless Crimes

Victimless crimes are acts that are considered illegal under the law but do not involve victims in the traditional sense. In many cases, the offenders engage in acts that are harmful only to themselves or that are consensual. For example, the use of illicit substances is considered illegal under the law. However, some question whether **drug use** is a victimless crime. As a stand-alone offense, drug use is harmful to an individual. However, addiction can have collateral consequences and lead to other criminal offenses to support a drug habit. Drugs can also have large-scale implications for communities. So it remains to be seen whether drug use is a victimless crime. Another crime that is often considered victimless is prostitution. **Prostitution** involves the exchange of sexual favors for money or other resources. While there are certainly acts of prostitution that are considered consensual, others involve the exploitation of individuals or compelling people to engage in sexual behaviors against their will (such as human trafficking). As with drugs, some scholars question whether prostitution is a victimless crime, as some may find themselves turning to these acts out of economic necessity or addiction. **Gambling** is also considered a victimless crime, as it involves a wager of money or other valuable goods in hopes of increasing one's financial status. Unlike most criminal acts, gambling is a regulated business and is legal under specific circumstances. For example, gambling is legal in states such as Nevada and New Jersey and is also allowed on tribal lands. However, gambling also occurs illegally and is considered a federal crime if the organization of gambling activities is part of a business. For example, it is legal to host a poker party in a private residence for your friends. However, if you charge a fee to play and end up making a profit on that fee or offer other gambling options in which the odds are in your favor (such as blackjack), then it is considered illegal.

Marginal Definitions

Status offenses
Refers to acts that are considered illegal for only certain groups of offenders based on their age.

Victimless crimes
Crimes that involve acts of self-harm or consensual behaviors.

Drug use
A crime that involves the use of illegal or illicit substances.

Prostitution
A crime that involves the exchange of sexual favors for money or other resources.

Gambling
A crime that involves the wager of money or other valuable goods in hopes of improving one's financial status.

White-collar crime
Describes a category of offenses that traditionally occur within the corporate field.

White-Collar Offenses

The term **white-collar crime** describes a category of offenses that traditionally occur within corporate and related fields and includes a diverse range of criminal and civil offenses—fraud, embezzlement, corruption, insider trading, malpractice, misconduct, tech-based offenses, extortion, bribery, and deception.[7] White-collar crimes are unique in a number of different ways from many of the other offenses that dominate our criminal justice system. First, white-collar

Martha Stewart was convicted of obstruction of justice related to the sale of her shares of ImClone stock. She was sentenced to 5 months in prison and 5 months house arrest. Though her case received extensive media attention, most white-collar cases do not. Why do you think that is?

crimes generally do not garner the same type of attention as street crimes. Second, white-collar crime usually involves significant amounts of money. Offenders tend to be adults from middle-class and upper-class backgrounds and often involved in large-scale corporate organizations. For example, the Enron energy scandal involved significant acts of corporate and accounting fraud, which led to inflated assets and stock profits for its natural gas and water utilities.[8] Similarly, the recent mortgage industry meltdown involved several banks, including JPMorgan Chase, Bank of America, and Citigroup.[9] Finally, white-collar crimes involve both criminal and civil law violations, although the criminal punishments typically involve significantly shorter sentences compared with traditional violent and property crime offenders. Several of the key players in Enron were sent to prison. Jeffrey Skilling, the ex-CEO of Enron, was originally sentenced to 24 years but later saw his sentence reduced to 14 years[10] while several others entered guilty pleas. Meanwhile, the settlements with the major banks in the subprime-loan crisis have been primarily limited to the financial arena.[11]

White-collar crimes often escape public attention because they are not violent events. However, these acts have significant financial costs, to both individuals and the larger economy. Consider the example above involving the Enron scandal. Many people who invested their savings and retirement plans in Enron stock, based on its inflated performance figures, saw their investments crash, which subsequently jeopardized their financial safety. Generally speaking, the financial effects of white-collar crime outnumber all other crimes. Research indicates that street crimes, such as violent and property crimes, cost $17.6 billion annually. Certainly, this is a significant amount of money. However, compare these costs with the estimated $250 billion each year that is lost as a result of white-collar crimes (Figure 3.1). In addition, white-collar crimes don't stop just because someone goes to prison, as the effects of this victimization are both widespread and long lasting.[12] You'll learn more about white-collar crime and its effects in the Current Controversy debate at the end of this chapter.

SAGE JOURNAL ARTICLE
The Trajectory of
White-Collar Crime

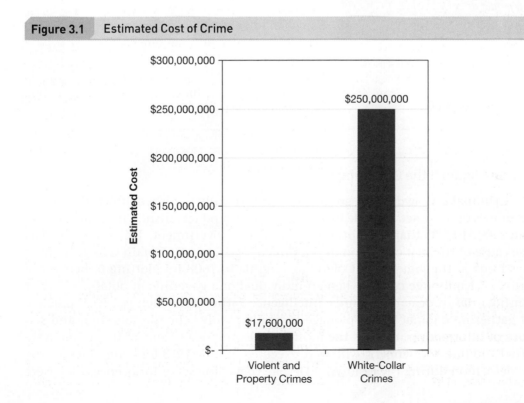

Figure 3.1   Estimated Cost of Crime

SPOTLIGHT

The Boston Marathon Bombing

On April 15, 2013, three people were killed and more than 260 were injured after two bombs exploded at the finish line of the Boston Marathon. In the days after the attacks, Tamerlan Tsarnaev and Dzhokhar A. Tsarnaev were identified as suspects. In their attempt to avoid the police, the Tsarnaev brothers robbed a gas station, killed Sean Collier (an MIT campus police officer), and carjacked an SUV. During a shootout with local police, Tamerlan Tsarnaev was shot several times and was run over by the stolen SUV by his brother Dzhokhar. Tamerlan died as a result of these wounds. In their attempt to locate Dzhokhar, the city was essentially shut down as residents were ordered to shelter-in-place and businesses closed their doors while law enforcement embarked on a search to find him. He was located the next evening by authorities and was taken into custody.[a]

In June 2013, Dzhokhar Tsarnaev was indicted on 30 counts related to using weapons of mass destruction to commit murder in an act of terrorism.[b] In January 2014, the Department of Justice announced that it would seek the death penalty against Tsarnaev. What makes this decision particularly interesting is that the state of Massachusetts is a strong advocate against the death penalty. There has not been an execution in the state since 1947, and the state's supreme court declared capital punishment unconstitutional in 1984.[c] A poll by the *Boston Globe* found that 57% of those surveyed support a sentence of life without the possibility of parole for Tsarnaev while only 33% favor the death penalty.[d] Federal prosecutors have only sought the death penalty in Massachusetts on three occasions, and only once has a case ultimately been tried as death eligible and resulted in a conviction. A federal jury sentenced serial killer Gary Lee Sampson to death in 2003. Tsarnaev was found guilty and sentenced to death by a federal jury in April 2015. Recently, his lawyers filed an appeal of his sentence, arguing that it was prejudicial to hold the trial in Boston.[e]

Boston Marathon bombing survivor Jeff Bauman throws out the first pitch at a Boston Red Sox game, one year after the bombing. Several individuals lost limbs in the bombing, and three died as a result of their injuries. Should victims and their families have a greater role in sentencing decisions?

Crimes Against the Government

Criminal acts against the government are typically punished under federal law. Examples of these acts include treason, espionage, and terrorism. The crime of **treason** refers to acts that attempt to overthrow the government. Treason is noted as the cause of the first execution in the United States, when Captain George Kendall was hung at the Jamestown Colony in Virginia in 1608 for plotting to betray the British.[13] **Espionage** occurs when an individual or a government obtains secret or confidential information. Unlike intelligence gathering, which is a legal practice of gathering data, acts of espionage typically involve the illegal search and seizure of information. Perhaps the most famous American icons of this crime were Ethel and Julius Rosenberg, who were executed in June 1953 for being spies for the Soviet Union during the Cold War. Despite their protests of innocence, they were

Treason
A crime that involves acts that attempt to overthrow the government.

Espionage
A crime that occurs when an individual or a government obtains secret or confidential information.

convicted of conspiracy to commit espionage for passing top-secret information to the USSR about the atomic bomb.[14] While these two crimes can sound very similar, espionage involves acting as a spy for or against the government, whereas treason refers to betraying one's country by working against the government. Depending on the nature of their actions, offenders can be charged with both treason and espionage.

AUDIO
Who Are America's "Homegrown Terrorists"?

While crimes such as espionage and treason appear to be relics of history, the crime of terrorism occupies a significantly greater space in the mind-set of Americans. Acts of **terrorism** involve acts of violence with the goal of instilling fear within residents. Such acts are perpetrated in the name of a political objective. While most people primarily associate terrorism with the acts of September 11, 2001, the reality is that acts of terror are far more common than we perceive. Prior to the events of 9/11, the bombing of the Alfred P. Murrah Federal Building in Oklahoma City, Oklahoma, on April 19, 1995, by Timothy McVeigh and Terry Nichols was the largest act of terrorism on American soil. One hundred and sixty-eight people were killed in the attack, and another 650 people were injured.[15] Other significant acts of terrorism in the United States include the first bombing of the World Trade Center in 1993; the acts of Theodore Kaczynski, otherwise known as the Unabomber; and the Boston Marathon bombing. Acts of terror against Americans have also occurred abroad, such as the bombing of the USS *Cole* in 2000 and the midair bombing of Pam Am Flight 103 in 1988, which was en route from London to New York when it exploded over Lockerbie, Scotland. You'll learn more about these events and the global response to terrorism in Chapter 14.

VIDEO
Terrorism Threats

UNIFORM CRIME REPORTS

In order to develop an understanding of the extent of criminal activity, it is important to look at how information about crime is gathered. While there is no one dataset that tells us everything that we want to know about crime, we can learn something from each source, as each represents a different point of view. Datasets vary based on the type of information collected (quantitative and/or qualitative), who manages the dataset (such as government agencies, professional scholars, or community organizations), and the purpose for the data collection. Finally, each dataset represents a picture of crime for a specific population, region, and time frame or stage of the criminal justice system.

> While there is no one dataset that tells us everything that we want to know about crime, we can learn something from each source, as each represents a different point of view.

The **Uniform Crime Reports** (UCR) represent one of the largest datasets on crime in the United States. Since 1930, the Federal Bureau of Investigation (FBI) has been responsible for collecting and publishing the arrest data from police agencies in the United States. These statistics are published annually and present the rates and volume of crime by offense type, based on arrests made by police. The dataset includes a number of demographic variables to evaluate these crime statistics, including age, gender, race/ethnicity, location (state), and region (metropolitan, suburban, or rural). UCR data give us a general understanding of the extent of crime in the United States and are often viewed as the most accurate assessment of crime. In addition, the UCR data allow us to compare how crime changes over time by comparing arrest data over a specific time frame or from one year to the next. Generally speaking, it is data from the UCR findings that are typically reported to the greater society through news media outlets, and they form the basis for headline stories that proclaim the rising and falling rates of crime.

Terrorism
A crime that involves acts of violence with the goal of instilling fear.

Uniform Crime Reports
One of the largest datasets on crime. Based on police arrest and reporting data.

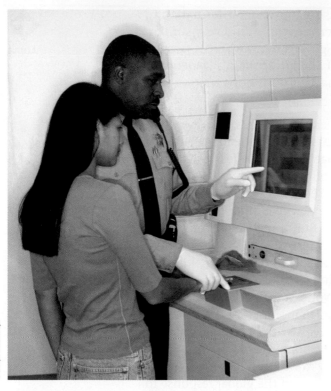

Most official crime statistics are based on arrest data. Here, a female is fingerprinted as part of the arrest process. Considering that not all individuals who are arrested are guilty of a crime, what are some of the challenges of using arrest rates to measure crime?

WEB LINK
Federal Bureau of Investigation (FBI) Uniform Crime Reports

Type 1 offenses
Also known as index crimes under the Uniform Crime Reports. Includes eight specific crime categories: murder, aggravated assault, rape and sexual assault, robbery, burglary, motor vehicle theft, larceny-theft, and arson.

Crime rate
A calculation that compares the number of crimes with the size of the population. Allows for standardized comparisons across time and space.

Data Collected

The Uniform Crime Reporting Program organizes its collection of crime data into two categories. Much of the focus of the UCR is on **Type 1 offenses**, also known as index crimes. Type 1 crimes include eight separate offenses that are divided into two categories: violent crime and property crime. Within the category of violent crime, data is collected on four crimes: murder, aggravated assault, rape and sexual assault, and robbery, whereas the category of property crime includes data on burglary, motor vehicle theft, larceny/theft, and arson. For each of these offenses, agencies report on the number of crimes known to the police, the number of arrests made, and the age, race, and sex of the offender. Arrest data is also collected on several lesser criminal events (known as Type 2 crimes). Definitions of each type of crime for which data are collected under the UCR Program can be viewed at https://www2.fbi.gov/ucr/cius2009/about/offense_definitions.html.

Rates of Crime

In addition to reporting the numbers of arrests, UCR data present the rates of crime. At the beginning of this chapter, you learned about how the number of murders in Chicago had increased, yet it had one of the lowest rates of crime in recent decades. A **crime rate** compares the number of occurrences of a particular crime with the size of the total population. Crime rates make it easy to understand trends in criminal activity and victimization over time, regardless of changes to the population. A crime rate is calculated by taking the number of crimes and dividing it by the population, or the number of residents of a specific region. Then, take this answer, and multiply it by 100,000. This will give you the standard rate of crime per 100,000 individuals. Crime rates can be used to compare the number of crimes across regions of different sizes or even across different time periods.

A review of arrest data from the UCR indicates that the rate of violent crime in 2014 was 365.5 per 100,000 inhabitants. While there was little change in this rate between 2014 and 2013 (369.1), a review of data over a 10-year period demonstrates that the violent crime rate fell 21.1% since 2004. We have also seen a reduction in the rate of property offenses. In 2014, the property crime rate was 2,596.1 per 100,000 individuals. Between 2013 and 2014, the rate of property crime decreased by 5.0% and has fallen 26.1% since 2004. In order to assess the reasons why these crimes have fallen, we need to take a deeper look at the individual offenses within the violent and property crime categories. Figure 3.2 illustrates the UCR data for each of the index crimes. Here, we note that while all crimes demonstrated a reduction in the crime rate since 2004 (except for rape where the definition changed between those years), some crimes represent a greater decrease than others. For example, a one-point decrease in the murder rate (from 5.5 in 2004 to 4.5 in 2014) is equal to an 18.8% reduction. Meanwhile, a 56-point reduction in the rate of aggravated assault is equal to a 19.4% reduction in the crime rate. Here, the 55-point difference is worth one half of a percent change in the crime rate.

Figure 3.2 Crime Rates for UCR Index Offenses, 2004 and 2014

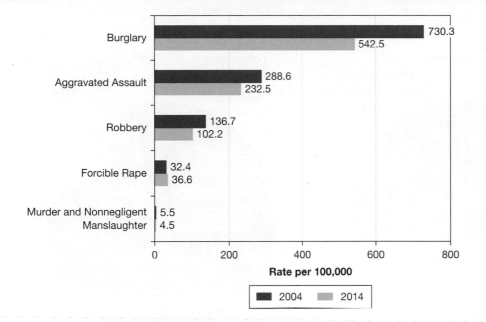

Offense	2004 Crime Rate	2014 Crime Rate	% Change
Murder and nonnegligent manslaughter	5.5	4.5	−18.8
Forcible rape[1]	32.4	36.6	+13.0
Robbery	136.7	102.2	−25.2
Aggravated assault	288.6	232.5	−19.4
Burglary	730.3	542.5	−25.7

Source: Crime in the United States, 2014. Uniform Crime Reports, FBI. Table 1.

1. References acts defined under the following: the carnal knowledge of a female forcibly and against her will. Attempts or assaults to commit rape by force or threat of force are also included; however, statutory rape (without force) and other sex offenses are excluded. As of January 1, 2013, the revised definition of rape is "Penetration, no matter how slight, of the vagina or anus with any body part or object, or oral penetration by a sex organ of another person, without the consent of the victim."

Data on Offenders

UCR data can also give us information about the perpetrators of these crimes. From this data, we learn that most offenders are White, male, and over the age of 18. Within each of these demographic categories, we learn about the differences between race, sex, and gender when it comes to offending. For example, Figure 3.3 demonstrates that larceny-theft is the most common crime for both men and women.

While the number of men involved in this crime is higher than women, this crime makes up a higher proportion of criminal activity for women compared with men. Meanwhile, the crimes of burglary and aggravated assault have a much greater proportion of men arrested for these crimes compared with women. What about age? Figure 3.4 illustrates the differences between adult and juvenile offenders in arrests for index crimes. Here, UCR data show us that the most common crime, regardless of age, is larceny-theft. However, it is interesting to note that the proportion of certain offenses is greater for juveniles than it is for adults. For example, just over 15% of

Figure 3.3 Sex Differences in UCR Index Offenses, 2014

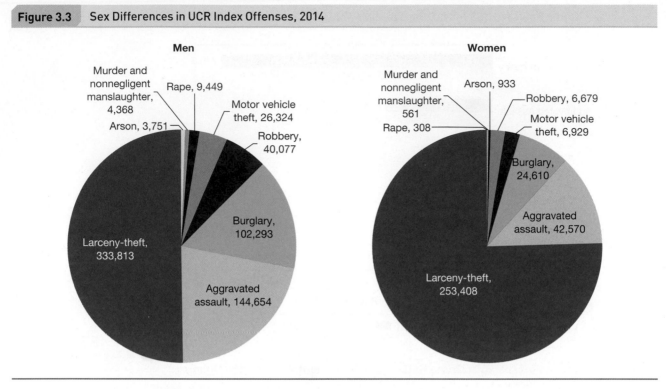

Source: Crime in the United States, 2014. Uniform Crime Reports, FBI. Table 33.

the arrests for the crime of burglary involve juvenile offenders under the age of 18. In comparison, burglary makes up approximately 12% of adult arrests. In contrast, arrests for the crime of aggravated assault involve a greater proportion of adults compared with juveniles (20% vs. 11%).

Finally, the UCR measures race by five categories: White, Black, Asian, Pacific Islander, and American Indian/Alaska Native. The UCR does not collect data on ethnicity; therefore, we do not have arrest data that will allow us to compare Hispanics with non-Hispanics. The proportion of Asian, Pacific Islander, and American Indian/Alaska Native arrests is less than 2% for each crime. A review of these findings in Figure 3.5 indicates that Whites make up the majority of arrests for six of the eight index crimes. Blacks represent a greater proportion of arrests for the two crimes of robbery, and murder and nonnegligent manslaughter, whereas Whites represent a much greater proportion of arrests for arson and larceny-theft.

Limitations of the UCR

While the UCR data can illustrate important trends in crime, the reporting of UCR data as the true extent of crime is flawed for the majority of the crime categories (with the exception of homicide), even though these data represent arrest statistics from approximately 95% of the population. Here, it is important to take several issues into consideration. First, the UCR data represent statistics on only those crimes that are reported to the police. As a result, the data are dependent on both what police know about criminal activity and how they use their discretion in these cases. If the police are not witnesses to a crime or are not called to deal with an offender, they cannot make an arrest. Arrests are the key variable for UCR data. This means that unreported crimes are not recognized in these statistics. Sadly, many criminal acts

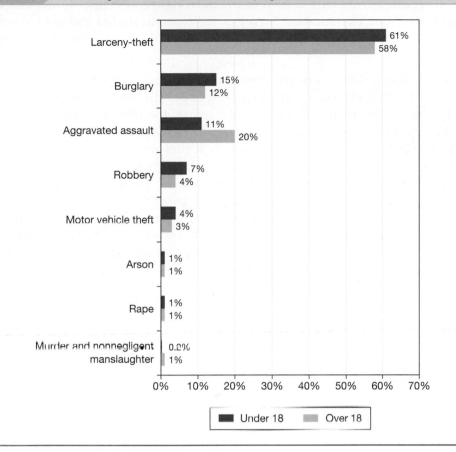

Source: Crime in the United States, 2014. Uniform Crime Reports, FBI. Table 32.

Figure 3.5   Arrests of Offenders by Race, 2014

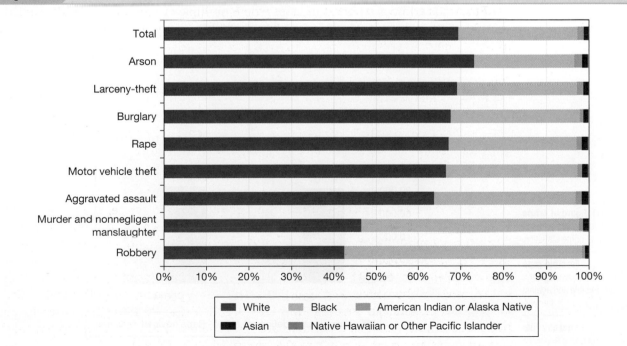

Source: Crime in the United States, 2014. Uniform Crime Reports, FBI. Table 43.

are significantly underreported and therefore do not appear within the UCR data. These unreported crimes are known as the **dark figure of crime**. Sources such as the National Crime Victimization Survey or self-reported studies attempt to capture some of this data to provide a greater understanding of the total extent of crime in the United States.

Second, the definitions of the crimes that are included within the UCR can be limited. Consider the category of **forcible rape**. Historically, the UCR defined forcible rape as "the carnal knowledge of a female forcible and against her will." This definition failed to capture the magnitude of sexual assaults, which may not involve female victims or may involve other sexual acts beyond vaginal penetration. In January 2012, the FBI announced a revised category to include crimes of rape and sexual assault with a definition to include "the penetration, no matter how slight, of the vagina or anus with any body part or object, or oral penetration by a sex organ of another person, without the consent of the victim."[16] This new definition went into effect in January 2013. Not only does the new law allow for both males and females to be identified as victims or offenders, but it also allows the UCR Program to include cases where the victim was either unable or unwilling to consent to sexual activity (for example, in cases involving intoxication). In addition, the new definition removes the requirement of force. As a result of these changes, the category of rape will now capture a greater diversity of sexual assaults. This new definition is more in line with the variety of state laws related to rape and sexual assault. With this change in how these sexually based offenses are counted, it is expected that we will see an increase in the UCR for this category in the following years. This does not mean that the crime of rape has increased dramatically in practice, only that we have changed the way we collect the data for these cases. Over time, these changes will help present a more accurate picture of the prevalence of rape and sexual assault in society.[17] Already, the change in the UCR Program's definition of rape has caused a change in the number of cases that are now counted as rape (Figure 3.6).

Third, the reporting of the crimes to the UCR Program is incomplete, as only the most serious crime is reported in cases where multiple crimes are committed during a single criminal event. This is referred to as the **hierarchy rule**. These findings skew

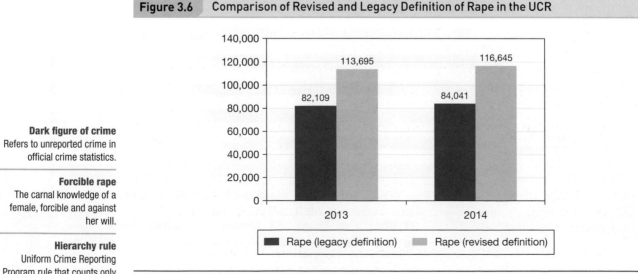

Figure 3.6 Comparison of Revised and Legacy Definition of Rape in the UCR

Rape (legacy definition) — 2013: 82,109; 2014: 84,041
Rape (revised definition) — 2013: 113,695; 2014: 116,645

Source: Crime in the United States, 2014. Uniform Crime Reports, FBI. Table 1.

Dark figure of crime
Refers to unreported crime in official crime statistics.

Forcible rape
The carnal knowledge of a female, forcible and against her will.

Hierarchy rule
Uniform Crime Reporting Program rule that counts only the most serious crime.

CAREERS IN CRIMINAL JUSTICE

So You Want to Be a Research Analyst?

Researchers play an important role in evaluating whether a criminal justice policy or program is effective. Depending on the environment that you work in, the job titles for this type of work include research analyst, research scholar, crime analyst, and criminal intelligence analyst. There are several different types of settings where you could perform this work. First, you could work for a college or university as a professor. Many institutions require full-time faculty to conduct research in addition to their teaching responsibilities. In order to pay for these research activities, faculty secure financial grants through foundations and government agencies.

You might also work directly for a research center, foundation, or government organization. In these settings, your primary role centers on reviewing data, analyzing the results, and publishing the data. For example, the Bureau of Justice Statistics, which is an agency within the Department of Justice, is involved in administering surveys about crime in a number of different settings, including jails and prisons. They also work with population data to determine how many individuals are housed in jails and prisons in a specific year or across several years. Research analysts might also work for a specific agency, such as a local police department. For example, the NYPD's Office of Management Analysis and Planning employs several research analysts and data analysts. These positions work with data to analyze both existing and proposed law and policies.

The education and training that is required to work as a research analyst varies depending on the type of agency or organization that you work for. Most positions require that candidates have a significant understanding of statistics and other analytical tools. In some cases, these positions will require that you have an advanced degree, such as a master's or doctoral degree. You may also need specialized training in things such as geographic information systems (GIS), crime mapping, and social-network analysis. Since you will likely be writing reports on a number of issues, you'll need to have strong writing skills as well.

As the need for research on crime continues to grow, so will the need for people to work in these positions. If you are someone who likes to solve problems and assess which types of policies and practices offer the greatest success in responding to crime, this may be an ideal career for you.

the understanding of the prevalence of crime, as several different offenses may occur within the context of a single crime incident. For example, a crime involving physical battery, rape, and murder is reported to the UCR by the most serious crime, murder. As a result, the understanding of the prevalence of physical battery and rape is incomplete because these crimes are not counted.

CAREER VIDEO
Crime Intelligence Analyst

Fourth, the reporting of these data is organized annually, which can alter our understanding of crime as police agencies respond to cases. For example, a homicide that is committed in one calendar year may not be solved with an arrest and conviction until the following calendar year. This might initially be read as an "unsolved crime" in the first year but as an arrest in the subsequent year.

Finally, the participation by agencies in reporting to the UCR Program has fluctuated over time. While there are no federal laws requiring agencies to report their crime data, many states today have laws that direct law enforcement agencies to comply with UCR data collection. However, this means that the analysts of crime trends over time need to take into consideration the number of agencies involved in the reporting of crime data. Failure to do so could result in a flawed analysis of crime patterns over time.[18]

These flaws of UCR data can have significant implications for members of society about the understanding of crime data. Most of us get our information about crime from news headlines or other media reports about crime. These 30-second clips about crime rates do little to explain the intricate nature of UCR data definitions and collection practices. Indeed, when the UCR Program was first assigned to the FBI, early scholars commented, "In light of the somewhat questionable source of the data, the Department of Justice might do more harm than good by issuing the Reports."[19]

NATIONAL INCIDENT-BASED REPORTING SYSTEM

In an effort to develop a better understanding of the extent of offending, the **National Incident-Based Reporting System** (NIBRS) was implemented in 1988. Rather than compile monthly summary reports on crime data in their jurisdictions, agencies now forward data to the FBI for every crime incident. The NIBRS catalog involves data on 22 offense categories and includes 46 specific crimes known as Group A offenses. Data on 11 lesser offenses (Group B offenses) are also collected. Unlike the UCR Program, which organizes its data into violent crimes and property crimes, the NIBRS divides its data into three themes: crimes against persons, crimes against property, and crimes against society. In addition to an increased diversity in the types of crimes that data are collected on, the NIBRS changed the hierarchy rule that was part of the UCR. This means that cases that involve more than one specific offense will now count toward all of the different offenses that are reported and not just the most serious event. In addition, NIBRS data are collected on both completed and attempted crimes. Overall, the NIBRS allows for a more comprehensive understanding of crime in the United States compared with the UCR.[20]

Data Collected

Data from the 2014 NIBRS report demonstrate how incident-based reporting provides a significantly greater detail of the types of crimes that are reported to police, compared with the UCR data. In addition to the greater number of offenses that are included in the NIBRS, the report includes information on the age, sex, and race of the offender and the victim, as well as data on the location and time of day of the offense and the type of force and weapons used in the crime. However, the reporting of data to the NIBRS remains incomplete. In 2014, only 6,520 law enforcement agencies reported their crime data to the NIBRS. This represents only one third of those agencies that report to the UCR Program. Table 3.1 illustrates data on the incidents, offenses, victims, and known offenders by offense category in 2014.[21]

A review of these data demonstrates how the NIBRS data paint a more detailed picture about crime. While there were 4.7 million incidents reported to police, there were almost 5.5 million offenses. This highlights that many criminal acts involve multiple offenses. At the same time, there are almost 5.8 million victims, indicating that some criminal acts involve multiple victims. We also learn that 4.4 million offenders commit these acts. This means that some offenders engage in multiple incidents of crime. These are data that are not included as part of the Uniform Crime Reports.

The NIBRS data also provide a unique insight as to the conditions under which crime occurs. For example, we learn about relationships that victims have with their perpetrators. In 2014, 21.8% of offenses involved a family member as the offender, compared with 57.2% who are known offenders and 10.2% that involve strangers. We also learn about when crimes are likely to occur. Figure 3.7 illustrates the different times of day that offenses against people, property, and society occur.[22] Across all three categories, NIBRS data indicate that crime is generally 40% to 50% higher between noon and 11:59 p.m. compared to between midnight and 11:59 a.m. For example, crimes against persons and crimes against society tend to fall during the

National Incident-Based Reporting System
System of crime data that offers expanded data categories of crime statistics. Removes the hierarchy rule of the UCR.

Table 3.1 — NIBRS 2014: Incidents, Offenses, Victims, and Known Offenders by Offense Category

Offense Category	Incidents[1]	Offenses	Victims[2]	Known Offenders[3,4]
Total	4,759,438	5,489,485	5,790,423	4,414,016
Crimes Against Persons	1,093,466	1,261,784	1,261,784	1,220,634
Assault Offenses	1,004,899	1,165,909	1,165,909	1,126,270
Homicide Offenses	3,599	3,854	3,854	4,649
Kidnapping/Abduction	13,744	15,552	15,552	16,172
Sex Offenses	66,008	70,928	70,928	68,105
Sex Offenses, Nonforcible	5,169	5,484	5,484	5,353
Crimes Against Property	3,493,904	3,493,904	3,794,240	2,246,790
Arson	12,951	12,951	15,446	9,128
Bribery	308	308	324	363
Burglary/Breaking & Entering	464,445	464,445	533,156	264,253
Counterfeiting/Forgery	71,959	71,959	79,433	64,716
Destruction/Damage/Vandalism	693,423	693,423	748,453	386,799
Embezzlement	18,885	18,885	19,729	20,188
Extortion/Blackmail	1,684	1,684	1,843	1,380
Fraud Offenses	294,160	294,160	324,057	184,525
Larceny/Theft Offenses	1,662,432	1,662,432	1,761,971	1,080,705
Motor Vehicle Theft	171,321	171,321	178,589	90,462
Robbery	66,487	66,487	88,038	96,699
Stolen Property Offenses	35,849	35,849	43,201	47,572
Crimes Against Society	733,797	733,797	734,399	946,592
Drug/Narcotic Offenses	640,727	640,727	641,181	832,208
Gambling Offenses	801	801	802	1,678
Pornography/Obscene Material	8,516	8,516	8,539	8,791
Prostitution Offenses	9,938	9,938	9,960	12,900
Weapon Law Violations	73,815	73,815	73,917	91,015

Source: NIBRS (2014). https://www.fbi.gov/about-us/cjis/ucr/nibrs/2014/tables/incidents_offenses_victims_and_known_offenders_by_offense_category_2014_final.pdf

1. The actual number of incidents is 4,759,438. However, the column figures will not add to the total because incidents may include more than one offense type, and each appropriate offense type is counted in this table.

2. *Victims* represents the number of victims associated with each offense type.

3. The term *Known Offender* does not imply the identity of the suspect is known, but only that an attribute of the suspect has been identified, which distinguishes him/her from an unknown offender.

4. The figures in the column *Known Offenders* do not include the 1,612,515 incidents with an unknown offender.

Figure 3.7 NIBRS Crimes Against Property, Persons, and Society by Time of Day, 2014

When are crimes against property most likely to occur? What about crimes against persons and crimes against society? How might this information be used by police departments?

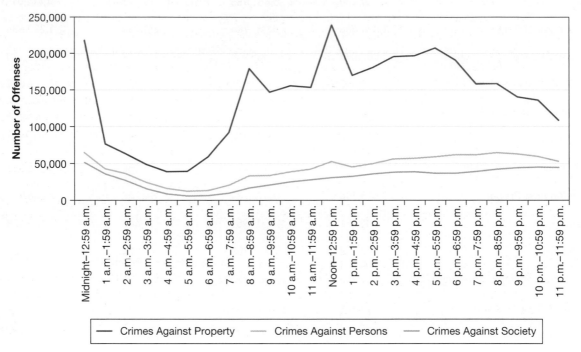

middle of the night and steadily climb as the day progresses, with the highest levels of these offenses occurring between midnight and 1 a.m. In comparison, property offenses are much more varied throughout the day, with spikes occurring during the afternoon and again at midnight.

Limitations of NIBRS

While the variability of NIBRS data is a great asset in understanding the extent and nature of crime in the United States, it remains an incomplete source due to the small number of agencies that are currently certified to submit their data. Hopefully, additional jurisdictions will be able to contribute to this rich data source, as it provides a more comprehensive way of looking at offending data compared with the Uniform Crime Reports. The transition of agencies to the NIBRS has been slow, as only 33 states were certified by the FBI as of June 2014. Eight additional states are currently testing the NIBRS in their jurisdictions, and seven more states or territories are in the process of developing plans for the NIBRS.[23] While the NIBRS is an improvement over the UCR Program, this system still carries over a fatal flaw from the UCR in that both are limited to reported crimes. In spite of this, it is hoped that the improvements in official crime data collection will allow for an increased understanding of the extent of offending patterns.

NATIONAL CRIME VICTIMIZATION SURVEY

National Crime Victimization Survey
The largest victimization study in the United States. Attempts to fill the gap of understanding between reported and unreported crime.

In contrast to the limitations of the UCR and NIBRS datasets, the **National Crime Victimization Survey** (NCVS) represents the largest victimization study conducted in the United States. National-level victimization data were first collected in 1971 and 1972 as part of the Quarterly Household Survey conducted by the Census Bureau. In 1972, these efforts evolved into the National Crime Survey (NCS), which was designed

AROUND THE WORLD

International Crime Data

While the UCR, NIBRS, and NCVS are examples of official data sources in the United States, there are several examples of international crime surveys that can shed light on the nature of crime in other countries. The Australian Bureau of Statistics (ABS) collects data on arrested individuals throughout Australia. Unlike the UCR Program, which collects data on a calendar year basis, the ABS data cycle runs from July 1 to June 30. In 2014–2015, there were 411,686 individuals ages 10 and older processed by the police for eight different offenses (homicide, assault, sexual assault, robbery, kidnapping, unlawful entry with intent, motor vehicle theft, and other theft).[a] Another example of an official source of crime statistics is the annual report produced by the Bundeskriminalamt (Federal Criminal Police Office of Germany). The Bundeskriminalamt (BKA) statistics includes data for all crimes handled by the police (Figure 3.8). In 2014, there were 6,082,064 crimes reported to the police, 3,336,398 of which were considered "cleared" or solved. Violent crime represents only 3% of crime in Germany. The largest crime category is theft, and it represents 40.1% of all criminal offenses. Men are much more likely to be considered a suspect by the police in these criminal activities—out of 2,149,504 suspects, only 14.4% are women. Men are also more likely to be victims of crime, as 59% of victims are male.[b]

Australia's and Germany's crime statistics agencies are just two examples of official international data sources on criminal offending at the country level. Due to the differences in laws and reporting practices, it is difficult to compare such statistics at a global level. However, there have been attempts to collect basic information on recorded crime across several jurisdictions. The United Nations Survey of Crime Trends and Operations of Criminal Justice Systems

| Figure 3.8 | Characteristics of Crimes Reported in Germany |

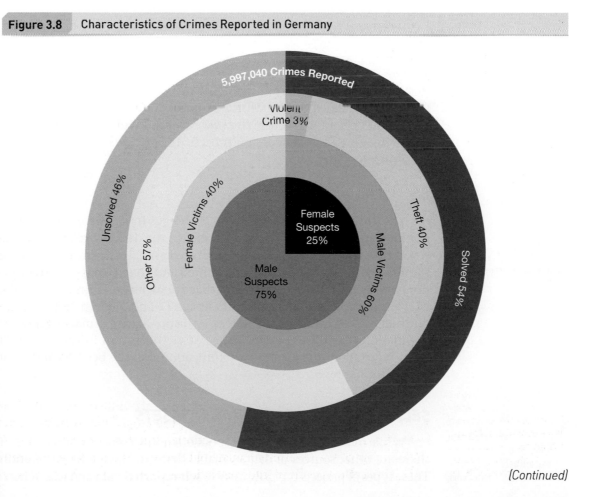

(Continued)

(Continued)

CRITICAL THINKING QUESTIONS

1. How are statistics about crime in other countries similar to and different from data on crime in the United States?

2. What are the challenges in comparing international statistics on crime with the types of data that are available about crime in the United States?

(UN-CTS) compiles crime data from a variety of different sources, including the World Health Organization, Eurostat, and national police organizations from individual countries (to name a few). Their data indicate that there were 378,776 global victims of homicide reported to the police in 2012, or a crime rate of 10 per 100,000.[c]

Table 3.2	Types of Data Collected Through the National Crime Victimization Survey			
Crimes Included	**Victim Demographics**	**Offender Demographics**	**Characteristics of the Crime**	**Crime Reporting**
• Rape or sexual assault • Robbery • Aggravated and simple assault • Personal larceny	• Age • Sex • Race/ethnicity • Marital status • Education level • Income	• Age • Sex • Race/ethnicity • Victim–offender relationship	• Time and place of the offense • Use of weapons • Nature of injury • Economic consequences	• Was the crime reported? • Reasons why the crime was reported • Reasons why the crime was not reported • Experiences with the criminal justice system

to supplement the data from the UCR and provide data on crime from the victims' perspective. The NCS was transferred to the Bureau of Justice Statistics (BJS) in 1979, and the BJS began to evaluate the survey instrument and the data collection process. Following an extensive redesign process, the NCS was renamed the National Crime Victimization Survey in 1991.

Data Collected

WEB LINK
National Crime Victimization Survey (NCVS)

The greatest achievement of the NCVS lies in its attempt to fill the gap between reported and unreported crime, described as the dark figure of crime. The NCVS gathers additional data about crimes committed and gives criminologists a greater understanding of the types of crimes committed and characteristics of the victims. Table 3.2 presents the different types of data that are included within the NCVS. In 2011, the NCVS interviewed 143,120 individuals age 12 and older in 79,800 households. Based on these survey findings, the Bureau of Justice Statistics makes generalizations to the population regarding the prevalence of victimization in the United States.[24] You'll learn more about the extent of victimization and the benefits and limitations of the NCVS in Chapter 5.

SELF-REPORTED OFFENDING DATASETS

Self-reported data
Refers to crime statistics that are based on personal disclosures.

While much of what we know about offending comes from the UCR and the NIBRS, there are other sources of data available that can shed light on offending behaviors. These types of projects typically involve **self-reported data** and researchers asking people

Behavior	Total	Males	Females	White	Black	Hispanic
Ever used alcohol	66.2%	64.4%	67.9%	65.9%	63.4%	72.4%
Current alcohol use[1]	34.9%	34.4%	35.5%	36.3%	29.6%	37.5%
Engaged in binge drinking[2]	20.8%	22.0%	19.6%	23.2%	12.4%	22.6%
Ever used marijuana	40.7%	42.1%	39.2%	36.7%	46.8%	48.8%
Current marijuana use	23.4%	25.0%	21.9%	20.4%	28.9%	27.6%
Ever used cocaine	5.5%	6.6%	4.5%	4.8%	2.1%	9.5%
Ever used hallucinogens	7.1%	8.8%	5.5%	7.6%	2.2%	8.4%
Ever used inhalants	8.9%	7.9%	10.0%	8.6%	6.8%	11.7%
Ever used heroin	2.2%	2.8%	1.6%	1.7%	1.6%	3.4%
Ever used prescription drugs	17.8%	18.3%	17.2%	18.8%	13.3%	19.2%
Ever used ecstasy	6.6%	7.6%	5.5%	5.8%	4.4%	9.4%
Ever used methamphetamines	3.2%	3.4%	3.0%	3.0%	1.3%	4.5%

1. Current use is defined as at least one experience in the past 30 days.

2. Binge drinking is defined as five or more drinks in a row (within a couple of hours) at least once in the past 30 days.

about the types of behaviors that they engage in. Generally speaking, these studies involve one of three populations: (1) studies of at-risk or general populations, (2) studies of offenders involved in the criminal justice process, and (3) convicted offenders who are either incarcerated or are participating in a community-based sanction.

Data Collected

Like the UCR, NIBRS, and NCVS, some self-reported studies are conducted on an annual or semiannual basis. The **Youth Risk Behavior Surveillance System** (YRBSS) began in 1991 and includes data on several categories of at-risk behaviors in youth. Organized by the Centers for Disease Control and Prevention, this study includes data from ongoing school-based studies as well as one-time national and special-population studies.[25] In 2013, 13,633 questionnaires were completed in 148 public and private high schools (Grades 9–12) across the nation. Along with health risk behavior data, this study also includes measures of at-risk and offending behaviors. In 2013, 17.9% of students surveyed had carried a weapon at least once during the previous month, and 5.5% brought a weapon to school. Boys (28.1%) were more likely to engage in these behaviors compared with girls (7.9%), and White males (33.4%) were more likely to carry a weapon compared with Black (18.2%) and Hispanic (23.8%) males. Almost a quarter of all students nationwide had been in a physical fight at some point during the previous year, and 8.1% of students were involved in an altercation on school property. Data is also collected on alcohol and drug use. Table 3.3 highlights some of the findings from this survey on the prevalence of teen use of controlled substances. Here, we learn that experimentation and use of illicit substances is quite common among the teen population. The most common substances used by youth are (1) alcohol, (2) marijuana, and (3) prescription drugs. Girls are more likely to use alcohol while boys are more likely to use marijuana and prescription drugs. Use of these substances

WEB LINK
Youth Risk Behavior
Surveillance System (YRBSS)

Youth Risk Behavior Surveillance System
Research study by the CDC that focuses on health and youth risk behaviors among high school students.

varies by race/ethnicity. While Whites are more likely to have a current history of alcohol use, as well as to engage in binge drinking, Hispanic youth have higher rates of ever having used alcohol. Black youth are more likely to use marijuana compared with White and Hispanic youth. Finally, Hispanic youth have higher rates of experimentation with all other substances compared with White and Black youth.[26]

Self-report studies may also reflect offending behaviors over a period of time. These studies are referred to as **longitudinal studies**. Typically, these projects select their subjects (based on the factors they are looking to study) and then follow this group of individuals over a specific time period. One of the most influential longitudinal studies on at-risk behaviors and youth is the **National Youth Survey Family Study** (NYSFS). The NYSFS began in 1976 and included 1,725 youth between the ages of 11 and 17 (and a parent) who were selected randomly from across the United States. In 2004, the National Youth Survey Family Study collected its 11th wave of interviews. In addition to interviewing 70% of the original participants, they also included interviews with 71% of their parents, 71% of their current spouses, and 77% of their adolescent children. What once began as a snapshot of youth at-risk and offending behaviors has transformed into an understanding of behaviors throughout the lives of the study participants and their families. To date, the NYSFS has produced hundreds of publications on topics such as violence, substance use, and causes and correlates of delinquent and criminal behavior.[27]

Limitations of Self-Reported Offending Datasets

Self reported studies such as these provide value as they measure things (both substantively and with particular detail) that are generally not provided by the official sources of data. While these studies often assure subjects that their identities and responses will be kept confidential, there is no way to ensure that the people who participate in these studies will be truthful in their responses. In addition, not all self-reported studies use a random sample. Many draw upon convenience-based samples, such as students in a college classroom. This means that the results from these studies cannot be compared with the population at large.

CONCLUSION

There are several ways to think about the prevalence of crime in society. Statistics about crime inform policymakers and the public alike. So the next time you are faced with the question of how much crime exists, remember to consider the following:

- What type of crimes are you looking for data on?
- Is there a particular stage of the criminal justice system that you are interested in?
- Are you interested in understanding rates of reported crime, unreported crime, or both?
- Are you looking for the presence of crime in a particular region? For a specific group of people? Or do you want to know about the estimated rates of crime for the population?

Your answers to these questions and more will determine which type of data source you should look for. Each source of data has its own strengths and weaknesses that you will need to keep under consideration. In many cases, you may pull together information from a variety of different sources to help answer your questions. Together, these types of crime data help us gain a better understanding of crime in society.

Longitudinal studies
Self-report studies that investigate crime over a period of time.

National Youth Survey Family Study
Longitudinal study of at-risk behaviors and youth.

CURRENT
CONTROVERSY
VIDEO
Where Do You Stand?
Cast Your Vote!

Is White-Collar Crime Harmful to Society?

—Henry N. Pontell, Gilbert Geis,
Adam Ghazi-Tehrani, and Bryan Burton—

INTRODUCTION

White-collar crime constitutes one of the more challenging problems confronting law enforcement in the United States and, indeed, throughout the world. The core difficulty is that these offenses, by definition, are committed by persons who have power in the worlds of business, politics, or the professions. The status of white-collar criminals is reflected in biases in criminal codes that favor them. In addition, efforts to discover and penalize white-collar and corporate crimes are largely in the hands of persons with the same background and beliefs as those who are perpetrating the offenses. To a certain extent, answering the question of whether white-collar crime is harmful to society requires us to ask, What do we consider harmful?

CON · White-Collar Crime Is Not Harmful to Society

Crime is often defined as acts such as the traditional street offenses perpetrated by low-status offenders or, in other cases, crimes of violence against society. In defending this definition, criminologist James Q. Wilson indicated that excluding white-collar offenses from the discussions about crime "reflects my conviction, which I believe is the conviction of most citizens, that predatory street crime is a far more serious matter than consumer fraud [or] antitrust violations . . . because predatory street crime makes difficult or impossible maintenance of meaningful human communities."[28]

White-collar offenses usually include acts such as forgery, embezzlement, and fraud. While one might consider these acts to be property crimes, information about these crimes is not included in the Uniform Crime Reports because these acts are not considered index crimes. Therefore, is it reasonable to assume that such acts are not considered as serious compared with other crimes. While we can locate data on these acts through the National Incident-Based Reporting System, not all agencies report their crime statistics to the NIBRS, making it difficult to understand the prevalence of these acts in society.[29]

In addition, upper-class violators are not persons on the outer rim of society, who commit burglaries and robberies in order to purchase another dose of an illegal drug or to secure funds to "keep the party going."[30] They are individuals and executives of entities who characteristically live in a style that is the envy of most of those of us who are less favored. They are likely to be well educated, which would presume that they are capable of making reasonably accurate linkages between causes and effects—that is, that they are or become aware that if they break the law and are caught doing so, this could possibly result in serious consequences for their lifestyle and reputation and the well-being of their family. The question is this: Does the criminal justice system inherently create these differences by treating these offenders differently? Or is the system simply responding to the perception of harm caused by these acts?

Given the current status of punishment in regard to these acts, one might assume that such acts are not as harmful as, say, other types of crimes. Perhaps the most appropriate word to describe the current state of policy in the United States with regard to individual and corporate white-collar crime is "erratic." As far as can be determined, it was decided in high government circles during the last part of the Bush administration and during the Obama presidency that bringing criminal charges against prominent businesspeople who had done woefully aberrant things (including actions that resulted in the meltdown of the mortgage industry during the first decade of the 21st century), acts that might reasonably be charged as criminal, was a matter best overlooked, since to prosecute them would undermine already skeptical views about those in power and the marketplace. In a major piece of investigative journalism, reports indicated that because of the seeming fragility of America's financial system, Timothy Geithner, the secretary of the treasury and a former star player in the world of high finance, had persuaded prosecutors to ignore Wall Street crimes. The aim, the reporters wrote, was "a desire to calm markets, a goal that could be compromised by a hard-charging attorney general."[31]

The most visible aspect of this approach was the use of civil suits launched by the Securities and Exchange Commission (SEC) against some of the more prominent malefactors and the companies they piloted. Bank of America, for instance, agreed to a fine of $155 million for its failure to notify stockholders that its acquisition of Merrill Lynch also involved the assumption of millions of dollars awarded to more than 100 employees of the near-defunct company. Yet none of the employees, including upper-level management, were held either civilly or criminally responsible. In their agreement to pay the fine, Bank of America insisted that the court acknowledge that the payment did not indicate guilt, a traditional dodge aimed at helping a company prevail against later lawsuits.

Given the perceptions of these acts in society and the response by the criminal justice system, these findings seem to suggest that acts of white-collar crime are not harmful to society.

PRO White-Collar Crime Is Harmful to Society

Certainly, predatory street crimes net their perpetrators far less loot than the bonuses that are obtained by corporate executives whose businesses have virtually or actually gone bust. But corporate crimes can have long-term financial consequences. One could observe that the great economic meltdown made it exceedingly difficult or impossible to maintain meaningful human communities in areas where a barrage of foreclosures had been fueled by sales tactics that resulted in the subprime crisis; home owners lost their homes as a result of poor business practices.

The lenders, who themselves profited handsomely, had readily unloaded the high-risk obligations on investment firms, which bundled them together and sold them to unwary investors.[32]

Consider one of the examples that was presented in the previous section. Bank of America agreed to a fine of $155 million. But what were the costs that resulted from their harmful practices? This is difficult, if not impossible, to measure, but we can look at some of the ripple effects. Unemployment rose, further making it impossible for home owners who had been gulled into absurd mortgage arrangements to meet payments. House values went "under water"—that is, a house often was not worth what the purchaser owed on it. This fueled a barrage of foreclosures. Banks became wary of making loans so that businesses that depended on such financing to meet payrolls gave up the ghost.

Many of these legal actions were settled with financial payments but without any admission of wrongdoing. In a related case involving Citigroup, the judge asked rhetorically why a company would pay a fine and, at the same time, insist that it was not guilty of having done anything that was against the law? Given the costs and consequences of these actions, should we devote greater attention to these crimes, as they may cause greater harm that we realize?

Many families were affected by the recent mortgage industry meltdown and lost their homes. Should banks be held criminally liable for the mortgage crisis?

DISCUSSION QUESTIONS

1. Given the perceptions of these acts in society and the response by the criminal justice system, are acts of white-collar crime harmful to society?

2. Should we devote greater attention to these crimes?

3. At the end of the day, how do these acts compare with the violent and property crimes that dominate our criminal justice system?

CURRENT CONTROVERSY 3.2

Is Burglary a Violent Crime?

—Phillip Kopp—

CURRENT
CONTROVERSY
VIDEO
Where Do You Stand?
Cast Your Vote!

INTRODUCTION

Burglary has historically been considered a nonviolent crime committed against the property of another. Under common law, the crime of burglary consisted of "a breaking and entering of a dwelling house of another in the nighttime with the intent to commit a felony therein."[33] While modern burglary statutes are generally broader than the common-law definition—usually dropping the requirement that entry into the house must have been forced, expanding the definition of target beyond residential property, and not limiting the time in which the crime is said to occur to the nighttime hours—constant, however, is that interpersonal violence is not an element of the offense. When violence does occur during a burglary, offenders are charged with a wholly separate criminal offense, in addition to burglary. Additionally, a review of state burglary statutes found that all of the 32 states that divide their criminal statutes by victim type (person or property) classify burglary as an offense against property.[34] Finally, burglary is counted as a property crime by the Uniform Crime Reporting Program and the National Crime Victimization Survey.

PRO · Burglary Is a Violent Crime

In contrast to the historical view of burglary, the Armed Career Criminal Act (ACCA) classifies burglary as a violent crime for the purposes of sentence enhancement. Created by the Comprehensive Crime Control Act of 1984, the ACCA is a federal career offender statute that provides a mandatory minimum sentence of 15 years to life in prison, in addition to a fine not to exceed $25,000, for individuals convicted of any felony while in possession of a firearm and who have three previous convictions for a violent felony or serious drug offense. Under the ACCA, a violent felony is defined as any offense that has as an element "the use, attempted use, or threatened use of physical force against the person of another" or is "burglary, arson, or extortion, involves use of explosives or otherwise involves conduct that presents a serious potential risk of physical injury to another."[35] Subsequent interpretation of the ACCA by the Supreme Court has applied the violent-felony classification to all classes of burglaries[36] and both attempted and completed burglaries.[37]

Review of the *Congressional Record* regarding the ACCA identified the following three beliefs underpinning the act's classification of burglary as a violent crime.[38] First, a small number of offenders are responsible for a disproportionate number of crimes of theft and violence, burglary being one of the most common. Second, legislators viewed burglary as one of the crimes most detrimental to society because it involves entry into the personal space of its victims, both at home and work, for the purpose of taking their—in some cases irreplaceable—property, shattering any feelings of privacy and security its victims might have previously enjoyed. Third, beyond the emotional trauma and financial loss incurred, burglary can also result in physical violence. Because of the potential interaction between victim and offender, burglary can rapidly transition from a nonviolent to a violent offense. Legislators argued that it was by mere chance that a burglary did not result in a violent confrontation between potential victim and burglar. When the U.S. Supreme Court expanded the ACCA's violent-crime classification to all attempted burglaries, they built upon this argument, reasoning that many attempted burglaries are never completed because of the intervention of another. The Court then went further, arguing that an attempted burglary may pose greater risk of violence than a completed burglary.[39]

 Burglary Is Not a Violent Crime

As a result of the contradiction between the traditional view of burglary and the ACCA's classification of burglary, scholars have worked to develop an understanding of the nature of the offense using data from the UCR, NCVS, and NIBRS. While all three data collections report the incidence of crime in the United States, differences in their respective designs and limitations can complicate how these datasets can be used. For example, between 1998 and 2007, the NCVS estimated that some 13 million more burglaries occurred than were reported to the UCR Program, indicating that roughly 72% of the burglaries that occurred in the United States were reported to the police.[40]

Second, the datasets contain varying levels of detail regarding the incidence of crime in the United States. While the UCR Program only reports summary totals of offenses, the NCVS and NIBRS provide extensive offense information. Without the detailed information contained in the NCVS and NIBRS, the study of the incidence of violence in burglary would be nearly impossible. As stated previously, when violence occurs during the course of a burglary, the offender has committed a completely separate offense that is charged in addition to the burglary. In these incidents, burglary has co-occurred with another, more severe crime. When crimes co-occur in this manner, the lesser offenses are effectively hidden by the hierarchy rule that is used by all three datasets. For example, a burglary/robbery incident is recorded as a robbery, and the incidence of burglary is not counted. Using data from the NCVS and NIBRS, researchers found that during the period 1998–2007, an estimated 2,880,735 violent burglaries occurred, representing 7.6% of all burglaries estimated to have occurred by the NCVS. In comparison, 31,094 violent burglaries were reported to the NIBRS by the police, or 0.9% of all burglaries for the same period.[41]

Third, the substantial difference between NCVS and NIBRS estimates illustrates an additional limitation of NIBRS data, the small-agency bias. As of 2013, only 38% of law enforcement agencies, covering 30% of the nation's population, reported to the NIBRS;

The crime of burglary involves the illegal entry into a building with the intent of committing a crime. Is this a crime against property or against a person?

only one agency serving a population of a million or more reported to the NIBRS. Because of this, when compared with the UCR, the incidents contained in NIBRS data represented only 29% of reported crime in 2013. More crime—and specifically, more violent crime—occurs in urban areas not covered by the NIBRS. As a result, the NIBRS is only representative of suburban and rural parts of the United States (populations of 250,000 or less), and results must be reported with this limitation in mind.[42]

Finally, information contained in the NCVS but not the NIBRS allowed researchers to identify the percentage (26%) of all burglaries that occurred while a victim was present. As well as the overall incidence of victim presence, researchers determined the incidence of actual physical violence (2.7%) and the incidence of victims being threatened or placed in fear but not physically harmed (4.9%). Finally, researchers found that completed burglaries (8.4%) were significantly more likely to result in violence than were attempted burglaries (3.4%).[43]

What does all this data mean? It means that when we look at the situations in which burglary occurs, we learn that acts of burglary do not involve acts of violence. Rather, there is very little incidence of physical violence with the crime of burglary, and few victims feel fearful as a result of these acts. Yet much of the way in which we collect and report data about this crime makes it appear more violent than it actually is.

SUMMARY

Certainly, there are valid arguments on both sides of this issue. Some would suggest that burglary can be a violent crime, given the nature of the offense as well as the potential for violence that exists within the act. At the same time, are there reasons why we should alter the way that we think about this crime? How might this alter not only our perceptions of the criminal justice system but also the manner in which it functions in relation to these types of crimes?

DISCUSSION QUESTIONS

1. Is the Armed Career Criminal Act's classification of burglary as a violent offense correct?

2. While the research highlighted addressed physical violence, none of the data sources discussed contain measures of the psychological aftermath of criminal victimization. Could the emotional harm done by an offense be worse and last longer than the physical harm done by the same offense?

3. What should researchers consider when comparing the crime of burglary across different data sources?

KEY TERMS

Review key terms with eFlashcards | ⑤SAGE edge™ • edge.sagepub.com/mallicoatccj

DISCUSSION QUESTIONS

Test your mastery of chapter content • Take the Practice Quiz | $SAGE edge™ • **edge.sagepub.com/mallicoatccj**

1. List the six general categories of crime and an example of each.

2. Discuss how the Uniform Crime Reports and the National Incident-Based Reporting System provide an understanding about the extent of crime in society.

3. How do self-reported datasets provide valuable information about crime and offending behaviors that are not captured by official data sources?

4. What are the strengths and limitations of the various datasets on crime?

LEARNING ACTIVITIES

1. Go to your state's criminal law legal code. Select a crime, and provide a definition of this act. Compare this definition with that from another state. What are the similarities and differences in how these crimes are defined?

2. Go to the Uniform Crime Reports website. Select an offense, and discuss how the occurrence of this crime has changed over the past decade.

SUGGESTED WEBSITES

- **Uniform Crime Reports:** http://www.fbi.gov/about-us/cjis/ucr/ucr
- **National Incident-Based Reporting System:** http://www.fbi.gov/about-us/cjis/ucr/nibrs/2012
- **National Crime Victimization Survey:** http://www.icpsr.umich.edu/icpsrweb/NACJD/NCVS
- **United Nations Office on Drugs and Crime:** https://www.unodc.org/unodc/en/data-and-analysis/statistics/data.html

STUDENT STUDY SITE

Review • Practice • Improve | $SAGE edge™ • **edge.sagepub.com/mallicoatccj**

Want a better grade?

Get the tools you need to sharpen your study skills. Access practice quizzes, eFlashcards, video, and multimedia at
edge.sagepub.com/mallicoatccj

4

CHAPTER

EXPLANATIONS OF CRIMINAL BEHAVIOR

LEARNING OBJECTIVES

- Describe how theories of crime are developed

- Evaluate the contributions of classical, biological, and psychological perspectives of criminal behavior

- Identify the differences between macro and micro theories of crime

- Compare and contrast the different features of strain theory, differential association theory, and labeling theory

- Discuss how social bond theory differs from other forms of macrolevel theories of crime

- Discuss the contributions of contemporary theories of crime in understanding criminal behavior

On December 14, 2012, Adam Lanza walked into Sandy Hook Elementary School in Newtown, Connecticut, and opened fire. In less than 11 minutes, Lanza shot and killed 20 children and six adults and wounded several others before turning the gun on himself.[1]

While the Sandy Hook tragedy rekindled the debate about issues such as mental illness and gun control, there have been few answers as to what led Adam Lanza to go to Sandy Hook Elementary and carry out such a violent attack. Reports indicate that Lanza was obsessed with mass-murder events, particularly those involving children. While he was diagnosed with Asperger's syndrome back in 2005, there was no indication that he had ever received any sort of mental health or other medical treatment.[2] While his parents had tried to get help for their son, they could not force these options on him once he turned 18.[3] The weapons used in the attack were purchased legally by Lanza's mother, who was killed that morning in the home she shared with her son.[4] Despite the evidence at the scenes of these crimes and an extensive background investigation on Adam Lanza, there has been no conclusive explanation as to why these acts occurred.

As the perceptions of violence in America's schools increase, many have called upon school officials and local police to find ways to keep children safe. Efforts have ranged from restricting public access to schools while classes are in session to allowing teachers to carry weapons on campus. One of the more common strategies has been to assign local police officers on school grounds. Which efforts do you think will be most effective?

Theory
A set of ideas used to explain
a particular phenomenon
or concept.

Micro theories of crime
Focus on individual
differences between law-
abiding and law-violating
behaviors.

Macro theories of crime
Focus on large-scale social or
structural explanations of crime.

**Classical school of
criminology**
Posits that people engage in
criminal behavior of their own
free will and that people choose
to engage in illegal acts.

**Positivist school of
criminology**
Perspective that involves
a data-driven approach
to understanding criminal
behavior.

Penology
A subfield of criminology
that focuses on punishment,
incarceration, and rehabilitation.

WHAT IS A THEORY OF CRIME?

Theories of crime help us understand what causes events such as the Sandy Hook tragedy. A **theory** refers to a set of ideas that is used to explain a particular phenomenon or concept. Criminologists look to theories to help explain what causes crime and, more specifically, why people engage in criminal behavior. Theories of crime are divided into two primary categories: micro and macro. **Micro theories of crime** focus on individual differences between law-abiding and law-violating behaviors. In contrast, **macro theories of crime** explore the large-scale social explanations for crime, such as poverty and community disorganization.

This chapter begins with a discussion about the classical theories of crime. The chapter then looks at biological and psychological explanations of crime, which historically have looked at factors such as biology and genetics to help understand criminal behavior. This chapter also looks at how external social factors such as poverty, family, and peers can help to explain crime. The chapter then moves to a review of some of the contemporary theories of crime, such as life course theory and feminist criminology. The chapter concludes with two Current Controversy debates: The first, by Kenethia McIntosh-Fuller, questions whether race and class can impact criminal behavior, and the second, by Jill L. Rosenbaum, investigates whether female offenders should be treated differently by the criminal justice system.

CLASSICAL THEORIES OF CRIME

The era of modern criminological theory is represented by two distinct schools of thought. The classical school began during the 18th century and was followed by the positivist school in the 19th century. The fundamental perspective of the **classical school of criminology** is that people engage in criminal behavior as a result of their own free will—that is, that people make a choice to engage in behaviors that are considered against the law. In contrast, the **positivist school of criminology** emerged out of a focus on the scientific method and involved a data-driven approach to understanding criminal behavior. While the theories that arose from these specific models have been heavily critiqued over the past several centuries, the roots of these perspectives have had a significant impact on the development and reinforcement of contemporary explanations of crime.

Cesare Beccaria

The works of Cesare Beccaria and Jeremy Bentham represent the most significant contributions of the classical school of criminology. Beccaria (1738–1794) was a professor of law from Italy. His book, *On Crimes and Punishment*, is considered to be one of the first works on the study of **penology**.[5] Penology is a subfield of criminology that specifically looks at the issues of punishment, incarceration, and rehabilitation. One of Beccaria's greatest contributions was the **pain–pleasure principle**. Here, Beccaria posited that individuals choose their behaviors based on how much pleasure they derive from them. Similarly, he believed that experiences

How did Jeremy Bentham's ideas on philosophy, punishment, and law influence correctional practices in 19th-century America?

SPOTLIGHT

Theories and Research on Crime

As a student of criminal justice, you'll learn about different research studies that scholars engage in. These research studies aim to investigate the causes and correlates of crime in an attempt to better understand these behaviors. Crime is inherently a complex phenomenon. As a result, it can be very difficult to say what causes crime, as **causation** implies that there is something that directly influences or is responsible for people engaging in criminal behavior. In contrast, many theories of crime investigate how different variables can be correlated with criminal behavior. **Correlation** means that two variables are linked together. When two variables are correlated, we will notice patterns; when one variable increases, so does the other. For example, the use of illegal drugs is often correlated with crime. While the mere possession of these substances is, in and of itself, a crime, the majority of these discussions look at how addiction to illicit substances can lead to criminal activity. Economic explanations for this relationship suggest that addiction may lead individuals into criminal acts (such as property offenses) in order to finance their drug habits.[a] However, this does not suggest that all people who use drugs will engage in crime, nor does it mean that all property offenders have issues with substance abuse. So we can't say that drug use causes crime (or the other way around), but we can say that there is a relationship between the two variables.

Sometimes, research attempts to test different relationships as a way to develop new theories of crime or to examine current theories of criminology in a different way. This process is called testing a hypothesis. A **hypothesis** frames a question that research is looking to answer. For example, a research study in criminology or criminal justice might pose the following hypothesis: As the number of arrests increases, the length of the prison sentence also increases. Here, the researcher is investigating whether there is a causal relationship between a defendant's prior criminal record and the length of a prison sentence. Similar to a hypothesis is a **research question**. While a hypothesis follows an "if *x* happens, then *y* will occur" format, research questions provide a path of inquiry to study. For example, a research question in criminology might ask, What are the effects of a criminal record on the likelihood of incarceration? While the presentation of a hypothesis and a research question varies, the intent is the same, as each sets out a direction for the research study and may reference the anticipated results of the study. It is then left up to the researcher(s) and their findings to determine whether they proved or disproved their hypothesis or if the results of their study provided an answer to their research question.

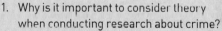

CRITICAL THINKING QUESTIONS

1. Why is it important to consider theory when conducting research about crime?

2. Why is it important to continue to investigate how different theories can explain crime in the 21st century?

As you learn about the various theories of crime and criminal behavior, keep in mind how research uses these theories to understand criminal behavior. Even though the majority of our theories of crime were first developed during the 19th and 20th centuries, scholars continue to test these theories in new arenas and new populations to determine how these theories can help explain criminal behavior around the world in the 21st century.

of pain would lead individuals to avoid other experiences. Beccaria's pain–pleasure principle is linked to the notion of **deterrence**. The theory of deterrence suggests that people will avoid potentially pleasurable acts (such as criminal behaviors) if the pain or fear of punishment is significant. You'll learn more about deterrence in Chapter 9. In his plea to revolutionize the punishment of criminals, Beccaria argued against the death penalty and the torture of criminals and suggested that offenders needed to be treated with care and dignity. He argued for the use of citizen juries and eliminating bias in the sentencing and punishment of offenders. Not only did his arguments lead

Pain–pleasure principle
Individuals choose their behaviors based on the amount of pleasure versus pain derived.

Deterrence
Suggests that people will avoid potentially pleasurable acts if the pain or fear of punishment is significant.

Jeremy Bentham's development of the panopticon had a significant impact on the architecture of prisons. In this photo of Presidio Modelo, the most famous Cuban prison, the panopticon allows guards to observe a large number of inmates simultaneously. What effect might this have on inmate behavior?

to significant reforms to the criminal justice systems in Europe; they also strongly impacted the development of the American criminal justice system.

Jeremy Bentham

While the principles expressed by Jeremy Bentham were similar to those of Beccaria, Bentham argued that the criminal justice system should take any mitigating factors into consideration when determining an appropriate punishment. For example, Bentham would argue that younger offenders should be treated differently than adult offenders as a result of their lower age, maturity, and decision-making abilities. He also suggested that lesser punishments can be equally, if not more, effective than extreme and harsh punishments. His most significant contribution to criminological theory came with the publication of his book *An Introduction to the Principles of Morals and Legislation* in 1789.[6] In addition, Bentham is known for his development of the **panopticon**.[7] The design of the panopticon was circular and was intended to be placed at the center of a larger complex. Here, the idea was to allow an individual or small group of people the ability to view the actions of the larger structure. One of the most unique features of the panopticon is its symbolic function. In the case of a prison environment, it was suggested that the mere presence of the panopticon would encourage good behavior, as the inmates could only assume that they were being observed at any time.

BIOLOGICAL AND PSYCHOLOGICAL THEORIES OF CRIME

Biological and psychological theories of crime focus on the characteristics of an individual to explain criminal behavior. While **biological theories of crime** look at genetic characteristics to explain offending, **psychological theories of crime** explore how factors such as early childhood experiences, cognitive development, and personality characteristics can help explain criminality. While many of these works were introduced during the late 19th and early 20th centuries, themes from this research have continued to inspire scholars in recent decades.

Foundations of Biological Theories of Crime

According to biological theories, crime occurs as a result of an inherited trait in an individual. To this extent, there is no action or free will of the individual to either engage in or desist from crime.

Cesare Lombroso

The works of Cesare Lombroso are perhaps the best representation of these biological theories of criminal behavior. As a medical doctor during the 19th century from Italy, Lombroso argued that there were several distinctive physical features that could be used to distinguish criminal offenders from law-abiding citizens. Lombroso's basic idea was that criminals are biological throwbacks to a primitive breed of man and can be recognized by various degenerative physical characteristics.[8] Lombroso was

---

Causation
Implies that there is something that directly influences or is responsible for people engaging in criminal behavior.

Correlation
Describes two variables or factors that are linked or related in some way.

Hypothesis
Term that describes the research process that investigates if a factor or variable causes an outcome.

Research question
Similar to a hypothesis but is not limited to investigating causation. Research questions provide a path of study or investigation.

Panopticon
A circular structure that is placed at the center of a larger complex that is under surveillance, such as a prison. Allows an individual or small group of people to set up an observation point and watch over the larger surrounding area.

Biological theories of crime
Looks at how genetic characteristics can be used to explain crime.

Psychological theories of crime
Explores how characteristics related to childhood development, cognitive development, and personality can be used to explain criminal behavior.

the first to use the scientific method to explain criminal behavior. Unlike scholars before him, who approached the understanding of crime from a philosophical perspective, Lombroso collected extensive amounts of data to help support his theory. While Lombroso's research has been highly criticized for how his data were collected, as most of his subjects came from Italian prisons, his efforts have led him to be recognized as the father of modern criminology.

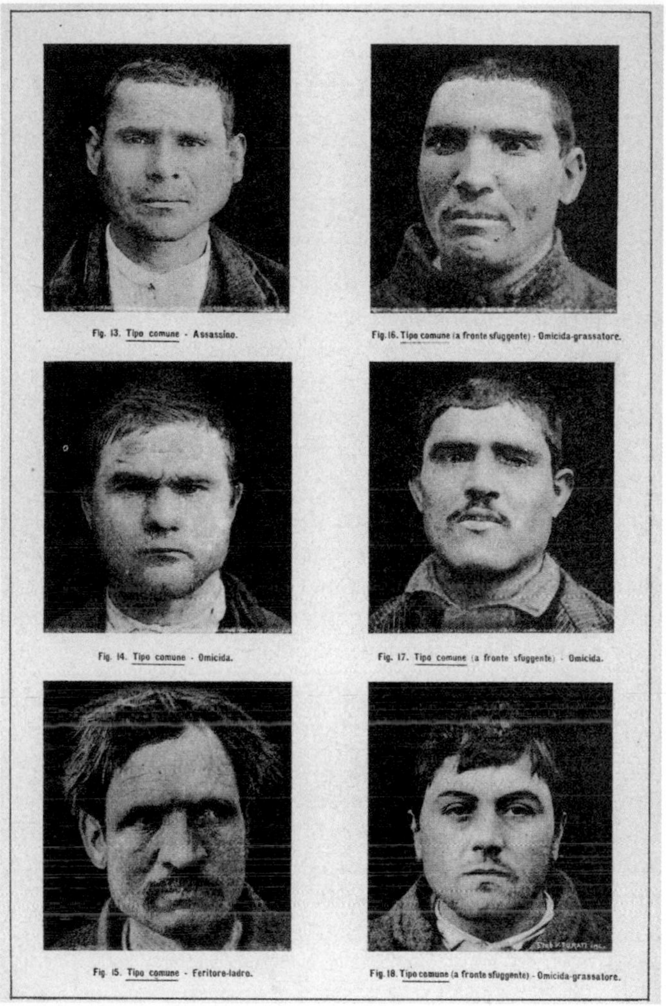

William Ferrero

Lombroso's work was not limited to the male offender, and he joined forces with William Ferrero to investigate the nature of the female offender. Lombroso and Ferrero went to women's prisons and noted the physical characteristics of the incarcerated women. They attributed a number of unique features to the female criminal, including occipital irregularities, narrow foreheads, prominent cheekbones, and a "virile" type of face. While they found that female offenders had fewer degenerative characteristics compared with male offenders, they explained these differences by suggesting that women, in general, are biologically more primitive and less evolved than men. They also suggested that the "evil tendencies" of female offenders "are more numerous and more varied than men's."[9] Female criminals were believed to be more like men than women, in terms of both their mental and physical qualities, suggesting that female offenders were more likely to experience suppressed "maternal instincts" and possess fewer "ladylike" qualities. They were convinced that women who engaged in crime would be less sensitive to pain, less compassionate, generally jealous, and full of revenge—in short, criminal women possessed all of the worst characteristics of the female gender while embodying the criminal tendencies of the male.

Fig. 13. Tipo comune - Assassino.

Fig. 16. Tipo comune (a fronte sfuggente) - Omicida-grassatore.

Fig. 14. Tipo comune - Omicida.

Fig. 17. Tipo comune (a fronte sfuggente) - Omicida.

Fig. 15. Tipo comune - Feritore-ladro.

Fig. 18. Tipo comune (a fronte sfuggente) - Omicida-grassatore.

Italian scholar Cesare Lombroso was the first criminologist to use the scientific method to explain the causes of criminal behavior, but this did not always lead him to accurate conclusions. He speculated that there was a link between physical deformities and criminal behavior. Why is this problematic?

WEB LINK
The Origins of Modern Criminology

Foundations of Psychological Theories of Crime

Like biological theories of crime, psychological theories of crime look at how individual factors can be used to explain criminal behavior. Psychologically based criminologists explain criminal behavior by individual factors, such as deficiencies in early childhood socialization or experiences, that lead to gaps in cognitive development. It is these gaps that these theorists suggest can explain why people commit crime. Psychological theories have also investigated how behaviors such as aggression, violence, and impulsivity are learned behaviors. Such theories also look at how mental disorders are related to criminality, a topic that you learned about in Chapter 1. However, psychological theories of crime still see criminal behavior as something that people are compelled toward, rather than an action of free will or rational choice.

WEB LINK
Deterrence

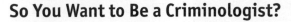

CAREERS IN CRIMINAL JUSTICE

So You Want to Be a Criminologist?

Criminologists investigate a number of different topics, including the causes of crime, criminal behavior, crime prevention, and how society responds to crime. Since criminology is a diverse field, people who work in this area approach the study of crime from a number of different backgrounds, including sociology, psychology, criminal justice, economics, and biology.

As a criminologist, you might be employed by a university, a government agency, a research institute, or a nonprofit organization. If you are employed by a university, chances are you might spend part of your day in a classroom—in fact, many of your faculty members in criminal justice are also actively engaged in research on criminal justice issues. Many universities also have faculty members who devote all of their time to research. As a government employee, you might work for organizations such as the Bureau of Justice Statistics (BJS), which is part of the Office of Justice Programs. The BJS conducts a number of different surveys on issues such as the mental health of inmates in solitary confinement or sexual assault in juvenile detention facilities. They also produce an annual report on trends of corrections, such as the number of individuals who are sentenced to probation or who are admitted to jails annually. Think tanks, such as the RAND Corporation or the Urban Institute, are also involved in research, such as evaluating whether police-worn body cameras reduce citizen complaints or whether the use of technology could improve parole supervision.

The education level needed for this job is dependent on where you will be working and the type of work that you will be doing. For those criminologists who teach at a college or university, the minimum degree is a master's degree, though many academics have a doctoral degree (PhD). Most of these positions require a master's degree or higher. In addition, you will likely need to have specialized training in statistics and research methods as part of the job requirements. Depending on the type of work that you are performing and your educational level and experience, the starting salary for these types of jobs ranges from $33,000 to $80,000.

CAREER VIDEO
Criminologist

Sigmund Freud

While his psychoanalytic theory was not specific to understanding criminal behavior, Sigmund Freud's work on the unconscious mind is often used to help explain criminality from a psychological perspective. Freud argued that an individual's personality is based on three parts: the id, the ego, and the superego. The id refers to one's instinctual wants and desires and is present at birth. The id does not have the ability to moderate itself, and as we grow, the id must be controlled. In comparison, the ego is more realistic and represents the part of the personality that deals with cognitive decision-making skills. The ego is the rational thinker of one's personality. If the id represents the passionate side of one's personality, then the ego is the reflection of common sense and morality. Finally, the superego refers to ability to create balance between the id and the ego. While the id is present at birth, and the ego evolves as part of one's development, the superego is the voice of reason. In many cases, this voice is instilled by influential individuals in our lives, such as parents, teachers, and other authority figures.

VIDEO
Exploring the Mind
of a Killer

How can Freud's concepts of the id, ego, and superego be used to understand criminal behavior? In some respects, the id can be thought of as the part of the personality that drives impulsive behavior. Given that many crimes are committed in the heat of the moment or are acts of opportunity, they would be considered to be driven by the id. In comparison, the ego is the side of the personality that would encourage law-abiding behavior, with the superego being the calculating rational thinker, making engaged decisions about whether to commit a crime.[10]

Contemporary Biological and Psychological Theories of Crime

Since the days of Lombroso and Freud, several other biologically and psychologically based theories have emerged to help explain criminal behavior on an individual scale. Psychological theories, such as **cognitive development theories**, were initially developed by Jean Piaget and were later refined by Lawrence Kohlberg and colleagues. Cognitive development theories posit that offenders have failed to develop the capacity to make moral judgments.

SAGE JOURNAL ARTICLE
General Multilevel Opportunity and Crime Events

Jean Piaget

Piaget's work identified four stages in the cognitive development of children. First, the sensorimotor stage refers to the first two years of life. During this stage, children learn about the world through their sensory explorations. The second stage is the preoperational stage, which lasts from ages 2 to 7. During this stage, children develop their language communication skills. They also build their imagination and play skills. It isn't until the third stage, the concrete operational stage, that children begin to develop their logic skills. They begin to understand how they relate to a larger community, such as a group of friends. They also begin to feel empathy for others. The concrete operational stage begins around age 7 and lasts until age 11. Finally, the formal operational stage begins at age 12 and continues into adulthood. During this fourth stage, children increase their logic development and begin to explore deductive reasoning skills. They also begin to diversify their thought and identify multiple solutions to a problem.[11]

Lawrence Kohlberg

The work of Lawrence Kohlberg applied Piaget's theory of moral development to the study of criminal behavior. Their six stages of development can be grouped into three levels, each with two steps. Level one is the **preconventional stage**. Here, children develop obedience and are first introduced to the notion of punishment. They also begin to determine their own self-interests. At this level, children may evaluate how they can avoid punishment. Level two is the **conventional level**. Here, youth identify with the social norms of law-abiding behavior and, as a result, avoid law-violating behaviors. Level three is the **postconventional level**. At this level, young adults begin to consider their worldview in light of their own moral compass. Kohlberg and his colleagues found that youth who engaged in violent behaviors had significantly lower levels of moral development, as illustrated by these three levels, compared with youth who were not involved in acts of violence.[12]

Contemporary studies on the psychology of crime have influenced the criminal justice system in a number of ways. One area in which such theories have had an instrumental effect is on our correctional system. While you'll learn more about this in Chapter 11 of this text, two of the most significant contributions include the classification of offenders and the use of cognitive-based therapies. For example, the use of risk assessment tools to predict the behavior of offenders has altered not only the sentencing of offenders but also how they are supervised in the community and how they are managed within a correctional institution.

Biosocial Theories

Just as psychological theories have evolved since the days of Freud, so have biological theories of crime. The works of Lombroso have inspired a new generation of biological and **biosocial theories of crime**. These individual-level theories began to reemerge following several decades of focus on sociological theories, which you'll learn more about in the next section. In some cases, scholars have combined the knowledge

Cognitive development theories
Suggests that offenders have failed to develop the capacity to make moral judgments.

Preconventional stage
Level one of Lawrence Kohlberg's theory of cognitive development and crime. Refers to the stage when children develop obedience and are introduced to the concept of punishment.

Conventional level
Level two of Lawrence Kohlberg's theory of cognitive development and crime, where youth begin to identify with the social norms of law-abiding behavior.

Postconventional level
Level three of Lawrence Kohlberg's theory of cognitive development and crime where young adults begin to consider their worldview in light of their own moral compass.

Biosocial theories of crime
Combines features of biological theories of crime and how they interact with social environments to produce criminological behaviors.

of biological factors of crime, such as genetics, with the understanding of social environments. These modern perspectives do not identify biological factors as the sole cause of crime (as early biological theories did). Rather, these works investigate how biological traits can contribute to crime and, in many cases, how these factors interact with social environments to produce criminological behaviors. For example, a number of biosocial explanations of crime have focused on how variance in brain chemistry can have an impact on criminal behavior. Here, scholars such as Adrian Raine and Diana Fishbein look at how variables such as neurotransmitters (chemicals that carry information to the brain)—for example, dopamine and serotonin—and hormones (like testosterone) can impact behavior. Research has linked higher levels of testosterone with aggression and antisocial behaviors.[13] Meanwhile, antisocial individuals are more likely to possess lower levels of serotonin.[14] Both aggression and antisocial behavior are correlates of criminal behavior.

Finally, research has also documented a relationship between environment and crime. One of the most studied variables in this realm is lead poisoning. During the 1920s, the use of lead paint increased. Similarly, gasoline from the 1940s to 1970s also had high levels of lead. While we can't conclude that violent-crime spikes during the 1930s and from the 1950s to the 1980s were a result of lead exposure, there is a corresponding pattern.[15] Research has noted that exposure to lead, particularly for young children, can increase the risk of learning disabilities, behavioral problems, and attention-deficit/hyperactivity disorder.[16] In 2015, the city of Flint, Michigan, was thrust into the national spotlight as a result of news that the public water source (Flint River) was heavily polluted by lead. Worse yet, documents indicate that government officials shifted to using the Flint River as a water source (versus Lake Huron, which is treated by anticorrosives) in an effort to save money. Even once the state learned that there were high levels of lead in the water, they failed to do anything about it.[17] Given what we know about lead exposure, will we see increased harm to a community that is already challenged by poverty and crime in future decades? You'll learn more about the challenges that communities such as Flint experience later in this chapter.

AUDIO

Flint Water Crisis

SOCIOLOGICAL THEORIES OF CRIME

Sociological theories of crime
Describes macrolevel theories that look at how larger social structures can help explain criminal behavior.

Biological and psychological theories focus on individual acts of crime. As a result, punishment for crime deals with how we can treat or reform an individual. These types of theories are considered microlevel theories. In contrast, **sociological theories of crime** are macrolevel theories, in that they look at how larger social structures, such as environments and institutions (for example, schools, peer groups, and the family), can help explain criminal behavior.

Social disorganization theory
Theory that investigates how neighborhood environments contribute to criminal behavior.

Social Disorganization Theory

Social disorganization theory investigates how neighborhood environments contribute to criminal behavior. Using the city of Chicago as their laboratory, Robert Park and Ernest Burgess suggested that as cities grow and prosper, residents are either forced out of the business zones or choose to exit in an effort to escape the chaos of city life.[18] This, in turn, leads to a deterioration of inner-city communities. Their work provided the foundation for Clifford Shaw and Henry McKay's discussion of social disorganization as an explanation for criminal behavior.[19] Shaw and McKay demonstrated how the expansion of factories in Chicago during the 1920s and 1930s, coupled with the rise of immigration and the creation of suburban communities for upper- and middle-class families, led

> " If we think of communities as a reflection of commonly shared values and norms for behavior and that these values help guide individuals toward law-abiding behavior, what happens when a community lacks cohesion?

to a breakdown in traditional communities. The communities around these factories were often the most affordable places to live and were often dominated by workers and those new to the area and in search of employment. This constant turnover of residents meant limited opportunities to develop a sense of community culture. Those who could afford to do so moved out of the area. As factories continued to expand, the migration of new residents into these working-class areas increased, and at the same time, the exit of those with greater financial resources accelerated. This led to a lack of community cohesion, and as a result, criminal behavior began to rise.

Social disorganization theory is a reflection of how crime is related to socioeconomic status, particularly for lower-class communities. Unlike previous theories of crime that focused on an individual's biological or psychological characteristics to explain offending, social disorganization theory was one of the first efforts

What elements of social disorganization are evident here? Based on social disorganization theory, do you think crime rates in this neighborhood would be low, average, or high?

to look at the effects of social structures on crime. If we think of communities as a reflection of commonly shared values and norms for behavior and that these values help guide individuals toward law-abiding behavior, what happens when a community lacks cohesion? When a community is characterized by a state of frequent migration, people don't get the opportunity to know their neighbors and to develop networks, which, in turn, leads to a breakdown in the informal social controls that can help prevent crime. Figure 4.1 illustrates how these sorts of factors can lead to social disorganization and its link to criminal behavior.

Figure 4.1   Shaw and McKay's Theory of Social Disorganization

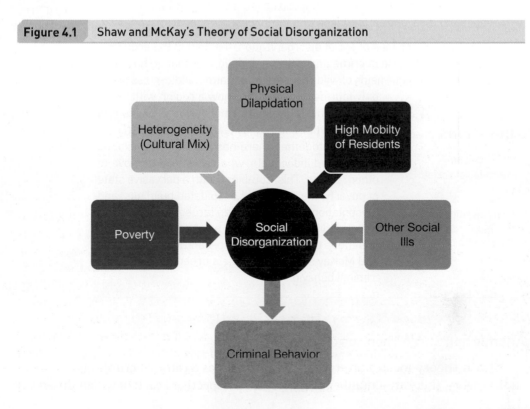

SPOTLIGHT

Flint, Michigan, and Social Disorganization Theory

The city of Flint, Michigan, is located 66 miles northwest of Detroit. During the 1960s, Flint was the second-largest city in Detroit, with almost 200,000 residents, and stood as an economic and political powerhouse for the state. As the home to numerous automotive factories, Flint was a town of employment, growth, and prosperity. However, beginning in the late 1960s, the city suffered from deindustrialization and urban decay. People began to leave the city as the factories began to close. Once a region dominated by companies such as General Motors (which, in 1978, provided jobs to more than 80,000 individuals in the region), changes to the automotive industry meant a significant hit to the city's employment rate. Today, fewer than 8,000 people are employed in this field.

The changes to the city were reflected in a mass exodus of middle-class communities from Flint. Such a phenomenon is not unique, and similar patterns emerged in other cities that saw a reduction in blue-collar jobs. Similar to the movement of communities from Chicago as described by Shaw and McKay in the 1920s and 1930s, the urbanization of the city and surrounding region reflected a time of rapid growth. Today, the population density in Flint is much greater than other parts of the state (3,065 residents per square mile, compared with 174 persons per square mile statewide). Alas, the downturn of the economy meant that people were soon left with an area where there was little social structure to help promote a positive community. Poverty and inequality soon became the new neighbors in the city. For example, the median household income in Flint today ($26,339) is nearly half of the per capita income for the state ($48,471). Similarly, many of the residents in Flint live below the poverty line (39.7% in Flint, compared with 16% statewide). The median value of Michigan homes is $128,600 while the median value of Flint homes is $50,500. Finally, the educational level of Flint residents further differentiates them from other state residents; while 25% of state residents hold a bachelor's degree or higher, only 11% of Flint residents do so. Considering that such shifts occurred over less than four decades, the effects have been significant for the community.

The effects of these experiences are reflected in the high levels of crime and violence in the region. Since 2007, Flint's violent-crime rate has been among the top five among cities of 100,000 or more, and the city has been ranked number one since 2011. In addition, it has been ranked as the sixth most violent city for women, had the highest per capita murder rate in the country (2012), and had the most per capita arson fires in the United States (2011). Aside from the issue of crime, Flint can be found in the top 100 cities with the oldest houses, top 100 least educated cities, and among cities with the highest number of infant deaths.

Looking at the city of Flint today through the lens of social disorganization, the shift in the economic climate of the city plays a significant role in the rise of crime and violence. Indeed, the change has been significant—what were once fields of wild raspberries or calm middle-class areas only four decades ago are now a region with crack houses where gunshots ring out near parks and schools. While community leaders work to bring the residents together, there has been a mass exodus of educated individuals, who can afford to move to other regions. This, combined with a pervasive state of poverty, the number of dilapidated buildings, and a population that is one of the largest for the region makes it difficult to establish a cohesive community. It is these types of social disorganization that Shaw and McKay suggested make a breeding ground for criminal behavior.

CRITICAL THINKING QUESTIONS

1. What makes communities such as Flint, Michigan, ideal examples of social disorganization theory?

2. Based on this theory, how can cities like Flint reduce their crime rate?

Anomie and Strain Theories of Crime

Strain theory focuses on stress and frustration as a cause of criminality. Within strain theory, there are a number of theoretical perspectives, each of which differs on

Strain theory
Focuses on stress and frustration as a cause of criminality.

the causes of this stress and frustration. Despite these differences, they all begin with the works of Robert Merton as their foundation.

Robert Merton's theory of strain was heavily influenced by Émile Durkheim's concept of anomie. **Anomie** refers to a sense of normlessness that societies experience as a result of a breakdown in the social cohesion of society. Individuals experience anomie when they lack guidance and structure for appropriate social behaviors. Here, criminal behavior is a consequence of anomie.[20]

According to Robert Merton, people experience strain when the socially approved goals do not mesh with the socially approved means to achieve those goals. Merton identified five different categories within his theory. The **conformist** is someone who accepts both the socially approved goals and the means to achieve them. Even though they may not always be successful in their quest, these individuals remain committed to this path by working hard to achieve success in their lives. A **ritualist** is someone who rejects the socially approved goals but engages in the processes that society mandates. Ritualists resign themselves to a particular life, in that they likely won't achieve high levels of wealth and status, thereby relieving strain. Conformists and ritualists are generally law-abiding individuals. In comparison, Merton's three other categories (the innovator, the retreatist, and the rebel) are more likely to engage in crime. An **innovator** is someone who embraces the socially approved goals but rejects the means to get there. The common example of an innovator is a drug dealer. This person wants the fruits of success in his or her life, such as money and status, but is either incapable of or not interested in doing what society says one should. Instead, the innovator finds a different way (even if it breaks the law) to get what she or he wants. A **retreatist** isn't interested in traditional measures of success, nor is this person willing to engage in hard work. Rather, these individuals tend to remove themselves from society entirely. For example, someone who engages in heavy drug use as a method of escape would be considered a retreatist. Finally, the **rebel** is someone who, in rejecting socially approved goals and means, develops new goals and means.[21]

General Strain Theory

While several theorists have made contributions to understanding how an individual's aspirations collide with the goals of society, the works of Robert Agnew represent perhaps the most modern of these applications, in terms of criminal behavior. While traditional theories of strain focused on the structural limitations of success, Agnew's **general strain theory** looks into individualized psychological sources as correlates of criminal behavior (Table 4.1). Agnew highlights three potential sources of strain: (1) failure to achieve positive goals, (2) the loss of positive influences, and (3) the arrival of negative influences.[22] In particular, strain-inducing events are most likely to lead to criminal behavior if they "1) are seen as unjust; 2) are seen as high in magnitude;

Table 4.1	Robert Merton's Adaptations to Strain	
Adaptation to Strain	**Society's Goals**	**Society's Means to Achieve Goals**
Conformity	Accepts	Accepts
Innovation	Accepts	Rejects
Ritualism	Rejects	Accepts
Retreatism	Rejects	Rejects
Rebellion	Develops New	Develops New

Anomie
Theory that refers to a sense of normlessness that societies experience as a result of a breakdown in social cohesion.

Conformist
Conformists are people who accept both the socially approved goals and the means to achieve them.

Ritualist
Someone who rejects socially approved goals but engages in the processes that society mandates.

Innovator
Someone who embraces the socially approved goals but rejects the means to get there.

Retreatist
Someone who is neither interested in the traditional measures of success nor willing to engage in hard work.

Rebel
Someone who rejects both the socially approved goals and means and replaces them with alternatives.

General strain theory
Looks at individualized psychological sources as correlates of criminal behavior.

3) are associated with low social control, and 4) create some pressure or incentive to engage in criminal coping."[23]

Research on strain theory highlights that some individuals are more likely to engage in criminal and delinquent behaviors than others as a result of their experiences with strain. For example, juveniles who experience strain within their relationships with their families, schools, and neighborhoods are more likely to engage in delinquent acts.[24] African Americans also experience strain in ways that are unique to their community. Efforts to cope with such strain may lead to increased risks for crime and delinquency. For example, victimization rates are higher in communities of color. This is particularly true for cases of violent victimization. These experiences of victimization impact not only individuals but larger social groups, such as families and communities. Fighting back against victimization becomes a way to deal with strain and, in turn, can lead to increased risks of offending.[25] General strain theory can be used to explain gender differences in crime. Girls are more likely to experience strain as a result of violence in the home (physical, emotional, and sexual), which, in turn, leads to delinquent acts such as running away and substance abuse. Second, boys and girls respond to strain differently. While strain can manifest as anger for both boys and girls, they exhibit this anger in different ways. For example, girls are more likely to internalize their feelings of anger, which can lead to self-destructive behaviors and depression. In contrast, boys tend to exhibit anger in physical and emotional outbursts.[26]

Differential Association Theory

Differential association theory focuses on the influence relationships have on crime, in particular, the influence of peer relationships on delinquent behavior. Developed by Edwin Sutherland, differential association theory is influenced by social learning theory. Differential association theory posits that learned behaviors about crime and delinquency are a result of peer associations. As youth spend time with people, these people then influence their knowledge, practices, and judgments of delinquent behavior. The more a person is exposed to these delinquent attitudes and behaviors, the more they influence this person.

Sutherland identified nine key principles for his differential association theory (Table 4.2). Each of these principles reinforces the idea that criminal behavior is a learned behavior. This perspective was a significant departure from many of the other theories about crime during this time period, as they were more likely to identify crime as an inherent or biological trait.

Differential association theory
Focuses on how relationships, particularly peer relationships, influence delinquent behavior.

Differential association theory suggests that criminal behavior is learned. Peer relationships represent one of the primary ways in which delinquent behaviors are shared among youth. What assumptions about causation does this theory make?

Since Sutherland first published his theory of differential association, there has been a substantial body of research highlighting the importance of peer relationships in crime. Recent research has highlighted how demographic factors such as race, ethnicity, and gender can impact how peer relationships affect delinquent behavior. For example, as girls spend more time with their delinquent peers, their likelihood of engaging in delinquent behaviors increases.[27] Meanwhile, other research indicates that the effect of delinquent relationships is stronger for males than females.[28] However, there have also been criticisms of differential association

Table 4.2	Sutherland's Principles of Differential Association
Principle 1	Criminal behavior is learned.
Principle 2	Criminal behavior is learned in interaction with other persons in a process of communication.
Principle 3	The principal part of the learning of criminal behavior occurs within intimate personal groups.
Principle 4	When criminal behavior is learned, the learning includes (a) techniques of committing the crime, which are sometimes very complicated, sometimes very simple; and (b) the specific direction of motives, drives, rationalizations, and attitudes.
Principle 5	The specific direction of motives and drives is learned from definitions of the legal codes as favorable or unfavorable.
Principle 6	A person becomes delinquent because of an excess of definitions favorable to violation of law over definitions unfavorable to violation of law.
Principle 7	Differential associations may vary in frequency, duration, priority, and intensity.
Principle 8	The process of learning criminal behavior by association with criminal and anti-criminal patterns involves all of the mechanisms that are involved in any other learning.
Principle 9	While criminal behavior is an expression of general needs and values, it is not explained by those general needs and values since noncriminal behavior is an expression of the same needs and values.

theory. One of the key criticisms involves the temporal order of criminal behavior. In this instance, it can often be difficult to determine whether an individual engages in crime because of her or his association with delinquent peers or whether someone seeks out like-minded individuals as a result of becoming involved in criminal behavior.

Labeling Theory

Labeling theory focuses on how people react to criminal behavior. In many ways, labeling offenders allows society to separate the law-abiding individuals from the deviant and delinquent ones. Edwin Lemert popularized labeling theory by creating a framework for understanding how people are labeled as delinquent or criminal and how this label can impact future behaviors. He distinguished between two different types of behaviors: primary deviance and secondary deviance. **Primary deviance** refers to minor acts that are often not serious. However, these acts are brought to the attention of police and the courts. As a result, the individual is labeled an offender. As the label of delinquent or criminal carries a negative association in society, an individual may then adopt this new identity. This process is known as a **self-fulfilling prophecy**. As a result, the individual, who may not have been engaging in serious acts initially, may subsequently be drawn to these negative behaviors. Here, the assumption becomes this: "Well, if I'm going to be looked at in a negative way, I might as well embrace it." In turn, individuals can find themselves engaged in acts of **secondary deviance**, which may often increase in frequency or severity.[29]

Social Learning Theory

According to Albert Bandura, **social learning theory** suggests that people learn from observing the behaviors of others around them. This is referred to as **modeling**—"from observing others one forms an idea of how new behaviors are performed, and on later occasions this coded information serves as a guide for action."[30] Bandura also suggested that there are multiple reinforcements of learning behaviors. Just as the larger social environment can reinforce the learning experience, there are also internal intrinsic rewards, such as experiencing personal satisfaction or pride from learning a new behavior. However, it is important to note that just because a behavior is learned, that doesn't

Labeling theory
Focuses on how being labeled as delinquent or criminal can influence future behaviors, regardless of the accuracy of the label.

Primary deviance
Refers to minor acts that are often not serious yet result in being labeled as an offender.

Self-fulfilling prophecy
Describes the process whereby individuals who may not have been engaging in serious acts initially may subsequently be drawn to these negative behaviors as a result of being labeled as an offender.

Secondary deviance
Refers to acts of deviance that occur as a result of assuming the identity of a label.

Social learning theory
Suggests that people learn from observing the behaviors of others around them.

Modeling
New behaviors are learned from observing others.

VIDEO
Self-Fulfilling Prophecy

mean that it will result in a change in behavior. We can think about these concepts in relationship to crime in the following way. Consider how popular culture can influence behavior as individuals mimic or model acts that they see on television, in movies, and even in music lyrics and video games. If such behaviors are perceived by some as "cool" or "popular," this can impact how people weigh out the costs and rewards of illegal activity. Another example is through peer relationships. If your peers are involved in shoplifting, and you want to be accepted by your peers, then the intrinsic rewards of being part of the group can outweigh the moral concerns about breaking the law. Ron Akers and Robert Burgess refer to this process as **differential reinforcement**. Differential reinforcement looks at behavior as a balance between increasing the rewards that come with engaging in deviant or criminal behaviors and minimizing the potential consequences and punishments. We learn this balance as a result of our relationships with those around us, such as parents and peers.[31] While differential reinforcement is an adaptation of Sutherland's differential association theory, it has been criticized for not acknowledging the differences between individuals and how such differences might alter the process of reinforcement in group settings.

Social Bond Theory

While most theories up to this point have focused on why offenders engage in crime, Travis Hirschi's work was unique in that he looked for explanations as to why people might desist from criminal behavior. His **social bond theory** focused on four criteria, or *bonds*, that prevent people from acting on potential criminological impulses or desires. He identified these bonds as (1) attachment, (2) commitment, (3) involvement, and (4) belief. *Attachment* refers to the bond that people have with family, friends, and social institutions (such as government, education, and religion) that may serve as an informal control against criminality. Hirschi posited that people refrain from criminal behavior as a result of these attachments, as they do not want to disappoint people in their lives. For example, youth who have positive attachments to parents or peers may limit their delinquent behavior because they do not want to disappoint these important people. The second concept, *commitment*, refers to the investment that an individual has in the normative values of society. In many ways, the concept of commitment embodies the spirit of rational-choice perspectives. For example, if one is committed to obtaining a college degree, and a violation of the law might limit one's ability to achieve that goal, one might decide not to engage in illegal behavior out of fear of jeopardizing his or her future. *Involvement* refers to the degree to which one participates in conventional activities such as studying or playing sports. The idea behind involvement is that youth who are more involved in these sorts of activities are less likely to engage in delinquent activities. Finally, *belief* refers to a general acceptance of the rules of society—"the less a person believes he should obey the rules, the more likely he is to violate them."[32]

Differential reinforcement Behaviors as a balance between increasing the rewards that come with engaging in deviant or criminal behaviors while minimizing the potential consequences and punishments.

Social bond theory Focuses on why people might desist from criminal behavior.

General theory of crime Focuses on self-control as the factor that explains delinquent and criminal behavior.

Hirschi's social bond theory suggests that attachment to conventional activities such as school or sports can serve as a protective factor against delinquency. Which of the four bonds could involvement in a sports team strengthen?

Control Theory

While Hirschi's social bond theory is considered a macrolevel perspective on criminal behavior, his **general theory of crime** (with Michael Gottfredson) is considered more of a microlevel theory. Gottfredson and Hirschi focus on

AROUND THE WORLD
Criminological Theory in a Global Context

Explanations of crime and criminal behavior are not limited to American soil. Indeed, many of our criminal justice processes originated in the United Kingdom, continental Europe, and Australia. At the same time, the experiences of crime in the United States and our justice system have influenced systems around the world. The same is true for understanding criminological theory. Many of the early criminologists were writing in Europe. For example, Cesare Lombroso was an Italian criminologist during the 19th century, and Michel Foucault was a French philosopher whose works during the mid-20th century had a significant impact on modern penology. While Adrian Raine is currently a professor in the United States, he was raised and trained in psychology in the UK.

In addition, the work of understanding criminal behavior looks at both national and international populations. For example, research on social bonds among Turkish youth indicates that social bonds have a stronger effect on the lives of female students. Given the heightened status of the family within Turkish culture, as well as differences in gender socialization between adolescent boys and girls in this region, it is not surprising that girls would be highly attached to the family unit. For boys, educational bonds, such as an attachment to teachers, are a stronger influence in preventing delinquency.[a]

Research on labeling theory in China demonstrates that labeling someone a delinquent can actually have positive effects because the stigma is a deterrent. As a result, a negative label can actually be a tool for rehabilitation. In addition, the effects of labeling are not limited to the individual but extend to the family and the general community. Consequently, there are significant sources of support for individuals to move away from a criminal identity. In this manner, families, neighborhoods, and schools are all active participants in cases of crime and delinquency.[b]

A final example of using criminological theory in an international context is the application of strain theory in a study of South Korean adolescents. The findings of this research indicate that stress related to academic performance on an exam and the emotional and physical abuse by teachers are two significant sources of strain for these youth. Even though these pressures are meant to encourage student success, they can have the opposite effect and encourage delinquent behaviors.[c]

CRITICAL THINKING QUESTIONS

1. Why is research on theories of crime in international contexts important to consider?

2. What are the challenges of using theory to understand criminal behavior in different countries? What are some of the other factors that you need to consider in this type of research?

self-control as the single explanatory factor for delinquent and criminal behavior. According to the general theory of crime, those individuals with high levels of social control will remain law abiding while those with low social control will be more likely to engage in deviant and criminal activities. But the question remains: What influences an individual's self-control? Gottfredson and Hirschi posit that the development of self-control is rooted in the family. The more involved parents are in their children's lives, the more likely they are to be aware of challenges to the development of their children's self-control. This awareness then leads to action, and parents are more likely to correct these issues at a young age. As a result, Gottfredson and Hirschi's general theory of crime suggests that early intervention efforts are the only effective tool to deter individuals from crime. From their perspective, variables such as gender, race, and class are irrelevant, as everything comes down to self-control.[33]

Since the development of Gottfredson and Hirschi's general theory of crime, many researchers have looked at the role of gender in this process using constructs such as impulsivity, risk-taking, and aggression as indicators of self-control. However, these findings demonstrate that the general theory of crime can explain the delinquency of boys but fails in its explanation for girls. For example, research on delinquent youth housed in the California Youth Authority indicates that while self-control measures are effective in predicting behavioral violations for incarcerated males, the misconduct in girls is more likely to be explained by other variables, such as age (younger girls are more likely to act out) and the presence of a psychiatric disorder.[34] The offense type can also make a difference in the role of self-control. While low self-control did predict offending behaviors for Latino boys and girls in terms of violent offenses, it did not predict the behaviors of girls who engage in property offenses (which generally compose much of female offending patterns).[35]

CONTEMPORARY THEORIES OF CRIME

Life Course Theory

While most theories look at a particular stage in life to explain delinquency and criminality, **life course theory** looks at how these behaviors begin during adolescence or young adulthood and either persist or desist throughout one's life and the factors or life events that may encourage these shifts in behavior. One of the most well-known theories within this field is Robert Sampson and John Laub's **age-graded developmental theory** (Figure 4.2).[36] Sampson and Laub's framework suggests that the events of one's life (from birth to death) can provide insight as to why one might engage in crime and highlights the importance of adolescence as a crucial time in the development of youthful (and ultimately adult) offending behaviors. Here, ties to conventional adult activities, such as family bonding and work, can serve as a protective factor in adulthood, even if the individual has engaged in delinquent acts during adolescence. Sampson and Laub suggest that it is a matter of how much social capital or how many positive relationships one has that can determine whether people continue to engage in crime or end up in a law-abiding lifestyle.

In developing their theory, Sampson and Laub returned to a dataset that was collected between 1949 and 1963 by Sheldon and Eleanor Glueck, who were early pioneers of longitudinal research. Of the 500 people in this sample, Sampson and Laub were able to follow up with 52 of the original study participants. Their research

Life course theory
Looks at how delinquent behaviors either persist or desist throughout one's life and how life events might encourage shifts in behavior.

Age-graded developmental theory
Explains how one might engage in crime as a result of one's life events.

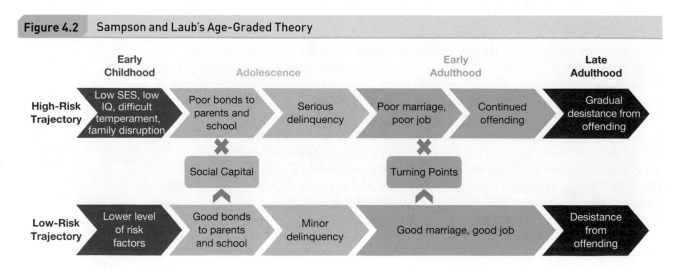

Figure 4.2 Sampson and Laub's Age-Graded Theory

indicated that regardless of whether participants were identified as having a low or high risk of offending, everyone had stopped engaging in criminal behaviors by age 70. Their theory demonstrates that eventually, everyone ages out of crime.

Feminist Criminology

Feminist criminology rose as an alternative to many of the traditional theories of crime. The majority of mainstream theories of crime failed to understand how female offenders differed from male offenders. In response, feminist scholars have sought out new perspectives to represent the female offender and her social world.

The emergence of feminist criminology builds upon the themes of gender roles and socialization to explain patterns of female offending. Here, scholars begin with a discussion on the backgrounds of female offenders in an effort to assess who they are, where they come from, and why they engage in crime. Feminist criminologists suggest that "feminist criminology began with the awareness that women were invisible in conventional studies in the discipline. . . . Feminist criminology began as a reaction . . . against an old established male chauvinism in the academic discipline."[37] While some criminologists suggested that traditional theories of crime could account for female offending, others argued that in order to accurately theorize about the criminal actions of women, a new approach to the study of crime needed to be developed.

Scholars point out that feminist discussions about crime aren't limited to "women's issues." They argue that it is important that any discussion of women's lives and criminality incorporates conversations on masculinity and patriarchy. Given the historical distortions and the casual assumptions that have been made about women's lives in relationship to their criminal behaviors, incorporating feminist perspectives can provide a richer understanding about not only the nature of female offending but also how women's experiences with victimization shape this process. In addition, feminist perspectives highlight that feminist criminology is not uniform but an opportunity to consider multiple influences when understanding issues of gender and crime.[38]

Feminist Pathways

The use of feminist theory, methodologies, and activism in discussions of criminology has led to a variety of new understandings about gender and crime. Perhaps one of the most influential perspectives to date on female offending is the **feminist pathways approach**. Feminist pathways research seeks to show how life events (and traumas) affect the likelihood to engage in crime. While the pathways approach has many similarities with other theories, such as life course or cycle-of-violence perspectives, these theories do not explain women's criminality from a feminist perspective. In comparison, the feminist pathways approach begins with a feminist foundation.[39] Within the feminist pathways approach, researchers have identified a cycle of violence for female offenders that begins with their own victimization and results in their involvement in offending behavior. One of the most significant contributions of feminist criminology is an understanding of the role of victimization in the histories of incarcerated women, as female offenders report substantially high occurrences of physical, emotional, and sexual abuse throughout their lifetimes. This is especially true of juvenile offenders, as shown in Figure 4.3. While such an explanation does not fit all female offenders (and also fits some male offenders), the recognition of these risks appears to be essential for understanding the etiology of offending for many girls and women. Yet this link between victimization and offending has largely been invisible or deemed inconsequential by the powers that be in criminology theory building and by those responsible for responding to women's and girls' victimizations and offenses.[40]

Feminist criminology
Alternative to traditional theories of crime, which often did not consider how the lives of women are different from men and, as a result, may explain the differences in offending behaviors.

Feminist pathways approach
Highlights how trauma and abuse contribute to offending behavior.

Figure 4.3 Prevalence of Adverse Childhood Experiences in Juvenile Offenders

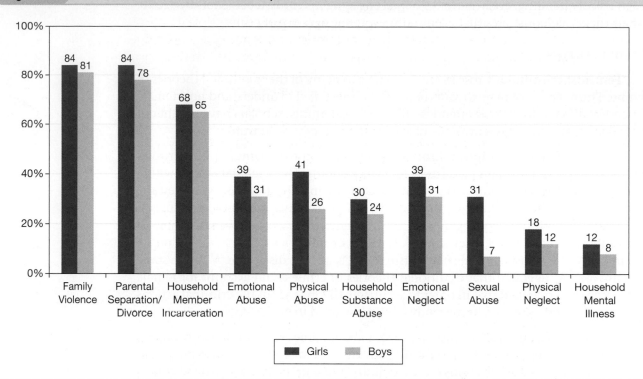

Source: Michael T. Baglivio et al. "Prevalence of Adverse Childhood Experiences (ACE) in the Lives of Juvenile Offenders." *OJJDP Journal of Juvenile Justice 3,* no. 2 (2014): 1–23, 8.

Figure 4.4 Time Line of Theories of Criminal Offending

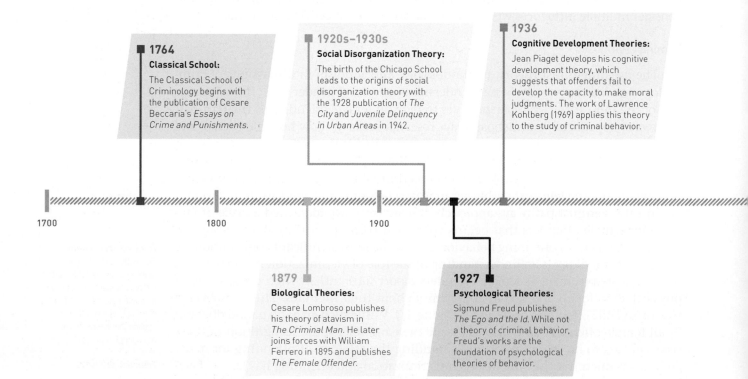

1764
Classical School:
The Classical School of Criminology begins with the publication of Cesare Beccaria's *Essays on Crime and Punishments.*

1920s–1930s
Social Disorganization Theory:
The birth of the Chicago School leads to the origins of social disorganization theory with the 1928 publication of *The City* and *Juvenile Delinquency in Urban Areas* in 1942.

1936
Cognitive Development Theories:
Jean Piaget develops his cognitive development theory, which suggests that offenders fail to develop the capacity to make moral judgments. The work of Lawrence Kohlberg (1969) applies this theory to the study of criminal behavior.

1879
Biological Theories:
Cesare Lombroso publishes his theory of atavism in *The Criminal Man.* He later joins forces with William Ferrero in 1895 and publishes *The Female Offender.*

1927
Psychological Theories:
Sigmund Freud publishes *The Ego and the Id.* While not a theory of criminal behavior, Freud's works are the foundation of psychological theories of behavior.

Feminist criminologists have also worked at identifying how issues such as race, class, and sexuality impact criminality (and the system's response to these offending behaviors). From this inquiry, we learn that women of color possess multiple marginalized identities, which, in turn, impact their trajectories of offending. Combining Black feminist theory and critical race feminist theory with feminist criminology allows for an enhanced understanding of how Black women experience crime. This perspective—*Black feminist criminology*—identifies four themes that alter the experiences for Black women in the criminal justice system. First, many Black women experience structural oppression in society. Second, the Black community and culture features unique characteristics as a result of their racialized experiences. Third, Black families differ in their intimate and familial relations. Finally, this perspective looks at the Black woman as an individual, unique in her own right.[41] Together, these unique dimensions lead to a different experience for Black women within the criminal justice system that needs to be recognized within theoretical conversations on women and crime.

Developments in feminist criminology have addressed the significant relationship between victimization and offending. A history of abuse not only is highly correlated with the propensity to engage in criminal behaviors but also often dictates the types of behaviors in which young girls engage. Often, these behaviors are methods of surviving their abuse, yet the criminal nature of these behaviors brings these girls to the attention of the criminal justice system. The success of a feminist perspective is dependent upon a theoretical structure that not only has to answer questions about crime and delinquency but also has to address issues such as sex role expectations and patriarchal structures within society.[42]

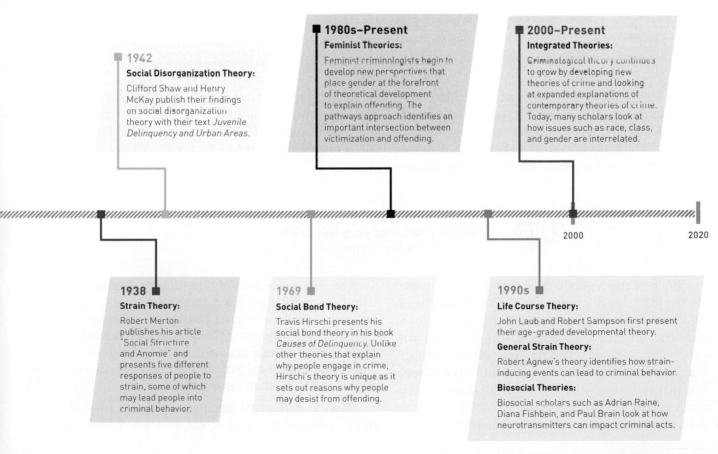

1942

Social Disorganization Theory:

Clifford Shaw and Henry McKay publish their findings on social disorganization theory with their text *Juvenile Delinquency and Urban Areas*.

1980s–Present

Feminist Theories:

Feminist criminologists begin to develop new perspectives that place gender at the forefront of theoretical development to explain offending. The pathways approach identifies an important intersection between victimization and offending.

2000–Present

Integrated Theories:

Criminological theory continues to grow by developing new theories of crime and looking at expanded explanations of contemporary theories of crime. Today, many scholars look at how issues such as race, class, and gender are interrelated.

2000   2020

1938

Strain Theory:

Robert Merton publishes his article "Social Structure and Anomie" and presents five different responses of people to strain, some of which may lead people into criminal behavior.

1969

Social Bond Theory:

Travis Hirschi presents his social bond theory in his book *Causes of Delinquency*. Unlike other theories that explain why people engage in crime, Hirschi's theory is unique as it sets out reasons why people may desist from offending.

1990s

Life Course Theory:

John Laub and Robert Sampson first present their age-graded developmental theory.

General Strain Theory:

Robert Agnew's theory identifies how strain-inducing events can lead to criminal behavior.

Biosocial Theories:

Biosocial scholars such as Adrian Raine, Diana Fishbein, and Paul Brain look at how neurotransmitters can impact criminal acts.

CONCLUSION

Whether it be micro theories or macro theories of crime, each perspective has added a new contribution to the understanding of criminal behavior. It is important to remember that no single theory can explain all acts of crime and that each theory has strengths and weaknesses. In addition, theories of crime continue to be tested to both provide a better understanding of criminal behavior and to expand upon the foundations of these schools of thought. Most notably, research on these theoretical perspectives today looks at how issues of race, gender, class, and sexuality might shift how we understand criminal behavior. Research on theories of crime has also taken on an international perspective; while most of the theories of criminal behavior originated in the United States, research on perspectives such as social bond theory and differential association are now looked at through an international context to explain at-risk and criminal behaviors in a global society. Figure 4.4 provides an overview of the development of these theories over time.

> "
> The success of a feminist perspective is dependent upon a theoretical structure that not only has to answer questions about crime and delinquency but also has to address issues such as sex role expectations and patriarchal structures within society.

CURRENT CONTROVERSY 4.1

PRO CON

CURRENT CONTROVERSY VIDEO
Where Do You Stand? Cast Your Vote!

Is There a Relationship Between Race and Class and Criminal Behavior?
—Kenethia McIntosh-Fuller—

INTRODUCTION

Race and social class are two very important divisions or classifications in American society. They are also two very controversial areas in the discussion of the causes of criminal behavior. At times, these variables are at the forefront of the discourse on crime, but at other times, they are the unexplored or ignored variables. But what are the core arguments around the relationship between race, social class, and crime?

RACE

PRO There Is a Relationship Between Race and Crime

Much of the research on race and crime focuses on the differences between Blacks and Whites, though the literature on Native Americans, Latinos, and other ethnic groups is increasing. Official statistics on crime show a difference in crime rates by race. Year after year, the UCR arrest data show that minorities are overrepresented for numerous offenses. This means that a group is arrested at a percentage higher than their percentage in the U.S. population.

The positivist school of criminology suggests that criminals are different from other citizens. It is those differences that induce an individual to engage in crime. To follow this line of thinking in reference to race would mean that there is something different about certain racial groups that compels them to engage in more criminal activities than other racial groups.

A wide variety of perspectives exist in positivist criminology. Biological and psychological criminology research has suggested that crime is actually a product of the biological makeup of certain human beings or their psychological characteristics. This research has a long tradition, starting with "the father of criminology," Cesare Lombroso. In his book, *The Criminal Man* (1876), Lombroso stated, "Criminals resemble savages and the colored races."[43] His work referred mainly to the differences among various groups in northern and southern Italy. However, in the second edition of his book, in 1878, Lombroso wrote that certain groups, such as tribes in Africa, "have no morality at all."[44] In addition, he stated that in Italy, the descendants of Arabs, Jews, and Gypsies were also more likely to be criminal.

Herrnstein and Murray wrote one of the most well-known studies on intelligence and crime, *The Bell Curve*.[45] One of the underlying assumptions of their research is that IQ is an accurate measure of intelligence and is inherited. The authors concluded that the people who struggle the most with social problems in society, such as poverty and criminal behavior, are also the groups that are more likely to have lower IQs. According to their research, of the groups studied, African Americans and immigrants are the groups most likely to be involved in crime, due to their low IQ scores.

Sociological perspectives on the relationship between race and crime also provide interesting insights. While most of the sociological criminology points to the conditions of an area as the main cause of crime, some research has examined the connection between neighborhoods and race. William Julius Wilson pointed out that Blacks and Whites live in different areas.[46] While many African Americans tend to live in areas with higher rates of poverty, African Americans who are the most successful move out of the poverty-stricken area, which leads to further decline. This results in *social isolation*, or the lack of interaction with mainstream society and mainstream values. Others have found support for this theory and suggest that this type of racial segregation leads to greater social and economic disadvantage. This, in turn, leads to increased crime.[47]

 ## CON   There Is Not a Relationship Between Race and Crime

Critical criminology suggests that crime is a social construct meant to oppress certain groups to protect the privileged position of groups in power. These theories realize that social inequality exists and is an inherent part of the criminal justice system.

There is a history of discrimination against minorities in the United States, particularly African Americans in the criminal justice system. These "systems of racial justice" set the foundations for racialized crime and justice policies that exist today.[48] Slave codes, Black codes, and Jim Crow were all forms of legal discrimination that served to keep African Americans from having any power or control in any arena. These laws severely restricted what African Americans could do and where they could go and outlawed behaviors that were completely acceptable and lawful for White citizens. Violation of these laws resulted in strict and severe punishments.

Discriminatory policies continued into more current times. Policies such as the war on drugs and the war on gangs in the 1980s and 1990s focused primarily on minority youth and resulted in harsher punishments for people of color.[49] Since then, other criminal justice practices have been called into question, such as racial profiling by law enforcement and sentencing disparities. Such practices have resulted in increased contact between minorities and the criminal justice system and harsher penalties. This may help explain the overrepresentation of minority offenders in official data.

A look at other data sources shows that race is not a significant factor in explaining differences in criminality. The UCR data show that Whites are arrested in greater numbers than any other group in the United States. Self-report studies have also consistently shown there are no significant racial differences in offending among different racial groups.

Are arrest rates accurate indicators of how much crime is committed and who is committing it? Why or why not?

SOCIAL CLASS

Generally, the public tends to think that crime is mostly committed by people within the lower classes of society. This perspective is understandable given that the UCR (which is supposed to be our best place for official data) focuses on street crimes as the index crimes or Part I offenses. That would indicate that these are the most important crimes and that these offenses happen more than other types of crimes. But is this an accurate statement?

PRO There Is a Relationship Between Social Class and Crime

There is some research support for a class–crime relationship. A lot of the support comes directly as a result of the introduction of some of our most influential crime theories. Park and Burgess studied the city of Chicago and found that cities expanded outward from the central business district. These concentric circles around the city formed zones. Zone two was referred to as the "slums," where crime rates were higher than anywhere else in the city.[50]

Merton proposed the idea of structural strain. According to Merton, crime is a result of the American desire for wealth. In an attempt to reach this highly valued cultural goal, some individuals will do whatever is necessary to achieve the goal, even if the methods to do so do not respect the law. Scholars have built upon Merton's work and referred to this goal as the "American Dream."[51] American society is focused on monetary gain and material possessions as the primary measure of success. All Americans are expected to reach for this goal in order to become successful. However, this focus leads to an imbalance of power in society and the devaluation of cultural norms, which then leads to crime.[52]

CON There Is Not a Relationship Between Social Class and Crime

As previously mentioned, according to the perspectives found in critical criminology, law is a social construct and social process. The law represents the values of the controlling classes of society. This means that when we talk about "crime," we talk about the perspective of crime presented by the "power elite" in society. This perspective is then publicized and reinforced by the media and internalized as fact by the general public.[53] Given this definition, social class is inescapably linked to political power.

Reiman and Leighton propose that some people do not think of white-collar crimes as negatively as other offenses because the problem is not as widespread, the harm is indirect, and the injuries are not as bad. In addition, if white-collar crimes were as bad as street crimes, the laws against and punishments for white-collar crimes would be harsher, and it would be more prevalent in the media.[54] Evidence for this argument is illustrated by the fact that the focus of the study of crime tends to be on street crimes, or the crimes of the lower classes. The index crimes of the Uniform Crime Reports focus on street crimes rather than white-collar crimes. Media representations of crime focus on "crime in the streets" and not "crime in the suites." Research on crime and justice tends to focus on the lower classes, property crimes, violent crimes, delinquency, and status offenses. The largest area of discourse in criminological theory is on the sociological explanations of offending, not on critical perspectives. The research and political agendas surrounding crime may (even if unknowingly) support the myth that crime is a lower-class problem.

SUMMARY

Given the research on race, class, and crime, we are left with the question of whether race and class status impact criminal behavior. At the same time, a look at our incarcerated population indicates that prisoners are disproportionately people from lower-class and minority communities. Here, the question remains: Are people of color and the poor more likely to engage in criminal activity, or are they more likely to be prosecuted and incarcerated for these offenses?

DISCUSSION QUESTIONS

1. How have criminological theories been used to support the idea that a relationship exists between race and crime?

2. How have policies led to the overrepresentation of minority offenders in our official data sources on crime?

3. How is our understanding about the relationships between social class and crime limited through our use of official crime data sources?

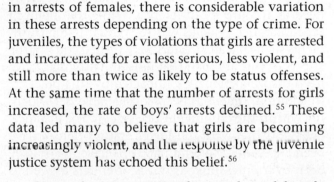

CURRENT CONTROVERSY 4.2

Should the Criminal Justice System Treat Female Offenders Differently?

—Jill L. Rosenbaum—

CURRENT
CONTROVERSY
VIDEO
Where Do You Stand?
Cast Your Vote!

INTRODUCTION

Historically, the study of criminal behavior was essentially the study of male criminal behavior. As a result, many policies and practices were designed to address the needs of male offenders. Because females were responsible for only a small amount of all known crimes, and their offending was believed to be predominately sexual in nature, they were seen as tangential to any serious study of crime.

Today, there is no dispute that the crime rates have increased considerably since the 1960s. If one looks at the Uniform Crime Reports, the data indicate that females accounted for 10% of all arrests in 1965 but increased to 27% in 2014. However, it must be noted that while there has been a huge increase in arrests of females, there is considerable variation in these arrests depending on the type of crime. For juveniles, the types of violations that girls are arrested and incarcerated for are less serious, less violent, and still more than twice as likely to be status offenses. At the same time that the number of arrests for girls increased, the rate of boys' arrests declined.[55] These data led many to believe that girls are becoming increasingly violent, and the response by the juvenile justice system has echoed this belief.[56]

Given this increase in the number of female arrests, the question arises: Should the criminal justice system treat female offenders differently?

 Female Offenders Should Not Be Treated Differently

Over the past four decades, the police and the courts changed the way they handled female offenders. Consider the following example: In 1968, a 17-year-old woman from California and her boyfriend took a bus to New York City. Once there, they used a weapon to rob a cab driver. Though the police report indicated that the cab driver reported to the police that the young woman held the knife, the police were skeptical of his story. They identified the young woman as a runaway, put her back on a bus to California, and charged the boyfriend with armed robbery. In today's society, the police's view of women is quite different, and the young woman would not be assumed to be guiltless and would also be charged. Herein lies the challenge of treating girls differently.

Today, there have been significant changes in how the system deals with the cases of female offenders. Many of these changes have resulted in treating females in the same way as males. For example, zero-tolerance policies in schools have significantly affected the number of youth being charged with crimes. Whereas schools used to handle these behaviors informally, they now make their way into the criminal courts. Such policies allow for like cases to be treated in similar ways.

Research has demonstrated that even though males and females can have different pathways to offending, they may, in some cases, receive the same sentences. This is one way of treating offenders the same, regardless of sex.[57] In addition, just as was true of theories explaining why people engage in criminal behavior, programs and policies in the criminal justice system were designed to protect and treat male offenders. As a result, the system has operated by treating males and females the same. Finally, others argue that maintaining gender-neutral programs is necessary. Proponents of gender-neutral policies argue that males and females should be treated equally. In addition, it is more cost-effective and allows programs to run seamlessly. For example, many facilities run programs that are coed. This allows for one set of programming and one set of staff members who can work with all of the program participants. All staff can receive the same training and can cover for one another whenever needed.

 PRO   **Female Offenders Should Be Treated Differently**

In addressing the argument that female offenders should be treated differently, it is important to note that this encompasses our criminal laws and policies, sentencing practices, and programs for offenders.

First, consider how our criminal policies may need to account for difference. While the intent of zero-tolerance policies was to standardize punishments such that all violators were treated equally, the effects of this are such that girls, in particular, have been disproportionately impacted by this practice. In addition, there has been considerable net widening within the criminal justice system. For instance, behaviors that were considered status offenses have been "upgraded" to criminal. Girls have historically been overrepresented as status offenders as well as family-based offenders. Many young women currently serving time in detention are there for domestic violence. The behaviors included under this charge can be throwing a phone at a parent or sibling. In the past, these behaviors were dealt with informally, through family counseling, but now they are dealt with in the criminal justice system. In this sense, trying to treat girls in the same way as boys has actually resulted in increased punishments. Consequently, it may be necessary to reform such laws to acknowledge that girls should be treated differently under the law.

As the number of female arrests increased, so did the number of girls sentenced to secure facilities and supervision/rehabilitation programs. Programs designed for males were replicated in female facilities without thought to the differences between males and females. Alas, we now know that these programs may not be as effective for females. This has led to the development of gender-responsive practices.

A key component to creating gender-responsive practices involves acknowledging the traumatic experiences of girls on their pathways to delinquency. You learned in this chapter that an overwhelming number of justice-involved girls report histories of multiple forms of trauma, such as abuse, neglect, witnessing violence, incest, rape, death of a parent or parents, and loss of a loved one to incarceration, at a higher rate than boys (see Figure 4.3). Some argue that to treat female delinquents in the same fashion as their male counterparts is ineffective because it fails to get at the heart of why girls engage in delinquent behavior and how the context of their lives informs their choices. These perspectives argue that acknowledging the differences and complexities of their experiences as girls and young women is crucial to implementing a gender-responsive program. Moreover, programs that use an integrative, cooperative, and holistic approach; foster empowerment; emphasize strengths; employ gender-responsive cognitive-behavioral elements; and build self-esteem, resiliency, and self-efficacy are the most effective at addressing girls' needs. Supporters of gender-responsive programs also recommend that a number of elements be considered when developing gender-specific correctional programming and factored into service delivery to women and girls. For instance, gender-specific programs must provide gender-relevant opportunities and not utilize programs designed for males in a female-only program. Female-only programs must recognize the fact that female needs and issues are very different from those of males and should be addressed in a safe, male-free environment. In addition, these programs should be culturally sensitive and build upon the strengths of women.[58]

SUMMARY

There has been significant debate as to whether girls should be treated the same or differently than their male counterparts. Let's take these two perspectives and apply them to the following example: An arts program was introduced to a detention facility in Michigan without regard to gender. The intent of the program was to encourage youth to express themselves in prosocial ways and serve as a coping mechanism.[59] Youth were housed in three separate wings—two all-male wings and one coed. Youth participated with their wing in both the spoken-word and visual-arts classes. The all-male classes worked extremely well; however, major problems were identified in the coed classes. First of all, some of the youth were more focused on other youth of the opposite gender than on the class. In addition, some of the females made attempts to gain the notice of the male teacher. It also became clear that males and females addressed different issues in their writing and were uncomfortable sharing their work in front of one another. Finally, it became clear that the males responded much better to the visual-arts component of the program, and the girls responded better to the spoken-word curriculum.

DISCUSSION QUESTIONS

1. Should female offenders be treated differently than male offenders?

2. What are the benefits and costs of adopting gender-responsive policies and practices?

3. As a program director, what types of changes do you think need to be made to design a curriculum that meets the unique needs of both male and female offenders? What implications does this have for the facility in terms of budget, scheduling, and training concerns for the staff? What do we learn from the Michigan example?

4. How can the lessons learned from gender-responsive programming inform the decisions of the criminal justice system as a whole, such as police and the courts?

KEY TERMS

Review key terms with eFlashcards | $SAGE edge™ • edge.sagepub.com/mallicoatccj

DISCUSSION QUESTIONS

Test your mastery of chapter content • Take the Practice Quiz | ⑤SAGE edge™ • edge.sagepub.com/mallicoatccj

1. What role does the scientific process play in the development of criminological theories?

2. What is the difference between causation and correlation? How can we use these terms to understand criminal behavior?

3. Compare the micro theories of crime with the macro theories of crime. Which do you believe best explain criminal behavior, and why?

4. How does social bond theory differ from other macrolevel theories of crime?

5. How might race, class, and gender differences in offending be explained by criminological theory?

LEARNING ACTIVITIES

1. Pick a newspaper article about a criminal act. Which theory best explains why the crime occurred?

2. Identify a criminal justice program in your community. Which theories are they using to help address criminal behavior, and how does the program use their information to punish or rehabilitate offenders?

3. Pick your favorite theory of crime. What types of information would you use to help prove that this theory is an effective perspective to understand criminal behavior?

SUGGESTED WEBSITES

- *Theoretical Criminology*: http://tcr.sagepub.com
- *Feminist Criminology*: http://fcx.sagepub.com
- *Critical Criminology*: http://link.springer.com/journal/10612
- *American Society of Criminology*: http://www.asc41.com

STUDENT STUDY SITE

Review • Practice • Improve | ⑤SAGE edge™ • edge.sagepub.com/mallicoatccj

Want a better grade?

Get the tools you need to sharpen your study skills. Access practice quizzes, eFlashcards, video, and multimedia at **edge.sagepub.com/mallicoatccj**

VICTIMS AND THE CRIMINAL JUSTICE SYSTEM

AP Photo/Jae C. Hong

LEARNING OBJECTIVES

- Assess the role of the just-world hypothesis in victim blaming

- Explain how routine activities and lifestyle theory helps to understand why people are victimized

- Compare and contrast the different typologies of crime victims

- Summarize the rights of crime victims

- Discuss how legislative efforts have improved the rights of crime victims

- Describe the extent of victimization in the United States

On May 6, 2013, three women were rescued from a home in Cleveland, Ohio. Amanda Berry, Georgina "Gina" DeJesus, and Michelle Knight had been held captive by Ariel Castro. Each of the women had accepted a ride from Castro, who then abducted them and forced them into his basement, where he kept the girls physically restrained. Michelle Knight was his first victim and was 21 years old when she was taken on August 22, 2002. His next victim, Amanda Berry, disappeared on April 21, 2003, just before her 17th birthday. Finally, Gina DeJesus was abducted next, on April 2, 2004. She was only 14. All three girls endured significant physical and sexual assaults throughout their captivity. Michelle Knight reported that she suffered several miscarriages, and Amanda Berry gave birth to a daughter in 2006 fathered by Castro.[1] Following a decade in hell, the women were rescued after garnering the attention of a neighbor, who helped them escape.[2]

While the prosecutors originally considered charging Castro with aggravated murder (in the cases of the forced miscarriages of Knight), he ultimately pled guilty to 937 counts of kidnapping, rape, and other crimes, such as child endangerment and gross sexual imposition.[3] In speaking at his sentencing hearing, Michelle Knight told Castro, "I spent 11 years in hell, where your hell is just beginning."[4] However, Castro served very little of his sentence before he hung himself by a bedsheet in his cell. Some might argue that

Michelle Knight reads her victim impact statement during the sentencing hearing for Ariel Castro. Castro was convicted on several counts of kidnapping and rape against Knight and her two covictims. Why is it important to include victims in the criminal justice process?

Castro's suicide cheats the justice system—"This man couldn't take, for even a month, a small portion of what he had dished out for more than a decade."[5]

While the victims in this case focus on moving on with rebuilding their lives following this tragedy, Ohio is trying to find ways to provide support to Berry, DeJesus, and Knight, as well as other victims of similar tragedies that may occur in the future. In October 2013, a victims' reparations bill (designed with Castro's victims in mind) was introduced and passed initial review. However, it subsequently died in committee. Had the legislation passed, it would have served victims who were held in involuntary servitude for at least eight years and provided compensation of $25,000 for each year that they were held in captivity, as well as free tuition, medical care, and living expenses at a state university.[6] In addition, the local community has demolished the home once owned by Castro where the three women were held after Castro signed over the deed as part of his plea bargain. The local community hopes that the lot will be used to develop a healing garden or some other peaceful space.[7]

This chapter looks at the role of victims in the criminal justice system. The chapter begins with a discussion of the history of the victims' rights movement. The chapter then turns to a review of the theories that help to explain criminal victimization. This follows with a discussion of the types of victims as well as the extent of victimization both within the United States and worldwide. The chapter concludes with two Current Controversy debates: the first, by Amy I. Cass, explores whether universities are best suited to respond to rape and sexual assault among college students; the second, by Kimberly J. Cook, investigates how a restorative justice model might help in the healing process for victims.

VICTIMS AND CRIME

When you think about crime, the majority of these acts involve a victim. A **victim** is someone who has been injured or harmed by the actions of another. While there are a few crimes that are considered victimless, most criminal acts involve an offender whose actions have, in some way, caused harm to another person or group. Why do victims seek out the criminal justice system? Do they desire justice? What does *justice* mean for victims of crime? Is it retribution? Reparation? Despite their presence in these criminal acts, victims have traditionally played a minor role in the criminal justice process. In many cases, human victims of crime are reduced to tools of the justice system or pieces of evidence in a criminal case. As a result, many of these victims experience frustrations about a system that seems to do little to represent their needs and concerns. In some cases, victims can even be further traumatized based on their experiences in dealing with the criminal justice system.

THEORIES OF VICTIMIZATION

Victim
Someone who has been injured or harmed by the actions of another.

In an effort to understand the victim experience, social science researchers investigate the characteristics of crime victims and the responses by society to these victims. While criminology focuses predominantly on the study of crime as a social phenomenon and the nature of offenders, the field of **victimology** places the victim at the center of the discussion.

Early Theories of Victimology

Early perspectives on victimology focused on how victims, either knowingly or unconsciously, can be at fault for their victimization, based on their personal life events and decision-making processes. One of the early scholars in this field, Benjamin Mendelsohn,[8] developed a typology of victimization that distinguished different types of victims based on the relative responsibility of the victim in his or her own victimization (Table 5.1). Embedded in his typology is the degree to which victims have the power to make decisions that can alter their likelihood of victimization. As a result of his work, the study of victimology began to emerge as its own distinct field of study.

Mendelsohn's theory of victimology is based on six categories of victims. The first category is the innocent victim. This distinction is unique in Mendelsohn's typology, as it is the only classification that does not have any responsibility for the crime attributed to the victim. As the name suggests, an innocent victim is someone who is victimized by a random and unprecipitated crime, such as a school shooting. Unlike the other categories in Mendelsohn's typology, the innocent victim is one with no responsibility for his or her victimization. In contrast, the other five categories assign a degree of blame or responsibility to the victim. Mendelsohn's second category is the victim with minor guilt. In this case, victimization occurs as a result of one's carelessness or ignorance. Victims with minor guilt are people who, if they had given better thought or care to their safety, would not have been victims of crime. An example of this is the case of a victim who is walking alone down the street in a high-crime area and is robbed. Mendelsohn's third category is a victim who is equally as guilty as the offender. This victim is someone who shares the responsibility for the crime with the offender and deliberately placed himself or herself in harm's way. An example of this classification is the individual who seeks out the services of a sex worker, only to contract a sexually transmitted infection as a result of their interaction. The fourth category represents the case wherein the victim is deemed "more guilty" than the offender. This is a "victim" who is provoked by others to engage in criminal activity. An example of this category

VIDEO
Man Robbed
While Meeting
Prostitutes at Ruth Motel

Victimology
A field of study within criminology that places the victim at the center of the discussion.

Table 5.1	Mendelsohn's Categories of Victims	
Category	**Definition**	**Example**
Innocent victim	No responsibility for the crime attributed to victim	Institutionalized victims, the mentally ill, children, or those who are attacked while unconscious
Victim with minor guilt	Victim precipitates crime with carelessness/ignorance	Victim lost in the "wrong part of town"
Voluntary victim	Victim and offender equally responsible for crime	Victim pays prostitute for sex, then prostitute robs victim ("rolling johns")
Victim who is more guilty than the offender	Victim who provokes or induces another to commit crime	Burning-bed syndrome: victim is killed by the domestic partner he or she abused for years
Victim who alone is guilty	Victim who is solely responsible for his or her own victimization	An attacker who is killed in self-defense; suicide bomber killed by detonation of explosives
Imaginary victim	Victim mistakenly believes she or he has been victimized	Mentally ill person who reports imagined victimization as real event

Source: Adapted from Sengstock, M. C. (1976, April 21–24). Culpable victims in Mendelsohn's typology. Paper presented at the annual meeting of the Midwest Sociological Society, St. Louis, MO.

is one who kills a current or former intimate partner following a history of abuse. The fifth category is a victim who is solely responsible for the harm that comes to him or her. These individuals are considered to be the "most guilty" of victims, as they engaged in an act that was likely to lead to injury on their part. Examples of the "most guilty" victim include a suicide bomber who engages in an act that results in his or her death or when a would-be attacker is killed by another in an act of self-defense. Mendelsohn's final category is the imaginary victim. This is an individual who, as a result of some mental disease or defect, believes that he or she has been victimized by someone or something when, in reality, this person has not been victimized.

While Mendelsohn focused on the influence of guilt and the responsibility of victims, Hans von Hentig's typology of victims looked at how personal factors, such as biological, psychological, and social factors, influence one's risk of victimization.[9] The categories in von Hentig's typology of victims include the young; the female; the old; the mentally defective and deranged; immigrants; minorities; dull normals; the depressed; the acquisitive; the wanton; the lonesome or heartbroken; the tormentor; and the blocked, exempted, or fighting. Table 5.2 provides a description of each of these categories.

AUDIO
Colleges Straddle Line Between Assault Prevention and Victim-Blaming

Just-world hypothesis
A hypothesis that suggests that society has a need to believe that people deserve whatever happens to them.

Just-World Hypothesis

To some extent, each of these perspectives places some degree of responsibility or blame on the victim. Why do we blame the victim? At its core, the process of victim blaming is linked to a belief in a just world. The **just-world hypothesis** suggests that society has a need to believe that people deserve whatever comes to them. Simply put, bad things happen to bad people, and good things happen to good people.[10] Under these assumptions, if a bad thing happens to someone, then that person must be at

Table 5.2	Hans von Hentig's Typology of Crime Victims
Category	**Description**
Young	Youth are seen as vulnerable to victimization as a result of their age.
Female	Women are at risk as they are physically weaker compared with men.
Old	The elderly have less physical strength due to age and greater financial resources.
Mentally defective	Mentally ill or intoxicated individuals are easy prey for attackers.
Immigrants	A new environment (culture, language, acculturation) may place someone at risk for victimization.
Minorities	Prejudice and discrimination can impact the victim experience.
Dull normals	These are vulnerable individuals who are easily exploited. Typically, they have lower-than-average IQs.
Depressed	Depressed individuals can be more submissive and less likely to fight off an attacker.
Acquisitive	One who is at risk of being taken advantage of due to a desire for financial advantage.
Wanton	One who is particularly vulnerable to stressors at various stages during the life cycle.
Lonesome/ heartbroken	One who is taken advantage of due to a fear of being alone.
Tormentors	The victim becomes the perpetrator of a crime, following years of abuse.
Blocked	One who is unable to help or defend himself or herself; he or she cannot get out of a negative situation.

Source: From Mallicoat, S. L., & Ireland, C. I. (2014). *Women and Crime: The Essentials.* Thousand Oaks, CA: Sage Publications. Originally adapted from Von Hentig, H. (1948). *The criminal and his victim: Studies in the sociobiology of crime.* New Haven, CT: Yale University Press.

fault for his or her victimization because of who he or she is and what he or she does.

A just-world outlook gives a sense of peace to many individuals. Imagining a world where crime victims must have done something foolish, dangerous, or careless allows members of society to distinguish themselves from this identity of victimhood—"I would never do that, so therefore I must be safe from harm." This, in turn, allows individuals to shield themselves from feelings of vulnerability and powerlessness when it comes to potential acts of victimization. However, there are several problematic assumptions surrounding the just-world hypothesis, namely, that it incorrectly (1) assumes people are able to change the environment in which they live, (2) implies only "innocent" victims are true victims, and (3) creates a false sense of security about the risks of crime and victimization.

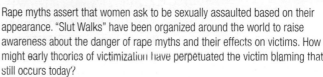

Rape myths assert that women ask to be sexually assaulted based on their appearance. "Slut Walks" have been organized around the world to raise awareness about the danger of rape myths and their effects on victims. How might early theories of victimization have perpetuated the victim blaming that still occurs today?

Given the nature of victimization patterns in society, few victims of crime meet the criteria for an "ideal" victim. Yet this process of subtle victim blaming allows society to diffuse the responsibility of crime between the victim and the offender. For example, the battered woman is asked, "Why do you stay?" or given the message that "I wouldn't put up with that!" The rape victim is asked, "What were you wearing?" or "Why did you let him come into your apartment if you didn't want sex?" The assault victim is asked, "Why didn't you fight back?" The fraud victim is chastised, "Why did you provide your credit card number online?" The burglary victim is asked, "Why didn't you lock the door?" Essentially, any victim who inadvertently puts herself or himself in harm's way is asked, "What were you thinking?" Each of these scenarios shifts the blame away from the perpetrator and assigns some degree of responsibility to the victim. **Victim blaming** enables people to make sense of the victimization and makes them feel somehow different from the person who is victimized. In many cases, the process of victim blaming allows people to separate themselves from those who have been victimized—"I would never have put myself in that situation"—and this belief allows people to feel safe in the world.

Victim blaming
Enables people to make sense of the victimization and makes them feel somehow different from the person who is victimized.

How does the just-world hypothesis work, and what are the implications for this application in the criminal justice system? Consider the crime of sexual assault. Under the just-world hypothesis, the victim often is assigned victimization responsibility for this violation in the eyes of the public. This can impact future reporting trends, as victims may be less likely to report their own victimizations after observing what happened to similar victims. The just-world hypothesis may also have an effect on potential offenders. For example, potential offenders who view media accounts of a crime that is not prosecuted or an offender who receives little punishment may adopt a belief that such acts are not criminal, particularly if these accounts engage in victim blaming.[11]

People walk by a memorial outside the gates of Marysville-Pilchick High School where Jaylen Fryberg opened fire on four of his classmates, killing two of them. It is unclear why Jaylen, a homecoming prince from a prominent tribal family, fired upon his friends and family members before turning the gun on himself.

Routine Activities and Lifestyle Theory

SAGE JOURNAL ARTICLE

Specifying the Influence of Family and Peers and Violent Victimization

While early theories of victimization provided a foundation to understand the victim experience, modern victimization theories expand from these concepts to investigate the role of society in victimization and to address how personal choices affect the victim experience. One of the most influential perspectives in modern victimology is Cohen and Felson's **routine activities theory**.[12] Routine activities theory suggests that the likelihood of a criminal act (and, in turn, the likelihood of victimization) occurs with the convergence of three essential components: (1) someone who is interested in pursuing a criminal action (offender), (2) a potential victim (target) "available" to be victimized, and (3) the absence of someone or something (guardian) that would deter the offender from making contact with the available victim. The name of the theory is derived from a belief that victims and guardians exist within the normal, everyday patterns of life. Cohen and Felson posit that lifestyle changes during the second half of the 20th century created additional opportunities for the victim and offender to come into contact with each other as a result of changes to daily routines and activities. Cohen and Felson's theory was created to discuss the risk of victimization in property crimes. Here, if individuals were at work or out enjoying events in the community, they were less likely to be at home to guard their property against potential victimization, and burglary was more likely to result.

Routine activities theory
Suggests that a criminal act is likely to occur when someone who is interested in committing a crime converges with a potential victim and there is an absence of something that would deter the offender.

Lifestyle theory
Theory that explores the risk of victimization from personal crimes whereby people place themselves at risk as a result of their lifestyle choices.

Routine activities theory has been used to understand a variety of different forms of crime, particularly related to demographic differences in victimization. For example, research tells us that girls are at a greater risk for cyberbullying than boys, even though boys engage in similar risky online behaviors.[13] Meanwhile, minority women are more likely to experience risk of victimization when riding public transportation while neighborhood factors can also have an effect on the odds of women's victimization.[14] Finally, while men are more likely to experience increased risks of violent victimization because they go out at night, women have an increased risk of theft based on increased shopping activities.[15]

Like routine activities theory, **lifestyle theory** seeks to relate the patterns of one's everyday activities to the potential for victimization. While routine activities theory was initially designed to explain victimization from property crimes, lifestyle theory was developed to explore the risks of victimization from personal crimes. Research on lifestyle theory suggests that people who engage in risky lifestyle choices place themselves at risk for victimization.[16] Based on one's lifestyle, one may increase the risk for criminal opportunity and victimization through both an increased exposure to criminal activity and an increased exposure to motivated offenders. However, crime is not the only factor that can place people at risk for victimization, as nonviolent deviant behaviors, mental health status, and substance use can increase the potential for victimization. For example, adolescent girls who have delinquent friends are

Based on routine activities theory, what are some "guardians" this homeowner is using to deter offenders?

CAREERS IN CRIMINAL JUSTICE

So You Want to Be a Victim Advocate?

With the increased attention on victims' rights throughout the 1970s and 1980s, the number of agencies that provided assistance to crime victims began to expand. While some of these groups were nonprofit community-based organizations, there was also a push for victims' services within local and state government bureaus. Today, there are a number of employment opportunities to work with victims of crimes. To work in this field, many agencies require formal education in fields such as victimology, psychology, criminology, social work, and sociology. Depending on the type of position, there may also be specialized training on issues such as domestic violence and sexual assault. The demand for services, particularly in these specialized areas, is high. Advocates in cases may provide a variety of services, such as counseling (or provide referrals for these services) and case management. These positions may also help victims secure temporary and transitional housing and provide support in legal cases. Depending on the type of agency, advocates may also be involved in community education, outreach, and fund-raising activities.

Working with crime victims can be a very rewarding experience. However, it is important to consider that victimization is a highly sensitive experience, and the people that work within these fields are often faced with high exposures to emotion within the context of their work. Over time, this can take its toll. For example, victims of intimate partner abuse often leave their abuser several times before they are able to completely sever their relationship. Over time, this can impact how an advocate feels about their position and lead to questioning whether one is able to be effective and successful in the position. In addition, it's important that people working in their field practice positive self-care strategies and develop peer support networks to prevent burnout and protect against stress.

In addition to paid career opportunities as a victim advocate, many agencies rely heavily on the contributions of volunteers. Since many of these organizations are run on small budgets within the community, volunteers can provide valuable support for related tasks. As a student interested in this work, you might want to consider donating some time to a local organization. Not only will the organization benefit from your contribution, but it may also give you better insight into whether this is the right career for you. Some agencies may also have formalized internship programs, which would provide you with greater experiences in the day-to-day activities of the organization.

more likely to participate in risky behaviors, such as substance abuse, sexual activity, and delinquency. These behaviors, in turn, increase the odds that they are victims of physical and/or sexual abuse in a dating relationship.[17]

CAREER VIDEO
Victims' Advocate

HISTORY OF VICTIMS' RIGHTS

The fight for victims began as a grassroots movement during the 1970s in response to the lack of attention by the criminal justice system to victims' issues. Groups such as Mothers Against Drunk Driving, Parents of Murdered Children, and the National Organization for Victim Assistance were developed.[18] In 1972, the first victim services organization was developed in St. Louis, Missouri (Crime Victim Advocacy Center), and it remains in operation today. At the same time, the women's movement led to the development of organizations such as rape crisis and domestic violence centers to provide services to victims of these crimes. Indeed, two of the three original victims' services organizations served this population—the Bay Area Women Against Rape in San Francisco, California, and the D.C. Rape Crisis Center in Washington, D.C. The general mission of these efforts was to raise awareness of the needs of victims and to provide support to them and their families.

WEB LINK
Crime Victims Fund

Lucia McBath receives a hug after reading her victim impact statement at the sentencing hearing for Michael Dunn. Dunn was convicted of first-degree murder for shooting 17-year-old Jordan Davis in Jacksonville, Florida, after a dispute over loud music. What rights are afforded to victims during the trial process?

In 1982, President Ronald Reagan established the **Presidential Task Force on Victims of Crime**. Composed of law enforcement officers, lawyers, and members of the judiciary, as well as victim advocates, their report included 68 recommendations to reform the experience of crime victims. Many of these recommendations have since been adopted into law. For example, the **Victim and Witness Protection Act of 1982** was passed by Congress to provide fair treatment to crime victims and witnesses. In 1983, the Office for Victims of Crime was established within the Office of Justice Programs to help implement the recommendations of the presidential task force and to provide resources and assistance to local professionals and jurisdictions. Perhaps one of the most significant recommendations that was incorporated into law was the passage of the **Victims of Crime Act** (VOCA) in 1984, which established the Crime Victims Fund. To date, the fund has deposited almost $19 billion.[19]

The Current State of Victims' Rights

Over the past three decades, there have been a number of different policies at the federal level focused on expanding the rights of victims and providing resources for training programs for criminal justice professionals and resources for community services. Table 5.3 highlights some of the policies that have been implemented at the federal level that have focused on victims. While each of these legislative actions has helped to increase resources and services for victims, it is the **Crime Victims' Rights Act of 2004** (18 U.S.C. section 3771) that currently provides victims with legal rights in federal criminal cases. These rights include the following:

1. The right to be reasonably protected from the accused.

2. The right to reasonable, accurate, and timely notice of any public court proceeding or any parole proceeding involving the crime, or of any release or escape of the accused.

3. The right not to be excluded from any such public court proceeding, unless the court, after receiving clear and convincing evidence, determines that testimony by the victim would be materially altered if the victim heard other testimony at that proceeding.

4. The right to be reasonably heard at any public proceeding in the district court involving release, plea, sentencing, or any parole proceeding.

5. The reasonable right to confer with the attorney for the government in the case.

6. The right to full and timely restitution as provided in law.

7. The right to proceedings free from unreasonable delay.

8. The right to be treated with fairness and with respect for the victim's dignity and privacy.

WEB LINK
Victims' Rights

Presidential Task Force on Victims of Crime
Task force created in 1982 by President Ronald Reagan to develop recommendations to reform the experience of crime victims.

Victim and Witness Protection Act of 1982
Passed by Congress to provide fair treatment standards to crime victims and witnesses.

Victims of Crime Act
Federal legislation that established the crime victims fund.

Crime Victims' Rights Act of 2004
Federal legislation that provides victims with legal rights in federal criminal cases.

Table 5.3	Examples of Federal Legislation for Victims' Rights
Legislation	**Description**
Student Right to Know and Campus Security Act (1990)	Requires colleges and universities to disclose statistics about campus crime
Hate Crime Statistics Act (1990)	Requires the collection of data on crimes that are motivated by prejudice as a result of race/ethnicity, sexual orientation, or religious identity
Victims' Rights and Restitution Act (1990)	Incorporates a bill of rights for victims in federal crime cases
Violent Crime Control and Law Enforcement Act (1994)	As part of larger legislation of criminal justice policy, the act included several provisions to provide funding for victims' services as well as enhanced sentencing and registry provisions for certain classes of offenders.
Violence Against Women Act (1994)	Provides funding for training of criminal justice personnel, funding for research on issues of intimate partner abuse, and resources for community-based services for victims
Megan's Law (1996)	Requires community notification in cases of convicted sex offenders
Crime Victims With Disabilities Awareness Act (1998)	Requires the collection of data on crimes involving people with disabilities
Trafficking Victims Protection Act (2000)	Increases resources to fight against trafficking and provides for increased penalties for offenders. Includes legal protections for victims and allows access to victims' services.

While there have been two attempts to introduce a federal amendment for victims' rights to the U.S. Constitution, these efforts have been unsuccessful, to date. However, several states have amended their individual constitutions to expand victims' rights. California was the first state to establish constitutional rights for crime victims and continues to have one of the most comprehensive bills of rights for victims in the nation.[20] Today, 35 states have amended their constitutions to provide rights to victims during the criminal justice process. While the laws vary from state to state, they generally allow for the victim to receive information about the process, attend court hearings, be heard, and receive restitution.[21] Figure 5.1 highlights one of the more common features of these individual state laws. In addition to the constitutional amendments for these jurisdictions, all 50 states, as well as the District of Columbia, the U.S. Virgin Islands, Puerto Rico, and Guam, have established programs to provide crime victims with compensation.[22]

In addition to efforts to increase the rights of victims, practices such as restorative justice have created alternative models of justice that provide increased opportunities for victims to have a voice in the criminal justice process. Not only are **restorative justice** (RJ) programs victim centered but they also provide offender-sensitive responses to crime. There are several different types of models of restorative justice programming, and they include both diversion and therapeutic-based interventions. You'll learn more about the pros and cons of restorative justice in the Current Controversy debate at the end of this chapter.

VICTIMS IN THE CRIMINAL JUSTICE SYSTEM

While the fight for the rights of victims has led to several improvements in the criminal justice system, the role of victims is often minimized. In Chapter 1, you learned about the criminal justice process. Now, consider how a case moves through the criminal justice system from the victim's perspective. In order for offenders to be

Restorative justice
Alternative model of justice that provides increased opportunities for victims to have a voice in the criminal justice process.

The right to confer with the prosecution may include the right to object or support plea agreements and/or sentences offered in a case and the right to review/comment on the presentence report. Should victims in all states have this right?

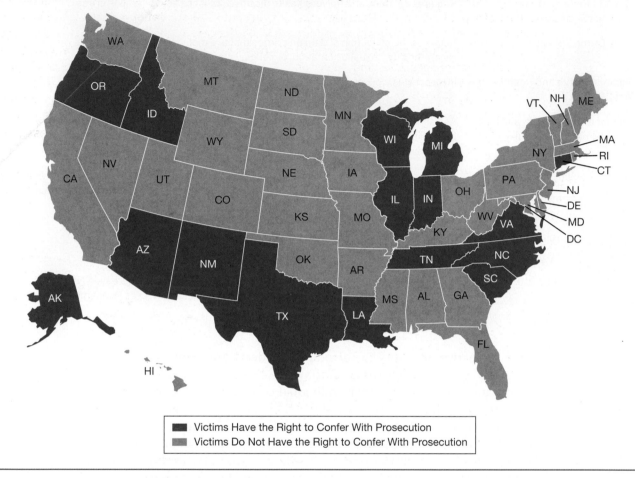

■ Victims Have the Right to Confer With Prosecution
■ Victims Do Not Have the Right to Confer With Prosecution

Source: Adapted from the National Center for Victims of Crime.

* The following states do not have a victims' rights amendment: Delaware, District of Columbia, Georgia, Hawaii, Iowa, Kentucky, Maine, Massachusetts, North Dakota, New Hampshire, New York, Pennsylvania, Rhode Island, South Dakota, West Virginia, and Wyoming. In those states that have a victims' rights amendment, all but Montana provide victims with the right to be informed, present, and heard during criminal proceedings.

Violence Against Women Act

Federal legislation that provided victims of intimate partner violence support through the allocation of federal funds to prosecute offenders, coordination of services for victims, and establishment of the Office of Violence Against Women.

held accountable for their actions, the police must be made aware of their crimes. At this point, police may exercise their discretion on whether or not to make an arrest. While many department policies allow for the victim to give her or his input into this decision, police are not required to follow the wishes of the victim. In many cases, mandatory arrest policies may require that an arrest is made, regardless of what the victim wants. Once a case reaches the court, criminal charges are filed by the district attorney or prosecutor. Victims do not get to choose whether charges are filed against an offender. Under criminal law, the criminal act is considered a violation of the laws of the state (or depending on the type of law violation, a municipality or the federal government). This is why the name of a criminal case is listed as the *State* or *U.S. vs. John Doe* and not *Jane Smith (victim) vs. John Doe*. The prosecutor is also in charge of determining whether a plea bargain will be offered to the offender. Finally, it is the judge who determines the sentence for the offender. While the push for victims' rights has allowed greater participation throughout this process, it is still the criminal justice system that controls the outcome.

SPOTLIGHT

Politics and Victims' Rights: The Violence Against Women Act

The fight for victims' rights is often a challenging one. Sometimes, this process can get tangled up as part of a political battle. Consider the most recent reauthorization efforts of the Violence Against Women Act in 2012. First passed in 1994, the **Violence Against Women Act** (VAWA) provided victims of intimate partner violence (IPV) support through the allocation of federal funds for prosecuting offenders, coordinated services for victims, and established the Office of Violence Against Women within the Department of Justice. Reauthorized with support from both sides of the political aisle in 2000 and 2005, the VAWA continued to expand the rights of victims in these cases. Each reauthorization also increased the support for research in the field, training for criminal justice professionals, and services for victims. Table 5.4 highlights the allocation of resources

Table 5.4	The Violence Against Women Act
1994	Violent Crime Control and Law Enforcement Act of 1994 Title IV: Violence Against Women • Allocated $1.6 billion in grant funds (1994–2000) for investigation and prosecution of violent crimes against women, community services for victims, and the creation of domestic violence help lines • Created new laws that target violators of civil restraining orders and made interstate domestic violence a federal crime • Allows offenders to use civil justice in cases that prosecutors decline to prosecute • Established the Office on Violence Against Women within the Department of Justice
2000	Victims of Trafficking and Violence Protection Act of 2000 Division B: Violence Against Women Act • Allocated $3.33 billion in grant funds (2001–2005) • Enhanced federal laws for domestic violence and stalking • Added protections for immigrant victims • Added new programs for elderly and disabled victims • Included victims of dating violence into VAWA protections and services
2005	Violence Against Women Act and Department of Justice Reauthorization Act of 2005 • Allocated $3.935 billion in grant funds (2007–2011) • Created repeat offender penalties • Added protections for trafficked victims • Provides housing resources for victims • Enhanced resources for American Indian and Alaska Native populations • Provides increased training for health care providers to recognize signs of domestic violence • Enhanced protections for undocumented immigrant victims
2013	Violence Against Women Act Reauthorization of 2013 • Allocated $3.378 billion in grant funds (2013–2018) • Continues funding for grants for research and services • Maintains and expands housing protections • Expands options for tribal courts to address domestic violence • Requires reporting procedures for dating violence on college campuses • Prohibits discrimination against LGBT victims in accessing services • Maintains and increases protections for immigrant victims

Sources: Seghetti, L. M., & Bjelopera, J. P. (2012). The Violence Against Women Act: Overview, legislation and federal funding. Congressional Research Service. Accessed at http://www.fas.org/sgp/crs/misc/R42499.pdf; National Coalition Against Domestic Violence. (2006). Comparison of VAWA 1994, VAWA 2000, and VAWA 2005 Reauthorization Bill. Accessed at http://www.ncadv.org/files/VAWA_94_00_05.pdf; Office of Violence Against Women. (n.d.). VAWA 2013 summary: Changes to OVW-administered grant programs. Accessed at http://www.ovw.usdoj.gov/docs/vawa-2013-sum.pdf

(Continued)

(Continued)

and the provision of services through the different reauthorizations of the VAWA. However, the 2012 attempts to reauthorize the bill were filled with partisan debates over the protections of victims of IPV for specific populations, such as same-sex victims, immigrants, and Native Americans. What had once been a joint collegial effort between Democrats and Republicans transformed into a hotly contested political debate. Alas, conservatives and liberal representatives were unable to find a compromise on the issues prior to the end of the 2012 congressional session.[a] The issue was once again raised at the outset of the 2013 congressional session. Despite holding a majority of representatives in the House, the GOP version of the bill, which advocated for narrower protections for certain population groups, ultimately failed. This paved the way for the House to pass the Senate's version of the bill in February 2013, which ensures that LGBT, Native American, and immigrant victims have access to federally funded programs and resources.[b]

Who Are the Victims of Crime?

In Chapter 3, you learned about the National Crime Victimization Survey (NCVS) and how it helps to reveal the dark figure of crime—those crimes that are not reported to the police. We can use this data to get a better understanding about the extent of victimization in the United States. Data from the NCVS is organized into two separate categories: personal crime and property crimes. Within the category of personal crime, the NCVS looks at the acts of rape and sexual assault, robbery, simple and aggravated assault, and pick-pocketing/purse-snatching. Within the category of property crime, the following four offenses are included: burglary, theft, motor vehicle theft, and vandalism.

According to the NCVS, the rate of violent crime has decreased over the past year. Figure 5.2 presents the rates of reported and unreported crime in 2013 and 2014.[23] Figure 5.3 highlights how the rate of violent crime has generally decreased. In many cases, it is specific criminal acts that are responsible for much of these changes in crime rates.

With only 49% of victims reporting violent crime and 37% of victims reporting property crime, the NCVS provides valuable insight about the dark figure of crime that is missing in official crime statistics. However, this dark figure of crime varies by offense, indicating that victims may be more likely or less likely to make a report to the police, depending on the type of victimization. For example, while 67% of cases of aggravated assault were reported, victims reported only 43% of simple assault cases. Similar patterns are observed in cases involving property crimes. While 83% of cases of motor vehicle theft were reported, other thefts were reported only 30% of the time.[24]

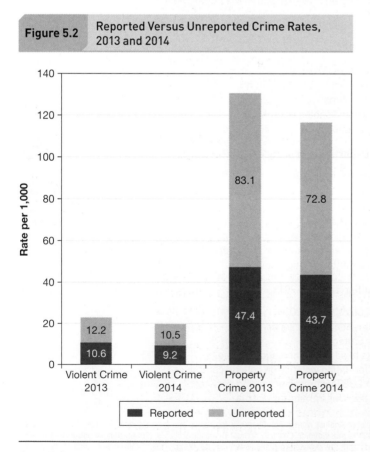

Figure 5.2 Reported Versus Unreported Crime Rates, 2013 and 2014

Source: Truman, J., Langron, L., & Planty, M. (2015). Criminal Victimization, 2014. Bureau of Justice Statistics.

Many crimes have seen a decrease in victimization over the past decade. Which crimes have experienced the greatest reductions? Which acts have stayed the same? How do you explain these patterns?

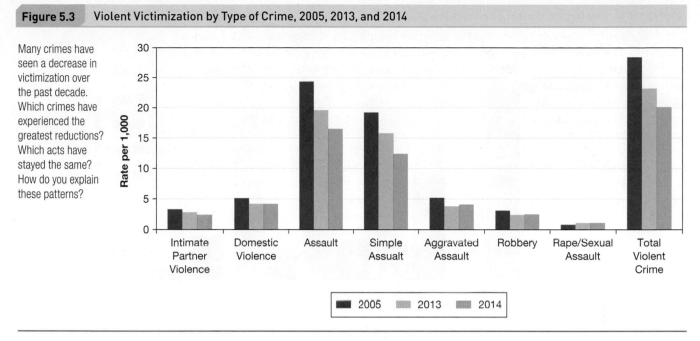

Souroo: Truman, J., Langron, L., & Planly, M. (2015). Criminal Victimization, 2014. Bureau of Justice Statistics.

Like other data sets, the NCVS has limitations that need to be considered when reviewing its findings. While the NCVS illuminates the dark figure of crime, the types of crime that it collects data on are different than the UCR data. This makes it difficult to make direct comparisons between the two datasets. For example, the NCVS does not include information on the crime of homicide, as the NCVS requires individuals to report those crimes that they personally experience. The NCVS also includes only individuals over the age of 12. This means that the data on childhood victimization are missing from the dataset.

From time to time, additional crime data may also be collected as a part of the National Crime Victimization Survey. This allows for researchers to look at a particular category of crimes that may not be generally covered within the NCVS. For example, an additional survey was administered in early 2014 to a subsample of the NCVS participants related to the crime of identity theft. While media outlets have suggested that the rates of identity theft have skyrocketed, what do we really know about this crime? If we look at the data from this survey, we learn that approximately 17.6 million people were victimized by acts of identity theft in 2014. The most common crime of identity theft involves the unauthorized use of a banking or credit card account (86% of all cases). While the majority of these cases involve a small amount of money, some cases are quite extensive. Figure 5.4 highlights the costs of identity theft in comparison with other acts of property crime. While the average incident of identity theft ($2,183) is similar to acts of burglary ($2,378), there are far more people victimized by identity theft. The overall losses from identity theft are far more expensive, with $24.7 billion dollars lost in 2014.[25] Luckily, most victims are often able to easily remedy the violation by working with their financial institution. However, not all cases are so easily resolved. Almost 2 million victims have a new account opened in their name or have their personal information used without their knowledge. For example, a person's identity might be used without his or her knowledge to rent an apartment or provided to law enforcement in an attempt to evade the police.

AUDIO
Victims of Social Security Number Theft Find It Hard to Bounce Back

Figure 5.4   The Cost of Identity Theft Victimizations, 2012*

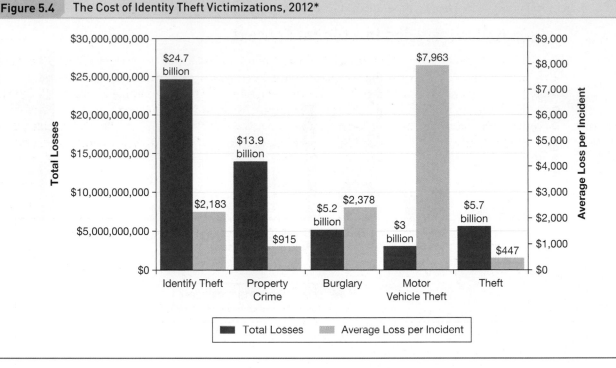

Source: Harrell, E., & Langton, L. (2013). Victims of identity theft, 2012. Bureau of Justice Statistics, U.S. Department of Justice. Retrieved at http://www.bjs.gov/content/pub/pdf/vit12.pdf. (Table 4)

*Most recent data available.

Unreported Crimes: Why Do Victims Not Report to the Police?

There are many reasons why victims might choose not to report their victimization to the police. Some victims feel embarrassed by the crime. Still others may decide not to report a crime to the police out of the belief that nothing could be done. In many cases, people don't report the crime because they believe that the crime was not serious enough to make a big deal over it while others believe it is a personal matter. For some victims, a fear of retaliation can affect their decision to make a report to the police.

However, a failure to report does not mean that victims do not seek out assistance for issues related to their victimization experience. In fact, victims often seek help from resources outside of law enforcement, such as family and friends, and many seek assistance through formal mental health services following a victimization experience.[26] While many victims may be reluctant to seek formal help, research suggests that victims who receive positive support from informal social networks, such as friends and family, are subsequently more likely to seek out formal services, such as law enforcement and therapeutic resources. In these cases, informal networks act as a support system to seek professional help and to make an official crime report.[27]

Secondary victimization
A process whereby victims feel traumatized not only as a result of their victimization experience but also by the official criminal justice system response to their victimization.

Victims may also choose not to report their crimes due to concerns about secondary victimization. The concept of **secondary victimization** refers to the practice whereby victims of crime feel traumatized as a result of not only their victimization experience but also by the official criminal justice system response to their victimization. For those cases that progress beyond the law enforcement investigative process,

AROUND THE WORLD

Criminal Victimization in a Global Context

While the National Crime Victimization Survey measures victimization in the United States, there are other surveys designed to look at these issues from an international perspective. Similar to the NCVS, the Crime Survey for England and Wales (CSEW) is administered to a random sample of households and is designed to develop estimates about the rate of crime and victimization in England and Wales. The Crime Survey for England and Wales first began as part of the British Crime Survey in 1984 and included data from Scotland and Northern Ireland. Today, these jurisdictions carry out their own victimization surveys,

| Figure 5.5 | International Rates of Crime Victimization |

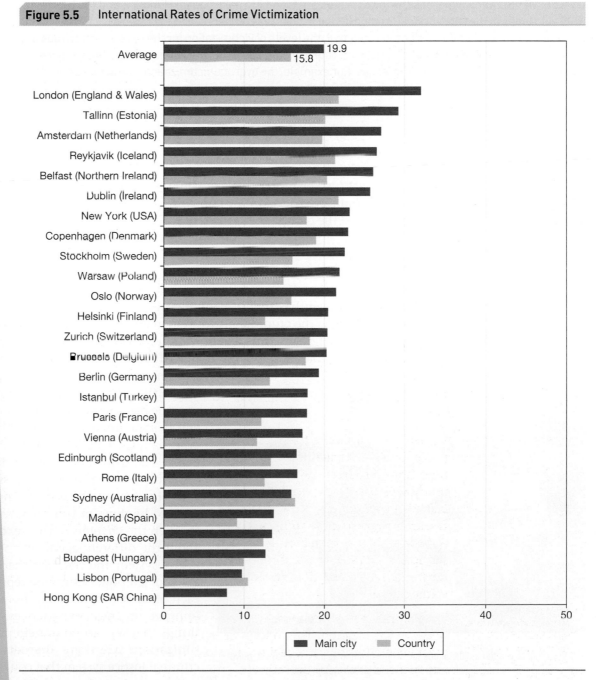

Source: European Survey of Crime and Safety (2005 EU ICS). Brussels, Gallup Europe.

(Continued)

(Continued)

though the design and intent of these data collections are similar. Like the NCVS, the CSEW attempts to shed light on the dark figure of crime by capturing victimizations that may not be reported to the police. In 2015, the CSEW estimated that there were approximately 6.6 million incidents of victimization against individuals and households. Not only were these findings 30% lower than 2010; they represent a 66% reduction since 1966. Sixty-five percent of these crimes (4.3 million) were reported to the police.[a]

Meanwhile, the International Crime Victims Survey (ICVS) compares levels of crime victimization on a global level.[b] The ICVS measures 10 common crimes (car theft, theft from a car, bicycle theft, burglary, attempted burglary, robbery, theft of personal property, sexual offenses, and assault and threat). These data indicate that the countries of Ireland, England and Wales, New Zealand, and Iceland have the highest levels of victimization, whereas the lowest rates are found in Spain, Japan, Hungary, and Portugal. The ICVS also looks at the rates of victimization in major cities, as compared with the rates of victimization for the country overall. For all 32 cities investigated, the levels of victimization for these common crimes are higher in the city compared with the national rate of victimization for the country as a whole. Figure 5.5 (page 119) demonstrates these differences. For example, the average victimization rate in these countries is 15.8 per 1,000 residents, compared with 19.9 in the major cities.[c]

few have charges filed by prosecutors, and only rarely is a conviction secured. Indeed, many victims indicate that had they known what was in store for them, they might not have reported the crime.[28]

CONCLUSION

While most criminal offenses involve a victim, much of the response by the criminal justice system has traditionally focused on the offender. As a result, victims may not feel like the criminal justice system effectively responds to their needs. According to the National Crime Victimization Survey, there may be as many as 3 million victims of violent crime and more than 15 million property crime victimizations in the United States annually.[29] While there has been significant progress over the past few decades, there are still several areas of unmet needs for victims. While criminal justice policies have attempted to bridge the gap for victims by increasing resources and improving processes within the criminal justice system, there is still work to be done in this area. As you read through the chapters of this text and learn about the different agents of the criminal justice system and the roles that they play, ask yourself how victims are represented in each of these processes and how we might improve on these experiences. Are there things that we can do to help prevent victimization? Are there alternatives to the criminal justice system that could provide a better experience for crime victims?

The trial process is often a difficult one for victims of crime as they may have to relive their victimization repeatedly. How can the criminal justice system better respond to victims?

CURRENT
CONTROVERSY
VIDEO
Where Do You Stand?
Cast Your Vote!

Should Colleges and Universities Respond to Campus Sexual Assault?

—Amy I. Cass—

Sexual assault is a reoccurring problem on campuses today. As many as 1 in 5 women will be sexually assaulted while in college in the United States. Data on male rape is harder to measure due to the low reporting rates. Some studies indicate that 1 in 71 men (1.4%) have experienced rape in their lifetime while other research finds that 6% of men have experienced some form of sexual coercion, including being forced to penetrate someone.[30] Given these rates of victimization, should colleges and universities respond to these events?

 College Campuses Should Respond to Cases of Rape on Campus

Title IX legislation was passed as part of the Education Amendments of 1972. It requires that colleges and universities that receive federal funding provide an environment free of discrimination based on sex. While the legislation is historically noted for requiring equity in high school and college athletic programs for girls, it has recently been used in cases of sexual assault and harassment. The Office of Civil Rights for the Department of Education has stated that "the sexual harassment of students, including sexual violence, interferes with students' right to receive an education free from discrimination and, in the case of sexual violence, is a crime." The OCR has also mandated that colleges and universities "take immediate and effective steps to end sexual harassment and sexual violence."[31]

Given the mandates of Title IX, colleges and universities must respond to these cases. Meanwhile, prosecutors have the discretion on whether they file a case, which means that not all cases will be pursued. From this perspective, the campus system provides a greater opportunity that a case will be considered. In addition, such cases are easier to prove through university processes, which use the standard of proof of preponderance of the evidence to make their rulings. This is a much lower burden of proof compared with the criminal justice system, which requires proof beyond a reasonable doubt.

Further, colleges and universities can reduce the rates of rape and sexual assault on campus by reducing opportunities for victimization by providing better guardianship and reducing the suitability of targets. As you learned in this chapter, routine activities theory proposes that victimization will occur when a motivated offender encounters a suitable target in the absence of capable guardians. In other words, when the offender and victim meet at a particular time and location without the risk of being caught by outsiders, opportunities for crime and victimization arise. College campuses provide an environment where these three elements can converge. For one, students are often in close proximity to one another while attending classes, parties, and/or other school events, thus bringing offenders and targets together, possibly with limited guardianship. Second, with the increasing number of people attending college, there is an increase in the supply of potential offenders and targets on campus who are no longer guarded or supervised by their parents. Third, the culture of alcohol and partying, as well as the use of other experimental drugs that materialize in college settings, makes victims more suitable, as they cannot easily protect themselves and they cannot guard their friends from victimization when they are in an inebriated state of mind. Research suggests that there are select activities that place individuals at greater risk of rape on campus, such as drinking and drug use. Furthermore, the risk for victimization is higher in fraternity houses and dorm rooms than in other locations on campus.

One of the most effective ways that colleges and universities can respond to campus rape and sexual assault is through the establishment of support services for students who have experienced rape and sexual assault. These may include a confidential consultant to help students identify therapeutic and legal resources. Many colleges throughout the United States have adopted several practical strategies in an attempt to prevent rape on campus. These strategies include offering self-defense classes to women, providing off-campus escort services for students, increasing the number of police officers on campus, requiring key card access into facilities, installing fences around campus, and establishing emergency alarm stations in designated areas on campus. While all of these are noteworthy attempts to prevent rape or, at the very least, reduce the rate of rape on campus, they are often not found to be effective empirically. As we know, rape often occurs in dorms or fraternity houses by known assailants. If rapes happen behind closed doors, manipulating the outside environment is not always useful. As a consequence, what is being done on campuses currently is not enough.

In addition, it would be worthwhile to create, implement, and evaluate programs focused on the offenders of rape. Routine activities theory, while extremely popular as a crime perspective, puts the focus of crime on the victim and, in some instances, blames the victim for his or her victimization, touting statements such as "She was drunk." The reality is that a person could restrict her movement on campus significantly and change her entire lifestyle to never drink, use drugs, or attend parties, but that doesn't mean she will never be raped. Routine activities theory doesn't really explain the root cause of rape. It assumes that if an opportunity presents itself, men may not be able to resist.

Finally, many colleges and universities have begun to implement programs in bystander intervention. These approaches focus on educating communities to recognize the signs of sexual violence and on building skills to intervene as well as to support one's peers when victimization does occur.[32] Some critics question whether such programs will lead people to think that someone is always looking out for them and will rescue them if they fall in harm's way.[33] However, research suggests that such programs have been shown to be effective in raising awareness among college students.[34]

 CON **Colleges Should Not Be Tasked With Responding to Cases of Rape on College Campuses**

While campuses are required to report sexual assault and harassment cases under federal law, a recent report notes that 64 schools are under investigation for their failure to comply. These failures range from issues with the adjudication process for offenders to a lack of training for faculty and staff on how to respond to cases of campus sexual assault. In addition, many schools lack meaningful protocols on how to work with local police in reporting these crimes.[35] Finally, many schools lack adequate staffing to respond to these cases. Given these failures, we can argue that colleges are not the best place to respond to cases of rape and sexual assault.

There are several reasons why campuses struggle in their response to these types of incidents. First, the lack of reporting complicates the ability of colleges and universities to respond to these cases. Research indicates that between 20% and 25% of women will be sexually assaulted at some point during their college experience. Yet few of these cases will become known to campus officials, as only 2% of college women report the crime to the police.[36] It has been estimated that 90% of campus women who are victims of these sexually based crimes know their perpetrator. This blurs the understanding both of consent and of assault and lessens the likelihood of reporting.

Second, the process by which campuses conduct their investigations can challenge the success of a criminal investigation. Title IX establishes many recommendations about the processing of cases. One of the most significant of these is that a school cannot wait for the conclusion of a criminal investigation in order to finish its own investigation. The Office of Civil Rights proposes that cases should be investigated within 60 days. Given that this time frame is significantly shorter than a typical criminal investigation, the question arises whether the involvement of the campus has a negative effect in the overall outcomes in such cases.

Related to this are the limitations in the types of punishments that colleges can hand down. While a criminal court can incarcerate individuals for such crimes or enforce other forms of community-based punishments, the college disciplinary process is rather limited in this regard. Campuses can suspend an individual for a period of time or expel someone from a particular campus or system.[37] In other cases, symbolic punishments such as being prohibited from attending graduation are used. There is also the tension between supporting the victims in this process and not violating the rights of those accused of such acts. Furthermore, in some cases, victims who have

brought forth cases are subsequently punished for violating the campus's honor code.[38]

Finally, while Title IX requires colleges and universities to provide these services to students, many of these requirements are unfunded, meaning that state and campus budgets are left trying to determine where the resources to provide these services will come from. As we have seen, the failure to provide these resources means that campuses become vulnerable to grievances and lawsuits from victims.

DISCUSSION QUESTIONS

1. What sort of resources does your campus have to prevent acts of rape and sexual assault? Do you believe these tools are effective?

2. How does your campus respond to allegations of rape and sexual assault? Do these responses address the needs of victims?

3. What sorts of reforms would you suggest to college officials on your campus to help improve prevention and intervention efforts?

CURRENT CONTROVERSY 5.2

PRO CON

Is Restorative Justice an Effective Tool for Victims?
—Kimberly J. Cook—

CURRENT
CONTROVERSY
VIDEO
Where Do You Stand?
Cast Your Vote!

INTRODUCTION

While some people correctly point to ancient traditions of indigenous cultures as the starting point for RJ, the modern application of this practice is fairly young. In the 1980s, New Zealand began implementing what they called *family group conferencing* as a means to address juvenile offending. The practice there stemmed from a Maori tradition (*whānau*) in which the extended family of offenders (and victims, whenever possible) would meet with the offenders to discuss what happened, why it happened, and how it could be repaired to the satisfaction of the community, the victim, and the extended families. Eventually, the practice became routine within the juvenile court system and adapted within the adult courts as well.

Australia adapted the practice in the 1990s and established *diversionary conferencing* programs in some limited jurisdictions that eventually spread throughout the country. The idea for diversionary conferences

was to "divert" juvenile offenders out of the formal court system by offering them an opportunity to take responsibility for their actions and make amends at the same time. This early Australian application of RJ was housed within local police departments and sessions were conducted by specially trained police officers. The sessions provided space for victims and their supporters to describe how the crime injured them so that the offender could hear it firsthand; it also provided offenders time to explain their behavior, take responsibility for it, and possibly apologize and then make amends.

In addition to diversion programs, some RJ initiatives are therapeutic in design. An example of a therapeutic RJ program is the postconviction Victim–Offender Mediated Dialogue program in Texas. It provides opportunities for victims and survivors of violent crime (including homicide) to meet with the

As part of a restorative justice program, victims and offenders meet to talk about the crime and experience of victimization. Research indicates that such programs can be a therapeutic and healing option in some cases. Under what circumstances might this not be a positive experience?

person convicted of those crimes. It generally takes months of preparation for the two sides to come together while a professional trained facilitator works with both to prepare for the meeting. Victims who are interested in this option can register with the state department of corrections, and the incarcerated offender can register his or her willingness to participate, provided the offender promises to take responsibility for the crime. Once both sides express their interest in this meeting, a facilitator meets with both and outlines a complex plan to prepare for the meeting. Preparations can take months and perhaps well over a year, depending on the case. Both offenders and victims can back out at any time should they desire to do so. Offenders gain no special advantages for participating.

PRO   Restorative Justice Is an Effective Tool for Victims

During this early phase of the development of restorative justice practices involving juvenile offenders, scholars such as John Braithwaite, Lawrence Sherman, and Heather Strang tested the program to determine whether RJ was an effective approach compared with those of conventional courts in cases involving nonviolent crime, some violent crime, and drunk driving. In order to be approved for this program, the young person responsible for the crime was required to admit responsibility and the injured persons had to be willing to participate. The tests documented that for the most part, victims of crime were much more satisfied with the diversionary conferences than victims whose cases went to the conventional court; also, young people responsible for the injuries were more satisfied than young people whose cases went to court as well. Typical resolutions included paying back the cost of what was lost or damaged during the offense, agreeing to stay out of trouble, and apologizing for the crime. These early findings inspired jurisdictions from around the world to build RJ programs within their communities.

Making amends in cases of severe violence, such as the rape and murder of a young woman, is impossible. Taking responsibility and offering genuine information to the victim's survivor is possible. In one case, a mother and her granddaughter (who was five when her mother was murdered) met with the man who killed their daughter/mother thirteen years after her death. The victims were able to talk about aspects of their daughter/mother's life that were important for them to share with the offender—her little daughter, the new baby she just found out she was carrying, their family's loss when she died, the pain of their grief, the loss of their

sense of security, and many other aspects of how this tragedy affected their lives. He was able to explain how messed up he was as a boy and as a teen when he did this, how he was abandoned by his parents to a series of abusive foster care situations, his attempted suicide when he was 8 years old, being in juvenile detention at a very young age, getting in trouble with the law, poor school performance, and no guidance throughout his sad young life. He also shared how deeply he had regretted that violent act every day of his life. The offender shared with them his victim's final words—"God will forgive you, and so do I"—which always haunted him. This knowledge was a gift of comfort to the victims because it affirmed for them that their family member's last act was peaceful and loving even as she faced the horrific reality of her own death. They spent about nine hours talking to each other, crying, being silent, holding hands, praying, and also laughing, hugging, and taking photos together. It seems incredulous to imagine such a meeting, but such is the capacity of restorative justice.[39]

Research into RJ programs shows promising results: Victims feel more satisfied and heard, and offenders have a place where they can take responsibility and genuinely offer their apologies to those who suffered from their actions. There are many organizations that promote restorative justice, and searching online will yield a wealth of information. Ultimately, as Professor Braithwaite says, "If crime is about injury, then justice should be about healing." Participants in restorative justice programs have stated that these meetings can create the space and the opportunity for healing to occur.[40]

CON   **Restorative Justice May Not Be the Best Option for Victims**

On the other hand, scholars and practitioners caution against using restorative justice in some cases. Concerns can hinge on whether the offender is truly remorseful for his or her actions. For instance, imagine a situation in which a battered woman might desire an RJ-based remedy for her needs and her children's needs, but her abusive (former) partner continues to be manipulative and emotionally abusive. During the meeting, he may behave in ways that trigger her continued trauma rather than provide opportunities for healing and moving forward. Such situations must be avoided, and facilitators need to be perpetually vigilant regarding the possibility of continued abuse of victims and survivors. Furthermore, some scholars and practitioners suggest that RJ may not be well suited for culturally specific situations. For example, some scholars argue that victims of gendered violence within Indian cultures would likely continue to be victimized given powerful cultural emphasis on women's submission and the patriarchal power of men.[41]

CONCLUSION

Restorative justice programs have been successful in many settings. Not only do such options provide crime victims and communities the opportunity to serve as active participants in the criminal justice experience, but programs can also provide avenues for healing. However, such a model does not fit all offenders and all victims. The challenge is understanding when and where such programs would be the most effective.

DISCUSSION QUESTIONS

1. Do you think restorative justice programs offer an opportunity for closure for victims of crime?

2. What are the challenges that exist in implementing these types of programs?

3. How might the criminal justice system learn from this approach?

KEY TERMS

Review key terms with eFlashcards | **⑤SAGE** edge™ • **edge.sagepub.com/mallicoatccj**

DISCUSSION QUESTIONS

Test your mastery of chapter content • Take the Practice Quiz | **⑤SAGE** edge™ • **edge.sagepub.com/mallicoatccj**

1. In what ways does the criminal justice system fail to meet the needs of victims?

2. How does the experience of secondary victimization and blaming the victim impact rates of reporting crimes?

3. How do perspectives such as routine activities theory and lifestyle theory help explain the risks of victimization?

4. How does the National Crime Victimization Survey add to our understanding about the presence of crime in society?

LEARNING ACTIVITIES

1. While many states have constitutional amendments that provide rights for victims of crime, attempts to create a federal victims' rights amendment have failed. Investigate these failed attempts, and highlight some of the challenges that these efforts have faced. How would you design a new campaign for a federal victims' rights amendment?

2. Compare the crime rates between (1) the National Crime Victimization Survey and (2) the Uniform Crime Reports and National Incident-Based Reporting System data. How are these data similar? How are they different? How can we use these different types of data together to develop an understanding about crime rates in society?

3. Research your campus policies on reporting and responding to acts of rape and sexual assault. How do these efforts compare with the requirements set forth by state and federal policies, such as Title IX?

SUGGESTED WEBSITES

- **National Center for Victims of Crime:** http://www.victimsofcrime.org
- **Office for Victims of Crime:** http://www.ovc.gov
- **Crime Victims United:** http://www.crimevictimsunited.com
- **California Victim Compensation Program:** http://vcgcb.ca.gov/victims/
- **Victims' Voices Heard:** http://www.victimsvoicesheard.org
- **Restorative Justice Online:** http://www.restorativejustice.org

STUDENT STUDY SITE

Review • Practice • Improve | ⑤SAGE edge™ • **edge.sagepub.com/mallicoatccj**

Want a better grade?

Get the tools you need to sharpen your study skills. Access practice quizzes, eFlashcards, video, and multimedia at **edge.sagepub.com/mallicoatccj**

CRIMINAL JUSTICE POLICY

AP Photo/John Minchillo

LEARNING OBJECTIVES

- Define how polices can be used in criminal justice

- Explain why we need criminal justice policies

- Describe how criminal justice policies develop

- Analyze how politics impact criminal justice policies

- Explain the importance of research in criminal justice policies

The war on drugs began in 1971 when President Nixon declared the abuse of illegal drugs as "public enemy number one." While the trend of decriminalization experienced a brief revival under President Carter in the late 1970s, the tides shifted back to drugs as a criminal justice issue during President Reagan's administration. The campaign to "just say no" led to stricter legislation and enhanced penalties. Throughout the 1980s, the public's fears about drugs grew exponentially.[1] In October 1986, Reagan signed the Anti–Drug Abuse Act. In addition to allocating $1.7 billion to expand prison facilities and provide drug education and treatment, the act established mandatory minimum sentences for the possession of crack and powder cocaine.[2] In crafting these regulations, a belief was perpetuated that crack cocaine was more dangerous than powder cocaine, which, in turn, led to differences in sentencing for the two substances. While the possession of 500 grams of powder cocaine led to a mandatory five-year incarceration sentence, the same five-year sentence was given for the possession of a mere 5 grams of crack. The 100 to 1 ratio is largely responsible not only for the rapid growth in the U.S. prison population throughout the end of the 20th century but also for contributing to significant racial disparities in the arrest, prosecution, and incarceration of men and women of color.[3]

With the signing of the Fair Sentencing Act in 2010, the sentencing disparity for violations involving crack cocaine and powder cocaine was reduced, but not eliminated. Some argue that since these are just different forms of the same drug there should be no differences in sentencing. Do you think a person charged with possession of crack cocaine should receive a longer sentence than someone in possession of powder cocaine?

Despite significant amounts of research on these disparate sentencing practices, it wasn't until 2010 that drug sentencing laws were amended. The Fair Sentencing Act of 2010 reduced the sentencing ratio between crack and powder cocaine to an 18:1 ratio. Under the new law, a conviction for the possession of 28 grams of crack or 280 grams of powder cocaine triggers a five-year mandatory sentence.[4] However, this change in policy was not retroactive, allowing those who had previously been sentenced under such draconian laws to remain incarcerated. To date, district and appellate courts have upheld this declaration.[5] While the Fair Sentencing Act of 2010 applies only to federal drug crimes, California recently passed a Fair Sentencing Act of its own (SB 1010). Prior to the passage of this new law, possession of crack cocaine led to a mandatory three-year sentence, and nearly every case involved a person of color. Under the new law, the possession of 28.5 grams of crack or powder cocaine carries the same sentence of two years in prison.[6]

Frank Loane, a gun shop owner in Maryland, stands in front of a wall of assault rifles at his store. In 2013, Maryland lawmakers passed a sweeping gun control bill, banning 45 types of guns like the ones featured at his store. The new law requires customers to submit their fingerprints and attend a gun safety course in order to purchase a handgun. Do you think this will reduce gun violence?

In this chapter, you will learn about how policy can shape—and is shaped by—the criminal justice system. The chapter begins with a discussion about the need for and function of criminal justice policies. The chapter then looks at how policies are developed and the role of politics in this process. The chapter concludes with two Current Controversy debates related to criminal justice policies. The first, by David Bierie and Sarah Craun, looks at whether sex offender registries are an effective tool for keeping the public safe. The second, by Shelly Arsneault, questions whether street-level bureaucracy is a good practice in criminal justice.

WHAT IS POLICY?

Policy is used in a variety of ways by the criminal justice system. Policies provide guidance to criminal justice officials. Policies can be particularly useful in cases where there are high levels of **discretion**. For example, sentencing guidelines have been used in a number of different states as well as by the federal government. These guidelines provide judges with a range that they can use to help make sentencing decisions for offenders. Policies are also used to facilitate and regulate action. In this sense, policies serve as the rules that workers in the criminal justice system use to do their jobs. For example, many jurisdictions use mandatory arrest policies in cases of intimate partner violence. Here, officers are required to make an arrest in these cases if called to a domestic dispute; an officer's discretion is significantly reduced, and it is policy that guides her or his action on the job.

Policy
Law or practice that is used to provide guidance to criminal justice officials.

Discretion
Refers to the power to make decisions by criminal justice officials.

WHY DO WE NEED CRIMINAL JUSTICE POLICIES?

Changes in criminal justice policy generally occur in response to a need or issue that faces the criminal justice system and society as a whole. Many of these needs are rooted in discussions about the levels of crime in society. Here, policy is seen as a way to deal with the presence of crime and the handling of offenders. The federal government has been an active player in the creation of crime control policies. Given the high level of policy implementation related to criminal justice issues, one might be led to believe that crime rates have spiraled out of control. After all, we have more police officers on the streets, our prisons are overcrowded, and we spend billions of dollars nationwide supporting the enterprise of criminal justice. In 2011, the Department of Justice's budget included $27.1 billion in discretionary funding.[7]

WEB LINK
Do Mandatory Domestic
Violence Arrests Hurt Victims?

WEB LINK
In Campaign for
Tougher Gun Laws,
Advocates Focus on States

HOW DO CRIMINAL JUSTICE POLICIES DEVELOP?

While there have been a number of different theories and discussions about the policy development process, we can generally organize this process into six stages: (1) problem identification, (2) policy demands, (3) agenda formation, (4) policy adoption, (5) policy implementation, and (6) policy evaluation. Figure 6.1 showcases how these six stages work together in the development of policy.

Planning a Policy

Before a policy can be developed, there must be an issue at hand. Issues can be identified by concerned citizens, the media, and advocacy groups, as well as politicians.

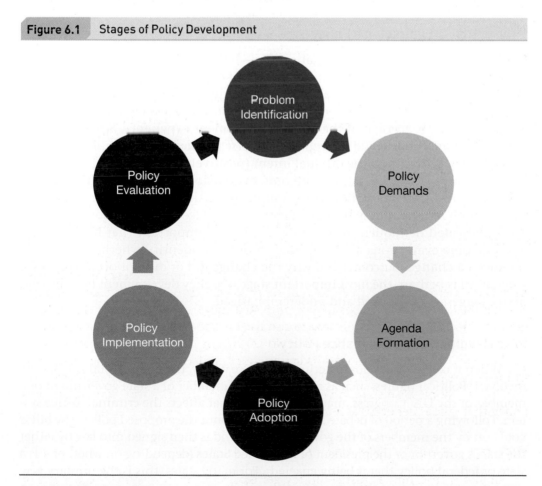

Figure 6.1   Stages of Policy Development

Source: Adapted from Cochran, C. E., Mayer, L. C., Carr, T. R., Cayer, N. J., & McKenzie, M. (2011). *American public policy: An introduction.* Boston, MA: Wadsworth Publishing.

SAGE JOURNAL ARTICLE
Variation in Criminal
Justice Policy Making

Issues in criminal justice might include rising crime rates, the need for drug and alcohol counseling in prisons, or concerns about the residency requirements for convicted sex offenders in the community. Once an issue is identified, there can be significant debate about the demands of the policy. What is the goal or objective of the policy? Is it to increase punishments? Is it to increase community safety? It is during this stage that the intent of the policy is put forward. Once this is decided, we move into the agenda formation process. This is perhaps one of the most politicized stages in policy development as it involves a variety of different voices—from government officials to special interest groups and individuals who will ultimately be affected by the policy—all of whom want to be heard.

Adopting and Implementing a Policy

The next stage involves the adoption of the policy. Depending on the nature of the policy, this could involve the passage of new laws or the signing of executive orders. Upon completion of this stage, the cycle moves to policy implementation. Implementation is all about spending money—from hiring more officers to increasing police presence in particular regions to allocating funds to supervise offenders in the community. This can present significant challenges—perhaps the law as it was written was too vague, or there isn't enough funding to effectively implement the policy, or there may be challenges to the policy that may stall or halt its implementation.

> "
> The ways in which a policy is implemented may differ significantly from the original intention of the authors of a policy.

Evaluating a Policy

Finally, the evaluation stage looks at the efficacy of the policy. Did the policy accomplish what it set out to do? What impact does the policy have?[8] Policy evaluation can be divided into two general categories: process evaluation and outcome evaluation. **Process evaluation** involves looking at the progression of the policy development experience. Are there areas where these methods could be improved or streamlined? If the implementation of the policy differs from the original intent (positively or negatively), how might this be resolved? In contrast, an **outcome evaluation** looks at the changes that occur as a result of the policy. For example, does the implementation of early intervention programming in elementary school reduce the number of youth who are adjudicated delinquent in juvenile court? It is important that both process and outcome evaluations are conducted in order to identify whether the policy produced a change (outcome) and why the change did or did not occur (process). Evaluation is perhaps the most important stage of policy development but one that many suggest is overlooked and underemphasized.

Process evaluation
Method of research that looks at the progress of the policy development experience to determine how the policy is developing and being implemented.

Outcome evaluation
Method of research that looks at the changes that occur as a result of a policy to determine whether it is effective.

Who Develops Criminal Justice Policy?

When it comes to developing criminal justice policy, there are several key players involved. Political figures, such as a congressional member of a state government or a member of the U.S. Congress, may sponsor a bill that affects the criminal justice system. Following a period of debate and discussion about the proposed policy, the bill is voted on by the members of the governing body and is then signed into law by either the state's governor or the president of the United States (depending on whether it is a state or federal policy that is being enacted). For many states, this is the primary way that new policies are developed and implemented.

Direct Democracy

Some states have an alternative method of creating new laws and policies. Under the practice of **direct democracy**, citizens in 17 states are empowered to make law through an initiative process. The **initiative** process begins with a petition for a new law. If a minimum number of signatures from registered voters is obtained, the measure is placed on the ballot for the citizenry to vote on. In states such as California, if a measure receives a majority of the votes, it is enacted into law. What makes the process of direct democracy unique is that it completely bypasses the traditional structures of lawmaking—that is, it does not require the support of elected officials in order to pass new laws. In addition, a policy enacted through the process of direct democracy does not necessarily endure the same rigorous process of vetting the budget in terms of implementing such a policy.[9] Many of California's most famous criminal justice policies were created through the citizen initiative process, including the habitual-offender law Three Strikes (Proposition 184, 1994, later amended through Proposition 36 in 2012); Jessica's Law (Proposition 83, 2006), which created new regulations for sexual offenders; and the diversion of low-level drug offenders from prison to drug treatment (Proposition 36, 2000).

The Goals of Criminal Justice Policies

In many cases, criminal justice policies are implemented to change the way in which offenders are processed by the criminal justice system. A review of recent history demonstrates that many of these policies are designed to be tougher on crime by increasing the penalties for various crimes and restricting the movement of offenders in the community. Despite the continued push toward retributive punishments, we do find examples of policies that seek to change the definitions of criminal behavior and the responses by police agencies to crime. In recent years, many states have attempted either to legalize the use of **marijuana** for medical purposes or to decriminalize marijuana use in general. For example, in 2010, California citizens introduced an initiative to legalize marijuana. While California's measure ultimately failed at the ballot box, other states have been successful in changing their laws. In 2012, voters legalized the use of marijuana in both Washington and Colorado. Washington State voters approved the possession of up to an ounce of marijuana for individuals over the age of 21. While the sale of marijuana remains illegal, the state is making plans to set up a system of state-approved growers (similar to having state-licensed liquor stores) within the year, a plan that could bring in hundreds of millions of dollars in revenue to the state.[10] A similar law passed in Colorado with 55% of voters in support.[11] In 2014, voters legalized marijuana in Alaska, Oregon, and Washington, DC.[12]

AUDIO
Cases Show Disparity of California's Three-Strikes Law

Direct democracy
Political process by which citizens are empowered to make law through an initiative process.

Initiative
Political process by which prospective laws are proposed for voters to approve during an election.

Marijuana
Drug derived from cannabis plant.

Criminal justice policies around the use of marijuana have evolved significantly in recent years as many states move to decriminalize or legalize the practice. How has this policy change come about?

Cost-Saving Measures

Attempts such as these have highlighted the fiscal concerns of states, as many are struggling to maintain the growing incarcerated populations stemming from the implementation of the tough-on-crime initiatives that have dominated the criminal justice landscape in recent times. However, the legalization of marijuana is not the only topic in this debate about dollars and cents. For example, the Savings, Accountability, and Full Enforcement (SAFE) for California Act (2012) highlighted the fiscal concerns of maintaining the death penalty. While public-polling data indicated that many California voters were in support of this initiative, it ultimately failed, with only 48% of the votes in favor of the measure.[13] In Maryland, legislators sought to introduce a graduated-sanctions program for technical parole violators. Rather than return these offenders back to prison, this program allowed for nonincarceration forms of punishment in cases such as missing a meeting with a parole officer or failing to complete community service hours. This change in policy would have freed up some of the one billion dollars that the state spends on its correctional system. Due to the high start-up costs of the program (versus focusing on its long-term savings), its implementation was scaled back to only three counties, instead of a statewide effort.[14]

POLITICS AND CRIMINAL JUSTICE POLICY

When we think about politics, we can generally divide beliefs into two separate camps: liberals and conservatives. **Liberal** politics tend to focus on the importance of due process, individual freedoms, and constitutional rights. Liberals also look to the government to help create equality in society and to solve problems. Socially, liberals believe that the government should help support those individuals who may suffer from various disadvantages in society. In terms of crime-related issues, liberals believe that society should fight against the racist, gendered, and classist disparities that exist in the system. When it comes to the punishment of offenders, liberals tend to lean toward a more rehabilitative focus.

In contrast, **conservative** politics lean toward less intervention by the government and focus on traditional values. "Conservatism also refers to a belief that existing economic and political inequalities are justified and that the existing order is about as close as is practically attainable to an ideal order."[15] On crime, conservatives see the actions of criminals as part of a rational-choice process whereby the offender makes a cognitive decision to participate in criminal activity. Conservatives follow more of a law-and-order philosophy and generally cite retributive values, or an "eye for an eye," in their perspective on punishing offenders.

Given these different philosophical foundations, it is not surprising that liberals and conservatives think differently about criminal justice policies. One example is Arizona's immigration law (called the Support Our Law Enforcement and Safe Neighborhoods Act, or SB 1070). Since the law was adopted in 2010, it has been debated by politicians and the public and challenged in the legal arena. One of the more controversial issues within the law calls for police officers to determine whether an individual is a legal U.S. citizen during a "lawful stop, detention or arrest" or any other form of "lawful contact" where there is reasonable suspicion that the person is an illegal immigrant. Supporters of SB 1070 (most of whom were conservative policymakers) argued that the federal government has failed to adequately police illegal immigration. For these conservatives, SB 1070 served to protect their communities from rising crime rates and other social problems (such as strains on educational resources and the state welfare system) that they perceived were directly related to illegal immigrants. However, opponents of the law (who generally identify as more liberal on the political spectrum) argued that Arizona's law

Liberal
A political perspective that tends to focus on the importance of due process, individual freedoms, and constitutional rights.

Conservative
A political perspective that follows more of a law-and-order philosophy and generally cites retributive values in punishing offenders.

SPOTLIGHT

Stand-Your-Ground Policy

Stand-your-ground laws exist in 24 states nationwide. Such laws are also referred to as the *castle doctrine*. These policies are based on the common-law doctrine that individuals have the right to protect themselves in their homes if they are under attack. Florida's use of the stand-your-ground policy has led to significant attention by the media and public alike.

Florida's stand-your-ground law was the first such law in the nation that reflected an expansion of the castle doctrine. Passed in 2005 and signed into law by Governor Jeb Bush, the stand-your-ground law only requires that the police and courts consider three basic criteria: (1) Was the individual entitled to be present, (2) was the individual engaged in a law abiding activity, and (3) could the individual reasonably believe that he or she was at risk for significant bodily harm or injury? Recently, there have been several controversial perceptions of the law related to some high-profile cases in which the offender alleged self-defense.

A recent high-profile critique of the stand-your-ground law involved the case of Trayvon Martin and George Zimmerman. Martin was walking in his gated neighborhood community following a trip to a local convenience store. Zimmerman, head of the neighborhood watch, contacted the police to report a suspi-

Sybrina Fulton, mother of Trayvon Martin, testifies before a subcommittee of the U.S. Senate Judiciary Committee on stand-your-ground laws. Should the stand-your-ground law in Florida be repealed?

cious individual (Martin) walking in the neighborhood. Zimmerman followed Martin and confronted him. Zimmerman alleged that Martin attacked him. In response, Zimmerman pulled out a gun and shot Martin, who died from his injuries.[a] While much was made of the stand-your-ground law, ultimately, Zimmerman did not use this option in his case. In July 2013, Zimmerman was acquitted of second-degree murder, admitting that he shot Martin in self-defense.[b] While Zimmerman did not expressly rely on the pretrial option of the stand-your-ground law, the public perception is that the law was used to acquit Zimmerman.

A case where stand your ground was used was that of Marissa Alexander. During a confrontation with her husband in August 2010, Alexander fired a bullet into the wall. She testified that she felt threatened. Luckily, no one was hurt in the incident. Even though Alexander used Florida's stand-your-ground law, the jury convicted her of aggravated assault with a deadly weapon, and she was sentenced to 20 years in prison, as her actions triggered a mandatory minimum gun law.[c] Her case was overturned on appeal, and in January 2015, she pled guilty to aggravated assault. She was sentenced to three years and received credit for the time she had already served.[d]

While several groups have called for the repeal of the stand-your-ground law in Florida, the state legislators are working on reforms to the law. One proposal currently under consideration would shift the burden of proof for the pretrial hearing to the prosecutor. The proposed changes

(Continued)

(Continued)

CRITICAL THINKING QUESTIONS

1. What challenges exist with stand-your-ground laws?

2. Given these examples, what recommendations for reform should states consider in relation to these policies?

also articulate that the stand-your-ground law "is not intended to encourage vigilantism or acts of revenge, authorize the initiation of a confrontation as a pretext to respond with deadly force, or negate a duty to retreat for persons engaged in unlawful mutual combat."[e] While high-profile cases have drawn a disproportionate amount of attention (and in many cases, attention based on incorrect facts about the law), it remains to be seen what changes the legislature will make to the law.

AUDIO
Another Florida Case Puts Crosshairs on "Stand Your Ground"

was unconstitutional and that the implementation of SB 1070 would divert important resources away from fighting violent crimes.[16] Ultimately, the U.S. Supreme Court held that the investigation of immigration status in cases of a lawful stop, detention, or arrest is permissible (*Arizona v. United States*).[17]

Even examples of crime policy that have traditionally represented bipartisan efforts to protect the interests of victims can be subjected to political controversy. In Chapter 5, you learned about the Violence Against Women Act. While this piece of legislation has traditionally been a bipartisan effort, its most recent reauthorization demonstrated a significant departure from previous efforts and became a battle between Republicans and Democrats. Ultimately, the bill did pass both the House and the Senate, but its journey was a rather political one.

Presidential Politics and Criminal Justice Policies

Regardless of values and ideologies, criminal justice issues are a hot topic for the body politic, including the White House. A focus on policing first began back in the 1930s with the creation of the Wickersham Commission (by President Hoover) and continued into the 1960s with research by groups such as the President's Commission on Law Enforcement and the Kerner Commission (President Johnson).[18] However, it wasn't until the 1970s that crime became a key component of the presidential platform when then president Richard Nixon declared a war on crime. The shift toward being tough on crime was highlighted during the 1988 presidential election when the Democratic candidate for president, Massachusetts governor Michael Dukakis, was heavily criticized by Republican candidate George H. W. Bush for Dukakis's support of weekend furlough releases for convicted offenders. This weekend furlough program was used by the Massachusetts State Prison as part of the state's rehabilitation program for offenders. Though Willie Horton was a convicted murderer who had received a sentence of life without the possibility of parole for his crime, he was still permitted to participate in the program. Unfortunately, Horton never returned from his furlough and instead traveled to Maryland, where he robbed a local couple, physically assaulted the male, and raped the woman.[19] As governor, Dukakis was held politically responsible for Horton's release (which led to these crimes) and declared soft on crime, a position that ultimately contributed to his loss in the election.[20] As a result of growing public concerns about crime, it seems that virtually every election

> As a result of growing public concerns about crime, it seems that virtually every election discussion on criminal issues results in candidates presenting a tough-on-crime stance in their attempts to garner public support.

discussion on criminal issues results in candidates presenting a tough-on-crime stance in their attempts to garner public support.

As the leader of our nation's government structure, the president has surprisingly little power when it comes to making policy. While each president enters the office with ideas for reforming policies such as health care, education, and social welfare, success in making these reforms is dependent on the actions of the House and the Senate. While it is up to the president to sign these acts into law, even this practice can be overruled by a two-thirds vote. Here, presidents have no direct ability to pass legislation; rather, their goal is to persuade members of Congress to introduce items that are consistent with their interests. (At the state level, similar processes occur between the governor and state senators and representatives.)

Congress and Criminal Justice Policies

Given that presidents have made criminal justice issues a part of their policy agenda for the past five decades, it begs the question of how much influence various presidents have had over Congress's ability to introduce legislation on crime-related issues. Between 1946 and 1996, 3,373 congressional hearings were held on crime-related issues, such as drug abuse and drug trafficking, juvenile crime, white-collar crime, and court administration. In comparing these data with the number of presidential speeches and conferences on crime related issues, we learn that the president has little influence over the actions of Congress when it comes to crime policy. In fact, research demonstrates that the only variables that appeared to influence crime policy discussions in Congress were the crime rate and whether it was an election year. Specifically, as the crime rate increased, the number of congressional hearings on crime-related issues increased. In addition, the number of congressional hearings on crime drops significantly during an election year. While presidential politics doesn't appear to impact congressional activity during that same year, it does appear to have an influence on the actions of Congress in the following year. This finding shows that it can take time to raise awareness of an issue within Congress and to effect behavioral changes.[21]

Public Perception and Criminal Justice Policies

At the same time, it's important to remember that criminal justice policies change over time. In some cases, this reflects changes in our government structure and the positions of those who hold political office. You'll learn more about the juvenile justice system in Chapter 13, but the laws surrounding juvenile crime are a great example

As the highest court in the land, the U.S. Supreme Court has been involved in deciding constitutional challenges to many criminal justice policies, such as habitual sentencing laws, sentencing guidelines, and capital punishment. What effect might a more liberal or more conservative Supreme Court have on criminal justice policies?

AROUND THE WORLD

Drug Policy in the Netherlands

While popular culture presents the image that drug use in the Netherlands is widely accepted, this is not an accurate reflection of drug policies throughout the country. Drugs are prohibited in the Netherlands. However, the Netherlands approaches drug use as a public health issue, accepts that drugs are an inevitable feature of a modern society,[a] and utilizes a harm reduction strategy.

Current drug policies in the Netherlands organize drugs into two separate categories. In the first category are substances that are viewed as harmful to individuals, such as heroin and cocaine. The second category includes soft drugs, such as marijuana and hashish. The division of drugs into these two separate categories allows the Dutch to approach the enforcement of hard drugs differently than soft drugs. Despite claims that marijuana is a gateway drug to more significant drug use, there is little research to substantiate this claim.[b] While there is no punishment for the simple possession of marijuana, possession of 15 to 300 grams of crack cocaine yields a six- to 18-month sentence. Compare this with mandatory minimum laws in the United States, where the possession of one ounce (28 grams) of crack will trigger a mandatory sentence of five years.[c]

Licensed coffee shops have historically been allowed to sell small amounts of marijuana for personal use to Dutch citizens only. The Bulldog coffee shop in Amsterdam first opened its doors in 1975 and is regarded as the first coffee shop to sell marijuana. Should the United States take a similar approach?

AP Photo/Peter Dejong

The Dutch also rely on a harm reduction model to deal with cases of addiction. Harm reduction policies argue that the best way to address drug use is to minimize the risks on both a social and an individual level.[d] In the Netherlands, drug treatment programs are widely available, and the costs are covered by the nationalized health care system. The Dutch were also the first to implement needle exchange programs for IV drug users. Such policies demonstrate a concern with reducing the personal harms (such as HIV transmission as a result of IV drug use) related to drug addiction.[e]

While policies in the United States have suggested that drug use can lead to criminal activity, crime rates in the Netherlands are significantly lower, as is the presence of violence related to drugs.[f] Indeed, the crime rates are so low in the Netherlands that Dutch officials recently announced the closure of eight prisons throughout the country due to low population levels.[g] Evidence also indicates that there are fewer users of such substances in the Netherlands than there are in regions where stricter drug policies exist. For example, research tells us that 41% of

Figure 6.2   Public Views on Drug Policy in the United States

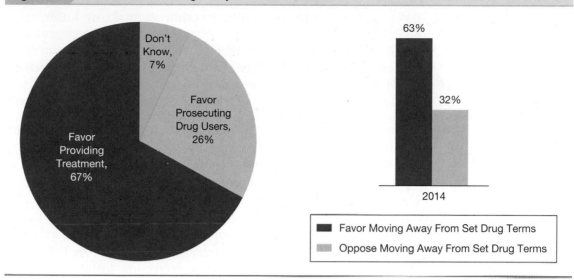

Source: PEW Research Center.

people in the United States have used marijuana in their lifetime while only 23% of people in the Netherlands have. Similar results are demonstrated with hard drugs, where 14.7% of Americans have used cocaine compared with 3.4% of the Dutch.[h]

The majority of Americans surveyed thought that when it comes to drug policy, the government should focus more on providing treatment than on prosecuting drug users and that courts should move away from mandatory minimum sentences for nonviolent drug crimes (Figure 6.2).

CRITICAL THINKING QUESTIONS

1. Given the challenges with the war on drugs in the United States, are there things we can learn from the policies in use under Dutch law? If so, what?

2. How could a harm reduction model, coupled with the decriminalization or legalization of soft drugs such as marijuana, provide opportunities for us to think differently about our drug laws in America?

of how our beliefs about offenders have evolved throughout history. For example, the juvenile court was founded on the notion that youth should be treated differently from adult offenders. Yet the rising crime rates and the involvement of youth in these activities led many policymakers to shift their thinking about how children who engage in at-risk and criminal behaviors should be treated. Indeed, the tough-on-crime practices that were common within the criminal justice system also influenced the juvenile court. Whereas youth were once seen as individuals capable of reform and change, laws during the late 20th and early 21st centuries began to view juveniles as similar to their adult counterparts, particularly in relation to violent crime. As a result, many young teen offenders saw themselves sentenced to significant prison terms (or even life sentences) as early as 14 years old. In 2012, the U.S. Supreme Court held that the use of mandatory juvenile life-without-the-possibility-of-parole sentences for certain crime categories was unconstitutional. At the time, this ruling only applied to future cases and left the current population of juvenile lifers with little recourse. In 2016, the U.S. Supreme Court held in *Montgomery v. Louisiana* that their decision in *Miller v. Alabama* (2012) was retroactive. This means that juveniles who received a mandatory sentence of life without the possibility of parole can now return to the courts to have a hearing on whether they should be sentenced to a term with the opportunity of parole.

RESEARCH AND CRIMINAL JUSTICE POLICIES

When it comes to responding to crime, how do we know what works? Alas, policymakers do not always know what the cutting-edge research says about the types of programs and strategies that are effective at reducing crime rates. While there are certainly examples that exist that reference research when creating or changing policy, these cases are often the exception rather than the rule. As a result, scholars are often left looking at whether a policy is effective after it has been implemented.

One of the initial efforts to share research findings on effective crime control strategies and prevention/intervention programming came with the passage of the Crime Control Act of 1973. Within this legislation, the government established the National Institute of Law Enforcement and Criminal Justice, which served as a clearinghouse for criminal justice information. Today, there are many federal agencies (such as the Office of Justice Programs, Community Oriented Policing Services, and the Office on Violence Against Women, to name a few) as well as private foundations and organizations (such as the Sentencing Project and the Police Foundation) that fund, conduct, and disseminate research on criminal justice policies and practices.[22]

VIDEO

Solutions in Corrections: Program Fidelity and Program Integrity

At the beginning of this chapter, you learned about the role of process and outcome evaluation with criminal justice policies. It is important to remember that the results of evaluations can vary across time and space. For example, what if a program evaluation demonstrates that a particular policy is effective at reducing crime? This is great news. But what if the next time someone implements the policy, they do so in a slightly different manner? Or in a community with different structures or needs? Are we to assume that if the program fails, it is a bad program? Consistency is important when it comes to replicating successful efforts in a new environment. This is called program fidelity. Program fidelity involves seven different factors. Table 6.1 highlights these factors and how they can impact the results when a program or policy is implemented.

Table 6.1	Program Fidelity Factors
Delivery	What strategies are used to deliver the material? • Lecture • Discussion • Active learning
Dosage	What are the number, length, and frequency of sessions in the program? • How many sessions do participants attend? • How long are the sessions? • How often are the sessions held?
Setting	Where does the program take place?
Target Population	Who are the intended participants of the program? • Gender • Age • Specific characteristics or risk factors • Prior history of exhibiting behavior
Materials	What are the written and audiovisual modules that are included in the program curriculum?
Provider Qualifications	What are the credentials or qualifications required of program providers?
Provider Training	What is the nature and length of training required to become a program provider?

Source: Adapted from the California Healthy Kids Resource Center. http://www.californiahealthykids.org/fidelity

CAREERS IN CRIMINAL JUSTICE

So You Want to Be a Policy Advocate?

There are a variety of career opportunities for someone interested in criminal justice policy. Although some of these jobs are found within governmental agencies and offices, others involve work with non-profit organizations.

Policy work within the government occurs at every stage and within a variety of different settings. At the local level, policy is made by a number of individuals and involves the criminal justice system in different ways. For example, as a chief of police you would be involved in setting policy and managing the organization. Your day-to-day activities might include meeting with the mayor or city manager, working with representatives from the police union, or talking with your managerial staff about issues facing your city and how the police are involved in responding to these concerns. Another example of policy work at the local level is the city council. City councils (also referred to as the board of supervisors or municipal legislature in some regions) are composed of several elected individuals who work together to propose policies and laws to help govern the city. In some cases, decisions are made in response to a public reaction. For example, the Greensboro, North Carolina, city council voted in May 2016 to release body camera footage of a shooting death of one of its residents after family members argued that the shooting was unjustified.[a] In some cases, the decisions made by these councils are financial. In 2011, Topeka, Kansas, debated whether to decriminalize domestic violence due to a lack of funds to handle such cases.[b]

Government-based policy work also occurs at the state and federal levels. As you've learned throughout this chapter, members of each state legislature and the U.S. Congress are elected officials who are responsible for the drafting and passage of new legislation. The requirements to serve as a member of the U.S. Congress are stated in Article I of the Constitution, which notes that senators must be at least 30 years old, citizens of the United States for the past nine years, and live in the state that they represent at the time of their election. To serve as a member of the House of Representatives you must be 25 years old and have been a citizen of the United States for the past seven years. Members of the House and Senate serve on a variety of different committees, and several of these groups focus on criminal justice issues. For example, the Senate Caucus on International Narcotics Control focuses on issues related to domestic and international drug trafficking. Committees hold hearings, issue reports, and draft legislation related to their areas of interest. However, there are other opportunities to work as a policy advocate without serving as an elected official. For example, each of these officials has staff members who work on research related to various policy issues. They may attend committee hearings and help members of Congress prepare items for discussion and debate.

There are also several non-government-based opportunities to engage in policy work. Perhaps you are interested in working for a nonprofit organization such as The Sentencing Project, the Police Foundation, or the Death Penalty Information Center. Each of these groups is involved in research and advocacy around criminal justice issues. Nonprofit organizations are also involved in local-level activities, such as domestic violence shelters and rape crisis organizations. These agencies work with local and state officials to provide training for the police and courts, as well as advocate for city and state funding to help support their organizations. In addition, research-based organizations focus on policy development and advocacy. Here, you might be involved in evaluating a local program designed to prevent at-risk youth from joining gangs, or in assessing whether police use-of-force tactics are effective in reducing injuries to officers in the line of duty. As a research policy analyst, you might work for organizations such as the RAND Corporation or the Urban Institute. These types of organizations often use their research findings to influence policymakers at the regional and national level.

The requirements for policy analyst positions vary dramatically. Some require sophisticated analytical skills, whereas others require strong interpersonal and networking skills. Some of these positions would be available to students with a bachelor's degree, while others would require advanced education and experiences in the field. Regardless of the type of position, people who work in these fields have a strong desire to engage in public service and advocacy.

As you review the Current Controversies at the end of this chapter, as well as policies that are presented throughout this text, ask yourself, What does the research show about whether these policies are effective at reducing crime rates, preventing future crimes, and reforming offenders? Or, as is the case in some examples, has the policy made matters worse?

CONCLUSION

From elected officials who utilize criminal justice issues as key components of their political platform to citizens who issue demands for safer communities and increased punishments for offenders, discussions about criminal justice policy invoke a variety of emotions across the ranks. Each of these policies has relied on political influence to pass and implement these practices. In many cases, the passage of such policies is intended to increase the safety of our communities. But is this actually the case? Or do these policies just make people think that they are protected? While politicians aim to reflect the values and ideals of their constituency, agents of the media can inflame the "threats" that criminal activity can represent. Is it possible that such threats lead to the retention of outdated policies and practices? Consider these questions as you read the following debates: Does the presence of these policies lead to reductions in crime? Is there the potential for unintended consequences as a result of such laws?

CURRENT CONTROVERSY 6.1

PRO CON

Are Laws Requiring Sex Offender Registries Effective?
—David Bierie and Sarah Craun—

INTRODUCTION

Sex offender registries first appeared in the United States in California during the mid-1940s. Registry laws provide for the creation of a database for law enforcement that contains personal identifiers, addresses, and criminal histories for convicted sex offenders. They have expanded significantly since that time and transitioned into national policy in 1994 via the Jacob Wetterling Act and Megan's Law in 1996. The most recent iteration of national policy was created in the Adam Walsh Child Protection and Safety Act of 2006.[23]

The fundamental premise of the registry is that people who have been convicted of a sex crime in the past are at a higher-than-average risk of committing a new sexual crime. Sex offender registries generally comprise two components: (1) the creation of a database for law enforcement that contains personal identifiers, addresses, and criminal history for convicted sex offenders (registration) and (2) the public display of portions of that information for some offenders (community notification) through a public sex offender registry website. There are numerous goals of the sex offender registry. However, two are particularly important from a law enforcement perspective: to prevent sexual crimes and to help law enforcement in responding to sexual crimes.

The first goal of registries is to prevent sexual crimes—primarily through enhancing guardianship of potential victims. In signing the Adam Walsh Act, for example, President Bush argued that a key intent was to make sure "parents have the information they need to protect their children

The Florida Department of Law Enforcement
FLORIDA SEXUAL OFFENDERS AND PREDATORS

Charting a Course for Public Safety

OFFENDER SEARCH
Click to search for Sexual Predators & Offenders

OFFENDER ALERT
Click to subscribe to e-mail notifications

FAQ
Click for Frequently Asked Questions

IMPORTANT
Information for Sexual Predators and Offenders

• Español • Home • Search • FAQ • Important • Legal • Links • Safety Tips • About Us • Contact Us • FDLE Home

PROXIMITY	PICTURE	NAME	STATUS	ADDRESS	ADDRESS SOURCE INFORMATION
0.8 Mile N		CHARLES, CLEVINS View Flyer Track Offender	Supervised - FL Dept of Corrections	10760 HOBBIT CIR APT 203 ORLANDO FL 32836 Show Map	Source: Registration Received: 11/24/2015 Type of Address: Temporary
2.2 Mile S		NORTON, ROBERT L. View Flyer Track Offender	Released - Subject to Registration	9560 VIA ENCINAS BONNET CREEK RESORT LAKE BUENA VISTA FL 32830 Show Map	Source: Registration Received: 12/02/2014 Type of Address: Temporary
2.5 Mile SE		RODRIGUEZ, LUIS E. View Flyer Track Offender	Released - Subject to Registration	13016 PLANTATION PARK CIR APT 1126 ORLANDO FL 32821 Show Map	Source: Registration Received: 07/08/2015 Type of Address: Permanent

The Florida Department of Law Enforcement

Sex offender registry laws provide options for community notification of convicted sex offenders. Websites such as this present residency and status information about registered sexual offenders. What are some of the benefits and drawbacks of having this information publicly available?

from sex offenders that might be in their neighborhoods."[24] Research suggests that nearly 80% of sexual assaults are committed by friends, acquaintances, neighbors, or people otherwise known to the victim.[25] In addition, a large portion of sexual predators target victims living within a 15-minute walk of a given crime location.[26] The hope, then, is that identifying known sex offenders in one's neighborhood allows citizens to better protect themselves and their children through limiting contact with those known offenders.

The second goal of registries is to assist law enforcement in solving a specific type of sexual crime (those committed by strangers). If a child is abducted,

for example, police might want to check whether the suspect's description matches any registered sex offenders who live or work in the area. This might lead to a higher clearance rate and, more importantly, a faster recovery of victims. The latter benefit (speed) is critical to law enforcement because the harm an abducted child experiences grows quickly as time passes. Research shows 75% of kidnapped children who are murdered are killed within the first three hours of their abduction.[27] Thus, "law enforcement officials realize that the faster the child is found, the greater the chance he or she will be unharmed."[28] The same is presumed with other types of sex crimes by strangers—a faster apprehension will reduce the total harm that person can inflict on the community.

CON   Sex Offender Registries Are Not Effective

Academic researchers have been deeply critical of registries and have articulated a broad number of potential costs or limitations associated with

them.[29] For example, they argue that registration may lead to unfair stigma placed on family members of registrants, vigilante justice, and money spent maintaining a registry instead of alternative policies. They worry that having a registry may give a false sense of security to families, as there are plenty of people who are sexually dangerous and not on the registry. Most importantly, however, critics warn that registries may actually increase danger to the public by making registrants more crime prone. They argue that being on the registry likely makes it difficult to get a job, obtain housing, or make friends. This might add stress that manifests in strain or defiance (motivation toward crime) and diminishes social control or prosocial values that might otherwise constrain or reduce that motivation.

With respect to the first key goal (reducing sexual assault), early research comparing sexual offense rates in communities before and after the enactment of a registry generally found no effect.

Regarding the second key goal (clearance rate), there is far less research available to consider. One of the only studies examining this question to date found a nonsignificant increase in clearance rates as a function of registries.[30] One might expect the effect of registries to be helpful in locating victims of abduction or rape by strangers (i.e., when the offender isn't already known at the time the crime is reported). But one wouldn't expect it to matter with the (approximately) 80% of sex crimes in which the offender is already known (e.g., those committed by family members against children or date rape).

There is no doubt that registries are controversial—informed people can and do disagree on what benefits and costs they generate and especially whether the benefits outweigh the potential costs. The scientific literature is not particularly persuasive in this debate. Opponents have generated a number of criticisms and found some evidence that there are unintended consequences of the registry (as noted above). On the other hand, there is some evidence that registries are associated with decreases in sexual offending. But in general, there are too few studies available, coupled with methodological limitations,[31] which collectively limit understanding about the effects of the registry on law enforcement outcomes.

 PRO **Sex Offender Registries Are Effective**

Despite these challenges, recent research on this issue showed that sexual crimes declined by an average of 13% in communities after the enactment of a registry.[32] Additionally, there are qualitative examples that illustrate the power of sex offender registries. For example, a woman in New Jersey opened the door to a census worker and recognized him from the registry as an offender who had multiple convictions for sexually assaulting children (though he gave a fake name when obtaining employment with the census). Concerned that the registrant was using a fake name and federal credentials to gain access to area homes, she contacted police. The registrant was arrested.[33] In another example, a former deputy in Colorado saw a man who appeared to be watching children from his car, which was parked outside an elementary school. The deputy recognized the man from his image on the sex offender registry. The registrant, previously convicted of sexually assaulting children, was interviewed by police. They determined he was there looking for the "perfect" girl to lure into his car. He was arrested.[34] It's not guaranteed that these offenders would have committed a sexual assault if not recognized. But is it possible that they were pursuing opportunities and access to potential victims? If so, it is unlikely these crimes would have been detected without the registry. This effect is difficult to measure.

DISCUSSION QUESTIONS

1. What are the goals of sex offender registries?

2. What are some of the criticisms of sex offender registries?

3. Do sex offender registries infringe on the rights of those accused and convicted of these crimes? Or are they important tools in evaluating and managing the risk of potentially dangerous offenders in the community?

4. Based on the evidence presented, are the laws that permit sex offender registries effective at preventing crime?

5. Do these laws go too far? Or not far enough?

PRO CON

Is Street-Level Bureaucracy a Good Thing?

—Shelly Arsneault—

CURRENT
CONTROVERSY
VIDEO
Where Do You Stand?
Cast Your Vote!

INTRODUCTION

A well-dressed couple in their mid-50s sits on a shady park bench talking and laughing. They pull out a bottle of champagne from a picnic basket and drink a toast. A police officer, recognizing the champagne as a clear violation of the city's ordinance against open alcohol containers, stops at the park bench. The couple explains that they were married under these trees 25 years ago and have come to celebrate. The officer congratulates them, reminds them to keep the champagne out of sight, and moves on. Now, imagine that on that same park bench two homeless people are sharing a bottle of Boone's Farm wine from a paper bag. What do you suppose the officer's reaction would be to the second couple? While both couples are engaged in the same illegal behavior, the people in these two scenarios will probably experience very different treatment from the police. This different treatment of a similar situation is an example of bureaucratic discretion. When an officer of the law has the authority to use her own judgments, opinions, experience, or reasoning to make decisions in the course of carrying out the law, he or she is exhibiting discretion.

You might think that it isn't fair for these two couples to be treated differently because they both violated the same law, or you may think that different treatment is perfectly logical and that the circumstances and characteristics of each couple should allow an exception to the law for the anniversary couple. Maybe you can see it both ways; if so, you are well on your way to understanding the complexity and ambiguity of bureaucratic discretion in the criminal justice system.

Before discussing the pros and cons of bureaucratic discretion, let us define some terms. **Bureaucracy** describes any large organization that is characterized by a defined structure and rules that allow it to pursue its mission and goals. In this case, bureaucracy is "the system" of the criminal justice system; it includes law enforcement agencies such as local police and sheriff's departments or the state highway patrol. Other bureaucratic agencies of the criminal justice system include criminal courts, county probation offices, or a state's department of prisons.

A bureaucrat in the criminal justice system, therefore, is someone who works in the criminal justice

Should police officers treat these two couples differently?

Chapter 6 • Criminal Justice Policy **145**

bureaucracy, such as a police officer, judge, district attorney, probation officer, or prison guard. We consider these people to be the **street-level bureaucrats** of the criminal justice system, those "who interact directly with citizens in the course of their jobs, and who have substantial discretion in the execution of their work."[35] These are the people at the front lines, carrying out the difficult, often dangerous work of the justice system.

CON Street-Level Bureaucracy Is Not a Good Thing

Criminal justice bureaucrats often have authority to use their own judgments, opinions, experience, or reasoning to make decisions in the course of carrying out the law. There are two key problems with this discretion. First, street-level bureaucrats have not been elected by anyone, and sometimes their discretionary decisions seem to ignore the laws written by democratically elected lawmakers. For example, if state law requires a minimum 10-year sentence in a drug case, should the county's prosecuting attorney have the authority to reduce the charges against a defendant to avoid the minimum sentence? This question is related to the second, more troubling aspect of bureaucratic discretion: the fact that it gives a high level of power to street-level bureaucrats. Especially in the criminal justice system, where police, prosecutors, judges, and corrections and parole officers have coercive power over citizens—including the right to kill—discretion can be used in ways that may appear to be discriminatory, unfair, political, and, at worst, abusive.

For example, individual bureaucrats often make decisions based on their perceptions of the "worthiness" of the citizens they encounter. We saw this concept with the couples enjoying alcohol in the park.[36] Many would argue that it is unfair for two equally guilty parties to be treated so *un*equally based upon one police officer's judgments.

Another example comes from California's three-strikes law, which requires 25 years to life for someone convicted of a third felony. An early study found that district attorneys and judges at the local level played an important role in implementation of the law because they were granted a fair amount of discretion over how prior "strike" violations were counted. In politically liberal regions of the state, such as the San Francisco Bay area, defendants were less likely to be subject to three strikes than in more politically conservative areas.[37] Some would argue that political ideology should not matter when charging or sentencing criminals and that this is a misuse of bureaucratic discretion.

The worst cases involve instances of racial profiling, violence, and excessive force experienced at the hands of prison guards or police officers. Although there are policies for escalation of physical force against suspects, what is appropriate use of force is left to the discretion of officers and their evaluation of the situation. A well-known case involving excessive force occurred in Los Angeles in 1991 when, after a high-speed chase, four White officers used batons and a Taser gun on an African American, Rodney King, in order to force him to comply with arrest. The videotaped beating left King hospitalized with multiple broken bones; however, the LAPD defended its officers, arguing that this was not an abuse of power but rather "a professional response to the seemingly dangerous situation."[38]

Although a jury acquitted the officers of excessive use of force, the verdict sparked six days of rioting in 1992 during which time 50 people were killed and more than 1,000 injured.[39] Later, King successfully sued the city of Los Angeles for $3.8 million, and in a federal trial, two of the officers were found guilty of federal civil rights violations and sentenced to two years in prison.[40] To this day, some argue that Rodney King's treatment was an appropriate use of professional police discretion while others say it was a racially motivated abuse of police power.

 PRO Street-Level Bureaucracy Is a Good Thing

Given all of the ways in which bureaucratic discretion at the street level can go wrong, why does the system allow for so much discretion? Those at the street level are granted discretion for a variety of reasons. First, although elected officials make the laws, putting those laws into practice in the criminal justice system often occurs in situations that lawmakers cannot imagine. Discretion allows street-level bureaucrats the freedom to carry out their duties and obligations in complex, often dangerous situations, such as a hostage-taking or domestic-violence case.[41] It would be impractical to provide detailed instructions on dealing with such complicated situations; instead, street-level bureaucrats must use their discretion—based on their training, education, experience, and moral judgments—to carry out their duties.

Second, those at the front lines in the criminal justice bureaucracy are typically professionals in their fields. There are training academies for law enforcement officers and law schools for lawyers and judges, and a great deal of experience and level of mastery is learned while on the job. For example, seasoned police officers often learn how to detect cues that lead them to successful discovery of illegal goods during discretionary citizen searches.[42] When we give a parole officer the discretion to assess a parolee's progress and recommend intervention

programs or allow a judge to sentence someone to the minimum rather than the maximum term in prison, we are acknowledging that they have the professional standing and experience to make a good decision.

Third, we must remember that while they enjoy a great deal of discretion, the behavior of street-level bureaucrats in the criminal justice system is constrained in many ways. These constraints include the following: basic rules and procedures that must be followed, monitoring and evaluation of performance, and sanctions for poor performance. Other constraints include professional norms and codes of conduct; for example, attorneys and judges who fail to uphold appropriate legal standards or engage in unethical behavior can be disbarred from the profession. Finally, those in the criminal justice bureaucracy usually view public service as a noble calling and dedicate themselves to it, reducing the odds that they will abuse their power.[43]

DISCUSSION QUESTIONS

1. As citizens, how do we ensure that street-level bureaucrats of the criminal justice system use their discretion wisely and fairly?

2. Should the powers of discretion be restricted? How do the various levels of discretion serve as a benefit to the criminal justice system?

KEY TERMS

Review key terms with eFlashcards | $SAGE edge™ • edge.sagepub.com/mallicoatccj

Conservative 134	Initiative 133	Outcome evaluation 132
Direct democracy 133	Liberal 134	Policy 130
Discretion 130	Marijuana 133	Process evaluation 132

DISCUSSION QUESTIONS

Test your mastery of chapter content • Take the Practice Quiz | $SAGE edge™ • edge.sagepub.com/mallicoatccj

1. How does fear of crime influence criminal justice policy decisions?

2. What are the six stages of policy development?

3. How have criminal justice policies led to unintended consequences for individuals and the larger system?

4. How might a criminal justice policy or practice be compromised or challenged due to political differences?

LEARNING ACTIVITIES

1. Review the six stages of policy development. Pick a criminal justice policy, and discuss how your example was developed through each of these stages.

2. Locate a criminal justice policy that has been implemented in your state. How has this policy assisted in reducing criminal behavior?

3. Review the efforts of states that have been successful in legalizing marijuana (Colorado and Washington) and those that have failed (California). What were the differences in these campaigns that led to their success or their failure?

4. Research a criminal justice policy or practice that is used internationally. What could the American criminal justice system learn from this international example?

SUGGESTED WEBSITES

- **Urban Institute Research Center:** http://www.urban.org/justice
- **Center for Evidence-Based Crime Policy:** http://cebcp.org
- **Center for Research on Direct Democracy:** http://c2d.ch
- **Initiative & Referendum Institute:** http://www.iandrinstitute.org

STUDENT STUDY SITE

Review • Practice • Improve | $SAGE edge™ • **edge.sagepub.com/mallicoatccj**

Want a better grade?

Get the tools you need to sharpen your study skills. Access practice quizzes, eFlashcards, video, and multimedia at
edge.sagepub.com/mallicoatccj

POLICING

©iStockphoto.com/Klaus Larsen

PART

II

POLICING ORGANIZATIONS AND PRACTICES

LEARNING OBJECTIVES

- Discuss the three eras of policing

- Identify the different types of police organizations

- Discuss the history of women in policing

- Explain the importance of racial and ethnic diversity in policing

- Explain the structure of a police organization and the various job functions that officers hold within the agency

- Distinguish between the various strategies and tactics of policing

On March 3, 1991, Rodney King was driving home with two friends from another friend's house, where they had been drinking. King noticed a California Highway Patrol police car driving behind him, and he panicked. King was on parole for a robbery conviction earlier that year, and he became afraid that he would be arrested and sent back to prison for violating the terms and conditions of his parole as a result of his drinking. He chose to try to flee the police in a high-speed chase but quickly realized that he could not outrun them. He stopped in front of some apartments in the hope that someone would see him in case an incident occurred between him and the police. King and his friends were pulled out of his car by officers from the Los Angeles Police Department. Both of King's friends were forced to the ground while King remained in the car. Upon exiting the vehicle, several LAPD officers approached King in an attempt to subdue him. The officers began to physically beat King.[1] George Holliday, a budding filmmaker who lived in one of the apartments, took his brand-new camcorder and began to record the event.[2]

The film was released on local television and quickly went viral. It showed three officers (Timothy Wind, Theodore Briseño, and Laurence Powell) using their batons repeatedly against King, who kept trying to rise up. Officers stated that they believed King was under the influence of PCP and was trying to attack them; King stated that he was simply trying to escape the abuse. In addition to the three officers who repeatedly used their batons against King at the order of their commanding officer Stacey Koon, King was also tased by Koon multiple times.[3] King's injuries were so severe that he was hospitalized and underwent five hours of surgery to repair his broken leg, facial fractures, and multiple broken bones at the back of his skull.[4]

The four officers were tried on multiple crimes related to their use of excessive force, including assault with a deadly weapon. On April 29, 1992, the four officers were acquitted of assault, and three of the officers were acquitted of excessive force (with the jury unable to make a decision on the fourth officer, Laurence Powell).[5] Following their acquittals, the city erupted into violence in protest of the decision. Over the next four days, more than 10,000 businesses were damaged by fire, vandalism, and looting. Thousands of people were injured, and 53 people died. Damages to the region cost almost a billion dollars.[6] Much of the struggle epitomized the strain that many Blacks in South Central L.A. felt toward the Korean and Hispanic communities.[7]

Sgt. Koon and Officer Powell were convicted of federal crimes for violating Mr. King's rights and were sentenced to 30 months in federal prison.[8] There were also several additional convictions from cases during the L.A. riots, most notably the trial of two Black men charged with the attempted murder and assault of a White truck driver, Reginald Denny.[9] While King received a $3.8 million settlement, he died at the age of 47.[10] In addition, the case led to a number of reforms within both the LAPD and police organizations nationwide.[11]

VIDEO
25 Years Later: How the Rodney King Beating "Banished" the Baton From the LAPD Arsenal

This chapter begins with a look at the historical roots of policing. The chapter presents the different types of police organizations and then turns to a review of the various styles of policing, such as order maintenance, community policing, and problem-oriented policing. The chapter concludes with two Current Controversy debates: the first, by Christine Gardiner, investigates whether intelligence-led policing can reduce crime while the second, by Alesha Durfee, asks whether mandatory arrest policies help victims of domestic violence.

A BRIEF HISTORY OF POLICING

The earliest example of policing in the United States is found back in 1631 in the city of Boston, with the development of a volunteer night watch (Figure 7.1).[12] Boston continued to make history with the first full-time paid law enforcement organization in 1712.[13] The U.S. Marshals was the first federal law enforcement organization and was created by Congress in 1789. Following its establishment, President George Washington appointed 13 officers to serve in this role. The Secret Service was established by President Abraham Lincoln on April 14, 1865 (which was, ironically, the day that he was assassinated by John Wilkes Booth).[14] Throughout the 1800s, other major cities followed suit and created their own police agencies, including New York, Chicago, and Los Angeles.[15]

These early police organizations were heavily influenced by their British counterparts and, in particular, the ideologies of Sir Robert Peel, who was responsible for creating the London Metropolitan Police Force in 1829. Table 7.1 identifies nine principles that have been associated with Peel and his model of policing (though is it widely believed that it was not Peel but his two commissioners who were the original authors of this philosophy). Not

National Photo Company Collection (Library of Congress)

Members of the White House police in 1923. The White House Police was first developed in 1922 and was responsible for the safety and security of the White House and the president. It was incorporated into the Secret Service in 1930. How did Peel's principles influence these early police organizations?

Figure 7.1 Development of Policing in Early America

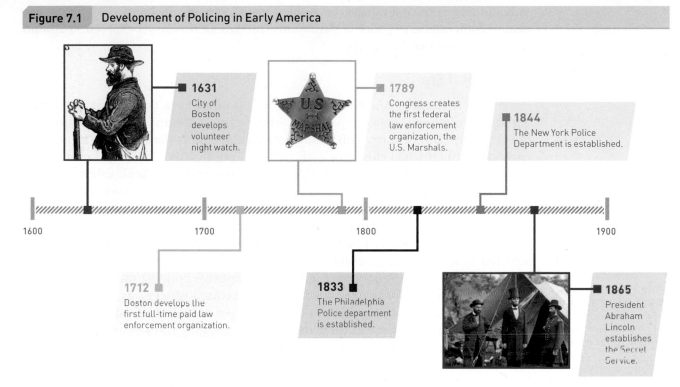

1631
City of Boston develops volunteer night watch.

1789
Congress creates the first federal law enforcement organization, the U.S. Marshals.

1844
The New York Police Department is established.

1712
Boston develops the first full-time paid law enforcement organization.

1833
The Philadelphia Police department is established.

1865
President Abraham Lincoln establishes the Secret Service.

1600   1700   1800   1900

Photo credits: 1631: © iStockphoto.com/duncan1890; 1789: © iStockphoto.com/spxChrome; 1865: Library of Congress, Mathew B. Brady

Table 7.1	Robert Peel's Nine Principles of Policing
Principle 1	"The basic mission for which the police exist is to prevent crime and disorder."
Principle 2	"The ability of the police to perform their duties is dependent upon public approval of police actions."
Principle 3	"Police must secure the willing cooperation of the public in voluntary observance of the law to be able to secure and maintain the respect of the public."
Principle 4	"The degree of cooperation of the public that can be secured diminishes proportionately to the necessity of the use of physical force."
Principle 5	"Police seek and preserve public favor not by catering to the public opinion but by constantly demonstrating absolute impartial service to the law."
Principle 6	"Police use physical force to the extent necessary to secure observance of the law or to restore order only when the exercise of persuasion, advice and warning is found to be insufficient."
Principle 7	"Police, at all times, should maintain a relationship with the public that gives reality to the historic tradition that the police are the public and the public are the police; the police being only members of the public who are paid to give full-time attention to duties which are incumbent on every citizen in the interests of community welfare and existence."
Principle 8	"Police should always direct their action strictly towards their functions and never appear to usurp the powers of the judiciary."
Principle 9	"The test of police efficiency is the absence of crime and disorder, not the visible evidence of police action in dealing with it."

Source: Reith, C. (1956). *A new study of police history.* London. Oliver & Boyd. http://www.civitas.org.uk/pubs/policeNine.php

only did these principles shape the modern system of policing; many of them remain central components of police organizations throughout the United States and around the world today (see Figure 7.1).

The Political Era

As the first era of American policing, the **political era** began with the emergence of professional police departments during the 1840s and continued throughout the early 20th century. This time frame was labeled as the political era, as these early departments had close ties with the local politicians. Police operations were generally conducted via foot patrols, and officers engaged in both crime fighting and social services. While officers engaged in investigative work, their efforts were usually centered not on solving crimes but on seeking information for local politicians. In many cases, these close relationships created opportunities for police corruption and abuses of power. Toward the end of this era, August Vollmer was selected as the first police chief of Berkeley, California, in 1909. He is considered the founder of professional policing for his innovative policing tactics during this time. He advocated for the hiring of college-educated officers, as well as women and minorities. He also introduced a number of technological advances to the field. Figure 7.2 highlights some of these innovations.

Reform Era

It was a result of these challenges during the political era, as well as the efforts of people like August Vollmer, that led to the rise of the **reform era**, beginning in the 1920s. Law, not politics, became the foundation for modern policing, and agencies focused on controlling crime by apprehending offenders and deterring would-be violators. One of the primary shifts during the reform era was the

Political era
Describes the first era of policing that existed from the 1840s to the early 20th century. Began with the emergence of professional police departments, which had close ties with local politicians.

Reform era
Began in the 1920s as the foundation for modern policing. Agencies focused on controlling crime by apprehending offenders and deterring would-be violators.

Figure 7.2   Contributions of August Vollmer to Policing

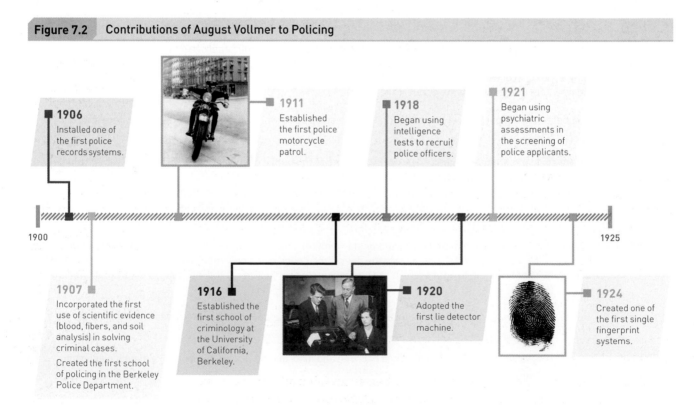

1906 Installed one of the first police records systems.

1911 Established the first police motorcycle patrol.

1918 Began using intelligence tests to recruit police officers.

1921 Began using psychiatric assessments in the screening of police applicants.

1900

1925

1907 Incorporated the first use of scientific evidence (blood, fibers, and soil analysis) in solving criminal cases.
Created the first school of policing in the Berkeley Police Department.

1916 Established the first school of criminology at the University of California, Berkeley.

1920 Adopted the first lie detector machine.

1924 Created one of the first single fingerprint systems.

Photo credits: 1911: Vintage Images/Getty Images; 1920: Keystone-France/Getty Images; 1924: © iStockphoto.com/imv

increased professionalism of policing organizations. Agencies engaged in public relations campaigns to help reform their image from corrupt and chaotic organizations to ones with the centralized mission of crime fighting. Police agencies became large, bureaucratic organizations with several levels of management. The emphasis on professionalism shifted officers away from providing social services to members of the community. The use of foot patrols was eliminated, and officers instead used marked automobiles and cruised randomly through the streets. Not only was the presence of police used as a visible deterrent to would-be offenders, but a centralized 911 system allowed for citizens to contact the police via telephone. Operators could then contact a local officer via radio and quickly dispatch him to an area in need of service.

Community Problem-Solving Era

While the reform era was successful throughout the 1930s and 1940s, the civil unrest throughout the 1960s and 1970s brought new challenges to policing. Rising crime rates and increased fears about victimization demanded a return to a more personal approach by officers. As a result, the **community problem-solving era** was born. Foot patrols were revived in an effort to better connect with community members. As a result of these interactions, officers were often able to gain information about criminal activities, which, in turn, increased the number of crimes solved. At the same time, officers were able to learn about citizen concerns and respond accordingly, which helped improve relationships between police and the community. However, not all communities felt that the police were interested in their needs, as issues such as discrimination, poverty, and corruption challenged police–community relations in many areas.[16]

Throughout this chapter, you'll learn how these three eras of policing have shaped how police agencies are organized and the strategies they use on the job. Technology and innovation continue to shape the daily lives of officers on the street, leading some scholars to suggest that we have moved into a fourth era of policing as we enter the 21st century: the **information era**.[17]

> " Technology and innovation continue to shape the daily lives of officers on the street, leading some scholars to suggest that we have moved into a fourth era of policing as we enter the 21st century: the information era.

VIDEO
See How Technology
Is Revolutionizing
Modern Policing

Community problem-solving era
A time period in which the primary strategy involved the use of foot patrols to better connect with community members, which allowed for increased numbers of crimes to be solved and improved relationships between the police and community.

Information era
21st-century policing with technological innovations that have altered the daily lives of officers on the street.

Jurisdiction
Determines when and how the criminal justice system can respond. Legal jurisdiction means that they have the legal authority to handle a particular matter, whereas geographic jurisdiction means that they are authorized to operate in a specific geographic location.

TYPES OF POLICE ORGANIZATIONS

There are several different types of police agencies. Police agencies are defined by their jurisdiction. **Jurisdiction** refers to two conditions: (1) Do the police have the legal authority to handle a particular matter? And (2) are the police authorized to operate within a specific geographic location? In terms of geographic jurisdiction, there are three levels of policing: federal, state, and local. There are also agencies that have jurisdiction over special areas, such as college campuses, transportation agencies, or special-subject enforcement agencies.

Federal Law Enforcement

Federal law enforcement has the authority to act when a federal law has been broken. Currently, there are 73 different federal agencies that incorporate officers who are authorized to carry a firearm and make arrests. Figure 7.3 presents the types of duties performed by these agencies.

The majority of all federal law enforcement agencies fall under two general categories. The Department of Justice (DOJ) and the Department of Homeland Security (DHS) contain several federal organizations, though each has four primary law

CAREERS IN CRIMINAL JUSTICE

So You Want to Be a Police Officer?

What do you need in order to get a job as a police officer? Generally speaking, you need to have a high school diploma or GED, though many jurisdictions require that applicants have completed either a certain number of hours of college coursework or, in some cases, hold a college degree. You must be a U.S. citizen and, for many agencies, be at least 21 years old. Applicants must pass several requirements as part of the application process, including a written exam, physical agility exam, interview board, psychological exam, medical exam, and background investigation. Generally speaking, a felony conviction will exclude you from being offered a job, and agencies vary on their position about experimental drug use. Some prohibit the use of all drugs in one's lifetime while others will accept a person if he or she experimented with marijuana as a youth. The median wage for a patrol officer in 2014 was $56,810 while detectives made $79,870. The demand for officers continues to grow even though crime rates are falling. However, factors such as job growth, officer retirement and attrition, and budget can all impact the availability of positions for a particular agency.[a]

As part of their training, police recruits must learn how to manage individuals who are under arrest. Here, an officer practices physically subduing an offender who is resisting arrest. What type of physical requirements might be necessary for this occupation?

Figure 7.3 Primary Functions of Federal Law Enforcement

The job duties of federal law enforcement officers are varied, but investigation and patrol remain the primary functions.

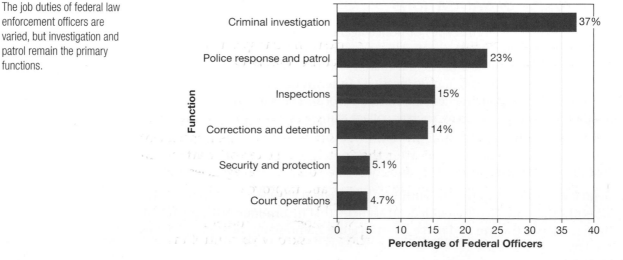

Source: Reaves, B. A. (2012). Federal law enforcement officers, 2008. U.S. Department of Justice. Retrieved at http://www.bjs.gov/content/pub/pdf/fleo08.pdf

Note: Most recent data available.

enforcement agencies.* The Department of Justice includes four law enforcement agencies: the Federal Bureau of Investigation (FBI), the Drug Enforcement Administration (DEA), the U.S. Marshals Service, and the Bureau of Alcohol, Tobacco, Firearms and Explosives (ATF). The Department of Homeland Security includes U.S. Customs and Border Protection (CBP), U.S. Immigration and Customs Enforcement (ICE), the Secret Service, and the security branch of the Federal Emergency Management Agency (FEMA). Together, the DOJ and DHS employ the majority of federal law enforcement officers.

Department of Justice

The Federal Bureau of Investigation was founded in 1908 with only 34 agents.[18]

An officer with the U.S. Customs and Border Protection agency conducts surveillance of an area near San Diego at the U.S.–Mexico border. Which branch would this officer fall under?

Today, it is the largest law enforcement agency within the Department of Justice, with more than 12,000 agents. The FBI is responsible for the investigation and enforcement of more than 200 different federal criminal and civil laws, targeting violent crime, organized crime, and white-collar crime, among other things. The Drug Enforcement Administration deals with crimes related to drug manufacturing and trafficking and employs more than 4,000 agents. The U.S. Marshals Service is the oldest law enforcement agency in the nation and provides security and transportation for federal inmates while they are awaiting trial. Today, it employs more than 3,300 agents. Finally, the Bureau of Alcohol, Tobacco, Firearms and Explosives handles acts of illegal possession and trafficking of these items, as well as incidents of arson, terrorism, and bombings, and employs more than 2,500 agents.[19] Together, these agencies work toward three primary goals:

CAREER VIDEO
Chief of Police

CAREER VIDEO
Police Officer

1. prevent terrorism and promote the nation's security consistent with the rule of law;

2. prevent crime, protect the rights of the American people, and enforce federal law; and

3. ensure and support the fair, impartial, efficient and transparent administration of justice at the federal, state, local, tribal and international levels.[20]

Department of Homeland Security

Meanwhile, the mission of the Department of Homeland Security is centered on protecting our nation's borders and preventing acts of terrorism. The Department of Homeland Security was created after the September 11 terrorist attacks in New York City and Washington, D.C., and consolidated 22 federal agencies under a central mission in an effort to streamline resources and improve communications among these federal agencies.[21] Four of these agencies are involved in law enforcement efforts. The largest of these agencies is U.S. Customs and Border Protection, which employs more than 37,000 officers who are tasked with controlling our

---

* Also included under the DOJ umbrella is the Federal Bureau of Prisons (BOP), which is charged with supervising inmates incarcerated in federal facilities. BOP officers are typically not armed while on duty but retain the right to carry a firearm and make an arrest during emergencies.

WEB LINK
Department of
Homeland Security

nation's borders by preventing the entry of illegal persons and contraband.[22] The origins of the U.S. Customs Service can be traced back to 1789 and the functions of the Border Patrol back to 1924.[23]

U.S. Immigration and Customs Enforcement handles investigations related to crimes such as illegal immigration, human trafficking, child exploitation, fraud, and financial crimes. ICE is the second largest law enforcement agency under the Department of Homeland Security and employs more than 12,600 officers.

The U.S. Secret Service is generally known as the protective detail of noted political dignitaries, including the president of the United States. In addition, it investigates crimes such as counterfeiting, financial crimes, and computer fraud.[24] The U.S. Secret Service was first created back in 1865 to deal with the problem of counterfeit currency. It wasn't until 1894 that agents' duties were expanded to include security detail. President Grover Cleveland was the first president to receive protection from the Secret Service, although it was only provided on a part-time basis. In 1902, the detail became a full-time responsibility, and it was expanded to include the family of the president as well as the vice president in 1951. Congress authorized the Secret Service to provide lifetime protection for former presidents in 1965.[25]

The smallest law enforcement agency under the Department of Homeland Security is the security branch of the Federal Emergency Management Agency (FEMA), which employs fewer than 100 officers.[26]

State Law Enforcement

Each state operates its own police agency. Recent data indicate that there are 93,149 officers working full time for the 50 **state law enforcement** agencies. Of these employees, 65.2% are sworn officers, and 34.8% are civilian employees. State law enforcement agencies are often defined as a **highway patrol**, though others also provide investigative and emergency assistance. The first state police agency was the Pennsylvania Constabulary, formed in 1905. Today, the largest state police agency is the California State Patrol, with more than 7,200 sworn personnel, while the smallest state police agency is North Dakota, with only 139 officers.[27]

Local Law Enforcement

The majority of people employed by law enforcement agencies work for local agencies. **Local law enforcement** agencies are defined as either (1) **county sheriffs** or (2) **municipal police**. County sheriffs are responsible for running the local county jail, providing security for the local courthouse, and serving warrants and subpoenas.

State law enforcement
Often defined as highway patrols. Provides investigative and emergency assistance to local agencies.

Highway patrol
Also known as state law enforcement agency.

Local law enforcement
Accounts for the majority of all law enforcement agencies.

County sheriff
Agency that is responsible for running the local county jail. Also provides security for the local courthouse, serves warrants and subpoenas, and provides patrol services.

Municipal police
Local-level police departments that have geographic jurisdiction limited to a specific city or region.

Cross-deputization
Refers to the practice whereby local law enforcement are given the power to enforce federal laws.

Arizona Senate Bill 1070
2010 legislative act in Arizona that allows for local and state law enforcement to use a lawful stop, detention, or arrest to try to determine whether the suspect is an illegal immigrant.

Table 7.2	Top Five Largest Sheriff Agencies	
County	Number of Full-Time Sworn Personnel	Percentage Assigned to Respond to Calls for Service
Los Angeles (CA)	9,461	31%
Cook County (IL)	5,655	4%
Harris County (TX)	2,558	25%
Riverside County (CA)	2,147	72%
San Bernardino (CA)	1,797	56%

SPOTLIGHT

Cross-Deputizing Officers

Cross-deputization refers to the practice whereby local law enforcement officers are given the power to enforce federal laws. Cross-deputization has been used in many instances, such as between local county sheriffs and the Bureau of Indian Affairs. In this case, cross-deputization allows for these local officers to assist tribal police with enforcing federal and tribal laws within Native American reservations and communities. In the absence of such agreements, local police have historically had limited jurisdiction in such cases.[a]

One area where the use of cross-deputization has been increasing in recent years is related to the issue of illegal immigration. While the practice was first permitted in 1996 as part of the Immigration and Nationality Act, it wasn't until the events of September 11, 2001, that agencies began to pursue the practice in earnest. The passage of the Support Our Law Enforcement and Safe Neighborhoods Act in 2010 (otherwise known as **Arizona Senate Bill 1070**) is perhaps one of the most significant acts of cross-deputization in recent history.

SB 1070 declares that state law enforcement officers are allowed to enforce federal immigration laws based on their reasonable suspicion during lawful stops, detentions, and arrests. Unlike most states, which do not require that law enforcement inquire about an individual's immigration status, Arizona's law mandated that officers do so. Proponents of the bill argued that the state was in need of stricter immigration enforcement due to the large numbers of undocumented individuals from Mexico.[b] Meanwhile, opponents of the bill raised concerns that the practice would increase the use of racial profiling when determining whether officers should initiate contact with an individual.[c]

The U.S. Department of Justice challenged Arizona's law and argued that SB 1070 was an attempt to trump the federal government's jurisdiction in regard to illegal immigration issues. Implementation of the law was blocked as a result of the legal challenges. Both the federal district courts and the Ninth Circuit Court of Appeals ruled in favor of the federal government. The case was ultimately appealed to the U.S. Supreme Court.

The decision by the Supreme Court in the case of *Arizona v. United States* (2012) struck down three of the provisions of SB 1070. The Court held that the requirement that legal immigrants be required to carry their registration documents at all times was unconstitutional. Arizona's law made it a misdemeanor crime and allowed for police to arrest individuals who failed to produce these documents at will. The Court also determined that the law's provisions that allowed police to arrest individuals who were suspected of being unauthorized immigrants and made it a misdemeanor to search for or hold a job without authorization in the state were unconstitutional. However, the Court upheld the portion of the law that permits police to investigate immigration status during a legal stop or interaction with individuals.

The permitted use of cross-deputization has, in many ways, altered the job duties of state and local police. Since the decision in *Arizona v. United States*, similar bills have been introduced in several states and passed in Alabama, Georgia, Indiana, South Carolina, and Utah.[d] The Court left the door open to future challenges of SB 1070 on the grounds of racial profiling, and the ACLU has begun to collect evidence of such practices.[e] Indeed, concerns about racism and policing can have widespread implications for the criminal justice system and can lead to a breakdown in public safety.[f] However, other community advocates are concerned about the unintended effects of the law. For example, will victims of intimate partner abuse, other victims of crime, or asylum seekers be less likely to contact the police for assistance if they fear that they will be questioned about their immigration status?[g]

CRITICAL THINKING QUESTIONS

1. What are the risks of cross-deputizing officers? Should there be limits placed on these powers?

2. What other examples can you identify in which the cross-deputizing of officers has been used to provide police support?

Bailiffs are members of the sheriff's department and are responsible for maintaining order and security in the courtroom. Is this a career that might interest you?

County sheriffs may also provide patrol services to unincorporated areas of the county or contract with local jurisdictions to provide policing services in the absence of a city agency. Table 7.2 (page 158) highlights the five largest sheriff agencies in the United States and their duties. Currently, sheriff agencies employ more than 353,000 personnel nationwide.

Local law enforcement accounts for the majority of all law enforcement agencies, with 12,326 agencies and 604,959 full-time employees (78.9% are sworn personnel) in 2013. While there are several agencies that employ a large number of officers, 48% of local police agencies employ fewer than 10 officers while only 4% of departments employ more than 100 officers.[28] Figure 7.4 shows the largest local police departments in the United States. With more than 36,000 sworn personnel, New York City has the largest metropolitan police department in the nation. However, it does not have the greatest number of officers proportionate to the population; that would be Washington, D.C.

Special Law Enforcement Agencies

There are more than 1,700 agencies and almost 57,000 sworn personnel that provide law enforcement to special regional or subject jurisdictions. The majority of these officers serve for university police agencies. There are also 250 departments that are responsible for providing law enforcement for public school districts. Unlike New

| Figure 7.4 | Largest Local Police Agencies by Number and Proportion |

Although New York City has the most full-time sworn officers, because the population of the city is so high, this amounts to only about 41 officers for every 10,000 residents.

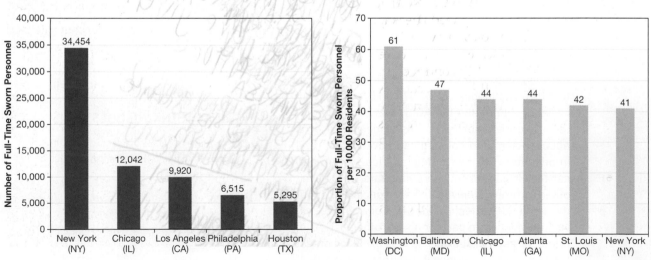

Source: http://www.bjs.gov/content/pub/pdf/lpd13ppp.pdf

York and Chicago, which draw from the local municipal police agency to provide security services for their public schools, school districts in Philadelphia, Los Angeles, and Houston have separate police forces for this purpose. There are also 167 agencies whose primary focus of enforcement is related to transportation. The largest of these is the Port Authority of New York and New Jersey, employing more than 1,600 officers. Several areas, including Los Angeles, Dallas/Fort Worth, and the Washington, D.C., metropolitan region, have their own airport police.[29]

WOMEN IN POLICING

An examination of the history of policing indicates that women did not enter the police force as bona fide sworn officers until the start of the 20th century. While there is some debate as to who was the first female police officer, most sources point to Alice Stebbins Wells, who was hired by the Los Angeles Police Department in 1910. Her philosophy centered on working with women and juvenile offenders and focused on preventative, rather than reactive, responses. Following in Wells's footsteps, many women sought out positions as police officers. The hiring of women by police agencies throughout the early 20th century did not mean that these women were assigned the same duties as male police officers. Rather, these policewomen were essentially social workers armed with a badge.

The mid-20th century saw significant growth in the numbers of women in policing. In 1922, there were approximately 500 policewomen in the United States; by 1960, more than 5,600 women were employed as officers.[30] Throughout this time, the majority of these policewomen remained limited in their duties, due in large part to a traditional policing (i.e., male) model. Policewomen were not permitted to engage in the same duties as policemen, out of fear that it was too dangerous and that women would not be able to adequately serve in these positions. Most importantly, the "all-boys club" that existed in most departments simply did not want or welcome women intruding on their territory. It was only during times of war that women found themselves placed in positions normally reserved for male officers, although these assignments were only temporary.[31]

As in many other fields during the 1960s, the civil rights and women's movements had a tremendous effect on the presence of women in policing. Legal challenges paved the way toward gender equality in policing by opening doors to allow women to serve in more active police capacities. However, they continued to face significant barriers in their field, such as low pay, limited opportunities for promotion, and a lack of family-friendly policies such as maternity leave.[32] Departments continued to resist calls to expand the role of women in policing, arguing that women lacked the necessary levels of physical fitness in order to effectively detain suspects. Subsequent legal challenges and new legislation continued to open more opportunities for women in policing.[33]

Over the past four decades, there have been significant increases in the number of

A group of female recruits taking the New York Police Department qualifying exam in 1947. Once hired, what might the duties of a female officer at this time be?

women employed as sworn law enforcement officers. By 1986, approximately 8.8% of municipal officers were female,[34] and this increased to 9.8% of sworn personnel in 1995 and 11.9% in 2014 (Figure 7.5). Women are more likely to be employed in larger jurisdictions (22%) and federal agencies (24%), compared with smaller jurisdictions (defined as departments with fewer than 500 officers), where women make up only 8% of all sworn personnel.[35] Meanwhile, few women have successfully navigated their way to the top position of police chief.[36]

Despite the significant advances that women in policing have made over the past century, research is mixed on whether the contemporary situation is improving for women in law enforcement. While legal challenges have required equal access to employment and promotion within law enforcement, research indicates that many women continue to be "passed over" for positions that are ultimately filled by male officers.[37] Sexual harassment by their male peers and superior officers has also been a continued part of the landscape of policing.[38]

Despite these challenges, the culture of policing has become more accepting of women throughout their careers. In particular, policewomen are noted for the positive traits that they bring to the profession. Research indicates that policewomen have been particularly successful within models of community policing due to their enhanced problem-solving skills through communication.[39] As a result, women officers have better relationships with members of their community, have fewer citizen complaints compared with their male counterparts, and are less likely to "jump" to

| **Figure 7.5** | Percentage of Males and Females Working in Law Enforcement in 1995 and 2014 |

Though the proportion of women who are employed by law enforcement agencies has not increased, the number of women who work as law enforcement officers, as opposed to civilian employees, has increased.

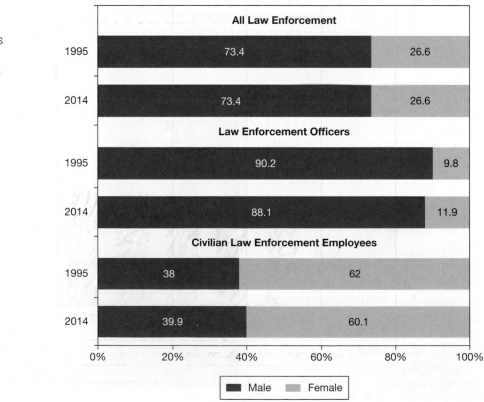

Source: Crime in the United States, 1995, 2014.

physical interventions.[40] Feminine traits such as care and compassion are also viewed as an asset, particularly when dealing with victims.[41] Finally, women officers are typically not involved in cases of police brutality and corruption. Research indicates that male officers are at least 8.5 times more likely than female officers to be accused of excessive force.[42]

RACIAL AND ETHNIC DIVERSITY IN POLICING

The first Black police officer was Wiley G. Overton, who was appointed to the Brooklyn Police Department in 1891.[43] Samuel Battle was the first Black NYPD officer in 1911 and rose through the ranks and became the first Black sergeant (1926) and the first Black lieutenant (1935).[44] In 1886, the LAPD hired its first African American officer (Robert W. Stewart). Yet it wasn't until 1992 that the LAPD saw its first African American chief of police with the appointment of Willie L. Williams.[45] Today, racial and ethnic diversity is reflected in a number of different departments.

In 2013, 27% of sworn police personnel identified as a racial or ethnic minority. This represents a significant growth since 1987, when racial and ethnic minorities made up only 14.6% of the sworn force. You've already learned about how federal law enforcement agencies have become more diverse in recent years. The Law Enforcement Management and Administrative Statistics (LEMAS) Survey collects data on state and local law enforcement agencies. Figure 7.6 shows how the representation of minorities in these agencies has shifted over the past three decades. In addition, the larger the department, the more racially and ethnically diverse are the sworn personnel.[46]

Figure 7.6   Racial and Ethnic Diversity in Local Police Agencies

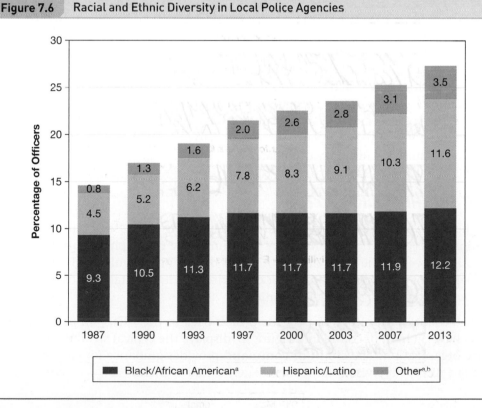

Why do you think it's important for minorities to be represented in a community's police force?

Source: http://www.bjs.gov/content/pub/pdf/lpd13ppp.pdf

a. Excludes persons of Hispanic or Latino origin.

b. Includes Asian, Native Hawaiian, or other Pacific Islanders; American Indian or Alaska Natives; and persons identifying two or more races.

The size of the department can impact the racial and ethnic diversity of its officers. The larger the department, the more racially and ethnically diverse are the sworn personnel. In addition, the size of the department also alters which racial and ethnic minorities are represented. For example, in departments that serve a population of 500,000 to 999,999, the representation of Black or African American officers is 23.2%, and Hispanic or Latino officers are 9.9% of the staff. In contrast, in departments that serve populations of 1 million residents or more, Black officers make up only 17.0% while Hispanic or Latino officers compose 24.7% of the sworn personnel. Meanwhile, smaller departments remain more homogeneous. For example, the racial and ethnic makeup of departments that serve populations of 2,500 to 9,999 residents are 89% White, 4.4% Black, and 4.4% Hispanic or Latino.[47]

The Importance of a Diverse Police Force

The diversification of police agencies is important. In 1965, President Johnson's Commission on Law Enforcement and the Administration of Justice suggested that minority officers would not only have a greater understanding of the needs of their communities but would also have greater credibility. One argument suggests that hiring a workforce that reflects the demographics of a neighborhood can help increase the positive relationships between the police and community, particularly under community-policing models. This is particularly the case among ethnic communities who have a history of distrusting the police, particularly immigrant and refugee populations. American history and modern-day events also play a role here as well, with the negative treatment of African Americans by the police.[48] Research by the RAND Corporation identifies several hiring barriers in diversifying police agencies. For example, some agencies have residency requirements that can limit who can apply for positions. The NYPD requires that officers must live in either one of the five boroughs or surrounding counties in order to be eligible. They cannot live in New Jersey or Connecticut. Similarly, members of Boston's police department must live in Boston. If these communities are not as racially diverse as the regions surrounding them, ethnic minorities may find themselves shut out of the hiring process. Meanwhile, the limited number of minorities in upper management not only can impact the number of officers of color seeking out these positions but could prevent some from applying to the police force in the first place. Such barriers to promotion could also impact the retention of qualified minority candidates.[49]

WHAT DO THE POLICE DO?

The duties of police can vary dramatically depending on the structure of the organization. The jurisdiction of an agency determines the geographic boundaries of its authority as well as the types of cases it might handle on a regular basis. Given that the majority of police officers work in local environments, let's take a look at the type of activities common to these organizations.

As a result of the efforts of police reformers back in the 1950s, all police departments have a chain of command. Figure 7.7 displays the typical structure of a local police organization. The **chain of command** provides guidance for each group by placing a direct supervisory rank immediately ahead of them.

Police Roles

A **police chief** is the leader of the organization and is generally appointed by the mayor, often in consultation with the city council. Some cities place a limit on how long someone can serve in this position. For example, the police chief for

Chain of command
Process that provides guidance for each group by placing a direct supervisory rank immediately ahead of them.

Police chief
Leader of the police organization. Chiefs are typically appointed by the mayor of a city, often in consultation with the city council.

Deputy police chief
Second highest ranking office that reports directly to the chief of police.

Assistant chief
Upper-level management position in policing in which the person is responsible for a specific subdivision of the police organization.

the city of Los Angeles is limited to two five-year terms.[50] In New York City, the police chief is called the commissioner. In some departments, the police chief is a sworn law enforcement officer, while other agencies have a civilian administrator as their top post. The police chief is responsible for maintaining the budget of the organization, working with local government entities such as the city council and the mayor's office on solving community issues, and setting policy priorities for the organization. The chief also serves as the public face of a department and communicates with local citizens and the media. Meanwhile, a **deputy police chief** is the second-highest-ranking officer in an organization and reports directly to the chief of police. The deputy police chief is essentially the "right hand" of the police chief and serves in the top position if the chief of police is unavailable. Meanwhile, the **assistant chief** is generally responsible for a specific subdivision of the organization, such as community affairs, internal affairs, or intelligence.

As you move down the chain of command, the duties of leadership are more narrowly defined, and these leaders are involved in more of the day-to-day activities of officers. For example, a **police captain** may be involved in the reviewing of personnel files and incident reports to ensure that officers are acting in compliance with the rules and regulations of an organization. She or he may also be tasked with interviewing and hiring new officers. In some instances, a police captain may be the lead officer for a specialized unit, such as narcotics, organized crime, or financial crimes. **Lieutenants** are responsible for ensuring that the appropriate number of officers are delegated to a particular neighborhood. As supervisors, they are tasked with many administrative functions, such as ensuring that the officers in their group have the equipment and training necessary to effectively perform their job. At the same time, they will also respond on site in serious cases. Finally, the **sergeant** is the first rank that carries supervisory duties. He or she may be in charge of creating the staffing schedule, providing training for new and continuing officers, and relaying information regarding important policies and practices.

The last category of police officers involves two subsets that are responsible for the hands-on aspects of policing. A **detective** is responsible for following a case throughout the investigation. Detectives begin at a crime scene, where they prepare a report of the incident. They are involved in the investigation of the crimes and prepare the case for the prosecutor. In many cases, they are called to testify in court about a crime. While many of the portrayals of policing in television shows and movies are based on detectives, it is the **patrol officers** that make up the majority of the sworn officers in a department. Patrol officers are typically assigned a transportation style, such as automobile, motorcycle, and even bicycle or foot patrol. Patrol officers are typically the first responders at the scene when a call for service is made. Patrol officers can interview suspects and witnesses of a crime and prepare reports on these experiences. They provide security and traffic control for community events. They are also responsible for arresting individuals and transporting them to the local jail.[51]

As you can see, the job of a police officer is quite diverse and varies based on the rank of an officer within an organization. However, it is important to keep in mind that local environments will have a significant impact on how police do their job. For example, a police officer in a small community will likely handle several different tasks as part of her or his daily duties. In comparison, larger agencies have the opportunity to allow officers to be more focused and specialized in their positions.

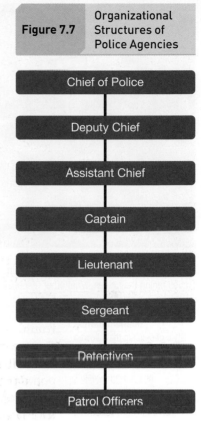

Figure 7.7 Organizational Structures of Police Agencies

Chief of Police

Deputy Chief

Assistant Chief

Captain

Lieutenant

Sergeant

Detectives

Patrol Officers

Police captain
Upper-level manager within the police organization; often serves as the lead officer for a specialized unit or may be involved in a specific administrative task, such as the hiring of new officers.

Lieutenant
Police supervisors who are tasked with many administrative functions for line officers, such as equipment, training, and staffing.

Sergeant
First rank in a police organization that carries supervisory duties.

Detective
A sworn police officer who manages a case throughout the investigative process.

Patrol officer
Most common classification of sworn officers. Serve as first responders.

Police chiefs often meet with division captains and other supervisory officers to review issues facing their cities. What other responsibilities does a police chief typically have?

STRATEGIES AND TACTICS OF POLICING

Throughout the evolution of policing, there have been a variety of different strategies used by officers. Such tactics not only provide guidance on the daily activities of police officers but also help guide their discretion when it comes to decision-making.

Random Versus Directed Patrols

What are the differences between random patrols and directed patrols, both of which were popular during the reform era? **Random patrols** allowed officers to cruise randomly throughout the streets. Here, the idea was that a visible police presence would serve as a deterrent to would-be criminals. At the same time, law-abiding citizens would feel safer knowing that the police were present. How do we know whether these sorts of random patrols are effective in curbing crime? In 1972, the **Kansas City Preventive Patrol Experiment** found that increasing (or decreasing) the level of police presence in a region did not have a significant effect on crimes such as burglary, theft, robbery, or vandalism. Such changes in patrol patterns also did not impact citizen satisfaction levels with their police or their fear of crime.[52]

In contrast to preventive patrols, **directed patrols** target a specific area of a city. In many cases, these regions are identified because either they have a high rate of crime in a particular area or the area is dominated by a particular type of criminal activity. **Hot-spots policing** (also called place-based policing) is an example of directed patrol. Research indicates that it is an effective strategy in reducing crime.[53] Generally speaking, hot-spots policing involves the use of **crime-mapping** technologies, such as **geographic information systems** (GIS), to help track geographic patterns in criminal incidents. The information is then used to predict future patterns of crime and make decisions about how to deploy officers. One example of how hot-spots technology is used to identify areas of high crime is **CompStat**. In 1994, NYPD police commissioner William Bratton implemented CompStat in his organization. Figure 7.8 presents the four core components of CompStat. As a result of this new technology, crime rates in New York City significantly decreased, in some cases by over 80%.[54] CompStat is not without its issues, though, and you'll learn more about the pros and cons of CompStat in the Current Controversy debate at the end of this chapter.

Order Maintenance Policing

Order maintenance policing directs police to handle minor incidents and crimes in an effort to prevent larger crimes in the future. The belief is that a focus on minor crimes, such as loitering, vandalism, and littering, can help create public order.[55] Order maintenance policing is influenced by the **broken-windows theory**, which suggests that when lesser acts of disorder are left unattended in a neighborhood, there is an increased risk for serious crime to breed. If communities (and the police) respond to these minor incidents, there will be more of a deterrent for would-be criminals.[56]

Random patrols
Style of policing that allowed officers to cruise randomly throughout the streets and provide a visible police presence.

Kansas City Preventive Patrol Experiment
Police study that found that changes to police presence did not have a significant effect on crime or change citizen satisfaction levels with the police.

Directed patrol
A police practice that targets a specific area of a city due to crime rates.

Hot-spots policing
Type of directed patrol with the use of crime-mapping technologies.

Crime mapping
Process by which information about crime locations is used to identify patterns of crime to assist in the deployment of officers.

Geographic information systems
A type of crime-mapping technology that is used to track geographic patterns in criminal activity that can, in turn, be used both to predict future patterns of crime and to make decisions about the deployment of officers.

Research indicates that order maintenance strategies have been effective in several jurisdictions. In New York City, which saw a high number of arrests for minor misdemeanors and ordinance violations, the rates of robbery and homicide decreased significantly.[57] However, critics have questioned whether it was the focus on broken-windows policing that was the cause of the drop in the crime rate. After all, misdemeanor arrests are only one aspect of maintaining order within a community.[58] While some have questioned whether the aggressive pursuit of these minor offenses results in a zero-tolerance model, research indicates that the pursuit of minor offenses is just one option for police officers under a model of order maintenance.[59]

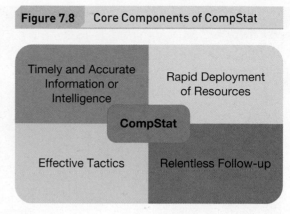

Figure 7.8   Core Components of CompStat

Source: Police Executive Research Forum. (2013). CompStat: Its origins, evolution, and future in law enforcement agencies.

Community Policing

At the same time that some departments were experimenting with order maintenance strategies, others were looking at models of community policing in an effort to reduce the crime rate. Agencies such as the San Diego and Santa Ana police departments were some of the early pioneers in implementing community policing during the early 1970s. The idea behind community policing was to establish better partnerships between the police and the neighborhoods they serve.

What is community policing? **Community policing** is "a philosophy that promotes organizational strategies, which support the systematic use of partnerships and problem-solving techniques, to proactively address the immediate conditions that give rise to public safety issues such as crime, social disorder, and fear of crime."[60] Community policing requires that police departments be proactive and develop partnerships with other community actors, such as schools, churches, business owners, and other community groups. These groups work together to identify and respond to issues of crime and disorder. In addition, the decision-making process is decentralized to allow street-level officers to make decisions about how to best respond to issues on a more immediate level. While there are many different variations of community-based policing in practice, the majority of police departments today have adopted characteristics of community policing as part of their organization.

The Office of Community Oriented Policing Services (COPS) was established within the Department of Justice in 1994 as part of the Violent Crime Control and Law Enforcement Act. It is responsible for providing training and funding to departments to help expand efforts in community policing. Over the past 20 years, the COPS office has awarded more than $14 billion to help hire additional officers and provide training and resources to departments that are engaging in community policing.[61]

While evidence indicates that community-policing efforts have been successful, there are several challenges that threaten its current stage. In particular, while many departments have adopted the language of community policing, not all have implemented the core strategies of the practice, which, in turn, can impact how successful a police department is in its efforts.[62] For example, research indicates that community-policing techniques do increase the levels of satisfaction that citizens have with their local police department. At the same time, community policing has been effective in reducing violent crime, but its effect on other types of crimes is mixed.[63] Some of the challenges to community policing include the following:

AUDIO
Community Policing Doesn't Sit Well With Everyone, Former Prosecutor Says

CompStat
A practice that first began in the NYPD that focuses on the comparison of different crime statistics to guide policing decisions.

Order maintenance policing
Policy that directs police to handle minor incidents and crimes in an effort to prevent larger crimes in the future.

Broken-windows theory
Theory that suggests that when lesser acts of disorder are left unattended in a neighborhood, there is an increased risk for serious crime to breed.

Community policing
A philosophy that promotes organizational strategies that support the systematic use of partnerships and problem-solving techniques to proactively address the immediate conditions that give rise to public safety issues, such as crime, social disorder, and fear of crime.

Members of the Atlanta Police Department's Homeless Outreach Proactive Enforcement Squad reach out to the city's homeless population to provide referrals and services to help people find food, shelter, and mental health care. What type of policing is this an example of?

1. Recruitment, hiring, and retention of service-oriented officers

2. Reinforcing the commitment to community policing by department supervisors

3. Inability to institute changes within the department

4. Dealing with disengaged communities

5. Budget and staffing shortages

6. Politics of public safety

7. Poor collaboration between police and other local government agencies

8. Local, state, and federal policies on criminal justice issues

9. Shifting the media's message on policing[64]

> Community policing requires that police departments be proactive and develop partnerships with other community actors, such as a schools, churches, business owners, and other community groups.

Given the current challenges that departments face, there is a great need to look at how community policing can help rebuild and strengthen relationships between residents and the police. New York City mayor Bill de Blasio has commented that community-policing efforts can help prevent events such as the deaths of Eric Garner and Michael Brown.[65] In December 2014, President Obama announced the establishment of a task force on 21st-century policing to help further research and strategies in this area.[66]

Problem-Oriented Policing

Like community policing, **problem-oriented policing** is a more proactive approach compared with order maintenance policing, which is a reactive model of policing. Problem-oriented policing (POP) encourages police officers not just to look at individual crimes or issues but rather to understand the root causes of crime. Problem-oriented policing strategies not only assist the police in fighting crime but also help to identify other issues within a community. Problem-oriented policing encourages departments to use a variety of tactics to identify and fight crime in their communities while, at the same time, helping to prevent future crime and disorder.[67]

Problem-oriented policing
Policy that encourages police officers not just to look at individual crimes or issues but rather to understand the root causes of crime. Problem-oriented policing strategies not only assist the police in fighting crime but also help to identify other issues within a community.

SARA
Policing model that is used to help identify problems. Stands for scanning, analysis, response, and assessment.

Many departments use the SARA model to help identify problems. **SARA** stands for scanning, analysis, response, and assessment. The first stage, scanning, asks for both the police and members of the community to identify issues that they are concerned with and the consequences of these problems. The analysis stage is heavily influenced by social science research methods. In order to understand the extent of an issue, it is important to develop an understanding about what is already known about the issue and identify the types of data available to investigate the issue. The response stage involves taking this new information and proposing potential interventions or solutions to the issue. The final stage is assessment. In many ways, this is the most important stage of problem-oriented policing because it looks at how the plan was implemented, gauges its successes and failures, and makes suggestions for the future.[68]

AROUND THE WORLD

Community Policing in Action

Community policing is not just an American phenomenon, and characteristics of this philosophy can be found in departments around the world. For example, the police de proximité is France's example of neighborhood policing, which provides specialized training for officers and encourages collaborations with other local partners to identify and implement crime prevention efforts.[a] These sorts of examples portray the movement toward community policing as a deliberate choice for change. Police in the Netherlands have embraced characteristics of community-oriented policing (COP) and have found great success in particular regions with the use of community patrols and partnerships.[b] For community officers in El Salvador, efforts such as painting over graffiti or digging a ditch to help prevent flooding are tasks that fall outside the realm of traditional police work, yet these efforts have gone a long way in building trust between officers and residents.[c] In other environments, community policing emerges as the only option to help reestablish public order. Countries throughout Africa, such as Kenya, Nigeria, and South Africa, have turned to community policing not only to help deal with corruption within the existing police ranks but, in some cases, to help establish new political and economic development within the region.

In order for these international efforts to be successful, countries must be realistic about both the issues within the community and the resources that the police have available to address such concerns. For some regions of the world, the desire to change may not be enough. Israel is a great example of this. Community policing was seen as a way to completely reform the police organization within the country. While COP did have positive effects, a lack of commitment by the organization to shift away from its military culture was a major barrier to success.[d] Attempts to incorporate community policing into these local settings must make sure that their efforts are culturally relevant for the specific community.[e]

CRITICAL THINKING QUESTIONS

1. What lessons can the United States learn from the adoption of community policing around the world?

2. What challenges do international police forces face when adopting a community-policing strategy?

In developing the model of problem-oriented policing, Herman Goldstein acknowledged that police departments not only will need to change the way that they go about their job on the street; they will also require a new level of analytical skills and resources in order to effectively identify problems and develop strategies to address these issues.[69] To date, research has shown that problem-oriented policing and SARA are effective models in reducing crime and disorder within communities.[70]

Many departments utilize problem-oriented policing as part of a community-policing model. However, there are several noted areas where problem-oriented policing differs from a traditional community-policing approach. Table 7.3 presents some of the similarities and differences that exist between these two approaches.

Predictive Policing

Predictive policing involves "taking data from disparate sources, analyzing them, and then using the results to anticipate, prevent and respond more effectively to future crime."[71] Predictive policing involves using several policing strategies in partnership with each other, such as community-oriented policing and problem-oriented policing.

Predictive policing
Policy that involves taking data from sources and using the analysis to anticipate, prevent, and respond more effectively to future crime.

Table 7.3 · Comparisons Between Problem-Oriented Policing and Community Policing

Principle	Problem-Oriented Policing	Community Policing
Primary emphasis	Substantive social problems within police mandate	Engaging the community in the policing process
When police and community collaborate	On a problem-by-problem basis	Always or nearly always
Emphasis on problem analysis	Highest priority given to thorough analysis	Encouraged but less important than community collaboration
Preferences for responses	Strong preference that alternatives to criminal law enforcement be explored	Preference for collaborative responses with community
Role for police in organizing and mobilizing community	Advocated only if warranted within the context of the specific problem being addressed	Emphasizes strong role for police
Importance of geographic decentralization of police and continuity of officer assignment to community	Preferred but not essential	Essential
Degree to which police share decision-making authority with community	Strongly encourages input from community while reserving ultimate decision-making authority for police	Emphasizes sharing decision-making authority with community
Emphasis on officers' skills	Emphasizes intellectual and analytical skills	Emphasizes interpersonal skills
View of the role or mandate of police	Encourages broad but not unlimited role for police, stresses limited capacities of police, and guards against creating unrealistic expectations of police	Encourages expansive role for police to achieve ambitious social objectives

Source: Scott, M. S. (2000). *Problem-oriented policing: Reflections on the first 20 years.* Washington, DC: U.S. Department of Justice, Office of Community Oriented Policing Services.

While predictive policing begins with approaches such as hot-spots technology, it involves the gathering of data from a variety of different sources to identify areas of future risk and help prevent these acts from occurring. Within predictive-policing models, crime data are not the only source of information, as models also include measurements such as demographics, neighborhood characteristics, environmental factors, and economic data. Once the different data are identified, computerized programs use sophisticated models to analyze the data and make predictions about areas of risk for future criminal acts. Police then use these results to make decisions about how to combat these areas that are at risk for future crimes. As a result, this technology can be used to predict the types of crimes that will occur as well as the place and time of these offenses, the typical perpetrator of these crimes, and the potential victims of these crimes.[72] Figure 7.9 illustrates the process of predictive policing.

Proponents of predictive policing indicate that the practice could be useful to help identify how to strategically deploy department resources, particularly given the tight budget constraints that many agencies face. Critics question whether the use of such data could violate the constitutional rights of potential suspects.[73] Since the use of data under predictive policing is a relatively new practice, there is limited evidence to understand whether these efforts are successful in improving how departments respond to such identified trends in crime. A review of the use of predictive policing within the Los Angeles Police Department indicates that the use of historical data has been successful in predicting burglaries. Similarly, the town of Modesto, California, has seen decreases in residential burglaries, commercial theft, and robbery.[74] Such successes have led several other cities to experiment with predictive policing, including San Francisco, Atlanta, and Chicago.

| Figure 7.9 | Predictive Policing |

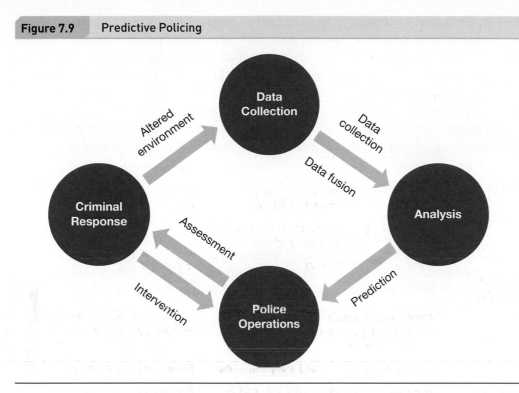

Source: Perry, W. L., McInnis, B., Price, C. C., Smith, S. C., & Hollywood, J. S. (2013). Predictive policing: The role of crime forecasting in law enforcement operations. RAND Corporation. Retrieved at https://www.ncjrs.gov/pdffiles1/nij/grants/243830.pdf

CONCLUSION

Police officers are the most visible component of the criminal justice system. As you learned in this chapter, the structure of law enforcement organizations and their duties vary dramatically. Without police officers to investigate crimes and make arrests, the other stages of our criminal justice system would not exist. Unlike the courts and correctional systems, police officers deal with not just offenders but everyday citizens as well. As you've learned in this chapter, the focus of these organizations has evolved significantly throughout history. Yet the core philosophy of policing has remained the same: to serve and protect members of the community.

CURRENT CONTROVERSY 7.1

PRO CON

Is CompStat a Good Policing Strategy?

—Christine L. Gardiner—

**CURRENT
CONTROVERSY
VIDEO**
Where Do You Stand?
Cast Your Vote!

INTRODUCTION

CompStat is one of several policing innovations that developed toward the end of the 20th century to address the failures of the professional era of policing. CompStat (which stands for "compare statistics") is different from the other innovations developed during this period because technically, it is a management system, not a police strategy. It has been adopted by more than one third of large police departments in the United States, as well as numerous agencies in the United Kingdom and Australia.[75]

Based on the premise "what gets measured, gets done," CompStat's driving features are information, accountability, and response. As part of the process, agency goals are identified, and numerous data are collected on a wide variety of performance measures (for example, the number of crimes committed, arrests made, citations issued, and citizen complaints). This information is compiled daily so district commanders can be aware of all developing issues and take appropriate action quickly. The feature that gets the most attention is the accountability meetings, where district commanders are presented with an analysis of current and past statistics and then grilled about the issues that command staff view as problems.

 ## PRO CompStat Is a Good Policing Strategy

CompStat is most celebrated for its capacity to reengineer a department to significantly improve performance and goal achievement and has made several significant contributions to policing. First, it renewed the vision that police can do something about crime. Second, it dramatically improves the availability of timely information. Third, it improves agency performance and has been associated with major crime reductions in New York City and elsewhere.

One of the most important aspects of CompStat is that it allowed police to believe in themselves and their power to reduce crime again. Police were beaten down with research during the 1970s and 1980s that concluded that police did not matter.[76] Reclaiming responsibility for crime was a watershed moment that changed the views of and invigorated police leaders around the nation.[77]

Another benefit is that CompStat improves police departments by making them smarter and more efficient than they had been in the past. Specifically, CompStat's reliance on timely and accurate information transformed the NYPD into an organization that was able to identify trends and allocate resources where they were needed most.[78] Without timely and accurate information, police would not know where to focus their efforts to prevent crime. Using CompStat means using a data-driven approach, which should lead to better policing tactics and less crime.

The New York crime decline of the 1990s, the largest and longest in the United States since World War II, has been the subject of many books and is synonymous (in some circles) with CompStat and broken-windows policing.[79] Research has demonstrated that the start of CompStat was correlated with a drop in firearm homicides[80] and a rise in some—but not all—broken-windows type arrests and decreases in property and total index crime.[81] Scholars have suggested that crime prevention effects come from the "focusing" that derives from the CompStat process.[82] CompStat is valuable because it can be used with any police strategy (community policing, problem-oriented policing, hotspots policing, broken-windows policing, pulling levers, and more) and does not favor one strategy over another.[83] From that perspective, it is a very effective crime prevention tool.

 ## CON CompStat Is Not a Good Policing Strategy

CompStat has some merits but there is one major criticism and a few smaller criticisms. First, the focus on statistics pressures managers to achieve goals at any cost, which encourages unethical reporting practices and police tactics that violate individuals' due process rights. Second, CompStat inhibits the agency's problem-solving capacity. Third, CompStat reinforces the traditional, paramilitary, hierarchical command structure for police departments.

The single most compelling argument against CompStat is that emphasizing statistics and crime reduction unintentionally encourages managers to use unethical practices to achieve set goals. For example, researchers have found that the pressure to show a reduction in crime can lead to unethical reporting practices, including downgrading felonies (serious crimes) to misdemeanors (minor crimes) or noncrimes (such as lost property or embezzlement).[84] Retired

Police Department
City of New York

Bill de Blasio
Mayor

William J. Bratton
Police Commissioner

| Volume 23   Number 24 | *CompStat* | Citywide |

Report Covering the Week
6/13/2016 Through 6/19/2016

Crime Complaints

	Week to Date			28 Day			Year to Date*			2 Year	6 Year	23 Year
	2016	2015	% Chg	2016	2015	% Chg	2016	2015	% Chg	% Chg	% Chg	% Chg
Murder	7	4	75.0	32	31	3.2	150	161	-6.8	11.1	-29.9	-82.5
Rape	28	36	-22.2	123	123	0.0	659	611	7.9	11.5	12.3	-56.2
Robbery	301	315	-4.4	1,149	1,272	-9.7	6,852	7,111	-3.6	-5.8	-17.4	-82.2
Fel. Assault	416	423	-1.7	1,688	1,639	3.0	9,161	8,696	5.3	-1.0	19.3	-50.1
Burglary	240	312	-23.1	948	1,197	-20.8	5,799	6,481	-10.5	-21.6	-28.5	-87.3
Gr. Larceny	828	832	-0.5	3,275	3,317	-1.3	19,544	18,855	3.7	0.4	19.0	-48.4
G.L.A.	150	140	7.1	585	569	2.8	2,726	3,120	-12.6	-15.8	-41.1	-94.7
TOTAL	1,970	2,062	-4.46	7,800	8,148	-4.27	44,891	45,035	-0.32	-5.20	-2.26	-76.93
Transit	45	39	15.4	175	188	-6.9	1,076	1,066	0.9	5.2	10.5	***.*
Housing	114	99	15.2	393	404	-2.7	2,290	2,137	7.2	0.2	27.0	***.*
Petit Larceny	1,645	1,803	-8.8	6,480	6,848	-5.4	36,327	35,774	1.5	-1.8	1.3	***.*
Misd. Assault	883	858	2.9	3,715	3,487	6.5	19,755	19,057	3.7	-2.3	-6.8	***.*
Misd. Sex Crimes	99	73	35.6	337	266	26.7	1,559	1,343	16.1	36.3	5.5	***.*
Shooting Vic.	27	31	-12.9	115	138	-16.7	481	591	-18.6	-12.9	-33.6	-81.4
Shooting Inc.	20	22	-9.1	91	113	-19.5	400	505	-20.8	-16.1	-32.8	-82.9

CompStat reports provide police departments with data on crimes within their region and help police leadership identify strategies for combating crime. How does this help measure police efficacy?

NYPD commanders reported that after CompStat was instituted, pressure to reduce index crimes increased significantly.[85] Importantly, before CompStat was instituted, the demand for integrity in crime statistics was greater than the pressure to reduce index crime. After CompStat, these were reversed. Media outlets have detailed numerous incidents of crime misclassification by U.S. police departments that use CompStat or a similar program, including New York, New Orleans, Philadelphia, Atlanta, Los Angeles, and Broward County, Florida.[86] Of course, the political pressure to downplay crime (and look good in national or international rankings) is not limited to departments that use CompStat. Such allegations of misconduct are disturbing and lead the public to lose trust in the police.

Second, CompStat has been said to inhibit an agency's problem-solving capacity.[87] Essentially, officers are too afraid to brainstorm during CompStat meetings because they do not want to appear to undermine supervisors, and commanders resist brainstorming during these meetings because they are afraid to fail. Ultimately, scholars have concluded that although there has been some innovation, "CompStat has done very little to change existing crime-fighting strategies."[88]

Third, rather than diffusing power and control throughout the ranks, CompStat actually reinforces the traditional, paramilitary, hierarchical structure that has defined policing for most of its formal existence.[89] This is the same model that came under attack in the 1960s and that scholars have urged departments to move away from. While this is not a major problem, it is one more piece of evidence that the police "innovations" that diffuse rapidly are those that reinforce the status quo, not the ones that challenge it.

Finally, studies claiming that CompStat reduces crime are unconvincing. One problem is that it is difficult (if not impossible) to untangle the effects of

CompStat (the managerial system) from the effects of both the particular policing strategy that is utilized to address the problems (broken-windows policing or hot-spots policing, for example) and the larger social changes that take place at the same time.[90] Some scholars argue that the credit for any crime reduction belongs to the effective treatment (hot-spots policing), not the diagnostic instrument (CompStat), as the treatment could have happened with or without that particular diagnostic tool.[91]

SUMMARY

CompStat is a major innovation in policing, no question about it. The management strategy has compelled agencies to set goals, collect data on performance indicators, make those data available to decision-makers in a timely manner, hold managers accountable for achieving goals, and use novel problem-solving tactics to achieve stated goals. It has helped create smarter, more effective, and more efficient public service agencies.

But does CompStat expect too much? A key issue that often gets forgotten is that police do not drive crime; criminals drive crime. Police respond to crime. While targeted, proactive police tactics can prevent crime, is it unreasonable to expect police to be wholly responsible for the extent of crime in a jurisdiction, even if that jurisdiction is using CompStat to identify and manage crime problems?

DISCUSSION QUESTIONS

1. Why is CompStat so popular?

2. Do you think the data-fixing issue is a problem of bad apples or a bad orchard? Why do you think so?

3. If you were a police chief, how would you balance the need to hold managers accountable for crime reduction with the need for crime stats that have integrity?

CURRENT CONTROVERSY 7.2

PRO CON

CURRENT
CONTROVERSY
VIDEO
Where Do You Stand?
Cast Your Vote!

Do Mandatory Arrest Policies Help Victims of Domestic and Intimate Partner Violence?

—Alesha Durfee—

INTRODUCTION

According to the Centers for Disease Control, nearly 36% of American women and 29% of American men will be victimized by an intimate partner at some point during their lifetime; each year almost 7 million women and 5.6 million men are victimized.[92] Intimate partner violence (IPV; violence that occurs between current or former dating, cohabiting, or married partners) can have serious physical and psychological impacts on victims; research shows that IPV survivors report higher levels of fear, stress, anxiety, and post-traumatic stress disorder and have higher rates of suicide than those individuals who have not experienced IPV.[93] IPV also impacts children; research suggests that domestic violence (DV)

and exposure to IPV can lead to cognitive delays, poor school performance, aggressive behavior, and higher rates of teenage pregnancy, alcohol/drug use, depression, and suicide.[94] Finally, the Centers for Disease Control estimates that the annual cost of IPV in the United States is more than $5.8 billion.[95]

Given the prevalence and impacts of IPV on victims, their families, and society as a whole, federal, state, and local governments have implemented a number of policies in order to prevent and intervene in IPV cases, including the removal of the spousal exemption for rape, enhanced police officer and judicial training, the provision of domestic violence civil-protection orders, the implementation of no-drop prosecution policies, and mandatory arrest and pro-arrest policies for DV.

First implemented in Oregon in 1977, mandatory arrest policies require police officers to arrest perpetrators in cases of DV; pro-arrest policies do not require officers to make an arrest but specify that arrest is the "preferred" option in these cases.[96] Discretionary arrest policies allow officers to make an arrest but do not require them to do so. As of 2016, 22 states and the District of Columbia had mandatory arrest laws, six states had pro-arrest laws, and 22 states had discretionary arrest laws.[97]

One common misperception about mandatory arrest policies is that officers have to make an arrest every time someone is abused. Mandatory arrest policies are limited to those cases that meet the legal definition of DV, which is far more restrictive than what most people consider to be DV. Officers use a two-part test to determine whether to make an arrest: (1) whether the victim and perpetrator have a "domestic" relationship and (2) whether a criminal act that can be legally classified as DV has occurred.

First, the perpetrator and victim must have a "domestic" relationship. Although the specific statutes vary by state, in most states, individuals who are related by blood, marriage, or cohabitation or who have a shared biological child have a "domestic" relationship. It is important to note that in 15 states, dating relationships are not considered "domestic" relationships,[98] and in three states, same-sex relationships are specifically excluded from the DV statutes.[99]

Second, in most states, an act that meets the legal definition of intimidation, stalking, criminal harassment, battery, unlawful imprisonment or kidnapping, sexual assault, rape, or homicide is legally considered to be DV. In addition, 33 states mandate arrest when a domestic violence civil-protection order has been violated.[100] However, mandatory arrest policies are often limited even further and in some jurisdictions apply only to cases that occurred within a particular time period and/or resulted in serious injury to the victim.

PRO Mandatory Arrest Policies Benefit Victims

Mandatory arrest laws may have a number of potential benefits for victims and their families. First and perhaps most importantly, mandatory arrest laws may increase the safety of victims and their children. Results from the Minneapolis Domestic Violence Experiment (MDVE) indicated that offenders who were arrested were less likely to recidivate (commit further acts of abuse) than were offenders in cases in which the police simply separated the parties or mediated the dispute.[101]

Furthermore, advocates of mandatory arrest policies argue that mandating arrest protects victims because the offender knows that the responding officer must make an arrest, regardless of the victim's wishes. Since the victim does not have a choice, offenders cannot avoid arrest by pressuring or intimidating the victim. If the offender confronts the victim later, the victim can claim that she or he asked for the offender not to be arrested but that the victim did not have a choice.

Mandatory arrest laws are also an important signal to law enforcement, victims, offenders, their families, other legal actors, and society as a whole that DV and IPV are crimes that will not be tolerated.

Abusers are not above the law simply because they assaulted a family member or partner. They force both police officers and the criminal justice system to treat DV and IPV as they would other types of criminal assaults and other offenses. This may also give victims a sense of "justice" and that their safety and well-being are important.

Finally, mandatory arrest policies were primarily intended to reduce the prevalence of DV and IPV in the United States through deterrence. The argument is that if perpetrators know that they will be arrested for DV and IPV reported to law enforcement, they will be less likely to abuse their victims. Since mandatory arrest laws were first implemented, arrest rates for IPV have risen from between 7% and 15% to between 33% and 57%, and this increase is directly attributable to mandatory and pro-arrest policies.[102] In this sense, mandatory arrest policies have been a success. Victims, advocates, and legal actors have also reported that mandatory arrest policies have been beneficial to victims and their families. However, these policies continue to be controversial, in large part due to the unintended negative consequences they have had on victims. A careful assessment of both the potential benefits and negative consequences of mandatory arrest policies may provide insights as to how the criminal justice and civil legal system can best support victims and their families in achieving safety.

 ## CON Mandatory Arrest Policies Have Negative Consequences for Victims

At the same time, mandatory arrest policies may have also had numerous unintended negative consequences for victims and their families. Other studies have indicated that arrest either has no effect[103] or increases the likelihood of re-abuse for some men.[104] Furthermore, the results of the MDVE do "not mean that arrest was . . . superior to more powerful alternatives; it only means that it worked better than the alternatives then in use"[105]—"such as on-the-spot marriage," counseling by police officers, or separating the parties.

There have also been some problems with the enforcement of mandatory arrest laws. In states with mandatory arrest policies, the arrest rates of women have increased faster than those of men,[106] victims have been arrested,[107] and women have been negatively impacted.[108] For example, because the police are required to make an arrest on a domestic call for service, they may ultimately arrest the victim, either because they cannot determine who the offender was or because the victim fought back against the abuse. These policies also disproportionately impact communities of color; "mandatory arrest laws will inevitably result in increased prosecution and consequently, increased oppression for Black men and women in the criminal justice system."[109]

Victims may also be financially dependent on their abusers, use them to provide child care for young children while the victim works, or live with their abusers. When an abuser is arrested, he or she may lose income, a job, or access to public housing and/or be unable to care for young children. If the abuser is an immigrant, he or she may be deported. This can result in a significant reduction or loss of the victim's income, housing, or job and/or lead to deportation. While there are some resources that can help victims, access to them takes time and is not guaranteed. Victims may also be reluctant to report as a result of limited access to assistance.

Finally, mandatory arrest policies remove agency from the victim, which is contrary to one of the primary goals of DV advocacy. Because abusers commit acts of DV and IPV in order to gain "coercive control" over their victim(s),[110] DV advocates work to disrupt that control by supporting victim decision-making.[111] Victims are the "experts" on their own situations, and advocates help victims identify and use their own resources to achieve safety rather than telling them what to do. By mandating arrest despite the victim's wishes, the state replicates the abusive relationship, with the state taking the role of the controlling abuser.

SUMMARY

More than 30 years after the widespread adoption of mandatory arrest and pro-arrest policies across the United States, there is still extensive debate about whether they are appropriate or effective responses to DV and IPV. Supporters of these policies argue that they protect victims and their families, but others have expressed serious concerns about the implementation, enforcement, and unintended consequences of these policies.

DISCUSSION QUESTIONS

1. Should victims be able to decide whether or not their abuser should be arrested when police respond to a case of intimate partner violence?

2. Do the potential benefits of mandatory arrest policies outweigh any unintended consequences of an arrest on a victim and abuser? Why or why not?

3. Which is more useful to victims: mandatory arrest or pro-arrest? Why?

4. Should mandatory arrest and pro-arrest policies be changed? Why or why not? If so, what changes would you make?

5. Are there other ways to improve the criminal justice response to intimate partner violence? If so, how would you improve it? If not, why not?

KEY TERMS

Review key terms with eFlashcards | ⓢSAGE edge™ • edge.sagepub.com/mallicoatccj

Arizona Senate Bill 1070   159

Assistant chief   165

Broken-windows theory   166

Chain of command   164

Community policing   167

Community problem-solving era   155

CompStat   166

County sheriff   158

Crime mapping   166

Cross-deputization   159

Deputy police chief   165

Detective   165

Directed patrol   166

Geographic information systems   166

Highway patrol   158

Hot-spots policing   166

Information era   155

Jurisdiction   155

Kansas City Preventive Patrol Experiment   166

Lieutenant   165

Local law enforcement   158

Municipal police   158

Order maintenance policing   166

Patrol officer   165

Police captain   165

Police chief   164

Political era   154

Predictive policing   169

Problem-oriented policing   168

Random patrols   166

Reform era   154

SARA   168

Sergeant   165

State law enforcement   158

DISCUSSION QUESTIONS

Test your mastery of chapter content • Take the Practice Quiz | ⓢSAGE edge™ • edge.sagepub.com/mallicoatccj

1. What indicators do we have that we are moving into the "information era"? How might it involve features from the three previous eras of policing?

2. How are Sir Robert Peel's principles of policing reflected in today's law enforcement organizations?

3. How are issues such as jurisdiction reflected in the various different law enforcement organizations?

4. What are some of the benefits of having a diverse police force?

5. According to research, which is more effective: random or directed patrols?

LEARNING ACTIVITIES

1. Interview a police officer in your city or at your university police department. What types of policing strategies do they use as part of their job duties?

2. Schedule a ride along with a local officer. How do officers use technology to perform their jobs?

3. Research the history of the Department of Homeland Security. How has the creation of this organization provided assistance to its agencies? What are some of the challenges of combining several agencies under one "roof"?

SUGGESTED WEBSITES

- **Discover Policing:** http://discoverpolicing.org
- **National Sheriffs Association:** http://www.sheriffs.org/content/about-nsa
- **International Association of Chiefs of Police:** http://www.theiacp.org
- **U.S. Department of Homeland Security:** http://www.dhs.gov

8

ISSUES IN POLICING

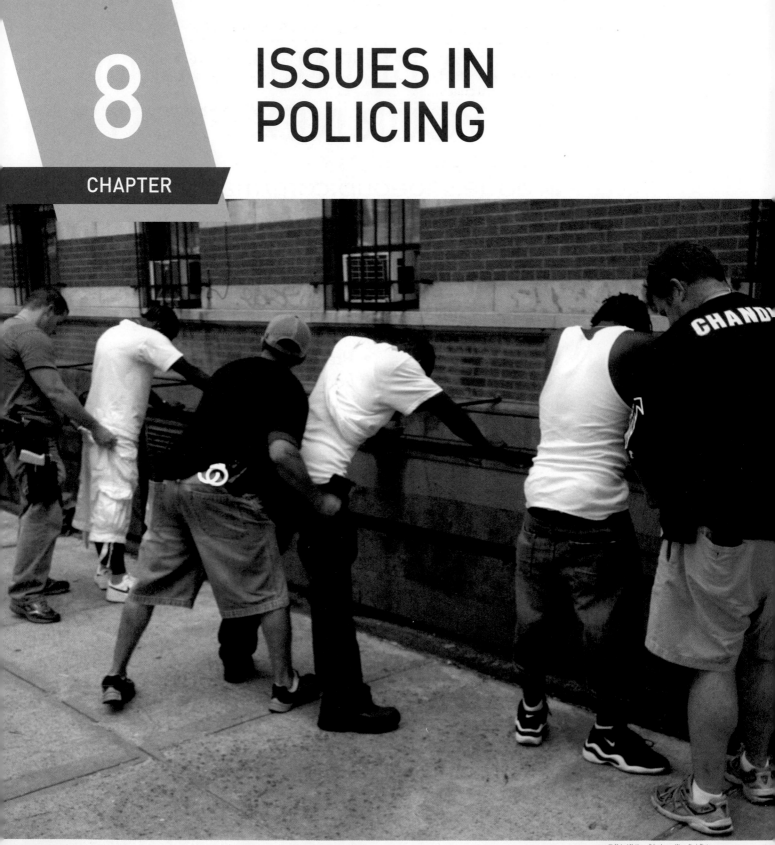

© Michael Matthews-Police Images/Alamy Stock Photo

LEARNING OBJECTIVES

- Discuss how the law has impacted the ways in which police carry out searches

- Identify the ethical challenges that police officers face as part of their job duties

- Discuss how actions by the police may involve the discriminatory treatment of certain groups in society

- List the different types of force used by the police

- Describe how police departments establish legitimacy in a community

- Identify sources of occupational stress for police officers

Stop-and-frisk policies allow for police to use their discretion to briefly detain an individual if they believe that he or she may be engaging in illegal behavior and pat down that person's exterior clothing if they believe that he or she may have a weapon. Stop-and-frisk practices were upheld by the decision in *Terry v. Ohio* (1968). In this case, an experienced detective noticed two men were alternating walking past a storefront and peering inside. After their viewing, the two would confer on the corner of the street out of view of the store employees. At one point, the two men were joined by a third individual for a brief conversation. The detective believed that the men were planning to rob the store and approached the individuals and proceeded to pat down their jackets. His search revealed that two of the men were in the possession of guns, and he subsequently arrested them. While the defense argued that the officer's pat down was an unreasonable search and seizure under the 4th Amendment, the Court held that the search, given the context of the officer's observations, was reasonable, and therefore, the search was conducted legally.[1]

Stop and frisk was adopted as a specific police strategy by the New York Police Department in 2003 as part of Mayor Bloomberg's fight against violent crime. In 2011, officers made 684,330 stops across the five boroughs.[2] Yet these stops led to the seizure of only 780 firearms—hardly a significant number given the volume of stops.[3] In addition, very few stops resulted in an arrest. Alongside concerns that the policy has not been effective, it has been challenged for unfairly targeting people of color. Data indicate that people of color are more likely to be the subjects of stop-and-frisk policies, when compared with Whites.[4] Figure 8.1 presents the racial breakdown of stop and frisks in New York City in 2011, compared with the demographics of the city. While Blacks and Latinos make up 52.7% of the city population according to U.S. Census data, they constitute over 86% of these stops. Concerns over racial bias led to legal challenges to the policy by groups such as the New York Civil Liberties Union and the Center for Constitutional Rights. In August 2013, U.S district court judge Shira Scheindlin declared that the use of stop and frisk by the NYPD was unconstitutional due to its discriminatory application.[5] As a result of this legal challenge, the NYPD has shifted away from the practice. In the first nine months of 2014, police engaged in 38,456 stop-and-frisk actions, a 79% decrease compared with the same time period in 2013.[6] While city officials such as former New York police commissioner Ray Kelly questioned whether a reduction in stop and frisk would lead to increases in the violent crime rate, it appears that the opposite trend has occurred, and crime in New York City was down 4.4% in 2014.[7]

Figure 8.1   NYPD, Race and Stop and Frisk Data

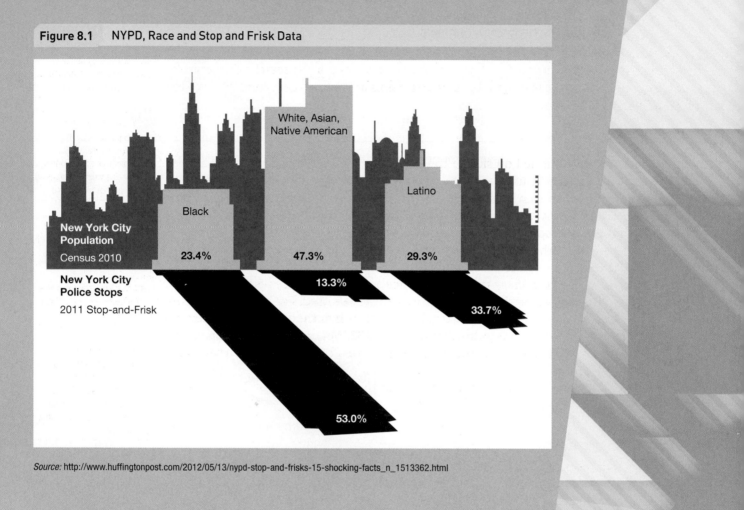

Source: http://www.huffingtonpost.com/2012/05/13/nypd-stop-and-frisks-15-shocking-facts_n_1513362.html

AUDIO
Top NYPD Cop:
Stop and Frisk Is Not "the Problem or the Solution"

Stop and Frisk
Policy that allows police to briefly detain an individual if they believe the individual may be engaging in illegal behavior and to pat down the individual's exterior clothing if they believe the individual may have a weapon.

In this chapter, you'll learn about some of the issues that the police face both as individual officers and as an organization at large. The chapter begins with a discussion of the legal issues in policing and the rules that impact how police officers do their job. The chapter turns to a discussion of how ethical challenges, corruption, racial profiling, and the use of force can have an effect on the public's perception of the police. The chapter then looks at the nature of police legitimacy and how these types of issues can threaten it. The chapter concludes with two Current Controversy debates: the first, by Bill Sousa, investigates how body cameras should be utilized in the line of duty; the second, by Lorenzo M. Boyd, asks if police discretion helps or harms our criminal justice system.

POLICING AND THE LAW

Much of the law that mandates how the police do their job comes from the 4th Amendment to the U.S. Constitution. The 4th Amendment protects individuals from unreasonable searches and seizures and requires the police to have probable cause to obtain a warrant in order to conduct most searches or make an arrest. But what does this mean?

Probable cause means that an officer believes that an offense has been (or is about to be) committed. Probable cause can be established based on the officer's own observations or information that the officer receives from others, such as witnesses. Probable cause is required in order to conduct a search. A **search** is when a person's reasonable expectation of privacy is violated. Generally speaking, an officer must have probable cause in order to obtain a warrant (although there are some exceptions). A **warrant** is a legal document that allows an officer to complete a search of a person's belongings. The police can then **seize**, or take, items and admit them into evidence to be used in a court case.

Search and Seizure

If evidence is obtained outside of the context of a warrant, such items must be excluded and cannot be used against someone in a court of law. This is called the **exclusionary rule**, and it was established by the U.S. Supreme Court case *Mapp v. Ohio* (1961). In addition, any evidence that is subsequently obtained as a result of this illegal search is also excluded. This is known as the **fruit of the poisoned tree** doctrine. The purpose behind the exclusionary rule is to ensure that the police follow the law and uphold the rights of the accused when gathering evidence. However, there are exceptions to the exclusionary rule. If the police act in accordance with the law but make an unintended error, then the evidence can still be used. For example, say the police are granted a warrant for 332 East 39th Street. When the warrant is processed into the computer system, the address is entered as 332 West 39th Street. Upon arriving at 332 West 39th Street, the officers seize 10 grams of crack cocaine that were sitting on the coffee table in the living room. Under the **good-faith exception** to the exclusionary rule, an arrest can be made, and the drugs can be used as evidence against this new offender.

Warrantless Searches

There are cases in which a warrant may not be required. For example, police can simply ask if they can search your home. If you say yes, then no warrant is required. This is considered a **consent search** because you agree to allow the police to conduct the search. As a result, anything that the police find that is considered illegal can be used in a case against you. Another example is that if the police legally stop you for a traffic violation and see, in plain view, a crack pipe sitting on the passenger seat, the police can legally seize this as evidence of criminal activity. Police can also exercise an **emergency exception** to the warrant requirement if they are concerned that waiting to secure a warrant could either jeopardize the safety of others or threaten the integrity of potential evidence.

Automobile Searches

What about automobile searches? Can the police search your car if you are pulled over for a lawful traffic stop? The answer to this specific question is no. If, however, you are placed under arrest, then the police can search a vehicle without a warrant if they have probable cause to arrest the occupants of the vehicle and if they have probable cause that the car contains illegal items. This is known as the **Carroll doctrine**, and it comes from the U.S. Supreme Court decision in *Carroll v. United States* in 1925.[8] The logic of the Court was that since an automobile can be moved (potentially out of a specific jurisdiction), a warrant is not required. Throughout the 20th century, the Court

VIDEO
Supreme Court: Police Need Warrant to Search Cell Phones

Probable cause
Legal standard that means that an officer believes that an offense has been or is about to be committed. Can be established by officer observations or information that is received by others.

Search
The process by which the criminal justice system is allowed access to your personal space and belongings to determine whether evidence of a criminal act is present.

Warrant
A legal document that allows an officer to complete a search of a person's belongings.

Seize
Practice that allows the police to take items and admit them into evidence.

Exclusionary rule
Established by the U.S. Supreme Court case *Mapp v. Ohio* (1961). It states that items obtained outside the context of a warrant cannot be used against someone in a court of law.

Fruit of the poisoned tree
States that any evidence that is obtained as a result of an illegal search is excluded and cannot be used against someone in a court of law.

Good-faith exception
If evidence is obtained without a warrant as a result of unintended error, then the evidence can still be used.

Consent search
A type of search that occurs when the individual gives permission to conduct a search.

Emergency exception
An exception to the warrant requirement that is invoked if police are concerned that waiting to secure a warrant could either jeopardize the safety of others or threaten the integrity of potential evidence.

A police officer has pulled over a motorist and is using a flashlight to check the backseat of his car. Would this be considered a legal search?

Carroll doctrine
Legal doctrine that allows the police to search a vehicle without a warrant if they have probable cause to arrest the occupants of the vehicle and if they have probable cause that the car contains illegal items.

Miranda warning
Used to inform people who are under arrest that the 5th Amendment provides protection against self-incrimination during an interrogation.

heard dozens of cases that limited the scope of warrantless automobile searches. The search of an automobile can include not just the basic interior of the car but also confined spaces if the officer believes that such spaces (such as a trunk) contain illegal property.[9] Meanwhile, *United States v. Chadwick* held that while the police could seize any containers found within the car (such as a suitcase), they could not open them without a warrant.[10] While the Court held that there is a lower expectation of privacy in an automobile compared with a residence,[11] cases involving "vehicles" such as mobile homes and motor homes were less clear about how a warrantless search could be conducted.

The confusion over when and how a warrantless search of an automobile can be conducted was addressed by the U.S. Supreme Court in 1991 in *California v. Acevedo*. The Court reinstated the Carroll doctrine as the primary rule of law and held that "police, in a search extending only to a container within an automobile, may search the container without a warrant where they have probable cause to believe that it holds contraband or evidence."[12] Despite the return to the Carroll doctrine, there are still some circumstances that limit when a warrantless search can be conducted. While it has been established that the police can conduct a reasonable search to ensure that there is nothing in the car that might place the officer or others at risk of personal harm, this provision is eliminated if it is unlikely that the driver would be able to gain entry back into the car. Consider the case of Rodney J. Gant, who was arrested in Tucson, Arizona, for driving on a suspended license. Mr. Gant was restrained by a pair of handcuffs and placed into the backseat of a patrol car. During a search of his vehicle, the police located a handgun and some cocaine. The U.S. Supreme Court held that since Mr. Gant was restrained and therefore unable to access the car or its contents, the search was illegal.[13]

The Miranda Warning

If you've ever watched a television show about police officers, you've probably heard the **Miranda warning**: *You have the right to remain silent. Anything you say can and will be used against you in a court of law. You have the right to an attorney. If you cannot afford an attorney, one will be provided for you. Do you understand the rights I have just read to you? With these rights in mind, do you wish to speak to me?*

> "You have the right to remain silent. Anything you say can and will be used against you in a court of law. You have the right to an attorney. If you cannot afford an attorney, one will be provided for you. Do you understand the rights I have just read to you? With these rights in mind, do you wish to speak to me?"

The Miranda warning is used to inform people who are under arrest that the 5th Amendment provides protection against self-incrimination during an interrogation. This warning comes from the 1966 U.S. Supreme Court decision in *Miranda v. Arizona*. In this case, Ernesto Miranda was accused of rape and kidnapping. After two hours of interrogation by the police, he confessed to the crime. Armed with his confession, the court convicted Miranda of these crimes. Miranda appealed his conviction on the grounds that he was not informed of his right to remain silent. The U.S. Supreme Court agreed with Miranda and overturned his conviction.[14]

CAREERS IN CRIMINAL JUSTICE

So You Want to Be a Criminal Investigator?

One of the more popular jobs in criminal justice, as a result of television shows about crime, has been that of the criminal investigator. However, the job on the streets is very different from what is portrayed on TV. Criminal investigators are usually sworn law enforcement officers. Criminal investigations may perform a number of different tasks, including gathering evidence, arresting and questioning suspects, working with crime victims, writing reports, and testifying in court.

In 2014, the average pay for criminal investigators was $79,620. With only a few opportunities available in each department, these are highly competitive positions. Criminal investigators can work for a variety of different agencies, including local police departments (where they typically serve as detectives) or the federal government.[a]

Most investigators are officers who have spent several years working for a police agency. Advancement to this rank often requires an exam and interview process that screens potential candidates for the job. Candidates selected for these positions receive specialized training on topics such as methods of interrogation and evidence or specific types of crimes (such as computer crimes, child abuse, or insurance fraud). In addition to their experience on the job, many investigators have met additional educational requirements, such as a bachelor's or master's degree.

Since *Miranda*, the Court has heard several challenges. In 1980, the Court heard the case of *Rhode Island v. Innis*, which sought to clarify the meaning of the term "interrogation." *Miranda* had held that the 5th Amendment protection existed during an interrogation. In the case of *Innis*, the suspect was read his Miranda rights and expressed a desire to speak to an attorney. The officers who were transporting him began to engage the suspect in a conversation about the crime but did not ask him any questions about the event. As a result of this conversation, the suspect disclosed the location of a weapon that was used in the crime. While the attorney for Innis moved to suppress the evidence, the motion was denied. In hearing the case, the Supreme Court held that an interrogation involves both directed questions and any conversations by the police with the accused that could elicit incriminating evidence.[15]

CAREER VIDEO
Crime Scene Investigator

ETHICAL DILEMMAS AND CORRUPTION

Ethics is the study of what is right or wrong, good versus evil. But how do we know what is right or wrong? Given their powerful position in society, we expect that police will have a high sense of ethics and that they will serve as representatives of fairness and justice in society. Most police departments have a code of ethics for their officers. Here is the Code of Ethical Conduct for the Oregon State Police:

As a peace officer, I am the image of penal law and its warden. If I am to be esteemed and the law I typify respected, I must know my authority well and use it wisely. I shall neither exceed nor abuse it.

During my private and public life, I shall conduct myself with the highest degree of integrity and honesty. I shall at all times conduct myself in a manner which consistently maintains the public trust.

I shall be intolerant of dishonorable or unethical conduct by any person in the criminal justice community. As an Oregon State Police officer, I shall strive to be courageous in my professional and everyday life, and will take prudent and judicious action when faced with danger, scorn, or ridicule.

DNA Collection

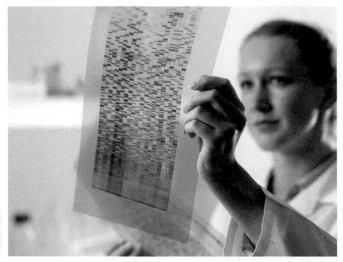

DNA is present in all forms of biological substances, including hair, skin, saliva, and blood. Here, a scientist examines a DNA map. Would you object to having your DNA in a police database?

When a suspect is arrested, it is standard procedure to take her or his photograph and fingerprints. While fingerprints have been used as a method to identify perpetrators since the late 19th century, technological advancements have opened the doors to other forms of identifying data. DNA, or deoxyribonucleic acid, was first identified in 1953. DNA is unique to every individual (except in cases of identical twins) and can be found in a person's bodily material, such as blood, saliva, hair, and semen. It has been used in criminal cases to (1) identify an offender who was otherwise unknown to the police, (2) confirm the identity of an offender, and (3) exonerate those who have been wrongfully convicted. During the 1980s, states began to pass laws that require the collection of DNA from offenders who are convicted of a sexual or violent crime.[a] Congress passed the DNA Fingerprint Act of 2005, which required that any adult who is arrested for a federal crime provide a DNA sample. This marked a departure from earlier laws, which limited the collection of DNA to only those convicted of an offense. In addition, 28 states have passed similar laws for state criminal offenses. Of these laws, 13 states require DNA collection in cases of any felony arrest, and seven states allow for DNA to be collected for misdemeanor cases. While 17 states allow for the DNA to be collected at the time of arrest, 11 states require that the court conduct a hearing to establish that there is probable cause that the offender engaged in the crime before DNA can be collected.[b] All 50 states, plus the District of Columbia, Puerto Rico, and the federal government, submit their data to the National DNA Index System (NDIS).[c] Data are then connected to other DNA laboratories through the Combined DNA Index System, or CODIS. To date, there have been almost 11 million offender and arrestee profiles entered into this system.[d]

The collection of DNA from arrestees and convicted offenders has been heavily debated. Supporters argue that the use of DNA databases (and their expansion) is a powerful crime-fighting tool. By collecting DNA data at the arrest stage, police may be able to link repeat criminals to unsolved crimes, even if they are not convicted on the current case. Opponents of these laws argue that the collection of DNA following an arrest is an unreasonable search and seizure and therefore against the 4th Amendment.[e] The U.S. Supreme Court addressed this issue in *Maryland v. King* in 2013 and held that the collection of DNA from an individual following a lawful arrest is constitutional. King was arrested for first- and second-degree assault. When his DNA was entered into the Maryland state DNA database, it matched evidence collected in an unsolved rape from 2003. Using the DNA match from his 2009 arrest, King was convicted for the 2003 rape. In a 5–4 decision, the Court noted that

CRITICAL THINKING QUESTIONS

1. What are some of the challenges that exist in the use of DNA as a form of evidence?

2. Review the laws about the collection of DNA from offenders in your state. Under what circumstances might your DNA be collected as a result of criminal activity?

when officers make an arrest supported by probable cause to hold for a serious offense and they bring the suspect to the station to be detained in custody, taking and analyzing a cheek swab of the arrestee's DNA is, like fingerprinting and photographing, a legitimate police booking procedure that is reasonable under the Fourth Amendment.[f]

Although the way I choose to conduct my private life is a personal freedom, I accept responsibility for my actions while on or off duty. I will not become a party to conduct that is likely to, or does bring disrespect to myself, my fellow employees, or the Oregon State Police. To that end, I shall not engage in personal conduct that affects, or could be perceived to affect, impartiality in my official capacity.

I shall not use my position or authority for any personal gain or benefit. I shall refrain from seeking or accepting any gift, gratuity, or favor that is tendered, or could reasonably be perceived as being tendered, as an attempt to influence impartiality in my official capacity.

As an Oregon State Police officer, I acknowledge the authority and responsibility entrusted to me and will use only the amount of force reasonably necessary to accomplish and fulfill my duties. I consider the use of deadly physical force as the final option to protect myself or another person from what I reasonably believe to be the infliction, or threatened infliction, of serious physical injury.

I shall bear faithful allegiance to the State of Oregon and the Oregon State Police and shall be loyal to the highest ideals of my profession. I will serve the public with due respect, concern, courtesy, and responsiveness without prejudice. I recognize the service to the public is beyond service to myself. As a police officer, I consider it a privilege, and the greatest honor that may be bestowed upon any person, to defend the principles of liberty.[16]

Police confront ethical dilemmas every day on the job. An **ethical dilemma** occurs when an officer is unsure about the right path of action, when following the right path is difficult, or when the wrong path becomes tempting to the officer.[17] Ethical dilemmas can occur in four different realms: discretion, duty, honesty, and corruption.

Discretion

You've already learned about how discretion is one of the most powerful tools of the criminal justice system. In policing, discretion allows for officers to determine when to stop an individual, when to issue a citation, and, in many cases, when to initiate an arrest. However, the power of discretion also has its challenges. In some cases, officers have limited discretion and have specific policies dictating how they should respond. In other cases, an officer's use of discretion can lead to either discriminatory or favorable treatment, which can lead to ethical violations. You'll have the chance to weigh in on the use of police discretion in Current Controversy 8.2 at the end of this chapter.

Duty

Ethical dilemmas involving **issues of duty** occur in two different ways. In some cases, officers are faced with challenges based on how they view their role as police officers. Is it to help prevent crime? Is it to help people? In other cases, the officer may know what is expected of him or her but may not be inclined to perform a particular aspect of the job. Each officer has her or his own perspective on duty, which can impact how the officer responds to ethical dilemmas in these cases.

Honesty

As a police officer, you are expected to be honest in your interactions with the public as well as fellow officers or other criminal justice professionals. Failures of honesty can not only impact how the public views the police but also lead to acts of corruption, such as bribery. What if you discover that an officer within your unit is

Ethical dilemma
Occurs when an officer is unsure about the right path of action, when following the right path is difficult, or when the wrong path becomes tempting to the officer.

Issues of duty
An ethical dilemma where officers are faced with challenges based on how they view their role as police officers. Also occurs when an officer knows what is expected of her or him but is not inclined to perform a particular aspect of the job.

involved in illegal behaviors? What do you do? Do you report him or her, or do you look the other way? Even if you don't approve of the behavior of your fellow officer, do you still support her or him as a member of the department?[18]

Corruption

Ethical challenges can lead to corruption. **Corruption** occurs when officers fail to make good ethical decisions (generally around the abuse of their authority as an officer), and the results of their actions lead to personal gain. The most common forms of corruption include acts such as theft (such as of drugs or other seized property) and selling information about police strategies and operations. Officers might also commit **perjury** by lying to cover up their wrongdoing.[19] Other acts of corruption include **mooching** or **bribery** (receiving free items in exchange of favorable treatment) and **shakedowns** (taking items without paying for them). The extent of corruption is difficult to measure because it occurs in every type of department: big, small, urban, and rural.

In their investigation of the New York Police Department in the 1970s, the Knapp Commission identified two categories of police corruption. Those officers who were described as **grass-eaters** were considered to be involved in corrupt activities in a passive sense. Here, officers would accept payoffs and opportunities that came their way. In contrast, **meat-eaters** would actively pursue corrupt activities that could result in significant and illegal gains. While it seems like a meat-eater would be the most problematic due to his or her overt illegal behaviors, the Knapp Commission suggested that it was the grass-eaters that were the more dangerous of the two, as they portray a culture wherein such behaviors are permissible as long as one doesn't actively seek them out.[20]

Since the 1970s, corruption has been more systematic in design. Previously, corruption was more of an individual effort and generally reflected that these officers deviated from department rules and norms. Today, corruption in American policing is generally conducted outside of the public eye in modern nations and is only exposed when officers and agencies are sanctioned for these behaviors.

Why Does Corruption Occur?

One perspective is the **rotten-apple theory**, which suggests that the corruption of a select few individuals can, in turn, shed negative light on a department. While some may perceive that corruption in these cases is easy to resolve through the removal of the few guilty individuals, others may believe that these few bad apples have spoiled the bunch.[21] In some cases, we have seen examples in which an entire division of a department becomes involved in corrupt and illegal activities, such as the Rampart Division of the Los Angeles Police Department. During the 1990s, more than 70 officers were implicated in and 24 officers were found guilty of wrongful activities. Acts of corruption can be costly to the department. To date, the city has faced more than 140 civil lawsuits and awarded $125 million in settlements in these cases.[22]

RACIAL PROFILING

Racial profiling occurs when "the race or ethnicity of an individual is used as the sole or primary determinant" by the police when making decisions.[23] The U.S. Supreme Court has stated that the police are prohibited from stopping an individual based solely on her or his racial or ethnic makeup.[24] However, race can be used in conjunction with other factors in describing a suspect in a crime.[25] While the decision in *Whren v. United States* (1996) permitted the police to stop motorists and search their vehicles if they had probable cause that the drivers were transporting contraband,

Corruption
An ethical dilemma that occurs when officers fail to make good ethical decisions and the results of their actions lead to personal gain.

Perjury
Lying to cover up wrongdoing.

Mooching
A form of corruption that involves receiving free items in exchange for favorable treatment.

Bribery
Involves the solicitation of something of value to influence the actions of another.

Shakedowns
A form of corruption that involves taking items without paying for them.

Grass-eaters
Officers who are considered to be involved in corrupt activities in a passive sense.

Meat-eaters
Officers who actively pursue corrupt activities that could result in significant and illegal gains.

Rotten-apple theory
Suggests that the corruption of a select few individuals can, in turn, shed a negative light on a department.

Racial profiling
Occurs when the race or ethnicity of an individual is used as the sole or primary determinant by the police when making decisions.

AROUND THE WORLD

Policing in the Middle East

Corruption among the police within developing nations is also a significant issue. Consider the challenges of developing nations. They often face authoritative challenges within the structure of the government, high rates of crime and poverty, and a great deal of pressure to establish a system of democracy. Police corruption is a significant issue for these countries. Examples of these activities can range from accepting bribes and kickbacks from individuals and local businesses to extorting money from citizens for protection and covering for criminal enterprises.

Consider the case of Afghanistan, a country that is struggling to establish a legal system. Several countries, including the United States, have contributed resources to help the nation reform its system of policing. At the time, there was no system of central control or a chain of command. Officers had limited training and even lacked uniforms to establish their official role within the community, which limited their ability to generate trust and support from residents. Low pay and ethnic tensions within the force contributed to the lack of cohesion within the units.[a] At the same time, the illegal drug trade fueled opportunities for corruption whereby police have accepted funds from drug traffickers in exchange for protection for their illegal activities.[b] We can see how these challenges can lead to corruption among the police force:

> It is not uncommon for police officers to buy their positions by paying bribes to superiors for unjustified promotions and for assignments that provide opportunities to extort truckers and merchants and engage in smuggling. Embezzling official funds and stealing gasoline to sell on the black market is common. Police officers are also reported to have sold their weapons and ammunition to the Taliban.[c]

The efforts to build a civilian police force have been threatened by limited opportunities for training as well as threats and violence against the police. While Germany provided significant training assistance to help build the infrastructure within the organization during the early years of the post-Taliban era, its efforts were restricted geographically. While an increase in resources from the international community (including significant contributions by the United States) meant that training for officers was expanded, the focus was on increasing the number of officers who received basic training rather than reviewing the quality of the training. As a result, many of these newly trained officers still had a limited skill set, which left them ill-equipped to do their jobs in an effective manner. This was further complicated by the fact that many of the individuals who were recruited to serve in these positions were illiterate, which limited the type of work that they could engage in. For many of these individuals, their training focused on applied skills, such as learning how to search for weapons and explosives at checkpoints.[d]

In an effort to support the establishment of a security force, the Afghan police system began to take on a military influence and focused on rebuilding regions that had been controlled by insurgents. This shift in training, coupled with an increase in compensation, helped to reduce the threats of corruption. Community-based policing was also introduced as a way to build trust.[e] However, there are still many reforms to be considered. Features such as citizen oversight bodies, a discussion of police powers, and the creation of internal policies and procedures will be necessary to establish the police as a legitimate security force within the community. There will also need to be an increased focus on community building while de-emphasizing the military roots of the police force.[f] Finally, scholars have recommended that the region focus on developing methods to research and analyze both the context of crime in the region and also the response by the police to these events.[g]

CRITICAL THINKING QUESTIONS

1. How has the changing political landscape in Afghanistan impacted the development of a legitimate police force?

2. How do on-the-job challenges threaten the status of police in the community?

3. What lessons from American policing could be useful to the reform of Afghan police organizations?

Figure 8.2 Gallup Poll Data on Racial Profiling

In 2013, 17% of Blacks who were surveyed said that they had been treated unfairly by the police within the last 30 days. While this number is down from recent years, it is still much higher than responses from Whites.

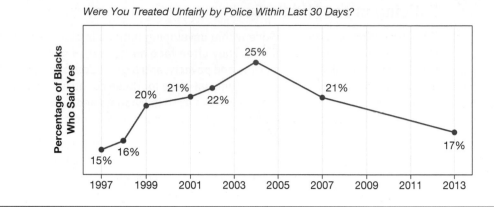

Were You Treated Unfairly by Police Within Last 30 Days?

Source: http://www.gallup.com/poll/163523/one-four-young-black-men-say-police-dealings-unfair.aspx?utm_source=racial%20profiling&utm_medium=search&utm_campaign=tiles

such as illegal drugs or weapons, scholars have suggested that this decision has given de facto permission to engage in racial profiling on the roadways.[26]

Research on Racial Profiling

VIDEO
Is "Driving While Black" a Systemic Problem?

The Gallup Organization has regularly conducted research about the issue of racial profiling to survey the public about their opinions on the issue. In 2013, their research found that 24% of young Black men surveyed stated that they had been treated poorly by the police during the past month. Meanwhile, women and those age 55 are more likely to believe they receive fair treatment. Overall, 17% of Black adults believe they have experienced unfair treatment by the police. These rates have continued to decrease since 2004. Figure 8.2 presents these data over the past 16 years.[27]

Much of the research on racial profiling is focused on traffic stops and whether minorities are disproportionately stopped by the police. The phrase *driving while Black or Brown* became synonymous with the practice of racial profiling and traffic stops. The Bureau of Justice Statistics indicates that in 2008, White, Black, and Hispanic/Latino drivers were stopped at similar rates. While there were no differences by race in terms of who was stopped, we do see demographic differences in the reasons why people were stopped, as well as the subsequent actions by the police. While 86.3% of Whites who were stopped by the police felt that it was for a legitimate reason, only 73.8% of African Americans believed their stop was valid. Figure 8.3 illustrates the actions by police made during traffic stops by race and ethnicity. Here, we can see that Whites are less likely to be ticketed by the police, and African Americans are more likely to be arrested when stopped by the police for a traffic violation.[28] Research has indicated that Black drivers are more likely to be searched than White drivers once a driver gives consent[29] or when officers have probable cause to conduct a search.[30] Scholars have also noted that African Americans are disproportionately stopped when driving through communities that are composed primarily of Caucasian residents, highlighting that police are more likely to stop minority individuals if they are perceived to be "out of place."[31]

Strategies to Reduce Racial Profiling

How can agencies reduce racial profiling? While it is important for agencies to develop policies that prohibit such behaviors, it is perhaps more important to develop guided procedures that mandate how officers should carry out traffic stops to help prevent the practice in the first place. While many agencies use dashboard cameras

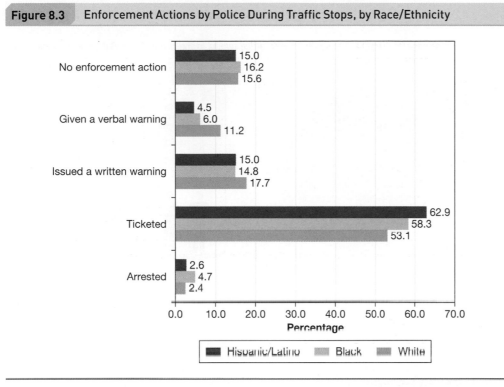

No enforcement action
- 15.0
- 16.2
- 15.6

Given a verbal warning
- 4.5
- 6.0
- 11.2

Issued a written warning
- 15.0
- 14.8
- 17.7

Ticketed
- 62.9
- 58.3
- 53.1

Arrested
- 2.6
- 4.7
- 2.4

Percentage (0.0, 10.0, 20.0, 30.0, 40.0, 50.0, 60.0, 70.0)

Legend: ■ Hispanic/Latino ■ Black ■ White

Hispanic drivers were more likely than White or Black drivers to be ticketed, but Black drivers were more likely to be arrested, and White drivers were more likely to be issued a written warning. Do these data show a pattern of profiling?

Source: http://www.bjs.gov/content/pub/pdf/cpp08.pdf

to document traffic stops, this is another area where body camera data could not only reduce the opportunities for officer misconduct but also protect officers and departments from fabricated claims of discrimination. Finally, it is important that states collect data on police stops and that scholars engage in independent analyses to assess the extent of racial profiling, as well as how such policies designed to prohibit the practice are being implemented on the streets.[32]

USE OF FORCE

Police often use force as part of their job. They may need to exert force to apprehend a suspect who is resisting arrest.

The use of force is a part of a police officer's duties. Even cases of deadly force, such as return-ing fire against someone who is shooting at the police while trying to flee the scene of a bank robbery, would be considered a reasonable expectation of an officer's duty. In the case *Tennessee v. Garner* (1985), the U.S. Supreme Court held that deadly force may be used to prevent the escape of a known offender if the officer's life or the lives of others around him or her are at imminent risk.[33] However, it is the issue of excessive use of force that is highly criticized. **Excessive use of force** is defined as "the application of amount and/or frequency of force greater than required to compel compliance from a willing or unwilling subject."[34] Despite what the public believes, the use of excessive force is incredibly rare (see Figure 8.4). Alas, the portrayal of these cases can dominate the media when they do occur. Given the

Police in riot gear prepare for the possibility of citizen unrest during a protest over the 2015 death of Freddie Gray in Baltimore. Three police officers are facing criminal trials in his death for using unreasonable force. At what point does the use of force become unreasonable or excessive?

Excessive use of force
Defined as the application of amount and/or frequency of force greater than required to compel compliance from a willing or unwilling subject.

Only a small percentage of the public's interactions with police results in the use of force. But these interactions are disproportionately with minority individuals.

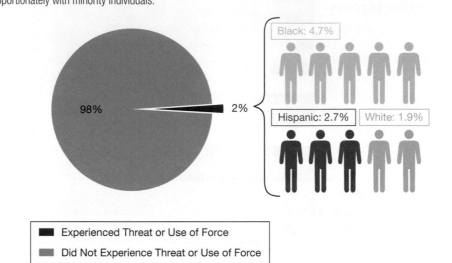
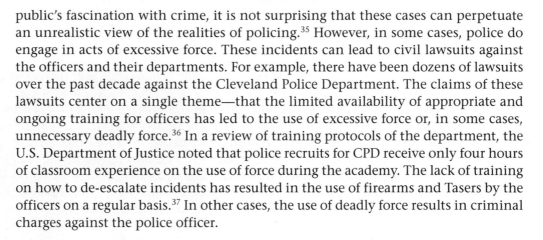

- Experienced Threat or Use of Force
- Did Not Experience Threat or Use of Force

public's fascination with crime, it is not surprising that these cases can perpetuate an unrealistic view of the realities of policing.[35] However, in some cases, police do engage in acts of excessive force. These incidents can lead to civil lawsuits against the officers and their departments. For example, there have been dozens of lawsuits over the past decade against the Cleveland Police Department. The claims of these lawsuits center on a single theme—that the limited availability of appropriate and ongoing training for officers has led to the use of excessive force or, in some cases, unnecessary deadly force.[36] In a review of training protocols of the department, the U.S. Department of Justice noted that police recruits for CPD receive only four hours of classroom experience on the use of force during the academy. The lack of training on how to de-escalate incidents has resulted in the use of firearms and Tasers by the officers on a regular basis.[37] In other cases, the use of deadly force results in criminal charges against the police officer.

Types of Force

There are five different types of force that can be used by officers:

- *Physical force:* Involves the use of physical restraint techniques such as wrist locks, bodily force, and choke holds.
- *Chemical force:* Chemical force involves the use of restraining substances, such as pepper spray or mace.
- *Electronic force:* Electronic force involves the use of electrical current to temporarily incapacitate an offender, such as the TASER.
- *Impact force:* Impact force involves the use of batons, flashlights, and other implements to deliver force against an individual.
- *Firearm force:* involves the pointing of or firing of a handgun.[38]

According to the Bureau of Justice Statistics, 1.6% of citizen contacts with the police involved either threats of force or the use of force. Males are more likely

WEB LINK
Police Use of Force

Physical force
Involves the use of physical restraint techniques, such as wrist locks, bodily force, and choke holds.

Chemical force
Force that involves the use of restraining substances, such as pepper spray or mace.

Electronic force
Force that involves the use of electrical current to temporarily incapacitate an offender, such as the TASER.

Impact force
Force that involves the use of batons, flashlights, and other implements to deliver force against an individual.

Firearm force
Force that involves the pointing of or firing of a handgun.

Kelly Thomas and the Fullerton Police Department

Kelly Thomas was a homeless man from Fullerton, in Orange County, California. Thomas was a diagnosed schizophrenic who was well known to the local police for a series of minor contacts and infractions throughout his years of living on the streets.[a] On July 5, 2011, Thomas was involved in an altercation with six Fullerton police officers, who were called amid reports that Thomas was vandalizing cars in the area. While video of the event initially shows Thomas responding to the officers' commands, reports of the incident indicated that Thomas failed to comply, and the officers engaged in a use of force against him. The video of the event shows Officer Ramos putting on latex

Orange County district attorney Tony Rackauckas presents video evidence in the Kelly Thomas beating case in Santa Ana, California. Two Fullerton police officers were ultimately acquitted in the case. Why do you think this case did not receive the level of attention from the public that similar cases have?

gloves and stating to Thomas, "See these fists? . . . They're getting ready to —— you up." Thomas was beaten by officers, who not only used their fists and batons to inflict damage but used a Taser against him at least five times.[b] Thomas died of his injuries on July 10, 2011.

Protests by community residents, including Kelly's father, Ron Thomas, urged the city to respond to this act of police brutality. The FBI was brought in to investigate the case, and in September 2011, the six officers were arrested on murder charges and placed on administrative leave with pay and benefits. In addition, the Fullerton police chief, Michael Sellers, departed on medical leave in August 2011 and resigned on February 18, 2012. Three city council members were also recalled in an election over concerns that they failed to respond adequately to the incident. Ultimately, the Orange Country district attorney ordered that two of the officers would stand trial for their involvement in Kelly Thomas's death. Officer Manuel Ramos was charged with second-degree murder and involuntary manslaughter, and Corporal Jay Cicinelli was charged with involuntary manslaughter and excessive use of force. Both officers were acquitted by a jury on January 13, 2014. A third officer, Joseph Wolfe, was also indicted on the charges of involuntary manslaughter and use of excessive force, but his case was dropped following the acquittal of Ramos and Cicinelli.[c]

In February 2015, Fullerton became the first department in Orange County to mandate the use of body cameras for every officer in the department. Several other departments in the region, including the Los Angeles Police Department, are also in the process of deploying this technology. Findings in other departments indicate that use of force by the police decreased by 60%, and the number of citizen complaints also fell by 88%, after the deployment of body cameras.[d] However, there are also several issues that have been raised about how to manage the use of body cameras within departments. You'll learn more about these issues in Current Controversy 8.1 at the end of this chapter.

CRITICAL THINKING QUESTION

1. What strategies should departments use to rebuild their communities following high-profile events?

to be involved in use-of-force incidents compared with women, as are African Americans compared with Whites and Hispanics. Fully 84% of those involved in these incidents believed that the police acted improperly, and 14% filed a complaint against the officer.[39]

POLICE LEGITIMACY

Establishing legitimacy within a police department requires that its community view a department as one with strong ethics that is committed to obeying and upholding the law. When the police lose their legitimacy, it is difficult to do their job in an effective way. After all, how do the police maintain order if the community does not support them in these efforts?[40]

At its core, the legitimacy of the police is dependent on how officers deploy their power and authority. This is referred to as procedural justice. Officers who are fair and transparent in their decision-making are viewed as being just, whereas officers who make decisions on factors such as race, gender, or age can be viewed in a negative light, which, in turn, can threaten the legitimacy of the police.[41] Research indicates that race can indirectly impact the levels of community satisfaction with the police. For example, neighborhoods with higher crime rates (which also tend to be disproportionately minority communities) are more likely to be dissatisfied with the police. Coupled with data that indicate that communities of color tend to have a high number of negative contacts with the police, we can say that these experiences can threaten the legitimacy of the police for certain communities.[42] The community of Ferguson, Missouri, is just one example of how police legitimacy can be threatened.

WEB LINK
Investigation of the Ferguson Police Department

On August 9, 2014, Michael Brown, an 18-year-old African American male, was shot and killed by Darren Wilson, a White officer for the Ferguson Police Department. The contested circumstances of the shooting, coupled with historical tensions between the police and the Black community, resulted in a series of protests and unrest not only within the region but across the United States. In the days following the shooting, tactical police officers were called to the region to manage the disturbances. Their efforts to disperse crowds included the use of tear gas against the protestors.

The protests returned in November after a St. Louis grand jury failed to indict Darren Wilson on any charges related to the shooting of Brown.[43] While a subsequent federal investigation cleared Wilson of any civil rights violations as a result of the shooting,[44] an additional investigation by the Department of Justice indicated that the police department in Ferguson routinely violated the constitutional rights of citizens through disparate treatment of Black members of the community. The report found that Black drivers were searched more than twice as often as White drivers, even though police were more likely to find contraband on White drivers when searches were conducted. Black residents

A woman pauses at a makeshift memorial where Michael Brown was fatally shot on August 9, 2014, by Darren Wilson, a Ferguson, Missouri, police officer. How do communities rebuild police–citizen relationships following events such as this?

AP Photo/Jeff Roberson

were also more likely to be subjects of municipal law violations, as they represented 95% of jaywalking cases, 92% of resisting-arrest charges, and 94% of failure-to-comply charges. Adding to these disparities by the police, the courts were more likely to dismiss charges against White defendants. While some have suggested that the police department may be too broken and may need to be dismantled completely, only time will tell how the relationship between the police and the community will be repaired.

POLICE OCCUPATIONAL STRESS

Police officers work in high-intensity environments where they must deal with stressful situations. What makes police occupational stress so different compared with job-related stress in other fields is that the typical day of a police officer can actually be rather mundane. Stressful situations tend to occur as a result of high-pressure incidents, which, contrary to the portraits painted by television and film, are not a regular component of the typical workday. However, the potential for stress can build over time, to the point that the anticipation of danger, in and of itself, can produce stress. In addition to the sources of stress that are unique to policing (e.g., violence), officers also experience stress that occurs as a result of work within a bureaucratic environment (e.g., shift work, limited opportunities for promotion, etc.).[45] Stress can also come from unexpected sources. For example, officers indicate that they experience stress as a result of the time and energy that they spend on issues of prejudice and bias.[46] This refers to dealing with these issues in their interactions not just with the community but also with other officers in their department.[47] Such stress can be enhanced, particularly if an officer is the only or one of a few minority police officers in the department.[48]

Occupational stress can have several implications for the lives of police officers, including physical and mental health problems, poor job performance, burnout, and the use of force.[49] For example, work stress is related to feelings of depression and experiences with intimate partner abuse.[50] Officers may also suffer from post-traumatic stress due to the types of issues that they confront on the job. However, job stress can be mediated by job satisfaction. Research demonstrates that higher job satisfaction is linked to positive relationships with peers and supervisors as well as a reasonable promotion system.[51] In addition, agencies should promote training, mentorship, and counseling opportunities for officers to develop positive coping strategies.[52]

> "
> Occupational stress can have several implications for the lives of police officers, including physical and mental health problems, poor job performance, burnout, and the use of force.

CONCLUSION

As the first responders to crime, the police are subjected to several legal and policy directives that impact how officers do their job on the streets. Here, the U.S. Supreme Court has been mixed on when, where, and how offenders should be identified and apprehended by the criminal justice system. Given the vast array of power that the police carry, there will always be the risk that an officer will do the wrong thing and fall into corrupt and illegal activities. While such practices are regularly portrayed on the nightly news, these cases represent a small number of officers within the larger scheme of those who work in their field on a daily basis. Alas, these few bad apples can indeed spoil the bunch and challenge the legitimacy of the police within the community.

PRO CON

Should Police Agencies Require Officers to Wear Body Cameras?

—William H. Sousa—

INTRODUCTION

The body-worn camera (BWC) is a relatively recent technological innovation that is now in use by American police agencies. Although there are different models of BWCs, most are small video- or audio-recording devices that are placed somewhere on an officer's uniform, usually in the chest area or on the lapel or collar. (Some models can also be mounted on a headband or on sunglasses.) BWCs are designed to record officer activities and encounters with citizens. Policies vary from department to department, but BWCs are generally activated when officers respond to emergencies or interact with members of the public. Videos that are recorded by a BWC are typically stored on the camera itself until the data are transferred to a larger storage device (such as a computer server) where they can be accessed at a later time.

BWCs are generally considered to be a technology that can help improve police practice. Many politicians, members of the public, and police themselves therefore support the use of BWCs. While BWCs do offer a number of potential advantages for policing, these benefits should be considered in light of several concerns that arise when video recording is in use.

Many departments are deploying body-worn cameras as a way to document police encounters with citizens. How might this change interactions between officers and the communities they serve?

PRO Police Agencies Should Require Officers to Wear Body Cameras

There are several benefits of requiring police to use body-worn cameras. These include the greater transparency of police activities with the general public, protections from police misconduct, protection of officer actions and decisions, and other improvements to police practices.

Greater transparency. One argument for BWCs is that they demonstrate a police agency's willingness to be open and transparent in terms of the activities of their officers. Since BWCs record officer behaviors, police can be held accountable for their actions. Greater transparency and openness on the part of police agencies can help improve police–community relations, build trust, and enhance legitimacy in the eyes of the public.

Protection of citizens. Many believe that BWCs can help protect citizens from acts of police misconduct. Officers, of course, are aware that BWCs record their activities. Since their superiors, the courts, the media, or the public could potentially review those recordings, officers will be more likely to act with integrity and professionalism when interacting with citizens. BWCs, therefore, can potentially reduce police misconduct, including unnecessary use of force, discourtesy, and abuse of authority.

Protection of officers. BWCs can also potentially help protect officers. Because BWCs record from an officer's point of view, the recordings provide a different perspective than what is often observed by bystanders. Some believe that video from an officer's perspective will help demonstrate that police actions are justified. Recordings can therefore be used to help exonerate officers who are falsely accused of improper actions. In addition, many

believe that citizens who are aware of BWCs on officers may be less antagonistic or confrontational when interacting with police.

Other improvements to police practice. There are other advantages to BWCs as well. For instruction and training purposes, video from BWCs can demonstrate examples of proper techniques that are performed in the field. BWCs can also make investigation practices more efficient. The audio and video capabilities of BWCs can record visual evidence, victim statements, and witness accounts at the scene of incidents, making it easier for police to gather and review information.

 Police Agencies Should Not Require Officers to Wear Body Cameras

Just as there are benefits to the use of body-worn cameras, there are also concerns. These include the limits of technology, issues of privacy, a threat that police organizations will return to a more bureaucratic and legalistic style of policing, and a reduction in the levels of proactivity among police officers.

Limits of technology. BWCs can provide more information about police–citizen interactions, but the recordings may not offer all of the answers concerning controversial police actions. First, although the video and audio capabilities of BWCs are generally good, numerous conditions can impact the quality of the recordings. Distortions can occur, for example, if the officer is running, scuffling with a suspect, or otherwise engaged in physical activity. Second, even if the recordings are clear, videos can still be open to interpretation. Several people, for instance, could view the same video of a contentious interaction between an officer and a citizen and reach very different conclusions regarding the appropriateness of the officer's actions.[53] In other words, just because there may be video of a controversial encounter between an officer and a citizen, this does not mean that the video will necessarily resolve the controversy to everyone's satisfaction.

Privacy issues. Although BWCs can capture potentially controversial interactions between officers and the community, many other types of police contacts with citizens will be recorded as well. Most events that gain public notoriety (such as police use of deadly force) are very rare given the number of contacts

that police have with citizens. Other types of police contacts are much more common, such as assisting people in distress, helping with medical emergencies, dealing with traffic accidents, managing family or neighborhood disputes, and aiding juveniles. This means that BWCs will record many events where people are very exposed and vulnerable—a concern for those who worry about government intrusion into the private lives of citizens.

Policing could become more legalistic and bureaucratic. One of the possible consequences of BWCs is that officers may shift to a more legalistic style of policing. For example, officers with BWCs may be more inclined to issue citations rather than warnings in situations that involve a high degree of discretion (such as minor traffic violations). This is because officers may feel more comfortable taking formal action—or feel pressure to take formal action—knowing that evidence of the violation is on video record.

Less proactivity. Another possible consequence of BWCs is that officers may become less proactive in terms of managing community problems. A good deal of research has demonstrated that when officers are reactive (i.e., mostly responding to 911 calls), they are not very effective at preventing larger neighborhood problems.[54] However, when police are proactive (e.g., communicating with citizens, working with juveniles, partnering with social services, managing quality-of-life offenses in neighborhoods, etc.), they can be much more effective at preventing crime and disorder.[55] Some believe that officers with BWCs will be less proactive because self-initiated police activities are often discretionary. Aware that their actions are being recorded, police may be reluctant to engage in self-initiated activities so as to avoid scrutiny over discretionary decisions. In addition, some believe that citizens will also be less proactive in terms of communicating with police. Knowing that the interaction could be recorded, citizens may be uncomfortable when approaching an officer or when providing confidential information to the police.

SUMMARY

BWCs offer a number of potential advantages for the practice of policing. One should, however, balance these potential advantages with potential concerns. To date, few research studies have examined the overall value of BWCs, and very little case law has been produced that can guide policies regarding the use of BWCs.[56] As a result, the use of BWCs by police remains a controversial issue in terms of its implementation and use.

DISCUSSION QUESTIONS

1. Should officers who wear BWCs be required to notify citizens that the interaction is being recorded?

2. Video storage is one of the major financial costs associated with BWC systems. Acknowledging that this is a major cost, should video of police interactions with citizens be stored indefinitely? If not, how long should it be stored? Under what circumstances should video be deleted?

3. BWC systems allow officers to activate and deactivate the technology. This is to protect the officer's privacy (such as during lunch or restroom breaks) and to save on the costs of video storage space. Under what circumstances should officers be required to turn the BWC on, and when should they be allowed to turn it off?

4. Who should have access to videos that are recorded by police BWCs? Many police records are available to the public and can be obtained through Freedom of Information Act (FOIA) requests. Should video records also be available to the public?

CURRENT CONTROVERSY 8.2

CURRENT CONTROVERSY VIDEO
Where Do You Stand? Cast Your Vote!

Does Police Discretion Help or Harm Our Criminal Justice System?

—Lorenzo M. Boyd—

INTRODUCTION

One of the most debated issues and biggest sources of contention within policing is the seemingly wide use of discretionary practices and decision-making. At all levels of justice, some form of discretion is used regularly. Admittedly, there are no two crimes or potential offenders that are exactly alike, but it would appear that there needs to be some sort of uniformity in the ways in which the criminal justice system deals with each situation. Because the police are the gatekeepers for the entire criminal justice system, the use of discretion by police can have sweeping and profound effects in latter parts of the criminal justice system. One side would argue that the overuse of discretion in dealing with citizens is a major cause of disparities within the system. The other side would assert that discretion is a necessary tool in the criminal justice system because *discretion* affords the criminal justice professionals a chance to be lenient and consider mitigating circumstances at each level of the system while tailoring appropriate responses for all concerned.

Levels of criminal justice discretion can include such situations as whether a driver will be stopped and ticketed, whether a suspect will be arrested or simply questioned and released, and the charge that an arresting officer will pass on to the courts. Police discretion weighs heavily in other parts of the system as well. The discretionary actions of the police may help determine whether a prosecutor will charge a suspect and with which charge, the negotiation of a plea arrangement, the amount of time a convicted offender will likely serve in prison, and whether a parole board is willing to accept treatment successes as a reason that an inmate will be released early. This nonexhaustive list is just a small sample of the levels of discretion that are afforded the police every day and the wide-reaching implications of that discretion. So the question at hand is whether discretion is a *discriminatory tool* wielded by the police or a *necessary evil* employed by criminal justice professionals in order to keep the criminal justice system moving in a more efficient manner.

Police discretion is the decision to act or not act based on an individual police officer's judgment regarding the best course of action to take in any given situation. Discretionary decisions are usually based on the officer's experience, training, philosophy, and knowledge, as well as situational factors such as type of crime, size and number of suspects, and damage done or injury to victims. Other factors may come into play, such as demographic considerations like gender, race, ethnicity, and social status and situational considerations like knowledge of suspect or victim and personal relationships.

When we have a discussion about criminal justice discretion, many times the conversation begins with a focus on the police. Many would argue that the occupational mandate of the police is to maintain order and keep the peace and that enforcing laws is secondary to order maintenance. Others would posit that enforcing laws is paramount in a police officer's job. Regardless of which view you subscribe to, each version of policing will have an incredible amount of discretion associated with it.

 ## PRO — Police Discretion Is Helpful to the Criminal Justice System

Police discretion gives the police the ability or option to handle community-level problems informally and help citizens work through disputes and work out informal resolutions that will be best for all parties involved, without bogging down the already overburdened criminal justice system. Sometimes, community-level officers are better suited to handle community-level issues without directing all problems formally into the courts system. A lack of police discretion amounts to having a zero-tolerance policy for all infractions. Discretion will allow an officer to give a stern warning and counsel a speeding driver to slow down instead of the officer issuing a ticket, which comes with additional court costs and a financial hit on a driver's car insurance.

Police use of discretion is often associated with the order maintenance role of the police. For instance, police discretion is often a technique utilized when mediating disputes instead of making arrests, or referring citizens to social service agencies instead of bringing them into the criminal justice system. The use of discretion can be seen when an officer chooses to commit a person with a mental illness to a health facility rather than arrest that person for disorderly conduct. Police officers are often forced to make discretionary decisions because many criminal laws are written too broadly. Many times, lack of specificity in written laws exists to encompass many different scenarios, but this leaves a lot of room for different interpretations and thus discretionary decision-making by the police.

 ## CON — Police Discretion Is Harmful to Our Criminal Justice System

Discretion in policing continues to be a major point of debate with community members and scholars alike. The presence of large-scale occupational discretion can be viewed as a double-edged sword. Discretion also has an ugly side that often rears its head

in policing. Discretion is not just a helpful tool for officers in effectively doing their jobs; often, it serves as a crutch for allowing officers to violate rules, laws, and civil rights. On one hand, discretion allows officers to use their authority appropriately to mitigate street-level disturbances. On the other hand, it also allows officers to use discriminatory practices against citizens on the basis of extralegal factors such as race, gender, or class.[57] Research shows that officers have ample opportunities for misconduct while on patrol, primarily because of the existence of large-scale occupational discretion and the ability of street-level officers to make decisions in the absence of any direct supervision.[58]

Empirical research has provided overwhelming support for the idea that police officers have a great deal of discretion in how they deal with a citizen's conduct and that both legal (seriousness of the crime, past criminal history, etc.) and extralegal (race, class, gender, etc.) criteria can influence the outcomes of police–citizen encounters.[59] Scholars note that the actions of the police are not at all based entirely on laws. Officers, for the most part, use extralegal factors as the basis for decisions in the course of performing their duties. Although, for the most part, they do work within the constraints of the law, they seldom actually invoke the law in performing their police duties.[60]

Police discretion sometimes manifests itself as racial profiling on the part of the police. The American Civil Liberties Union (ACLU) published a 2014 report that asserts that police officers often engage in widespread racially biased stop-and-frisk practices, targeting people of color at far greater rates than White people. The report also states that Black citizens in the city studied were subjected to 63% of these encounters, even though they made up just 24% of that city's population. Moreover, the report shows that controlling for neighborhood-level crime rate does not explain this racial disparity. The report further shows that as the Black population in this city increased as a percentage of the total population, so did the number of police encounters.

The ACLU reports that even after controlling for crime, police officers were more likely to initiate encounters in Black neighborhoods and to initiate encounters with Black people. When questioned about this disparity, police officials gave no justification for 75% of these encounters, simply stating that they were investigatory in nature. More than 200,000 of these stop-and-frisk investigative encounters over a four-year period yielded no arrests, and only 2.5% led to seizure of contraband of any kind.

SUMMARY

So you can see that discretion in the realm of policing can be both useful and troublesome. Often, that discretion appears to occur in the form of biased policing, and without proper oversight, it can wreak havoc on disenfranchised communities. Where there is discretion, there is the possibility of discriminatory practices and biased policing. But without some level of personal discretion in policing, we run the risk of moving toward a situation in which zero-tolerance policing is the outcome. We have to decide whether we want to have a firmer hold on and oversight of police officers' daily decision-making or to become willing to allow levels of professional discretion in policing and all that comes with it. The hard part will be balancing levels of potential discrimination with the need for occupational efficacy in the criminal justice system.

DISCUSSION QUESTIONS

1. What are the benefits and consequences of the use of police discretion?

2. What suggestions would you offer to prevent abuse and misconduct that can occur under the umbrella of police discretion?

KEY TERMS

Review key terms with eFlashcards | $SAGE edge™ • edge.sagepub.com/mallicoatccj

Bribery 188	Corruption 188	Excessive use of force 191
Carroll doctrine 183	Electronic force 192	Exclusionary rule 183
Chemical force 192	Emergency exception 183	Firearm force 192
Consent search 183	Ethical dilemma 187	Fruit of the poisoned tree 183

DISCUSSION QUESTIONS

Test your mastery of chapter content • Take the Practice Quiz | §SAGE edge™ • edge.sagepub.com/mallicoatccj

1. How does the 4th Amendment protect individuals from unreasonable searches and seizures by the police? When are there exceptions to this rule?

2. How do issues such as racial profiling and use of force challenge the legitimacy of the police?

3. How can lawsuits against police departments lead to changes in policies and practices?

4. What types of ethical dilemmas do police officers face?

5. What types of force can police officers use?

6. Why is legitimacy important when it comes to policing?

7. What are some sources of occupational stress for police officers?

LEARNING ACTIVITIES

1. Select a case from the U.S. Supreme Court from the most recent term that deals with a 4th Amendment issue. What was the decision by the Court? How does this decision impact the on-the-job experience for police officers?

2. Identify a case in which officer misconduct led to policy changes within a police department. What is the new policy, and how is it designed to protect against similar events in the future?

SUGGESTED WEBSITES

- **Center for Problem-Oriented Policing:** http://www.popcenter.org
- **Police Executive Research Forum:** http://www.policeforum.org
- **Police Foundation:** http://www.policefoundation.org

STUDENT STUDY SITE

Review • Practice • Improve | §SAGE edge™ • edge.sagepub.com/mallicoatccj

Want a better grade?

Get the tools you need to sharpen your study skills. Access practice quizzes, eFlashcards, video, and multimedia at **edge.sagepub.com/mallicoatccj**

HEAR IT FROM THE PROFESSIONALS

▶ edge.sagepub.com/mallicoatccj

HEAD TO THE STUDY SITE WHERE YOU'LL FIND

- **Exclusive video interviews** with professionals in the criminal justice field.

COURTS

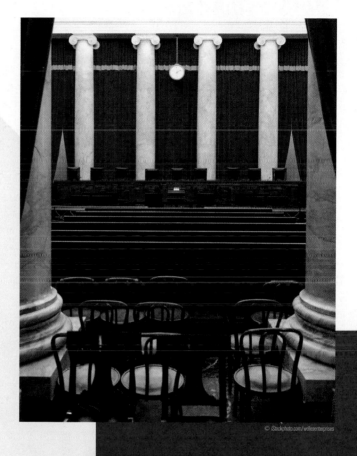

PART

9

COURTS AND CRIME

LEARNING OBJECTIVES

- Discuss the differences between the criminal courts and the civil courts

- Identify the different types of jurisdiction that impact how courts hear cases

- Describe the typical structure of the state and federal court systems

- Discuss the various actors in the court system and their duties

- Explain how a case moves through the trial process

During the 2014 term, the U.S Supreme Court heard the case of *Riley v. California*,[1] which asked whether the police are allowed to search the cell phone of an arrestee without a warrant.

On August 22, 2009, David Leon Riley was pulled over by a police officer in San Diego, California, because the registration tags on his car had expired. Upon making contact with Mr. Riley, the officer noted that he was driving on a suspended license. In response to department policy, Mr. Riley was arrested, his car was towed, and the contents of his car were cataloged. During this process, the officers discovered two handguns that were located under the hood of the car. Mr. Riley was placed under arrest, and his personal belongings, including his cell phone, were confiscated by the police as part of the arrest process. His cell phone was subsequently searched, and officers learned that he had ties to a local gang. They also discovered photos on his phone, including one of him with a car that was used in a gang-related shooting. Based on the evidence on the phone, in conjunction with ballistics testing that indicated that the two guns found in his car were used in the shooting, police filed charges in the gang-related shooting. Riley was convicted and received an enhanced sentence, based on his gang involvement, of 15 years to life.

Riley appealed his conviction to the California court of appeals on the grounds that the evidence from his phone was obtained illegally and therefore should not have been used against him in his trial. While the court of appeals affirmed his conviction, the U.S. Supreme Court granted certiorari to hear the case. In June 2014, the Court unanimously ruled that police must obtain a warrant in order to search a cell phone of someone under arrest. In the majority opinion, Justice Roberts stated that people have a reasonable expectation of privacy with their cell phones given the particularly large amount of personal information that is generally stored on their devices.

AUDIO
Supreme Court Considers
Limits on Warrantless
Cell Phone Searches

In this chapter, you will learn about the structure of the American courts system and its relationship to the criminal justice system. The chapter begins with a discussion about how courts are organized. The chapter then looks at the different participants in the courtroom and their roles. This is followed by a discussion of the stages of a criminal court case. The chapter concludes with two Current Controversy debates related to the criminal courts system. The first, by Julius (Jay) Wachtel, asks whether physical evidence should be required in serious criminal cases. The second, by G. Max Dery, asks whether we should limit the use of plea bargains in criminal cases.

CRIMINAL VERSUS CIVIL COURTS

In Chapter 2, you learned about the differences between criminal law and civil law. As a result of these primary differences in law, we also have differences in the courts—criminal courts hear issues of criminal law while civil courts hear matters of civil law. You also learned how the decision-making in these cases varies. Criminal law requires that a criminal court satisfy a burden of proof of beyond a reasonable doubt. Meanwhile, the burden of proof in civil courts is a lower standard: preponderance of the evidence. Generally speaking, cases are heard either in criminal court or in civil court. However, there are some occasions when a case may involve violations of both criminal and civil law. The murders of Nicole Brown Simpson and Ronald Goldman are perhaps one of the most well-known examples of this. Nicole Brown Simpson was the ex-wife of football star O. J. Simpson, and Ronald Goldman was her friend. The two were found murdered on June 12, 1994. Mr. Simpson was arrested and tried for their murders. After a long trial, he was found not guilty of criminal murder by a Los Angeles jury. Their verdict indicated that the jury was not able to find O. J. Simpson guilty beyond a reasonable doubt. The families of Ms. Brown and Mr. Goldman subsequently filed a wrongful death case against O. J. Simpson. They won their case with the lower burden of proof of preponderance of the evidence. The judgment in the case totaled $33.5 million.[2]

VIDEO
2/4/1997: O.J. Simpson
Civil Trial Verdict

A more recent example of a case involving both the criminal and civil court can be found in the legal cases against Jameis Winston. Winston was a student at Florida State University (FSU) in 2012 when Erica Kinsman accused him of rape that December. The case made national headlines when Winston won the 2013 Heisman Trophy, and FSU won the national college football championship. There was limited investigation of the criminal complaint by the Tallahassee police. For example, the police failed to interview any witnesses or even the accused until several weeks after the case was reported. The lead detective took over two months to write his report. By the time the case was handed to the prosecutor, key pieces of evidence had gone missing. As a result, no criminal charges were filed. But two cases were filed in civil court. First, Kinsman filed a civil case in which she asked for $15,000 in damages against Winston on the grounds of sexual battery, false imprisonment, and emotional distress.[3] The second case involved a Title IX lawsuit against Florida State over how it mishandled her complaint. Title IX provides several educational rights to students, including a requirement that colleges and universities investigate allegations of rape and sexual assault. In January 2016, FSU settled the lawsuit for $950,000.[4]

Although there was not enough evidence to convict O. J. Simpson in a criminal court, a civil court did rule against him. Why is it significant that there is a lower burden of proof in civil courts? Should the burden of proof be lower?

JURISDICTION AND THE COURTS SYSTEM

Geographical Jurisdiction

Following an arrest, a criminal case moves to the courts system. The jurisdiction of a court depends on several factors (Table 9.1). First, does the court have **geographical jurisdiction**? In order to answer this question, we need to know what type of law was broken. Say you are arrested by a local police officer for trespassing on private property. This crime is likely a local offense, and therefore, this case would be heard by a local municipal court. The most common type of criminal act is a violation of state law. As a result, these cases are brought to the court by the state, so a criminal court case would be heard in state court. These cases are presented as the State of New York (or whatever state that the crime occurred in) vs. the name of the defendant. Finally, there are several offenses that are considered a violation of federal law. As a result, these cases would be heard in federal court. While federal law applies to all 50 states, state law applies only to the jurisdiction of that particular state. In some cases, federal law and state law contradict each other. The recent legalization of marijuana by Washington and Colorado are examples of this situation. While users would not be subject to any punishments for possessing marijuana in these two states, they could face punishment under federal law. In addition, laws of one state are limited only to that state. So it would be illegal to possess marijuana under Texas state law, even if it was purchased legally in another state.

> **While federal law applies to all 50 states, state law applies only to the jurisdiction of that particular state.**

Concurrent Jurisdiction

A recent example of a federal case is the prosecution of Dzhokhar Tsarnaev for the bombings during the 2013 Boston Marathon. Why was this case heard in federal court and not the state court of Massachusetts? Certainly the crimes for which he was charged are illegal under both state and federal law. When acts are illegal under both federal law and state law, this is referred to as **concurrent jurisdiction**. As a result, it is up to the federal government to decide whether it will prosecute a case or whether it will allow the state to do so. While Tsarnaev could certainly have been charged for the events that ultimately killed three people and injured 260 others under Massachusetts state law, several of his acts also fell under federal law violations, such as conspiracy to use a weapon of mass destruction resulting in death. In 2015, Tsarnaev was found guilty on all 30 crimes that he was charged with and was sentenced to death. While such punishment is allowed under federal law, it is not an option under Massachusetts state law, which some argue influenced the decision to charge him in federal court.[5]

VIDEO
Dzhokhar Tsarnaev Indicted on Criminal Charges for Boston Marathon Bombing

Table 9.1	Different Types of Jurisdictions
Jurisdiction	**Cases Are Sent to . . .**
Geographical Jurisdiction	A court based on the geographical location in which the crime was committed
Concurrent Jurisdiction	Either a state or federal court; both have jurisdiction
Subject Matter Jurisdiction	A court based on the type of crime that was committed
Appellate Jurisdiction	A court that hears appeals

Geographical jurisdiction
Jurisdiction determined by the physical location of a crime.

Concurrent jurisdiction
Allows a case to be heard in either state or federal courts (or adult and juvenile courts).

The courtroom represents the place in the criminal justice system where legal decisions about criminal and civil cases are made. Based on the layout of the courtroom, who is the central figure during the proceedings?

In some cases, both the federal and state governments will pursue a criminal case against a defendant. For example, Terry Nichols was prosecuted by the federal government for his involvement in the Oklahoma City Bombing of the Alfred Murrah Federal Building with Timothy McVeigh in 1995. While the federal government successfully convicted Mr. Nichols in 1997 for conspiring to build a weapon of mass destruction, as well as eight additional counts of involuntary manslaughter of federal officers, the jury in that case sentenced Nichols to life in prison without the possibility of parole. The state of Oklahoma then subsequently tried Nichols for 161 courts of first-degree murder in an effort to sentence him to death. The jury in that case was deadlocked on whether to sentence Nichols to death. As a result, the judge handed down 161 consecutive sentences of life in prison without the possibility of parole.[6]

Subject Matter Jurisdiction

The jurisdiction of a court is also based on the type of case that it is allowed to hear. This is known as **subject matter jurisdiction**. At the lowest level, courts of **limited jurisdiction** handle misdemeanor cases. Limited jurisdiction courts may also handle specific types of cases, such as drug courts, domestic violence courts, and mental health courts. In contrast, courts of **general jurisdiction** do not have any restrictions on the types of cases that they can hear. In the criminal courts, general jurisdiction courts hear the most serious felony cases. A criminal case begins in a court of **original jurisdiction** or a **trial court**, where a case is heard for the first time. Trial courts are concerned with issues of fact. In these courts, evidence is presented, and decisions of guilt are made.

Appellate Jurisdiction

Meanwhile, courts of **appellate jurisdiction** are concerned with issues of law and whether there were errors made by the trial court. In criminal court, only the accused can file the first appeal. If a prosecutor loses at trial, there is no option to appeal the decision. Unlike a trial court, which may use a jury to make a decision, appellate courts use a judge or a panel of judges to render a decision. The decision at this level can either reverse or uphold the verdict of the lower court.

STRUCTURE OF THE COURTS

As you have just learned, we have laws at both the federal level and the state level. In order to prosecute these crimes, the federal court system handles cases that violate federal law. While there are offices and courtrooms located throughout the United States, they all operate under the same system. At the same time, each state has its own separate court system. Together, these make up our **dual court system**. Figure 9.1 demonstrates how these two systems work in a separate yet similar fashion.

The Federal Court System

The federal court system is responsible for managing criminal, civil, and administrative cases under federal law. The jurisdiction for the court not only covers all 50

Subject matter jurisdiction
Courts that hear specific types of cases based on their topic.

Limited jurisdiction
Courts that handle misdemeanor cases or specific types of cases.

General jurisdiction
Courts that do not have any restrictions on the types of cases that they hear but generally hear the most serious felony cases.

Original jurisdiction
Courts that hear cases for the first time. Also called trial courts.

Trial court
A court of original jurisdiction that hears issues of fact and makes decisions based on the law.

Appellate jurisdiction
Level of the courts that is concerned with issues of law and whether an error was made by the trial court.

Dual court system
Explains how the state and federal court systems work in separate yet similar fashions.

states but includes U.S. territories and the District of Columbia. The federal courts also handle matters of local law for the U.S. territories. Figure 9.1 shows the structure of the federal court system. Within the federal system, most judges are appointed by the president, confirmed by the Senate, and serve a life term.

WEB LINK
U.S. Courts

Magistrate Courts

The first level of courts in the federal system is the **U.S. magistrate courts**. These courts have limited jurisdiction and generally hear misdemeanor cases. They can also be involved in pretrial matters for more serious cases. Their duties for criminal matters include authorizing search and arrest warrants and conducting detention hearings, initial appearances, and arraignments. However, the bulk of their work involves civil cases. In 2015 magistrate judges were involved in more than 1 million matters, including 192,593 felony pretrial matters, 94,906 Class A misdemeanor and petty-crimes cases, and 25,959 cases of prisoner litigation.[7] Magistrate judges are the only judges in the federal system who are appointed in a manner that is different from other federal judicial appointments. In addition, these positions have term limits. Magistrate judges are selected by the district court judiciary and serve a term of eight years. In 2015 there were 573 magistrate judges.[8]

District Courts

U.S. district courts are courts of general jurisdiction. There are 94 district courts that are spread throughout the 50 states, the District of Columbia, and the U.S. territories. These courts hear cases, review evidence, and apply legal reasoning in deciding a case. In 2015, there were 80,069 criminal filings in U.S. district courts, which were heard by 677 judges. Federal judges are nominated by the president and confirmed by the Senate.[9] The most common offense heard by these courts involves drugs (32%). Immigration cases make up 26% of the court's caseload, a majority of which involve cases of illegal border entry.[10]

U.S. magistrate courts
First level of courts in the federal courts system. Courts of limited jurisdiction, and they generally hear misdemeanor cases.

U.S. district courts
Courts of general jurisdiction in the federal courts system.

Figure 9.1   The Dual Court System

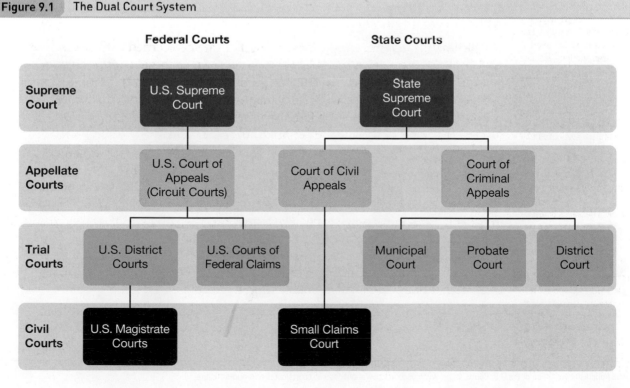

A panel of appellate judges hears arguments in a case to determine whether there was a legal violation that altered the decision by a lower court.

Appeals Courts

The **U.S. courts of appeals** are intermediate courts that hear appeals from the U.S. district courts or from the federal administrative courts. There are 13 courts of appeals, called **circuit courts**. Figure 9.2 presents a map of the U.S. federal judicial circuits. As appellate courts, the circuit courts hear cases to determine whether there was an error in how the law was applied. In 2015, the U.S. courts of appeals heard 52,698 cases, 22% of which involved criminal matters. There were also 13,900 petitions by prisoners.[11] Cases are typically heard by a three-judge panel, though in rare instances, a case may be heard **en banc**, meaning that the full bench hears the case. In 2015 judges from the circuit courts issued 3,794 published opinions.[12]

Supreme Court

The **U.S. Supreme Court** is the highest court that can hear cases on criminal law. The Court comprises nine justices. Justices are selected by the president of the United States and are confirmed by the members of the Senate. An appointment to the bench of the U.S. Supreme Court is a lifetime appointment. The Court generally hears only cases that involve a constitutional question—that is, that a defendant's constitutional rights were violated as a result of her or his criminal conviction. Table 9.2 highlights some of the notable Supreme Court decisions on issues of criminal law.

U.S. courts of appeals
Intermediate courts of appeals that hear cases of law from the U.S. district courts or from the federal administrative courts.

Circuit courts
Another names for the federal courts of appeals.

En banc
A hearing of the full bench of a U.S. circuit court.

Figure 9.2	United States Federal Judicial Circuit Courts

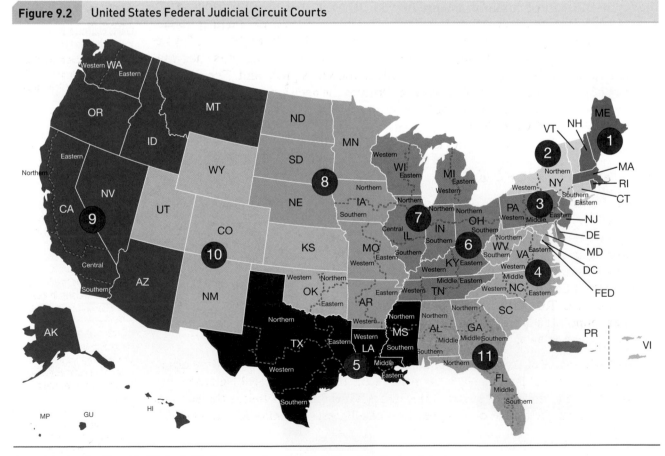

Source: Administrative Office of the U.S. Courts. http://www.uscourts.gov/about-federal-courts/court-role-and-structure

Table 9.2	Landmark U.S. Supreme Court Cases on Criminal Law
Case	**Ruling**
Mapp v. Ohio (1961)	Evidence that is obtained as a result of an illegal search cannot be used as evidence in a court case.
Gideon v. Wainwright (1963)	Defendants are entitled to an attorney if they are accused of a crime. If they cannot afford an attorney, they will be appointed one by the government.
Miranda v. Arizona (1966)	Police must advise arrestees of their constitutional rights to remain silent, to speak to a lawyer, and to have a lawyer appointed on their behalf if they cannot afford one.
Katz v. United States (1967)	Police must obtain a warrant to search and seize evidence in any instance where the defendant has a reasonable expectation of privacy.
Terry v. Ohio (1968)	Police may stop and search a person if they have a reasonable suspicion that the person is armed and is about to engage in a criminal act.
Strickland v. Washington (1984)	In order to successfully appeal on the basis of ineffective assistance of counsel, defendants must prove that the lack of a qualified and competent attorney negatively prejudiced their case.
Batson v. Kentucky (1986)	Prosecutors cannot use a peremptory challenge to exclude a potential juror solely on the basis of race.

In order for a case to reach the Supreme Court, all appeals in the lower courts have to be exhausted.* Then, appellants—those who are appealing—must petition the Court to hear the case. This is called a **writ of certiorari**. However, the Court hears only a select few of the cases that it is asked to review each year. Generally speaking, the Court will accept between 100 and 150 cases, even though there are more than 7,000 requests annually.[13] In order to hear a case, four of the nine justices must vote in its favor. If a case is granted certiorari, both sides will submit a **brief** that outlines the legal arguments of their case. Briefs may also be submitted by outside parties that have an interest in the case. These briefs are called **amicus curiae**, or "friend of the court," briefs. The parties will then appear before the nine justices for **oral arguments**. Following the oral arguments, the justices meet to discuss the case and cast their votes to make a decision. Decisions are written down in an opinion, which is then used to guide future decisions in similar cases. This is known as precedent. The **majority opinion** of the court and its legal reasoning becomes the decision in the case. In some cases, a judge who agrees with the decision of the majority but perhaps differs in the reasoning provided by the Court may choose to write a **concurring opinion**. Finally, any justice who disagrees with the decision can write a **dissenting opinion**.

Women and Minorities on the Supreme Court

The U.S. Supreme Court is an institution unlike any other in the nation. The first court was established in 1789 with six members: a chief justice and five associate justices. Today, the law states that the Court is composed of nine justices—eight associates plus the chief justice. In 2016, the death of Justice Scalia left the Court with only eight justices, as well as a significant battle within Congress over the confirmation of a new justice. Over the past 211 years, there have been 112 justices and 17 chief justices. Turnover on the Court is a slow process, as members of the Supreme Court are appointed for life (and many serve until death).[14] A historical review of the court finds that 80% of the justices have been White, male, and Protestant.[15]

The first justice of color was Thurgood Marshall in 1967. Prior to his time on the court, Marshall spent 25 years as an attorney with the NAACP Legal Defense Fund. During that time, he argued several important civil rights cases before the Supreme Court, including the educational segregation case *Brown v. Board of Education* (1954).

U.S. Supreme Court
Highest court that can hear cases. Makes decisions based on issues of law. Decisions are used to establish precedent in subsequent cases.

Writ of certiorari
A petition to the U.S. Supreme Court to hear a case.

Brief
Document that is submitted by the parties in an appellate case that outlines their legal arguments.

Amicus curiae
Describes "friend of the court" briefs that are submitted to appellate courts in support of a legal argument.

Oral arguments
Arguments presented by the parties to the court in an appellate case.

Majority opinion
Legal reasoning that is used to make a decision in a case, which becomes precedent.

Concurring opinion
An opinion provided by the court that agrees with the outcome of the majority but has different reasoning for the decision.

Dissenting opinion
A written opinion by a justice who disagrees with the majority decision.

---

* The Court also holds original jurisdiction on cases involving disputes between states.

In 2016, the U.S. Supreme Court was faced with a vacancy due to the death of Antonin Scalia. This photo displays the remaining eight justices serving on the Court.

AUDIO

Miranda's Foundation and Today's Rights

Marshall was appointed to the Court by President Johnson in 1967. During his 24 years on the court, his liberal philosophy concentrated on strong protection for the rights of individuals. It was during his tenure on the Court that several landmark decisions on the rights of offenders were handed down.[16]

The only other African American justice has been Clarence Thomas. Thomas was appointed by President George H. W. Bush in 1990 and was confirmed the following year. Unlike Marshall, Thomas is very conservative in his legal ideology. He is a strong supporter of states' rights.[17]

The presence of women on the Supreme Court is a newer development. It wasn't until 1981 that the first female justice was appointed to the Court. To date, only four women have served on the Supreme Court: Sandra Day O'Connor, Ruth Bader Ginsberg, Sandra Sotomayor, and Elena Kagan.

In 1981, President Ronald Reagan appointed Sandra Day O'Connor as the first woman to grace the Supreme Court's bench. At the time of her appointment, there were few women in high-ranking judicial positions at the state and federal level. O'Connor began her tenure on the Court as a conservative voice, and she voted with her conservative colleagues in the overwhelming majority of her decisions.[18] While she was initially appointed as a conservative voice on the Court, she was not always aligned with the political right and became the swing vote, alongside more liberal justices, in some high-profile cases before the Court. She retired in January 2006.

In 1993, President Bill Clinton appointed Ruth Bader Ginsburg to serve as the second female justice. During her tenure as a lawyer, she appeared before the Court on six separate occasions in cases involving women's rights. As a justice, Ginsberg has presented a balanced view in her decision-making—sometimes voting with her liberal colleagues and other times serving as the swing vote for the conservative voice.

Recently, Ginsberg has been joined by two additional female justices: Sonya Sotomayor, in 2009, and Elena Kagan, in 2010. Their appointments mark a shift in the judiciary of the highest court in the land. Sotomayor is the first woman of color, a Latina, to serve on the Supreme Court, and the inclusion of Kagan created a historical first, as this is the first time in history that three women have served simultaneously on the Court. Both Sotomayor and Kagan were appointed by President Obama. Sotomayor has been involved in several landmark decisions, including health care reform and immigration laws. On the Court, she has served as a liberal voice and is often viewed as a champion for the rights of the downtrodden.[19] In 2010, Elena Kagan was appointed by President Obama.[20] While some viewed her lack of experience in the judiciary as a negative, she has posited herself as one of the more influential leaders on the Court.

The State Court System

The purpose of the state criminal courts is to try cases that allege violations of state criminal law. The majority of criminal cases are heard in state courts, rather than federal courts. Indeed, given the size of some states in the United States, the caseload of one state can exceed that of the entire federal system. Like the federal courts, most state court systems are organized into four tiers based on their subject matter jurisdiction. The majority of cases involving criminal matters are heard in the trial courts (both limited- and general-jurisdiction cases). While most states divide their original jurisdiction cases into two categories (limited and general jurisdiction), some states combine all cases into a single court. In 2013, state courts across the United States heard 94.1 million cases. Figure 9.3 highlights the different types of cases that are

| Figure 9.3 | Incoming Caseload Composition in State Trial Courts |

How does jurisdiction (general, limited, and single) affect the types of cases that a court will hear?

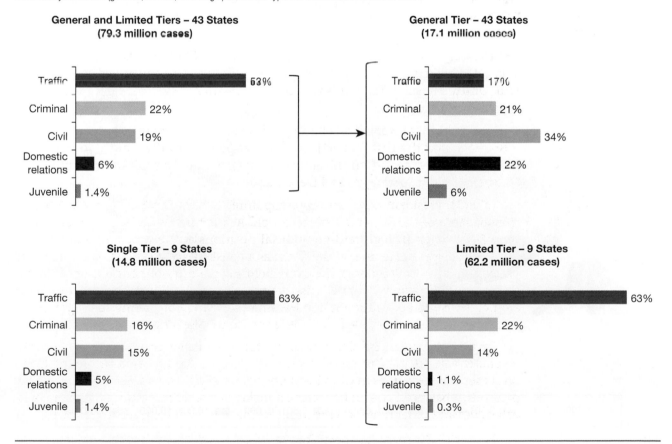

General and Limited Tiers – 43 States
(79.3 million cases)

- Traffic: 63%
- Criminal: 22%
- Civil: 19%
- Domestic relations: 6%
- Juvenile: 1.4%

General Tier – 43 States
(17.1 million cases)

- Traffic: 17%
- Criminal: 21%
- Civil: 34%
- Domestic relations: 22%
- Juvenile: 6%

Single Tier – 9 States
(14.8 million cases)

- Traffic: 63%
- Criminal: 16%
- Civil: 15%
- Domestic relations: 5%
- Juvenile: 1.4%

Limited Tier – 9 States
(62.2 million cases)

- Traffic: 63%
- Criminal: 22%
- Civil: 14%
- Domestic relations: 1.1%
- Juvenile: 0.3%

Source: http://www.courtstatistics.org/~/media/Microsites/Files/CSP/EWSC_CSP_2015.ashx

handled by state courts. The majority of these cases are heard by limited-jurisdiction courts, meaning that these offenses tend to be less serious in nature. Figure 9.4 presents data on the criminal rates for all state courts. Texas handles significantly more cases than anywhere else in the nation, with more than 3 million criminal filings in 2014. Even when you consider the population of the state, this number is disproportionately high compared with other state courts. While the rate of criminal filings in Texas exceeds 11,000 cases per 100,000, other states have a very low rate of criminal filings, such as Kansas (1,684 per 100,000) and Wisconsin (1,921 per 100,000).[21]

Judicial Selection

The selection process for state court judges varies from state to state. There are five primary ways in which state judges are selected. While most states have adopted one of these practices, some states use a combination of methods. Some states use either a partisan or nonpartisan election. A few states use an appointment system whereby either the governor of the state or the legislature appoints someone to the bench. The majority of states use a combined process called the **Missouri plan**. The Missouri plan involves three steps. First, candidates are nominated by a citizen committee. The nominees are presented to either the governor or the head of the state's judicial system, who then makes a selection. Once the appointed judge has served a year in the post, his or her name appears on a ballot as part of a retention election, which allows for the residents of the state to determine whether the individual should remain in the position. Figure 9.5 presents a map showing the different methods of judicial selection that are utilized by each of the 50 states.

Missouri plan
A three-step plan of judicial selection. Candidates are nominated by a citizen committee and selected by either the governor or the head of the state's judicial system. After a year, a retention election is held.

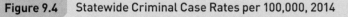

| Figure 9.4 | Statewide Criminal Case Rates per 100,000, 2014 |

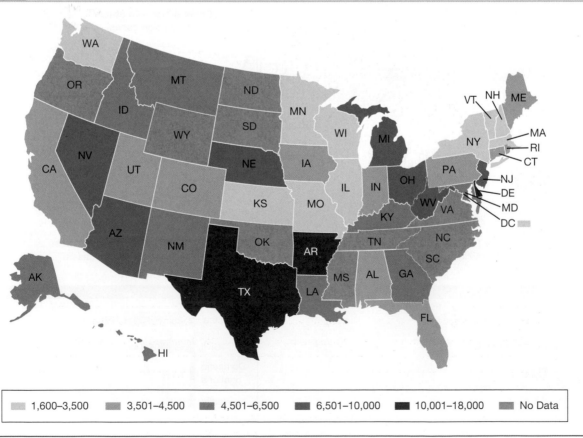

Source: Data from http://www.ncsc.org/Sitecore/Content/Microsites/PopUp/Home/CSP/CSP_Intro

State Appellate Courts

For the majority of states, the appellate level is divided into intermediate courts of appeals as well as a court of last resort, also known as the state supreme court.* In 2013, state appellate courts heard 262,230 cases nationwide. State appellate courts hear four different types of cases. **Appeals by right** are cases the appellate court must hear. The majority of cases heard in state intermediate appellate courts involve appeals-by-right cases, whereas the courts of last resort generally involve appeals-by-permission cases. **Appeals by permission** involve reviews of lower decisions that the court may choose to accept. Appellate courts will also hear cases in which the death penalty was imposed, as well as cases where they hold original jurisdiction. Criminal cases make up the majority of all cases heard in both intermediate courts of appeals and courts of last resort.[22]

COURTROOM PARTICIPANTS AND THEIR DUTIES

There are several players in a courtroom who work together to hear cases and make decisions. The courtroom workgroup is made up of the judge, the prosecutor, and the defense attorney. These three individuals are the primary members of the group.

Appeals by right
Involve cases that the appellate court must hear.

Appeals by permission
Involve reviews of lower level decisions that the court may choose to accept.

Figure 9.5	Methods of Judicial Selection in State Courts

What do you think are some of the pros and cons of having judges appointed versus being elected?

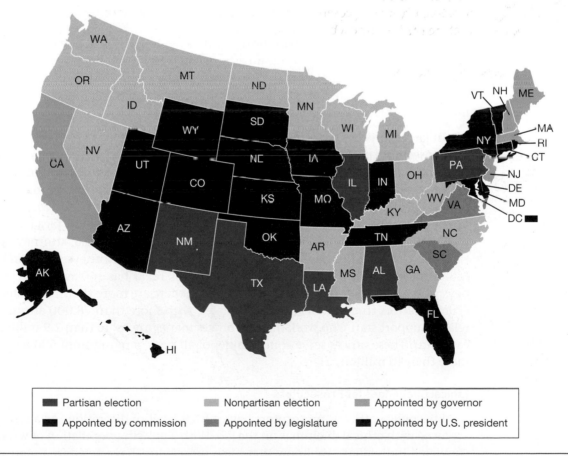

- ■ Partisan election
- ■ Appointed by commission
- ▨ Nonpartisan election
- ▨ Appointed by legislature
- ▨ Appointed by governor
- ■ Appointed by U.S. president

Source: https://ballotpedia.org/Judicial_selection_in_the_states

*Eleven states do not have an intermediate level of appeal—Nevada, the District of Columbia, West Virginia, New Hampshire, Delaware, Maine, Montana, Vermont, Rhode Island, South Dakota, and Wyoming. These states direct all appellate cases to the state supreme court.

Ancillary Members

In addition, there are three ancillary members: the bailiff, the clerk of the court, and the court reporter. The bailiff provides security for the courtroom, escorts the defendant in and out of the courtroom if he or she is in custody, and provides assistance to members of the jury. The clerk of the court manages all of the paperwork for the courtroom and works closely with the judge. The court reporter prepares the transcript of the trial and other official hearings.

Judges

The judge presides over the courtroom. The judge is the primary decision-maker throughout the process. She or he listens to the information presented by the prosecutor and defense counsel and makes decisions by applying the law. For example, the judge decides whether probable cause exists in a case, determines bail for the accused, rules on pretrial motions, and ensures that the rights of the defendant are upheld. During a trial, the judge officiates over the proceedings and rules on any objections raised by the prosecutor or defense. When a jury is involved, the judge provides instructions to the jury and answers questions about the law. In the absence of a jury, the judge listens to the evidence presented and makes a determination of guilty or not guilty. If a defendant is found guilty, the judge hands down a sentence.

Prosecutors

The prosecutor is tasked with bringing the case to the court. She or he represents the state in criminal cases. Unlike an attorney in a civil case, who represents an individual, a prosecutor represents the larger community. In most jurisdictions, the lead prosecutor is an elected official. As a result, he or she has to consider the needs of many individuals when determining how to proceed in a case.

In larger jurisdictions, the lead prosecutor serves in a supervisory role while deputy prosecutors carry out the daily tasks of the office. These tasks include conducting trials and hearings, negotiating plea bargains with defendants, and interviewing witnesses and victims. Prosecutors have a high degree of discretion in many of their duties. They determine whether charges will be filed against someone who is arrested by the police. They also decide whether an offender will be offered a plea bargain and the details of this negotiation. At the federal level, there are 93 U.S. attorneys, one for each office. Each office then employs several assistant U.S. attorneys. For example, the U.S. Attorney's Office for the Southern District of Texas has 160 assistant U.S. attorneys working in their office.[23] At the state level, there are more than 2,300 state prosecutors' offices throughout the United States, with more than 78,000 attorneys and related support staff who work in these offices managing more than 2.9 million cases each year. These offices serve communities of all sizes, ranging from 500 residents to more than 10 million.[24]

Ethical Challenges for Prosecutors

Like police officers, prosecutors have a high level of discretion. As a result, they are faced with ethical dilemmas on the job. With a growing population of wrongfully convicted individuals, we know that some prosecutors have acted in a manner that blurs the line of what is right and wrong in their pursuit of justice.

The American Bar Association Model Rules of Professional Conduct provides guidance for prosecutors. They state that prosecutors should (a) only file cases in which probable cause exists; (b) make a reasonable effort to ensure that the accused has been

CAREERS IN CRIMINAL JUSTICE

So You Want to Be a Prosecutor?

In order to work as a prosecutor, you have to have a law degree and pass the bar for the state where you want to work. But beyond the minimum qualifications, it takes a certain personality to work in this field. As a prosecutor, you are interacting with many different types of people, from defense attorneys to judges, and victims to offenders. As a prosecutor, you will also interact with the public when you are in trial on a case. As a prosecutor, you will spend a lot of time in courtrooms, which is generally not true for those who practice other types of law. But in addition to your legal skills and your ability to argue a case, prosecutors must be able to be fair and show compassion. As a prosecutor, you will hold a great deal of power in determining when to file charges or when to offer a plea bargain in a case. As a result, you need to have strong ethics—a clear sense of right and wrong.

If you are interested in becoming a prosecutor, you should spend a fair amount of time observing a courtroom to see the type of work that a prosecutor does on a daily basis. You may also want to seek out internship opportunities with your local prosecutor's office, either as an undergraduate student or once you are enrolled in law school. Internships can give you valuable experience to help you decide whether this is the type of career for you.

It is important to note that the job of a prosecutor is a busy one, and as a public servant, most of these positions have lower salaries than positions in corporate and private law firms. However, most individuals who work in these fields find satisfaction in knowing that they have helped achieve justice for victims.

advised of his or her right to an attorney; (c) not pressure an unrepresented defendant to waive his or her pretrial rights; (d) disclose evidence in a timely manner to the defense, particularly information that might show that the defendant is not guilty of the crime or information that mitigates the defendant's role in the offense; (e) exercise care when communicating details about the case to the public, the media, or other criminal justice personnel; and (f) disclose any new evidence in a case that might vindicate a convicted offender and assist the authorities in remedying the issue.[25] The case of *Brady v. Maryland* (1963) requires that prosecutors must disclose any exculpatory evidence to the defense.[26] **Exculpatory evidence** is evidence that is favorable to the defense and may exonerate a defendant from any criminal wrongdoing.

When a prosecutor engages in conduct that violates these ethical codes, the results can be catastrophic for the lives of individuals and the community at large. Consider the case of Ron Williamson, whose story is told by popular author John Grisham in his book *An Innocent Man*. Williamson was convicted of the murder of Debra Carter in 1988 and was sentenced to death by the state of Oklahoma. After spending 11 years in prison and even coming within five days of being executed, Williamson was released with his codefendant Dennis Fritz in 1999. While Williamson was exonerated by DNA evidence that showed that he did not commit the crime, the truth was also shrouded by prosecutorial misconduct, as the district attorney failed to turn over evidence that could have altered the outcome of the trial. In particular, the prosecutor failed to provide the defense a videotaped statement by Williamson after he had completed a polygraph examination.

In addition to failing to turn over exculpatory evidence, **prosecutorial misconduct** can include behaviors such as the use of perjured testimony, failing to disclose preferential treatment given to a jailhouse informant, or misstating the law to the jury, which then impacts their decision-making process.[27] The case of Williamson is just one example where prosecutorial misconduct has had an effect on the outcome of a case. According to the Innocence Project, prosecutorial misconduct was a factor in 36% to 42% of cases in which an offender was ultimately exonerated by DNA.[28]

CAREER VIDEO
Legal

Exculpatory evidence
Evidence that is favorable to the defense and may exonerate a defendant from any criminal wrongdoing.

Prosecutorial misconduct
Can include behaviors such as the use of perjured testimony, failure to turn over exculpatory evidence, failing to disclose preferential treatment to a jailhouse informant, or misstating the law to the jury, which then impacts their decision-making process.

While most cases of prosecutorial misconduct go unrecognized or unpunished, the state of Texas recently brought charges against a local prosecutor for concealing evidence. In November 2013, Ken Anderson, who was once named prosecutor of the year by the Texas State Bar Association, was convicted of evidence tampering in the case of Michael Morton. Morton was convicted in 1986 for the murder of his wife. After serving nearly 25 years in prison, Morton was exonerated by DNA. For his crimes, Anderson was sentenced to 10 days in jail, ordered to complete 500 hours of community service, and was disbarred.[29] You'll hear more about this case in Current Controversy 9.1 at the end of this chapter.

Dennis Fritz and Ron Williamson listen as Judge Tom Landrith dismisses murder charges against them. After serving 12 years in prison, DNA proved that the two did not commit the crime. What role did prosecutorial misconduct play in this case?

Defense Attorneys

While the prosecutor represents the state in a criminal case, the defense attorney represents those who have been accused of a crime. The 6th Amendment of the Constitution states that persons who have been accused of a crime have the right to an attorney to assist in their defense. If a defendant cannot afford an attorney, the government will provide one to him or her. This right was established as a result of the U.S. Supreme Court case *Gideon v. Wainwright* (1963).[30] In order to satisfy this burden, most jurisdictions have established an office of the public defender. There are also cases in which the court will appoint private counsel to represent a defendant. This occurs in those districts and states where an office of the public defender has not been established. Private appointed counsel or an alternative defender is also used in cases where a codefendant is already represented by the public defender's office. Due to a conflict of interest, this office cannot represent the defendant and the codefendant. In some jurisdictions, there is a separate office that is funded to support these cases. In others, private counsel is appointed by the judge to provide the defendant with an attorney at the expense of the local or state government. In cases where the defendants are deemed to have adequate resources to afford an attorney, they can hire a private attorney to defend their case in court. In some cases, the defendant may decide to act as her or his own attorney or to proceed through the case without the assistance of counsel.

The work of a defense attorney centers on protecting the rights of the accused, most notably their 4th, 5th, and 6th Amendment rights. The 4th Amendment protects against unreasonable searches and seizures. Defense attorneys may petition the court to have evidence against their client excluded if they believe that it was obtained illegally. The 5th Amendment protects individuals against self-incrimination, as well as protecting them against double jeopardy. This means that people cannot be compelled to testify against themselves, nor can they be tried for the same crime twice. The 6th Amendment includes several

Though the media often portrays lawyers as unscrupulous individuals, like Saul Goodman from *Breaking Bad*, most public defenders work very hard to represent their indigent clients. What are some other ways the media represents (or misrepresents) lawyers?

SPOTLIGHT

The 50th Anniversary of *Gideon v. Wainwright*

The year 2013 marked the 50th anniversary of the U.S. Supreme Court decision in *Gideon v. Wainwright* and the declaration that counsel must be provided for all indigent defendants. The mission of *Gideon* was a significant one, as it set forth to provide equal access for all to legal assistance. However, providing such services continues to challenge jurisdictions across the United States in several ways.

The first challenge of *Gideon* is ensuring that those accused of a crime have access to qualified and competent counsel. The first public defender's office was established in 1914 in Los Angeles, California. Today, this office has more than 700 licensed attorneys as well as hundreds of support staff and an annual budget of $186 million.[a] Nationwide, estimates indicate there are more than 15,000 court-appointed attorneys.[b] However, the demand for assistance exceeds their availability. Clients can spend months in jail while they wait for an attorney to be appointed in their case. This is a direct result of a system that is overstretched in terms of available resources.

The American Bar Association recommendation indicates that the caseloads for public defenders should not exceed 150 felony cases annually. However, the reality in many jurisdictions is that public defenders can represent more than 300 clients each year.[c] Research on the workloads of public defenders in Missouri indicates that attorneys are able to spend only 8.7 hours on a typical high-level felony case, 4.4 hours on a lower level felony, and 2.3 hours on a misdemeanor case. This is a sharp departure from what attorneys feel they should expect to spend on such cases.[d]

The second challenge of *Gideon* is the financial cost to provide public defense systems. In 2012, state governments spent $2.3 billion nationwide on indigent-defense systems.[e] While many of these offices are supported as part of the state budget, 18 states leave it to the local counties to fund indigent defense.[f] As a result, there can be significant regional disparities. Disparities in funding also exist between the district attorney and public defender offices. Consider Orange County, California, which has well-funded public and alternative defender systems. In 2014, these offices received $78 million. In comparison, the O.C. District Attorney's Office received $123 million to prosecute cases. Given that 80% of all defendants nationwide are represented by appointed counsel, these discrepancies in funding can limit the abilities of public defenders.[g]

While *Gideon* held that counsel must be provided to indigent defendants, the 21st-century realities of the criminal justice system question its implementation. The Court held in *Strickland v. Washington* (1984) that in order to prove ineffective assistance of counsel, the defendant must show not only that his or her attorney failed to perform in a reasonable manner but that these deficiencies significantly impacted the outcome of the case. While some cases that are successful under *Strickland* highlight examples where attorneys were intoxicated or asleep, many others highlight what has become the reality for many jurisdictions: systems that are significantly underfunded to meet the demands and attorneys who are so overwhelmed that their ability to provide an adequate defense is challenged. In 2013, the Florida Supreme Court held that public defenders had the right to refuse to accept new assignments due to overburdened caseloads, a decision which may mark a shift in how resources for indigent-defender systems are prioritized within the criminal justice system.[h]

CRITICAL THINKING QUESTIONS

1. Why is the holding in *Gideon v. Wainwright* important?

2. What are the challenges for upholding the decision of *Gideon* in the 21st century?

due process protections for the accused, such as the right to an attorney, the right to a speedy trial, the right to confront witnesses against her or him, and the right to have one's case heard before a jury of one's peers. As a case proceeds, the defense attorney is focused on preparing for a trial and managing any pretrial motions to the court.

She or he represents the client in any court hearings and negotiates with the prosecutor on potential plea bargain opportunities. In those instances where a case proceeds to trial, the defense attorney cross-examines prosecution witnesses and calls his or her own witnesses to testify on behalf of the defendant. The defense attorney also conducts investigations to challenge the evidence presented by the prosecutor or to identify **mitigating evidence** for her or his case. Mitigating evidence is any evidence that serves to either explain the defendant's involvement in the crime or reduce his or her potential sentence.

Juries

The jury is a group of citizens who are responsible for determining whether someone is guilty of an offense. Juries are used in both criminal and civil cases. There are two different types of juries that are used as part of the criminal process: grand juries and trial juries.

Grand Juries

A **grand jury** is composed of a group of citizens who are called to serve for a specific period of time. In the federal system, grand juries serve for a period of one year. A prosecutor presents his or her case to the grand jury, which then reviews the evidence to determine whether an indictment should be issued. The accused and her or his attorney do not have a right to appear, present witnesses, or cross-examine witnesses in a grand jury proceeding. The **indictment** is the official declaration that there is probable cause to charge the accused with a crime.

Trial Juries

However, when most people think of serving on a jury, they are referring to a trial jury. A **trial jury** is selected through a process of questioning by the prosecutor and the defense attorney, known as **voir dire**. In the federal system, there are 12 people selected to serve on a criminal jury. Alternate jurors may also be selected to serve in case someone falls ill or is unable to complete his or her jury service. Jurors in federal court are paid $40 a day, though the rate for state and local jurisdictions can be as little as $5. While employers are not required to continue to pay regular salary while one serves on a jury, the Jury Act prohibits them from firing someone for missing work as a result of jury duty.[31] To serve on a jury, one must be a U.S. citizen 18 years or older, be proficient in the English language, reside in the jurisdiction that calls one for service, and have never been convicted of a felony.[32]

During the voir dire process, the prosecutor and the defense question potential jurors to determine who should be selected to serve. Potential jurors can be excused for three general reasons. First, potential jurors can request that they be excused from service. Here, individuals may suggest that serving on a jury would present a hardship on either their work or their family life. In these cases, it is up to the judge to determine whether a juror will be excused. Second, jurors can be excused for cause. A **challenge for cause** is granted in cases where the court believes that a potential juror may be unfair or biased in her or his decision-making. Finally, jurors can also be

Mitigating evidence
Any evidence that serves to either explain the defendant's involvement in the crime or reduce her or his potential sentence.

Grand jury
Describes a group of citizens who review the evidence presented by a prosecutor to determine whether an indictment should be issued.

Indictment
An official declaration that there is probable cause to charge the accused with a crime.

Trial jury
A group of citizens who are charged with listening to the evidence that is presented by the attorneys and making a judgment of whether someone is guilty or liable.

Voir dire
The process of questioning by the prosecutor and the defense attorney that is used to select a trial jury.

Challenge for cause
Allows attorneys to exclude a potential juror in cases where the court believes that the individual may be unfair or biased in her or his decision-making.

The right to trial by a jury of one's peers is guaranteed in the Constitution, yet there are many controversies around jury service. Should jurors be paid more? Should attorneys have the ability to select a jury based on race or ethnicity?

AROUND THE WORLD

Juries in a Global Context

The use of juries to render an impartial verdict in a criminal case is not a new phenomenon, nor is it limited to the American justice system. The roots of the modern jury system come from medieval England. In particular, it was under the reign of Henry II that the use of juries began to develop. Today, these influences can be found not only throughout the U.S. system but in many other modern democratic countries as well.

Under King Henry II's rule, the courts of assizes would travel to local regions to hear cases involving criminal matters four times a year. The judge would summon 12 "free and lawful men" to determine whether the accused was guilty or innocent of the crime. These early juries were self-informing, which meant that they were not neutral participants in the process and were expected to come to the court with personal knowledge about the crime. Over time, this feature shifted to one where jurors were expected to be neutral in their opinions and would base their decisions only on the information presented within the court proceedings.[a]

Today, more than 40 countries use citizen juries as part of their criminal court process.[b] Generally speaking, these countries use juries for only the determination of guilt while the declaration of a sentence is left to the judge. The major exception to this rule is the United States in death penalty cases. In 2002, the U.S. Supreme Court decision in *Ring v. Arizona* held that a defendant has the right to have a jury, rather than a judge, decide his or her fate when it comes to the death penalty. While countries such as Australia and New Zealand rely on citizen juries, other countries, such as Germany and France, use a combination of lay and professional panels to make decisions. Some countries, such as Thailand and Croatia, require particular areas of topical expertise from their jury members in order to serve.[c]

What about those jurisdictions that do not use a jury to make decisions? Consider the case of South Africa, which abolished the use of juries in 1969. During the early 20th century, laws were adopted that allowed defendants to choose to have their case decided by a judge rather than a jury. Over time, the law was amended, which further limited their use. Ultimately, South Africa ended its use of the citizen jury, partly in response to concerns about racial prejudice. Between 1948 and 1991, the country was divided under a system of apartheid whereby Whites and non-Whites lived separately, maintained separate facilities, and had limited contact with each other.[d] In many ways, South African apartheid mirrored Jim Crow laws in the United States. While apartheid ended near the close of the 20th century, the use of juries has not reemerged. Instead, cases, such as that of Oscar Pistorius (which you learned about earlier in this text) are decided by a judge. However, the judge is not the only decision-maker in the case. In South Africa, judges are joined by assessors, who offer expert advice to the judge and provide assistance with the facts of the case.[e]

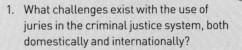

CRITICAL THINKING QUESTIONS

1. What challenges exist with the use of juries in the criminal justice system, both domestically and internationally?

2. How might international examples of juries improve the American jury system?

Some scholars have questioned whether the jury experience should remain a part of the criminal justice system. On one hand, a jury of one's peers is fundamental to the American justice system and many others. Yet several issues have challenged the modern jury experience. For example, the rise of popular-culture television shows has created what scholars call the CSI effect whereby jurors believe that advanced technology, such as DNA analysis, should be required in all cases. As a result, jurors may be faced with making a decision in a case but lack the training or background to adequately understand the evidence as it is presented.[f]

excused by the choice of the prosecutor or the defense. Each side has a limited number of **peremptory challenges** whereby an attorney can reject a juror without having to give a specific reason. It is important to note that the U.S. Supreme Court held in *Batson v. Kentucky* that peremptory challenges cannot be used against a potential juror solely on the basis of his or her race or ethnicity.[33] Alas, some have questioned whether the use of peremptory challenges on the basis of race has continued into the 21st century.

In order to find someone guilty in federal court, all 12 jurors must agree on the **verdict**, or decision. If a jury is unable to come to a unanimous decision, it results in a **hung jury**. In these cases, it is up to the prosecutor to determine whether she or he will refile charges against the defendant or let him or her go free. While most states also require a unanimous jury decision, Oregon and Louisiana allow for guilty verdicts when 10 of the 12 jurors vote to convict. While such a practice has been challenged in front of the Supreme Court in the past, the Court declined to hear a case on this issue in 2014.[34]

STAGES OF A CRIMINAL COURT CASE

In Chapter 1, you learned about how a case moves through the criminal justice system. During the court process, there are several stages that a case moves through.

Pretrial

During an **initial appearance**, the defendant is officially notified by the court of the charges that are pending against her or him. It is during this stage that the court will appoint an attorney for an indigent defendant. Earlier in this chapter, you learned about the grand jury proceeding. The **preliminary hearing** is another option for the court to establish whether probable cause exists for the case to move forward. In some cases, the defense will waive their right to a preliminary hearing. If the defendant is in custody, he or she may have a bail hearing to determine whether the accused is eligible for bail.

Bail is a promise to return for future court appearances in exchange for one's release during the pretrial stage. During the bail hearing, the court hears arguments about whether someone is a risk if released. When someone is released on bail, he or she has provided the court with a financial promise to appear. In some cases, defendants will use a bail bondsperson to help secure their bond. In this case, the defendant pays a fee to the bail bondsperson along with some form of collateral (such as the deed to a home or a car) in exchange for the bondsperson putting up the remaining amount of the bail. In these cases, if a defendant fails to appear, the bail bondsperson will seize the asset to pay the debt.

In some cases, a defendant is held in custody until trial. This is called preventative detention. **Preventative detention** is used in cases where the court believes that the person may be a danger to the community or would flee the jurisdiction if she or he were allowed out of jail during the pretrial stage. In other cases, defendants may be **released on their own recognizance**. This type of release means that the defendant promises to appear for all future court dates but does not have to provide the court with any sort of financial guarantee.

Arraignment

The arraignment is the formal reading of the charges. It is during the arraignment that the defendant enters a plea. In most cases, the defendant will enter a plea of either guilty or not guilty. In some cases, the court may allow the defendant to enter

Peremptory challenge
Allows attorneys to reject a juror without having to give a specific reason.

Verdict
A decision in a case.

Hung jury
Occurs when a jury is unable to make a unanimous decision.

Initial appearance
First appearance by a defendant where she or he is officially notified by the court of the charges that are pending against her or him. If the defendant is indigent, it is during this stage that an attorney is appointed for her or him.

Preliminary hearing
One option for the court to establish whether probable cause exists for the case to move forward.

Bail
A promise to return for future court appearances in exchange for one's release during the pretrial stage.

Preventative detention
Used in cases where the court believes that the person may be a danger to the community or would flee the jurisdiction if she or he were allowed out of jail during the pretrial stage.

Released on their own recognizance
Type of release where the defendant promises to appear for all future court dates but does not have to provide the court with any sort of financial guarantee.

Figure 9.6 Types of Pleas Entered at the Arraignment

The arraignment is an important step in the court process and determines whether a case will move on to sentencing or if a trial will be carried out.

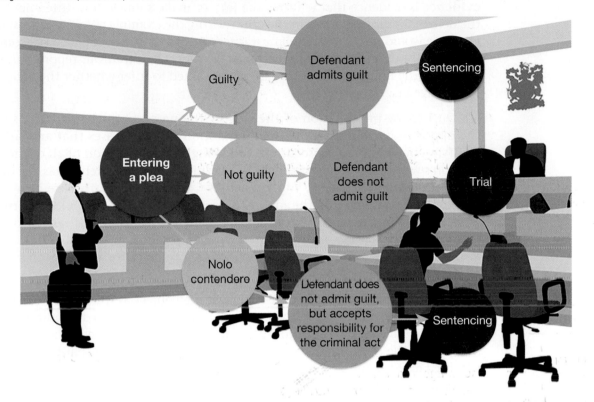

a plea of **nolo contendere**. A nolo contendere plea is a no-contest plea. In this case, the defendant is not admitting guilt but accepts responsibility for the criminal act. Nolo contendere pleas mean that the defendant is not required to address his or her crimes (Figure 9.6). **Allocution** occurs when a defendant appears before the court and publicly admits involvement in the crime. This can be an important variable in any subsequent civil actions that may be filed following the conclusion of the criminal case.

At any point during the process, the defendant can plead guilty to the charges and waive her or his right to a trial. By pleading guilty, the defendant admits wrongdoing in the case. The prosecutor may also offer a plea bargain to the defendant. A **plea bargain** is a reduction in charges (and punishment) in exchange for a guilty plea. Plea bargains are an essential part of the criminal justice system because they provide a way to resolve cases in an efficient manner. You'll learn more about the use of plea bargains in Current Controversy 9.2 at the end of this chapter.

Trial

Only a small percentage of cases go to trial. A trial is when a prosecutor presents her or his case to either a judge or a jury. The burden of proof during a criminal trial falls on the prosecutor to prove that the defendant committed the crime in question. The trial has eight stages. During the first stage, both the prosecution and defense attorney present their **opening statements** to the court. During the opening statement, each side presents their core arguments to the judge and jury. After the opening statements, the prosecution begins by calling witnesses to provide testimony about what they believe happened during the offense. A witness is someone who can provide information about the case. He or she will introduce evidence to support his or her position. There are two different types of evidence.

SAGE JOURNAL ARTICLE
Is Plea Bargaining a Rational Choice?

Nolo contendere
A no-contest plea in which the defendant does not admit guilt but accepts responsibility.

Allocution
Occurs when a defendant appears before the court and publicly admits his or her involvement in a crime.

Plea bargain
A reduction in charges (and punishment) in exchange for a guilty plea.

Opening statement
The first stage of the trial, when each side presents their core arguments to the judge and jury.

Direct evidence refers to evidence that is directly linked to the defendant's involvement in the crime. For example, a witness who says that she or he saw the offender enter the home illegally is providing direct evidence. In contrast, **circumstantial evidence** is evidence that requires the jury to make some sort of inference about the defendant's involvement in the crime. Using the example above, circumstantial evidence would be if the defendant was seen with a new piece of jewelry. Combine this with testimony that the jewelry matches a necklace that was reported missing following the home invasion, and the jury is asked to infer whether the defendant could have taken the jewelry.

During the presentation of the case by the prosecutor, the defense is given the opportunity to cross-examine, or question, the witnesses that are called to testify on behalf of the prosecution. Following the presentation of all of the prosecution's witnesses, they rest their case. At this point, the defense has the opportunity to put on their case. You learned in Chapter 2 about the use of insanity as a defense strategy. It is the job of the defense counsel to provide alternative explanations for the theories presented by the prosecution. Just as the defense can question any witnesses presented by the prosecution, the district attorney also is provided with the opportunity to cross-examine any witnesses that testify on behalf of the accused.

In some cases, the prosecution or defense may object to the information that is presented by the other side. In these cases, it is up to the judge to determine whether the jury should consider this information under the law. For example, a witness may indicate on the stand that she or he was told by someone else that the defendant admitted to the home invasion. This is an example of hearsay. In most cases, hearsay evidence is not admissible, though there are some exceptions to this rule.

Once each side presents their case, they both have the opportunity to make a summary statement to the court. This is called a **closing argument**. It is then up to the jury to make their decision. Forty-eight states use standardized **jury instructions** that provide guidance to the members of the jury about how to apply the law to the facts that were presented during the trial. In order to find a defendant guilty, they must agree that the facts of the case prove that the defendant committed the crime beyond a reasonable doubt. If the jury believes that there is reasonable doubt, then the defendant is found not guilty. Sometimes, the jury may not be able to agree on a decision. This is called a hung jury. In some cases, the jury may decide not to convict a defendant even though the evidence would support a guilty verdict. This is called jury nullification. **Jury nullification** occurs if the jury believes that the defendant should not have been charged with a crime or if they disagree with the law as it is written.

CONCLUSION

Our criminal courts are tasked with perhaps one of the most important functions of our criminal justice system: to weigh the evidence of a case and determine whether an offender is guilty of violating the law. The courts provide an important filter between those who arrest alleged violators and those who carry out the punishments for these acts. Despite jurisdictional differences, most criminal cases are processed in a similar manner throughout a complex system involving a number of different professionals, all of whom are tasked, in one way or another, with managing the justice process. Indeed, many of the decisions of our courts have helped to shape how the criminal justice system operates on a daily basis.

Direct evidence
Refers to evidence that is directly linked to the defendant's involvement in the crime.

Circumstantial evidence
Evidence that requires the jury to make some sort of inference about the defendant's involvement in the crime.

Closing argument
Stage of a case in which each side makes a final summary statement to the court once all the evidence has been presented.

Jury instructions
Provide guidance to the members of the jury about how to apply the law to the facts that were presented during the trial.

Jury nullification
Occurs when the jury may decide not to convict a defendant even though the evidence would support a guilty verdict.

Should Physical Evidence Be Required in Serious Criminal Cases?

—Jay Wachtel—

CURRENT
CONTROVERSY
VIDEO
Where Do You Stand?
Cast Your Vote!

INTRODUCTION

It seems that not a week goes by without news of yet another wrongfully convicted person's release from prison. In a criminal justice system that's supposedly the envy of the world, how can such things happen? Experts who have studied the problem attribute it to various factors, including false and coerced confessions, mistaken eyewitness testimony, lying by witnesses and informers, junk science, sloppy investigation, and, more generally, the dilemma faced by those accused who do not have the funds to marshal an adequate defense.[35]

Ninety percent or more of criminal cases are disposed of through plea bargains. But many of the safeguards that were designed to protect the innocent take effect only at trial. Hearsay cannot be used as evidence unless it fits into an approved category,[36] expert testimony must be based on "sufficient facts or data" and produced by "reliable principles and methods,"[37] and so on. Trials also bring into play the adjudicative system's ultimate safeguard: that an accused cannot be convicted unless a judge rules (in trials before the bench) or a jury unanimously finds that guilt was proven beyond a reasonable doubt.

Of course, absolute certainty is often beyond reach. Evidence varies in quantity and quality and can point in different directions. Jurors are instructed to apply "common sense and experience" to resolve conflicts in testimony.[38] But life experiences

CSI technicians are used to collect and preserve physical evidence at crimes. Forensic investigation is a growing field in criminal justice. Is this a field you might be interested in?

vary, and disagreements about what is "common sense" are, well, common. Suffice it to say that as miscarriages of justice continue to accumulate, one's faith in the system's ability to arrive at the truth—*to do justice*—suffers.

Even if errors can't be wholly prevented, how can the likelihood of an unjust verdict be minimized? One approach is to require objective proof of guilt. And there is nothing supposedly more "objective" than physical evidence.

PRO

Physical Evidence Should Be Required to Convict a Defendant of a Crime

On August 13, 1986, Michael Morton left for work. Later that day, a neighbor stopped by and discovered the body of Morton's wife. She had been beaten to death. Morton was charged with her murder. Evidence at trial focused on the couple's quarrels and Michael Morton's dissatisfaction with his sex life. Morton was convicted and drew a life sentence. He served 25 years before DNA positively linked his wife's murder—and a similar killing committed two years later—to another man.[39]

Morton's conviction rested on circumstantial evidence. Actually, there *was* physical evidence, a bloody bandanna found near the crime scene, but its presence was ignored by authorities. A quarter century later, DNA from the bandanna identified the real killer. (He was tried and convicted in 2013.[40]) Morton's prosecutor ultimately gave up his law license and spent 10 days in jail for withholding other evidence that would have cast doubt about Morton's guilt from the very start.[41]

On September 28, 1990, a 16-year-old girl was attacked by a masked man in a Dallas motel room. She identified her assailant as Michael Phillips, a maintenance worker at the motel, and later picked him out from a photo lineup. Phillips protested his innocence. But he had an old burglary on his record, so his public defender suggested he plead guilty to avoid a life sentence. That's what Phillips did. He served his full term—12 years—and had to register as a sex offender.[42]

Five years after his release, the Dallas D.A.'s office tested all unprocessed rape kits, including the one in Phillips's case. It turned out that DNA from the kit excluded Phillips but matched a motel resident who physically resembled him. (That man could not be prosecuted because the statute of limitations had lapsed.) Phillips was exonerated and, under Texas law, awarded financial restitution for life. "Hang on to your faith," he told reporters. "The Father works in his own time, and like the good song says: He may not come when you want to, but He's always on time."[43]

Rare events such as home invasions can lead fact finders astray. Morton was at work when his wife's body was discovered. His only possible defense—that she had been murdered by an intruder—seemed implausible to jurors, who, no doubt, dutifully applied their "common sense and experience" but reached the wrong conclusion. Had physical evidence been required, authorities would have probably paid more attention to the bandanna and perhaps even caught the real killer before he struck again.

Phillips was done in by careless detectives and eyewitness misidentification. Lacking the means to hire investigators, he gave up and, like others have done in his shoes, pled guilty. Had authorities tested the rape kit using techniques then available, they might have thought to look for another suspect, and a bit of sleuthing would have led them to the perpetrator. But they didn't, and a man needlessly lost more than a decade of his life while the real rapist roamed free.

 Physical Evidence Should Not Be Required to Convict

Shoddy policing and overzealous prosecution were the culprits in the wrongful convictions of Morton and Phillips. What these examples teach is that authorities must use great care when targeting suspects and not simply accept the quickest or most convenient solution. What they *don't* teach is that physical evidence is always essential. Physical clues are often absent or lacking, and insisting that it's either that or nothing would be a public policy disaster—literally, an invitation to break the law. Consider these examples (the first two are composites, and the third is an actual case):

- Witnesses record the license plate of a vehicle used in a drive-by shooting. Hours later, police find the car and detain its sole occupant. He denies involvement. Two witnesses identify him as the gunman from a photo lineup. No gun or other physical evidence is recovered.

- A woman pedestrian fights off an attacker. Police locate him nearby, and the witness identifies him as her assailant. But he denies everything, and there is no DNA.

- As happened in New York City, a man is purposely pushed into the path of an oncoming subway train. He is instantly killed. A detective connects the blurry video image of a possible perpetrator with a suspect who allegedly shoved someone on the street in an earlier incident. Police arrest the man for both crimes.[44]

If defendants must be physically linked to a crime, police might as well ignore all episodes such as these, where tangible proof of guilt is lacking.

Actually, our obsession with "scientific" evidence has already created perverse incentives to stretch the truth. That, indeed, is how so-called "junk science" came to be. Consider, for example, the case of

Cameron Todd Willingham. Forensic scientists now concede that Willingham was wrongfully executed for setting a house fire that killed his three children. In fact, the fire was accidental, and Willingham, who protested all the way to the end, was really innocent.[45] Years later, scientists thoroughly debunked the testimony of a fire marshal who misused burn patterns to incorrectly conclude that accelerants had been used, meaning that the fire was deliberately set. In its landmark 2009 report, the National Academy of Sciences contested the validity of burn patterns and a host of other commonly accepted techniques, including the analysis of bite marks, bloodstain patterns, shoeprints, and tire tracks.[46]

Unreliable and improperly used forensic science has caused incalculable harm to innocent persons.[47] Of course, physical evidence *is* important. Sometimes it's critical. But *reliable* physical evidence that ties in a suspect is not always available. To insist that only physical evidence will do is a terrible idea that could only tarnish law enforcement and frustrate justice.

DISCUSSION QUESTIONS

1. Why does the public believe that physical evidence is required in order to convict someone? Where does this belief come from?

2. What are the risks of convicting someone without physical evidence that directly ties her or him to the crime?

3. Identify a case of wrongful conviction. How was the evidence used to convict this individual? What errors existed in this case?

CURRENT CONTROVERSY 9.2

PRO CON

CURRENT CONTROVERSY VIDEO
Where Do You Stand? Cast Your Vote!

Should We Limit the Use of Plea Bargains?

—G. Max Dery—

INTRODUCTION

Plea bargaining is controversial and can provoke intense emotion from competing interests.[48] Deciding whether this hotly debated process is good or bad for our criminal justice system requires an understanding of what plea bargaining is in the first place. Plea bargaining involves negotiation between the prosecution and the defense (and sometimes the trial judge) to reach an agreement about a case's outcome without going through a trial.[49] In the bargaining process, officials offer the defendant incentives, such as a chance to plead to a lesser offense or to serve a shortened sentence, to encourage a plea of guilty or nolo contendere ("no contest").[50]

Courts recognize two fundamental kinds of plea bargaining: (1) *charge bargaining* and (2) *sentence bargaining*.[51] Charge bargaining can involve negotiations about reducing the severity of the crime charged.[52] For example, a prosecutor might offer to reduce a kidnapping charge to the typically less serious crime of false imprisonment. Charge bargaining can also deal with an offer to reduce the number of charges, or *counts*, a defendant is facing.[53] For instance, if a defendant is charged with Count 1: Drug Sales, and Count 2: Possession for Sale of Drugs, a prosecutor will commonly offer to drop Count 2 if the defendant will agree to plead guilty to Count 1.

Sentence bargaining involves the prosecution making a concession dealing directly with the amount of time the defendant will serve in jail or prison. In sentence bargaining, the prosecutor will agree to recommend a shorter sentence or to not argue for a longer or maximum sentence.[54]

In debating whether plea bargaining should be abolished or limited, you should consider five key questions.

The first question is this: Does plea bargaining prevent jury trials and undermine the adversarial process of our courts system? Plea bargains short-circuit the truth-finding process. Those who find plea bargaining desirable or even inevitable have forgotten the crucial importance of guaranteeing each person the chance to present his or her case in open court to a trial jury. The 6th Amendment to the U.S. Constitution guarantees that "in all criminal prosecutions, the accused shall enjoy the right to a speedy and public trial, by an impartial *jury*."[55] To guard against "oppression and tyranny,"[56] the Supreme Court has ruled that "only the jury can strip a man of his liberty or his life."[57] Plea bargains trade away the open and fair jury trial and therefore undermine the adversarial process itself. Instead of acting as zealous advocates for their clients' interests, the prosecutor and defense attorney are reduced to little more than a seller and a buyer arguing over the "worth" in prison time of a case.

The second question is this: Do plea bargains encourage prosecutors to overcharge defendants? A defendant who negotiates a plea often does so under circumstances of enormous pressure. The process of reaching a bargain, in which each side moves from his or her original position toward the middle, encourages prosecutors to start by overcharging defendants with more crimes than the case truly merits.[58] So a case might, from its very beginning, be distorted by the incentives created by the plea-bargaining process. When defendants are facing a long list of charges, they might feel compelled to plead guilty to one crime in order to avoid a long prison term.

The third question is this: Do plea bargains force innocent defendants into pleading guilty and allow guilty defendants to receive lenient sentences? Anyone, especially if overcharged by the prosecutor, might feel that he or she cannot win, regardless of the actual merits of the case. In order to avoid the "massive risk" of a jury trial, an innocent defendant might be compelled to plead guilty.[59] Not only can plea bargaining unfairly punish the innocent; it also can fail to adequately punish the guilty.[60] A guilty defendant, having little to lose in forcing the government into risking an acquittal or a hung jury at a costly trial, can bargain for a sentence "discount."

The fourth question is this: Do plea bargains make cases like a commodity rather than an individual matter of justice? One of the selling points of plea bargaining is that it enables the courts to process many more cases with less time and resources. The speed at which the lawyers can resolve cases makes plea bargaining feel like an assembly line. As the lawyers bargain dozens of cases a day over the years, the very repetition of cases leads to lumping defendants into groups, each having a case "worth" a certain "value" in terms of time in prison or jail. This process drains each defendant of his or her own individuality. A lawyer who too quickly categorizes a case based on experience in earlier bargains is in danger of missing important questions in the case.

The fifth question is this: Do plea bargains create a public perception of backroom deals rather than justice? Justice Scalia, in discussing plea bargaining, compared a court to a "casino-operator,"[61] and the Court itself has called plea bargaining "horse trading."[62] The game-playing atmosphere of plea bargaining is furthered by the way it is carried out. Rather than having all matters decided in open court, as would occur at a public trial, the lawyers and judge emerge from a closed-door meeting in chambers to announce a guilty plea. Both the manner and result of such bargaining harms the public's trust.

 CON Plea Bargaining Is Necessary and Should Be Retained

In arguing that plea bargaining is necessary and should be retained, there are four issues to consider.

First, plea bargaining is a necessity because it enables the courts to handle huge and continually increasing caseloads. The criminal justice system is so overwhelmed with cases that plea bargaining is a necessity.[63] Noting that "ninety-seven percent of federal convictions and ninety-four percent of state convictions are the result of guilty pleas,"[64] the Supreme Court has bluntly concluded that plea bargaining "is not some adjunct to the criminal justice system; it *is* the criminal justice system."[65] Also, plea bargaining removes the straightforward cases from the system. By focusing resources on where they are genuinely needed, plea bargaining actually promotes justice in the real world.

Second, plea bargaining allows victims and witnesses the chance to avoid the trauma, expense, and inconvenience of going to trial. Victims of crime sometimes feel they are victimized twice—once at the time of the crime and again at the time of trial, where they are forced to confront the criminal and undergo a defense lawyer's hostile cross-examination. If the parties agree that the defendant is guilty, no practical reason exists to force victims to undergo the ordeal of going to trial.[66]

Third, plea bargaining enables defendants to show remorse and embark on rehabilitation as soon as possible. When a defendant stands up and takes responsibility for the crime, the offender shows that he or she is ready to change his or her criminal ways. A plea allows the sentence to be carried out quickly, improving the chance of rehabilitation.[67]

Fourth, plea bargaining provides certainty and finality to the criminal justice system. Even when a jury convicts a defendant at trial, matters can be dragged out by numerous appeals, and all the while the defendant may be out of prison awaiting a final ruling. Although pleas resulting from bargains can lead to appeals, cases ending due to plea bargains usually reach a conclusion more quickly and therefore have greater "finality."[68]

SUMMARY

Is plea bargaining good, bad, or simply unavoidable? Even justices of the highest court in the land cannot agree on the answer to this question. Justice Scalia called plea bargaining "a somewhat embarrassing adjunct to our criminal justice system."[69] Chief Justice Burger urged that plea bargaining was "an essential component of the administration of justice" which should be "encouraged."[70] Perhaps an answer is best reached by considering plea bargaining's impact on the goals of the criminal justice system and the values that we give to each of these goals.

DISCUSSION QUESTIONS

1. Given the arguments presented, should the use of plea bargains be eliminated, reduced, or retained?

2. What are the consequences of eliminating or reducing the use of plea bargains in our criminal justice system?

3. How does the use of plea bargains support the goal of punishing offenders for their crimes?

4. How does the use of plea bargains challenge the deterrent value of punishment?

5. How might you reform the system to reduce our reliance on plea bargains?

KEY TERMS

Review key terms with eFlashcards | ⑤SAGE edge™ • edge.sagepub.com/mallicoatccj

DISCUSSION QUESTIONS

Test your mastery of chapter content • Take the Practice Quiz | $SAGE edge™ • edge.sagepub.com/mallicoatccj

1. What are the key differences between criminal and civil courts?

2. What is jurisdiction, and what is the difference between the five different types of jurisdiction discussed in this chapter?

3. Describe the similarities and differences between the federal court system and the state court system where you live.

4. What is the difference between a finding of not guilty and a finding of innocent?

5. What are the different methods for selecting judges? What's problematic about these selection processes?

6. Why would someone enter a nolo contendre plea?

7. Describe the three key stages of a criminal court case.

LEARNING ACTIVITIES

1. Visit a local courtroom, and observe a hearing. What do you notice about how a courtroom functions?

2. Identify a U.S. Supreme Court decision related to a criminal justice issue from the most recent term. How did the court reach its decision? What implications does this decision have for the system?

3. Explore how jury members are selected for your county. How would your life be affected if you were selected to sit on a jury?

SUGGESTED WEBSITES

- **American Bar Association:** http://www.americanbar.org/aba.html
- **National Center for State Courts:** http://www.judicialselection.us
- **United States Courts:** http://www.uscourts.gov
- **U.S. Supreme Court:** http://www.supremecourt.gov

STUDENT STUDY SITE

Review • Practice • Improve | $SAGE edge™ • edge.sagepub.com/mallicoatccj

Want a better grade?

Get the tools you need to sharpen your study skills. Access practice quizzes, eFlashcards, video, and multimedia at **edge.sagepub.com/mallicoatccj**

CHAPTER

10

PUNISHMENT AND SENTENCING

LEARNING OBJECTIVES

- Discuss the different sentencing philosophies

- Compare the differences between indeterminate, determinate, and mandatory sentencing

- Explain how federal sentencing guidelines are used

- Identify the current methods of execution and legal challenges to capital punishment

While most ordinary crimes rarely make news headlines, this changes when a celebrity is involved in a crime. As a result of their social status, these cases dominate the headlines regardless of the offense. In 2009, Chris Brown was arrested for felony assault against his then girlfriend Rihanna following a domestic dispute. In an effort to avoid jail time, he pled guilty and received five years of probation, one year of domestic violence counseling, and six months of community service. However, his involvement with the criminal justice system didn't end with this incident. Over the next five years, Brown continued to have run-ins with the law, including a hit-and-run accident in California and an aggravated assault outside a Washington, D.C., hotel in 2013.[1] As a result, Brown's probation was revoked, and he spent 90 days in an inpatient anger management treatment program. However, he was kicked out of the program for noncompliance and, as a result, spent two and a half months in jail. In 2015, he was released from probation.[2] Meanwhile, Justin Bieber's involvement in at-risk and criminal behavior has been escalating since 2013. While his official record highlights a DUI arrest in 2014, media accounts list events such as reckless driving throughout his neighborhood, bar scuffles, marijuana use, and vandalism, which have occurred both in the United States and abroad.[3] However, the punishments for these bad acts have been limited. In 2014, the DUI case was resolved with a charitable donation and by enrolling in anger management classes. He also accepted a plea deal in the vandalism case that sentenced him to two years probation plus $80,000 in restitution. In 2015, the Canadian courts found him guilty of assault and careless driving. His punishment for this crime was a $600 fine.[4]

Do celebrities receive preferential treatment in the criminal justice system as a result of their status? In some instances, the punishments in these cases do little to sanction the offenders, particularly when the punishment is a small fine. Some groups were highly critical of the sentence that Brown received for his domestic assault, arguing that it was not proportional to the injuries that he inflicted to his victim. Meanwhile, others express concerns about what sort of message is received by youth who might look up to these superstars and how they are treated by the criminal justice system.

In this chapter, you will learn about the types of sentencing practices that are used by the criminal justice system. The chapter begins with a discussion about the various philosophies that guide sentencing practices. The chapter then looks at the different types of sentences. The chapter concludes with two Current Controversy debates related to the criminal court system. The first, by Kimberly Dodson, asks whether habitual sentencing laws deter offenders. The second, by Scott Vollum, looks at whether there is a risk of executing an innocent individual.

> "
> The most effective punishments from the perspective of deterrence theory are those that are certain, severe, and swift.

CORRECTIONAL PHILOSOPHIES

What is the purpose of punishment? Is it to prevent someone from doing the same thing again? Or do we punish someone to send a message that certain behaviors will not be tolerated? There are five different philosophies that have helped guide our sentencing and correctional practices, and each of these philosophies has been popular at different points throughout history. In order to understand these different practices and how they are used by the criminal justice system, we must first understand the foundations of these practices.

Deterrence

The theory of deterrence suggests that offenders will be discouraged from committing crime if they fear the punishments that are associated with these acts. There are two different ways in which deterrence theory works. First, there is the concept of specific deterrence. **Specific deterrence** looks at how individual behaviors are curbed as a result of Becarria's pain–pleasure principle. If the individual decides that the threat of punishment (such as a prison sentence) is undesirable, then specific deterrence suggests that that particular individual will make the decision not to engage in the criminal behavior. Specific deterrence is limited to a particular individual. In contrast, the theory of **general deterrence** suggests that if people fear the punishments that others receive, they will, in turn, decide not to engage in similar acts, as they do not want to risk the potential punishment for themselves.[5]

In order for deterrence theory to be effective, a punishment must possess three characteristics. The first of these characteristics is **certainty**. This means that offenders need to be reasonably aware that if they engage in a criminal act, they will be apprehended and punished. Consider that parents generally teach their children not to touch a sharp object (such as a knife), or else, they will likely get hurt. This works because the punishment (getting hurt) is relatively certain. When it comes to crime and punishment, this level of certainty doesn't exist because crimes occur every day that are not reported to the police, and offenders are not punished for these acts. Second, the punishment must be severe. If the punishment is not harsh enough, offenders may not be deterred from engaging in the criminal behavior. The **severity** of a punishment can limit the certainty of that punishment—as the severity of a punishment increases, the likelihood of that punishment being implemented decreases.[6] Finally, the potential punishment must be swift. This is also referred to as the **celerity** of punishment. Celerity of punishment references the amount of time between the criminal act and the punishment for said act. If the punishment does not occur in a timely fashion, the deterrent effect is reduced. Therefore, the most effective punishments, from the perspective of deterrence theory, are those that are certain, severe, and swift. The problem with deterrence is that punishments rarely operate in this manner. For example, most people do not engage in crime with the expectation that they will be caught, which negates the certainty principle. And what is considered

SAGE JOURNAL ARTICLE
Do More Police Lead to More Crime Deterrence?

Specific deterrence
Looks at how an individual may avoid criminal behavior if the potential punishment is viewed as undesirable.

General deterrence
Suggests that if people fear the punishments that others receive, they will decide not to engage in similar acts to avoid punishment.

Certainty
The notion that individuals need to be reasonably aware that if they engage in a criminal act, they will be apprehended and punished.

Severity
The notion that punishment must be harsh enough to deter people from criminal behavior.

Celerity
The notion that potential punishment must occur in a timely fashion.

SPOTLIGHT

Deterrence and the Death Penalty

Once upon a time, deterrence used to be the leading reason as to why people expressed support for the death penalty. According to a Gallup poll, 62% of those surveyed in 1985 believed that the death penalty acts as a deterrent against murder and that having the death penalty leads to lower murder rates. Today, people are most likely to support capital punishment for retributive reasons, and people no longer believe that it serves as an effective deterrence (see Figure 10.1).[a]

Research on capital punishment as an effective deterrent has long been cited by policymakers and politicians. One of the most notable contributions on deterrence and the death penalty was published during the 1970s by Isaac Ehrlich, an economist from the University of Chicago. His work indicated that for every execution, the number of homicides decreased by eight. These findings were in sharp contrast to the previous studies in the field, and many jumped to embrace deterrence as a plausible justification for the practice of execution. Even the U.S. Supreme Court cited Ehrlich's work in their decision to reinstate the death penalty in 1976.[b] However, Ehrlich's research methods have since been highly criticized, and many studies since have failed to find evidence of a deterrent effect.[c] While there are certainly a number of factors that scholars use to investigate the effects of deterrence from the death penalty, opponents of the death penalty often begin with a review of murder rates between those states that have laws that permit executions and those states that have abolished the death penalty. Here, we can see that states that have retained the death penalty have higher murder rates compared with those states without it.

While many politicians continue to suggest that the death penalty saves lives, we simply don't know what would-be murderers think about before they decide whether to engage in violent crime. Given that only 2% of those convicted of death-eligible crimes actually receive the death penalty, it is fair to say that there is little certainty that a would-be murderer will receive the death penalty.[d] The issue as to whether the death penalty is the most severe form of punishment is also debated. Of those who favor the

---

Figure 10.1   Murder Rates in Death Penalty and Non–Death Penalty States

Murder rates in states that impose the death penalty have been consistently higher than in states that do not impose the death penalty. How does this relate to the idea that the death penalty acts as a deterrent?

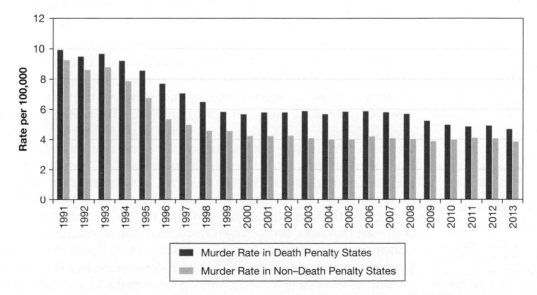

Source: http://www.deathpenaltyinfo.org/deterrence-states-without-death-penalty-have-had-consistently-lower-murder-rates

(Continued)

(Continued)

CRITICAL THINKING QUESTIONS

1. Why do people believe that the death penalty serves as an effective deterrent?

2. If deterrence is not a valid reason to support the death penalty, what are some of the reasons why individuals are in favor of the practice? What are some of the reasons why individuals are opposed to the practice?

death penalty, 37% say that life in prison without the possibility of parole would be a worse punishment.[e] Finally, it is difficult to argue that the length of time between sentencing an offender to death and carrying out an execution is swift. Nationwide, the average time spent on death row is 14.8 years.[f] In some states, such as California, 37% of offenders have spent more than 20 years waiting for their execution.[g] Indeed, inmates are more likely to die of natural causes than to be executed by the state.

So if we look at the death penalty through the eyes of the certainty, severity, and celerity of punishment, it is questionable as to whether this practice is an effective example of deterrence.

a severe punishment is a subjective concept—while some offenders might feel that six months in jail is an extreme punishment, others may feel that it's not a big deal. Finally, in an era of crowded court systems and legal challenges, how often are punishments delayed?

Rehabilitation

Many of the rehabilitative ideals that are reflected in the modern-day criminal justice system began during the early 20th century. Prior to this, rehabilitative efforts were tied to religious reforms.[7] It was from this focus that we saw the development of practices such as probation, parole, and the juvenile justice system.[8] The concept of **rehabilitation** focuses on reforming criminal behavior so that the offender does not need or want to engage in future acts of crime. Rehabilitation was used within the prison walls not only as a way to treat prisoners and help transform their behaviors but also to assess whether offenders were prepared to return to the community.

During the 1970s, rehabilitation became less popular as a result of a belief that "nothing works." In his 1974 article "What Works?—Questions and Answers About Prison Reform," Martinson reviewed more than 200 programs, from counseling to education, and noted rather dismal results.[9] However, he noted that these results may reflect the efficacy of the specific programs.[10] Alas, the stone was cast, and Martinson's research became part of the quest to turn against rehabilitation in favor of a tougher approach.[11] In political circles, support for rehabilitative programming became the equivalent of being soft on crime. Consider the 1988 presidential election in which presidential candidate Michael Dukakis was heavily criticized by the Republican candidate, George H. W. Bush, for Dukakis's support of weekend furlough releases for convicted offenders. The debate centered on the case of Willie Horton, who was a convicted murderer. Even though he had received a sentence of life without the possibility of parole (LWOP) for his crime, he was still permitted to participate in the program. Unfortunately, on one occasion, Horton never returned from his furlough. Instead, he traveled to Maryland, where he robbed a local couple, physically assaulted the male, and raped the woman.[12] As governor, Dukakis was held politically responsible for Horton's release (which had led to these crimes) and was declared to be "soft on crime," a position that ultimately contributed to his loss in the election.[13]

Rehabilitation
Focuses on reforming criminal behavior so that the offender does not need or want to engage in future acts of crime.

Today, we have evidence that programs can work when they are targeted toward the needs of the offender (compared with a general approach), are provided with the financial support to offer programs in a manageable way, and have staff that are adequately trained and supportive of the rehabilitative mission.[14] When implemented with these ideals in mind, rehabilitative efforts that focus on changing the way individuals think about crime and criminal behavior can reduce recidivism.[15]

Incapacitation

Incapacitation refers to the practice of removing offenders from society so that they will not engage in criminal behaviors for a certain period of time. Generally speaking, we think of the prison as a way to incapacitate offenders. However, technology has made it possible to utilize some of the features of incapacitation in other settings. This is particularly useful given the current issues of overcrowding in prisons. For example, few celebrity cases, such as the one you learned about at the beginning of this chapter, lead to time behind bars. The concept of incapacitation has been used for low-level offenders as well as serious offenders. Sentencing practices such as mandatory minimums and three-strikes laws are examples of how incapacitation is used to ensure public safety.

Today, most sentencing practices combine the use of incapacitation with other theories of punishment, such as deterrence and retribution, which can make it difficult to determine whether incapacitation is an effective tool in preventing crime. For low-level offenders, research indicates that the benefits of increasing public safety through the use of incapacitation are often superseded by the challenges that come with the "ex-convict" label in society, prompting some to question whether incapacitation does more harm than good in the long run for certain groups of offenders.[16] Indeed, studies find that prison may actually increase the likelihood of future offending.[17] Even in the case of parole violators, research demonstrates that community-based sanctions are more effective in preventing crime compared with the use of jail time as a punishment.[18]

Retribution

Retribution is a punishment philosophy that reflects the idea that offenders should be punished for their bad acts purely on the basis that they violated the laws of society. Retribution does not take into consideration whether the punishment will lead to future change in the offender's behavior (like deterrence or rehabilitation philosophies do). The theory of retribution embodies the concept of lex talionis from ancient law and is even referenced in biblical texts with the discussion of punishment as *an eye for an eye*. Retribution is a way for offenders to *pay* for the harms that they have

In some states, inmates have the opportunity to work with training service dogs for visually impaired persons. Such programs can have a transformative experience for the inmates, who learn about dealing with anger and developing patience, and provide opportunities for empathy and responsibility. Should these types of programs be available to inmates?

Incapacitation
Refers to the practice of removing offenders from society so that they will not engage in criminal behaviors for a certain period of time.

Retribution
A punishment philosophy that reflects that offenders should be punished for their bad acts purely on the basis that they violated the laws of society.

Electronic monitoring is often used as a way to track offenders and monitor their whereabouts while being supervised in the community. How does this work to incapacitate offenders?

CAREERS IN CRIMINAL JUSTICE

So You Want to Be a Drug and Alcohol Counselor?

As a drug and alcohol counselor, you will work with individuals who are struggling with addiction. Careers in this field are tied to many different academic backgrounds, including criminal justice, social work, human services, and psychology. Some states require a bachelor's degree while others allow for workers to qualify for these careers with a certificate program in substance abuse counseling. Such careers also may require you to pass an exam in order to qualify with the state department of health.

People in this field work in many different environments. For example, you might work as part of a program providing counseling to inmates who have been incarcerated as a result of their addiction or whose crimes are related to their substance abuse. You might work in a residential treatment or out-patient treatment center in the community. You might also work providing educational outreach for the purposes of prevention or intervention. Within the context of your job, you will deal with emotional environments as people navigate their sobriety. In many cases, the damage caused by addiction is not limited to just the individual but can span across their family members and friends. Like other human service fields, this work can be challenging because people have to want to change their behavior. Not all who seek treatment want or are willing to change their behaviors that create the environment for addiction. In these cases, it can be challenging for workers to identify successful outcomes with their work, and it can lead to questions about their job satisfaction and burnout.

This field is considered a growth industry, particularly as more people find themselves covered by health insurance under the Affordable Care Act. This policy requires that plans provide coverage for mental health programs and may include support for addiction services. In addition, many states are looking at reducing their prison populations and have directed more offenders to community-based services, which may include treatment for substance abuse.

CAREER VIDEO
Drug and Alcohol Counselor

perpetuated against society. Under this philosophy, there is no justice if the offender is not punished under the law.

The use of retribution draws on the concept of **just deserts**. The theory of just deserts argues that a punishment for a crime should be proportional or equal to the crime itself. Under this perspective, a serious crime would result in a serious punishment and a minor crime would result in a low-level punishment. While retribution often invokes a discussion about vengeance or revenge, this is not an appropriate response under retributive theory. However, the use of retribution can be a way to express the emotional or value-centered beliefs of the public on issues such as the death penalty or terrorism.[19]

Unlike other philosophies, retribution is not about improving public safety or other utilitarian functions. Retribution is about looking back at the act and enacting a punishment for that violation. This key feature is often confused with many of the policies developed under the tough-on-crime model that dominated the late 20th century in the United States. For example, mandatory minimum sentences were developed during the modern retributive era, which began in the 1970s and continues today. One of the most popular uses of mandatory minimum sentencing was the war on drugs, which began with the passage of the Anti–Drug Abuse Act of 1986. One of the more notable features of the law was that it mandated a sentence of five years for the possession of 500 grams of powder cocaine yet gave the same sentence for only 5 grams of crack cocaine. While this 100:1 sentencing disparity was reduced to an 18:1 ratio with the passage of the Fair Sentencing Act in 2010, the war on drugs has made a significant contribution to the rise in prison populations nationwide.

Just deserts
Argues that a punishment for a crime should be proportional or equal to the crime itself.

Restoration

The theory of **restoration** is the only punishment philosophy that places the victim at the core of all decision-making. This feature is very different compared with other theories, which view crime as a violation against the state. The theory of restoration is best reflected in restorative justice practices, which you learned about in Chapter 5. While restoration has often been positioned in opposition to a retributive model, some scholars suggest that the two may actually have some common themes, as both strive for justice. In particular, it is important to note that a restorative philosophy does not mean that offenders are not punished for their crimes. Instead, the decision-making on how the crime should be punished involves a joint process between the victim, the offender, and the community. Justice becomes an opportunity for healing. Research demonstrates that victims who participate in restorative justice programs generally have higher rates of satisfaction with the process compared with victims whose cases are handled through traditional criminal courts.[20] Evidence also suggests that offenders whose cases are handled in this fashion are also less likely to recidivate, making restorative justice a cost-effective model in reducing future offending.[21]

Each of these punishment philosophies impacts the different types of sentences that are handed down by the courts. For example, under a model of deterrence or incapacitation, sentences may be more likely to feature time in a jail or a prison. In contrast, sentences handed down under a model of rehabilitation will be more likely to emphasize counseling and treatment. While these theories of punishment can influence how a judge will make a decision, these decisions are somewhat limited by the laws that are created by the legislature. In the next section, you will learn about some of the different sentencing structures that have been adopted by various states and the federal government.

DETERMINATE SENTENCING

How does a judge decide on a sentence for an offender? In some cases, the law dictates what type of punishment should be handed down for a specific crime. Many jurisdictions have passed **determinate sentencing** structures. Determinate sentencing is when the offender is sentenced to a specific term. While the law may allow for an offender to be released early due to good-time credits, these releases are incorporated into the law. This means that there is no opportunity for an early release based on the behavior of the offender, also known as **parole**. You will learn more about parole in Chapter 12.

Throughout most of history, judges have had discretion in handing out sentences to offenders. In most cases, judges were free to impose just about any type of sentence, from probation to incarceration. Essentially, the only guidance for decision-making came from the judge's own value system and beliefs in justice. This created a process whereby there was no consistency in sentencing, and offenders received dramatically different sentences for the same offenses, whereby the outcome depended on which judge heard their case. While this practice allowed for individualized justice based on the needs of offenders and their potential for rehabilitation, it also left the door open for the potential of bias based on the age, race, ethnicity, and gender of the offender.

Sentencing Guidelines

During the 1970s, the faith in rehabilitation as an effective correctional approach began to wane and was replaced with the theory of "just deserts," a retributive philosophy that aimed to increase the punishment of offenders for their crimes against society. In an effort to reform sentencing practices and reduce the levels of discretion

VIDEO
Thousands Released
Early From Prison Under
New Sentencing Guidelines

Restoration
The only punishment philosophy that places the victim at the core of all decision-making.

Determinate sentencing
A sentencing structure in which the offender is sentenced to a specific term.

Parole
Early release based on the behavior of the offender. Provides supervision and a system of accountability for offenders for a period of time once they are released from prison.

This table guides federal judges when determining the length of an offender's sentence. They factor in the level of the offense as well as the offender's past criminal history. Do you think these guidelines are helpful, or do they hinder the discretion of federal judges too much?

	Offense Level	Criminal History Category (Criminal History Points)					
		I (0 or 1)	II (2 or 3)	III (4, 5, 6)	IV (7, 8, 9)	V (10, 11, 12)	VI (13 or more)
Zone A	1	0–6	0–6	0–6	0–6	0–6	0–6
	2	0–6	0–6	0–6	0–6	0–6	1–7
	3	0–6	0–6	0–6	0–6	2–8	3–9
	4	0–6	0–6	0–6	2–8	4–10	6–12
	5	0–6	0–6	1–7	4–10	6–12	9–15
	6	0–6	1–7	2–8	6–12	9–15	12–18
	7	0–6	2–8	4–10	8–14	12–18	15–21
	8	0–6	4–10	6–12	10–16	15–21	18–24
	9	4–10	6–12	8–14	12–18	18–24	21–27
Zone B	10	6–12	8–14	10–16	15–21	21–27	24–30
	11	8–14	10–16	12–18	18–24	24–30	27–33
Zone C	12	10–16	12–18	15–21	21–27	27–33	30–37
	13	12–18	15–21	18–24	24–30	30–37	33–41
	14	15–21	18–24	21–27	27–33	33–41	37–46
	15	18–24	21–27	24–30	30–37	37–46	41–51
	16	21–27	24–30	27–33	33–41	41–51	46–57
	17	24–30	27–33	30–37	37–46	46–57	51–63
	18	27–33	30–37	33–41	41–51	51–63	57–71
	19	30–37	33–41	37–46	46–57	57–71	63–78
	20	33–41	37–46	41–51	51–63	63–78	70–87
	21	37–46	41–51	46–57	57–71	70–87	77–96
	22	41–51	46–57	51–63	63–78	77–96	84–105
	23	46–57	51–63	57–71	70–87	84–105	92–115
	24	51–63	57–71	63–78	77–96	92–115	100–125
	25	57–71	63–78	70–87	84–105	100–125	110–137
	26	63–78	70–87	78–97	92–115	110–137	120–150
	27	70–87	78–97	87–108	100–125	120–150	130–162
Zone D	28	78–97	87–108	97–121	110–137	130–162	140–175
	29	87–108	97–121	108–135	121–151	140–175	151–188
	30	97–121	108–135	121–151	135–168	151–188	168–210
	31	108–135	121–151	135–168	151–188	168–210	188–235
	32	121–151	135–168	151–188	168–210	188–235	210–262
	33	135–168	151–188	168–210	188–235	210–262	235–293
	34	151–188	168–210	188–235	210–262	235–293	262–327
	35	168–210	188–235	210–262	235–293	262–327	292–365
	36	188–235	210–262	235–293	262–327	292–365	324–405
	37	210–262	235–293	262–327	292–365	324–405	360–life
	38	235–293	262–327	292–365	324–405	360–life	360–life
	39	262–327	292–365	324–405	360–life	360–life	360–life
	40	292–365	324–405	360–life	360–life	360–life	360–life
	41	324–405	360–life	360–life	360–life	360–life	360–life
	42	360–life	360–life	360–life	360–life	360–life	360–life
	43	life	life	life	life	life	life

Source: http://www.ussc.gov/sites/default/files/pdf/guidelines-manual/2015/Sentencing_Table.pdf

within the judiciary, many jurisdictions developed sentencing guidelines to create systems in which offenders would receive similar sentences for similar crimes. At the heart of this campaign was an attempt to regulate sentencing practices and eliminate racial, gender, and class-based discrimination in courts. As part of the Sentencing Reform Act of 1984, the U.S. Sentencing Commission was tasked with crafting sentencing guidelines at the federal level. Several states have also adopted sentencing guidelines as part of their determinate sentencing structure. One of the key features of this act was the abolition of parole boards at the federal level.

Since their implementation in November 1987, these federal guidelines have been criticized for being too rigid and unnecessarily harsh. In many cases, these criticisms reflect a growing concern that judges are now unable to consider the unique circumstances of the crime or characteristics of the offender. Table 10.1 presents the federal sentencing guidelines.

Each federal crime is classified on the basis of its severity level and is ranked on a scale of 1 to 43. Depending on the specific circumstances of the crime and the defendant's role in the offense, this value may be increased. Examples of these enhancements include characteristics about the victim (such as whether the victim was a government employee or a member of law enforcement), the crime (such as a hate crime or serious human rights offense), and the offender (mitigating factors and acceptance of responsibility by the offender). These categories are reflected along the left side of the table. The number of prior convictions is organized into six categories and is listed along the top of the table. To determine the sentencing range (in terms of months), you would find the intersection of the criminal history category and the offense classification plus any enhancements. For example, the crime of aggravated assault carries a base level of 14. If a firearm was discharged during the crime, the score increases by five levels. If the victim sustains bodily injury as a result of the crime, the score increases by an additional three levels. But if the offender accepts responsibility for the crime, the score decreases by two levels. As a result, the sentencing of this act is rated at a value of 20. If the offender has no prior history, the sentencing range for this offense is 33 to 41 months. If, however, the offender has five prior offenses, the sentencing range increases to 41 to 51 months.

Opposition to Sentencing Guidelines

In 2004, the U.S. Supreme Court heard the case of *Blakely v. Washington*.[22] The Court held that while the state sentencing guidelines that were used by Washington State were intended to serve as a mandatory sentencing scheme, they violated a defendant's 6th Amendment right to a trial by jury. *Blakely* states that only those facts that are either admitted by the defendant or proved beyond a reasonable doubt may be used to determine an appropriate sentence for the offender. The case of *United States v. Booker* applied this ruling to the federal sentencing guidelines.[23] Even though the federal sentencing guidelines now serve as an advisory practice rather than a mandatory one, research by the U.S. Sentencing Commission indicates that the majority of sentences fall within the ranges specified by the guidelines.[24] Others note that sentence severity has been reduced dramatically since *Booker*.[25] However, minority offenders continue to receive slightly higher sentences than white offenders, as shown in Figure 10.2.[26]

INDETERMINATE SENTENCING

In comparison with determinate sentencing structures, **indeterminate sentencing** practices generally set a minimum sentence length. The maximum sentence is reflected in the laws set forth by the legislature, though a judge may set a maximum

WEB LINK
United States
Sentencing Commission

Indeterminate sentencing
A sentencing structure in which the offender is sentenced to a minimum and maximum sentencing range. The actual time served is determined by a parole board, which evaluates release based on rehabilitation and behavior while in prison.

Parole board hearings provide the opportunity for officials to assess the inmate's rehabilitative efforts and evaluate whether he or she should be released from prison. What factors does a parole board consider when determining if an inmate should be released?

sentence that is lower than the legal provision. Indeterminate sentencing was first featured during the progressive era of the late 1800s. It was during this time that new innovations in corrections such as probation and parole first appeared. Indeterminate sentencing structures fit within the rehabilitative focus of this time period. The theory of indeterminate sentencing was that offenders would be released based not only on their time served but also their efforts toward reforming their criminal selves. As a result, the length of time that an offender served was determined by a parole board, which would consider factors such as the types of programming that an offender participated in and his or her institutional behavior and plan for reintegration in determining whether someone would be released. While the 1970s saw a shift toward determinate and mandatory sentencing structures, many states still retain some form of indeterminate sentencing and the use of parole boards today.

MANDATORY SENTENCES

Mandatory sentencing
A type of sentencing structure where the law, not the judge, determines the length of punishment for specific offenses.

While determinate sentences were designed to limit the discretion of judges, mandatory sentences have effectively eliminated judicial discretion from the criminal justice system. Under a **mandatory sentencing** scheme, the law prescribes the specific punishments. Earlier in this chapter, you learned about how the Anti–Drug Abuse Act of 1986 created mandatory minimum sentences for the possession of certain illicit drugs. Congress has also created mandatory sentencing practices for certain gun-related crimes, sexually based offenses (including pornography), and white-collar crimes.[27] However, we have seen several other examples of mandatory sentences, some

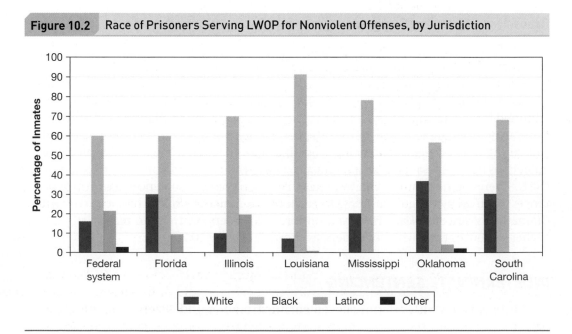

Figure 10.2   Race of Prisoners Serving LWOP for Nonviolent Offenses, by Jurisdiction

Source: https://www.aclu.org/sites/default/files/assets/141027_iachr_racial_disparities_aclu_submission_0.pdf

AROUND THE WORLD

Criminal Sentencing in China

Unlike the United States, the criminal justice system in China is a relatively new phenomenon. As a result, it has embarked on several revisions and reforms over the past four decades. In some ways, the features of China's criminal justice system are similar to those in the United States, and in others, there are marked differences between the two.

While several jurisdictions in the United States are shifting the way they look at some drug offenses, nonviolent drug-related crimes are ranked as severe crimes in China (along with acts of violence, such as murder and robbery). Research on drug trafficking in China demonstrates that judges are most likely to make their sentencing decisions in these cases based on the amount of drugs involved. Since many smuggling cases involve high quantities of drugs such as heroin, the sentences are quite significant as most offenders are sentenced to either more than 10 years in prison, a life sentence, or even death. However, Chinese law allows for offenders to express remorse for their crimes, which, in turn, can significantly reduce the length of the sentence that an offender will receive, even for these serious crimes.[a] Finally, the country has also relied less on the death penalty in recent years. During the "strike hard" era of punishment, China was a consistent user of the death penalty and even carried out more than 1,000 executions in a month.[b] While China still leads the world in the number of executions, some scholars have suggested that China may begin to shift its thinking on the issue as other Southeast Asian countries abolish the death penalty in law or in practice.[c]

In addition to punishments by the judiciary for criminal offenses, China allows for individuals to be sent to a labor camp for up to three years. These decisions are based on administrative law and do not allow for judicial interventions. This means that an individual can be sent away for a "re-education through labor" sentence (referred to as *laodong jiaoyang*) without any criminal charges filed or being processed by the criminal court. This is particularly interesting in that many of the students of such camps are sent there as a result of their involvement in minor crimes, such as vandalism, drug use, and theft. The labor camp is designed to rehabilitate first-time offenders, and following the completion of their service, they do not have a criminal record.[d]

The current sentencing practices in China have been pushed by a desire to "balance leniency and severity." In one high-profile incident, an offender offered a victim financial restitution in exchange for a reduced sentence.[e] While some suggest that this reflected a restorative justice model, others believed that the case was so minor that it would never have been considered for prosecution under the new reforms.[f] Others still questioned whether preferential treatment was given to this offender because of his financial status.[g] Indeed, white-collar offenders who have privileged status (such as a government official) are less likely to receive a sentence of incarceration than are offenders of low social status.[h] Given that the modern judicial system in China is a relatively new one, it is likely that they will continue to experience efforts to reform and revise sentencing practices.

CRITICAL THINKING QUESTIONS

1. Given that China's criminal justice system is relatively new, what can they learn from the experiences of the American criminal justice system?

2. What are some of the ways in which the Chinese system of justice is similar to that of the United States? In what ways does it differ?

of which have been declared unconstitutional by the courts. For example, the U.S. Supreme Court held that mandatory death sentences in cases of first-degree murder were unconstitutional because they did not allow for a jury to weigh in on the aggravating and mitigating factors when making a sentence recommendation (*Woodson v. North Carolina*).[28]

Opposition to Mandatory Sentences

AUDIO
Judge Regrets Harsh
Human Toll of Mandatory
Minimum Sentences

One of the major criticisms of mandatory sentencing practices is that they prevent the judge from considering the unique characteristics of the offense or the offender in handing down a sentence. In effect, the power of sentencing is shifted to the prosecutor, who determines whether a charge that carries a mandatory sentence will be filed against an offender. Mandatory sentencing has been tied to the dramatic increase in prison populations throughout the late 20th and early 21st centuries. As a result, many states have begun to repeal their mandatory sentencing laws (Figure 10.3). South Carolina and Pennsylvania have eliminated their use of mandatory sentences for school zone drug cases. Others, such as Ohio and California, have replaced mandatory prison sentences for first-time drug offenders with drug treatment programming.[29] The U.S. Supreme Court recently held that sentencing enhancements for violent felonies under the Armed Career Criminals Act are unconstitutional on the grounds that defendants were denied their right to due process and that the law was vague in its application (*Johnson v. United States*).[30] Mandatory sentencing laws have

Figure 10.3	State Sentencing and Correction Trends

Many states are undertaking reforms of their sentencing and corrections practices. What reform efforts has your state undertaken?

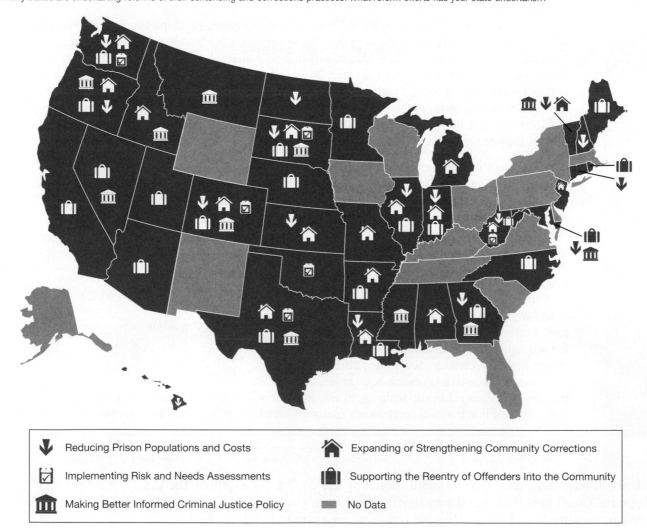

⬇ Reducing Prison Populations and Costs

🏠 Expanding or Strengthening Community Corrections

☑ Implementing Risk and Needs Assessments

💼 Supporting the Reentry of Offenders Into the Community

🏛 Making Better Informed Criminal Justice Policy

▬ No Data

Source: Vera Institute of Justice. (2014, July). *Recalibrating justice: A review of 2013 state sentencing and corrections trends.*

also been used to deal with habitual offenders. You'll learn about these types of sentences in Current Controversy 10.1 at the conclusion of this chapter.

CAPITAL PUNISHMENT

The death penalty has been referred to as the ultimate punishment, reserved for the worst of the worst offenders. However, the United States is one of the last remaining developed countries to engage in executions as a form of punishment. And its implementation throughout the United States varies dramatically. Currently, there are 31 states (as well as the federal government and the military) that allow for the use of the death penalty. Figure 10.4 shows states that currently allow and prohibit the use of capital punishment.

Since the death penalty is aimed for the worst of the worst offenders, states have restricted its use to crimes of first-degree murder with special circumstances. A first-degree murder is defined as one in which the crime was premeditated, meaning that the offender planned the attack on the victim. States vary on the types of special circumstances that can make a case death penalty eligible; examples of this include a murder that was committed during a felony (such as rape, kidnapping, or burglary) or involved a particular type of victim, such as a police

AUDIO
Supreme Court Strikes Down Florida's Death Penalty System

| Figure 10.4 | Implementation of Capital Punishment by State |

Does the state you live in permit the death penalty? If so, what methods of execution can it legally employ?

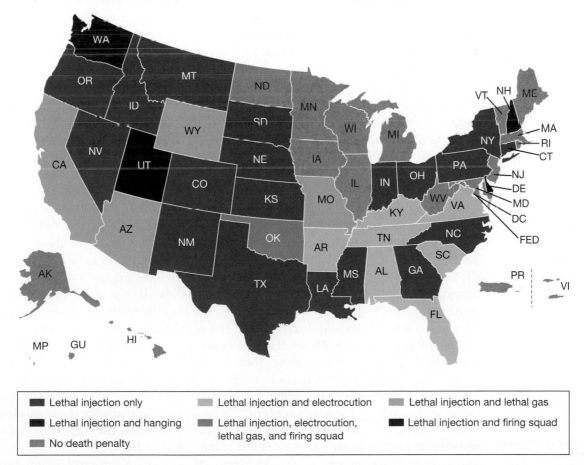

Lethal injection only
Lethal injection and electrocution
Lethal injection and lethal gas
Lethal injection and hanging
Lethal injection, electrocution, lethal gas, and firing squad
Lethal injection and firing squad
No death penalty

Source: U.S. Department of Justice, Bureau of Justice Statistics, Capital Punishment Series; http://www.bjs.gov/content/pub/pdf/cp13st.pdf and http://www.deathpenaltyinfo.org/methods-execution

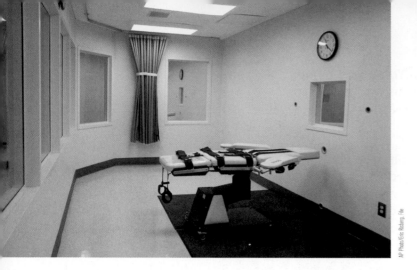

California's new death chamber at San Quentin Prison has sat unused since its completion in 2010. California has the largest death row in the nation but has executed only 13 individuals since the death penalty was reinstated. Legal challenges have prevented the state from carrying out an execution in the past decade. Are you for or against the death penalty?

WEB LINK
Death Penalty
Information Center

VIDEO
2015 Was a Historic Year for
the Death Penalty in America

Aggravating factors
Circumstances that increase
the severity of the crime, such
as torture, excessive violence,
or premeditation.

Mitigating factors
Circumstances that minimize
or explain the actions of the
offender or the crime.

officer or government official. The federal government permits the use of the death penalty in cases of treason or espionage.

The first use of the death penalty in the United States involved the execution of Captain George Kendall in 1608 for acts of treason against the government. Since then, there have been an estimated 16,000 executions over the past four centuries.[31] Throughout history, our system has been plagued with sentencing practices that were often disproportionate and arbitrary. As a result, the U.S. Supreme Court determined in *Furman* (1972) that the administration of the death penalty at that time constituted cruel and unusual punishment and violated the 8th Amendment of the Constitution. As a result, 629 death sentences in 32 states were overturned.[32]

Legal Challenges

Following the *Furman* decision, several states developed new death penalty statutes to address these constitutional violations and bring the death penalty back to life. In an attempt to resolve the issue of arbitrary administration, North Carolina and Louisiana designed laws requiring mandatory death sentences for capital crimes. These states posited that such laws would eliminate the unregulated discretion of the jury decision-making process that concerned the *Furman* court. The justices held that mandatory death sentences would violate "the fundamental respect for humanity" and declared these laws unconstitutional.[33] However, the Court approved the statutes presented in the cases of *Gregg v. Georgia* (428 U.S. 153), *Jurek v. Texas* (428 U.S. 262), and *Proffitt v. Florida* (428 U.S. 242). Known as the *Gregg* decision, these cases developed a new system by which offenders could be sentenced to death. The provisions in these cases created three new procedures that dramatically altered the administration of capital sentences. First, the *Gregg* decision separated the guilt and sentencing decisions into two trials. As a result, juries must first determine whether the defendant is guilty of capital murder and then decide in a separate trial if the convicted person should receive the death penalty. For all states that have the death penalty, the alternate option is a life without the possibility of parole. This means that regardless of the sentence, the offender will die behind prison walls. Second, an automatic appellate process was created, which mandated that the highest court of each state review all convictions and death sentences to protect against constitutional errors. Finally, states implemented guided discretion statutes to help juries weigh the effects of aggravating and mitigating factors in applying a death sentence. **Aggravating factors** are circumstances that increase the severity of the crime, such as torture, excessive violence, or premeditation. **Mitigating factors** include references to the defendant's background that may explain the defendant's behavior but that do not constitute a legally relevant defense. In order for a death sentence to be handed out under these guided discretion statutes, a jury must determine that the value of the aggravating factors outweighs any mitigating factors. If the value of the mitigating factors exceeds any aggravators, then life without the possibility of parole (or a similarly designated sentence of incarceration) is given. Since the reinstatement of the death penalty, there

Figure 10.5   Executions in the United States, 1976–2015

The number of executions has been declining, in part due to legal challenges related to issues such as the use of lethal injection drugs.

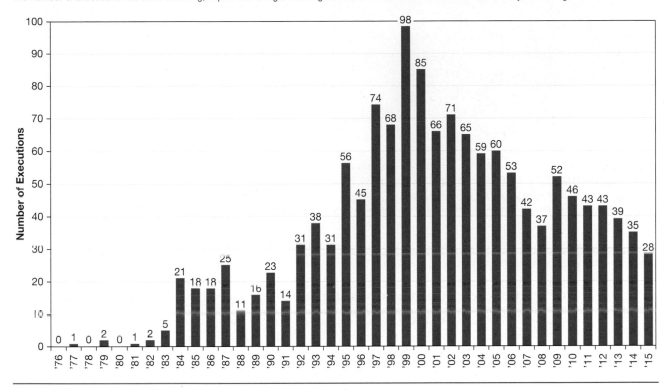

Source: Vera Institute of Justice. http://www.deathpenaltyinfo.org/executions-year

have been more than 1,400 executions in the United States. Figure 10.5 illustrates the executions that have been carried out over the past 40 years.

Methods of Execution Under the 8th Amendment

Recent execution history in the United States has involved five methods of execution: hanging, firing squad, electrocution, lethal gas, and lethal injection. While each had its day of popularity, most of these methods have drifted into obscurity in light of constitutional challenges. Today, the primary method of execution for all states is lethal injection, though, as you saw in Figure 10.4, several states still allow these other methods.

Firing Squad

The **firing squad** involves strapping the offender into a chair and placing a white cloth over the offender's heart. Five shooters are armed with rifles, although only four of the weapons are loaded with live ammunition. The cause of death is dramatic blood loss as a result of a rupture of the heart and/or lungs.[34] The use of the firing squad was made famous in modern times with the execution of Gary Gilmore in January 1977, the first execution following the reinstatement of the death penalty in *Gregg v. Georgia* (1976).[35] With the introduction of lethal injection in Utah in 1980, the state legislature retained the choice of the firing squad "in case the man who was going to die wanted his blood to be shed, as a bid for salvation."[36] In 2004, the Utah legislature enacted a provision that eliminated the option of the firing squad.[37]

Firing squad
A form of execution involving the death of an individual by a gunshot to the heart. Death occurs as a result of rapid blood loss.

Historically, the death penalty has been used as a deterrent for crime. Executions were typically public to serve as a warning against those who may consider committing similar crimes. Do you think this was effective?

However, Utah recently reauthorized the use of the firing squad if other methods were found to be unconstitutional.[38] The firing squad is also an accepted form of execution in Oklahoma but can only be used if lethal injection is found to be unconstitutional.

Hanging

Like the firing squad, **hanging** remains a constitutionally valid method of execution, even as many states have eliminated its use. Historically, hangings account for the majority of all executions throughout the history of the United States.[39] Today, hanging is utilized as an option for execution in New Hampshire and Washington. Death by hanging is designed to occur when the offender is dropped through a trap door, causing the person's body to fall and his or her neck to break, resulting in death. However, this method has seen a variety of botched executions, ranging from decapitation to strangulation.[40]

Electrocution

During the late 1800s, **electrocution** was developed as a more humane option than hanging. Death occurs from a high dose of electricity over a 30-second period that is administered to the body through electrodes that are attached to the skull and the leg. In some cases, multiple attempts are required to cause death. While the Court upheld the use of the electric chair in *In re Kemmler* (1890), many states have since outlawed its use, with Nebraska being the most recent state to declare the electric chair unconstitutional in 2008. Eight additional states (Alabama, Arkansas, Florida, Kentucky, Oklahoma, South Carolina, Tennessee, and Virginia) still permit the use of electrocution under law, though no states have carried out an execution in this manner since the adoption of lethal injection. Justice Brennan argued in 1985 that the practice of electrocution is "a cruel and barbaric method of extinguishing human life, both per se and as compared with other available means of execution."[41] In recent history, several cases of botched executions via electrocution have made headlines. In the state of Florida, the executions of Jesse Tafaro in 1990 and Pedro Medina in 1997 resulted in flames erupting from their heads due to the improper use of sponges designed to conduct electricity to their brains.[42] In both cases, the men did not die quickly. The state responded to these issues, stating that the botched executions were a result of human-related error.

Hanging
A method of execution that involves breaking the neck of an offender by suspending him or her with a rope around his or her neck.

Electrocution
A form of execution where death occurs from a high dose of electricity that is administered to the body.

Lethal gas
A method of execution that uses cyanide gas to suffocate an individual.

Lethal Gas

As the public grew concerned with the potential for pain in execution methods, several states looked toward technological advances in their search for humane execution. For many states, the move to lethal cyanide gas was the answer, and it was first introduced by the state of Nevada in 1921.[43] While **lethal gas** is an option in Arizona, California, Missouri, Oklahoma, and Wyoming, the practice is rarely utilized today. In 1996, the Ninth Circuit Court of Appeals, in the case of *Fiero v. Gomez*, held that the use of the cyanide gas was unconstitutional.[44] Recently, Oklahoma passed legislation allowing for a lethal dose of nitrogen gas as an alternative to lethal injection.[45]

Lethal Injection

Currently, the primary method of execution is **lethal injection**. First adopted by the state of Oklahoma in 1977 (with the first execution by lethal injection carried out by the state of Texas in 1982), lethal injection represents the concept of the most humane medicalized method of execution to date. Since its acceptance as a method of execution, lethal injections have accounted for the majority of all executions carried out during the modern era of the death penalty.[46]

The constitutionality of the use of lethal injection has been challenged in the courts and involves not only the petitions of death row inmates but also the opinions of medical professionals. This challenge is based on the administration of the drugs used during the execution process and inquires whether (1) the chemicals cause unnecessary pain and (2) whether the lethal injection "cocktail" masks the true levels of pain experienced by the inmate during the execution. In 2008, the Court heard the case of *Baze v. Rees*, which challenged the lethal injection process in the state of Kentucky. The Court held that the use of sodium thiopental as a sedative, which was designed to render the inmate unconscious while drugs designed to stop the heart and lungs from functioning were administered, did not constitute cruel and unusual punishment. Since then, several manufacturers of this and similar drugs have either halted production or prohibited their use in lethal injection. As a result, states have been left to seek out alternative options for use in either a one- or three-drug protocol. One option that has been used by several states is midazolam. Several inmates challenged the use of this drug after executions in Oklahoma and Arizona were identified as botched because it was unclear whether the inmate was appropriately sedated before other drugs were administered. In *Glossip v. Gross* (2015), the Court held that the use of midazolam was constitutional.[47]

> The constitutionality of the use of lethal injection has been challenged in the courts and involves not only the petitions of death row inmates but also the opinions of medical professionals.

In addition to concerns over the way in which people are executed, the Court has heard several challenges over the past three decades about who can be executed (such as juveniles and the intellectually disabled) as well as procedural issues, such as juror selection, racial bias, and ineffective assistance of counsel. In addition, public opinion polls show that support for the death penalty has declined significantly over the past two decades and that individuals are leaning more toward support for life without the possibility of parole for offenders due to the high financial costs of the death penalty. Another key debate in this issue is whether there is a risk of executing an innocent offender. You'll learn more about this debate in Current Controversy 10.2 at the conclusion of this chapter.

CONCLUSION

As you have learned in this chapter, our correctional system is tied to how and why offenders should be treated under the law. Whether it is rehabilitation or retribution that guides our practices, these foundations have a significant effect on the programs and practices that extend from our courts to our correctional system. As you read the next two Current Controversy debates, consider which correctional philosophies are best represented in these practices. Are these policies an accurate representation of what our criminal justice system should stand for? Are there alternatives that our criminal justice system should consider that would better serve our communities?

Lethal injection
A method of execution that involves the injection of drugs designed to stop the heart and lung functions, resulting the death.

Do Habitual Sentencing Laws Deter Offenders?

—Kimberly Dodson—

INTRODUCTION

In the 1970s, there was an antirehabilitation movement adopted by policymakers and legislators across the United States. The final blow to rehabilitative efforts came in the form of a report that declared "nothing works" to reduce recidivism.[48] Rehabilitation gave way to the "get tough" movement of the 1980s and 1990s. The more punitive approach toward offenders included the development and implementation of policies to punish offenders through incapacitation, bolster victims' rights, and address public safety concerns. Habitual-offender laws were an outgrowth of this policy shift.

Habitual-offender statutes target individuals who repeat the same or similar types of criminal offenses. Under these laws, habitual offenders receive harsher legal penalties because of their continued involvement in criminal behavior. Most states have statutes that include provisions for sanctioning both habitual misdemeanor and felony defendants. Being classified as a habitual offender can lead to additional criminal penalties, including greater fines and the loss of certain rights and privileges (e.g., driver's license revocation, inability to purchase or own firearms, or termination of parental rights). However, the most common type of sanction is a sentencing enhancement that allows or requires a judge to increase the term of incarceration for repeat or habitual offenders.

Three-strikes legislation is arguably the most well-known habitual-offender law in the United States. In California, if an offender has two prior felony convictions, a third felony offense (or strike) triggers a mandatory sentence of 25 years to life. California's three-strikes law is one of the harshest in the country.[49] The rationale for habitual-offender laws is deterrence.

As you recall from earlier in the chapter, deterrence consists of three primary components: certainty, severity, and celerity (i.e., swiftness). Certainty refers to the likelihood an offender will be punished for wrongdoing. If an offender believes the certainty of apprehension and punishment is great, he or she is more likely to be deterred. The severity of the punishment should not be excessive but rather proportionate to the crime committed to have the greatest deterrent effect. Swift punishment sends a message to would-be offenders that the consequences of criminal behavior will be immediate. Theoretically speaking, when these three components are applied properly, deterrence can be achieved. Deterrence is based on the premise that individuals are rational, calculating actors who make behavioral choices that maximize pleasure and minimize pain. If the consequences of criminal offending are sufficiently painful, individuals will likely choose not to engage in it. Following this logic, habitual-offender laws may have the potential to deter individuals because the consequences for repeat offenders are substantial.

 Habitual Sentencing Laws Deter Offenders

Proponents of habitual-offender laws believe repeat offenders are unable or unwilling to adhere to the laws of society and, as a result, should receive severe sanctions. They argue that certain and severe punishment will deter the future offending of habitual criminals and send a message to would-be repeat offenders that if they choose to break the law, they will face serious consequences.

The certainty of punishment is the most important element under deterrence theory.[50] To be deterred, individuals must calculate that the certainty of apprehension and punishment are relatively high. Therefore, policymakers and criminal justice practitioners must increase the public perception that those who choose to violate the law will be caught and sanctioned.

Policymakers and criminal justice practitioners have successfully heighted the public's awareness regarding habitual-offender laws. In California, for example, the highly publicized cases of Kimber Reynolds and Polly Klaas led to the passage of three-strikes legislation, which was followed by an intense media blitz. In all, 25 states have established three-strikes and/or similar habitual-offender laws, and the prosecution of two- and three-strikes cases across the country has increased dramatically since the first legislation was passed in 1993.[51] Thus, it stands to reason that the certainty of punishment for repeat offending has significantly increased, and it is difficult to imagine that the public is unaware of the potential consequences of violating habitual-offending laws. Additionally, research consistently demonstrates that the certainty of punishment is a deterrent to criminal behavior.[52]

Deterrence theory states that the severity of the punishment should be proportionate to the crime committed, or the "punishment should fit the crime." The penalties under habitual-offender statutes for repeat offenders seem to meet this criterion. Most habitual-offender laws are designed to punish serious criminal offending, especially violent crimes such as robbery, rape, and murder. It seems reasonable that harsh sanctions like life in prison for repeated acts of violence are proportionate and thus warranted. As previously mentioned, habitual-offender laws, including potential punishments, have received a great deal of media attention in the last two decades. Knowing that the sanctions for repeat offending are serious, the public has been put on notice regarding the possible consequences. Rational individuals should be able to weigh the benefits of repeat offending against the costs, resulting in deterrence.

 ## CON Habitual Sentencing Laws Do Not Deter Offenders

Opponents of habitual-offender laws are skeptical about the deterrent effect of these laws. Some policymakers believe that it is unrealistic to assume that habitual criminals are knowledgeable about these laws.[53] If this is true, then the decision to commit future crimes is made without regard to the potential consequences of violating habitual-offender statutes because the offender lacks the knowledge to conduct a cost–benefit analysis. Research shows a significant portion of offenders suffer from mental illness, including depression, bipolar disorder, and schizophrenia.[54] Mentally ill individuals often lack the intellectual capacity to make rational decisions, so it is unlikely habitual-offender laws will act as a deterrent for this population of offenders. Taken together, it appears that not all offenders rationally weigh and consider the possible costs and benefits of their behavior. On the contrary, there is a significant body of research that indicates they make decisions impulsively.[55]

Although supporters contend that habitual-offender laws ensure the certainty of punishment, there is evidence to suggest otherwise. For example, research indicates that prosecutors frequently decline to pursue charges under habitual-offender laws.[56] Prosecutors can move to dismiss or strike prior felony convictions from consideration during sentencing. There also is evidence to suggest habitual-offender

laws are not uniformly applied across jurisdictions.[57] When the probability of punishment is uncertain, the chances individuals will commit additional offenses is much more likely.

Opponents also argue that habitual-offender laws are overly severe. The public has been led to believe that these laws are directed at deterring serious habitual offenders, especially those with violent criminal histories. However, some estimates indicate that about 70% of defendants charged under habitual-offender statutes are nonviolent.[58] Habitual offenders also may trigger prosecution even if their third offense is a misdemeanor. For example, Robert Fassbender had two prior felony robbery convictions, and he faced life in prison for his third offense—stealing a pack of donuts valued at less than one dollar.[59]

One unintended outcome of habitual-offender laws is a backlog of criminal cases. Because the penalties under habitual-offender laws are so severe, more and more defendants are choosing to go to trial rather than plea bargain. Jury trials significantly slow down the courts' ability to process cases quickly. Deterrence theory states that the punishment should be swift so that the offender will associate actions with consequences. Delays in court processing hinder the deterrent effect of habitual-offender laws.

SUMMARY

Proponents of habitual-offender laws argue that certain and severe punishment should be imposed on habitual or repeat offenders to deter criminal behavior. In addition, there are some who claim that their states experienced a significant decline in serious crime in the wake of the implementation of habitual-offender laws.[60] Opponents maintain that habitual-offender laws have not had the deterrent effect that their supporters claim. Although supporters argue that crime rates decline after the implementation of habitual-offender laws, others claim that this was merely part of a downward trend in crime rates across the United States, even in states without habitual-offender laws.[61] Below are some questions to consider.

DISCUSSION QUESTIONS

1. What are some of the arguments that indicate that habitual-offender laws deter crime? Give specific examples.

2. What are some of the arguments that indicate that habitual-offender laws are not a deterrent to crime? Give specific examples.

3. Do you think habitual-offender laws deter criminal behavior? Why or why not?

California has had one of the most significant implementations of a three-strikes policy, with thousands of individuals receiving 25-years-to-life sentences. In 2012, voters approved a revision to the law that requires that the third strike to be a serious or violent felony. Is this an improvement to the law?

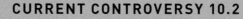

CURRENT CONTROVERSY 10.2

PRO CON

Is the Risk of Executing Innocent People Acceptably Low?

—Scott Vollum—

INTRODUCTION

Most agree that executing innocent people is the worst thing that could happen in a criminal justice system. But there is vast disagreement about whether this is likely to happen. As former Supreme Court justice Antonin Scalia has said, if an innocent person had ever been executed (in the contemporary death penalty period[62]), people would be "shouting from the rooftops" and calling for an end to the death penalty.[63] The question here is whether the risk has been sufficiently minimized so as to be acceptably low or is the risk still unacceptably high, warranting serious concerns about the use of the death penalty in the United States.

PRO The Risk of Executing an Innocent Person
Is Acceptably Low

In spite of any acknowledged risk of wrongful execution, the fact remains that there has been no officially recognized (meaning by criminal justice or governmental authorities) case of an innocent person being executed in the modern era of the death penalty. Justice Scalia made this point in *Kansas v. Marsh*, declaring that in the modern death penalty era, there has never been "a single case—not one—in which it is clear that a person was executed for a crime he did not commit. If such an event had occurred in recent years, we would not have to hunt for it; the innocent's name would be shouted from the rooftops."[64] However, even those who reject any notion of innocent people having been executed in the modern death penalty era acknowledge some risk—that it could possibly happen. But, they argue, this risk is present in all criminal justice endeavors, and to eliminate any risk would mean bringing all crime control efforts to a screeching halt. Given that the death penalty enjoys the most rigorous procedural safeguards to ensure only the right person is being executed, the risk is sufficiently low.

As you learned earlier in this chapter, the changes to the death penalty in the 1970s meant that states needed to use "super due process" in cases where an offender was facing the death penalty. The intent of these procedural safeguards was to ensure the proper and fair application of the death penalty and minimize any risk of executing an innocent person. One of the outcomes of this is a lengthy appeals process that often spans decades before an individual is executed. The exonerations that have occurred since the 1970s provide evidence that these safeguards are working, and by extension, it can be argued that the risk of executing an innocent person is kept sufficiently low.

Some take this argument one step further and note that the risk of executing innocent people must be weighed against the risk of not having the death penalty. In other words, the benefits that are gained by having the death penalty outweigh any small risk that exists of executing an innocent person.

The argument in terms of public safety takes the form of either general deterrence (that the death penalty stops other people from committing murder) or incapacitation (that the death penalty physically prevents the particular offender from causing any further harm). Most famously, Isaac Ehrlich conducted such an analysis in the early 1970s and concluded that for each execution, eight murders were prevented.[65] If this is true, it is argued, the minimal risk of executing an innocent person is acceptable given that substantially more innocent lives are being saved than lost. Similarly, if we assume that the death penalty is eliminating people who would otherwise cause further harm (whether in prison or if/when they return to society), including possibly committing more murders, the argument can be made that the death penalty is reducing harm to and the death of innocent people at a greater rate than the minimal risk of wrongful execution would yield.

 CON The Risk of Executing an Innocent Person
Is Unacceptably High

Of course, the aforementioned arguments rely on the assumption that the risk of wrongful execution is very low and that execution of innocent people, if it happens at all, is an extremely rare event. Contrary to this assumption, there is evidence that death penalty cases are particularly susceptible to errors and carry a heightened risk of wrongful conviction and execution. This is primarily due to two things: the nature of the crimes and the nature of capital trials. First, the death penalty is intended only for the most serious and heinous murders. Capital murders are typically very brutal crimes that evoke outrage and horror. This reaction by the public and officials alike puts great pressure on police to apprehend and arrest the perpetrator and on prosecutors to secure a conviction. It is argued that this creates a situation primed for overzealous investigation and prosecution. This, in turn, spawns events and factors known to contribute to wrongful convictions, such as false confessions, faulty eyewitness testimony, and prosecutorial misconduct.[66] Second, the jury selection process is unique in capital murder trials as juries are responsible for determining both the guilt of and sentence for the offender. As a result, juries must be *death qualified*. That is, individuals who could under no circumstances sentence someone to death (even if that's what the law and evidence require) must be excluded from the jury. Research has shown that the death qualification process predisposes jurors toward guilt by injecting the presumption of guilt into the voir dire (jury selection) process. Prospective jurors are asked to assume a determination of guilt in answering the question of whether they then would be able to vote for a death sentence under the appropriate circumstances. Research has shown that this creates a conviction-prone jury and increases the likelihood of convicting an innocent person and possibly sending that person to his or her death.[67]

Those who believe that the risk of executing an innocent person is unacceptably high often cite the large number of exonerations as evidence. As of 2015, there have been 156 individuals wrongfully sentenced to death and eventually formally exonerated since 1973.[68] Given this number, we are talking about more than one exoneration for every 10 executions (as of February 2016, there have been 1,429 executions in the United States). A recent study examined all cases in which offenders were sentenced to death and concluded that there was an error rate of 4.1%, meaning that about 1 in 25 individuals sentenced to death were actually innocent.[69] In addition, there have been several heavily documented cases (such as Carlos DeLuna and Cameron Willingham) in which the evidence strongly suggests that a person who was executed was indeed innocent.

In regard to the suggested benefits of the death penalty, some call into question the incapacitative value of the death penalty because capital murderers typically present no greater threat of further harm than other offenders.[70] Additionally, the option of true life without parole sentences can accomplish the same level of incapacitation as the death penalty without the risk of executing an innocent person.

SUMMARY

Others would say that it is just one among many historical examples of the heightened and endemic risk of killing an innocent person when you use the death penalty. We are compelled to acknowledge that there is *some* risk that innocent people will be executed as long as the United States continues to use the death penalty. Whether this risk is too great and the consequences too grave or whether it is as minimized as possible and worth the benefits of maintaining the death penalty will continue to be debated. On both sides is a sincere desire to save innocent lives.

DISCUSSION QUESTIONS

1. Do you agree with Justice Scalia that if an individual had been wrongfully executed, people would be shouting from the rooftops in calling for an end to the death penalty?

2. Do you think that the United States would stop using the death penalty if there were an officially acknowledged execution of an innocent person?

3. Do you think that there is an acceptable risk of wrongful execution in terms of the benefits of the death penalty outweighing this potential cost? If so, how many wrongful executions are acceptable? If not, on what grounds do you base your answer?

KEY TERMS

Review key terms with eFlashcards | SAGE edge™ • edge.sagepub.com/mallicoatccj

Aggravating factors 246	Hanging 248	Mitigating factors 246
Celerity 234	Incapacitation 237	Parole 239
Certainty 234	Indeterminate sentencing 241	Rehabilitation 236
Determinate sentencing 239	Just deserts 238	Restoration 239
Electrocution 248	Lethal gas 248	Retribution 237
Firing squad 247	Lethal injection 249	Severity 234
General deterrence 234	Mandatory sentencing 242	Specific deterrence 234

DISCUSSION QUESTIONS

Test your mastery of chapter content • Take the Practice Quiz | ⓢSAGE edge™ • edge.sagepub.com/mallicoatccj

1. How have sentencing philosophies evolved throughout history? What features suggest that retribution continues to dominate our sentencing practices? What signs exist that indicate that we may be moving away from retribution?

2. Compare and contrast indeterminate and determinate sentencing. What are the benefits and drawbacks of each?

3. What are some reasons for opposing mandatory sentencing?

4. What is required in order for deterrence to be an effective sentencing philosophy? In which cases is deterrence successful? In which cases does it fail?

5. What are sentencing guidelines, and why are they problematic?

6. What are the five methods of execution in the United States? Which is used most frequently now?

LEARNING ACTIVITIES

1. Review some of the criminal laws in your state. Identify which of the five sentencing philosophies best describes the types of punishments that are used for perpetrators of these crimes.

2. Research your state's laws on capital punishment. Discuss how these practices fit within your state's general sentencing practices.

3. Identify a case from the most recent term of the U.S. Supreme Court on sentencing practices. How will this decision alter how offenders are sentenced in your state? What challenges do you believe will arise as a result of this decision?

SUGGESTED WEBSITES

- **United States Sentencing Commission:** http://www.ussc.gov
- **The Sentencing Project:** http://www.sentencingproject.org
- **Death Penalty Information Center:** http://www.deathpenaltyinfo.org

STUDENT STUDY SITE

Review • Practice • Improve | ⓢSAGE edge™ • edge.sagepub.com/mallicoatccj

Want a better grade?

Get the tools you need to sharpen your study skills. Access practice quizzes, eFlashcards, video, and multimedia at **edge.sagepub.com/mallicoatccj**

CORRECTIONS

© iStockphoto.com/thagee

PART

IV

11
CHAPTER

PRISONS AND JAILS

- Discuss the historical significance of prisons and their influence on today's institutions
- Discuss how jails are similar to and different from prisons
- Compare the differences between federal, state, private, and military prisons
- Identify the different security levels of prison institutions

- Discuss how issues such as racial disproportionality, overcrowding, and prison misconduct impact the management of prisons
- Discuss how the Supreme Court has interpreted the Bill of Rights for inmates
- Identify the challenges that correctional officers face on the job

Prison riots have been in existence since the emergence of the modern prison. Early research on the causes of prison riots indicated that they occurred as a result of either shifts in prison authority or changes to the conditions behind the prison walls.[1] Consider the events at Attica in September 1971. More than 1,000 inmates took control of the facility and held 42 correctional officers and other staff members hostage as they made demands to the state about the treatment of inmates, lack of medical treatment, and general prison conditions. In the early hours of the riot, a correctional officer by the name of William Quinn died as a result of his injuries sustained from being beaten by the inmates and thrown from a second-story window. After four days of unsuccessful negotiations, Governor Rockefeller issued orders for state police to take back control of the prison by force. After dropping tear gas and firing more than 3,000 rounds, the police were successful in regaining control but not without injury and casualties to the inmates as well as the hostages. While early reports from the authorities indicated that the inmates had slit the throats of 10 hostages, the autopsies found that each of these officers died as a result of gunfire by the police. Twenty-nine inmates were also killed, and another 89 suffered from injuries as a result of the actions by the state police.[2] Alas, the riot did little to stem the violent abuses of the inmates by the staff, and only one officer was indicted for his abusive treatment toward the inmates.[3] Yet 62 prisoners were indicted for their actions during the riot. While a lawsuit representing the inmates was filed against the prison and state officials in 1974, it wasn't until 2000 that the suit was settled for $8 million. Indeed, it has taken more than four decades for many of the details about the riot and the abuses that followed to be made public.[4]

Since the days of Attica, prison riots have continued to occur. The 1980 riot at the New Mexico State Penitentiary was a result of changes in the management of the prison, combined with a shift in prison culture that eliminated inmate employment opportunities and related programs. Tensions between inmates began to increase as there remained few incentives for prisoners to comply with the rules of the facility. The breakdown of communication between the inmates and the prison administration further contributed to the rising tensions.[5] The riot at the New Mexico State Penitentiary stands as one of the most violent events in prison history, with more than 200 inmates injured and 33 killed.[6] Recent events across the nation, including one at a private prison in Arizona in July 2015, indicate that poor prison conditions, coupled with over-worked officers who have limited training, lead to inmate uprisings.[7]

Racial tensions and gang violence have also led to several riots across prisons in California. Yet despite the rate at which these events make the news, the number of prison riots and the deaths that result from such events are actually decreasing. Much of this decline can be attributed to the changes in who is incarcerated. Over the past three decades, we have significantly increased the number of individuals who are incarcerated for nonviolent crimes. It is these inmates who make up the majority of prison populations nationwide and reside in minimum- and medium-level secure facilities. Meanwhile, those violent inmates who once ruled the prison yard are today housed in facilities and units where there is far less freedom of movement.[8] Despite these shifts, prison overcrowding continues to be a major risk factor and contributor to prison violence.[9] Indeed, as resources for inmate programming and space continue to decrease, we may see an increase in violence within the walls of these institutions.

Prison
A facility that is designed to house individuals for a period of time as a form of punishment for breaking the law.

Jail
Correctional facility that is used to hold people until their punishments are carried out. Also offers incarceration for misdemeanor offenders and specialized programs.

In this chapter, you will learn about the structure of prisons and jails in the United States. The chapter begins with a historical review of how prisons and jails developed. The chapter then looks at the current state of jails and the different types of populations that these facilities serve. The chapter then turns to a review of prisons and highlights how issues such as security levels impact the design and organization of a facility. You'll then learn about life behind bars and how issues such as violence, programming, and health care can impact the quality of life of inmates. You'll also learn about the legal rights of prisoners and how landmark Supreme Court cases have impacted the prison environment. Finally, you'll hear about the role of correctional officers in the prison. The chapter concludes with two Current Controversy debates. The first, by Brett Garland, investigates whether we should use supermax facilities to control violent offenders. The second, by Jason Williams, looks at whether prisons should be segregated.

HISTORY OF JAILS AND PRISONS

A **prison** is a facility that is designed to house individuals for a period of time as a form of punishment for breaking the law. The concept of the prison is a relatively new one in approaches to punishment. Historically, **jail** facilities were used to hold people until their punishment was to be carried out.

Jails began to emerge in the Americas at the same time that the English settlers first arrived (Figure 11.1). Incarceration was not the typical form of punishment for much of history, and the preferred forms of punishment included whip-pings, fines, the stocks, and sentences of physical

Walnut Street Jail in Philadelphia was the first penal institution to use individual cells and work details for inmates. What role did labor play in these early correctional facilities?

labor. Given their limited use, jails were rather small in size. For example, the city of Philadelphia built its first jail in 1683—a five-by-seven-foot cage.[10] Another of the earliest jails was the Old Gaol in Massachusetts. Built in 1690, the jail was in use until 1820 and remains standing today as the oldest wooden jail in the United States.[11] Jails, such as the Old Gaol, were used as pretrial detention facilities, not as places of incarceration.

WEB LINK
Eastern State Penitentiary:
A Prison With a Past

The conditions of these early jails were very poor. They were often overcrowded, and prisoners were required to pay their own way, including food. Facilities lacked adequate space and often did not have basic necessities, such as heating, water, or plumbing. There was no form of segregation among the prisoners, and everyone was housed together, regardless of sex, health, or crime. Due to the high levels of death and disease within the jail walls, reformers set out to change the poor conditions of these facilities. For example, the Walnut Street Jail in Philadelphia first opened in 1776 and was designed to serve as a workhouse. However, this purpose was short-lived, as it was reappropriated as a military prison until 1784. By 1789, the jail was being used more as a prison for offenders serving out their sentences. As a result, the facilty became known for its use of solitary confinement and hard labor.[12]

The Pennsylvania System

Meanwhile, the birth of the American prison was the first time that the idea of imprisonment, in and of itself, was used as a source of punishment. During the early 19th century, two penitentiary systems developed. The **Pennsylvania system** was characterized by larger cells that allowed inmates to remain isolated from each other. This system of solitary confinement was developed to prevent inmates from corrupting one another. Hard work and religious reformation were the key features of this system. The cells at **Eastern State Penitentiary** in Philadelphia were large enough so that inmates could engage in work within their cells. Religion was a significant component of the rehabilitative efforts in the Pennsylvania system. Prayer and reflection were viewed as ways in which inmates could reform themselves. Alas, these facilities quickly began to fill to capacity and beyond. In addition, officials noted that the regular use of solitary confinement had a significant and negative impact on the mental health of the inmates.[13]

The New York System

While the **New York system** featured many of the same components of Pennsylvania's separate and silent system, there were also some notable differences. The cells at **Auburn Prison** were smaller than those at Eastern State, and inmates engaged in **congregate labor systems**, which allowed them to work side by side, although they were prohibited from communicating with each other. As more states began to experiment with penitentiary systems, the New York system was more popular, as it allowed facilities to house more individuals and benefit from prison labor on a larger scale. However, it wasn't long before even these penitentiaries found themselves struggling with issues of overcrowding and disciplinary issues.[14] As a result, New York and others began to scramble to build more prisons. In 1826, a group of inmates from Auburn were sent to the banks of the

Pennsylvania system
An early model of prison that focused on solitary confinement, silence, and work in cells.

Eastern State Penitentiary
The first penitentiary designed within the Pennsylvania system model.

New York system
Used the system of silence that was popular in the Pennsylvania system but adopted congregate labor systems.

Auburn Prison
The first facility under the New York model.

Congregate labor systems
Form of labor first used in the New York model that organized prison labor as a group process.

Eastern State Penitentiary was one of the first penal facilities in the United States. Inmates were kept in solitary confinement for the length of their sentence. What was the goal of this treatment?

Library of Congress Prints and Photographs Division Washington, D.C. 20540 USA

Figure 11.1   Early History of Jails and Prisons in the United States

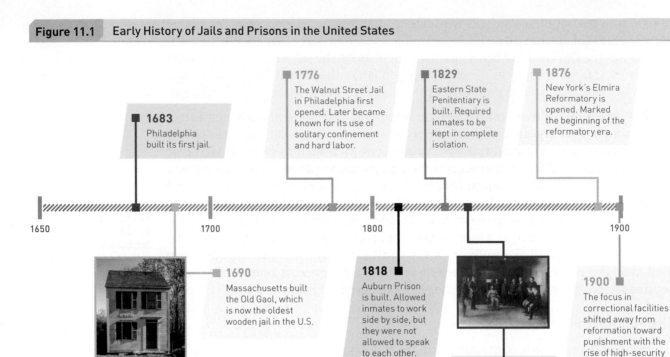

1683
Philadelphia built its first jail.

1776
The Walnut Street Jail in Philadelphia first opened. Later became known for its use of solitary confinement and hard labor.

1829
Eastern State Penitentiary is built. Required inmates to be kept in complete isolation.

1876
New York's Elmira Reformatory is opened. Marked the beginning of the reformatory era.

1690
Massachusetts built the Old Gaol, which is now the oldest wooden jail in the U.S.

1818
Auburn Prison is built. Allowed inmates to work side by side, but they were not allowed to speak to each other.

1831
Sing Sing is first opened. Relied heavily on the use of the electric chair for executions.

1900
The focus in correctional facilities shifted away from reformation toward punishment with the rise of high-security facilities like San Quentin, Stateville, and Alcatraz.

1650   1700   1800   1900

Photo credits: 1690: Kenneth C. Zirkel. Creative Commons Attribution-Share Alike 4.0 International license. https://creativecommons.org/licenses/by-sa/4.0/deed.en; 1831: William Vander Weyde/Getty Images

---

Hudson River, north of New York City, to build the next prison. This facility was Sing Sing, and it first opened in 1831, with 800 cells. Over time, more units were added to increase the number of inmates that could be housed. The days at Sing Sing were filled with corporal punishment and abuse of the prisoners in the name of "rehabilitation."[15] Sing Sing was also made famous by its use of the electric chair, which executed 614 people between 1891 and 1963.[16]

The Reformatory Era

Amid concerns that the penitentiary was unsuccessful, a new group of reformers suggested that the key features of solitary confinement and fixed sentences were ineffective and provided little incentive for inmates to rehabilitate. The **reformatory era** emerged in 1876 at New York's **Elmira Reformatory**. Elmira utilized features such as **good-time credits**, which allowed inmates to earn time off of their sentence for good behavior. Led by Zebulon Brockway, Elmira was dramatically different compared with the institutions of the past. When an inmate arrived at the institution, he was evaluated not only to determine what led to his criminal behavior but also to assess his aptitude for work and rehabilitation. This information was used to develop an individualized plan for his time behind bars. Brockway used an incentive system to motivate offender behavior changes. For example, inmates were allowed to earn statuses, which allowed them greater freedom of movement as well as privileges such as access to the mail and prison libraries.[17] This era also saw the introduction of parole as an early release program to reward inmates' rehabilitative efforts. Despite all its

Reformatory era
Emerged in 1876 in response to concerns that the penitentiary was unsuccessful.

Elmira Reformatory
The first facility during the reformatory era.

Good-time credits
Allow inmates to earn time off of their sentence for good behavior.

positive gains, the system came under fire at the turn of the century for its continued use of corporal punishment.

In addition to the emergence of reformatories, many states retained the use of custodial institutions during this period. In custodial institutions, inmates were simply warehoused, and little programming or treatment was offered. The custodial institution was more popular with southern states. In cases where a state had both a reformatory and a custodial institution, the distribution of inmates was made along racial lines; custodial institutions were more likely to house inmates of color who were determined to have little rehabilitative potential while reformatories housed primarily White inmates.[18] Black inmates were also sent to work on state-owned penal plantations under conditions that mimicked the days of slavery in the South. Louisiana State Prison at Angola (which is still in operation today) was originally a slave planation back in the 1840s. Its name references the origin of many African slaves, who arrived from Angola, a country in southern Africa. In a postslavery United States, many regions in the South used convicts in areas where slaves once worked. The convict lease system allowed states to manage a large number of inmates without bearing the high cost of their incarceration. While the convict lease system was very profitable, as workers received very little compensation, inmates were often treated very poorly.[19]

The Punishment Era

The failures of the reformatory era sent the pendulum swinging back to a focus on punishment over rehabilitation. Between 1900 and 1940, the **punishment era** dominated the prison landscape. Prison labor became popular once again, particularly in the South, where convicts were leased to local farms and plantations. The number of prisons continued to grow, and high-security facilities such as San Quentin, Stateville, and Alcatraz began to emerge. By the 1940s, a post–World War II America had once again decided that a punishment model did little to curb the rising rates of criminal behavior. The next four decades saw a return to rehabilitation, with the introduction of therapeutic treatments and education. However, as crime rates increased during the 1980s, rehabilitation once again fell out of favor with the public, and punishment once again returned to center stage.

JAILS

Today, jails are used to house individuals who are awaiting criminal prosecution and either are not eligible for bail or cannot afford it. Jails can also house individuals on shorter term sentences or serve as a transfer facility for juvenile offenders, individuals with mental health issues or immigration violations, and individuals who are being held for a probation or parole violation. Jails can also operate community-based programs such as work release, day reporting, and other alternatives to incarceration. Unlike prisons, which are run by a state or the federal government, jails are managed by local city or county governments and are often staffed by the local police or sheriff.

Jail Inmates

At the end of 2014, there were an estimated 744,600 individuals housed in local jails. California housed the largest number of jail inmates nationwide, with 81,547 over the year. Indeed, the number of inmates in just this one state is almost as large as the number of inmates held in jail facilities throughout the entire northeastern United States (87,026) and makes up over half of the jail population in the West. Much

SAGE JOURNAL ARTICLE
Revisiting the Total
Incarceration Variable

Punishment era
Emerged between 1900
and 1940, when corporal
punishment and prison labor
were used to punish offenders.

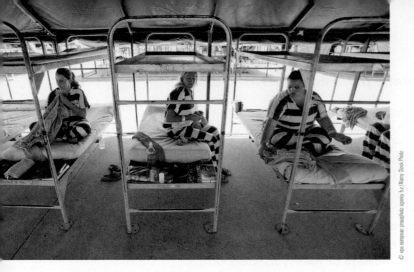

Maricopa County's Tent City was built in 1994 by Sheriff Joe Arpaio to house inmates convicted of low-level offenses. Arpaio's tough law-and-order perspective has inmates wearing pink underwear and spending their days in 120-plus-degree heat in the summertime. What type of punishment philosophy is being employed?

of the growth in California's jail population is a result of its prison realignment plan, which you'll learn more about later in this chapter. While the female inmate population increased 18.1% between 2010 and 2014, the male population decreased by 3.2%. Whites make up the majority of all inmates (47%) in local jails, compared with 35% for Blacks and 15% for Hispanics (Figure 11.2).[20] Additionally, 7% of jail inmates are veterans.[21] However, these data capture only a snapshot of a specific day. If we look at the total number of inmates who were housed in local jails between June 2013 and June 2014, we see that more than 11.4 million persons were admitted to local jails over the course of a year. While 37% of inmates in local jails have been convicted of a crime and are serving out their sentence, the remaining 63% are waiting for their cases to proceed through the system. In addition to these populations, there is another group of offenders that often falls under the jurisdiction of the jail but is not housed within the facility. This group is enrolled in various programs, which include weekend incarceration programs, forms of alternative monitoring, work release, and treatment-based programs, all of which will be covered in greater detail in Chapter 12.[22]

In addition to jails that are run by local authorities, there are 79 jails that are operated by tribal authorities and the Bureau of Indian Affairs. These facilities house individuals who are arrested or sentenced for crimes that occur on tribal land. These are generally short-term facilities, as the average length of a stay in 2014 was six days.

Figure 11.2   Jail Inmate Characteristics

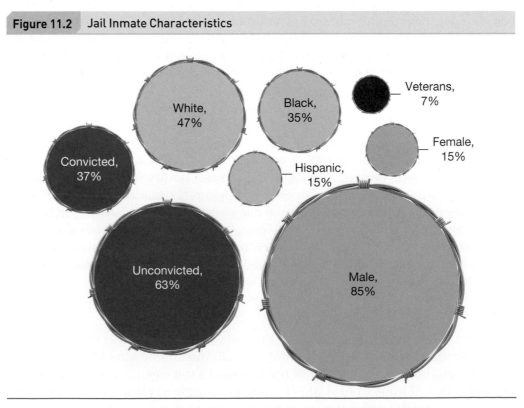

Source: Data from http://www.bjs.gov/content/pub/pdf/jim14.pdf; barbed wire photo: © istockphoto.com/RakicN

Like regional jail facilities, the majority of offenders housed in tribal facilities are male. Twenty-seven percent of inmates are in custody for violent crimes, and cases of domestic violence make up the majority of these offenses. Fifty-one percent of those housed in Indian country jails have been convicted of a crime.[23] There is also a small number of federal facilities that function as jails. In 2013, there were 12 jails that held 11,864 individuals, the majority of whom are male and Hispanic.[24]

Jail Challenges

There are several significant challenges that jails must face. As short-term facilities, their population is constantly changing. In 2013, the average amount of time that an offender spent in jail was 23 days. In states such as Idaho, Oregon, and South Dakota, the average stay was only 12 days.[25] Given these short time frames, it can be difficult to provide meaningful management of these offenders, many of whom have significant issues that have impacted their trajectory to jail. For example, 40% of jail inmates report at least one disability. These disabilities, which include limitations in hearing and vision and cognitive deficiencies, as well as compromised independent-living skills, can have a significant impact on inmates. Jail inmates with a disability are 2.5 times more likely to have experienced serious psychological distress in the month prior to their time in jail. The presence of a disability often co-occurs with other chronic conditions, like mental disabilities, such as depression, anxiety, and schizophrenia. Female inmates are more likely to report a disability than male inmates, and women are more likely to suffer from a cognitive disability. These can include issues such as learning disorders, dementia, or traumatic brain injuries.[26]

> " The U.S. Supreme Court has held that the use of excessive physical force against a prisoner may constitute cruel and unusual punishment if the force is deliberate and malicious.

Recently, there have been a number of high-profile cases in which inmates have died in custody. In 2013, 967 inmates died while in the custody of local jails, an increase over previous years. The most common cause of death in custody is suicide, accounting for over a third of all jail inmate deaths. Twenty-eight cases are characterized as homicide, either by other inmates, as a result of staff use of force, or from injuries sustained prior to being admitted to the facility.[27] The U.S. Supreme Court has held that the use of excessive physical force against a prisoner may constitute cruel and unusual punishment if the force is deliberate and malicious.[28]

TYPES OF PRISONS

There are several different types of prisons. Federal prisons house individuals convicted of violations of federal law. In addition to the federal prison system, each state maintains its own prison system. While the majority of offenders are held in government facilities, both the federal and state prison systems have used private prisons to help deal with the prison overcrowding crisis over the past four decades. There are also military prisons that house individuals who are members of the armed forces who engage in criminal behavior. Finally, there are psychiatric prisons that house offenders that either have significant mental health issues or were found guilty but mentally ill by a court of law.

State Prisons

At the end of 2014, there were 1,350,958 inmates in **state prisons** nationwide. The rate of incarceration was 612 adults per 100,000 residents. While this is the lowest incarceration rate in more than a decade, the number of individuals incarcerated in

State prisons
Prisons used to hold offenders convicted of state criminal law violations.

AROUND THE WORLD

Prisons in Russia

During the Soviet era, prisons were not only used as a source of workers that could help support the development of the economy; the experience of incarceration was used as a tool for political indoctrination. Under Stalin's rule, the Soviet Union utilized forced labor camps, known as the Gulag. These labor camps were generally located in rural areas. The conditions were so harsh that the experience of incarceration during these times amounted to a significant violation of basic human rights.[a] The end of the Communist government led to changes in the ecology of the Russian prison. New laws aimed at reforming the prison were designed to provide better conditions in the facilities as well as increased attention to the rights of prisoners. In particular, there have been significant changes to the Russian legal system since the country joined the Council of Europe in 1996. As a result, there has been increased attention on the development of criminal law and constitutional rights for all citizens.[b] However, one of the consequences of the development of a new social system has been the rise of illegal behavior, which, in turn, has led to significant growth in the number of incarcerated individuals.[c]

Despite a recent downturn, Russia has one of the highest rates of incarceration in the world. In 2015, the Russian prison population was 644,696, and the rate of incarceration was 446 per 100,000 residents. This was a significant departure from 2000, which saw 729 people incarcerated.[d] Indeed, the current level of incarceration is similar to the population in 1990, which saw 698,900 inmates incarcerated. Pretrial detainees make up 18% of the prison population. Russian prisons are predominantly male, with women making up only 8.1% of the prison population. While the percentage of women in prison has increased from 5.8% in 2002, the rate of women incarcerated remains the same. Youth in prison are also quite rare, with less than 1% being under the age of 18.

Currently, there are 992 institutions across the country. Of these, 218 facilities are reserved for pretrial detainees while 729 facilities are identified as corrective colonies. Many of these facilities resemble minimum- or medium-security prisons in the United States, and inmates are organized by security level. However, some of these corrective colonies function as open communities. Designed for first-time low-level offenders, these facilities house inmates in dormitories or apartments under prison control. In some cases, families live with the inmate. There are also 37 colonies designed specifically for juvenile offenders. Finally, there are 13 prison facilities, which are similar in design to the medium- and maximum-security facilities in the United States. The perimeter of the facility is patrolled by armed guards. Inmates are housed in cells with 5 to 30 people, and they remain in their cells unless they are working.[e] One of the most notorious Russian prisons is known as the Black Dolphin Prison, and it houses some of the most violent offenders in the country. In many ways, it is the counterpart to the supermax prisons in America.

One of the most significant concerns in Russian prisons today is the presence of tuberculosis. Over 10% of inmates suffer from TB, and the majority of these cases are not only chronic but also resistant to many of the drugs that are available to treat TB.[f] While facilities attempt to isolate cases of those who are infected, there is a higher demand for these resources compared with their availability. In addition, these confinement units are typically not available in pretrial detention centers, which places both healthy inmates and guards at risk. Left untreated, these infected inmates pose a risk not only within the prison walls but also to the general population.[g]

While work is still a central component for Russian prisoners, there are also opportunities for rehabilitation. Illiterate prisoners are sent to school to learn how to read. Inmates also participate in recreational activities, including organized sports.[h] As in a select number of states, there are a few facilities

CRITICAL THINKING QUESTIONS

1. In what ways is the Russian penal system similar to that of the United States? In what ways is it different?

2. What are some of the challenges that Russia is experiencing with its penal institutions and inmates?

within the Russian system that allow for young children under the age of 3 to reside with their mothers.[i] However, the system still has significant challenges. Many facilities suffer from high rates of overcrowding. One intake center near Russia was so overwhelmed by the masses that inmates were required to eat and sleep in shifts.[j] The work conditions remain particularly harsh, and inmates spend 16 hours a day making police uniforms.[k] Such conditions are further compromised by the fact that many of these facilities are old and have significantly deteriorated, which leads to poor ventilation, limited lighting, and overwhelmed sewage systems.[l] As the country continues to determine the role of prisons in its society, it will need to find a way to balance these challenges with the limited available resources.

prisons has increased substantially since the 1980s, and 92.6% of all state inmates are male. Texas has the largest number of people incarcerated in the United States, with 166,043 inmates. Between 2013 and 2014, Mississippi saw the greatest decrease in its prison population as a result of new policies that encourage community-based programs in lieu of incarceration. In states with small prison populations, the increase of just a few inmates resulted in a significant representative growth in their institutions. For example, between 2013 and 2014, North Dakota had 140 additional inmates at year's end, which represented a 9% increase in its prison population.

In terms of severity, 53.2% of all inmates are in state prison for violent offenses, compared with 19.3% for property crimes, 15.7% for drug crimes, and 11.0% for public-order offenses. While men are more likely to be incarcerated for violent crimes, women are more likely to be incarcerated for property and drug-related offenses (Figure 11.3). In terms of race and ethnicity, Blacks have higher rates of incarceration (56.8%) for violent offenses than Whites (47.85%), and Hispanics (59.2%) have slightly higher rates compared with non-Hispanics (47.8%). In comparison, Whites have higher rates of incarceration for property crimes compared with Blacks and Hispanics. For drug and public-order crimes, we see that there are similar rates of incarceration across all racial and ethnic groups.[29]

Indeed, much of the growth in our national prison population is related to changes in state policy. Figure 11.4 shows how the incarceration rate has changed dramatically in recent decades. Many states continue to see growth in their prison

Figure 11.3   State Prison Populations by Offense, 2014

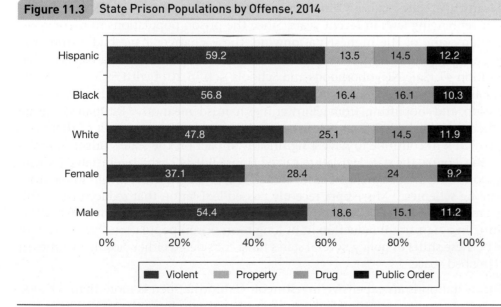

Women are more likely than any other group to be incarcerated for drug offenses. What other differences in sex and race stand out to you?

Source: http://www.bjs.gov/content/pub/pdf/p14.pdf

Figure 11.4   State Policy Drives Mass Incarceration

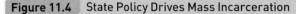

Since the 1970s, states have greatly increased their policy efforts on issues within the criminal justice system, which has had a significant effect on incarceration rates. Review some of the criminal justice policies that have been implemented in your state in the last four decades. What effect have these had on incarceration in your state?

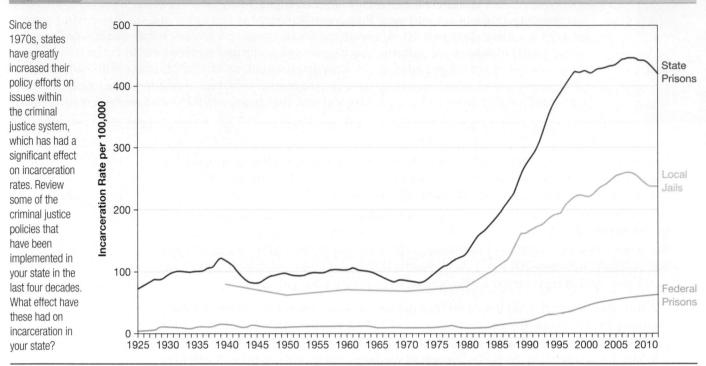

Source: Prison Policy Initiative.

populations. States such as Alabama have always incarcerated offenders at a higher rate than other states, and this number continues to grow. Louisiana incarcerated more of its male residents than any other state (1,577 per 100,000 male state residents). Oklahoma incarcerates women at the greatest rate nationwide (142 per 100,000 female state residents).[30] Such expansions are costly, as states spent more than $37 billion on institutional operations in 2010. This is a dramatic increase compared with 1982, when costs nationwide amounted to only $9.7 billion. This effective increase means that prison operating costs have increased 384% over the past three decades.[31]

Meanwhile, states such as California and New York have made significant changes to their sentencing laws in recent years. Since the prison populations in these states have been some of the highest nationwide, these changes have had a dramatic impact on the nationwide rate of incarceration. For example, California voters passed Proposition 47 (Safe Neighborhoods and Schools Act) in 2014 with 59% of the vote. This policy changed several nonviolent offenses, such as writing bad checks, drug possession, and shoplifting, from felony crimes to misdemeanors.[32] Estimates indicate that there will be 40,000 fewer felony convictions each year as a result of this measure, which will continue to have a significant impact on the state's prison population.[33] In Georgia, the state legislature passed House Bill 349, which reinstated judicial discretion for some drug-related cases and allows judges to depart from mandatory sentencing schemes.[34] Mississippi recently passed legislation that reduced the minimum amount of time served of a sentence for nonviolent offenders from 85% to 25%, resulting in a significant reduction in its long-term prison population.[35] As a result of some of these shifts in policy, several states have considered either closing facilities or reducing bed space.

Incarceration is an expensive investment. California spends more than $47,000 a year to incarcerate each inmate. Security costs make up more than $19,000 of this amount. Inmate health care is also expensive, with costs of more than $12,000 a year per person. Alas, rehabilitation costs make up the smallest portion of the budget, with only $1,612 spent on each inmate for academic education, vocational training, and substance abuse programs.[36] New York spends the most per inmate, with an average annual cost per inmate of $60,076. In addition to the costs of caring for an inmate behind bars, taxpayers are also faced with the administrative costs of staffing. Here, New York residents paid more than $3.5 billon, including $179 million in contributions to prison guard pensions and $223 millon toward the health care of retired correctional employees. In contrast, the average annual cost per inmate in Kentucky state prisons is $14,603.[37] A recent study of 40 state correctional budgets indicates that almost $39 million is spent each year incarcerating inmates in state-run facilities.[38]

> ""
> A recent study of 40 state correctional budgets indicates that almost $39 million is spent each year incarcerating inmates in state-run facilities.

Federal Prisons

Federal prisons are designed to hold people convicted of federal crimes. The Bureau of Prisons (BOP) was established in 1930. At the time that the BOP was established, there were only 11 federal prison facilities. By 1980, there were 44 institutions. However, many of these facilities were small, and the total number of inmates in these facilities was less than 25,000. Over the next two decades, the number of institutions and the inmate population exploded as a result of laws such as the Sentencing Reform Act of 1984, which not only introduced determinate sentencing practices but also abolished parole and reduced the availability of good-time credits that inmates could earn toward their release. Subsequent laws introduced minimum sentencing practices for a number of crimes, including drug-related crimes.[39]

In September 2015, there were 198,953 inmates housed in federal prisons. Eighty-one percent of inmates were housed in facilities run by the Bureau of Prisons while 12% were housed in privately managed facilities. An additional 7% of inmates are housed in community-based facilities.[40] The majority of inmates are male (93.3%) and White (58.9%), though Blacks make up 37.7% of inmates. Thirty-four percent of inmates identify as Hispanic, and 28% of federal inmates are not U.S. citizens. The majority of offenders are between the ages of 31 and 40 (36.4%).[41] Table 11.1 presents the representation of the different offenses among the federal prison population. Notice that the majority of offenders are incarcerated for drug-related crimes. In addition, the majority of these drug offenses were for crimes related to powder or crack cocaine. Crack cocaine offenders are likely to be sentenced to 10 years or more as result of mandatory minimum sentences and are predominantly Black (88%).[42] Prior to the crime that resulted in a federal prison sentence, 35% of inmates had a limited criminal history and had never been incarcerated. In addition, the majority of offenders are sentenced to five to 10 years (25.5%). Only 2.8% of offenders (5,387) are incarcerated for life. Another 57 offenders have been sentenced to death, though the last federal execution was in 2003.[43]

Federal prisons
Prison facilities used to hold offenders convicted of federal crimes.

As more offenders receive life sentences, prisons must deal with the health issues that come from an aging prison population, including the cost of medical care and even burial. Here, inmates place a coffin in a grave on prison grounds. What challenges do you think exist in managing the needs of elderly and dying inmates behind bars?

Table 11.1	Offenses of Federal Prison Inmates	
Offense	**# of Inmates**	**% of Inmates**
Drug Offenses	93,821	48.4%
Weapons, Explosives, Arson	31,676	16.3%
Immigration	17,725	9.1%
Sex Offenses	14,034	7.2%
Extortion, Fraud, Bribery	12,267	6.3%
Burglary, Larceny, Property Offenses	8,079	4.2%
Robbery	7,146	3.7%
Homicide, Aggravated Assault, and Kidnapping Offenses	5,590	2.9%
Miscellaneous	1,586	0.8%
Courts or Corrections	818	0.4%
Banking and Insurance, Counterfeit, Embezzlement	666	0.3%
Continuing Criminal Enterprise	444	0.2%
National Security	76	<0.1%

Private Prisons

In 2014, 131,300 inmates were housed in privately run facilities in 30 states.[44] While several states housed at least 20% of their inmates in **private prisons**, New Mexico is the leader in this category, as they send 44% of their state prison population to such facilities.

VIDEO
Prisons for Profit

The largest entity of private prisons is Corrections Corporation of America (CCA). CCA's largest state client is the state of California, which houses more than 8,000 of their inmates in facilities in Arizona, Mississippi, and Oklahoma. For this service, the state pays $214 million to CCA. In comparison, the federal government paid $752 million to house inmates for the U.S. Marshals Service, the Federal Bureau of Prisons, and Immigration and Customs Enforcement.[45] There are currently about 130 private prisons nationwide that offer 157,000 beds for hire.[46]

The need for private prisons resulted from the dramatic growth in prison populations during the late 20th century. States could simply not keep up with the number of inmates that they needed to house. The lack of bed space in state and federal prisons means that inmates can be sent to these privately run facilities, which can engage in competitive-bidding practices to build and manage facilities. Private prisons are also not subjected to the same levels of bureaucracy that state and federal facilities are.[47] Finally, private prisons can be built and house inmates on an individual basis and, in turn, charge a state or the federal government for this cost. This practice means that these governments do not have to provide the startup costs of building a facility. While the federal government does not collect data on whether private prisons are more cost-efficient than government prisons, some have conducted their own analyses. In one study, supported by the National Institute of Justice, researchers indicated that the cost to incarcerate a federal inmate at Taft Correctional Institution, a private prison, ranged between $33.25 and $38.37 per

Private prisons
Prisons that are used to house inmates when bed space is unavailable in state or federal facilities.

day per inmate. In comparison, housing an inmate in a publicly run facility cost between $39.46 and $46.38 per day per inmate. The average cost savings at Taft CI were about 15% lower than the government facility.[48] Yet not all states have the same experience. Arizona paid $10 million more to incarcerate its own state prisoners in private facilities.[49]

There is an incentive for private prisons to maintain their inmate populations. In 2012, CCA offered all mainland states the opportunity to sell their prison facilities to them. In exchange, states would pay CCA a per-inmate cost to run the facility. One of the largest pitfalls of CCA's offer was that it was contingent on a 20-year contract and required that states maintain a 90% occupancy rate. While no one accepted its offer, the use of guaranteed fill rates is not uncommon in the private-prison sector. In these cases, states are required to pay for unused beds.[50]

There is no guarantee that inmates will be housed in a facility that is located in their own state. For example, Hawaii sends a number of its inmates to a private prison in Arizona, paying $60 million a year to house and rehabilitate these offenders. The Saguaro Correctional Center in Eloy, Arizona, was built primarily to house Hawaiian prisoners. In designing the prison, CCA consulted with cultural advisers to incorporate traditional Hawaiian foods, holidays, and ceremonies into the culture of the facility.[51] Yet there have been several lawsuits against the facility. Two families have filed wrongful death lawsuits against the facility for failing to control gang violence in the prison, failing to classify inmates appropriately, and failing to adequately staff the facility.[52] Another class action lawsuit alleges that the facility violated the inmates' rights to their religious practice.[53] Following several inmate charges of abuse, 243 inmates were returned to the islands to serve out the remainder of their sentences.[54]

The Saguaro Correctional Center is not the only private prison in Arizona that is experiencing problems. Between 2008 and 2010, there were more than 28 riots in six private prisons in Arizona.[55] Research on private prisons indicates that they are more likely to have problems in maintaining the safety and security of the facility. A prison escape is generally a rare event, and private prisons have seen more of these incidents compared with their public counterparts. A prison escape is often symbolic of several failures within the prison. However, other studies have found a higher number of escapes at government-run facilities.[56] Private prisons also have a higher turnover rate. This means that much of the line and supervisory staff in private prisons are relatively inexperienced.[57] Certainly, much of the news reporting on private prisons is critical and highlights individual negative events. However, the limited research in this area makes it difficult to grasp whether private prisons in general are problematic or if the issues are concentrated in specific facilities.

Military Prisons

Military prisons are facilities designed to house individuals who are convicted of a crime while a member of the armed forces. In 2014, 1,409 members of the armed forces were incarcerated in military prisons for sentences greater than one year. The majority of individuals in military prison were from the army (54% of inmates). Forty-three percent of military inmates were incarcerated due to a violent crime, 24.4% of offenders were convicted of a violent sexual offense, and an additional 37.2% were convicted of a nonviolent sex offense. This means that 61.7% of all offenders in military prisons for all branches were incarcerated for sexually based crimes.[58]

Military prisons
Prisons that are designed to house individuals who are convicted of a crime while a member of the armed forces.

Military prisons can house inmates from all service branches, but each branch can also coordinate separate institutions. There are six consolidated facilities in the United States and one in the United Kingdom. The U.S. Army has two independent institutions—one in South Korea and one in Germany. The U.S. Marine Corps operates two facilities—one in Japan and one at Camp Pendleton, which is located in California. The U.S. Navy operates the largest number of facilities both in the United States and abroad. And these facilities are not located only on land; several ships have their own brigs to isolate and punish offenders.

Prior to its use as a federal prison, Alcatraz Island was a military prison, which housed both military inmates and also citizens accused of treason during the Civil War. The island served in this capacity from 1850 to 1933.[59] Fort Leavenworth, in Leavenworth, Kansas, is perhaps the most widely known current military prison in the United States. In addition to housing a U.S. penitentiary on its grounds, it houses 671 inmates between two different military facilities: the United States Disciplinary Barracks and the Midwest Joint Regional Correctional Facility. There are also six offenders who have been sentenced to death housed on the grounds. One of these individuals is Nidal Hasan, who was an army psychiatrist stationed at Fort Hood, Texas. In 2009, he killed 13 individuals and injured several others.[60] There have been no executions under military authority since 1961. The Midwest Joint Regional Correctional Facility is also home to Chelsea Manning, who was sentenced to 35 years for releasing more than 750,000 pages of classified documents in 2013. At the time of the crimes, Manning went by the name Bradley.[61] Following her conviction, Chelsea Manning successfully sued for the right to receive treatment for gender dysphoria, which included psychological counseling and hormone treatments.[62]

PRISON SECURITY LEVELS

WEB LINK
Prison Security Levels

States and the federal government have a variety of different types of prisons. These are typically organized by security level. Generally speaking, there are four categories of prison security. This refers to how restrictive the security of a facility is. Each of these categories differs in terms of the physical design of the facility, how it is staffed, and the types of operational policies that are in place.

Alcatraz Prison, which sits in the San Francisco Bay, is perhaps one of the most famous historical federal prisons. It was operated as a federal maximum security prison between 1934 and 1963 and housed some of the nation's most notorious offenders. In what way did Alcatraz represent a shift in correctional focus?

Built in 2010 to hold inmates in solitary confinement, Colorado State Penitentiary II was mothballed just 2 years later as officials moved away from the practice and the inmate population sharply declined. The prison's 948 single-bed cells now sit empty, and supporters say filling them with Guantanamo detainees would be a perfect use for the shuttered prison that still costs $20 million each year. What would be the pros and cons of moving Guantanamo detainees here?

A **minimum-security prison** is the least restrictive level of incarceration. Minimum-level prisons are designed to give inmates the highest degree of movement and autonomy and acknowledge that these inmates, while subjected to punishment for their crimes, are generally not a violent risk to the community. Many minimum-level facilities have limited or no fencing around the perimeter of the institution. Minimum-security prisons may have dormitory-style housing where several inmates reside in a space. In some states, minimum-security inmates are required to participate in rehabilitative programming to help prepare them for their return to community. The majority of prisons in the United States are classified as minimum-level prisons.

Medium-security prisons have an increased level of security compared with minimum-level prisons. There is less freedom of movement, and inmates are more likely to be housed in cells with another offender or in smaller dormitory-style units. Institutions may have a guard tower that serves to keep watch over the perimeter of the facility. The increased security of the facility means that the inmate-to-staff ratio is higher than a minimum-level prison. These inmates may have a history of violent behavior or be an escape risk. As a result, these facilities tend to have increased physical barriers to maintain the safety and security of the community.

A **maximum-security prison** is designed to house serious and violent offenders. Inmate movement and autonomy is significantly restricted. Inmates housed in maximum-security prisons are often a risk to themselves, other inmates, and staff. Figure 11.5 highlights the security levels of the current federal inmate population. Finally, some facilities and units are designated as **supermax** and are designed to house the worst of the worst. Inmates housed in supermax facilities are generally locked up in individual cells for 23 hours a day and are kept in solitary confinement, with limited interaction with others. You'll learn more about supermax prisons in Current Controversy 11.1 at the end of this chapter.

ISSUES IN INCARCERATION

Racial Disproportionality

Racial disproportionality exists when inmates of color are overrepresented in the prison population, compared with their representation in society in general. If we look at prison populations across the United States, Black men make up 37% of the male prison population, compared with 32% of White men and 22% of Hispanic males. For young inmates, Black males have the greatest disparity of incarceration, as they are 10 times more likely to be in prison compared with similarly aged White men.[63] Women of color are also overrepresented among prison populations.[64] In particular, Black women are between 1.6 and 4.1 times more likely to be imprisoned than White women.[65]

In Chapter 6, you learned about how policies about criminal justice issues have impacted incarceration rates. While many of these policies were intended to create a race-neutral system, they have had the opposite effect and have resulted in significant racial disparities among the prison population. The loss of men and women of color to the prison system also has a significant impact on communities.

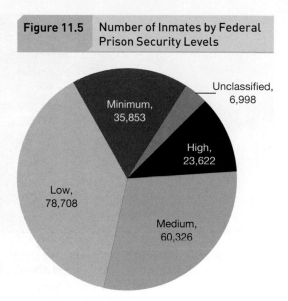

Figure 11.5 Number of Inmates by Federal Prison Security Levels

Unclassified, 6,998
Minimum, 35,853
High, 23,622
Low, 78,708
Medium, 60,326

Minimum-security prison
The least restrictive level of incarceration that is designed to give inmates the highest levels of movement and autonomy and that acknowledges that these inmates, while subjected to punishment for their crimes, are generally not a violent risk to the community.

Medium-security prison
A prison that has an increased level of security compared with a minimum-security prison and has less freedom of movement.

Maximum-security prison
A prison that is designed to house serious and violent offenders. Inmate movement and autonomy is significantly restricted.

Supermax
Prisons designed to house the worst of the worst offenders. Inmates are confined to their cells for 23 hours a day.

Racial disproportionality
Occurs when inmates of color are overrepresented in the prison population, compared with their representation in society in general.

Individuals of color are overrepresented in our jail and prison populations. Thinking back to Chapter 4, how might different criminologists account for this?

AUDIO

Doubling Up Prisoners in "Solitary" Creates Deadly Consequences

Overcrowding
Occurs when there are more individuals in prison than a facility is designed to house.

Overcrowding

Overcrowding occurs when there are more individuals in prison than a facility is designed to house. Both the Bureau of Prisons and at least 18 states are currently dealing with issues of prison overcrowding.[66] Data indicate that the total number of inmates that the federal system is rated to hold is 132,731. Yet with its current population, these facilities are operating at 128% of capacity. While California was once one of the worst offenders, recent changes to its state policy have moved the prison population to within 93% of its operational capacity. Yet other states remain large offenders. For example, Delaware prisons housed 6,730 inmates, even though these facilities were designed to house only 4,161 inmates. Similarly, Illinois prisons currently house 48,278 inmates, which is 171.1% of their design capacity. On the flip side, some state prison populations, such as those of Mississippi and New Mexico, are at only half of their organizational capacity.

Overcrowding has a number of significant consequences for both inmates and staff. As inmate populations increase, facilities may struggle to provide adequate space to house offenders. This, in turn, often leads to two or three offenders sharing a cell that was meant to house a single individual. Larger spaces such as gyms are repurposed to create open dormitories. The number of inmate jobs decreases, and options and availability for rehabilitative programming, such as school programs, job training, and drug treatment, can be reduced. Overcrowding also can lead to increased tensions between inmates, which, in turn, can increase the levels of misconduct. Not only can this threaten the safety of the inmates but it can also impact the health and welfare of the prison staff.

In 2011, the U.S. Supreme Court ruled that the current state of overcrowding and the resulting conditions of California's state prisons were a violation of the prisoners' 8th Amendment protection against cruel and unusual punishment. As a result, the California Department of Corrections was required to substantially reduce the state's prison population. To bring the prison population to 137.5% of the institutional design capacity, the state needed to reduce its prison population by 40,000 prisoners.[67]

As part of the efforts to reduce the population in the state prison, correctional officials have shifted much of the correctional supervision of lower level offenders, parolees, and parole violators to the local governments. In particular, the state legislature has altered how the state punishes felony crimes. Historically, felons were sent to the state prison, and only misdemeanor

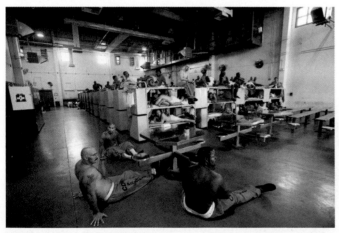

Due to tough-on-crime policies such as the war on drugs, the number of people incarcerated has grown significantly, to the point that many facilities are overcrowded. Many facilities are faced with converting spaces that were never meant to house inmates into dormitory-style housing. What steps are being taken to address this issue?

offenders served their time in local jail facilities. The introduction of Assembly Bill 109 reclassified certain felonies (nonviolent, nonserious, and nonsexual offenses) to permit offenders to serve their time in county jails. Additional legislation allows offenders to receive good-time credits based on time served as well as participation in specialized programming.[68]

As a result of California's realignment plan, the state prison population has seen dramatic changes in 2011 and 2012, both in terms of its overall size and also in terms of the types of offenders who remain housed in these state prison facilities. While there have been noted changes in the prison population for both male and female offenders, women have seen proportionally greater reductions. Not only has the number of inmates decreased significantly, but the types of offenders who remain in prison are also more likely to be violent offenders. As a result of realignment practices, nonviolent and drug offenders are now no longer housed in California's prison facilities.

Prison Misconduct

The U.S. Constitution requires that prisons make a reasonable effort to keep inmates safe. **Prison misconduct** can threaten the safety and security of a facility. There are several different forms of misconduct behind bars. These include violence, drug use, rule violations, and security-related violations.[69]

There are several factors that predict higher levels of prison misconduct. For example, younger inmates tend to have higher rates of prison misconduct compared with older inmates. Inmates with longer sentences are also more likely to engage in acts of misconduct, as are inmates sentenced to medium- or maximum-level facilities. Finally, gang members, sex offenders, and those who have a history of mental health issues have higher rates of violence behind bars.[70] Factors such as criminal history, facility security, overcrowding, racial tensions between inmates, and administrative practices can also contribute to incidents of misconduct.

Prison misconduct
Refers to acts of violence, drug use, rule violations, and security-related violations that can threaten the safety and security of a facility.

Prison Gangs

Prison gangs are a constant threat to the safety and management of the facility. Prison gangs first emerged in California facilities during the 1950s. Research estimates that 12% to 16% of inmates are gang involved.[71] Prison gangs are organized primarily by race and ethnicity. Some of the most prominent organizations include the Mexican Mafia (La Eme), the Aryan Brotherhood, the Black Guerrilla Family, La Nuestra Familia, and the Texas Syndicate.[72] Prison gangs are primarily involved in the underground drug market in prison, and the majority of prison violence is attributed to these activities.

Sexual Misconduct

Sexual misconduct is also another threat within the prison. One of the more significant efforts to combat this form of victimization is

Prison gangs are a common feature in state and federal prisons. Individuals often use tattoos to identify their membership. This photo features inmates from organized White supremicist groups in Texas, such as Aryan Nation and Aryan Circle. How might a gang threaten the security of a prison?

the Prison Rape Elimination Act of 2003. The Bureau of Justice Statistics annually collects data on the characteristics of prison rape. One of the challenges of understanding the extent of sexual violence in prison is that these acts often go unreported. The Bureau of Justice Statistics surveys former prisoners who are released on parole. The most recent data indicate that 9.6% of former prisoners reported at least one incident of sexual misconduct during their most recent incarceration period. About half of these experiences occurred between inmates, and the other half occurred between staff and inmates. In the majority of the staff–inmate experiences, these former inmates characterized these events as consensual. In comparison, the majority of inmate-on-inmate acts were nonconsensual. Women were 3 times more likely than males to experience inmate-on-inmate victimization. Race and ethnicity statistics also show differences in victimization, as White, non-Hispanic male inmates and multiracial male inmates had higher rates of this form of victimization compared with Black, non-Hispanic inmates. Finally, those who identified as bisexual and homosexual were more likely to be victimized than heterosexual inmates.[73]

While the National Prison Rape Elimination Commissions have made a number of recommendations to reduce the extent of abuse within confinement facilities, many of these reforms are costly and out of reach. Public officials have also argued that conducting annual reviews of abuse would be too costly. However, allowing such abuse to continue is also an expensive burden, as the emotional experience of victimization impacts inmates long after they have departed the facility. In addition, the failure to respond to systemic abuse within the prisons places facilities at risk for lawsuits by youth and their families. In 2007, Alabama paid a $12.7 million settlement in response to a class action lawsuit by 48 girls who served time at a state youth correctional facility.

LEGAL RIGHTS OF PRISONERS

AUDIO
California Prisons to Limit Number of Inmates in Solitary Confinement

In addition to due process rights and protections for those who are accused of a crime, prisoners also retain several constitutional rights. However, this hasn't always been the case. It was once the prevailing legal philosophy that prisoners forfeited their constitutional rights as a consequence of their crimes. *Cooper v. Pate* (1964) shifted this philosophy and opened the floodgates on prisoner litigation. Thomas Cooper filed suit saying that he was denied his right to practice his religion as a Black Muslim. Not only did the Court agree that the prison violated Cooper's 1st Amendment rights, but in handing down their decision, they established the rule that state prison inmates could sue the state in federal court.[74]

Over the past 60 years, the Court has heard numerous challenges in the name of prisoner rights. For example, while the 4th Amendment contains a basic right to privacy, inmates have very few legitimate expectations of privacy. Correctional officials may conduct searches (including strip searches) in the name of security[75] and do not need a warrant in order to search an inmate's cell or to seize materials and use them as evidence against the inmate.[76] Just as those who are accused of a crime are entitled to be represented by legal counsel, inmates are also provided this right. In cases where a professional attorney is not available, the Court has held that prisoners have the right to consult inmate lawyers.[77] In addition, prisons must provide adequate legal-library facilities so that inmates can exercise their right of access to the courts.[78] While prisoners do have the right to due process in disciplinary hearings,[79] the right to counsel does not extend to these proceedings.[80]

SPOTLIGHT

The Incarceration of the Mentally Ill

During the late 1950s, more than a half million individuals were housed in state psychiatric facilities. Over time, the move to deinstitutionalize these individuals meant that very few remained in mental hospitals while the majority transitioned into the community.[a] Yet the failure to provide viable resources meant that many went untreated. Over time, shifts in criminal justice policies meant that jails and prisons became the new asylums for the mentally ill.

By 2005, research indicated that over half of prisoners in state and federal prisons had a mental health issue. A review of state prisoner mental health issues found that 43% of state prisoners experienced symptoms of mania, 23% reported symptoms of clinical depression, and 15% of inmates met the DSM criteria for a psychotic disorder.[b] Figure 11.6 demonstrates the extent of mental health care both prior to and since their admission to prison. Many of these cases are left untreated, as only 38% of state prison inmates had used prescription medications, and only 35% received therapy from a mental health professional prior to their incarceration. Inmates with mental health issues are more likely to have issues with substance abuse and are more likely to be homeless prior to their arrest. The backgrounds of those with mental health issues are also dramatically different than those of individuals who do not have a history of mental health problems. For example, inmates with a mental health issue were more likely to have a family member incarcerated during their lifetime, were more likely to receive public assistance while growing up, and were more likely to have a history of physical or sexual abuse.[c]

Not only is the number of inmates with mental health issues increasing, but the severity of these illnesses is intensifying as well. Prisons now house more individuals with significant mental health issues than state psychiatric facilities. Alas, many of the traditional methods that prisons use to control the inmate population, such as restraining devices or solitary confinement, can increase the harm to inmates with these issues.[d] The pains of imprisonment, including separation from family and adapting to the prison environment, can exacerbate mental health conditions. In addition, many offenders with life sentences (45%) often experience suicidal ideation upon receiving this sentence.[e]

Figure 11.6 Mental Health Treatment of Offenders in Prison or Jail

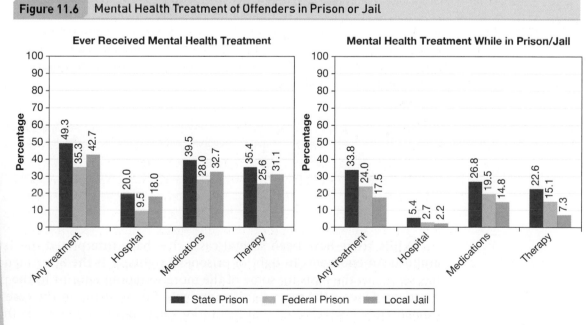

State Prison   Federal Prison   Local Jail

(Continued)

(Continued)

Data demonstrate that once inmates enter a correctional facility, their access to mental health treatment decreases. Unfortunately, the standard course of treatment in many facilities involves prescription psychotropic medications. Often, these medications are prescribed in excess and often in lieu of counseling or other therapeutic interventions. For example, one study indicates that 21 of the 22 participants were given the prescription Seroquel,* which is used to treat bipolar disorder. Yet only one of the women was actually officially diagnosed with bipolar disorder. While the manufacturer of Seroquel recommends that people who take this medication be reassessed at regular intervals, few of these inmates actually received such treatment while in prison. While some drugs were readily available, the same did not hold true for all psychotropic medications. In some cases, prison doctors would prescribe new drugs to the inmates rather than continue to offer prescriptions for drugs that had been effective in the past. "Prison doctors just do whatever they want; the opposite of what you were getting before you went in so that they can show you who's boss. It's just a way for them to show you how much control they have."[f] Not only can the failure to comply with a prescribed medication protocol be grounds for a disciplinary action while in prison but such behaviors can also be used against an offender during a parole hearing.

Some inmates believe that their mental health status improves during incarceration because they were appropriately medicated, were no longer using illicit substances, and were engaged in therapeutic support programs. However, the majority of inmates believed that incarceration exacerbated their mental health issues and that a number of variables contributed to this. First, incarceration is a stressful experience, and stress can increase feelings of anxiety and insecurity. Second, the majority of resources for mental health were focused on crisis intervention, not therapy. In particular, "lifers" felt that they were often placed at the end of the list and were denied services due to their sentence. Finally, many of the inmates felt degraded and abused by the staff, which added to their trauma.[g]

CRITICAL THINKING QUESTIONS

1. What challenges do prisons face in dealing with mentally ill inmates?

2. How can prisons improve inmate treatment access and options behind bars?

Research has made several recommendations for reforming the experience of mentally ill prisoners. First, we need increased options in the community to help stabilize individuals before they become involved in the criminal justice system. Second, we need to implement diversion-style programs in lieu of incarceration. Third, facilities need to develop better screening tools for mental health issues and expand their services beyond traditional efforts, which are often limited to suicide prevention. Finally, states need to allocate adequate financial resources to provide appropriate levels of care for these individuals during their incarceration.[h]

---

*The manufacturer of Seroquel indicates that "Seroquel is an anti-psychotic medication, useful as a mono-drug therapy or as an adjunct to the drugs lithium or divalproex for the treatment of schizophrenia and the acute manic and depressive episodes in bipolar disorder" (Kitty, 2012, p. 168).

While there have been several cases that have interpreted the 1st, 4th, 5th, and 6th Amendments in light of prisoners' rights, it is the 8th Amendment that has served as the basis for some of the more sweeping reforms to the prison environment. One of the most significant decisions occurred in the case of *Estelle v. Gamble* (1976), which held that institutions may not be deliberately indifferent to

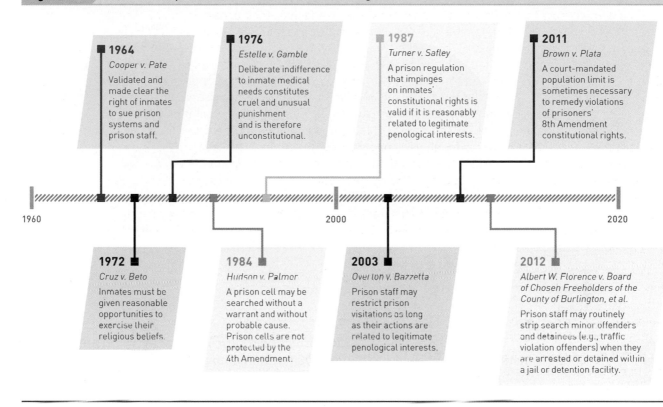

the serious medical needs of inmates (Figure 11.7).[81] In fact, recent decisions by the Court require prisons to provide adequate medical care within the prisons, though the Court does not go so far as to define what this might look like.[82] While practices such as double celling are not unconstitutional on their own,[83] prison administration may not also be deliberately indifferent to the negative conditions of confinement, such as facility overcrowding, poor lighting and ventilation, and unsanitary conditions.[84] Indeed, several states have active lawsuits filed by inmates alleging that the conditions of confinement violate the 8th Amendment. In 2012, the Southern Poverty Law Center filed suit against the Alabama State Correctional System claiming that the state failed to provide basic medical and mental health care to inmates.[85] However, relief from the courts will not likely be swift, as a similar lawsuit in Florida was settled 19 years after it was filed.[86]

CORRECTIONAL OFFICERS

Correctional officers (COs) are a central component of the criminal justice system. Responsible for the security of the correctional institution and the safety of the inmates housed within its walls, correctional officers are involved with every aspect of inmate life. Indeed, correctional officers play an important part in the lives of the inmates as a result of their constant interaction. Contrary to other work assignments within the criminal justice field, the position of the correctional officer is integrated into every aspect of the daily lives of prisoners. Duties of the correctional officer range from enforcing the rules and regulations of the facility to responding to inmate needs to diffusing inmate conflicts and supervising the daily movement and activities of the inmate.[87]

Correctional officers
Criminal justice officials who are responsible for the security of the correctional institution and the safety of the inmates housed within its walls.

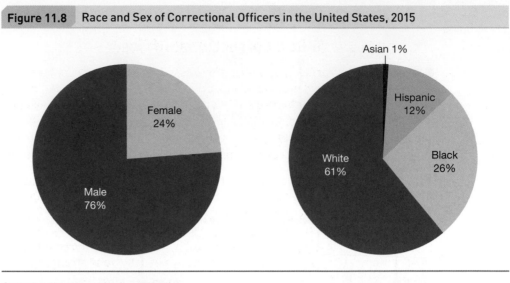

Figure 11.8   Race and Sex of Correctional Officers in the United States, 2015

Female 24%

Male 76%

Asian 1%

Hispanic 12%

White 61%

Black 26%

Source: http://www.bls.gov/cps/cpsaat11.pdf

VIDEO
Alarming Number of Corrections Officers Driven to Suicide

In 2013, there were 434,420 correctional officers working in prison facilities nationwide.[88] With more than 49,000 positions, Texas employs the largest number of correctional officers in the country. While the majority of correctional officers are men, women make up 37% of correctional officers in state adult facilities and 51% of juvenile correctional officers (Figure 11.8).[89] Within these facilities, both men and women are assigned to same-sex as well as cross-sex supervision positions. In addition, more women are working as correctional officers in exclusively male facilities, where they constitute 24.5% of the correctional personnel in these institutions.[90]

Many choose corrections as a career out of interest in the rehabilitation services, as well as a perception that such a career provides job security.[91] However, work as a correctional officer can be quite stressful. There is a high degree of bureaucracy within the prison walls, which can contribute to feelings of job dissatisfaction. On-the-job stress is also a significant issue. There is always a risk of harm from the inmates. Officers may also feel dissatisfied with their roles if they lack the resources to perform their jobs or don't see adequate progress in the rehabilitation of the inmates. In addition, many officers may feel stuck in their roles as they perform the same duties day in and day out.[92] As one CO describes it, life on the job is like "serving a life sentence in eight-hour shifts."[93] Stress and burnout also can extend beyond the prison walls and impact the personal lives of these officers.

CAREER VIDEO
Correctional Officer

CONCLUSION

The management of jails and prisons composes a significant part of state and federal correctional budgets. Due to our current criminal justice policies and practices, institutions are faced with large numbers of offenders. In many cases, prisons are overcrowded, which not only complicates the delivery of inmate services but can threaten the safety and security of the facility, the residents, and the staff. As prisons continue to represent a dominant force in our criminal justice system, policymakers will need to reevaluate how these institutions will be used as a form of punishment and who will be housed within their walls.

CAREERS IN CRIMINAL JUSTICE

So You Want to Be a Correctional Officer?

The boom in prison populations has also led to a significant increase in the number of jobs in these facilities. In order to work as a correctional officer, you must be at least 18 years old (though many states set a minimum age of 21 years old), a U.S. citizen, and have a clean criminal background. Generally speaking, most facilities do not require more than a high school diploma for an entry-level position. However, some states and the federal government require a bachelor's degree. Some positions will accept active or reserve military experience in lieu of college coursework.

Recent reductions in the prison population mean that the current job outlook for this career field is slower than it once was. The median pay in 2014 was $44,910,[a] though in states such as California and New Jersey, the salaries are significantly higher ($68,800 and $71,660 respectively). In comparison, the average wage in Mississippi is just $26,430.[b] Since facilities are open 24 hours a day, 365 days a year, there are often significant opportunities to earn overtime pay. In addition, the medical and retirement benefits for these positions are usually quite strong, particularly for those working in state or federal facilities.

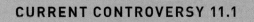

CURRENT CONTROVERSY 11.1

Should We Use Supermax Prisons to Control Offenders?

—Brett Garland—

CURRENT
CONTROVERSY
VIDEO
Where Do You Stand?
Cast Your Vote!

INTRODUCTION

Supermax, in correctional language, is short for *super maximum* and refers to "a highly restrictive, high-custody housing unit within a secure facility, or an entire secure facility, that isolates inmates from the general prison population and from each other due to grievous crimes, repetitive assaultive or violent institutional behavior, the threat of escape or actual escape from high-custody facility(s), or inciting or threatening to incite disturbances in a correctional institution."[94] The typical supermax facility houses these noncompliant and disruptive offenders for 23 hours a day with little opportunity for shower and exercise.[95] Other supermax features vary across jurisdictions, such as the stringency of procedures to move from the supermax to a less secure location inside prison, the availability of inmate-to-inmate contact, and the opportunity to participate in programs and receive library services. Ultimately, the supermax functions as a segregation unit, which is a concept that has existed in American prisons for many decades. What makes supermax

confinement unique is that supermax offenders are normally housed for lengthier periods than in regular segregation units, and entire prison facilities may serve as a supermax.[96]

The emergence of the modern-day supermax was ignited by the murder of two correctional officers by inmates at the federal prison in Marion, Illinois. These incidents fueled an extended lockdown at the prison and made Marion a full-scale supermax facility and a model for future supermax units. Violence in American prisons had always been a deep concern, with inmate riots and rebellions flourishing during the middle of the twentieth century. The deaths of the officers at Marion also happened at a time when criminal justice policy was growing more stringent, and tolerance for crime and disorder was rapidly declining. State and federal legislation reflected a "lock'em up" mentality, and this new attitude seeped into correctional practice, with a renewed emphasis on tough punishment and a de-emphasis on offender treatment and reform.

One of the most popular arguments in favor of supermax facilities is that extended stays in segregation units, by definition, isolate dangerous and unruly prisoners and thereby prevent supermax inmates from directly committing serious misconduct against the general prisoner population.[97] This strategy is called incapacitation and is routinely advocated as a justification for using imprisonment as a punishment in the criminal justice system. The logic goes that if bad, harmful people are locked up in prison, they cannot hurt anyone out in society while incarcerated. The supermax then serves as a type of prison within the prison system. The supermax lockdown approach assumes that prison staff will be able to maintain control of prisoners in these ultra-high-security environments and not be victimized themselves. In addition, the enhanced supermax security should protect violent and disruptive prisoners placed there from inflicting harm on one another because typically, they are securely separated by formidable physical barriers.

Advocates of the incapacitative function also point out that many prisoners housed in supermax units had previously facilitated violence and disorder by directly influencing inmate behavior in the general population.[98] Prison systems in states like California have placed a substantial number of gang leaders into supermax facilities, believing that by severing the head of the gang organization, lower ranking members will no longer receive orders to carry out gang business and consequently will become less disruptive. Prison gangs, such as the Aryan Brotherhood and Mexican Mafia, have hierarchical organizational structures, which implies that lower ranking members are guided heavily by gang leadership. Isolating problem inmates, not necessarily gang members, in a supermax may also create a better prison environment by removing the relatively small number of "bad apples" who cause serious disruptions and threaten institutional order. With troublemakers removed, more compliant inmates have fewer opportunities to feed into episodes of misconduct. The placement of problem offenders into a supermax might also make institutional programs like education classes, stress and anger management sessions, and trade skill courses function more efficiently with inmate distractions contained. In turn, this should lead to greater institutional order and less violence since offender programming provides positive ways for inmates to occupy time and cope with the daily grind of prison life.[99]

In addition to potential incapacitative benefits, some proponents of supermax confinement believe that the deprivations imposed by isolation will deter the person experiencing the supermax and others who may fear facing supermax time from future misbehavior.[100] Serving time in an isolated setting is often portrayed as an extremely unpleasant experience. Physical movement is severely restricted, and boredom can be extreme and agonizing. The experienced or perceived misery of the supermax, then, should dissuade offenders from engaging in conduct that might lead to a supermax placement.

 We Should Not Use Supermax Prisons to Control Offenders

Opponents of the supermax challenge the claims that it successfully achieves incapacitative and deterrent goals. To reduce violence through incapacitation via supermax placements, prison administrators will need to isolate offenders who would otherwise commit violent acts and serious disruptions if left in the general prisoner population. Although identifying those who will reoffend sounds like a simple task, correctional risk assessment instruments sometimes inaccurately predict who will continue engaging in misconduct during a prison term.[101] If the intent is to reduce violence and disorder through incapacitation, but the inmate has already decided not to engage in further misconduct, the supermax placement will have no direct incapacitative impact. Critics also note that supermax units create potential hot spots of violence since prisoners with serious records are concentrated in close quarters.[102] Even if supermax offenders are kept separate and unable to conspire together or attack one another, the frustration experienced in supermax deprivation may motivate already volatile and disruptive offenders to lash out aggressively and defiantly at staff.

Others question whether supermax confinement can significantly hinder the influence of prisoners who facilitate prison disorder through their leadership positions.[103] Inmates are creative and have found methods to communicate with the general prisoner population when held in high-security environments, such as sending encoded written messages and manipulating staff and other offenders to communicate on their behalf. Removing leaders of prisoner groups and gangs from the general population might also backfire by creating power vacuums. Gang members may compete physically against one another in a prolonged struggle to fill vacant leadership roles. In addition, leaders of inmate organizations can be very influential in keeping other inmates in line, and their controlling influence may enable the aggression of lower ranking gang members to be unleashed during their absence.[104]

The deterrent value of the supermax is also debated. The certainty of receiving a specific punishment is critical for that punishment to achieve a deterrent effect. One study has found that prisoners view supermax placements as quite arbitrary, meaning that for a serious prison violation warranting supermax isolation, an offender might get placed there or might get a different sanction, such as the loss of good time.[105] Without a high degree of certainty of receiving supermax placement for serious misconduct, there is little reason to expect that inmates will be dissuaded from disruptive behavior. Moreover, critics charge that the unpleasantness and loneliness of a supermax stay takes a tremendous psychological toll and has serious mental health consequences. Studies indicate that solitary confinement can cause severe anxiety, cognitive dysfunction, and suicidal ideation, which may impair one's ability to function when released into the general prison population and back into society and thereby make supermax inmates more likely to misbehave and reoffend.[106]

SUMMARY

Unfortunately, studies on the effectiveness of supermax facilities are few in number and provide mixed results.[107] Nonetheless, the idea of segregating violent and seriously disruptive prisoners from the general prison population is not new. If problem inmates can be handled effectively through traditional prison segregation units, there is no need for a supermax. The financial costs of prison space rise as the level of security increases, so a supermax unit is a waste of money if a clear need is not established for it.

If the traditional segregation units prove inadequate, then either the supermax or some alternative is necessary. Prior to the emergence of supermax facilities, a dispersion strategy was common, which consisted of transferring extremely difficult prisoners to other prisons within a correctional system. The effectiveness of this strategy is just as unclear as the supermax approach. Hopefully, new research will emerge in coming years and provide greater clarity regarding this controversial correctional practice.

DISCUSSION QUESTIONS

1. Is the supermax an effective deterrent against institutional violence?

2. How might the supermax experience be harmful to inmates?

3. What alternatives could be used to manage the safety and security of an institution in lieu of the supermax?

CURRENT CONTROVERSY 11.2

PRO CON

Is Segregating Prison Populations a Good Policy?
—Jason M. Williams—

CURRENT
CONTROVERSY
VIDEO
Where Do You Stand?
Cast Your Vote!

INTRODUCTION

Segregating prisoners is a very controversial and complex issue. Prison officials must take extreme precaution to ensure that prisoners and correctional workers are protected. However complicit they are in this practice, officials are often led to engage in certain controversial maneuvers to ensure the tranquility and safety of their institutions. Segregation has been used as a management tool to exert discipline over inmates.[108] This debate will critically examine whether or not prison segregation is a useful tool.

Earlier in this chapter, you learned about how the use of segregation was debated between the Pennsylvania and New York prison systems. While the origins of segregation can be found in our early prisons, its use today varies. There are some forms of segregation that are disciplinary, whereas others are protective. There are four main forms of segregation practiced within most U.S. prisons: (1) disciplinary segregation, a form of segregation that punishes inmates for violating codes and rules within the prison; (2) administrative segregation, a tactic used to remove prisoners who pose a threat to other inmates and prison workers from the general population (this form of segregation can also be used during long-term investigatory processes); (3) protective custody, a form of segregation that seeks to protect those who are at risk within the general population; and (4) temporary confinement, a tactic used during the process of investigating an active incident, which is usually short in contrast to administrative segregation. These forms of segregation are highly controversial and are used for various reasons.[109]

 PRO   **Segregation Is a Good Policy**

There are many instances where prison segregation can be viewed as a positive. For example, in contemporary society, prisons have become hazardous spaces where anything is to be expected, and the expectation of danger within the prison has caused many prison officials to adapt to these new emerging issues to maintain the safety of inmates and prison workers. Furthermore, the prison is also a holding space for all of the ills of society—a harsh and hard reality for anyone to control. For instance, not only does the prison hold criminals, but it is also overflowing with mentally ill individuals and those with other kinds of medical abnormalities who may belong in a hospital instead of a prison. Some prisons may also hold juvenile offenders and other protected classes of individuals, who, by the nature of their offenses, gender, or sexuality, may need to be quarantined from the general population. To this extent, prison segregation has become commonplace to maintain peace and the safety of the many kinds of inmates who are incarcerated.

The mentally ill population is one such group that benefits from segregation, as they are often segregated from the general population due to their psychological conditions. If the mentally ill were included in the general population, they would become a major risk not only to themselves but also to other inmates and prison workers. Also, those with developmental, intellectual, and physical disabilities are annexed in spaces that are conducive to their special needs. Thus, quartering these populations into specialized housing units within the prison is not only logical but it is also crucial to the well-being of all individuals within the prison.

Gender is another area where segregation is reasonable. For example, incarcerating males and females within the same prison space may present serious hazards to inmates and prison workers. Therefore, preventing the genders from intermixing helps to preemptively prevent in-prison sex offenses, the hypertransmission of sexually transmitted diseases, unplanned pregnancies, and a host of other costly complications that would normally exist outside of the prison.

Moreover, sexuality is also a crucial component of segregation. Inmates who identify as gay are often considered high risk and are quarantined from the general population for their own protection.[110] Gay men are stereotypically conceived as weak to many within the general population, and as a result, these false conceptions may lead to victimization. Thus, segregation via the use of protective custody serves to protect gay men from being perpetually victimized (mentally, physically, and sexually) and preyed upon by heterosexuals, who dominate the general population. Postallegation protective custody also exists for those who have been sexually assaulted and are subsequently in need of protection from their abusers.

Another group that would normally be segregated within the prison is juvenile offenders. Many states allow for the transfer of juveniles to the adult court, which can result in juveniles being admitted to adult prisons. As a result, many prison officials segregated these juvenile offenders from the general population under the concept of protective custody. These kinds of policies are positive because they help to prevent many dangers that juvenile offenders would likely face if placed in the general population.[111] Thus, based on these examples, one can ascertain that prison segregation is a useful tool for prison officials, as segregation ensures tranquility and protection; however, there are some cons to the use of segregation.

 ## CON Segregation Is Not a Good Policy

While some may advocate for the use of prison segregation, there are some core cons that deserve attention. An infamous example within the state of California is segregation by race. One might argue that segregating races engenders an atmosphere of isolation that fuels racism and xenophobia that presents additional potential safety risks in the prison. The racial battles within many of California's prisons are well documented.[112] Furthermore, many prisons also segregate gang members. While segregating gang members may seem suitable at the surface level, similar to race, keeping gangs in a state of isolation can potentially fuel gang warfare within the prison. An opponent to segregating gangs may advocate for safe spaces, within which gang members may come together to settle tensions and positively socialize with each other. In-prison programming aimed at the long-term rehabilitation of gang members may be better suited for ameliorating the problem of gangs.

Moreover, the use of segregation (including the four forms listed in the prior section) has dire consequences. While many people support segregation, little is generally known about the conditions that the segregated often have to face. For example, segregated prisoners are often treated hyperpunitively, even in cases where their segregation is a protective measure (i.e., juvenile, gay, or mentally ill offenders). Segregation often includes intense isolation, as "prisoners in segregation are taken out of their cells for only one hour out of every twenty-four hours, either for recreation or a shower."[113] The impact isolation has on the human psyche is tremendously negative, and in some instances, to heighten

punishment, medical services are even limited for segregated inmates. Furthermore, segregated inmates are more likely to develop psychological abnormalities while isolated.[114] The use of segregation is also disproportionately aimed against inmates with preexisting psychological illnesses, which often worsen during isolation. As a result, the use of segregation can create broken inmates who will pose new sets of problems to both prison officials and society once returned to the general population and freed from the prison. There have been countless reports of suicides and suicide attempts by those in segregated housing, too. Further, the use of segregation is costly,[115] as it requires additional staff to monitor the cells and the inmates' needs (e.g., showering, exercise, appointments, etc.).

Segregating those who are medically disabled can have an adverse effect on inmates, too. For example, in 2012 a federal judge ordered the state of Alabama to put an end to segregating HIV-positive inmates because it violated the Americans With Disabilities Act.[116] Opponents to this form of segregation argued that the policy was inhumane and discriminatory— that isolating inmates with HIV had a rejecting effect on the inmates. Incidentally, these inmates were forced to wear armbands that identified their condition; this visible layer served as an additional punishment, meted out because of their condition. Thus, segregation, in this context, shames inmates and has the potential to create additional risks for prison workers. Such shaming can also create psychological abnormalities that are likely to develop as a consequence of shaming.

SUMMARY

While prison segregation has its pros, it also has its cons. Contemporary issues in U.S. prisons today require prison officials to be adept and armed with the knowledge that enables them to protect inmates and prison workers while also ensuring that inmates' rights are not jeopardized. Nevertheless, old processes like segregation (and others) are increasingly becoming a moral issue for

many politicians, criminal justice professionals, and citizens. However, despite the backlash against segregation as a safety and disciplinary tool, there is still a void as to what a replacement system may look like that would ensure peace and safety in U.S. prisons. A process of reconciliation between the pros and cons of segregation must be sought if the debate is ever to be settled.

DISCUSSION QUESTIONS

1. What are the historical traces of prison segregation?

2. Are there any benefits to prison segregation? Explain.

3. Are the consequences of prison segregation so dire that segregation should be outlawed? Why, or why not?

4. Create a new system that would account for special inmate populations if segregation were to be abolished.

KEY TERMS

Review key terms with eFlashcards | $SAGE edge™ • edge.sagepub.com/mallicoatccj

Auburn Prison 261

Congregate labor systems 261

Correctional officers 279

Eastern State Penitentiary 261

Elmira Reformatory 262

Federal prisons 269

Good-time credits 262

Jail 260

Maximum-security prison 273

Medium-security prison 273

Military prisons 271

Minimum-security prison 273

New York system 261

Overcrowding 274

Pennsylvania system 261

Prison 260

Prison misconduct 275

Private prisons 270

Punishment era 263

Racial disproportionality 273

Reformatory era 262

State prisons 265

Supermax 273

DISCUSSION QUESTIONS

Test your mastery of chapter content • Take the Practice Quiz | $SAGE edge™ • edge.sagepub.com/mallicoatccj

1. How do issues of prison misconduct threaten the safety and security of institutions? How can prison administrators and others alleviate these problems?

2. How are jails different from prisons?

3. What are the different security levels in a prison?

4. How does the security level of a prison facility alter the quality of life of inmates and efforts at rehabilitation?

5. What are some of the key Supreme Court decisions that have affected inmates' rights?

6. How can prisons address issues of racial disproportionality within their facilities?

7. What are some challenges that correctional officers face on the job?

LEARNING ACTIVITIES

1. Investigate the use of private prisons in your state. How many private facilities operate in your state? How are they similar to and different from state-owned institutions? How many inmates in your state are housed in a private prison? What challenges does this present for these inmates?

2. Identify a recent U.S. Supreme Court decision on the rights of offenders. How might this ruling be applied to individuals in custody? How will prison officials need to respond to this ruling in order to ensure that inmate rights are not violated?

SUGGESTED WEBSITES

- **Bureau of Prisons:** http://www.bop.gov
- **Bureau of Justice Statistics:** http://www.bjs.gov
- **Prison Policy Initiative:** http://www.prisonpolicy.org
- **Corrections Corporation of America:** http://www.cca.com

STUDENT STUDY SITE

Review • Practice • Improve | **$SAGE** edge™ • **edge.sagepub.com/mallicoatccj**

Want a better grade?

Get the tools you need to sharpen your study skills. Access practice quizzes, eFlashcards, video, and multimedia at **edge.sagepub.com/mallicoatccj**

COMMUNITY CORRECTIONS

LEARNING OBJECTIVES

- Discuss the function of pretrial services

- Identify how diversion programs differ from other forms of community corrections

- Compare the five different types of probation sentences and the role of the presentence investigation report

- Discuss the different forms of intermediate sanctions

- Compare the two different ways that the term *parole* is used

- Discuss the issues that ex-offenders face during the reentry process

n the late 1960s, the charismatic Charles Manson lived with a few dozen followers on an abandoned ranch/movie lot near Topanga Canyon in L.A. County, engaging in free love and drug experimentation. He called these followers his "family." Among his more radical ideas, Manson believed a race war called Helter Skelter was coming, and he developed a plan to initiate this inevitable race war. He convinced several of his followers to commit murder, thereby testing their loyalty and sparking Helter Skelter. Several members of his "family" followed his request, including the "Manson women": Susan Atkins, Leslie Van Houten, and Patricia Krenwinkel.

Susan Atkins and Patricia Krenwinkel participated in the now infamous murder of the pregnant actress Sharon Tate and her houseguests on August 8, 1969. They, along with another follower of Manson, Charles "Tex" Watson, stabbed the five victims at Tate's house more than 100 times, smearing blood on the walls of the home. Atkins reportedly wanted to cut out Sharon's Tate's unborn baby, but there wasn't time. Two days later, Van Houten joined as Atkins, Krenwinkel, and Watson stabbed a wealthy grocer, Leno LaBianca, and his wife, Rosemary, leaving another gruesome crime scene in their wake.

During their arrest, trial, and initial incarceration, the Manson women remained loyal to Manson and appeared as the monsters depicted in the media, often chanting and behaving in a bizarre fashion, presumably at Manson's instruction. All three were convicted and sentenced to death for committing murder. Their death sentences were commuted in 1972 to life sentences with the possibility of parole when state and federal courts declared capital punishment unconstitutional.

A psychiatrist who performed an evaluation of Susan Atkins shortly after she entered prison expressed his belief that Atkins would eventually change her worldview in opposition to Manson's, suggesting she would no longer be a danger to society. As early as her first parole hearing in 1975, doctors recommended Atkins for release. It was never granted. For the next 30 years, her parole petitions were denied. She was a model prisoner who got along well with the other

inmates and the correctional staff throughout her imprisonment; she participated in many prison programs and even started a prison choir. When she was diagnosed with brain cancer in March 2008, her husband, James Whitehouse, petitioned for a compassionate medical release; his petition was denied. In September 2009, the parole board once again held a hearing on whether or not to grant Atkins parole. The board denied parole for the 13th time, stating that Atkins was still a danger to society. At this time, Atkins was living in a skilled nursing facility inside a prison compound, near death from terminal brain cancer. She died three weeks later on September 24, 2009, as an inmate in the California prison system.

Leslie Van Houten speaks before the board at her 20th parole board hearing. After 44 years behind bars, the board voted in favor of parole in April 2016. What might be some factors contributing to her inability to obtain release?

Leslie Van Houten is also described as a model prisoner. She denounced her ties with Manson months before being sent to death row. She is currently working toward a master's degree and is very active in the Prison Pups program, which allows inmates to train service dogs for the disabled. Van Houten was granted parole in 2016 after 20 rejections.

Patricia Krenwinkel was very involved in taking care of the Manson family children before she committed murder. She is also described by prison staff as a model inmate. In January 2011, Krenwinkel was denied parole for the 13th time at the age of 63. The parole board set her next hearing date for 2018.

All three of these women were described by the prison staff at the California Institute of Women, where they served most of their sentences, as model prisoners. They have perfect prison records, never having been written up for any disciplinary reason. All three earned college degrees while serving their time. They were each in different prison programs: Krenwinkel helped other inmates learn to read, and Van Houten worked as a college tutor for other inmates. The prison staff continually recommends to the parole board that these women be released, and the parole board has generally denied their requests, saying these female murderers remain a danger to society nearly half a century after their murderous summer of 1969.

Community corrections work with two distinct populations: those who have been sentenced for a crime and those who have been charged with offenses and are waiting for their cases to be resolved by the criminal justice system. One group has been found guilty while the other group is presumed innocent throughout the process. As a result, programs are designed either to reintegrate offenders back into the community or to provide an alternative to incarceration. In addition, these programs allow for the supervision of offenders to retain a rehabilitative focus rather than a punitive one.

While probation and parole are perhaps the most well-known programs in community corrections, there are several other options, including diversion, pretrial supervision programs, electronic monitoring and house arrest, day-reporting centers, and work release programs. In this chapter, you will learn about each of these programs and how they balance the safety and security of the community with the needs of the offender. You'll also learn about the process of reentry after prison and the role of parole. The chapter concludes with two Current Controversy debates. The first, by Krista Gehring, looks at whether risk assessment tools can accurately identify the needs of offenders. The second, by Christine Scott-Hayward, looks at whether parole is an effective correctional strategy.

VIDEO
Youngest Charles Manson Follower Receives Parole Recommendation

PRETRIAL RELEASE

Bail

Historically, the only way to be released from custody before one's case was settled was to post a bond or bail. Bail is a financial commitment provided to the court, usually as either property or money, in exchange for the promise to appear at a later date. Bail allowed those who were accused of a crime to remain at home while they waited for their court date, instead of in jail.

> **"** While there is no right to bail, the 8th Amendment of the U.S. Constitution does specify that excessive bail is unconstitutional.

The topic of bail has always been a discussion for the American criminal justice system. While there is no right to bail, the 8th Amendment of the U.S. Constitution does specify that excessive bail is unconstitutional. One of the first efforts to reform bail was the Manhattan Bail Project. Established in 1961, the project interviewed defendants to assess their ties to the community and investigate the likelihood that they would appear at their court hearings if they were released from custody on their own recognizance. The results of this project indicated that defendants with ties to family and employment were more likely to return to court under a personal promise than individuals who satisfied a monetary bail requirement. As a result of these findings, ROR (release on own recognizance) programs are now in place in most jurisdictions in the nation.[1]

VIDEO
Pretrial Services May Show Promise, but Savings May Take Longer

Release on Own Recognizance

ROR programs have several benefits. As the financial burden of bail can be difficult to meet, many people who are accused of a crime cannot afford to pay these fees (Figure 12.1). Research from New York City's misdemeanor cases indicates that bail is set in 22% of cases while the rest of defendants are released on their own recognizance. Alas, only 13% of those who are ordered to pay bail can afford it. The remaining 87% of individuals remain behind bars. In many of these cases,

Community corrections
Collection of programs that works with two distinct populations: those who have been sentenced for a crime and those who have been charged with offenses and are waiting for their cases to be resolved by the criminal justice system.

Figure 12.1   Average Bail Amount for Felonies in California

High bail costs limit options for numerous individuals in the pretrial stage. Many are forced to remain in jail while awaiting trial, even though they are technically presumed innocent until proven guilty.

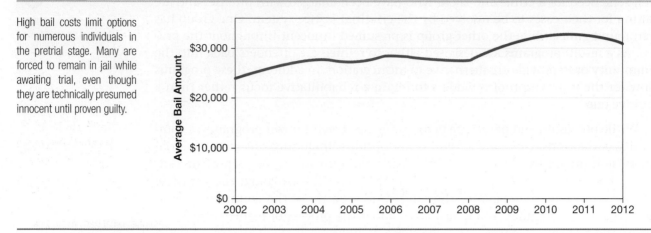

Source: Public Policy Institute of California.

Note: Most recent data available.

the bail is less than $1,000. As a result, they spend an average of 15.7 days behind bars. Seventy-one percent of these cases involve nonviolent, non-weapons-related charges.[2] Research has indicated that failure to make bail has other consequences. For example, offenders that are detained prior to trial are more likely to receive harsher sentences compared with those who remained free on bond.[3] This has a significant impact, particularly for people of color, who are more likely to be detained prior to trial compared with White defendants.[4] Men are also more likely to be detained at the pretrial stage than women.[5] Offense type also plays a role, as women who are charged with drug or property crimes are less likely to be detained prior to trial compared with women who engage in crimes against persons.[6]

Pretrial Release Programs

Pretrial detention occurs when offenders either are denied bail or are financially unable to make bail and must remain in custody until their case is resolved or their status changes with the court. This has a negative impact on employment, as people may lose their jobs, further jeopardizing their status with the courts. It also impacts defendants with minor children, particularly if they are the primary or sole caregiver. The length of pretrial detention is also related to recidivism, as those who remain in custody longer prior to trial are more likely to recidivate following the conclusion of their case.[7]

Pretrial detention
Correctional practice that occurs when an offender either is denied bail or is financially unable to make bail and must remain in custody until his or her case is resolved or his or her status changes with the court.

Pretrial release programs
Programs that supervise offenders in the community prior to their court proceedings in lieu of detention. Serves as an alternative to preventative detention and saves jurisdictions money.

The field of pretrial services emerged to bridge the gap between pretrial detention and bail programs. The concept was tested at the federal level in 1974 under the Speedy Trial Act, which authorized pretrial agencies in 10 judicial districts throughout the country. These agencies were tasked with supervising offenders who were released from custody prior to their court appearances and helping individuals accused of a crime find services and support within the community. Their efforts were viewed as a success, and in 1982, President Ronald Reagan signed the Pretrial Services Act to extend these services to all federal districts.[8]

Pretrial release programs save a significant amount of money for jurisdictions. Consider that it costs $161 per day to house someone in jail in New York City. If we apply these costs to the bail example above, this means that the city spent $42 million over the course of the year on pretrial incarceration for these cases.[9] Such programs also help offenders maintain ties to the community. Despite the introduction of pretrial services as an alternative to preventative detention, bail is still used in many cases. The Bail Reform Act of 1984 states that defendants should be released unless they have a risk of failure to appear for a future court date or if their release would place the community at risk of harm. Since its introduction at the federal level, the majority of states have adopted similar measures.[10] While the risk of failure to appear has been a key consideration in bail programs, this policy shifted practices such that the court also considered the needs of safety and security in the community in determining the eligibility and amount of bail. In making their decision, the act held that the courts should also consider the following:

Businesses that provide bail bond services are often organized around local courthouses. What is the purpose of bail?

the history and characteristics of the person, including the person's character, physical and mental condition, family ties, employment, financial resources, length of residence in the community, community ties, past conduct, history relating to drug or alcohol abuse, criminal history, and record concerning appearance at court proceedings; and whether, at the time of the current offense or arrest, the person was on probation, on parole, or on other release pending trial, sentencing, appeal, or completion of sentence for an offense under Federal, State, or local law.[11]

DIVERSION

The goal of **diversion** is to refer offenders to a program instead of processing the case through the system. The most common type of diversion program is used with first-time low-level juvenile offenders, though some jurisdictions also have options for adults. Rather than formally process these cases through the system, these programs often involve classes such as anger management or substance abuse education, coupled with service to the community. Offenders who complete the tasks as assigned have their cases dismissed.[12]

Diversion programs have four primary benefits. First, diversion programs help reduce the number of cases that are formally processed by the criminal justice system. Second, diversion programs can provide skills that aid in the rehabilitation of the offender. Third, the offender is able to avoid the stigma associated with a criminal conviction. Finally, these programs have significant cost benefits as they are generally less expensive to administer.[13]

While diversion programs do offer several benefits, there are also negative consequences to consider. First, the presence of diversion programs can lead to **net widening**. Net widening refers to the practice of bringing more offenders under the jurisdiction of the juvenile and criminal justice systems. In many cases, the use of diversion can bring cases within the reach of the system that historically were not targeted.[14] Second, there is little evidence that demonstrates that diversion programs serve as an effective deterrent or help prevent recidivism.[15] Still, despite some of their overall failures, there is evidence that diversion programs can be more successful than traditional court interventions.[16]

AUDIO
In 2016, States Expected to Ramp Up Ideas to Solve Opiate Abuse

Diversion
An approach that refers offenders to a program instead of processing their cases through the system.

Net widening
Refers to the practice of bringing more offenders under the jurisdiction of the juvenile and criminal justice systems.

Youth courts use peers from the community to sentence low-level acts of delinquency. How might this aid all of the juveniles involved?

Juvenile Programs

Even though one of the more popular types of diversion programs focuses on juveniles, there are several different types of diversion programs that are used with this population. Case management programs involve supervision at various levels. In some cases, juveniles are required to check in with their diversion officer on a weekly or monthly basis, whereas others provide intensive supervision, whereby youth are monitored on a daily basis. Individual treatment diversion programs provide counseling to offenders to encourage changes to their at-risk or delinquent behavior. Family-based treatment diversion programs provide a therapeutic approach not only for the offender but for the parents and siblings as well. These programs are designed to provide not just the youth but the whole family with skills and tools to prevent delinquent behavior. Youth court programs use peers from the community to "sentence" offenders for low-level acts of delinquency. The concept is that a sentence handed down by one's peers can be more meaningful by sending a message to youth from other youth that certain behaviors are not condoned. Restorative justice diversion programs use a victim- and community-centered approach designed to repair the harms caused by the delinquent behavior. Research indicates that some programs are more effective at reducing recidivism than others. Here, we find that programs that provide case management are the least effective at preventing recidivism, whereas family intervention and restorative justice diversion programs demonstrate the strongest promises of reform for participants.[17]

Specialized Courts

There are also diversion programs that target specialized populations. For example, diversion programs are a popular option for mentally ill offenders. Mental health courts are a valuable option to work with this category of offenders for a number of reasons. First, the professionals that work in these programs (such as the judge, prosecutor, and case manager) are specifically assigned to this courtroom, which allows these professionals to develop a specialized knowledge base about the needs of individuals in this community. Second, the focus of these courts is not on proving an offender's guilt; rather, they aim to provide treatment and services for the offender. Finally, any "punishments" are designed to weigh the needs of offenders and promote their reform while maintaining the safety of the community. Research indicates that these programs are more effective at preventing recidivism among mentally ill offenders compared with traditional court interventions.[18]

Like mental health courts, drug courts are used to target specific offenders and provide specialized resources to this category of offenders. The first drug court was set up in 1989 in Miami-Dade County, Florida. Cases were eligible based on the type of drug-related offense the offender was arrested for, such as possession of, purchasing, or solicitation to purchase drugs. Individuals with a history of violence, who have been arrested for the sale or trafficking of drugs, or who have two felony non-drug-related convictions are not eligible to participate in the drug court program. Like mental health courts, drug courts have a different philosophy compared with the criminal justice court experience. Instead of an adversarial process, drug courts are a supportive environment geared toward rehabilitation and reform. Drug courts function as a form of diversion; the processing of a case is set aside for a year while the offender is placed in a treatment program. His or her progress is tracked by the court, and participants are required to submit to regular drug screenings. If they complete the program successfully, the charges are dismissed. The process can be long and difficult, and not all participants will be successful in the intervention. In some cases, individuals may be sanctioned for their relapse or noncompliance but be allowed to remain in the program. Such sanctions may include community service or jail time.[19] If they are terminated from the program, offenders will return to the criminal court, where they will be sentenced for the crime.

Research on drug court programs indicates that adult participants are less likely to recidivate after participation in this type of programming, compared with traditional criminal justice interventions.[20] Similar results are demonstrated by drug courts for juvenile offenders.[21] Despite the number of individuals who have entered the criminal justice system on drug-related charges, drug court programs have been unable to serve as an effective way to reduce the jail and prison population. Many of these programs do not have the adequate budget to meet the demand. In addition, the eligibility requirements to participate in these programs potentially eliminate many individuals.[22] While many of these programs target low-risk individuals, individuals who have a high risk of recidivism can also benefit from the therapeutic environment. Research indicates that high-risk offenders are more successful in a drug court program compared with traditional probation supervision.[23]

> Research on drug court programs indicates that adult participants are less likely to recidivate after participation in this type of programming, compared with traditional criminal justice interventions.

PROBATION

Probation involves the supervision of offenders in the community in lieu of incarceration. The origins of probation date back to the Middle Ages and English criminal law.

A Brief History of Probation

In the United States, John Augustus became the first volunteer probation officer in 1841 (Figure 12.2). In this role, he helped offenders (often first-time offenders) reform their lives by helping them post bond and find jobs and housing and by providing support during the period between arrest and sentencing. His belief was that "the object of the law is to reform criminals and to prevent crime, and not to punish maliciously or from a spirit of revenge."[24] Most of his charity cases involved drunk men and abandoned children. He continued his work for more than 18 years until his death and helped more than 1,900 men and women. Historical records indicate that he was successful in getting all but 10 of these cases to honor their bond to the court.[25]

The first probation statute was passed in Massachusetts in 1859, and the practice of probation began to spread to other states. The first probation law was adopted to provide services for juveniles in 1878. In 1880, Massachusetts established the first statewide probation agency. Over the next 40 years, several others states followed by creating their own agencies, and by 1930, every state had laws for juvenile probation except Wyoming.[26] Acceptance of probation for adults was slower in its development. The first state law permitting probation for adult offenders was passed by New York in 1901. In 1925, the federal government passed the National Probation Act and established the U.S. Federal Probation Service.[27] In 1927, the first federal probation officer was appointed in Massachusetts. By 1951, probation departments were established in every state, and in 1955, the first professional organization for probation was formed.

Probation
Form of punishment that involves the supervision of offenders in the community in lieu of incarceration.

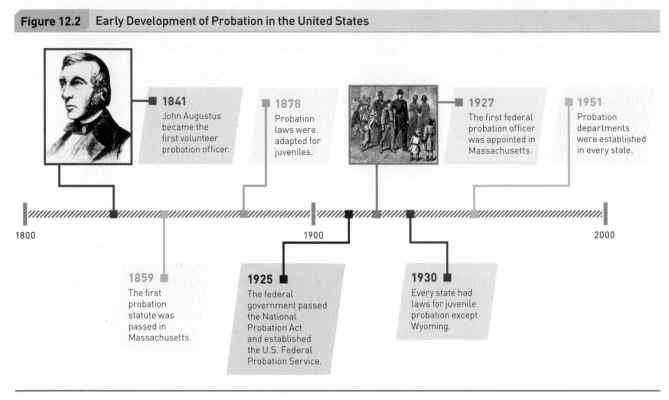

The Federal Probation and Pretrial Officers Association was developed to provide policy analysis and advocacy on a variety of issues, including officer safety, training, and staffing.[28] Over the next few decades, probation departments struggled to find their place in the criminal justice system. While the workload and expectations of departments continued to increase, the financial support for these tasks remained stagnant.[29] These challenges, coupled with a general shift from a rehabilitative philosophy to a more punitive one, led many to question whether probation was an effective correctional tool. In 1974, Robert Martinson, a correctional researcher, published an article titled "What Works? Questions and Answers About Prison Reform." While his review focused on both probation and other forms of rehabilitation, he concluded that very few of these interventions were effective at preventing recidivism. This finding became translated to politicians and the public as "nothing works" and provided lawmakers and others with the fuel to shift away from rehabilitation.[30] However, Martinson never stated that nothing works. Instead, he noted that there was no "one size fits all" program that meets the needs of all offenders.

Since then, research has noted that there are many successful programs that help to reform offenders and prevent reoffending.[31]

Probation in the 21st Century

In 2014, 3,864,100 adults were on probation. Demographics of adults on probation indicate that 25% of probationers are female; 53% are White, non-Hispanic while 30% are Black, and 13% are Hispanic. Probationers account for the greatest proportion of all individuals in community corrections. The average length of a probation sentence is just under two years (21.9 months). Fifty-six percent of those sentenced to probation were convicted of a felony, and 42% were for misdemeanor crimes. The remaining 2% were for other infractions. Nineteen

SPOTLIGHT

Recidivism

Recidivism means that a person returns to criminal behavior after he or she has been punished by the criminal justice system. This return is measured by a re-arrest, reconviction, or return to prison. In a recent study of 30 states, the Bureau of Justice Statistics found that 76.6% of the 405,000 prisoners who were released were arrested at least once within five years of their release. More than half of these arrests occurred within the first year of their freedom, and this highlights the challenges that offenders face during the reentry experience. Those offenders who were released without some form of community supervision (such as parole) were more likely to reoffend, compared with those who were on a conditional release. Male inmates were more likely to reoffend than women. Younger inmates were also more likely to reoffend. Property offenders were the most likely to be rearrested (82.1%), compared with drug offenders (76.9%) and violent offenders (71.3%).[a]

Research tells us that programs and treatment can be effective, particularly for specific groups of offenders. For example, sex offenders who successfully complete a treatment program are less likely to recidivate compared with those who do not.[b] Successful completion of a drug court program is also likely to protect against recidivism.[c] Interestingly, while offenders with mental health issues have a higher risk of recidivism in general, they are re-arrested just as often as their counterparts without mental illness. However, once they are arrested, offenders with mental illness are more likely to be sentenced to prison.[d]

Research also tells us that prisons do not deter offenders.[e] Instead, findings indicate that prison can produce a criminogenic effect. This means that prison can actually encourage offenders to engage in crime, rather than prevent it, at least in terms of particular offenses. Time in prison is more likely to increase property and drug crimes for male offenders, and incarceration for women increases their recidivism for property offenses.[f] Prison may actually have the highest risk of increased recidivism for lower level offenders.[g] These results indicate that the "most punitive" punishment may be the least effective in terms of rehabilitation and that reentry efforts need to consider these factors when providing support.

CRITICAL THINKING QUESTIONS

1. Is prison the best tool to prevent recidivism? Why or why not?

2. Why do you believe that so many offenders have issues with recidivism?

3. What should the criminal justice system do to reduce the levels of recidivism?

---

percent of these cases involved violent crimes, 28% were property crimes, 25% drug-related crimes, and 16% public-order crimes.[32] On average, probationers served 21.9 months on probation. Figure 12.3 presents the rate of probation exits for 2014.

Types of Probation

There are several different types of probation sentences. These vary by jurisdiction and the needs of the offender. Each type of probation typically involves specific terms and conditions that are assigned by the court that the offender must follow. The most common type of probation is **supervised probation**. Under a supervised-probation sentence, the offender is required to check in, either face to face or by telephone, on a particular schedule. Depending on the type of case, offenders may be required to check in on either a monthly or a weekly basis.

Recidivism
When a person returns to criminal behavior after he or she has been punished by the criminal justice system.

Supervised probation
A type of probation sentence where the offender is required to check in either face to face or by telephone on a particular schedule.

Figure 12.3 Exits From Probation, 2014

While the majority of inmates complete their probation, 35% do not, for various reasons, and many end up incarcerated.

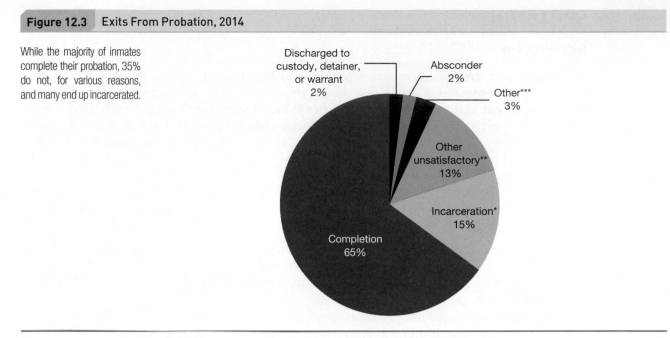

Discharged to custody, detainer, or warrant 2%

Absconder 2%

Other*** 3%

Other unsatisfactory** 13%

Incarceration* 15%

Completion 65%

Source: http://www.bjs.gov/content/pub/pdf/ppus14.pdf

* Includes probationers who were incarcerated for a new offense and those who had their current probation sentence revoked.

** Includes probationers discharged from supervision who failed to meet all conditions of supervision.

*** Includes, but not limited to, probationers discharged from supervision through a legislative mandate because they were deported or transferred to the jurisdiction of Immigration and Customs Enforcement; transferred to another state through an interstate compact agreement; or had their sentence dismissed or overturned.

AUDIO

After Thousands of Inmates Released Early, Probation Officers Will Be Watching

Below are some of the most common conditions that are assigned by the court:

- Report to probation officer as directed

- Obtain permission to change residence

- Report any arrests or contact with the police to probation officer

- Maintain employment or attendance in school

- Follow curfew as ordered by the court

- Not possess any weapons if on probation for a felony offense

- No contact with individuals on probation or parole or who have a criminal record

- Maintain sobriety from drugs and alcohol

- Submit to reasonable searches and seizures of person, property, and residence

- Submit to breath, blood, or urine testing for substance use as directed

- Follow house arrest procedures

- Participate in specific programs as ordered, such as substance abuse, anger management, or mental health treatment

- Pay any fines to the court as ordered

- Pay restitution to the victim

- Complete community service hours

- No contact with the victim

Intensive probation (also referred to as community control probation) is a more intensive form of supervision. Under this type of sentence, probation officers closely monitor the daily activities of their offenders. As a result of this high-intensity supervision, caseloads are typically kept smaller than those of traditional supervised probation. Under an intensive probation supervision sentence, offenders may also be outfitted with an electronic monitor or GPS tracker. You'll learn more about these options later in this chapter.

Split-sentence probation involves the use of a short-term incarceration sentence in conjunction with a traditional probation sentence. Also referred to as **shock probation**, these sentences are designed to serve as a stronger deterrent against criminal behavior and encourage greater compliance with a probation sentence.

Probation officers provide supervision for offenders in the community. What are some of the specific duties of a probation officer?

Crime-specific supervision organizes a probation officer's caseload by specific offense types. In these cases, probation officers may be in charge of a caseload of just sexual offenders, drug offenders, or mental health cases. This specialization allows for probation officers to focus on the unique needs of a specific population and have an increased awareness of the treatment options that are the most effective. Crime-specific supervision is often a type of intensive probation, and caseloads are kept smaller so that probation officers can give greater attention to their clients.

Finally, individuals on **unsupervised probation** are generally not required to check in with a probation officer but are required to meet certain terms and conditions set forth by the court. Unsupervised probation is also referred to as informal probation and is typically only used in cases of minor-level offenders. Individuals on unsupervised probation may be recalled by the court if they reoffend during their term of probation. If they remain out of trouble, their cases are closed as a successful completion term.

Duties of the Probation Officer

While many think of probation as something that is involved toward the end of the criminal justice process, the reality is that probation officers can be involved throughout every stage of the system. Figure 12.4 highlights how probation officers can be involved in either a primary or secondary role. For example, some jurisdictions rely on probation officers to make recommendations on whether someone should be released on her or his own recognizance during the pretrial stage. If released, the probation officers may be involved in supervising the accused as part of her or his pretrial supervision. If chosen to participate in a specialized program, such as a drug court, a probation officer is actively involved in the management of an offender's case as part of the program. Finally, they are responsible for managing the community sanctions or probation sentence of the offender as part of a plea-bargaining or sentencing process.[33]

The Presentence Investigation Report

One of the primary tasks of the probation officer is to prepare the **presentence investigation report (PSI)**. Following a guilty plea or finding, the probation

Intensive probation
A form of probation sentence where probation officers closely monitor the daily activities of their offenders.

Split-sentence probation
Form of punishment that involves the use of a short-term incarceration sentence in conjunction with a traditional probation sentence. Also referred to as **shock probation**.

Crime-specific supervision
Organizes a probation officer's caseload by specific offense types.

Unsupervised probation
A type of probation where individuals are generally not required to check in with a probation officer but are required to meet certain terms and conditions set forth by the court.

Presentence investigation report (PSI)
A report to the court that makes a recommendation for a sentence based on the individual's criminal history, nature of the offense, and needs. In some cases, it involves interviews with parents/guardians, school officials, treatment providers, and social services.

Probation officials are involved in decision-making even before sentencing and can be involved as early as the point of a crime being noted by the police.

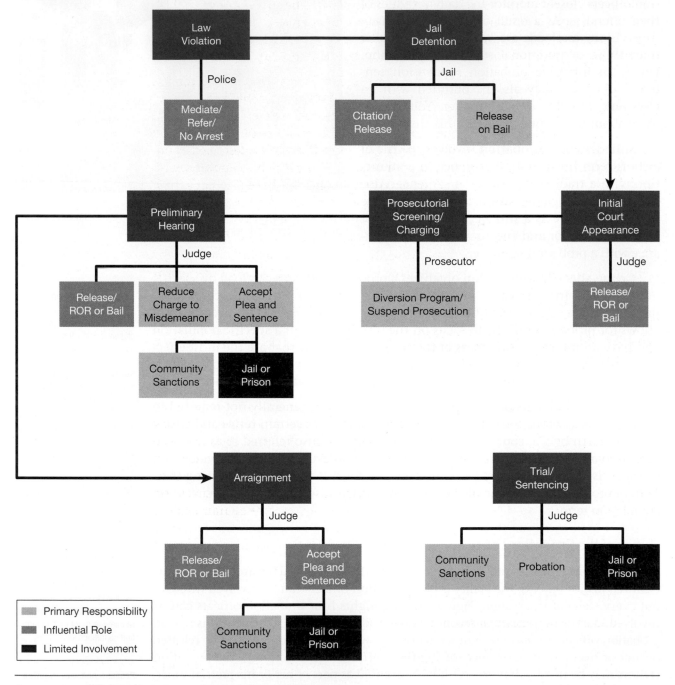

Source: http://www.appa-net.org/eweb/Resources/PPPSW_2013/docs/sp98pers30.pdf

officer conducts an interview with the offender. In cases involving juveniles, the probation officer may also include interviews with parents, legal guardians, school officials, treatment providers, and social service agents. This report provides the court with detailed information regarding the background of the offender. For example, the report can include demographic information and personal data on education, employment, mental health, substance abuse history, history of personal violence and abuse, and peer relationships. It includes information about the offense, victim impact statements, and restitution, as well as opinions by the probation officer on the likelihood that the offender will be successfully rehabilitated. Presentence reports may also include narrative data reflecting the demeanor of the offender. They also include an assessment of the offender's needs and a recommendation to the court about the appropriate sentence for the offender.[34]

Research on presentence investigation reports finds that probation officers can use different language in describing different categories of offenders, which can impact how they are viewed by the court. Males and females are often described differently, even when they engage in the same types of crimes. The nature of offending and causation of the crime also varies.[35] Girls are much more likely to be described as not criminally dangerous, suffering from a poor relationship with their families, lacking support from their parents, and out of parental control.[36] Race also alters how offenders are described. Blacks are more likely to be described using negative identifiers about things such as their personality and disposition, whereas Whites are more likely to be described using negative contexts about their environment or situational characteristics. As a result, Black youth were more likely to be described as violent and not remorseful for their crimes, whereas White youth were viewed as victims of circumstances and in need of treatment.[37] The way that people are described relates to how responsible they are perceived for their crimes. Those whose crimes are seen as a result of individual characteristics tend to be viewed as more responsible for their behavior and more dangerous than those who engage in crime as a result of their social environment.[38]

Probation Revocation

If defendants violate the terms and conditions of their probation or if they commit a new crime, they are subject to having their probation sentence revoked by the court. Under the law, any **probation revocation** must occur via a prompt hearing by the court, and the probationer is entitled to basic due process rights. The U.S. Supreme Court established this rule in its decision in *Gagnon v. Scarpelli* (1973). The Court also held in this case that probationers are not guaranteed the right to appointed counsel during these hearings. Instead, representation is offered on a case-by-case basis.[39] Here are some of the rights of the offender during the revocation hearing:

- written notice of the alleged violation;

- disclosure of the evidence against the person;

- an opportunity to appear, present evidence, and question any adverse witness unless the court determines that the interest of justice does not require the witness to appear;

- notice of the person's right to retain counsel or to request that counsel be appointed if the person cannot obtain counsel; and

- an opportunity to make a statement and present any information in mitigation.[40]

In considering revoking a sentence of probation, courts generally have two options. First, the court can decide to continue the offender on probation. Second, the court can revoke the sentence of probation and resentence the offender to a new

Probation revocation
Court hearings where offenders receive due process protections if they are to have their probation sentence rescinded and are resentenced as a result of violating the terms and conditions of their probation or if they commit a new crime.

punishment. In most cases, probation is used as an alternative to incarceration. As a result, a new sentence could involve jail or prison time. While most decisions to revoke probation are based on the discretion of the probation officer, some jurisdictions require mandatory revocations. **Mandatory revocation** also occurs in cases where an offender refuses to comply with drug testing or tests positive for a controlled substance three times within a year.[41] Federal law requires the revocation of a probation sentence in cases where the offender is found in possession of a controlled substance or a firearm. These types of cases are called **technical violations**, as they violate the terms and conditions of probation and do not generally result in an arrest for a new offense. However, the U.S. Supreme Court has held that people on probation cannot be jailed for failing to satisfy their financial punishment, such as failure to pay a fine.[42]

How often is probation revoked? Studies indicate that between 13% and 23% of probationers have their probation revoked for engaging in a new crime. If data on technical violations are included, the number of offenders who have their probation revoked can be as large as 50% of cases.[43] Research tells us that not everyone has their probation revoked for the same reasons. For example, Black probationers in some regions are more than twice as likely to have their probation revoked compared with White and Hispanic probationers. We also learn that younger probationers are more likely to have their probation revoked than older adults. Women are also less likely to experience a probation revocation.[44] In some cases, these three variables—age, race, and gender—join together: young, Black men often have the highest rates of revocation.[45] Research also indicates that there are both legal and extralegal factors that predict whether someone will be incarcerated for probation revocation. For example, those who have previously been incarcerated are more likely to be resentenced to an incarceration term for violating their probation. Here, probation officers may feel that a harsher sentence is required for those who have previously served time. Men are also more likely to be sent to jail or prison for a probation violation than women. Finally, those who are employed or attending school are less likely to be sent to prison as a result of violating their probation, as officers are likely to show leniency toward those who are working at improving their lives, whereas they respond more harshly toward those who are unemployed.[46]

INTERMEDIATE SANCTIONS

There is no one clear definition of what constitute an **intermediate sanction**. The term is generally used to reference the category of intervention between probation and incarceration. In many cases, these interventions are used in conjunction with probation or parole supervision. Intermediate sanctions rose to popularity during the 1990s, an era when the public was growing increasingly concerned with the supervision of offenders in the community. Coupled with the rising incarceration rates and prison overcrowding, there was great concern that individuals on probation and parole were often unsupervised or undersupervised due to the large caseloads of the officers or the lack of viable rehabilitative options in the community. These concerns were only fueled by the increasing rates of recidivism during this time period. Intermediate sanctions also provided judges with additional sentencing options, which allowed them to better tailor these sentences to the unique needs of the offender. Finally, the rise of new technologies created increased ways that offenders could be better supervised in the community without dramatic increases in costs or staff.[47] This section highlights some of the commonly used forms of intermediate sanctions: house arrest and electronic monitoring, day-reporting and work release programs, and halfway houses.

SAGE JOURNAL ARTICLE
Extralegal Disparity in the Application of Intermediate Sanctions

Mandatory revocation
Revocation of a probation sentence as a result of specific violations.

Technical violation
Refers to violations of the terms and conditions of probation.

Intermediate sanction
A category of interventions that are used between probation and incarceration.

AROUND THE WORLD

Probation in Italy

Probation first emerged in Italy in 1975 as part of Penitentiary Act 354. Probation services are part of the Department of the Penitentiary Administration. As in many regions, probation services receive a small portion of the budget in Italy. In 2005, the budget for probation services represented only 2% of the total budget of the Penitentiary Department.[a]

In 2005,[b] the total number of offenders sentenced to probation services was 88,697. There are 1,170 probation workers employed, with an additional 486 managers and administrative and other staff that provide assistance.[c] However, there are more than 200 different volunteer groups that also assist with the rehabilitation of offenders. With more than 7,000 volunteer personnel, it is a fair assumption that they play a significant role in this process. The probation service also interacts with several other agencies, including hospitals for the mentally ill and treatment programs for those with drug and alcohol addiction issues.

Under Article 47 of the Italian Penitentiary Act, offenders can be sentenced to probation as an alternative to detention as part of the final disposition in a criminal case. Unlike probation officers in the United States, the probation service in Italy is not involved with the presentencing investigative report. Probation is typically used in lieu of incarceration and is generally available to certain first-time and nonviolent offenders. Individuals are sentenced to probation for three years or less, and the term of probation is the same as what one would have been sentenced to prison for. Probation officers work both within and outside the prison walls. Unlike the United States, which separates these roles into probation (for community supervision in lieu of significant incarceration) and parole (community supervision following a period of incarceration), Italy combines both of these tasks into a single agency.

Offenders can also be sentenced to probation if they engaged in criminal behavior as a result of addiction or being under the influence. In these cases, probation is given to those who are willing to participate in a rehabilitation program. These offenders are eligible if they were sentenced to prison for less than six years. Here, treatment is used as a way to prevent recidivism. As a result, this form of probation is only available twice at the discretion of the supervisory court. The public health care system is responsible for the management of the treatment program while the probation officer serves as a liaison between the program and the court.

Many of the terms and conditions of probation in Italy are similar to those in the United States: limitations on who probationers can associate with and where they can congregate and the requirement to work. However, there are also some unique features as well. For example, a probationer in Italy is required to "regularly fulfil his/her family obligations" and to "do his/her best in favour of the victim of his/her crime."[d] Probationers can be assigned to pay restitution in cases of property damage or to perform community service. The focus on the family is a unique feature. Under Italian law, probation supervision with home detention can be used specifically for mothers of children under the age of 10.[e]

Probation supervision in Italy can also be used as a form of split sentence. For some offenders, supervision on probation represents a *semiliberty*, meaning that offenders will spend their day outside of the prison to work, go to school, or participate in rehabilitative programming. At the end of the day, they return to prison. This feature is generally used for those who are already serving time in prison and are in the process of being reintegrated back into the community. Semiliberty was recently made available to Rudy Guede, who was convicted in 2008 of murdering Meredith Kercher. While he was initially sentenced to 30 years, his

CRITICAL THINKING QUESTIONS

1. Identify the similarities and differences between probation in Italy and the United States.

2. Discuss the concept of *semiliberty*. How is this similar to some of our programs in the United States?

(Continued)

(Continued)

sentence was significantly cut by an appeals court to just 16 years. The case made international head-lines, as Amanda Knox and Raffaele Sollecito were also convicted. Knox and Sollecito were ultimately exonerated for their crimes after several trials and appeals. After serving just over seven years of his sentence, Guede was approved to participate in a semiliberty program in which he could attend a local university to study history. Initially, Guede declined to participate in the program out of fears of harass-ment by the media. But with Italy facing significant issues of prison overcrowding, many offenders are taking advantage of these sorts of programs. In order to receive this type of probation—day release—a surveillance judge approves the eligibility and conditions of an offender's release and monitors her or his participation in the program. Probationers also have the option of early release. Under Article 54 of the Penitentiary Act, prisoners who exhibit good behavior in prison have their prison sentence reduced 45 days for every six months that they are incarcerated.[f] In the case of Guede, if he maintains good behavior, he could be released from prison in 2018.[9]

House Arrest and Electronic Monitoring

House arrest is a form of sanction that requires that offenders remain in their homes in lieu of jail or prison. The offender is permitted to leave his or her residence only for short-term approved purposes, such as going to work or school. House arrest serves a dual purpose: Not only does it punish the offender but it also helps keep the community safe. House arrest can be used as a pretrial release as a condition of one's bond or as a postconviction or early release program.

In many cases, house arrest programs are used in conjunction with electronic monitoring. **Electronic monitoring** involves the use of technology to follow the loca-tion of an offender. In some cases, electronic monitoring involves an ankle bracelet that is placed on the offender. Any time that the offender travels outside of a desig-nated area, the bracelet emits a signal that notifies the supervision officer that she or he is out of compliance. Recent advances in technology have allowed for **Global Positioning System (GPS) monitoring** to provide greater opportunities to locate and track the movement of offenders. GPS technology is often used to monitor the transit of convicted sex offenders. However, there have been criticisms about how the tech-nology is used to supervise offenders. A recent case in Orange County, California, used GPS technology to link two convicted sex offenders to the rape and murder of five women. However, the devices did not note that the two offenders were spending time together, which would have been a violation of the terms and conditions of their release.[48] Critics of this case have questioned whether the presence of GPS technology creates a false sense of security as a result of the types of supervision that the offender may or may not be subjected to.

Perhaps one of the more famous cases of house arrest in modern times involved Martha Stewart. Stewart was an icon in American culture, building a billion-dollar empire of books, magazines, products, and media specials on social entertaining. In 2004, she was convicted on federal charges (conspiracy, obstruction of justice, and making false statements to federal investigators) related to her sale of ImClone stock based on insider-trading knowledge from her broker, Peter Bacanovic. While she staunchly maintained her innocence and even took out a full page ad in *USA Today* to this effect, she was sentenced to five months in federal prison. She served her time at the Alderson Federal Prison Camp in West Virginia.[49] Following her release, she served an additional five months on house arrest at her Bedford, New York, home. As part of the conditions of her release, she was permitted to leave her home for up to 48 hours a week to buy groceries, go to the doctor, or attend work or religious events. Her house arrest was extended for three additional weeks after the court held that

House arrest
A sanction that requires that offenders remain in their homes in lieu of a jail or prison.

Electronic monitoring
Form of supervision that involves the use of technology to follow the location of an offender.

Global Positioning System (GPS) monitoring
A type of electronic monitoring that allows for greater opportunities to locate and track the movement of offenders.

she violated the terms and conditions of her home confinement by attending a yoga class and riding an off-road vehicle around her estate.[50]

Day-Reporting Centers and Work/Study Release Programs

A **day-reporting center** requires offenders to attend a program or center during the day but allows them to live in their own homes during the evening. Many of these centers provide job assistance, such as resume writing, job search, and other life skills programming. The goal of a day-reporting center is to create a system of accountability for the offender while enforcing his or her sentence. These programs can be used as either a pretrial or a postconviction form of supervision. During the pretrial stage, day-reporting centers are used to help reduce the likelihood that an offender will fail to appear for her or his court date. As a postconviction sentence, day-reporting centers can be used as a transition period for a split sentence or as a way to provide enhanced supervision for certain offenders.[51]

House arrest is used to restrict the freedom and movement of offenders while allowing them to remain in the community. Does this seem like a light sentence? How would your life be affected if you were not allowed to leave your home for several months?

In contrast, a **work/study release** program is used for offenders that are currently housed in a local jail. These programs allow for offenders to leave the facility during the day to go to work or school. Remaining in the jail during the evenings and weekends allows for these offenders to also take advantage of any training or rehabilitative programs that might be available at the facility. These types of programs were first popularized during the 1960s and 1970s, when support for rehabilitation was high. Work/study release programs are most effective for low-level offenders. In order to be eligible to participate in these programs, offenders are typically nearing the end of their incarceration sentence. They are selected on the basis of their positive behavior and progress in prison. In addition, program participants are typically subjected to regular drug testing. Research indicates that offenders who participate in work release programs are more likely to find and maintain employment upon release, which, in turn, leads to lower rates of recidivism. Work release programs are also cheaper to operate compared with traditional correctional programs.[52] Such programs can also provide intrinsic benefits to offenders as they serve as a positive reinforcement of good behavior.[53]

Halfway Houses

A **halfway house** is designed to provide a transitional living arrangement for ex-offenders upon their release from jail or prison. These residences also provide supervision of offenders and require that residents participate in programs to aid in their reentry process. Halfway houses first appeared during the early 1800s. In the early days, there was no system of parole, and halfway houses provided a supportive place for offenders to reestablish themselves in the community. However, others feared that congregating several offenders together would actually increase the risk of recidivism. The emergence of parole, coupled with the Great Depression of the 1930s, essentially eliminated these programs. During the rehabilitative era, from the 1950s to the 1970s, such programs returned to popularity as they provided individualized treatment and supervision for offenders. Many of these programs were run by faith-based organizations and focused on rehabilitation and redemption. The movement

Day-reporting center
Requires an offender to attend a program or center during the day but allows him or her to live at home during the evening.

Work/study release
A type of program that allows offenders to leave the facility during the day to go to work or school and return in the evenings and weekends to take advantage of training and rehabilitative programs.

Halfway house
Designed to provide a transitional living arrangement for ex-offenders upon their release from jail or prison.

was legitimized during the 1960s, when Congress provided financial support for programs targeting juvenile offenders. Government support of these programs continued until the tough-on-crime philosophy of the 1980s shifted the priorities of corrections to more of a retributive model. Today, halfway houses continue to exist, though they are supported primarily though private foundations and contracted funding.[54]

PAROLE

A Brief History of Parole

Parole was first developed during the 19th century. Its rise as a correctional strategy is credited to the work of Alexander Maconochie and Sir Walter Crofon. Maconochie was the leader of the English penal colony at Norfolk Island in 1840, which was located off of the coast of Australia. Maconochie was not in favor of prison terms and developed a system whereby inmates could earn credits based on their behavior in custody, which could then be used toward their release. While he was appointed in 1849 to serve as the head of the new prison in Birmingham, England, his philosophy was viewed as too lenient, and he was dismissed from his position in 1851. However, Sir Walter Crofton was inspired by Maconochie's efforts and implemented his practice in the Irish prison system in 1854. In addition to providing release credits to offenders based on their behavior, Crofton also developed a supervision program for offenders once they left prison. Individuals were required to provide a report each month to the police. In addition to providing supervision and a system of accountability for the offender, these police officers also helped offenders secure jobs in the community.[55]

Parole in the 21st Century

VIDEO
WKYT Investigates: State Senator Wants Parole Board Abolished

Today, the term **parole** invokes different meanings, which reflect the contributions of both Maconochie and Crofton. On one hand, offenders in prison can be up for parole and have their file reviewed by a board of officials to determine whether they should be released back into the community. In determining whether someone should be released from prison, the board considers a number of different factors. Some of the common characteristics that parole boards look at when making this decision include the following:

- Nature of the offense
- Criminal history of the offender
- Institutional behavior of the offender (e.g., disciplinary infractions or participation in rehabilitative programming)
- Potential for recidivism
- Remorse for one's behavior and insights into causes of one's behavior
- Plan for reintegration

Parole
Term used to describe both a form of early prison release and the post-incarceration supervision of offenders in the community.

The passage of the Sentencing Reform Act of 1984 abolished parole at the federal level. While many states followed this trend, others retained the right to operate parole boards to determine whether someone should be released from custody prior to the completion of her or his sentence. The Michigan Department of Corrections uses a three-member panel to decide most cases. The board uses a numerical scoring system in making their decision.[56] In other states, parole eligibility is based on how much time an offender has served. In Oklahoma, an individual convicted of a violent crime must serve at least 85% of the sentence prior to being considered for parole. Nonviolent offenders must serve only one third of their sentences before they can be declared eligible for parole. If they are denied parole, they must wait one to five years before being reconsidered. The amount of time that they have to wait is dependent on the severity of their crime.[57]

Each state varies on how its **parole boards** are organized and how decisions are made by this body. For example, Iowa state law requires that the board be composed of five individuals. State law specifies the categories of individuals that must be represented on the panel. In Iowa, a parole board is composed as follows:

- Members must be of good character and judicious background
- Must include a member of a minority group
- May include a religious leader from the community
- Must meet at least two of the following:
    - Contain one member who is a disinterested layperson
    - Contain one member who is an attorney licensed to practice law in this state and who is knowledgeable in correctional procedures and issues
    - Contain one member who is a person holding at least a master's degree in social work or counseling and guidance and who is knowledgeable in correctional procedures and issues[58]

At the same time, parole also refers to the supervision of offenders following their release from prison. In 2014, there were 856,900 individuals on parole. Between 2007 and 2014, the number of individuals on parole has increased by 3.7%. Comparatively speaking, the number of individuals on probation during the same time decreased by 10%. As with probation, the majority of offenders on parole are male (88%), though men make up a larger proportion of parolees (Figure 12.5). Forty-three percent of those on parole are White, compared with 39% Black and 16% Hispanic. Thirty-one percent were sentenced to prison for a violent offense, 22% for a property offense, 31% for a drug offense, 4% for a weapons-related offense, and 12% for other crimes.[59]

WEB LINK
U.S. Parole Commission

Parole boards
A group of officials who determine whether someone should be released from custody prior to the completion of her or his sentence.

Figure 12.5	Characteristics of Parolees

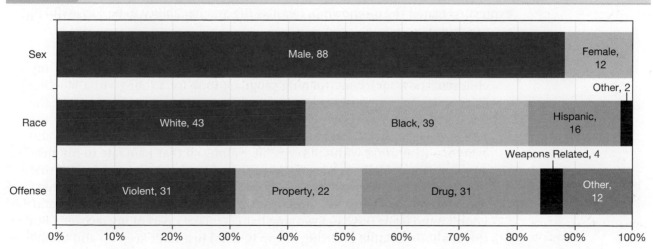

CAREERS IN CRIMINAL JUSTICE

So You Want to Be a Probation or a Parole Officer?

The jobs of a probation officer and a parole officer are similar in a number of ways. Both positions involve the supervision of offenders in the community. Both require officers to manage dual functions in their job. On one hand, you are there to ensure the safety and security of the community. In this way, officers fulfill a law enforcer role of sorts. At the same time, probation and parole officers are involved in supporting offenders in their rehabilitation. They assist with locating options for employment, housing, and treatment. Here, their jobs take on characteristics similar to a social worker. Officers also appear before the court to report on the status of offenders and whether they are in compliance.

One of the key differences between probation and parole officers is their supervision population and the type of agency they work for. Most probation agencies are organized by local and regional governments. Their caseload is predominantly lower level offenders, who are supervised in the community in lieu of an incarceration sentence. Several states, such as Georgia and Tennessee, have privatized some of their probation services. In contrast, parole officers supervise offenders who are released from prison. The offenders were usually convicted of a felony, and many of them may have a criminal history involving serious and/or violent crimes. Since parole is an extension of the prison system, these jobs are usually at the state level. In addition, there are probation and parole officers who work for the federal government to supervise offenders in these types of cases.

Work in these fields is very popular with students in criminal justice and related areas. To supervise these offenders, there are approximately 90,300 probation and parole officers in the United States. To work in these fields, applicants are required to have at least a bachelor's degree (though some jurisdictions require a master's degree). The median pay is $48,190 annually. Much of the job growth in this field is related to job turnover and not an increase in the number of positions, which are highly competitive.

CAREER VIDEO
Probation/Parole Officer

Role of Parole Officers

While parole supervision was once intended to help offenders successfully transition back to the community, the role of parole officers has shifted. Due to the high caseloads that many parole offices face, the opportunities to provide individualized care to these offenders are limited. Instead, the majority of their time is spent monitoring offenders, waiting to respond if and when an offender violates the conditions of his or her release. One woman shares the struggles in meeting the demands of parole, expressing fear of the unknown in her new life and her ability to be successful in her reentry process:

> I start my day running to drop my urine [drug testing]. Then I go see my children, show up for my training program, look for a job, go to a meeting [Alcoholics Anonymous], and show up at my part-time job. I have to take the bus everywhere, sometimes eight buses for 4 hours a day. I don't have the proper outer clothes, I don't have the money to buy lunch along the way, and everyone who works with me keeps me waiting so that I am late to my next appointment. If I fail any one of these things I am revoked. I am so tired that I sometimes fall asleep on my way home from work at 2:00 a.m. and that's dangerous given where I live. And then the next day I have to start over again. I don't mind being busy and working hard. . . . That's part of my recovery. But this is a situation that is setting me up to fail. I just can't keep up and I don't know where to start.[60]

ISSUES IN REENTRY

The needs of the incarcerated returning to their communities are high. While much of the research on **reentry** issues has focused on whether offenders will reoffend and return to prison (recidivism), recent scholars have shifted the focus on reentry to discussions on how to successfully transition offenders back into their communities. This process can be quite traumatic, and a number of issues emerge in creating a successful reentry experience.

Consider the basic needs of offenders who have just left prison. They need housing, clothing, and food. They may be eager to reestablish relationships with friends, family members, and, in some cases, their children. In addition, they have obligations as part of their release—appointments with their parole officer and treatment requirements. Furthermore, the majority of offenders find themselves returning to the same communities in which they lived prior to their incarceration, where they face the same problems of poverty, addiction, and dysfunction. Finding safe and affordable housing is challenging, and many of the available options place them at risk for relapse and recidivism.[61] For those few offenders who were able to receive some therapeutic treatment in prison, most acknowledge that these prison-based intervention programs provided few, if any, legitimate coping skills to deal with the realities of the life stressors that awaited them upon their release.

> For those few offenders who were able to receive some therapeutic treatment in prison, most acknowledge that these prison-based intervention programs provided few, if any, legitimate coping skills to deal with the realities of the life stressors that awaited them upon their release.

WEB LINK
Prisoner Reentry Center

Employment Challenges

On top of all these struggles, offenders have a new identity upon their release from prison: the ex-offender status. This identity can present significant challenges for offenders and threaten their ability to be successful upon release. Consider the number of employment opportunities that require applicants to disclose whether they have ever been arrested for a crime. In many cases, this automatically excludes the applicant from consideration. Many also reference how their lack of education or training makes it difficult to secure legal and stable employment.[62] A recent campaign to "**ban the box**" has many agencies and companies changing the way they handle ex-convicts' applications for employment. In Minnesota, recent legislation makes it illegal for state employers to ask about an offender's criminal history on a job application. Similar laws exist in an additional 18 states. As one of the largest retailers, Target has reformed its hiring policies such that questions about any criminal history are not raised until an applicant has been granted an interview.[63] In November 2015, President Obama announced a new policy to "ban the box" on applications for jobs in federal agencies.[64]

Reentry
Refers to the period of time when an offender is released from prison and returns to the community.

Ban the box
Policy that asks or mandates that potential employers eliminate from initial hiring applications the check box that asks individuals if they have a criminal record.

Disenfranchisement

Many states deny individuals the right to vote if they have been convicted of a felony. Figure 12.6 highlights this phenomenon and notes that while some states disenfranchise individuals only while they are incarcerated, others continue to disenfranchise individuals even after they have successfully completed their sentence. Nationwide, this means that 5.85 million Americans are unable to

An inmate leaves prison after the completion of his sentence. What challenges will he likely face as an ex-offender?

Figure 12.6 Felony Disenfranchisement Restrictions by State, 2016

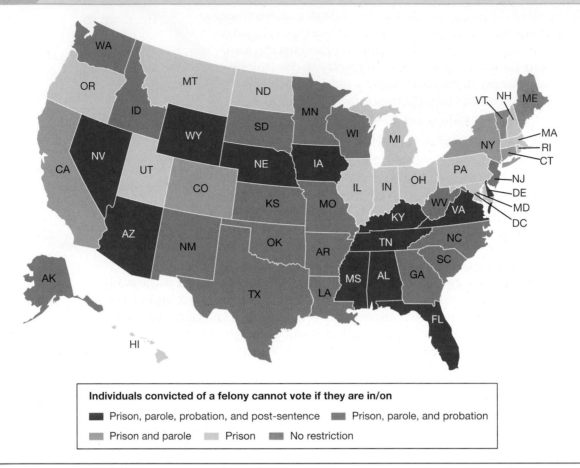

Individuals convicted of a felony cannot vote if they are in/on

- Prison, parole, probation, and post-sentence
- Prison, parole, and probation
- Prison and parole
- Prison
- No restriction

Source: http://www.sentencingproject.org/publications/felony-disenfranchisement-a-primer/

participate in the political process, 2.2 million of whom are African American.[65] This has a particularly profound effect on communities of color, which lack the political power to elect officials who represent the voice of these often marginalized communities. In fact, research indicates that felony disenfranchisement policies have had a significant impact on several national-level elections.[66]

While all states have a process that allows for offenders to reinstate their voting rights, the process is often so difficult that many are discouraged. Recently, several states have revisited these policies to determine whether individuals should have their right to vote reinstated based on their rehabilitative efforts. In 2007, Maryland's legislature eliminated the lifetime voting ban that was previously in place. Today, all individuals receive an automatic restoration of their rights once they have completed their sentence. Similarly, Nebraska's legislature overturned the lifetime ban for felons in their state and replaced it with a policy that bans felons from voting for two years following the completion of their punishment. Several other states, including Tennessee and Washington, require that offenders satisfy all fees and restitution orders prior to having their voting rights reinstated.[67]

Drug Addiction

In addition to the challenges of returning home from prison, many offenders continue to battle the demons that led them to criminal activity in the first place. Drug addiction is one of the primary reasons why many offenders are involved in criminal activity and ultimately sent to prison. Given the limited availability of treatment options both behind bars and within the community, issues of addiction can lead to recidivism.[68] Drug addiction has a multiplying effect in the lives of offenders; not only can addiction threaten their status on parole, but it impacts their ability to maintain stable employment and secure housing. Without community-based resources, many offenders will return to the addictions and lifestyles in which they engaged prior to their incarceration. Throughout the reentry process, ex-offenders also struggle with gaining access to these services. Without these referrals by probation and parole, most women are denied access to treatment due to the limited availability of services or an inability to pay for such resources on their own.

Access to Health Care

Many offenders have limited access to physical and mental health care, often due to a lack of community resources, an inability to pay, or lack of knowledge about where to go to obtain assistance. Given the status of mental and physical health needs of incarcerated men and women, the management (or lack thereof) of chronic health problems can impede an ex-offender's successful reentry process.[69] Unfortunately, mental health services within the community overemphasize the use of prescription psychotropic medications. Coupled with the limited availability of therapeutic interventions, these health interventions resemble more of a Band-Aid than a comprehensive, stable approach for offenders.[70]

Access to Resources

While many ex-offenders may turn to public assistance to help support their reentry transition, many come to find that these resources are either unavailable or significantly limited. The welfare reform bill of 1996—titled the Personal Responsibility and Work Opportunity Act—not only imposed time limits on the aid that individuals can receive but it also significantly blocked the road to success by denying services and resources for those with a criminal record, particularly in cases involving felony drug-related charges.[71] Section 115 of the welfare reform act called for a lifetime ban on benefits, such as Temporary Assistance for Needy Families (TANF) and food stamps, to offenders convicted in the state or federal courts for a felony drug offense. In addition, offenders convicted of a drug offense are barred from living in public housing developments, and in some areas, a criminal record can limit the availability of Section 8 housing options.[72] Drug charges are the only offense type subjected to this ban—even convicted murderers can apply for and receive government benefits following their release.[73] Indeed, the limits of this ban jeopardize the very efforts toward sustainable and safe housing, education, and drug treatment that are needed in order for women to successfully transition from prison. Figure 12.7 presents state-level data on the implementation of the ban on welfare benefits for felony drug convictions.

Since its enactment in 1996, a majority of states have rescinded the lifetime ban on resources for felony drug offenders, either in its entirety or in part. In 2015, senators Cory Booker, D-NJ, and Rand Paul, R-KY, introduced legislation titled the Record Expungement Designed to Enhance Employment (REDEEM) Act. In addition to allowing nonviolent federal offenders the option to have their criminal records sealed (thus making it easier for ex-convicts to successfully reintegrate back into society), this proposed legislation would lift the lifetime Supplemental Nutrition Assistance Program (SNAP) and TANF bans for nonviolent drug offenders.[74]

But even offenders without a drug conviction still face significant issues in obtaining public assistance. TANF carries a five-year lifetime limit on assistance. This lifetime limit applies to all residents, not just those under the criminal justice

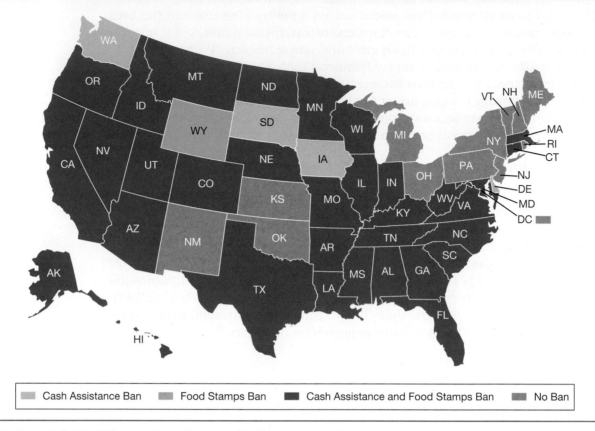

Cash Assistance Ban   Food Stamps Ban   Cash Assistance and Food Stamps Ban   No Ban

Source: The Sentencing Project, *A lifetime of punishment: The impact of the felony drug ban on welfare benefits.* http://sentencingproject.org/wp-content/uploads/2015/12/A-Lifetime-of-Punishment.pdf

system. In addition, the delay to receive these services ranges from 45 days to several months, a delay that significantly affects the ability of parolees to put a roof over their children's heads, clothes on their bodies, and food in their bellies.[75] Ultimately, these reforms are a reflection of budgetary decisions that often result in the slashing of social service and government aid programs while the budgets for criminal justice agendas, such as incarceration, remain supported by state and government officials. Despite the social stigma that comes with receiving welfare benefits, women in one study indicated that the receipt of welfare benefits represented progress toward a successful recovery and independence from reliance on friends, family, or a significant other for assistance. A failure to receive benefits could send them into a downward spiral toward homelessness, abusive relationships, and relapse:

> We still need welfare until we are strong enough to get on our feet. Trying to stay clean, trying to be responsible parents and take care of our families. We need welfare right now. If we lose it, we might be back out there selling drugs. We're trying to change our lives. Trying to stop doing wrong things. Some of us need help. Welfare helps us stay in touch with society. Trying to do what's right for us.[76]

Clearly, ex-offenders who make the transition from prison or jail back to their communities must achieve stability in their lives. With multiple demands on them (compliance with the terms and conditions of their release; dealing with long-term issues such as addiction, mental health, and physical health concerns; and the need for food, clothing, and shelter), this transition is anything but easy. Here, the influence of a positive mentor can provide significant support for women as they navigate this journey. Several key pieces of legislation have focused on the need for support and mentorship throughout the reentry process and have provided federal funding to support these networks. For example, the Ready4Work Initiative (begun in 2003), the Prisoner Reentry Initiative (2005), and the Second Chance Act (2007) all acknowledged the challenges that ex-offenders face when they exit the prison environment. These initiatives help support community organizations that provide comprehensive services for ex-offenders, including case management, mentoring, and other transitional services.[77]

CONCLUSION

Community correctional programs support offenders in the community, either in lieu of an incarceration sentence or following a sentence in jail or prison. However, this benefit comes with a price of net widening and increased supervision of offenders. In some cases, it's unclear whether this increased supervision helps to prevent crime. However, when effective, these programs represent a significant cost savings to the state and federal criminal justice systems. While the use of community corrections has come a long way, there is still significant progress to be made to help support offenders and lead them away from a criminal lifestyle.

CURRENT CONTROVERSY 12.1

PRO **CON**

CURRENT
CONTROVERSY
VIDEO
Where Do You Stand?
Cast Your Vote!

Should We Use Risk/Needs Assessments to Identify Offender Needs?

—Krista S. Gehring—

INTRODUCTION

The concept of assessment is not a new one; individuals are assessed on several occasions throughout their lives. For example, when a person visits the doctor, the doctor asks a series of questions about the individual's symptoms in order to assess what is wrong with the patient. The doctor may also conduct a physical exam to gather more information beyond the answers the patient has given. The information then helps the doctor to implement the proper treatment or write the correct prescription. Another example is when a person brings her automobile to the mechanic. She will tell the mechanic what is wrong with her vehicle, and the mechanic may ask questions or connect the vehicle to a computer to assess what is wrong prior to performing any maintenance. Assessment is about gathering as much information as possible in order to make an informed judgment about what to do next.

Over the past several decades, the practice of offender assessment has evolved from subjective judgments and "gut feelings" to the use of actuarial assessments that objectively predict risk and identify crime-producing needs that should be targeted with programs.[78] Currently, many risk/needs assessments use a combination of both static and dynamic risk factors to predict offender risk. Static risk factors are characteristics about an offender that do not change. Examples of these include number of prior arrests, age at first arrest, or other criminal history variables that are good predictors of risk. Dynamic risk factors, also known as criminogenic (crime-producing) needs, are characteristics or situations involving the offender that can change. These needs also predict risk and give criminal justice professionals something to target with programs. For example, if an offender has a substance abuse problem, and research has determined that substance abuse is related to criminal behavior, placing the offender in a substance abuse program to address that need may reduce the likelihood that that offender would recidivate. So for these instruments, risk is determined by identifying not only static factors but also "needs" that are, in fact, dynamic risk factors.

There are several needs (i.e., dynamic risk factors), which have been identified through research, that are related to criminal justice outcomes, such as recidivism, escape, or institutional misconduct. These risk factors have been deemed the Big Four and the Central Eight. The Big Four are four risk factors that

research has found to be most related to criminal behavior. These include (1) criminal history; (2) antisocial attitudes, values, and beliefs; (3) antisocial associates; and (4) antisocial personality. The Central Eight include all of the risk factors from the Big Four, as well as four additional needs: (1) substance abuse, (2) poor family/marital relationships, (3) poor performance at school/work, and (4) lack of prosocial leisure and/or recreational activities. Excluding criminal history (because it is a static risk factor and cannot change), these seven criminogenic needs are worth assessing and targeting with interventions.

 PRO Risk/Needs Assessments Are Effective Tools for Identifying Offender Needs

Many believe that the use of validated risk/needs assessment tools is a major advancement in offender management and treatment. Indeed, there are many reasons why risk/needs assessments are important for criminal justice professionals. First, the information gathered by the assessment can help guide and structure decision-making. It aids criminal justice personnel in determining who goes where, whether it is custodial placement for prison inmates or a supervision level for individuals in the community. Second, it helps reduce bias by eliminating extralegal factors, such as race or gender, from consideration in the determination of risk. Third, it aids in legal challenges, as individuals have a right to be placed in the most appropriate housing or treatment. If we do not assess offenders accurately, we may place them in housing which is more restrictive than necessary or assign (or fail to assign) them to treatment programs without a legitimate basis for doing so. Fourth, using assessments helps utilize resources better because when we are able to place the individual in the best possible treatment environment, we are able to get the most for the money that is spent on treatment. Finally, assessments enhance public safety because they allow us to know which individuals are higher risks and thus place those people in more restrictive environments so we may decrease the likelihood of future victimization.[79]

Several risk/needs assessment tools have been developed in the past several decades that use a

combination of both static and dynamic risk factors (i.e., criminogenic needs). These instruments consist of numerous questions that tap into domains linked to criminal behavior. Typically, these domains reflect the Central Eight risk factors discussed above. Examples of these assessments include the Level of Service Inventory–Revised (LSI-R),[80] the Northpointe Correctional Offender Management Profiling for Alternative Sanctions (COMPAS),[81] and the Ohio Risk Assessment System (ORAS).[82] These instruments are used in agencies across the country to determine supervision and custody levels for offenders, as well as identify which needs should be targeted with programs and interventions.

Extensive research has examined these tools to determine if they effectively identify who the high-, medium-, and low-risk individuals in the criminal justice populations are and what needs should be targeted for these individuals. Numerous validation studies have shown that these instruments are indeed valid and appropriate to use with offender populations.[83] When an instrument is valid, this means that it measures what it is supposed to measure. In the case of risk/needs assessments, valid assessments predict that high-risk individuals will have a higher recidivism rate than low-risk offenders. Some validation studies have also shown that these instruments predict recidivism when race and gender are taken into account.[84]

 CON Risk/Needs Assessments Are Ineffective Tools for Identifying Offender Needs

While risk/needs assessments have begun to be used throughout the country to identify offenders'

risk and needs, some argue that these instruments are missing important aspects that may cause them to not identify the needs of everyone who is assessed. The crux of this argument rests on how these tools were initially developed. Most of the risk/needs assessment tools that are currently used were developed and validated by male researchers using samples of male offenders; because of this, some scholars argue that inattention to gender and culture raises concern as to whether these are appropriate tools to use with all offenders.[85] For example, many claim that the aforementioned risk/needs assessment tools are gender neutral; that is, these instruments are valid for both men and women. While research has indeed shown that these instruments are valid for women, some argue that they are missing important needs that contribute to female offending.[86]

Although the Central Eight may seem like a comprehensive list of risk and need factors, some scholars note the absence of assessment scales pertaining to relationships, depression, parental issues, self-esteem, self-efficacy, trauma, and victimization, which they argue are important for women offenders.[87] These needs have been called *gender-responsive* risk factors, as it is believed they contribute to women's offending behavior. Since risk/needs assessment instruments serve as a guide to program recommendations, scholars are troubled by the possibility that omission of factors from current assessments may risk inattention to essential programming for women.[88]

This belief has contributed to the development of gender-responsive risk/needs assessments for women offenders. One example of this type of risk/needs assessment is called the Women's Risk/Needs Assessment (WRNA) instrument. This instrument combines both gender-neutral and gender-responsive needs in order to collect comprehensive information about women offenders. Validation studies of this instrument indicate that it is valid in predicting the recidivism and institutional misconduct of women and that subsets of the gender-responsive scales made significant contributions to gender-neutral models. This means that when the gender-responsive risk factors were added to gender-neutral risk/needs assessments like the LSI-R,

prediction of risk improved compared with using the LSI-R alone.[89]

Some scholars argue that not only are risk/needs assessments not sensitive to gender, but they do not account for cultural differences as well. It is possible that needs are not uniform across all individuals; different races or ethnicities may have risk factors that impact them differently. However, like gender, these assessments were not developed with cultural differences in mind, so failure to attend to this issue may lead to misidentification of risk for some individuals. While research has shown that these risk/needs assessment tools are valid for racial and ethnic minorities, this validation was done after these risk/needs assessments were created. Like gender, it is possible that these instruments are missing important needs that are important predictors in a particular culture, and omission of these factors from current assessments may risk inattention to essential programming for a specific cultural group. Indeed, some research has emerged suggesting that with some risk/needs assessments, the predictive validity differs by offender race or ethnicity.[90]

Following from this, risk/needs assessments have yet to address the concept of intersectionality. Intersectionality is a concept often used in critical theories to describe the ways in which oppressive ideologies (racism, sexism, classism, etc.) are interconnected and cannot be examined separately from one another.[91] For example, according to this concept, we cannot assume that the needs of middle-class White women will be the same as lower class African-American women. Since these needs may be different, risk/needs assessment instruments should be cognizant of and attend to these differences. Assuming that needs are the same for everyone might mask important differences that may appear when the offenders are separated into groups and researchers tap into the concept of intersectionality. If this is not done, individuals may be overclassified (put at a higher risk level than is warranted), or they may not be placed in programs or treatment interventions that could address their needs.

SUMMARY

Although the practice of risk/needs assessment is one of the many components of evidence-based practices in the criminal justice system, there is an ongoing debate as to whether these instruments are effective in identifying offender needs. Advocates of risk/needs assessment instruments claim they are valid instruments that adequately identify needs that are

related to recidivism, but others have expressed serious concerns that important needs are missing from these instruments, especially in relation to gender and culture. If these needs are missing, then these instruments are not effectively identifying them, and this could contribute to misplacement (or no placement) in important treatment programs for offenders.

DISCUSSION QUESTIONS

1. What are the risks of not using an objective risk/needs assessment to determine offender risk?

2. What are some issues of using a risk/needs assessment instrument that does not account for risk factors that are unique to a particular criminal justice population (e.g., women)?

3. Should there be different risk/needs assessment instruments for different types of criminal justice populations? That is, should there be separate instruments depending upon the offender's gender, race, ethnicity, class, or other special issues he or she might have? Or should we just use the same risk/needs assessment for everyone? Explain your answer.

4. If someone were to say to you, "Assessment is the engine that drives effective correctional programs," what would you interpret that to mean? Do you agree or disagree with this statement?

CURRENT CONTROVERSY 12.2

CURRENT CONTROVERSY VIDEO
Where Do You Stand?
Cast Your Vote!

Is Parole an Effective Correctional Strategy?
—Christine Scott-Hayward—

INTRODUCTION

Parole supervision refers to the period of time that an individual serves in the community after release from prison. Parole supervision is considered *conditional* supervision because people on parole supervision are subject to a list of conditions with which they must comply or risk being sent back to prison. Although some jurisdictions have changed how they refer to this type of supervision and use terms such as *community supervision* or *supervised release*, there are few significant differences in what happens to a person once he or she is on postprison supervision: Individuals are supervised by a parole or probation officer, subject to similar conditions, and subject to revocation should they violate one of these conditions. Therefore, I use the term *parole supervision* to refer to all forms of conditional postrelease supervision. Generally, parole supervision has two goals: protecting public safety and assisting with reentry or reintegration.

Although the number of people released onto parole supervision in the United States has declined over the last five years (from 74% of releases in 2008 to 64% of releases in 2013),[92] most people released from prison are still released onto some form of conditional, postcustody supervision. In 2013, there were more than 850,000 people on parole supervision in the United States.[93] People reentering society from prison face a variety of challenges, ranging from finding a job and a place to live to reconnecting with family and, of course, avoiding criminal activity. Approximately half of those released from prison will be returned to prison within three years, either for committing a new crime or for violating a condition of supervision.[94] Despite the fact that every state relies on some form of parole supervision, it is unclear whether it is an effective correctional strategy to address these issues.

PRO — Parole Supervision Is an Effective Correctional Strategy

The role of a parole officer is unique. Given the two roles of parole, officers are expected to exercise both social work and law enforcement functions, and balancing those two roles can be difficult. Parole officers can help individuals get back on their feet by helping them find and apply for jobs, access education, and so forth. However, parole officers are also responsible for ensuring that individuals comply with their supervision conditions and have the authority to recommend revocation, which could result in a return to prison. Although some scholars have expressed doubt as to parole's overall effectiveness, there has also been a considerable amount of research that shows what kinds of supervision programs and practices are effective. Based on this research, there is a considerable consensus among academics, policymakers, and practitioners as to the strategies that make parole effective.[95] Instead of focusing on surveillance and enforcement, this framework emphasizes "reducing reoffending through changing offender behavior."[96]

First, as a general matter, research shows that effective correctional treatment should focus on three major principles: risk, needs, and responsivity, collectively known as RNR.[97] Applied to parole supervision, these principles call for assessing the risk of recidivism and the criminogenic needs of individuals

exiting prison and then using this information to develop individualized parole plans. A key element in this is to involve clients in developing these plans to enhance their engagement while on supervision. Resources should be directed to those at a moderate or high risk to reoffend and front-loaded in the period soon after release from prison. Further, conditions of supervision should be tailored to the client's individual needs.[98]

Other promising strategies include incorporating incentives and rewards into the supervision process, employing graduated responses to violations of supervision conditions, and implementing earned-discharge programs, similar to good time in prison, as a way for clients to be rewarded for successfully adhering to their supervision requirements.[99] Together, this research suggests that if parole supervision targets the right people and is done well, it can be an effective correctional strategy.

CON Parole Supervision Is Not an Effective Correctional Strategy

Despite the promising practices outlined previously, overall, there is little evidence that parole supervision is effective at either of its two goals—protecting public safety and assisting with reentry or reintegration. If parole supervision were an effective correctional strategy, we would expect to see lower recidivism rates for people on parole than people released from prison without any supervision. Similarly, we would expect to see parole supervision having a positive impact on the reentry process.

There is no dispute that the recidivism rates for people released from prison are high. However, there is a lack of evidence that people who are released from prison onto parole supervision have lower recidivism rates than people who are unsupervised. A 2005 study found that parole supervision had very little effect on overall recidivism rates.[100] The authors found that people released under discretionary parole, as opposed to mandatory parole or unsupervised release, were slightly less likely to be arrested within two years of release but that those released under mandatory parole were no more likely to be arrested than those released without any supervision at all.[101] A recent meta-analysis of 15 studies published between 1980 and 2006 that examined the effectiveness of community supervision (both probation and parole) supports these findings, concluding that "on the whole community supervision does not

appear to work very well."[102] The authors found only a very small decrease in overall recidivism associated with community supervision and no relationship at all between community supervision and violent recidivism.[103]

Recent state-specific studies are mixed but fail to clearly demonstrate the effectiveness of parole supervision. For example, 2010 data from Texas show that outcomes for people released without supervision are actually slightly better than for those released onto parole.[104] In 2011, Kentucky passed legislation requiring a mandatory period of reentry supervision for

An officer places an individual under arrest for failing to check in with his parole officer. This form of recidivism is called a technical violation.

everyone leaving prison. A recent evaluation found that although parolees in the supervised group were less likely to be returned to prison for a new crime, when including technical violations, 28% of the supervised population were returned to prison within a year, compared with just 8% of the prepolicy comparison group.[105] Similarly, a 2013 study of releases from New Jersey prisons in 2008 compared outcomes for individuals released on parole with those for individuals who "maxed out," or served their entire sentence and were released without any community supervision.[106] Although the study did find that parolees were significantly more likely to return to prison as a result of a new crime than max-outs, these differences were offset by the number of parolees returned to prison as a result of a technical violation.

In addition to protecting public safety, parole supervision should also assist prisoners with reentry into the community. Although there is limited research in this area, few studies have found that parole supervision helps with reentry. For example, although most participants in the Urban Institute's Returning Home study expected their supervision officer would assist with their transition, after release, just half reported that their officer had actually been helpful.[107] Another study involving interviews with people on parole supervision in Washington State found that few people leaving prison thought of their supervision officers as a resource in the reentry process.[108] A more recent study by this author of people on parole in New York State concluded that parole supervision didn't help people with reentry and, in fact, sometimes hindered them: "For most people, parole officers were service brokers at best, and at worst, participants found that parole added barriers to reentry."[109]

SUMMARY

Parole supervision after release from prison remains extremely common, and although numerous studies have been conducted to determine supervision best practices, overall, there is still little clear evidence showing that parole supervision is an effective correctional strategy.

DISCUSSION QUESTIONS

1. Should parole officers be responsible for providing reentry services to people leaving prison?

2. Should all people leaving prison be placed on conditional supervision?

3. Should people on parole supervision be returned to prison for technical violations?

KEY TERMS

Review key terms with eFlashcards | $SAGE edge™ • edge.sagepub.com/mallicoatccj

DISCUSSION QUESTIONS

Test your mastery of chapter content • Take the Practice Quiz | $SAGE edge™ • edge.sagepub.com/mallicoatccj

1. How do community corrections programs serve to widen the net of the criminal justice system?

2. What are the primary benefits of diversion programs? How are they different from other forms of community corrections?

3. What makes an intermediate sanction different than probation? How might these programs be used in conjunction with probation supervision?

4. What is the role of the presentence investigation report? In what ways is it problematic?

5. What are the five rights that probationers are entitled to during a probation revocation hearing?

6. How might parole supervision provide better support for offenders during the reentry process?

LEARNING ACTIVITIES

1. Imagine you are a parole officer. Design a reentry strategy for an offender exiting from prison. How will you meet the needs of this offender and support a successful transition?

2. Using your library resources, locate a community-based program that is effective in reducing recidivism.

Why does this program work? How would you implement a similar program in your community?

3. Research parole in your state. How is the parole board organized? Which offenders are considered eligible for parole?

SUGGESTED WEBSITES

- **American Probation and Parole Organization:** http://www.appa-net.org/eweb
- **Federal Probation and Pretrial Officers Association:** http://fppoa.org
- **U.S. Parole Commission:** http://www.justice.gov/uspc
- **Federal Probation Journal:** http://www.uscourts.gov/statistics-reports/publications/federal-probation-journal

STUDENT STUDY SITE

Review • Practice • Improve | $SAGE edge™ • edge.sagepub.com/mallicoatccj

Want a better grade?

Get the tools you need to sharpen your study skills. Access practice quizzes, eFlashcards, video, and multimedia at **edge.sagepub.com/mallicoatccj**

SPECIAL TOPICS IN CRIMINAL JUSTICE

PART
V

13

CHAPTER

JUVENILE JUSTICE

LEARNING OBJECTIVES

- Discuss the history of the juvenile justice system

- Compare the two different case types that the juvenile court has jurisdiction over

- Discuss the process of cases in the juvenile court

- Identify the U.S. Supreme Court cases and decisions that established due process in the juvenile court

- Explain the different types of juvenile waivers

- Identify some of the challenges for juvenile incarceration

Sara Kruzan's childhood was anything but perfect. Her mother was abusive and addicted to drugs. Her father was in and out of jail for most of her childhood. She was sexually assaulted by several of her mother's boyfriends, and her mother kicked her out of their home when she was just 11.[1] In 1995, Sara Kruzan was only 16 years old when she was convicted of first-degree murder in California and sentenced to life without the possibility of parole (LWOP). The victim was her pimp, a 31-year-old man named G. G. Howard who had begun grooming Sara when she was only 11 years old and had been sexually trafficking her for the past four years.[2] Even though her age made it possible for the case to be tried in juvenile court (where the maximum sentence would have resulted in her incarceration until age 25), prosecutors transferred her case to criminal court, where she was tried as an adult. In January 2011, new state legislation was enacted that allowed for the reconsideration of juvenile cases in which life sentences were handed down. Following the new law, then-governor Schwarzenegger granted clemency to Kruzan and commuted her LWOP sentence to 25 years with the possibility of parole. Additional legislation signed into law by Governor Jerry Brown required parole boards to give special consideration in parole decisions involving juvenile offenders who were tried as adults and who had served at least 15 years of their sentences. After serving 19 years, Kruzan was paroled, in part due to these new policies.[3]

In this chapter, you will learn about how the juvenile justice system functions as a separate but similar counterpart to the criminal justice system. The chapter begins with a discussion of the history of the juvenile justice system. The chapter then turns to a review of the structure of the juvenile court and highlights some of the differences between the juvenile and criminal courts. You'll learn about how legal challenges in juvenile justice have changed the way in which youthful offenders are treated by these courts and how due process in juvenile cases has evolved. You'll also be exposed to some of the issues that face these young offenders in the juvenile justice system today. The chapter concludes with two Current Controversy debates. The first, by Alicia Pantoja, Sanna King, and Anthony Peguero, asks whether zero-tolerance policies have made schools safer. The second, by Schannae Lucas, addresses whether the juvenile court should be abolished.

> " While the adult penitentiary focused on punishment, these reformers believed that an institution for youth should not just be focused on rehabilitating these offenders but also target those who were at risk of engaging in delinquency.

Pauperism
Belief that certain classes of the poor were dishonest, lazy, and manipulative individuals.

Parens patriae
Legal doctrine that translates to "the best interests of the child" and was used to justify the removal of youth from their families and their placement under the care of institutions.

HISTORY OF THE JUVENILE JUSTICE SYSTEM

During the early 19th century, there was a growing concern about **pauperism**. Unlike issues such as crime or poverty, paupers were seen as the "undeserving poor," meaning that they were poor because they were dishonest, lazy, and manipulative individuals. During the early 19th century, the upper elite of New York believed that pauperism was destroying the city. Several of these prominent community members organized themselves into the Society for the Prevention of Pauperism and set out to develop policy recommendations on how to combat this growing problem. At the same time, these reformers realized that there were no separate facilities for youthful offenders. While the adult penitentiary focused on punishment, these reformers believed that an institution for youth should not just be focused on rehabilitating these offenders but also target those who were at risk of engaging in delinquency. This shift in philosophy led to the foundation of the New York House of Refuge in 1825.[4]

Houses of refuge began to develop in many of the major cities, including Boston and Philadelphia. These early institutions focused not only on young offenders but also on children whose parents were unable to care for them due to disease, neglect, or death. The doctrine of **parens patriae** was an important legal principle that was used to justify removing youth from their families and placing them under the care of these institutions. Parens patriae refers to "the best interests of the child." It was assumed that the state (and, therefore, these institutions) could provide a better environment for these youth, who were believed to be lacking discipline and supervision. As a result, states were permitted to remove children from the family home without due process protections.[5]

While the focus of these early institutions was to educate and reform these wayward youth, corporal punishment was a common feature and was used as a way to control the youth and instill discipline. Alas, their efforts often failed amid growing concerns that there was little reform

Houses of refuge were used to help provide for delinquent and dependent youth. The Virginia K. Johnson Home was a house of refuge in Dallas, Texas, for unmarried mothers under 21 years old. What effect did these early institutions have on the development of juvenile justice?

going on behind the walls of these institutions. During the late 19th century, a new reform effort called the child savers developed. Unlike the members of the Society for the Prevention of Pauperism (and later, the Society for the Prevention of Juvenile Delinquency), who were members of the upper-class elite, the child savers comprised primarily middle-class educated women. While their involvement created new career opportunities for women, it also allowed for the maintenance of the status quo and institutionalized a belief system that focused on traditional definitions of family life and child-rearing.

> What seemingly began as a movement to humanize the lives of adolescents soon developed into a program of moral absolutism through which youth was to be saved from movies, pornography, cigarettes, alcohol, and anything else which might possibly rob them of their innocence.[6]

Their efforts were perhaps one of the most significant contributions in the development of the first juvenile court.[7]

The first juvenile court was established in 1899 in Chicago as a result of the passage of a new child welfare law in Illinois. The intent of the law was to allow cases involving delinquent youth to be heard outside of the criminal courts. It also provided a venue to manage cases involving dependent and neglected children. By bringing these cases together under one institution, the courts were given a large degree of discretion to handle cases of youth who were a potential threat to the current social order. Like the reform schools that were created during the early 19th century, the doctrine of parens patriae continued to influence the philosophies and functions of the juvenile court. Their efforts were so successful that by 1925, all but two states had adopted juvenile courts. Over the next four decades, the juvenile court continued its efforts under the best-interests-of-the-child perspective.[8]

VIDEO
Affluenza Teen Ethan Couch May Be Jailed for Nearly Two Years

Delinquency
Refers not only to those acts that would be considered criminal under the law but also to status offenses.

STRUCTURE OF THE JUVENILE COURT

When we think about the juvenile justice system, we often think about youth who engage in criminal behaviors. However, this is a rather narrow view, as the juvenile courts handle more than just these types of cases. The juvenile justice system has jurisdiction over two different populations.

Delinquency Cases

First, the court is responsible for cases involving charges of **delinquency**. Delinquency refers not only to those acts that would be considered criminal under the law but also to status offenses. A status offense is an act that is prohibited under the law only for individuals under a certain age. For example, it is perfectly legal to consume alcoholic beverages if one is age 21 or older in the United States. However, it is illegal to do so if you are under the age of 21. Other examples of status offenses include truancy and running away from home. States vary significantly on how they

Ethan Couch was convicted of four counts of intoxication manslaughter. The case made headlines when Couch's defense attorney argued that his client suffered from *affluenza* and would be more suitable for rehabilitation than prison. He was sentenced to 10 years of probation. In December 2015, out of fear that he was going to be sentenced to prison for violating his probation, Couch and his mother fled the United States. They were found a few weeks later in Puerto Vallarta, Mexico, and were returned to the United States to face charges.

CAREERS IN CRIMINAL JUSTICE

So You Want to Work in Juvenile Justice?

As in the criminal justice system, there are a variety of occupations in which you can work with offenders. In this case, you are working with people under the age of 18. In many instances, you will find similar jobs. For example, you might find work as a member of a local police agency as a school resource officer. As a school resource officer, you have the same responsibilities and duties as a regular police officer, except that your "beat" is a school campus. In addition to participating in public safety and awareness initiatives for the general student body, you are the responding police officer for all infractions and crimes that happen on school grounds. You might also be interested in working as a juvenile probation officer. In this role, you will not only act as a liaison and provide presentencing and status reports to the juvenile court but you'll also provide services and support to youth who have been sentenced to probation in lieu of a confinement sentence. Finally, you might decide to work in a juvenile institution providing supervision and custodial care for incarcerated youth.

In addition, there are several jobs that are unique to the juvenile justice system. For example, a *guardian ad litem* is an individual that is appointed by the court to represent a juvenile's best interests. In many instances, these individuals are attorneys and can serve as a legal guardian. While this role can be found in delinquency courts, they are most commonly used in dependency courts, in cases where youth are housed in foster care because of instances of abuse or neglect. Another job related to the dependency court is a case manager. In this field, you might be assigned to work with children and families involved in the child welfare system. Children in these situations have often experienced abuse and neglect, and it is the job of the case manager to coordinate services such as housing, educational needs, therapy, and medical care. You also prepare reports to the court to make recommendations on issues such as guardianship and residency. Finally, you might work as a program manager in any of these settings to provide services and support to youth and families in need.

CAREER VIDEO
Juvenile Court Counselor

respond to status offenses. Some laws require juveniles and their families to participate in intervention programming. Here, the goal is to improve family functioning and divert youth away from potential delinquent behaviors. Meanwhile, other states approach status offenses as a way to place youth in a secure detention facility. Even though such cases are considered *predelinquent*, these youth are often treated the same as their offending counterparts, which can actually be more harmful to youth over the long run.[9]

Dependency Cases

The second type of case managed by the juvenile justice system is dependency cases. **Dependency** cases involve youth who have been harmed or neglected by their parents. When parents either cannot or are unwilling to care for their child, the juvenile court steps in to accept legal custody of the youth. **Legal custody** means that the court is now responsible for all the decisions made about the child. In some cases, the court will also take **physical custody**, and the youth will be sent to live in a temporary home or with a foster care family. In other cases, the court may assign physical custody to another family member or friend of the family. In a dependency case, the court considers information from a variety of different sources, including social workers, teachers, police, doctors, and family members, as well as the parents and child. Separate attorneys are appointed by the court to represent the child(ren) as well as the parent(s). Depending on the outcome of the case, the child(ren) can (1) remain under the custody of their parent(s), perhaps with some supervision provided by a social worker or requirements that the family undergo counseling or other

Dependency
Refers to cases that involve youth who have been harmed or neglected by their parents and therefore are being removed from the parents' custody.

Legal custody
Legal status in which the court is now responsible for all the decisions made about the child.

Physical custody
When a youth is sent to live in a temporary home, such as a group home, foster family, or with another family member.

types of therapeutic programming; (2) be moved to another family member or group home while the parent(s) work(s) with social services to reunite the family; or (3) be removed from the parent's or parents' custody while the court determines whether parental rights should be terminated.[10]

Juvenile Justice Process

Intake

As in the criminal justice system, most cases enter the juvenile justice system via a referral by the police. Unlike adults who are arrested, juveniles enter the system through the **intake** branch. Intake officers review the report submitted by the police and determine what should happen in each case. Intake officers have a high degree of discretion in their decision-making for many types of cases. In 2013, intake officers dismissed 191,800 cases, which was 18% of all cases referred by police.[11] For lower level acts of delinquency, an intake officer may refer a case to diversion (see Figure 13.1). Diversion allows for a youth to complete a set of require

Intake
Entry point for juvenile cases.

ments in lieu of being processed by the juvenile court. Twenty-seven percent of all cases were handled informally in this manner.[12] For example, youth may be required to attend anger management counseling or a drug/alcohol class, depending on the nature of their offense. They may also be required to complete some hours of service to the community. If they successfully complete their assigned tasks, the case is dismissed, and there are no formal notes on their juvenile record. In order to make her or his decision, the intake officer often conducts an interview to initially identify whether the youth can be released or should be detained. This can involve conversations with the both the youth and his or her parents about topics such as school attendance and performance, peer relationships, family dynamics, at-risk behaviors such as drug/alcohol use, and mental health concerns.

If the intake officer determines that it is in the best interests of the youth to not be released back into the care of her or his parent(s) or guardian(s), there are a couple of options available. If the intake officer is concerned about either the nature of the current charge or the likelihood of additional delinquent behaviors, the youth may be placed in juvenile detention for a short time until his or her court appearance (usually 24 to 72 hours). If the intake officer is concerned that one or more parents or guardians are unable to provide adequate supervision for the youth or if there are concerns about the residential environment, she or he may elect to place the youth in a temporary shelter or detention facility for a short period of time until the court reviews the case. In many

Although a juvenile's first point of contact with the criminal justice system is through a police officer, it is the intake officer who has the most influence over each case. What are the responsibilities of the intake officer?

Figure 13.1 Difference Between the Juvenile and Criminal Courts

What are the stages of delinquency case processing in the juvenile justice system?

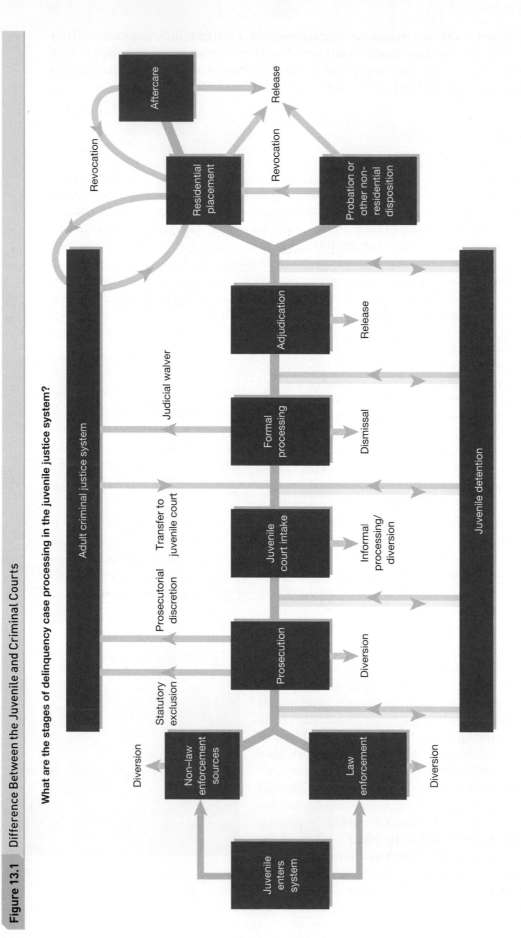

ways, the intake officer has discretionary power similar to that of both a police officer and a prosecutor in that he or she can decide how a case will be handled (formally or informally) and whether or not a youth needs to be initially remanded to custody or released to a parent's or parents' care.[13] In 2013, the majority of juveniles were not detained (79%).[14]

VIDEO
Cuyahoga County Starts New System for Booking and Processing Juvenile Offenders

Processing

While many cases are handled on an informal basis or are sent to diversion, some cases will be referred to the juvenile court. The majority of these youth will remain in the custody of their parent(s) or guardian(s) until they have to appear before the court. However, as you learned above, some cases will be remanded to some form of custodial care for a short time until they appear before the juvenile court judge. Unlike judges in criminal courts, juvenile court judges are much more active in the process. They can request information about the youth or their parents and even inquire about things such as school performance, family dynamics, and physical or mental health as part of the **adjudication hearing**. The conclusion of this hearing is to determine whether a **delinquency petition** will be filed. This allows for the juvenile court to retain jurisdiction over a case.

Adjudication

Since juveniles do not have the constitutional right to a trial by jury, it is the judge that renders the decision in a case. Like cases in the criminal court, juvenile cases must be proved beyond a reasonable doubt. Whereas an adult offender is declared guilty, a juvenile offender is adjudicated as a delinquent. The different terminology of the juvenile court helps to distinguish the differences between how cases are handled compared with the adult court. Table 13.1 highlights some of these differences in terminology between the juvenile and criminal court.

Fifty-five percent of all cases were adjudicated delinquent in 2013 (Figure 13.2).[15] If a youth is adjudicated delinquent, the court holds a **disposition hearing** to determine the plan of action for the case. Unlike the criminal court, this stage is not always about punishment but instead balances the issues of community safety with the best interests of the child. For example, a judge can decide to send a juvenile to a secure facility

Table 13.1	Differences in Terminology Between the Juvenile and Criminal Courts
Juvenile Court	**Criminal Court**
Taken into custody	Arrested
Petition	Charged
Delinquency proceeding	Criminal case
Detention hearing	Bail hearing
Adjudication hearing	Trial
Adjudicated	Guilty
Disposition	Sentencing
Commitment	Incarceration
Aftercare	Parole

Adjudication hearing
Similar to a trial in the adult court.

Delinquency petition
Legal filing that allows for the juvenile court to retain jurisdiction in a case.

Disposition hearing
Similar to a sentencing hearing in adult court, this is held to determine the plan of action for the case once a juvenile is adjudicated delinquent.

Figure 13.2 Case Flow for Cases in 2013

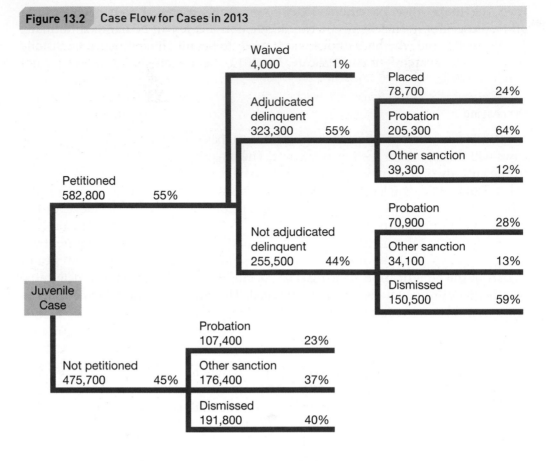

Juvenile Case

Petitioned 582,800 — 55%

Waived 4,000 — 1%

Adjudicated delinquent 323,300 — 55%
- Placed 78,700 — 24%
- Probation 205,300 — 64%
- Other sanction 39,300 — 12%

Not adjudicated delinquent 255,500 — 44%
- Probation 70,900 — 28%
- Other sanction 34,100 — 13%
- Dismissed 150,500 — 59%

Not petitioned 475,700 — 45%
- Probation 107,400 — 23%
- Other sanction 176,400 — 37%
- Dismissed 191,800 — 40%

Figure 13.3 Landmark Cases for Juvenile Offenders

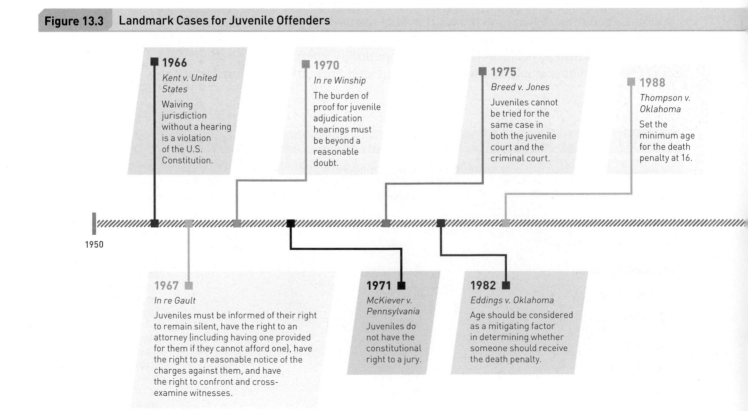

1966 *Kent v. United States* — Waiving jurisdiction without a hearing is a violation of the U.S. Constitution.

1970 *In re Winship* — The burden of proof for juvenile adjudication hearings must be beyond a reasonable doubt.

1975 *Breed v. Jones* — Juveniles cannot be tried for the same case in both the juvenile court and the criminal court.

1988 *Thompson v. Oklahoma* — Set the minimum age for the death penalty at 16.

1950

1967 *In re Gault* — Juveniles must be informed of their right to remain silent, have the right to an attorney (including having one provided for them if they cannot afford one), have the right to a reasonable notice of the charges against them, and have the right to confront and cross-examine witnesses.

1971 *McKiever v. Pennsylvania* — Juveniles do not have the constitutional right to a jury.

1982 *Eddings v. Oklahoma* — Age should be considered as a mitigating factor in determining whether someone should receive the death penalty.

for a specific time. Washington State uses a determinate sentencing structure that looks at the offenses, together with the delinquency history and the age of the youth in order to determine a range of time that the judge can use in sending a youth to the Juvenile Rehabilitation Administration (JRA).[16] However, judges in many states have wide discretion when handing out their dispositions. For example, Boulder County, Colorado, provides the option of a wilderness work program in lieu of time in a detention facility. Under this program, youth are sentenced to 10 days in a highly structured outdoor work program, which incorporates physical labor as well as therapeutic activities.[17] Youth might also be sentenced to write an essay about their behavior or a letter of apology to the victim, participate in targeted therapies based on their unique needs, or even be required to participate in opportunities such as sports or mentoring programs, such as Big Brother/Big Sisters. The court may also determine that while a detention or other locked facility may not be an appropriate placement, the family home environment is not appropriate either. In these cases, youth may become a temporary or permanent ward of the court and be provided support services, such as therapeutic interventions, life skills courses, or parenting classes in cases of youth who are pregnant or teen parents.

In Chapter 9, you learned about how due process is guaranteed by the 5th Amendment of the Constitution. In addition, the 14th Amendment extends the protections related to criminal prosecutions under the 6th Amendment. However, the early juvenile courts were designed to treat youth, not to punish them. As a result, they did not include the same due process protections as those for adults in the criminal courts. By the mid-20th century, the juvenile court began to function more as a tool of punishment. As a result, several Supreme Court decisions during the 1960s highlighted the need for due process protections in the juvenile court (see Figure 13.3).

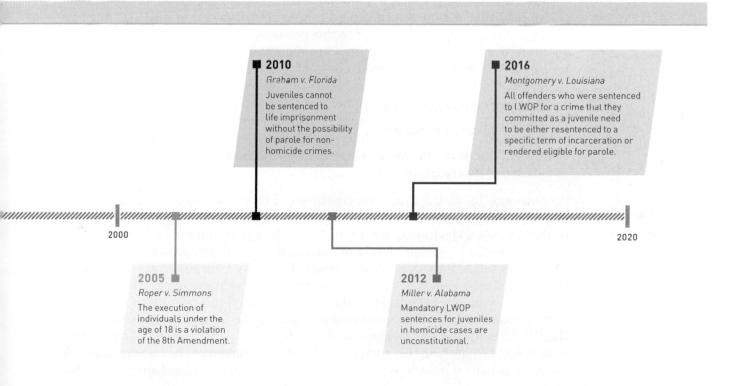

2010
Graham v. Florida
Juveniles cannot be sentenced to life imprisonment without the possibility of parole for non-homicide crimes.

2016
Montgomery v. Louisiana
All offenders who were sentenced to LWOP for a crime that they committed as a juvenile need to be either resentenced to a specific term of incarceration or rendered eligible for parole.

2000

2020

2005
Roper v. Simmons
The execution of individuals under the age of 18 is a violation of the 8th Amendment.

2012
Miller v. Alabama
Mandatory LWOP sentences for juveniles in homicide cases are unconstitutional.

The first case to reach the court was *Kent v. United States* (1966).[18] At age 16, Morris Kent was sentenced to 30 to 90 years for his involvement in a robbery and subsequent rape. Even though his attorney filed for a hearing to assess whether the case should be heard by the juvenile or criminal court, the judge waived the jurisdiction in the case without holding a hearing. As a result, the case was transferred to the criminal court. The Supreme Court held that to waive jurisdiction without a hearing was a violation of the U.S. Constitution. This finding was significant because it was the first time that the structure of the juvenile court was successfully challenged by the Court. In many ways, this decision provided the foundation for subsequent cases to fight for due process rights for juveniles.

Perhaps one of the most well-known U.S. Supreme Court cases involving juvenile offenders is *In re Gault* (1967). Gerald Gault was 15 years old and made what was considered to be an obscene phone call to his neighbor. He was arrested by the local sheriff and taken to juvenile hall. His parents were not notified of his arrest or that he was scheduled for a detention hearing the following day. While his mother did eventually find out about the hearing, no witnesses were present, no records were kept of the proceedings, and Mr. Gault did not have an attorney present. Had he been charged as an adult, his maximum punishment would have consisted of a $50 fine and a two-month jail sentence. Instead, the judge sent Gerald Gault to a state reform school for six years, a sentence that, under the law, he had no right to appeal. The Supreme Court held that the denial of due process was a violation of the 14th Amendment. In particular, the justices commented that in cases where juveniles are under arrest for a charge that could result in being removed from their homes and placed in an institution as a result of an act of delinquency, they must be informed of their right to remain silent, right to have an attorney present (including having one provided for them if they cannot afford one), right to a reasonable notice of the charges against them, and right to confront and cross-examine witnesses.[19] Following the *Gault* decision, the Court heard three additional cases that continued to refine the rights of delinquent juveniles. The case of *In re Winship* (1970) held that the burden of proof for juvenile adjudication hearings must be beyond a reasonable doubt.[20] Prior to this decision, courts were determining cases based on the lower standard of proof of preponderance of the evidence. *Breed v. Jones* (1975) stated that a juvenile could not be tried for the same case in both the juvenile court and the criminal court—to do so would violate the protection against double jeopardy.[21] As a result of these decisions, the majority of due process protections that were enjoyed by adults in the criminal court were extended to the juvenile court. The primary exception to this rule is the right to a trial by jury. The Court held that juveniles do not have the constitutional right to a jury in the case of *McKiever v. Pennsylvania* (1971).[22]

Since the 1970s, the Court has continued to be concerned about issues related to juvenile offenders. In 1988, the Court heard the case of *Thompson v. Oklahoma*. In their decision, the justices determined that age was an important factor in determining whether a juvenile should be subjected to the death penalty. At the time, 19 states, as well as the federal government, did not have a minimum age by which an offender could be sentenced to death. However, many of these same states did allow for some 15-year-olds to be tried as adults, which opened the gates for the possibility that such offenders could be sentenced to death. At the same time, the Court noted that 18 states had set the minimum age for the death penalty at 16. Based on this evidence, the Court held that a national consensus existed that the minimum age for the death penalty should be 16. As a result, the Court rendered illegal any statutes that

AROUND THE WORLD

Juvenile Justice in Japan

Japan's juvenile law during the 20th century was largely modeled after the laws in the United States, whereby the doctrine of parens patriae served as the foundation for managing juvenile delinquency. Family courts were established to manage cases of juvenile delinquency for youths between the ages of 14 and 20 who engaged in criminal offenses. Cases involving youth under the age of 14 were sent to child welfare agencies. Cases were most commonly referred to the family court by the police, although prosecutors could also direct cases to the court as well. Once a case was assigned to the family court, a report similar to the presentence investigative report was prepared. The report contained information about the youth's background, family environment, and the needs of the juvenile. This report was then used to identify the types of services that would be tied to the disposition of the case. The core philosophy in disposing of these cases was to rehabilitate the youth and divert him or her away from the criminal justice system.[a]

In 2000, the Act Revising Part of the Juvenile Act was passed, which represented the first reforms to the juvenile law in more than 50 years. These reforms were initiated in response to several high-profile murders involving juvenile offenders, as well as a perception that juvenile crime in general was increasing.[b] What is particularly interesting is that while there were several graphic crimes that made the headlines, the number of juvenile arrests has actually decreased substantially. According to Japan's Statistics Bureau, there were 65,448 juvenile offenders who were arrested in 2012. This is a significant departure from 1990, which saw 154,168 juvenile arrests, and 2000, which saw 132,336 juvenile arrests. Of these 65,448 arrests, only 836 were for the top-four felony crimes: homicide, robbery, arson, and rape. The majority of cases involved larceny offenses.[c]

Under the new juvenile act, the minimum age of criminal responsibility (meaning, the youngest age that an offender could be sent to the criminal court) was lowered from 16 to 14. In addition, the new law allows for all youth aged 16 and older who commit a premeditated crime resulting in death to be automatically sent to the criminal courts. Under these practices, we see a strong influence from the American juvenile-waiver process, which sends juvenile cases to adult criminal courts.

Recently, the Liberal Democratic Party has proposed new legislation that would lower the maximum age of juvenile jurisdiction to 17. The rationale behind lowering the age of juvenile jurisdiction follows recent legislation that lowered the eligible voting age in the country from 20 to 18. The logic is that if someone is old enough to vote, she or he is old enough to be treated as an adult if she or he engages in acts against the law. Critics of the proposal question whether the shift from rehabilitation to punishment for these offenders will limit access to education and medical and mental health treatment, as well as other therapeutic interventions that are often utilized under the juvenile system but that are absent under the criminal system. Should this policy be implemented, people aged 18 and 19 who commit crimes would automatically be treated by the criminal courts regardless of offense. As a result, the number of family court cases would decrease by an estimated 40%.[d] The clear trend here is that like the United States during the late 20th century, the modern juvenile court in Japan is distancing itself further away from the rehabilitative model of the juvenile courts in favor of a more punitive option.

CRITICAL THINKING QUESTIONS

1. How is the structure of Japan's juvenile court similar to the American juvenile court? Are there any noted differences?

2. How would you explain the reduction in the number of arrests of juvenile offenders between 1990 and 2012? How might the proposed policies impact the number of youth in the juvenile courts?

did not specify a minimum age of at least 16. In the following year, a subsequent case held that there was no national consensus prohibiting the death penalty for juvenile murderers who were either 16 or 17 years old at the time of their crime (*Stanford v. Kentucky* [1989]). Even though the court set minimum ages by which offenders could be sentenced to death, they also held that age should be considered as a mitigating factor in determining whether someone should receive such a punishment (*Eddings v. Oklahoma* [1982]).

The juvenile death penalty remained unchanged on a nationwide level for 16 years. During that time, 19 individuals in six states were executed for crimes that they committed at either 16 or 17 years old, and an additional 72 offenders who were awaiting their execution and were housed on death row in 12 states. By 2005, several states had changed their laws such that 31 jurisdictions prohibited the death penalty for juveniles; 19 states (plus the federal government and the U.S. military) set a minimum age for the punishment at 18, and an additional 12 states prohibited the practice for all individuals. In addition, public support for the execution of juveniles had fallen dramatically. Finally, the court considered the evidence presented by professional medical and psychological organizations that pointed to findings that juveniles may lack the appropriate brain development to be able to appreciate the consequences of their actions. As a result of these shifts, the Court held in *Roper v. Simmons* (2005) that the execution of individuals under the age of 18 was a violation of the 8th Amendment protection against cruel and unusual punishment.

In recent years, the Court has begun to consider other forms of criminal sentences as cruel and unusual punishment. For example, in *Graham v. Florida* (2010), the Court held that juveniles cannot be sentenced to life imprisonment without the possibility of parole for nonhomicide crimes. At the time, there were 129 individuals serving an LWOP sentence for nonhomicide acts that they had committed under the age of 18. While these offenders were scattered across 10 different states, the majority of these offenders (*n* = 77) were sentenced under Florida state law. A few years later, the Court held in *Miller v. Alabama* that mandatory LWOP sentences for juveniles in homicide cases were unconstitutional. At the time, this decision impacted only future cases and left an estimated 2,300 offenders under an LWOP sentence. Recently, the Court determined that the ruling in *Miller* must be retroactive, meaning that all offenders who were sentenced to LWOP for a crime that they committed as a juvenile need to be either resentenced to a specific term of incarceration or rendered eligible for parole (*Montgomery v. Louisiana* [2016]).

DEMOGRAPHICS OF JUVENILE OFFENDERS

Who are the youth who appear before the juvenile court for cases of delinquency? In 2013, juvenile courts nationwide managed more than 1 million cases. However, this is a reduction from previous decades. For example, the number of delinquency cases increased between 1985 and 1997 by 62%. Then, from 1997 to 2013, the number of cases decreased by 44%. Given these rises and falls, what do we know about the number of delinquency cases over the past three decades? In 2013, the juvenile courts actually handled 9% fewer cases than they did in 1985. Table 13.2 demonstrates how the number and types of cases in the juvenile courts have changed over the years.[23]

In 2013, girls made up 28% of delinquency cases while boys made up 72%. Girls were most likely to be involved in crimes against persons (31% of cases) and least likely to be involved in drug-related crimes (20%) (Figure 13.4).

Table 13.2	Juvenile Delinquency Cases			
		Percent change		
Most serious offense	**Number of cases**	**10 year 2004–2013**	**5 year 2009–2013**	**1 year 2012–2013**
Total delinquency	1,058,500	−37	−29	−7
Person offenses	278,300	−34	−24	−6
Criminal homicide	900	−30	−33	−1
Forcible rape	7,500	−16	−5	−1
Robbery	22,000	2	−25	4
Aggravated assault	26,900	−42	−32	−7
Simple assault	186,400	−37	−25	−6
Other violent sex offenses	9,700	−18	−6	−3
Other person offenses	25,000	−28	−12	−11
Property offenses	366,600	−42	−35	−10
Burglary	65,300	38	32	−11
Larceny-theft	183,400	−38	−34	−10
Motor vehicle theft	11,600	−65	−38	0
Arson	5,000	−42	−29	−10
Vandalism	54,200	−46	−40	−13
Trespassing	29,900	44	−38	−11
Stolen property offenses	10,200	−48	−34	−7
Other property offenses	7,100	−59	−38	−6
Drug law violations	141,700	−23	−14	4
Public order offenses	271,800	−38	−30	−7
Obstruction of justice	132,000	−33	−28	−5
Disorderly conduct	74,500	−43	−32	−9
Weapons offenses	21,700	−44	−33	−7
Liquor law violations	9,000	−47	−47	−23
Nonviolent sex offenses	10,600	−25	−8	−2
Other public order offenses	24,000	−38	−28	−3

Notes: Data may not add to totals because of rounding. Percent change calculations are based on unrounded numbers.

Source: http://www.ojjdp.gov/pubs/248899.pdf

We also see differences in the types of offenses by race. In 2013, 62% of the youth involved in delinquency cases were White. Blacks made up 35%. American Indian/ Alaskan Native youth were 2% of all cases, and Asian/Pacific Islander youth were 1%. While White youth are most likely to be involved in drug-related cases (72%),

Figure 13.4 Sex and Age Differences in Delinquency Cases

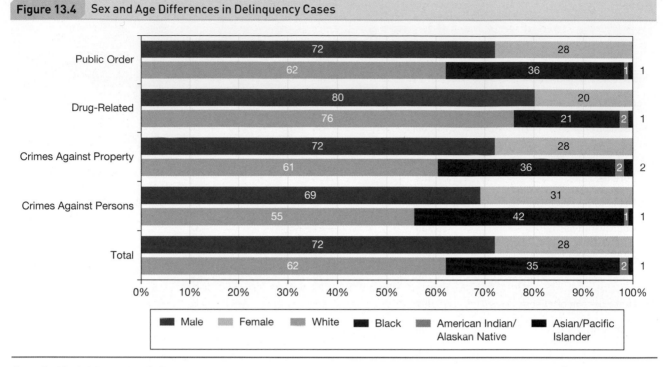

Source: Furdella, J., & Puzzanchera, C. (October 2015). Delinquency cases in juvenile court, 2013. U.S. Department of Justice, http://www.ojjdp.gov/pubs/248899.pdf

they make up only 55% of crimes against persons. In comparison, the most common category for Black youth is crimes against persons (42%). Indeed, most of the cases involve either White or Black youth, as American Indian and Asian youth make up only 1% to 2% of cases across all offense types. Finally, youth under the age of 16 made up 53% of all delinquency cases. For the very youngest of offenders (under the age of 13), they are most often referred to the juvenile court for crimes against persons (11% of all cases) and are less commonly referred for drug-related cases (4%).[24]

ISSUES IN JUVENILE JUSTICE

SAGE JOURNAL ARTICLE
A Preliminary Assessment of the Impact of Plea Bargaining Among a Sample of Waiver-Eligible Offenders

As a result of the legal challenges over the past seven decades, the juvenile justice system today provides youth with many of the same legal rights and protections that are used in the adult criminal courts. Over the past three decades, there has been a push to treat serious and violent juvenile offenders more like their adult counterparts, regardless of their age, though. The push to be tough on juvenile crime began in the mid-1990s. One influence on these policies was the work of John DiIulio, a political science professor from Princeton University. DiIulio's work coined the term **superpredator** to describe what he predicted was a new wave of "kids that have absolutely no respect for human life and no sense of the future. . . . These are stone-cold predators."[25] The linking of this perspective to the rising rates of juvenile violence led DiIulio and a prominent criminologist, James Q. Wilson, to predict that by the year 2000, "there will be a million more people between the ages of 14 and 17 than there are now. . . . Six percent of them will become high rate, repeat offenders—thirty thousand more muggers, killers and thieves than we have now."[26] While such predictions never materialized, this myth of the juvenile superpredator had a significant impact on the public's fear of potential future crime; it influenced policymakers to introduce stricter laws against juvenile offending. As a result, not only did these laws alter which cases would be heard by the juvenile court, but they shifted the court to a more punitive model.

Superpredator
A term created by DiIulio that predicted a new wave of kids who would not have any sense of remorse for their crimes. Predictions about the superpredator had a significant impact on policies and practices related to juvenile crime.

Juvenile Waiver

As you learned at the start of this chapter, juvenile justice professionals determine whether a case should be formally processed in the juvenile court. But what happens in those cases where a juvenile is of a certain age and either engages in repeated acts of delinquency or is involved in a serious or violent offense? In these instances, the juvenile court may decide that they are not the appropriate place to manage a case. As a result, cases are then transferred to the adult criminal court for processing. This is called a **juvenile waiver**.

Chris Bay, a teenager sentenced to 40 years for murder, shares a small cell with his roommate at the Clemens Unit prison in Texas. The state of Texas sentences juvenile offenders convicted of serious crimes to adult prisons run by the Department of Corrections. What challenges might they face as youth in an adult prison?

Legislative Waiver

There are three different types of juvenile waivers. The first is a **legislative waiver**. In response to concerns over the rising rates of serious and violent crime, many states passed laws during the late 20th and early 21st century. As a result of these new laws, cases involving youths of a particular age, combined with a specific category of offense (usually involving serious and violent felonies), were automatically sent to criminal court.[27] Some states have determined that youth as young as 14 can be waived to the adult court. Figure 13.5 highlights the minimum age whereby youth can be transferred to the criminal court as a result of statutory law. This map highlights that several states do not set a minimum age for juvenile transfer. These policies reflect a philosophy that became popular during this era: Do the crime, do the time. In addition, many states have "once waived, always waived" policies, which mean that once a youth is sent to the criminal court, any subsequent cases that occur, even if those cases happen before the youth's 18th birthday, will be handled by the adult court, regardless of their severity.[28]

Prosecutorial Waiver

The second type of waiver is the **prosecutorial waiver**. In these types of cases, it is up to the prosecutor to decide whether to file the case in the juvenile court or in the criminal court. Since the law allows for these cases to be tried in either court, this is referred to as concurrent jurisdiction. As a result, the prosecutor holds a high degree of power in determining which court to file a case in. When a prosecutor decides to pursue the case in the criminal court instead of the juvenile court, this is called a **direct file**. This means that the traditional practices and sentencing options that are normally available to juvenile offenders are eliminated, and the proceedings are more focused on the philosophy of punishment instead of rehabilitation.[29]

Judicial Waiver

The final type of waiver is the **judicial waiver** or a **discretionary waiver**. In many ways, the judicial waiver has always been a part of the juvenile system. It was this practice that was formalized as a result of the U.S. Supreme Court decision in *Kent v. United States* (1966). The judicial waiver process requires that before a youth can be sent to the criminal court, the juvenile court must hold a hearing to assess whether the youth could still benefit from the resources available in the juvenile court. In some cases, the hearings are rather limited. These cases are referred to as mandatory waivers, and it is the court's job to determine whether the juvenile meets the legally proscribed

Juvenile waiver
Legal process whereby cases are transferred to the adult criminal court for processing.

Legislative waiver
A method of juvenile waiver that involves laws specifying a minimum age at which cases are automatically sent to criminal court for certain crimes.

Prosecutorial waiver
A method of juvenile waiver that relies on the decision of the prosecutor whether to file charges in the juvenile or criminal court.

Direct file
The process by which a prosecutor files a case involving a juvenile offender in criminal court.

Judicial waiver
Legal process that requires the juvenile court to hold a hearing to determine whether the youth could still benefit from the resources of the juvenile court in its decision to transfer a case to the criminal court. Also known as a **discretionary waiver**.

Figure 13.5 Minimum Transfer Age for Legislative Waivers

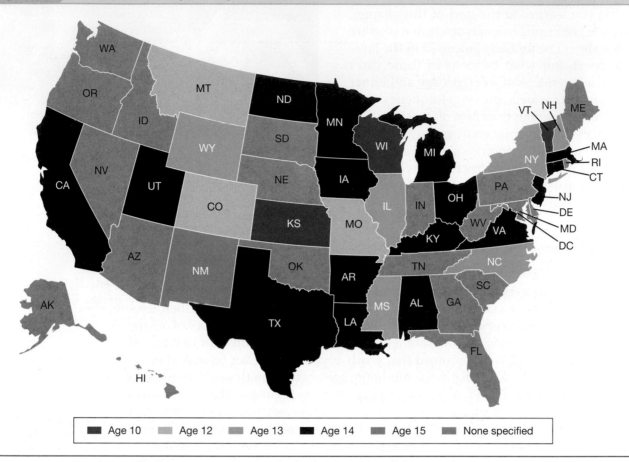

| ■ Age 10 | ■ Age 12 | ■ Age 13 | ■ Age 14 | ■ Age 15 | ■ None specified |

Source: OJJDP Statistical Briefing Book. Available online at http://www.ojjdp.gov/ojstatbb/structure_process/qa04105.asp?qaDate=2011

characteristics—such as age, delinquency history, and probable cause for the current offense—in order to have his or her case waived to the criminal court. In other cases, the judge has greater discretion whereby the defense attorney can argue to the court that the juvenile's needs would be best served by the juvenile court.[30]

How many cases are waived to the adult court? These data are difficult to compile. While we can determine how many youth are waived under the judicial waiver process, we don't know how many waivers occur based on either statutory exclusions or direct filing practices.[31] According to the Office of Juvenile Justice and Delinquency Prevention, the number of juvenile waivers peaked in the mid-1990s and has declined ever since. In 1985, 5,800 youth were judicially waived. By 1994, this number grew to 13,600 cases. Yet by 2011, the number of cases rebounded, as only 5,400 cases received judicial waivers. However, this does not necessarily reflect that fewer cases are being moved to the criminal courts. Instead, these trends may reflect the number of states that passed laws that permitted cases to be waived via legislative or prosecutorial waivers.[32] Figure 13.6 presents the demographics for these cases over these three time periods.

Research tells us that the waiver practice has disproportionately impacted youth of color.[33] Not only are youth of color more likely to be waived to the criminal court, but they face disproportionately harsher sentences compared with their White counterparts.[34] In fact, juveniles can receive even harsher punishments than some of their adult counterparts for the same offenses. For example, juveniles receive longer prison sentences than adults under the age of 30. However, their sentences are similar to those received by offenders who are older than 30. This means that judges likely see

Figure 13.6 Demographics of Judicial Waiver Cases

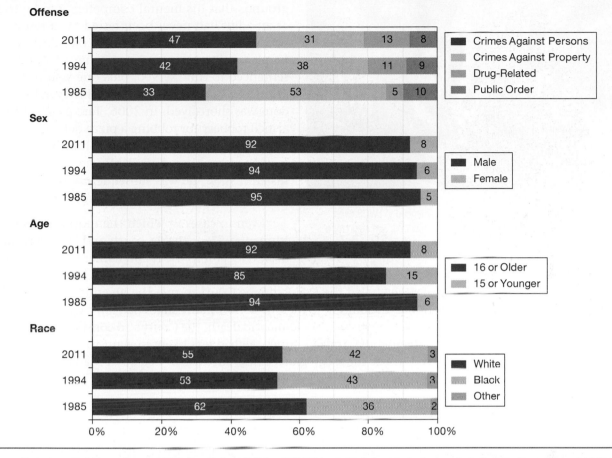

Source: Hockenberry, S., & Puzzanchera, C. (2015). *Juvenile Court Statistics, 2013.* Pittsburgh, PA: National Center for Juvenile Justice. http://www.ojjdp.gov/ojstatbb/njcda/pdf/jcs2013.pdf

juvenile offenders as more dangerous and therefore in need of increased punishments, compared with adults between the ages of 18 and 30.[35] Indeed, we find that even in states that use sentencing guidelines, sentences for juveniles tried as adults are 15% to 20% greater than those for their young-adult counterparts.[36]

Juvenile Sentencing

Whether tried as adults or retained as children, it is clear that for juveniles, the laws have fallen in line with the larger movement to be tough on crime. The superpredator myth not only led many youth to be waived to the adult criminal court but even resulted in sentences such as life without parole for young offenders. Consider the case of Lionel Tate. Tate was convicted of first-degree murder at just 12 years old for killing 6-year-old Tiffany Eunick in 1999. Tate's mother was babysitting Tiffany, and the two children were playing upstairs in the Tate home in Pembroke Park, Florida. Eunick suffered significant injuries, including a fractured skull, lacerations to her liver, broken ribs, and internal bleeding.[37] While prosecutors argued that Tate was a cold and callous murderer, the defense argued that Tate was imitating professional wrestlers and didn't know that he could cause harm, despite the 130-pound difference between them. Despite an earlier offering of a plea deal by prosecutors, the defense sought a trial, believing that Tate would be acquitted, as his age limited his ability to understand the significance of his actions. Instead, the judge sentenced him to LWOP, making him the

> Not only are youth of color more likely to be waived to the criminal court, but they face disproportionately harsher sentences compared with their White counterparts.

Lionel Tate was just 12 years old when he was sentenced to LWOP. Even though this conviction was later overturned, he is now in prison again for a separate crime. Do you think his initial conviction and time in prison had any bearing on his later crime?

youngest person ever to receive such a sentence. In 2004, his conviction was overturned on the grounds that his mental competency to be tried as an adult had never been tested. As a result, he was able to return to the original plea deal, where he pled guilty to second-degree murder and was sentenced to time served, plus one year of house arrest and 10 years' probation.[38] However, his freedom was short-lived. In 2006, Tate pled guilty to armed robbery for robbing a pizza delivery worker with a gun.[39] The case involved four pizzas with a value of less than $35. While he later retracted his admission, he was subsequently sentenced to 30 years in prison for violating probation.

Even in cases in which the most serious punishments were available, courts and juries have also been reluctant to use them. Earlier in this chapter, you learned about how changes to the evolving standards of decency led the U.S. Supreme Court to rule the juvenile death penalty unconstitutional. In addition to looking at how many states had laws, either in theory or practice, on sentencing such offenders to death, the Court also considered how such laws were implemented. Indeed, juries seemed less likely to want to sentence youth to death, even in the most egregious cases. The case of Lee Boyd Malvo provides an example of this.

Juvenile Confinement

The best way to understand how many youth are in custody is to take a snapshot of a typical day across the country. Data from October 26, 2011, demonstrated that 61,423 youth were incarcerated. This was a dramatic departure compared with data from 1997, which indicated that 116,701 youth were incarcerated. While the number of youth in custody has declined 42% since 1997, the United States still has one of the highest rates of youth incarceration in the world (Figure 13.7).[40]

AUDIO
Juvenile Incarceration Rates Are Down; Racial Disparities Rise

The majority of youth incarcerations involve acts of delinquency, though there remains a small percentage (4%) of youth who are institutionalized for status offenses, such as running away and truancy. The majority of youth in these facilities have been committed by the court following an adjudication hearing, though in some cases, youth are detained prior to their disposition.

Youth can be committed to a variety of different facilities. The majority of youth are held in detention (short-term residential) facilities or long-term, secure residential facilities. Another common placement, particularly for committed offenders, is a group home. Depending on the type of the facility, a group home can be either a secure or nonsecure facility and, in some cases, can provide specialized or targeted interventions (such as drug and alcohol counseling or treatment for sex offenders). **Boot camps** have also been used as an option to confine adjudicated youth. Juvenile boot camps are short-term interventions that have been modeled after military-style basic-training programs. The purpose of a boot camp setting is to incorporate physical training, discipline, and leadership training with other traditional treatment resources, such as counseling and education. While boot camps have been very popular with both policymakers and the public for their tougher approach in dealing with juvenile delinquency, researchers question whether boot camps offer long-term results in terms of altering future delinquent and criminal behaviors. In some cases,

Boot camps
A form of short-term intervention that has been modeled after military-style basic-training programs.

youth viewed the boot camp environment as more positive compared with a traditional locked facility, as they felt safer and received greater support from these highly structured environments. However, the boot camp setting is not an appropriate intervention for all youths. For example, placing a youth with a history of abuse in a boot camp setting is not only ineffective in reducing at-risk behaviors but it also may actually be psychologically harmful to the youth.[41] In addition, boot camps appear to have no greater effect on youth recidivism compared with traditional programs.[42] This may be due to the lack of attention to **aftercare** (similar to parole in the adult system) programs for youth exiting these types of environments. In particular, even youth who perform very well in these structured settings may return to a dysfunctional community and/or family environment, which can quickly defeat any of the positive skills that the youth may have learned during the program.[43]

Aftercare
Similar to parole in the adult system.

Juvenile Justice and Delinquency Prevention Act
Federal legislation that called for the deinstitutionalization of status offenders and requires states to address issues of disproportionate minority contact and gender-responsive services.

In 1974, Congress passed the **Juvenile Justice and Delinquency Prevention Act** (JJDPA). In addition to creating the Office of Juvenile Justice and Delinquency Prevention, the act called for a deinstitutionalization of juvenile delinquents and specifically targeted the incarceration of status offenders. It also provided mandates to remove youth from adult lockup facilities, as well as to ensure that youth are not housed next to adult cells or sharing public spaces where they may come into contact with adult offenders. The JJDPA also requires that states address issues of disproportionate minority contact of youth of color at all stages of the juvenile justice process.

Figure 13.7	Youth Commitment Rate per 100,000 by State, 2013*

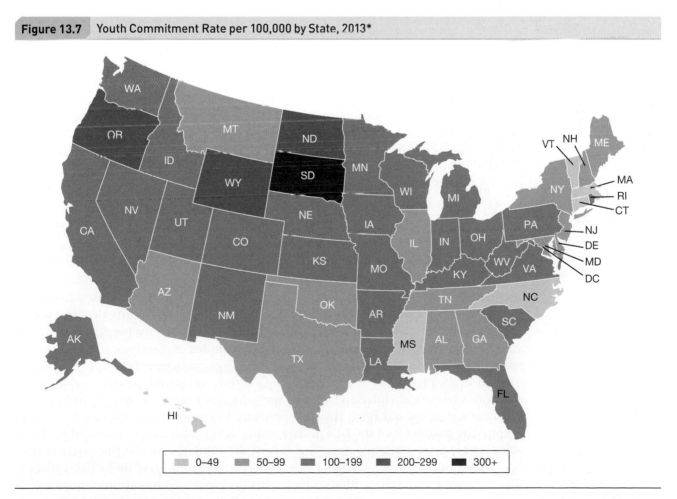

0–49   50–99   100–199   200–299   300+

Source: http://sentencingproject.org/doc/publications/Youth-Commitments-and-Facilities.pdf

*Most recent data available

SPOTLIGHT

The D.C. Snipers

Lee Boyd Malvo and his codefendant, John Muhammad, were involved in several sniper shootings throughout the D.C. beltway region during October 2002. While prosecutors could have chosen to try the pair in several different state and federal courts given the wide region covered by their crimes, Virginia was chosen because not only was it one of the most active death penalty jurisdictions for adult offenders (Muhammad was sentenced to death and was executed in 2009), but it was the only state that permitted the death penalty for juveniles. Despite the calculated, premeditated nature of the attack, the jury failed to sentence Lee Boyd Malvo to death for his involvement in the murder of FBI analyst Linda Franklin. He was sentenced to life without the possibility of parole for this crime and subsequently received multiple, consecutive life sentences across several states for his involvement in shootings that claimed more than 20 additional victims. In an interview 10 years after his crimes, Malvo expressed deep regret for his actions and admitted he was under the abusive psychological control of John Muhammad.[a]

CRITICAL THINKING QUESTIONS

1. Why do you believe that the jury decided to not sentence Lee Boyd Malvo to death for these crimes?

2. Should Lee Boyd Malvo have the option of parole, given the young age and circumstances under which he committed his crimes?

> **African American youth are incarcerated at a rate 4.5 times greater than White youth.**

Since its introduction, the JJDPA has been reauthorized several times. In 1992, the JJDPA highlighted the need for gender-responsive services in response to the rising number of girls entering the juvenile justice system. The last major revision to the JJDPA occurred in 2002. Since then, there have been significant developments over the past decade in what we know about youth and offending behaviors. The bill was reintroduced for reauthorization by Congress in 2015, but it remains to be seen how the law might take the latest research into account.[44]

Despite the reduction in the number of youth in custody over the past 15 years, as well as a requirement of JJDPA to evaluate these issues, youth of color are still disproportionately represented in these facilities. African American youth are incarcerated at a rate 4.5 times greater than White youth.[45] Technical violations account for a larger proportion of these committed offenders than crimes-against-persons offenses. A technical violation means that the youth did not commit a new crime; rather, she or he was punished for breaking the terms and conditions of community supervision. Examples of a technical violation are failure to complete required treatment (such as anger management), failing to check in with one's probation officer, violating curfew, or testing positive for drugs or alcohol. A technical violation can also include status offenses, which many scholars have suggested has been the new pathway to incarcerate youth for these acts despite the mandates of the JJDPA. As a result, acts that were once treated as status offenses are now processed as minor acts of delinquency due to the expansion of the discretionary power available to schools, police, and juvenile justice officials. The replacement of status offenses by probation violations has allowed justice officials to recommit youth who are deemed to be out of control by the courts to these residential facilities.[46]

WEB LINK
Office of Juvenile Justice and Delinquency Prevention

CONCLUSION

Over the past century, the juvenile justice system has seen significant growth and change. From a system where youth had few due process protections, and dispositions were made in the best interests of the child, to an era of "do the crime, do the time," concerns over juvenile crime have always been at the forefront of our society. Today, the pendulum appears to be shifting back toward a sentiment of supervision and support, in some cases, and more states are involved in issuing calls for alternatives to detention. Alas, the desire to punish is strong, and states face an uphill battle in rolling back some of these laws that were passed during an era driven by fear. Indeed, as our Current Controversy debates indicate, there are still many varying opinions on these issues.

A youth shows painted banners that he and his fellow inmates made at an art show at the Hillcrest Youth Correctional Facility in Salem, Oregon. Though the youth at the facility may have limited resources and limited space to express themselves, its new 10-month art workshop program is giving them an opportunity to make art and grow as individuals. Research indicates that such programs can be effective as a tool for rehabilitation.

CURRENT CONTROVERSY 13.1

PRO CON

CURRENT
CONTROVERSY
VIDEO
Where Do You Stand?
Cast Your Vote!

Have Zero-Tolerance Policies Made Schools Safer?

—Alicia Pantoja, Sanna King, and Anthony Peguero—

No other school antiviolence policy has received as much scrutiny as zero tolerance. Zero-tolerance school antiviolence policies attempt to eliminate school violence by establishing clear and transparent guidelines for student punishment. The intent of zero tolerance is to restrict the discretion of school administrators and faculty in order to ensure an unbiased application of punishments for violent acts within school.

It is clear that the historical roots of zero tolerance stem from when the United States Customs Agency developed zero tolerance in the 1980s to target the booming drug trade. The language of zero tolerance sparked the public imagination to apply this ideology to a broad range of issues, from environmental pollution and trespassing to skateboarding, homelessness, and violence within schools. Beginning in 1989, school districts across the United States started implementing zero-tolerance antiviolence school policies. Very quickly, zero tolerance expanded as a policy not just for drugs and weapons but also for minor forms of misbehavior, such as smoking, school disruption, and disrespect. In 1994, this zero-tolerance philosophy and policy was legislatively indoctrinated into this nation's public school system during President Clinton's administration with the Gun-Free Schools Act. Congress passed this law to address the issue of school violence, requiring schools to institute a zero-tolerance policy for students and enforcing a minimum of one year of expulsion for students who bring a firearm on campus. Over the past two decades, the pervasiveness of such zero-tolerance policies has grown exponentially.[47] The question is this: Are they effective in reducing violence in schools?

 PRO   Zero-Tolerance Policies Have Made Schools Safer

Since the Gun-Free Schools Act of 1994, the implementation and prevalence of zero tolerance has become a fixture of the educational experience. It is also important to consider the increase in the implementation of security measures in schools, such as metal detectors, surveillance, checkpoints, law enforcement, and the like, all associated with the Gun-Free Schools Act of 1994 and zero tolerance. The philosophy and intent of zero tolerance is to have uniform standard of behavior for all students, regardless of their demographics, background, and social status. As a result, it is widely believed and argued that schools have become one of the safest environments for children.[48]

Evidence indicates that zero-tolerance policies can curb criminal behaviors, such as rape, aggravated assault, vandalism, and destruction of school property, through the use of mandatory student suspension or expulsion. Indeed, research demonstrates that the rates of homicides, gun possession, drug-related crimes, and violent felonies in schools have steadily declined since 1994. On these grounds, can we argue that such policies have made schools safer for students?

CON Zero-Tolerance Policies Have Not Made Schools Safer

While zero-tolerance policies were implemented to create a standard of uniform behavior and unbiased distribution of punishment for misconduct, the implementation of such practices indicates otherwise. There has been an emergence of disproportionate distribution of punishment for violations of policies based on race, ethnicity, socioeconomic status, culture, gender, language, sexual orientation, and immigration status, which is leading some students to disregard the effectiveness and seriousness of zero-tolerance policies.[49] In addition, the increase in harsh school punishments resulting from zero-tolerance policies has deteriorated school climates and decreased academic achievement, as teachers and administrators are led to focus more on behavior management and standardized test scores than teaching.[50] Furthermore, the zero-tolerance policies have a strong potential to alienate students from adults at their schools by making students feel they cannot approach adults or school officials if they are experiencing a hardship due to fear of punitive repercussions rather than assistance.[51] This form of alienation can be especially harmful for students who have or are currently experiencing trauma from poverty, abuse, or sexual assault. This particularly affects girls who have a higher rate of experiencing trauma from abuse, particularly sexual abuse.[52]

As the implementation of zero-tolerance policies is increasing school misconduct and exclusion, it is also increasing student dropout rates. Moreover, schools that have policies that enforce truancy can increase school disengagement and push students out of schools. Examples of this include police officers who are stationed near bus stops or subway stops in front of schools to enforce truancy by issuing summonses to students or escorting them to campus.

This practice may lead students who are late to school to avoid attempting to attend school, as they would rather stay home than risk a police encounter.[53]

As zero-tolerance policies have increased in popularity, many schools are using school resource officers on campuses to respond to incidents involving disorderly conduct. Should conduct-related issues in school be handled by police instead of school administrators?

COMPLEXITIES TO CONSIDER

There are number of complexities to consider when studying zero-tolerance policies. As noted in the prior section, the disproportionate punishment of minority students is apparent. Moreover, zero-tolerance policies are implemented in ways that are argued to be culturally biased and marginalize minority youth. In other words, minority youth often get punished for "subjective reasons," like disrespect, while White youth are punished less and get punished for "objective" reasons, like smoking.[54] This biased implementation brings into question whether it is possible, given the parameters of these policies, to treat all students equally. What makes a behavior "disrespectful," and who decides that definition? Can children and youth be treated equally and fairly when the "norm" of acceptable behavior is not inclusive of the cultural and social context of the school and community where zero-tolerance policies are implemented?

It is also clear that the sources and factors associated with the vulnerability and marginalization of youth punished at school intersect. Intersectionality is a conceptual approach to studying the relationships across multiple dimensions and modalities of subject formations, such as race, ethnicity, gender, sexual orientation, language, age, religion, immigration, and socioeconomic status.[55] The concept of intersectionality is particularly pertinent to the growing body of research on youth violence at school, as well as the associated disciplinary practices, because it allows researchers to study whether and how zero-tolerance policy implementation differs across and according to students' intersecting social-identity categories.

Finally, it is important to note that there are arguments indicating disproportionate punishment patterns are reflective of disproportionate levels of misconduct and misbehavior within schools. Some researchers argue that the overall reduction in the occurrence of violence and disorder in schools is directly related to increased control and security within schools—in other words, that many youth were indeed misbehaving, and sanctioning has kept that in check. The question that often arises is whether zero-tolerance suspension and expulsion are effective at addressing misbehavior for youth or whether they are exacerbating engagement in delinquency and contributing to educational failure, which can have long-lasting detrimental consequences.[56]

SUMMARY

Some critical questions to keep in mind when reviewing zero-tolerance policies and related research are these: What are the ideological origins of zero-tolerance policies? Whose experiences and voices have been included and whose are excluded in the design of, implementation of, and research on zero-tolerance policies in schools? What research methodologies and related frameworks have been applied to research this issue, and how do these approaches shape what is known about zero-tolerance policies? What evidence is there that these policies are the only reason for a decrease of school crime rates since 1994?

Further inquiries to engage throughout an analysis of this issue are as follows: What behaviors are criminalized by zero-tolerance policies, and why? What are the short- and long-term consequences of zero-tolerance policies on the lives of students across race, ethnicity, socioeconomic status, culture, gender, language, sexual orientation, and immigration status? What explains the disproportionate punishment that minority students experience? Finally, when seeking to grasp the big picture of this topic, it is crucial to consider the following: What conceptualizations of a "safe school" and of educational equity are supported by zero-tolerance policies, and what conceptualizations of a "safe school" and educational equity are supported by alternative school policies and practices?

DISCUSSION QUESTIONS

1. What was the original intent of zero-tolerance policies? Were they successful in meeting their goal?

2. How have zero-tolerance policies increased the rate of juvenile crime?

3. How do zero-tolerance policies negatively impact youth of color?

Should the Juvenile Court Be Abolished?

—Schannae Lucas—

Ever since the pendulum of justice has swung toward the tough-on-crime movement, scholars have debated the degree to which judicial punitive practices have impacted the juvenile justice court system. As you learned in this chapter, the primary goal of the early juvenile court grew from a parens patriae doctrine, for which the state sought to adopt the role of a surrogate parent in order to resocialize and discipline youth into a proper and moral lifestyle. Are the goals and rationale established for the creation of the juvenile court movement in the 1890s still relevant in the 21st century? Or has society's perception of the role of and need for the juvenile court system changed? As the rate of juvenile crime has changed over the years, are the current needs of social control and perception of public safety taking precedence over the rehabilitation and protection of minors?

 ## The Juvenile Courts Should Be Abolished

Juvenile courts, designed to deal with youth who violate social norms and crime statutes, commonly discourage applying the criminal law jurisprudence approaches of guilt, blameworthiness, and punishment to juveniles. However, many of the original goals and beliefs held have deteriorated as the juvenile system adopted more punitive systemic changes. As juveniles are seen as more "criminal-like" or as committing more "adult-like" crimes, it "becomes easier to convert to aggressive punitive measures towards juveniles and take common institutional forms of social policies to control and incarcerate youth rather than to enhance their emotional and psychological development through rehabilitation approaches."[57] Advocates for abolishing the juvenile justice system argue, "Increasingly the juvenile courts function as a system of criminal social control to protect society from young offenders, rather than a welfare agency to nurture and protect vulnerable children from a wrathful community."[58] This current state of the juvenile court has prompted many scholars to seek reform.

As states adopted get-tough crime policies, many youth were deprived of certain protections and safeguards. Advocates assert that minors should receive many of the judicial constitutional safeguards that adults are provided as the juvenile courts adopt more criminal court approaches. Punitive judicial decisions, legislative amendments, and administrative changes have transformed the juvenile court system from a "normatively rehabilitative welfare agency into a scaled-down, second class criminal court for young people."[59] The expansion of juvenile-waiver laws are one example of this. These reforms lowered the minimum age for transfer, increased the number of transfer-eligible offenses, expanded prosecutorial discretion, and reduced judicial discretion in transfer decision-making.[60]

Juvenile courts provide some constitutional rights, but they are lacking in some important areas. The due process rights afforded to juveniles in the *In re Gault* (1967) ruling are the 5th Amendment right against self-incrimination and the 6th Amendment rights to confront witnesses, receive timely notification of charges, and be represented by an attorney. However, researchers have found inconsistencies with these protections in a range of cases. Studies show some youth are not represented by counsel, and when they are represented, the counsel are not adequately trained and fail to provide competent representation. In an adult criminal court, the same juvenile case would be in jeopardy of dismissal.[61] Even more pressing, juveniles do not have the constitutional rights to a jury trial, bail, or public hearings. The dilemma exists because juveniles have been detained and adjudicated under judicial circumstances that would not hold up in court for adults. Increasingly, courts are treating juveniles more like adults but not providing those constitutional rights that adult offenders are afforded.[62]

An integrated court system would provide juveniles with constitutional rights and allow a more just and equitable process. An integrated court could formally recognize adolescence as a developmental continuum that should effectively address the problems created by our binary conceptions of youth and social control.[63] The court could offer a "youth discount" in the form of sentencing guidelines. It would consider the youth's age and apply it toward their crime. For example, a 14-year-old offender might receive 25% to 33% of the adult penalty, a 16-year-old offender might receive 50% to 66% of the adult penalty, and an 18-year-old offender would receive the full penalty. A deeper discount would be applied based on the needs of the youth (i.e., mental capability). The youth discount introduces more uniformity and consistency in court processing between male and female, urban and rural, Black and White.[64] With the youth discount in the integrated court, youth

During a juvenile court hearing, juvenile court professionals discuss the best disposition that reflects the needs of the youth. What are some notable differences between this courtroom and courtrooms in the adult system?

will have enhanced legal protections, obtain the same constitutional rights as adults, and receive more humane and publicly accountable decisions from judges.

 CON **The Juvenile Courts Should Not Be Abolished**

States created a separate court system for juveniles specifically to provide a system of youth-based service delivery different from services provided to adults. The juvenile justice system is better able to deal with the social and emotional problems that youth offenders face. Juveniles at these critical stages of growth are different from adults. They have different stages of social and emotional development, they are less blameworthy for their behavior, and they should not be held to the same level of culpability as adults.[65] Due to these fundamental differences, the juvenile court system believes that juveniles have a greater capacity for change. They are designed to give a second chance to youth in order to correct their behavior through court-guided forms of education, rehabilitation, and transformation. Juvenile courts should not be abolished because youth are still in need of being treated as youth, and the premise of the juvenile court has not changed, even in the midst of laws and polices becoming more punitive.

Proponents of juvenile courts would agree that the juvenile justice system has already passed the threshold into criminal court approaches. Juvenile get-tough polices have provided short-term relief and long-term detriment. Scholars recognize that punitive changes stem from the need to control the rise in youth crime in the 1980s and early 1990s.

However, juvenile crime has steadily decreased since the early 1990s, and the system has not adjusted to this change. Instead, when juveniles commit an "adult crime" like robbery, theft, or a drug offense, the quick fix is to incarcerate that individual like an adult to punish him or her and protect society. This may work for adults, but it is not appropriate for juveniles. Juveniles in the adult system are deprived of the educational and rehabilitative programs designed and geared to assist them at various levels of the juvenile court system.

The system is meant to hold youth accountable, reduce recidivism, help youth with their struggles, and integrate them back into the community. It strives to reduce the criminal stigma and labeling that are often associated with crime. A juvenile's exposure to the adult criminal court robs her or him of childhood and unnecessarily exposes her or him to the harms of adult criminal processes. Many studies have found that significantly harsher punishments are meted out to juveniles in adult courts when compared with juveniles in juvenile courts.[66] The idea that sentencing youth to a jail or prison will "scare them straight" is not proven to be effective in reducing recidivism.[67] It may instill fear, but it can often be emotionally and physically dangerous for youth when they are exposed to adult serious offenders who prey upon youth in adult-centered environments. The juvenile court process allows our youth to be successful by providing them with a supportive structure to deal with the consequences of violating the law in a rehabilitative and educational manner. It is likely to give youthful offenders a more desired outcome traveling through the criminal justice system.

SUMMARY

Should the juvenile court be abolished, or should the juvenile court be retained? One side would argue that youth receive fewer procedural safeguards than adults convicted of comparable crimes. In order to enhance the protection and the rights of youth, they should be provided with the same due process rights provided to adults within an integrated court system. The opposing side claims that the juvenile courts are designed for youth—they seek to provide them with the tools needed to rehabilitate, educate, and reintegrate back into their community—and that the adult criminal court system subjects youth to unnecessary exposure to adult criminality.

DISCUSSION QUESTIONS

1. Would abolishing the juvenile courts and creating youth-based adult-court sentencing guidelines produce equal treatment in the courts among gender, race, and class?

2. Which approach will achieve the goals of juvenile crime deterrence and rehabilitation: retaining the juvenile justice system or abolishing it? What are the short- and long-term effects of each?

3. What are the likely consequences of keeping the juvenile courts as they are, and what are the likely consequences of creating an integrated court system? Who benefits?

KEY TERMS

Review key terms with eFlashcards | SAGE edge™ • edge.sagepub.com/mallicoatccj

Adjudication hearing   329

Aftercare   341

Boot camps   340

Delinquency   325

Delinquency petition   329

Dependency   326

Direct file   337

Discretionary waiver   337

Disposition hearing   329

Intake   327

Judicial waiver   337

Juvenile Justice and Delinquency Prevention Act   341

Juvenile waiver   337

Legal custody   326

Legislative waiver   337

Parens patriae   324

Pauperism   324

Physical custody   326

Prosecutorial waiver   337

Superpredator   336

DISCUSSION QUESTIONS

Test your mastery of chapter content • Take the Practice Quiz | SAGE edge™ • edge.sagepub.com/mallicoatccj

1. Describe the similarities and differences between the juvenile justice system and the criminal justice system.

2. What is the difference between a delinquency case and a dependency case?

3. How did the historical roots of the juvenile justice system influence today's juvenile court?

4. Describe three of the key U.S. Supreme Court cases that affected due process in juvenile cases.

5. What are the three types of juvenile waivers?

6. How did the tough-on-crime movement impact the juvenile court?

LEARNING ACTIVITIES

1. Interview a local professional who works in the juvenile court. Identify the differences in his or her job compared with a similar job in the criminal court.

2. Locate a program in your community that serves the needs of at-risk youth. What types of services and support does it provide? How might these resources help prevent and intervene in these cases?

SUGGESTED WEBSITES

- **Office of Juvenile Justice and Delinquency Prevention:** http://www.ojjdp.gov
- **Juvenile Justice Geography, Policy, Practice and Statistics:** http://www.jjgps.org
- **Coalition for Juvenile Justice:** http://www.juvjustice.org
- **Children's Defense Fund:** http://www.childrensdefense.org/policy/justice
- **National Council of Juvenile and Family Court Judges:** http://www.ncjfcj.org

STUDENT STUDY SITE

Review • Practice • Improve | $SAGE edge™ • **edge.sagepub.com/mallicoatccj**

Want a better grade?

Get the tools you need to sharpen your study skills. Access practice quizzes, eFlashcards, video, and multimedia at **edge.sagepub.com/mallicoatccj**

EMERGING ISSUES FOR THE 21st CENTURY

LEARNING OBJECTIVES

- Define the different forms of terrorism

- Discuss the functions of homeland security

- Identify the features and criticisms of the USA PATRIOT Act

- Discuss the use of drones and their challenges to privacy and security

- Highlight how issues of immigration, transnational crime, human trafficking, organized crime, and drugs and arms trafficking threaten the security of our borders

On December 2, 2015, a mass shooting occurred at the Inland Regional Center in San Bernardino, California. Syed Rizwan Farook and his wife, Tashfeen Malik, opened fire at a holiday party filled with many of Syed's coworkers from the San Bernardino County Department of Public Health. Fourteen people were killed, and 22 others were injured. By the end of the day, Farook and Malik were killed following a shootout with police.

In the aftermath of the shooting, authorities and community members alike were questioning why two people would engage in such acts of violence. As the story began to unfold in the weeks following the attack, authorities learned that Syed was radicalized prior to meeting Tashfeen and showed interest in developing a terrorist attack as early as 2011.[1] While there did not appear to be any direct relationship between the shooters and ISIS, many have suggested that Syed and Tashfeen were inspired to engage in a high-profile act of terrorism in support of the Islamic State of Iraq and Syria (ISIS). On the day of the attack, Tashfeen posted her support of ISIS leader Abu Bakr al-Baghdadi on Facebook. A search of the family home found pipe bombs, more guns, and thousands of rounds of ammunition.[2] Two of the guns used in the attack were purchased legally by Syed's neighbor and brother-in-law, Enrique Marquez.[3] Marquez was indicted by a federal grand jury for providing material support to an act of terrorism.[4]

As the authorities continue to develop the backstory on this violent tragedy, the local and national communities have responded in both positive and negative ways. In the four days following the attack, local Muslim organizations raised more than $100,000 for the families of the victims of the attack.[5] Meanwhile, some local residents rushed to gun stores to purchase firearms as a way to protect themselves from future acts of violence.[6] In her speech to the Royal Institute of International Affairs in London, England, Attorney General Loretta Lynch stated that the attack was carried out "with a single, repugnant purpose: to harm, frighten and intimidate anyone who believes in open and tolerant societies; in free and democratic governments; and in the right of every human being to live in peace, security and freedom."[7] Meanwhile, Republican presidential candidate Donald Trump inflamed many with his comments that the United States is "at war with Islamic terrorism" and that Muslims should be barred from entering the country.[8] As San Bernardino continues to heal and honor the victims of this tragedy, the community leaders, elected officials, law enforcement, and the religious community have called on residents to practice forgiveness, healing, and reconciliation and not engage in acts of backlash and violence.[9]

AUDIO
Friend of San Bernardino Shooter Charged With Aiding Terror Plot

The criminal justice system is faced with a number of emerging issues in the 21st century. This chapter introduces some of these issues and discusses the challenges that criminal justice agencies will face as they navigate their way through these issues. The chapter begins with a discussion of terrorism. The chapter then turns to look at homeland security. You'll also learn about some of the privacy threats that exist with the use of drones. Finally, the chapter turns to a discussion of border control. The chapter concludes with two Current Controversy debates. The first, by Gus Martin, asks whether enemy combatants should be denied due process rights. The second, by Zahra Shekarkhar, asks if immigration impacts crime.

TERRORISM

Terrorism is described as an event that is designed to elicit fear or terror in a particular group of people. What makes terrorism different from other crimes is that it is often linked to a political agenda. Terrorism can be an act of physical violence as well as emotional violence. The Federal Bureau of Investigation defines terrorism as a violent or dangerous activity that violates state and/or federal law and "appear[s] to be intended (i) to intimidate or coerce a civilian population; (ii) to influence the policy of a government by intimidation or coercion; or (iii) to affect the conduct of a government by mass destruction, assassination, or kidnapping."[10]

Types of Terrorism

The FBI divides terrorism into two different categories: domestic terrorism and international terrorism. **Domestic terrorism** refers to those acts that occur within the jurisdiction of the United States (including U.S. territories). The acts of Ted Kaczynski (aka the Unabomber) are one example of domestic terrorism. Between 1978 and 1995, Kaczynski mailed or delivered 16 bombs that ultimately killed three individuals and injured 24. Because many of his targets included members of universities and airlines, he was branded by the FBI as the UNABOM. However, efforts by the authorities to identify him were unsuccessful. In 1995, he mailed several letters to major media outlets and several of his victims, demanding that his 35,000-word essay titled "Industrial Society and Its Future" be published. In an effort to learn the true identity of the author, his manifesto was published by the *New York Times* and the *Washington Post* on September 19, 1995.[11] Family members of Kaczynski had previously wondered whether the Unabomber and Ted were one and the same. However, it was the words of his manifesto that confirmed their suspicions. They contacted the FBI, which conducted its own investigation and subsequently issued a search warrant for Kaczynski's residence, a remote cabin outside of Lincoln, Montana. He was arrested on April 3, 1996, when the search of his residence discovered bomb components, a live bomb, and thousands of pages of writings similar to the manifesto. While the federal government

Domestic terrorism
Acts of terrorism that occur within the jurisdiction of the United States.

initially sought the death penalty against Kaczynski, he ultimately pled guilty in order to avoid such a punishment. He was sentenced to eight life-without-the-possibility-of-parole sentences and is currently housed at the Federal Administrative Maximum Facility in Florence, Colorado.

In comparison, acts of **international terrorism** "occur primarily outside the territorial jurisdiction of the U.S., or transcend national boundaries in terms of the means by which they are accomplished, the persons they appear intended to coerce or intimidate, or the locale in which their perpetrators operate or seek asylum."[12] The bombing of Pan Am Flight 103 is an example of an act of international terrorism. On December 21, 1988, Pan Am Flight 103 was traveling from London to New York with 243 passengers and 16 crew on board when it exploded over Lockerbie, Scotland.[13] It wasn't until 1999 that Abdelbaset al-Megrahi and Lamin Khalifah Fhimah were turned over to Scottish authorities as suspects. In 2001, Megrahi was convicted of murder while Fhimah was acquitted. While Megrahi was sentenced to three life sentences, he applied for compassionate release in 2009 due to his diagnosis of prostate cancer.[14] He died in 2012.[15] In 2003, Libya admitted responsibility for the bombing and provided $2.7 billion in restitution to the family members of the victims.[16] The bombing of Pam Am Flight 103 is often referred to as an example of **state-sponsored terrorism**, as it was widely believed that Libyan leader Muammar Gaddafi specifically ordered the bombing in response to military action against Libya.[17]

The FBI released this sketch of the suspected "Unabomber," Ted Kaczynski. UNABOM stands for UNiversity & Airline BOMber.

In addition to state-sponsored terrorism, there are two other primary forms of terrorism that typically fall under the category of international terrorism. **Dissident terrorism** refers to acts that are committed by nonstate groups against governments, religious entities, and citizens. Generally speaking, acts of dissident terrorism occur because of deep-seated frustrations with how society functions. Acts such as those perpetuated by al Qaeda and ISIS are examples of a form of dissident terrorism known as **religious terrorism.** Religious terrorism refers to terrorist acts that are based on one's religious belief system. ISIS claimed responsibility for the November 2015 terrorist attacks in Paris, which killed approximately 130 and injured hundreds of others in shootings and bombings in six locations around the city. Seven of the 10 attackers killed themselves in suicide bombings connected to the attacks. An eighth suspect was killed in a raid of an apartment by the police. Two additional suspects remained at large following the events.[18]

Prevalence of Terrorism

The National Consortium for the Study of Terrorism and Responses to Terrorism (START) maintains the Global Terrorism Database on all known domestic and international terrorist incidents. To date, this database contains information on

International terrorism
Acts that occur primarily outside the territorial jurisdiction of the United States or transcend national boundaries in terms of the means by which they are accomplished, the persons they appear intended to coerce or intimidate, or the locale in which their perpetrators operate or seek asylum.

State-sponsored terrorism
Acts of terrorism that are ordered by government officials.

Dissident terrorism
Acts of terrorism that are committed by nonstate groups against governments, religious entities, and citizens.

Religious terrorism
Refers to terrorist acts that are based on one's religious belief system.

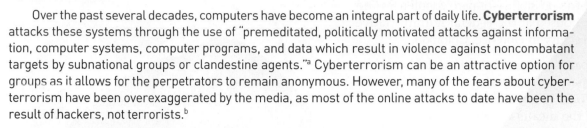

SPOTLIGHT
Cyberterrorism

Over the past several decades, computers have become an integral part of daily life. **Cyberterrorism** attacks these systems through the use of "premeditated, politically motivated attacks against information, computer systems, computer programs, and data which result in violence against noncombatant targets by subnational groups or clandestine agents."[a] Cyberterrorism can be an attractive option for groups as it allows for the perpetrators to remain anonymous. However, many of the fears about cyberterrorism have been overexaggerated by the media, as most of the online attacks to date have been the result of hackers, not terrorists.[b]

Acts of cyberterrorism can also be used in conjunction with a traditional form of terrorism. For example, a terrorist group could detonate a bomb in a public area and then use a cyberattack to hinder the communications system, which could limit the ability for first responders to arrive on scene quickly.[c] Researchers have also identified that the U.S health care system could be at risk due to the high degree of private information that medical records contain.[d] Terrorists will continue to search for new ways to attack America's infrastructure, and cyberterrorism is one of our country's biggest threats. In recent years, several prominent government computers around the world, including the CIA's main computer and French, Israeli, and British defense agency systems, have also seen hacking attempts.

In an attempt to build up our infrastructure against potential cyberterrorist threats, each military branch is developing "cyberwarriors," who will be tasked with defending our defense information systems online.[e] In addition, the National Cyber Investigative Joint Task Force brings these individuals together with affiliates in law enforcement and intelligence agencies to prevent cyberattacks.[f] As the risk of cybercrime and cyberterrorism continues to grow, so will the need for our response to these acts.

CRITICAL THINKING QUESTIONS

1. How might agencies at different levels of the government (local, state, and federal) think about their response to cyberterrorism? What issues should they consider?

2. What are some of the challenges that exist in both preventing acts of cyberterrorism and identifying and apprehending perpetrators of these crimes?

---

more than 140,000 terrorist attacks, including 58,000 bombings, 15,000 assassinations, and 6,000 kidnappings between 1970 and 2014.[19] In 2014, there were more than 43,500 deaths and 40,900 injuries worldwide as result of 16,800 terrorist events (Figure 14.1). While many Americans identify the acts of September 11, 2001, as the most prominent event of terrorism, these data demonstrate that terrorism has existed long before this date and continues to exist today in events around the world (Figure 14.2).

Terrorism is not a new phenomenon, and the 21st century has seen many prominent cases of terrorism. Included in these is the Moscow theater hostage crisis in October 2002, in which approximately 50 Chechen rebels stormed the theater and took more than 700 people hostage. They demanded that Russia remove its troops from Chechnya. Due to the layout of the building, it was feared that it would be too difficult to effectively restrain the rebels and that they would likely detonate their explosives. Following a 57-hour standoff, Russian authorities pumped a narcotic gas into the theater in hopes of gaining control over the rebels and rescuing the hostages. Most of the rebels and 120 hostages were killed during the raid as a result of the toxic gas.[20] In addition to the more recent events in Paris and Indonesia, there

Cyberterrorism
Acts of terrorism that involve premeditated, politically motivated attacks against information, computer systems, computer programs, and data.

Figure 14.1   Deaths Related to Terrorist Attacks

The majority of terrorist incidents are highly centralized. In 2014, 57% of all attacks occurred in five countries: Iraq, Pakistan, Afghanistan, Nigeria, and Syria. However, the rest of the world suffered a 54% increase in terrorist incidents in 2013.

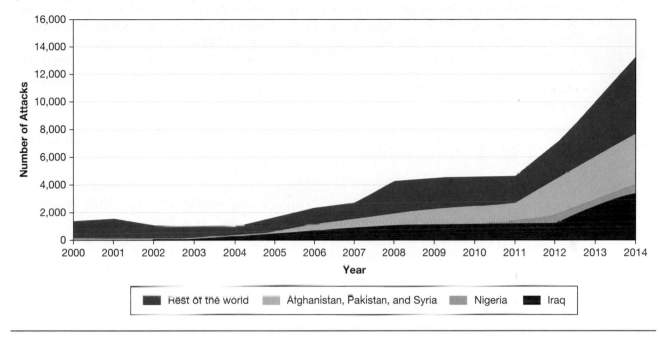

Source: Institute for Economics and Peace. http://economicsandpeace.org/wp-content/uploads/2015/11/Global-Terrorism-Index-2015.pdf

Figure 14.2   Global Impact of Terrorism

While terrorism is highly concentrated in a small number of countries, the number of countries that have had a terrorist attack is also increasing. In 2014, terrorism impacted more countries than ever before.

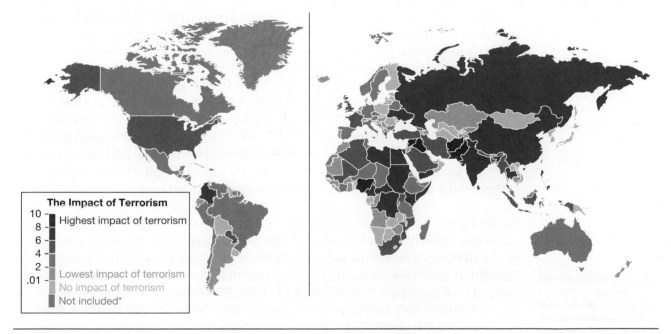

Source: Institute for Economics and Peace. http://economicsandpeace.org/wp-content/uploads/2015/11/Global-Terrorism-Index-2015.pdf

have been several attacks and suicide bombings in 2016 in areas such as Belgium, Iraq, Nigeria, Syria, and Turkey. In January, 32 people were killed and 58 were injured following a car bomb explosion at a shopping center in Baghdad. The same day, a suicide bomber killed 42 people at a café in the Diyala province, which is located 50 miles northwest of Baghdad.[21] In March, two female suicide bombers killed 22 and wounded 18 at a mosque in Maiduguri, Nigeria.[22] In the same month, bombings at a metro station and the airport in Brussels killed 32 and injured 340.[23] Meanwhile, Turkey has seen six terrorist attacks during the first three months of 2016. The targets in these attacks have included military personnel, civilians, and tourists.[24]

Groups such as al Qaeda and ISIS continue to be primary threats of both organized acts of terrorism as well as the foundation for individual offenders. Research indicates that there are four trends that are likely to threaten the safety of both national and foreign soil. These include

1) a continuing interest in attacking hard targets, but an increased focus on soft, civilian-centric venues; 2) an ongoing emphasis on economic attacks; 3) continued reliance on suicide strikes; and 4) a desire to use chemical, biological, radiological, and nuclear weapons but little ability to execute large-scale unconventional attacks.[25]

HOMELAND SECURITY

WEB LINK
Department of Homeland Security

The term **homeland security** is referenced in a number of different ways, but generally speaking, it refers to a coordinated government and private-sector effort that provides security against and responses to specific and general threats. While the concept of homeland security is often used in conjunction with the discussion of terrorism and other threats to national security, it is important to note that homeland security isn't just about fighting terrorism and also includes issues such as cybersecurity, border control, and natural disasters. In addition, homeland security does not imply that these efforts will guarantee absolute protection from such episodes.[26]

Responses to Terrorism Before 9/11

Prior to the events of 9/11, the investigation of terrorist acts in the United States was managed by a number of different agencies, which made it difficult to share information across these agencies. The prosecution of these crimes was handled through the criminal justice system. Indeed, there were few opportunities to coordinate a response, as acts of terrorism on American soil were fairly rare. Prior to 9/11, most of what we identified as terrorism occurred outside of the United States. Many of these attacks occurred against our military or embassies (such as the bombing of the U.S. embassies in Kenya and Tanzania in 1998 and the bombing of the USS *Cole* in 2000) or against airlines. The procedures for handling these events were often managed by agencies whose jurisdictions and job duties overlapped. In many ways, the existing legal structure significantly hampered the efforts of these agencies to effectively respond to these attacks.

Homeland security
Refers to a coordinated government and private-sector effort that provides security against and responses to specific and general threats.

Exchange of information collected by foreign and domestic agencies was determined by a strict set of rules that was (perhaps somewhat incorrectly) interpreted as forbidding pure "intelligence" information from being collected for law enforcement purposes, and—conversely—made it difficult to share criminal justice–derived information with other agencies. When terrorists were apprehended either in the United States or abroad, they were accorded the treatment of any other criminal defendant, including receiving warnings about the right to silence, and a full-blown criminal jury trial.[27]

AROUND THE WORLD

Terrorism in Indonesia

Indonesia has seen a number of terrorist attacks over the past three decades. Many of these events have been focused on the bombings of businesses, religious sites, and other public spaces. For example, Christmas Eve 2000 saw a series of explosions that targeted Christian churches in eight different cities.[a] One of the deadliest attacks was the Bali bombings in October 2002, where 202 people were killed, and an additional 209 were injured. In 2005, a similar attack involving a series of suicide and car bombs killed 20 people and injured 100.

The cause of terrorism in Indonesia is difficult to identify. Indonesia transitioned to a democratic state in 1998. Issues such as religious radicalization, ethnic violence, and the displacement of communities are major threats to this process. Islamic terrorist groups, such as Jemaah Islamiyah (JI), which has significant ties to al Qaeda, were responsible for a number of the violent attacks. Some of the bombings were believed to be directed by Osama bin Laden in retaliation for the U.S. war on terror. While the efforts of JI have been weakened in recent years, several smaller affiliated cells remain active throughout the region.[b] Insurgent groups have been effective in recruiting individuals who feel alienated by the new democracy.[c] Indeed, many of these attacks focus on tourist and business areas, as a statement of rebellion against these westernized ways.[d] Government agencies, such as the police, have also been targeted.[e]

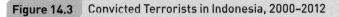

Figure 14.3   Convicted Terrorists in Indonesia, 2000–2012

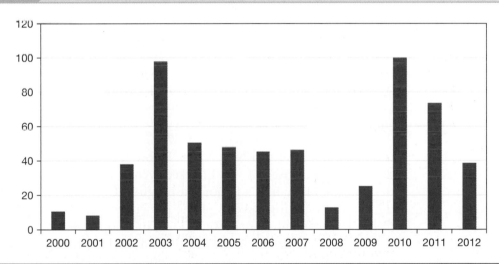

Source: http://www.cfr.org/councilofcouncils/global_memos/p32772

In the past decade, Indonesian authorities have embarked on a number of counterterrorism efforts. The country's military has recently unveiled a plan to establish a task force to help gather intelligence and combat insurgent networks. However, the police remain the primary resource against terrorism. Since 2000, they have been actively involved in the investigation and apprehension of hundreds of terrorism suspects. Figure 14.3 illustrates the number of terrorists who have been convicted between 2000 and 2012. Unlike neighboring countries such as Malaysia and Singapore, whose laws permit the arrest and incarceration of suspected terrorists outside of the legal process, Indonesia's system requires that the detention of those suspected of holding links to terrorist organizations must follow the legal procedures that have been set forth under the law. This means that offenders are entitled to a formal trial and other protections. While prison is certainly an appropriate punishment in these cases (and in some circumstances, offenders have been sentenced to death and executed for their crimes), others are sent

(Continued)

(Continued)

CRITICAL THINKING QUESTIONS

1. How have terrorist activities in Indonesia impacted the surrounding countries? Have there been any collateral effects?

2. How can collaborative teams both help and harm the investigative efforts in these cases?

to a government-sponsored "deradicalization" program, which is designed to direct individuals away from their connections with terrorist groups. The results of this program are mixed, and there is a need for the country to reform its correctional system and improve prison conditions to help support this process.[f] While the number of events has decreased in recent years, the risk of a terror attack remains high. Most recently, authorities thwarted a suicide bomb attack that was set for New Year's 2016. Their efforts reflected a collaborative investigation among Indonesian, Australian, and U.S. authorities. As a result of their investigation, six members of an alleged ISIS-inspired network were arrested.[9]

As a result, the United States was generally unprepared to respond to the type of large-scale attack that occurred on September 11th. On that day, 19 men affiliated with al Qaeda hijacked four planes. Willing to die for their cause, these men had trained in how to fly planes. American Airlines Flight 11 originated from Boston and was scheduled to fly to Los Angeles. The hijackers took control of the plane and flew it into One World Trade Center in New York City at 8:46 a.m. The second plane, United Airlines Flight 175, also departed from Boston Logan Airport and was scheduled to fly to Los Angeles. The hijackers flew this plane into Two World Trade Center (South Tower) at 9:03 a.m. American Airlines Flight 77 departed Washington Dulles Airport and was scheduled to fly to Dallas. The hijackers deliberately crashed the plane into the Pentagon at 9:37 a.m. Finally, United Flight 93 was hijacked from Newark airport in New Jersey. Before it could arrive at its scheduled destination in San Francisco, it was hijacked. While it is believed that terrorists intended to crash the plane into a major Washington, D.C., site such as the White House or the Capitol building, several of the passengers attempted to retake control of the plane. The plane ultimately went down in an open field in Pennsylvania. Together, the death toll of these four crashes, including the passengers on board as well as the lives of people on the ground at the Pentagon and the collateral damage as a result of the collapse of three of the towers at the World Trade Center, was 2,996 people, with injuries to more than 6,000 additional people.

Responses to Terrorism After 9/11

Following the terror attacks of September 11th, the federal government responded 11 days later with the establishment of the Department of Homeland Security. Over the next year, Congress worked to pass two key acts of legislation that changed both the infrastructure for investigating cases and also the methods by which such investigations could be conducted. The **Department of Homeland Security Act of 2002** consolidated several federal agencies that had previously worked independently of each other. Figure 14.4 highlights the organizational structure of the Department of Homeland Security. Only the Federal Bureau of Investigation and Central Intelligence Agency remained as stand-alone agencies.

Department of Homeland Security Act (2002) Federal legislation that consolidated several federal agencies that had previously worked independently of each other prior to 9/11.

Figure 14.4 Department of Homeland Security

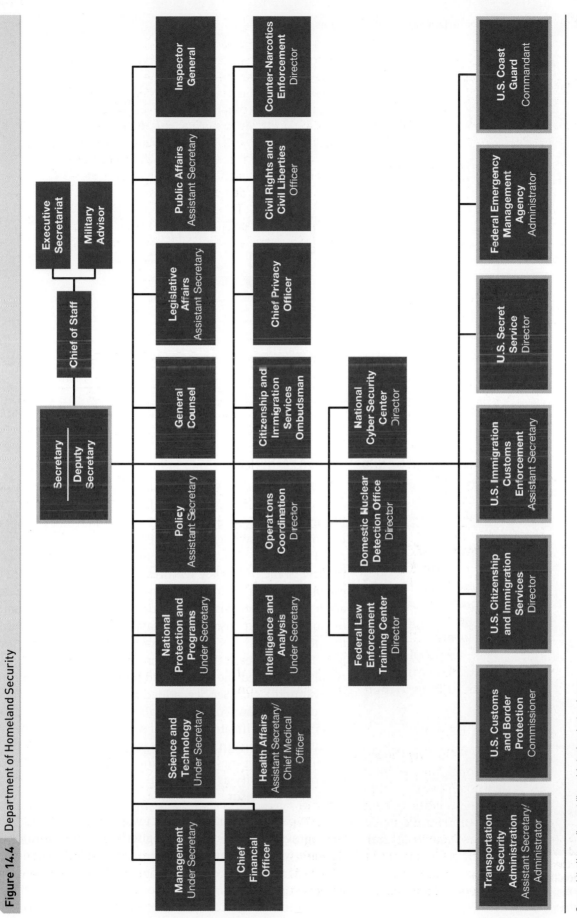

Source: http://www.dhs.gov/xlibrary/photos/orgchart-web.png

Figure 14.5 Key U.S. Antiterrorism and Related Statutes, 1961–2007

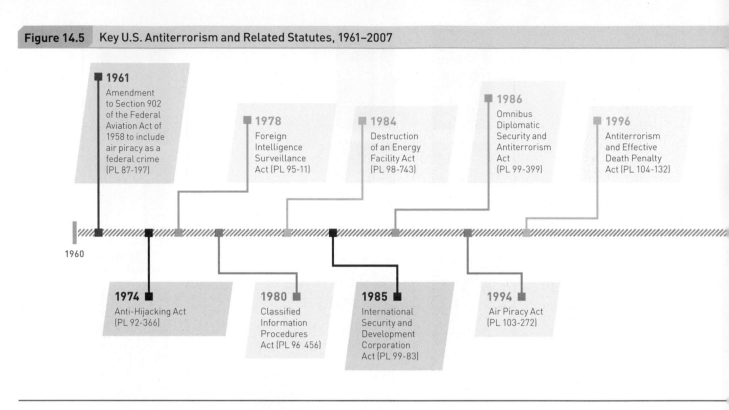

Source: Capron, T. A., & Mizrahi, S. B. (2016). *Terrorism and homeland security: A text reader*. Thousand Oaks, CA: Sage Publications.

Protestors voice their opposition to the U.S. Patriot Act. Do you think the Patriot Act was necessary for security or a gross violation of privacy?

The USA PATRIOT Act

The other major piece of legislation passed was the Uniting and Strengthening America by Providing Appropriate Tools Required to Intercept and Obstruct Terrorism Act of 2001, more commonly known as the **USA PATRIOT Act**, or the Patriot Act (Figure 14.5). The act made a number of revisions to existing law. Some of the key features of the Patriot Act were the establishment of a fund for counterterrorism efforts, the creation of new methods for gathering intelligence information (including the expansion of wiretapping and surveillance), and an increase in the record-keeping requirements for banks in an effort to increase the detection of money laundering. The act also expanded the powers and budget of the Immigration and Naturalization Service, added new provisions to mandatory detention laws for individuals who either engage in acts of terrorism or threaten national security, and expanded the monitoring of foreign student visas. Finally, the act expanded the numbers of crimes that were included under the definition of terrorist activity as well as acts that may be related to the support of terrorism.

The passage of the Patriot Act was controversial from the beginning. Some criticized the legislation on the grounds that its reach was too intrusive and could threaten civil liberties as protected under the Constitution. While supporters argued the sharing of information between intelligence agencies and the government increased the efficacy of agencies to detect

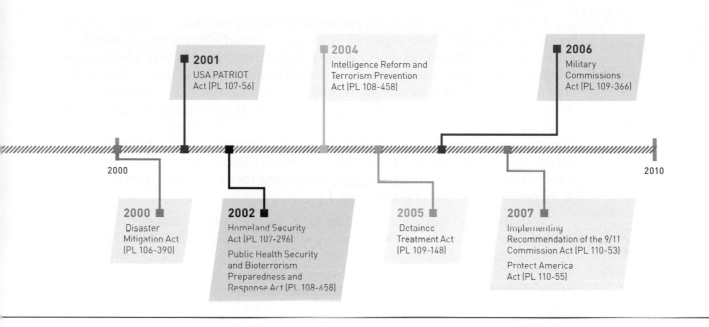

2001 USA PATRIOT Act (PL 107-56)	**2004** Intelligence Reform and Terrorism Prevention Act (PL 108-458)	**2006** Military Commissions Act (PL 109-366)	

2000   2010

2000
Disaster
Mitigation Act
(PL 106-390)

2002
Homeland Security
Act (PL 107-296)

Public Health Security
and Bioterrorism
Preparedness and
Response Act (PL 108-458)

2005
Detainee
Treatment Act
(PL 109-148)

2007
Implementing
Recommendation of the 9/11
Commission Act (PL 110-53)

Protect America
Act (PL 110-55)

potential terrorist actions, opponents raised concerns that these provisions might lead to the development of databases of law-abiding individuals and the collection of data not related to a criminal investigation. Similarly, supporters posited that the provisions to permit "sneak and peek" warrants, which allowed for officers to search spaces without providing notice to potential terrorists, could assist in retrieving sensitive information, whereas opponents feared that such practices could be extended beyond terrorism cases, even into situations involving minor crimes.[28] Indeed, the core of many of these criticisms was that the Patriot Act gave too many freedoms to investigative and police agencies. In June 2015, the Senate passed the USA Freedom Act, which ended a key controversial provision of the USA PATRIOT Act by changing the way that phone data are collected by authorities. As a result of this new law, phone companies will retain the data about phone records and require the government to receive permission from the courts to obtain information about targeted individuals.[29] However, the use of roving wiretaps to follow suspected terrorists and the ability to use national security resources against lone-wolf suspects were retained under the law.[30]

AUDIO
Americans Say They Want the
Patriot Act Renewed . . .
but Do They Really?

DRONES AND THE LAW

A **drone** is an unmanned, remotely piloted aircraft that is used in a variety of ways. Drones have been used by commercial and recreational photographers to take pictures from the sky, by farmers to monitor their livestock, and by geologists to survey landslide areas. The online-shopping giant Amazon has suggested that packages could be delivered via drones, and Switzerland has tested a similar idea with its postal service. Drones are also becoming more commercialized and are marketed to the average individual for entertainment purposes, as companies such as GoPro are developing products for consumer use. However, the emergence of these aircraft in the public

USA PATRIOT Act (2001)
Federal legislation that focused
on tactics to investigate
terrorist activities and
apprehend terrorists.

Drone
Unmanned, remotely piloted
aircraft that is used in a variety
of ways.

zone has created a new category for legislators and policymakers to discuss the limitations of how such equipment should be used. At the same time, concerns over privacy issues have dominated the discussion about the government's use of drone and related technology.

VIDEO
FAA May Ease Restrictions on
Drone Flying

While the use of drones in the private sector has expanded in recent times, these types of aircraft have been deployed by government and military organizations for many years. Radio-controlled devices were used during World War II. The German military was the first to use a remote-controlled weapon with the Fritz X. During the 1980s, drones were used by Israel in its conflict with Syria. The MQ-1 Predator became a significant force in military intelligence after 9/11. Indeed, it was this drone that helped locate Osama bin Laden in Afghanistan in 2000.[31] Today, the use of drones by the military provides sophisticated analysis to assist troops both on the ground and in the air. They are equipped with live-feed video cameras, heat sensors, and radar. Drones can also be armed with weapons, eliminating the danger of military personnel to be on site at the time of deployment.

With the recent expansion of drones to the general public, estimates by the FAA indicate that as many as 30,000 drones could be taking up airspace by 2020.[32] By 2035, we could be looking at more than 1 million drone flights a day within the United States.[33] Indeed, our current laws are ill-equipped to deal with how this new technology should be regulated. Current regulations divide drone flights into three categories: (1) public operations, which covers drones for government use; (2) civil operations, which covers drones for nongovernment usage; and (3) model aircraft operations, which covers the recreational use of drones.[34] Drones that are used for public operations are subject to FAA licensing regulations. For civil-operation flights, drones can be used in environments that are controlled and considered low risk. Meanwhile, recreational use of drones is regulated by a series of guidelines by the Federal Aviation Administration. Some of these regulations include the following:

- Fly below 400 feet and remain clear of surrounding obstacles
- Keep the aircraft within visual line of sight at all times
- Remain well clear of and do not interfere with manned aircraft operations
- Don't fly within 5 miles of an airport unless you contact the airport and control tower before flying
- Don't fly near people or stadiums
- Don't fly an aircraft that weighs more than 55 lbs
- Don't be careless or reckless with your unmanned aircraft—you could be fined for endangering people or other aircraft[35]

What distinguishes recreational use from civil use? For example, if someone is using a drone to take aerial photographs for her or his personal use, it is considered a hobby and falls under the regulations for model aircraft operations. However, if these same photographs are used as part of a business, the use of the drone falls under the category of civil operations.[36]

Drone Concerns

Some of the concerns over the use of drones are related to issues of security and privacy. For example, the National Park Service has declared that all national parks are considered no-fly zones out of safety concerns. Indeed, we have seen cases where the use of drones has actually hindered rather than helped emergency efforts. In July 2015, several drones were flying over a wildfire that had crossed a major freeway. Several cars were set on fire, and many folks were stranded. Helicopters were unable to get near the site to drop water buckets out of concern that the smoke was limiting visibility, and pilots could be at risk of colliding with one of these unmanned aircraft.[37] After several security breaches around the White House, the FAA is working on outlawing the use of drones throughout Washington, D.C.[38] Several other jurisdictions throughout the United States have also made flying illegal out of privacy concerns. For example, Texas has restricted the use of drones by private citizens while Idaho prohibits their use entirely. Several states, including Oregon and Montana, require law enforcement to obtain a warrant in order to collect data on private citizens via drones.[39] Such laws are becoming more popular as residents and legislators are increasingly concerned with indi-

Drones have several uses, ranging from personal entertainment to government interests. Here, agents with the secret service test out a drone to use during surveillance exercises. How might the use of drones change policing strategies?

viduals' privacy rights. However, many of these laws provide an exception to the warrant requirement in emergency cases, as the use of this technology can bring information that was previously unavailable under traditional methods of surveillance. For example, the FBI recently used drones to monitor a hostage situation.[40] However, current laws prohibit the use of drones to observe large public events. In order to obtain a warrant, law enforcement would need to provide probable cause that a crime was likely to occur.[41]

WEB LINK
Should We Freak Out About Drones Looking in Our Windows?

BORDER CONTROL

Border control refers to the efforts that a country takes to regulate and maintain its borders. Discussions about border control have also increased significantly since 9/11. Indeed, the control over our borders was not a national priority prior to the events of September 11th. In the years since, such conversations have been a mainstay of both political and popular commentary. As these discussions morph into policies and practices, the criminal justice system is tasked with determining how to respond to these issues, from a systemic as well as an individualized level. At the heart of border control are three issues: terrorism, transnational crime, and immigration. Earlier in this chapter, you learned about the role of terrorism and how it changed the political landscape of criminal justice in many ways. This section highlights that while terrorism has dominated much of the focus, transnational crime and immigration remain core discussions within border control.

Immigration

Immigration refers to the act of entering a country for the purposes of work or residency. Criminal justice agencies at both the local and national level are involved with immigration control. There are three primary federal agencies that are tasked with responding to immigration. The first agency, the Customs and Border Protection Agency, was established in 1924 to combat illegal immigration. After 9/11, the agency was incorporated as part of the Department of Homeland Security. It is the largest federal law enforcement agency, with more than 60,000 sworn and nonsworn employees.[42] The Office of Border Control is housed within the Customs and Border

Border control
Refers to the efforts that a country takes to regulate and maintain its borders.

Immigration
Refers to the act of entering a country for the purposes of work or residency.

CAREERS IN CRIMINAL JUSTICE

So You Want to Be an Interpreter?

In the United States and abroad, our criminal justice system comes into contact with a diverse group of people. Interpreters and linguists are used to help translate information about crimes into English so that our system can best determine how to respond to these offenses, offenders, and any potential victims. For example, police agencies may recruit officers that are bilingual in order to better engage with members of the local community who may not speak English. Courts also use interpreters to translate the legal proceedings into the native language of the accused so that they can best understand their rights under the law. For example, New York courts provide certified interpreters for 24 different languages. For those who provide interpretation services for common languages such as Spanish, full-time jobs with the courts are often available. For example, the salary for a senior court interpreter in New York is $60,650 per year. For other languages, many interpreters work on an as-needed basis, meaning that they only get paid when someone is in need of their services. These interpreters are paid a flat fee of $250 a day or $140 for a half day of work.[a]

Federal agencies such as the Federal Bureau of Investigation and the Central Intelligence Agency also use interpreters to translate foreign documents and recordings as part of criminal investigations. Such jobs are very difficult to obtain due to the detailed screening and security process that applicants undergo. In order to work for the FBI as a linguist, an individual must possess a bachelor's degree and be able to (1) read and comprehend formal and stylized text in a foreign language; (2) understand and interpret at least one or more dialects of a foreign language; (3) possess superior English skills in listening, reading, writing, and speaking; (4) possess basic or higher computer operation skills; (5) produce translations of written or audio samples in a foreign language as it is produced and in a timely manner; and (6) conduct interviews or interrogations in English and a foreign language.[b] Some of the primary languages for which linguistic agents are employed by the FBI include the following: Arabic, Chinese, Farsi, Korean, Punjabi, Russian, Spanish, Urdu, and Vietnamese.

While some FBI linguists work full time and earn between $33,000 and $78,000 per year, the majority of these employees work as contractors and are hired at an hourly wage.

CAREER VIDEO
Interpreter

Protection Agency. With more than 21,000 officers, its primary task is to patrol our primary borders between the United States and Mexico and Canada. In 2015, agents apprehended 337,117 individuals nationwide.[43] The second agency is Immigration and Customs Enforcement, or ICE, which was established in 2003 as part of the Homeland Security Act. The duties of ICE are focused on the investigation of illegal immigration. In 2015, agents apprehended 235,413 individuals who were either attempting to illegally enter or were currently residing in the United States without authorization.[44] ICE is also tasked with managing the detention of individuals who are either awaiting legal proceedings for violations of immigration law or awaiting deportation. Finally, the third agency is the Bureau of Citizenship and Immigration Services, which is charged with the administrative functions related to visa and citizenship applications.

At the local level, agencies are also involved in issues related to immigration. In areas such as California and Texas, where there is a large number of undocumented immigrants, local and state police interact with immigration cases in a number of ways. They may come into contact with suspects and victims who do not have a legal immigration status. They can also provide regional support for federal agencies during investigations and apprehensions. Finally, they may also help with the detention of individuals, as the majority of immigration violators (67%) are housed in local and state facilities.[45]

There are several entry areas that are regulated by the government that thousands of people pass through each day to enter the country legally. With more than 88 million individuals arriving into our gateway airports each year and millions of others entering through our borders with Mexico and Canada, the task of ensuring compliance with our entry laws is significant. Individuals who wish to enter the United States from a foreign country must obtain a **visa**. There are several different types of visas. While some may come to the United States on a tourist visa, others may come to attend school or work. There are specific types of visas for certain occupations, such as a doctor or a professor, as well as specific programs that recruit temporary workers for particular fields (such as agriculture). There are also specific visas for crime victims. U visas are granted to individuals who have suffered significant mental or physical abuse and are providing assistance to law enforcement to investigate or prosecute these crimes. Meanwhile, T visas are used specifically for victims of human trafficking who wish to remain in the United States.[46] In 2014, 613 victims and 788 family members were granted T visas, and 17 victims received U visas.[47]

> " Despite several attempts to reform our immigration process, it remains a long and challenging system to navigate. As a result, many still choose to enter the country illegally.

While almost 10 millions visas were granted in 2015, there are many others who are unable to obtain a visa.[48] Some of these individuals choose to enter the country illegally. Estimates indicate that 11.3 million individuals reside in the United States illegally.[49] Figure 14.6 shows the distribution across the United States of undocumented immigrants. The majority of undocumented immigrants are from Mexico and Central America (71%), with the second largest group coming from Asian countries (13%).[50] Almost 40% of these individuals have minor children. Many of these children spent the majority of their lives in the United States, never knowing that their parents entered the country illegally. The Development, Relief, and Education for Alien Minors (DREAM) Act was designed to provide a pathway for conditional and permanent residency for youth. While features of the act were introduced several times in both the House and the Senate, they failed to receive a majority of the votes. In 2012, Deferred Action for Childhood Arrivals (DACA) was implemented by the Department of Homeland Security to provide a renewable exemption from deportation for youth who are not U.S. citizens. In order to be eligible, applicants must meet several criteria. Estimates indicate that as many as 1.2 to 2.1 million individuals would be eligible.[51] In 2014, President Obama expanded the program to provide a three-year renewal timeline. In addition, a related policy—Deferred Action for Parents of Americans and Lawful Permanent Residents (DAPA)—was also introduced. Research indicates that the fiscal effects of DAPA and DACA are significant. Undocumented but employed immigrants often fill important yet low-skilled positions and contribute to the local, state, and federal tax base. Nationwide, DAPA- and DACA-eligible workers pay almost $50 billion in taxes.[52] These programs would protect such workers from potential deportation, allowing them to continue to contribute to the economy. While the original policy under DACA is still active, the implementation of its expansion, as well as the DAPA program, have been stalled as a result of a legal challenge. In April 2016, the U.S. Supreme Court heard arguments in the case *United States v. Texas* to determine whether DACA and DAPA violate the U.S. Constitution or the Administrative Procedures Act (APA).[53]

Despite several attempts to reform our immigration process, it remains a long and challenging system to navigate. As a result, many still choose to enter the country illegally (see Figure 14.6). Throughout the 21st century, there have been several bills introduced that are designed to address concerns over illegal immigration. In Chapter 7, you learned about Arizona's Senate Bill 1070 and its subsequent legal

Visa
A document that is required to enter, reside, work, or study in a country.

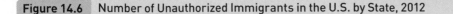

Figure 14.6 Number of Unauthorized Immigrants in the U.S. by State, 2012

California has by far the largest number of unauthorized immigrants, followed by Florida, Illinois, New Jersey, New York, and Texas.

U.S. Total: **11,200,000**

| < 25,000 | 25,000–70,000 | 75,000–160,000 | 170,000–725,000 | > 750,000 |

Source: PEW Research Center.

WEB LINK
Number of Unauthorized
Immigrants in the U.S.
by State, 2012

Transnational crimes
Acts that (1) occur across
the boundaries of different
countries; (2) involve migration
between borders as part of the
criminal activity; (3) take place
in one country but involve a
group that engages in similar
activity in several regions; or
(4) take place in one country
but have a significant effect on
another region.

challenges. In 2005, the House of Representatives passed the Border Protection, Anti-Terrorism and Illegal Immigration Control Act. The bill was the product of several of the major discussions among Republicans about how to combat illegal immigration. For example, the bill sought to build additional fencing along the U.S.-Mexico border and to investigate the feasibility of a similar fence along the U.S.-Canada border. The bill would also have shifted much of the enforcement of federal immigration law violations to local authorities. Beyond that, the measure would have established an employment verification system and have required employers to participate.[54] Critics of the bill expressed concerns that the proposed legislation would violate due process protections for individuals.[55] The bill failed by a majority vote in the Senate and thus was not implemented as law. This measure is but one example of the types of legislation that have been introduced over the past decade, and similar themes about restricting access through our borders and punishing violators have remained in subsequent conversations on the issue.

TRANSNATIONAL CRIME

Defining transnational crimes can be challenging because there is no one specific definition. Generally speaking, **transnational crimes** are acts that (1) occur across the boundaries of different countries; (2) involve migration over borders as part of the criminal activity; (3) take place in one country but involve a group that engages in similar activity in several regions; or (4) take place in one country but have a significant effect on another region. Transnational crime is not a new phenomenon, as such acts have been a regular feature of the criminal landscape. However, the focus on transnational crime is a relatively recent practice, and the role of criminal justice agencies in combating these acts represents a new priority for many of these agencies. Here, intelligence sharing and on-the-ground efforts in apprehending and prosecuting offenders

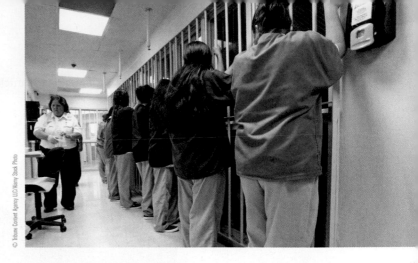

Immigrant detainees spend time in custody as they await the conclusion of legal proceedings that may result in their deportation. How should the United States respond to illegal immigration?

between jurisdictions are effective ways to help battle these types of criminal activity. Examples of transnational crime include human trafficking, organized crime, and drug and arms trafficking.

Human Trafficking

Human trafficking involves the abduction of individuals for the purposes of exploitation and is the second largest criminal activity and the fastest growing criminal enterprise in the world. Estimates by the United Nations suggest that approximately 2.5 million people from 127 countries are victims of trafficking.[56] Due to the nature of these crimes, it is difficult to determine a precise number of human-trafficking victims worldwide. According to data provided by the U.S. State Department, between 600,000 and 820,000 men, women, and children are trafficked across international borders every year. These numbers do not include the thousands—and potentially millions—of individuals who are trafficked within the boundaries of their homelands.[57]

Trafficking can involve cases within the borders of one country as well as transport across international boundaries. Thailand is a well-known location for the sex trafficking of women and girls who migrate from other Southeast Asian countries, such as Cambodia, Laos, Myanmar (Burma), and Vietnam, as well as other Asian countries and territories, such as China and Hong Kong. Others find their way to Thailand from the United Kingdom, South Africa, the Czech Republic, Australia, and the United States.[58] However, examples of trafficking are not limited to countries from the Southeast Asian region. The trafficking of women and children is an international phenomenon and can be found in many regions around the world, even in the United States.

There are several ways in which victims are trafficked. **Forced labor** typically involves immigrants and migrant workers who are in need of employment. Due to their illegal status, they are often taken advantage of, threatened, and, in some cases, physically abused. Estimates indicate that forced labor generates more than $30 billion annually.[59] In contrast to forced labor, **debt bondage** requires victims to pay off a debt through labor. Debt may be inherited as a result of the actions of other family members or may be acquired in return for employment, transportation, housing, or board.[60] In some cases, the costs of these debts are so high that it is impossible for the victim to ever depart the situation. While men, women, and children are all at risk for being victimized, women are disproportionately represented in these cases.[61]

It is **sex trafficking** that receives the greatest amount of attention within the discussion of human trafficking. Between January 2007 and September 2008, there

VIDEO
U.S. Releases Human Trafficking Report

Human trafficking
Involves the abduction of individuals for the purposes of exploitation.

Forced labor
Form of human trafficking that involves immigrants and migrant workers who are in need of employment.

Debt bondage
A form of human trafficking that requires victims to pay off a debt through labor.

Sex trafficking
Victims of human trafficking who are required to participate in acts of prostitution and other forms sexual slavery.

Figure 14.7   Victims of Human Trafficking

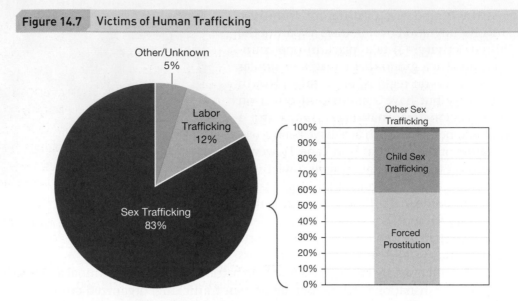

were 1,229 documented incidents* of human trafficking in the United States. An astounding 83% of these cases were defined as alleged incidents of sex trafficking (such as forced prostitution and other sex crimes), of which 32% of these cases involved child sex trafficking, and 62% involved adults (see Figure 14.7).[62]

Sex-trafficked victims may find themselves working in a variety of settings, including brothels, strip clubs, and sex clubs. They also appear in pornographic films, live Internet sex chats, and on the streets, where they solicit money in exchange for sexual services. Traffickers use several methods to manipulate women and girls into the sex trade and prey on their poor economic standing and desires for improving their financial status. In some cases, women may be kidnapped or abducted, although these tactics are rare compared with the majority of cases, which involve lies, deceit, and trickery to collect victims.[63] In some cases, young children are recruited by "family friends" or community members or may even be intentionally sold into servitude by their own parents. Victims are dependent on their traffickers for food, shelter, clothing, and safety. They may be trafficked to a region where they do not speak the language, which limits opportunities to seek assistance. They may be concerned for the safety of their family members, as many traffickers use threats against loved ones to ensure cooperation.[64]

Despite being aware of trafficking as a social issue, many jurisdictions have failed to effectively address the problem in their communities. Much of the intervention efforts against trafficking involve nongovernmental organizations (NGOs), national and international antitrafficking agencies, and local grassroots organizations. While several countries have adopted legislation that criminalizes the sale and exploitation of human beings, many have yet to enact antitrafficking laws. In some cases, countries may have laws on the books but have limited resources or a low priority for enforcing such laws. Still other countries punish the victims of these crimes, often charging them with crimes such as prostitution when they seek out assistance from the police. While grassroots and antitrafficking organizations have developed policies and practices designed to punish traffickers and provide assistance to the victims, few of these recommendations have been implemented effectively or on a worldwide scale.

---

* The Human Trafficking Reporting System (HTRS) is part of the Department of Justice and tracks incidents of suspected human trafficking for which an investigation, arrest, prosecution, or incarceration occurred as a result of a charge related to human trafficking.

In the United States, legislation known as the Trafficking Victims Protection Act (TVPA)* is designed to punish traffickers, protect victims, and facilitate prevention efforts in the community to fight against human trafficking. Enacted by Congress in 2000, the law stipulates that traffickers can be sent to prison for up to 20 years for each victim. In 2013, the Department of Justice prosecuted 208 cases of human trafficking against 335 defendants. The majority of these cases (91.3%) were focused on acts of sex trafficking. The DOJ obtained 184 convictions. They also provided victim services to more than 2,782 cases. Meanwhile, there were an estimated 10,051 prosecutions and 4,443 convictions involving 44,462 victims around the world in 2014.[65]

> While grassroots and antitrafficking organizations have developed policies and practices designed to punish traffickers and provide assistance to the victims, few of these recommendations have been implemented effectively or on a worldwide scale.

Organized Crime

Organized crime is one of the most common forms of transnational crime and involves the coordinated efforts of individuals for the primary purpose of engaging in criminal activity. Many of their activities are about creating opportunities for financial gain. Organized-crime syndicates typically have a developed structure of leadership, and each actor fills a role within the organization. The typical image of organized crime involves people such as Al Capone during the Prohibition era, or the Gambino family, with characters such as Carlo Gambino and John Gotti, during the mid- to late 20th century. Modern-day examples of organized crime include the following eight groups, which have been identified by the National Institute of Justice as well-known and powerful entities:

- *Russian Mafia:* Around 200 Russian groups that operate in nearly 60 countries worldwide. They have been involved in racketeering, fraud, tax evasion, gambling, drug trafficking, arson, robbery, and murder.

- *La Cosa Nostra:* Known as the Italian or Italian-American mafia. The most prominent organized crime group in the world from the 1920s to the 1990s. They have been involved in violence, arson, bombings, torture, loan sharking, gambling, drug trafficking, health insurance fraud, and political and judicial corruption.

- *Yakuza:* Japanese criminal group. Often involved in multinational criminal activities, including human trafficking, gambling, prostitution, and undermining licit businesses.

- *Fuk Ching:* Chinese organized criminal group in the United States. They have been involved in smuggling, street violence, and human trafficking.

- *Triads:* Underground criminal societies based in Hong Kong. They control secret markets and bus routes and are often involved in money laundering and drug trafficking.

- *Heijin:* Taiwanese gangsters who are often executives in large corporations. They are often involved in white-collar crimes, such as illegal stock trading and bribery, and sometimes run for public office.

- *Jao Pho:* Organized crime group in Thailand. They are often involved in illegal political and business activity.

- *Red Wa:* Gangsters from Thailand. They are involved in manufacturing and tracking methamphetamine.[66]

Organized crime
One of the most common forms of transnational crime, it involves the coordinated efforts of individuals for the primary purpose of engaging in criminal activity, often related to acts of financial gain.

---

* Reauthorized by Congress in December 2008.

Though Hollywood films and television shows such as *The Sopranos* tend to glamorize organized crime, it presents a serious problem for the criminal justice system.

While some of these groups have been linked to terrorist activities, they are also involved in a variety of other crimes. As these organizations expand their efforts, many of these crimes threaten our national security. This is particularly true for those organizations that have successfully infiltrated legitimate businesses and government organizations. The more obvious challenges arise when bribery and corruption occurs within these groups. However, there are also subtle ways that such efforts can challenge both American and foreign stability. Earlier in this chapter, you learned about how cybercrime is an emerging problem for criminal justice. Agents of organized crime can use technology to threaten personal networks and cause significant financial damage. Intellectual-property damage is another avenue in which organized crime can threaten the stability of businesses. For example, counterfeit products and the piracy of movies, music, and video games represent significant financial losses to these industries.[67]

Efforts to combat organized crime are diverse and rely significantly on collaborative efforts between agencies, both within the United States and abroad. The United Nations Convention Against Transnational Organized Crime calls on member countries either to create new offense categories or to pursue charges under existing criminal law to punish perpetrators of these activities. Examples of these categories include making it a crime to participate in an organized criminal group or obstruction of justice. In addition, it is important that law enforcement and related agencies receive the necessary training and technical support to help in their identification, investigation, and apprehension of these offenders.[68] One of the most commonly used laws within the United States to punish individuals affiliated with organized crime is the RICO statute. RICO, or the Racketeer Influenced and Corrupt Organizations Act, provides for criminal and civil penalties for acts that are conducted as part of a criminal organization. This federal law allows for law enforcement to pursue legal actions against individuals who order others to perform criminal activity, effectively closing the loophole that historically allowed many individuals who didn't "do the crime" to avoid prosecution. Today, the RICO statute has been applied to a number of different settings outside of organized crime, including police departments, street gangs, and professional sports organizations.

Drug and Arms Trafficking

SAGE JOURNAL ARTICLE
Classifying the Variety of Drug Trafficking Organizations

Drug trafficking
Type of transnational crime that involves the cultivation, manufacturing, distribution, and sale of illegal drugs.

Arms trafficking
Involves the illegal transport of guns and ammunition.

Drug trafficking involves the cultivation, manufacturing, distribution, and sale of illegal drugs. For example, the United Nations Office on Drugs and Crime has identified that much of the global heroin trade originates in either Afghanistan and its surrounding regions or in Myanmar and Laos in Southeast Asia. With more than 450 tons of heroin distributed each year, just the trafficking of this substance alone is a $33 billion enterprise. Cocaine is used by an estimated 17 million people around the world and represents a value of $88 billion.[69] Meanwhile, 70% of all methamphetamine in the United States is trafficked through the U.S.–Mexico border in San Diego, California.[70] These examples illustrate how financially lucrative the global illicit drug trade is.

Meanwhile, **arms trafficking** involves the illegal transport of guns and ammunition. While the trafficking of weapons is a smaller industry than drug smuggling, it is still a billion-dollar annual enterprise.[71] Identifying the number of illegal weapons is a difficult task. In some cases, weapons that are illegal in one region may be legal in another. In addition, many of these weapons can have a legitimate and legal

The use of our waterways to smuggle drugs remains a popular method of transport. Here, members of the U.S. Coast Guard review approximately 3,500 pounds of cocaine seized outside of Miami, Florida. What efforts are being made to reduce drug smuggling?

purpose, such as small-scale weapons that are frequently issued to members of law enforcement and the military. One method of identifying the extent of illegal-weapons smuggling is to measure the seizure of weapons by customs officials. In 2013, more than 1.4 million weapons were seized by customs officials around the world.[72] Local, state, and federal law enforcement throughout the United States are also active in investigating and seizing illegal firearms. In August 2013, the NYPD was involved in the largest raid in the city's history, which resulted in the confiscation of more than 250 illegal firearms and the arrest of 19 people.[73] At the federal level, Homeland Security agents have been actively involved in the investigation of the illegal exportation of weapons. In December 2015, a Texas man was sentenced to three years in prison for the illegal smuggling of guns to the Middle East. Agents discovered that a network of individuals would hide weapons in used cars that were purchased at auction and arrange for the cars to be exported to Jordan.[74]

Like other acts of transnational crime, combating drug and firearms smuggling requires a coordinated effort of law enforcement in order to successfully apprehend offenders. We have also seen early intervention policies implemented designed to stop the manufacturing of drugs and the possession of illegal guns. For example, the Combat Methamphetamine Epidemic Act of 2005 requires that retailers limit the sale of pseudoephedrine (the primary substance used to manufacturer methamphetamine) to individuals to no more than 7.5 grams of product over a 30-day period. In addition, nonprescription medications that contain pseudoephedrine must be kept behind the counter under lock and key. Meanwhile, California has taken a unique approach in the seizure of illegal weapons by tracking down more than 20,000 guns that were purchased legally but whose owners have since been disqualified from ownership. Senate Bill 140 provides for $24 million to hire additional agents who will be tasked with locating the weapons of individuals who either have failed to re-register them or who failed to surrender their weapons following a criminal act.[75]

> **"**
> Perhaps one of the greatest challenges is the speed at which crime continues to expand and evolve, and our justice and legal systems can be unprepared to deal with these issues. As a student of criminal justice, you may be faced with many of these issues, as well as other threats that are currently unknown.

CONCLUSION

The nature of criminal justice in the 21st century involves both domestic and international challenges. As you have seen from the topics in this chapter, there are many unique and diverse threats that our system is faced with. One of the greatest fallacies is that international crimes don't have an impact on the American criminal justice system. But they do. Not only are American officials called to provide assistance around the world, but such crimes can impact Americans, both domestically and abroad. Perhaps one of the greatest challenges is the speed at which crime continues to expand and evolve, and our justice and legal systems can be unprepared to deal with these issues. As a student of criminal justice, you may be faced with many of these issues, as well as other threats that are currently unknown.

PRO **CON**

Should Enemy Combatants Be Denied Due Process Rights?

—Gus Martin—

INTRODUCTION

The modern war on terrorism began in the aftermath of the September 11, 2001, terrorist attacks on the U.S. homeland and involved large-scale military suppression campaigns, selective military strikes, and covert special-operations missions. During the prosecution of the war, the United States captured thousands of suspected enemy fighters. Hundreds of these prisoners were detained indefinitely at U.S.-managed detention centers, such as the Guantánamo Bay Naval Base in Cuba and covert facilities in allied countries.

Legal and policy debates arose concerning the status of enemy detainees and protocols for their treatment during detention. The principal areas of concern centered on due process questions, including how to frame their status, methods for capturing

suspects, treatment during detention, and access to legal counsel and judicial review. Regarding the status of suspects, prisoner-of-war status was not afforded to detainees. Regarding how suspects were captured, many were detained using unconventional tactics, such as *extraordinary renditions*, in which suspects were covertly captured and "rendered" to U.S.-managed detention centers. Regarding conditions during detention, critical debate centered on the civil-liberties implications of the use of coercive "enhanced interrogation" techniques such as waterboarding. And finally, regarding access to legal counsel and judicial review, due process proponents argued that all persons held by American authorities should receive counsel and review.

PRO   Enemy Detainees Should Be Afforded Due Process Protections

The question of a suspect's official status when he or she is taken prisoner is critical because it determines whether or not certain recognized legal or political protections will be observed by U.S. captors. For this reason, official designations and labels of individual suspected terrorists are a central legal, political, and security issue. From the inception of the war on terrorism, the status of enemy detainees was never sufficiently defined. In fact, the process of defining the status of detainees was intentionally designed to be an arbitrary, bureaucratic, and quasi-legalistic process. There was never a status designation that would have afforded enemy detainees rights guaranteed under international or domestic laws. Government attorneys rendered legal opinions that specifically created a special status for the detainees to justify how they were treated. This poses very troubling policy, legal, and moral questions for the United States.

During conventional wartime, enemy soldiers who are taken prisoner are traditionally afforded legal protections as *prisoners of war*. This is well recognized under international law. During the unconventional war on terrorism, many suspected terrorists were improperly designated by the United States as *enemy combatants* and were not afforded the same legal status as prisoners of war. Because of these designations, they were deemed ineligible to enjoy due process rights. Such practices are hotly debated among proponents and opponents for good reason: They violate principles of due process. Basic legal and humanitarian protections should be granted to prisoners regardless of their designation. This was not done, so under enemy combatant status, conditions of confinement in Guantánamo Bay and elsewhere were designed by military and intelligence agencies. As a result, due process protections were circumvented because of arbitrary status definitions.

Another example of circumvention of established due process guarantees is the inappropriate use of extraordinary renditions. Extraordinary renditions involve an uncomplicated procedure: Find suspects anywhere in the world, seize them, transport them to the United States, and force their appearance before a state or federal court. "Such compulsory appearances before U.S. courts have long been accepted as procedurally valid and as not violating one's constitutional rights. The doctrine that permits these abductions and appearances is an old one, and it has come to be known as the 'Ker-Frisbie Rule.'"[76] In the case of rendered terrorist suspects, no appearances before U.S. courts occurred after capture. Instead, "unlike previous renditions in which suspects were seized and brought into the U.S. legal system, most antiterrorist abductions placed suspects in covert detention centers" managed by military and intelligence agencies.[77] A significant number of abductions were conducted by Central Intelligence Agency operatives, who rendered abductees to cooperative allies for intensive interrogation. The CIA also established *black sites* in allied countries, which were covert detention facilities that held suspects for indefinite periods of time.

Allegations arose and findings were made that these enemy detainees were tortured.

In the United States, due process protections prohibit the use of coercive interrogation methods to elicit information from suspects in custody. Unfortunately, enemy detainees incarcerated in detention centers were reported to have been regularly subjected to intensive physical and psychological interrogation techniques, including repeated waterboarding. Officials attempted to draw definitional lines between permissible "enhanced interrogation" methods and torture. However, such interrogation techniques, under any definition, constitute torture and are therefore unconstitutional.

Legal and judicial review of detainees has been inadequate. Rendered prisoners were at first denied status review by impartial review tribunals, and after challenges in federal court, they were only afforded access to newly created Combatant Status Review Tribunals and later an Administrative Review Board. These are administrative commissions, rather than judicial tribunals, and do not provide an adequate degree of impartial due process to enemy detainees.

CON   Enemy Detainees Should Be Denied Due Process Rights

According to the protocols of the third Geneva Convention, prisoners who are designated as prisoners of war and are brought to trial must be afforded the same legal rights in the same courts as soldiers from the country holding them prisoner. This is a reasonable practice, and under these conditions, prisoners of war held by the United States *should* be brought to trial in standard military courts under the Uniform Code of Military Justice and *should* have the same rights and protections (such as the right to appeal) as all soldiers. However, the modern war on terrorism is extraordinarily unconventional, and captured terrorists are not soldiers who are entitled to prisoner-of-war status. Nor do they have automatic recourse to judicial review.

The practice of capturing terrorists using extraordinary renditions is appropriate during wartime, especially during unconventional conflicts. When captured, suspected terrorists do not have a right to appear before U.S. courts after capture and may be placed in covert detention centers managed by military and intelligence agencies.

Because captured terrorists are not prisoners of war, designations such as *enemy combatants*, *unlawful combatants*, and *battlefield detainees* are necessary to differentiate them from prisoners of war. This is a reasonable practice because terrorists are

The Guantánamo Bay detention facility located on the U.S. naval base in Cuba is used to house enemy combatants and other prisoners from the wars in Iraq and Afghanistan. What are some of the pros and cons of closing this facility?

not soldiers fighting for a sovereign nation and are therefore not eligible for prisoner-of-war status. When the United States detains prisoners at facilities such as the Guantánamo Bay Naval Base and elsewhere, it may legally do so because persons designated as enemy combatants are not subject to the Geneva Conventions. Such individuals may be held indefinitely, detained in secret, transferred at will, and sent to allied countries for more intensive interrogations.

Regarding the treatment of terrorists in custody, it is perfectly reasonable (and indeed necessary) to discuss whether physical and psychological stress methods are acceptable. During the modern war on terrorism, the extraction of information from enemy detainees is necessary to successfully predict and preempt possible terrorist incidents. In

this regard, coercion is justifiable to save innocent lives. Assuming the application of coercion is justifiable, to some degree, to break the resistance of suspects, the question becomes whether physical and extreme psychological coercion are also justifiable. In this regard, if interrogations produce actionable intelligence, then the methods used to elicit the information are justifiable because this information may save lives.

Review of the status of enemy detainees has been adequate. They are not prisoners of war, nor under arrest, and therefore do not have an automatic right to judicial review. Appropriate administrative review of prisoner status has been conducted since the inception of the Combatant Status Review Tribunals, and annual reviews were conducted by the Administrative Review Board.

DISCUSSION QUESTIONS

1. Which capture and interrogation techniques are acceptable from a due process perspective?

2. Should terrorists be afforded the same due process rights as prisoners of war or suspects held in judicial custody?

3. Who should have primary custody and jurisdiction over enemy detainees?

CURRENT CONTROVERSY 14.2

PRO CON

CURRENT CONTROVERSY VIDEO
Where Do You Stand? Cast Your Vote!

Does Immigration Impact Crime?
—Zahra Shekarkhar—

INTRODUCTION

For more than 100 years, the relationship between immigration and crime has been debated. With the large influx of mostly European immigrants in the late 1800s and early 1900s, U.S. natives feared that newcomers were criminal and would destroy the social fabric of American society. After decades of assimilation and acculturation into American society, the image of the criminal immigrant mainly subsided until the next large influx of immigrants entered the United States beginning in the 1960s. This wave of immigration coincided with increases in the crime rate in general, including an increase in the U.S. homicide rate between 1960 and 1990.[78] Once again, immigrants were being viewed as criminals.

While some politicians and interest groups have argued that the influx of immigrants has negative consequences for American society, others have described data that run counter to this position. On the one hand, nearly a century of research confirms that foreign-born immigrants residing in the United States are less criminal than their native-born peers.[79] On the other hand, there is much research that shows that children of immigrants living in the United States (i.e., second- and third-generation immigrants) are at greater risk of engaging in criminal behavior than first-generation immigrant children.[80]

One argument for how immigration may increase crime centers on population increase. Between 1965 and 2015, new immigrants (first-generation immigrants), their children (second generation), and grandchildren (third generation) accounted for 55% of U.S. population growth.[81] In 2015, the foreign-born population (first-generation immigrants) made up 13.9% of the country's population.[82] It is projected that over the next 50 years, the foreign-born population will account for 88% of the country's population increase.[83] The increase in this population may be of concern given the demographic similarities between criminal offenders and recent immigrants. Like criminal offenders, recent immigrants tend to be young, male, poorly educated, and from a racial or ethnic minority group.[84] Perhaps by increasing the numbers of the most crime-prone demographic, immigrants could contribute to increases in the crime rate.

Immigrant generational status has also been shown to influence crime rates. Historically—and still today—studies find that first-generation immigrants are less criminal than their U.S.-born counterparts. However, crime involvement appears to increase through successive generations. Research shows that second- and third-generation youth (U.S.-born individuals) exhibit a number of negative social and behavioral outcomes compared with their foreign-born parents. Second- and third-generation youth have, on average, lower self-control, more delinquent peers, and less parental supervision; spend more time in unstructured activities with peers; and report more parent–child conflict at home compared with first-generation youth.[85] These findings suggest that length of time in the United States increases crime among immigrant groups.[86] Similarly, studies that differentiate between first-generation immigrants who arrived in the United States at a young age (before 12 or 13) and those who arrived at a later age show that those who came at a young age tend to report greater crime involvement than those who came at a later age.[87] This finding suggests that age of arrival can also influence criminal outcomes.

Another argument for how immigration increases crime suggests that immigration may influence the criminal involvement of members of the native U.S. population. In particular, one study found a strong relationship between immigration, Black employment rates and wages, and Black incarceration rates.[88] This analysis suggests that the increase in immigrant workers (in certain sectors) lowered the wages and employment rate of Black workers in those sectors, which indirectly increased the incarceration rate for Blacks.

 Immigration Does Not Increase Crime

Increases in both the immigrant population and the U.S. crime rate occurred simultaneously during the 1960s through the 1990s. Given this finding, it is not surprising that much of the public believed immigrants were responsible for the increase in crime. However, crime dramatically decreased in the 1990s while the immigrant population continued to grow.[89] This prompted a number of researchers to examine if increases in immigration increased crime. The same pattern emerged from those studies: Immigration did not contribute to the crime increase, and in some areas, immigration may have actually lowered or decreased the crime rate.[90]

Official records from the 1980s suggest that many cities with large immigrant populations also experienced high crime rates. If the immigrants were the cause of increased crime rates, then it would be expected that any change in the immigrant population would change the crime rate in that city. However, numerous studies reported no relationship between changes in the immigrant population and changes in the overall crime rates.[91] Analyses looking at changes in the 1990s also indicate decreases in the crime rate, especially the violent crime rate, as the immigrant population increased.[92] The same pattern was seen in the early 2000s. Violent victimization rates hit a record low in 2002 despite the growing immigrant population. Additionally, cities with the largest concentration of immigrants experienced the greatest drops in the violent crime rate.[93]

In an argument made in the preceding section, it was suggested that immigrants may influence the crime rate of native populations. In some areas, however, living in a neighborhood with a large concentration of immigrants has been shown to result in lower violence, even among the native-born population of Blacks and Whites.[94]

Even though studies discussed in the previous section suggest that the second- and third-generation youth are more crime prone, those same studies also find that overall, these youth tend to be less involved or equally involved in crime compared with their native-born counterparts.[95]

SUMMARY

There are three main patterns that have emerged in immigration and crime research. First, foreign-born individuals report less involvement in crime compared with their native-born counterparts. Second, the children of immigrants, namely the second and third generations, show greater involvement in crime than their foreign-born counterparts (i.e., first generation). Third, neighborhoods with large and/or growing immigrant populations tend to witness declines in the overall crime rates, especially for violent crimes.

Some scholars suggest that immigrant communities can protect residents and youth from adopting a deviant lifestyle through a common ethnic subculture that helps create social ties among residents.[96] Thus, the concentration of immigrants may act as a protective factor against crime, particularly violence.[97]

The issue of why second- and third-generation immigrants have higher crime rates than the first generation remains unsolved. Some suggest that immigrants are more likely to live in two-parent households, which acts as a protective factor, especially for newly arrived immigrants.[98] Others suggest that living in a neighborhood with a large concentration of immigrants provides new immigrants with an extended social network that provides job opportunities and social support.[99] Yet still the possibility exists that there is something unique about U.S. culture that increases the propensity for crime among second- and third-generation immigrants. Future research is needed to address these remaining questions.

DISCUSSION QUESTIONS

1. In your opinion, what factors are most likely to influence involvement in crime by second- and third-generation immigrants? Is there anything unique about American culture that would increase criminality across immigrant generations?

2. Why do you think the general public continues to believe that immigration causes crime, despite evidence to suggest the opposite?

3. What are some possible ways to help reduce criminal involvement among second- and third-generation immigrants?

KEY TERMS

Review key terms with eFlashcards | ⑤SAGE edge™ • edge.sagepub.com/mallicoatccj

Arms trafficking 370	Drone 361	Organized crime 369
Border control 363	Drug trafficking 370	Religious terrorism 353
Cyberterrorism 354	Forced labor 367	Sex trafficking 367
Debt bondage 367	Homeland security 356	State-sponsored terrorism 353
Department of Homeland Security Act (2002) 358	Human trafficking 367	Transnational crimes 366
Dissident terrorism 353	Immigration 363	USA PATRIOT Act (2001) 360
Domestic terrorism 352	International terrorism 353	Visa 365

DISCUSSION QUESTIONS

Test your mastery of chapter content • Take the Practice Quiz | $SAGE edge™ • **edge.sagepub.com/mallicoatccj**

1. How does domestic terrorism differ from other forms of terrorism?

2. How do acts of cyberterrorism differ from traditional acts of terrorism?

3. How might Homeland Security respond to events other than acts of terrorism?

4. What are some of the pros and cons of the Patriot Act?

5. In what ways does the use of drones present challenges to privacy and security?

6. How does the local response to immigration differ from the national-level response?

7. How do events of transnational crime threaten the security and safety of the United States?

LEARNING ACTIVITY

1. Review the most recent *Trafficking in Persons* report from the U.S. Department of State. What did you learn about how acts of human trafficking are perpetrated around the world and about the strategies that are used to prevent and respond to such crimes?

SUGGESTED WEBSITES

- *Trafficking in Persons* **Report, U.S. Department of State:** http://www.state.gov/j/tip/rls/tiprpt/
- **Polaris Project:** https://polarisproject.org/human-trafficking
- **Global Terrorism Database:** http://www.start.umd.edu/gtd/about/
- **Department of Homeland Security:** https://www.dhs.gov
- **United Nations Office on Drugs and Crime:** https://www.unodc.org

STUDENT STUDY SITE

Review • Practice • Improve | $SAGE edge™ • **edge.sagepub.com/mallicoatccj**

Want a better grade?

Get the tools you need to sharpen your study skills. Access practice quizzes, eFlashcards, video, and multimedia at **edge.sagepub.com/mallicoatccj**

GLOSSARY

Actus reus: Latin for "evil act." One of the four required components of a criminal act.

Adjudication hearing: Similar to a trial in the adult court.

Administrative law: Body of law that governs the creation and function of state and federal government agencies.

Aftercare: Similar to parole in the adult system.

Age-graded developmental theory: Theory that explains how one might engage in crime as a result of one's life events.

Aggravating factors: Circumstances that increase the severity of the crime, such as torture, excessive violence, or premeditation.

Allocution: Occurs when a defendant appears before the court and publicly admits his or her involvement in a crime.

American Law Institute standard: See *model penal code test*.

Amicus curiae: Describes "friend of the court" briefs that are submitted to appellate courts in support of a legal argument.

Anomie: Theory that refers to a sense of normlessness that societies experience as a result of a breakdown in social cohesion.

Appeals by permission: Involve reviews of lower level decisions that the court may choose to accept.

Appeals by right: Involve cases that the appellate court must hear.

Appellate jurisdiction: Level of the courts that is concerned with issues of law and whether an error was made by the trial court.

Arizona Senate Bill 1070: 2010 legislative act in Arizona that allows for local and state law enforcement to use a lawful stop, detention, or arrest to try to determine whether the suspect is an illegal immigrant.

Arms trafficking: Involves the illegal transport of guns and ammunition.

Arson: A crime that involves the destruction of a physical structure or item by fire.

Assault: A crime that involves the physical harm (or threat) to a victim.

Assistant chief: Upper-level management position in policing in which the person is responsible for a specific subdivision of the police organization.

Attendant circumstances: The relationship between mens rea and actus reus. Refers to what happens within the context of the act that makes it a crime.

Auburn Prison: The first facility under the New York model.

Bail: A promise to return for future court appearances in exchange for one's release during the pretrial stage.

Ban the box: Policy that asks or mandates that potential employers eliminate from initial hiring applications the check box that asks individuals if they have a criminal record.

Beyond a reasonable doubt: In order to convict a defendant of a crime, the court must find that there is little doubt according to the reasonable-person standard.

Biological theories of crime: Collection of theories that look at how genetic characteristics can be used to explain crime.

Biosocial theories of crime: Theoretical perspective that combines features of biological theories of crime and how they interact with social environments to produce criminological behaviors.

Boot camps: A form of short-term intervention that has been modeled after military-style basic-training programs.

Border control: Refers to the efforts that a country takes to regulate and maintain its borders.

Bribery: Involves the solicitation of something of value to influence the actions of another.

Brief: Document that is submitted by the parties in an appellate case that outlines their legal arguments.

Broken-windows theory: Theory that suggests that when lesser acts of disorder are left unattended in a neighborhood, there is an increased risk for serious crime to breed.

Burglary: A crime that occurs when someone enters a building or other physical space with the intent of taking property without permission.

Carroll doctrine: Legal doctrine that allows the police to search a vehicle without a warrant if they have probable cause to arrest the occupants of the vehicle and if they have probable cause that the car contains illegal items.

Case law: Law that is created as a result of legal decisions by the court.

Causation: Implies that there is something that directly influences or is responsible for people engaging in criminal behavior.

Celerity: Refers to the notion that potential punishment must occur in a timely fashion. One of the three characteristics that is required in order for deterrence to be effective.

Certainty: Refers to the notion that individuals need to be reasonably aware that if they engage in a criminal act, they will be apprehended and punished. One of the three characteristics that is required in order for deterrence to be effective.

Chain of command: Process that provides guidance for each group by placing a direct supervisory rank immediately ahead of them.

Challenge for cause: Allows attorneys to exclude a potential jury in cases where the court believes that the individual may be unfair or biased in her or his decision-making.

Chemical force: Force that involves the use of restraining substances, such as pepper spray or mace.

Circuit courts: Another name for the federal courts of appeals.

Circumstantial evidence: Evidence that requires the jury to make some sort of inference about the defendant's involvement in the crime.

Civil law: Law that governs disputes between individuals or private parties and generally involves the violation of private acts.

Classical school of criminology: Posits that people engage in criminal behavior as a result of their own free will and that people make a choice to engage in illegal acts.

Closing argument: Stage of a case in which each side makes a final summary statement to the court once all the evidence has been presented.

Cognitive development theories: Group of theories that suggests that offenders have failed to develop the capacity to make moral judgments.

Community corrections: Collection of programs that work with two distinct populations: those who have been sentenced for a crime and those who have been charged with offenses and are waiting for their cases to be resolved by the criminal justice system.

Community policing: A philosophy that promotes organizational strategies that support the systematic use of partnerships and problem-solving techniques to proactively address the immediate conditions that give rise to public safety issues, such as crime, social disorder, and fear of crime.

Community problem-solving era: A time period in which the primary strategy involved the use of foot patrols to better connect with community members, which allowed for increased numbers of crimes to be solved and improved relationships between the police and community.

CompStat: A practice that first began in the NYPD that focuses on the comparison of different crime statistics to guide policing decisions.

Concurrence: One of the four required components of a criminal act. Occurs when the mens rea and actus reus join together in a crime.

Concurrent jurisdiction: Allows a case to be heard in either state or federal courts (or adult and juvenile courts).

Concurring opinion: An opinion provided by the court that agrees with the outcome of the majority but has different reasoning for the decision.

Conformist: One of the five components of Merton's strain theory. Conformists are people who accept both the socially approved goals and the means to achieve them.

Congregate labor systems: Form of labor first used in the New York model that organized prison labor as a group process.

Consent search: A type of search that occurs when the individual gives permission to conduct a search.

Conservative: A political perspective that follows more of a law-and-order philosophy and generally cites retributive values in punishing offenders.

Constitutional law: Law that is specified by either a state or the U.S. Constitution.

Conventional level: Level two of Lawrence Kohlberg's theory of cognitive development and crime, where youth begin to identify with the social norms of law-abiding behavior.

Correctional officers: Criminal justice officials who are responsible for the security of the correctional institution and the safety of the inmates housed within its walls.

Corrections: One of the three major components of the criminal justice system. The corrections system carries out the punishment as ordered by the court.

Correlation: Describes two variables or factors that are linked or related in some way.

Corruption: An ethical dilemma that occurs when officers fail to make good ethical decisions (generally around the abuse of their authority as

officers) and the results of their actions lead to personal gain.

County sheriff: Agency that is responsible for running the local county jail. Also provides security for the local courthouse, serving warrants and subpoenas and providing patrol services.

Courts: One of the three major systems of the criminal justice system. The courts are responsible for determining whether an offender should be charged with a crime and also manage the process to determine whether the offender should be held criminally responsible for the crime.

Crime: An act that is against the law and causes a punishment.

Crime control model: Model of criminal justice that advocates for the suppression and control of criminal behavior as a function of public order in society.

Crime mapping: Process by which information about crime locations is used to identify patterns of crime to assist in the deployment of officers.

Crime rate: A calculation that compares the number of crimes to the size of the population. Allows for standardized comparisons across time and space.

Crime-specific supervision: Organizes a probation officer's caseload by specific offense types.

Crime Victims' Rights Act of 2004: Federal legislation that provides victims with legal rights in federal criminal cases.

Cross-deputization: Refers to the practice whereby local law enforcement are given the power to enforce federal laws.

Cyberterrorism: Acts of terrorism that involve premeditated, politically motivated attacks against information, computer systems, computer programs, and data.

Dark figure of crime: Refers to unreported crime in official crime statistics.

Day-reporting center: Requires an offender to attend a program or center during the day but allows him or her to live at home during the evening.

Debt bondage: A form of human trafficking that requires the victim to pay off a debt through labor.

Defendant: Someone who has criminal charges filed against her or him.

Defense: A strategy to justify, explain, or excuse criminal behavior.

Delinquency: Refers not only to those acts that would be considered criminal under the law but also to status offenses.

Delinquency petition: Legal filing that allows for the juvenile court to retain jurisdiction in a case.

Department of Homeland Security Act (2002): Federal legislation that consolidated several federal agencies that had previously worked independently of each other prior to 9/11.

Dependency: Refers to cases that involve youth who have been harmed or neglected by their parents and therefore are being removed from the parents' custody.

Deputy police chief: Second highest ranking office that reports directly to the chief of police.

Detective: A sworn police officer who manages a case throughout the investigative process.

Determinate sentencing: A sentencing structure in which the offender is sentenced to a specific term.

Deterrence: Theory of punishment that suggests that people will avoid potentially pleasurable acts if the pain or fear of punishment is significant.

Differential association theory: Theory that focuses on how relationships, particularly peer relationships, influence delinquent behavior.

Differential reinforcement: Theory that looks at behavior as a balance between increasing the rewards that come with engaging in deviant or criminal behaviors while minimizing the potential consequences and punishments.

Direct democracy: Political process by which citizens are empowered to make law through an initiative process.

Direct evidence: Refers to evidence that is directly linked to the defendant's involvement in the crime.

Direct file: The process by which a prosecutor files a case involving a juvenile offender in criminal court.

Directed patrol: A police practice that targets a specific area of a city due to crime rates.

Discretion: Refers to the power to make decisions by criminal justice officials.

Discretionary waiver: See *judicial waiver*.

Disposition hearing: Similar to a sentencing hearing in adult court, this is held to determine the plan of action for the case once a juvenile is adjudicated delinquent.

Dissenting opinion: A written opinion by a justice who disagrees with the majority decision.

Dissident terrorism: Acts of terrorism that are committed by nonstate groups against governments, religious entities, and citizens.

Diversion: An approach that refers offenders to a program instead of processing their cases through the system.

Domestic terrorism: Acts of terrorism that occur within the jurisdiction of the United States.

Drone: Unmanned, remotely piloted aircraft that is used in a variety of ways.

Drug trafficking: Type of transnational crime that involves the cultivation, manufacturing, distribution, and sale of illegal drugs.

Drug use: A crime that involves the use of illegal or illicit substances.

Dual court system: Explains how the state and federal court systems work in separate yet similar fashions.

Due process model: Model of criminal justice that believes that the protection of individual rights and freedoms is the most important function of the system.

Duress: A defense strategy that describes people who are forced to violate the law out of fear for their own safety or the safety of others around them.

Eastern State Penitentiary: The first penitentiary designed within the Pennsylvania system model.

Electrocution: A form of execution where death occurs from a high dose of electricity that is administered to the body.

Electronic force: Force that involves the use of electrical current to temporarily incapacitate an offender, such as the TASER.

Electronic monitoring: Form of supervision that involves the use of technology to follow the location of an offender.

Elmira Reformatory: The first facility during the reformatory era.

Emergency exception: An exception to the warrant requirement that is invoked if police are concerned that waiting to secure a warrant could either jeopardize the safety of others or threaten the integrity of potential evidence.

En banc: A hearing of the full bench of a U.S. circuit court.

Entrapment: A defense strategy that describes when an individual is deceived by a government official to engage in an act that is against the law.

Espionage: A crime that occurs when an individual or a government obtains secret or confidential information.

Ethical dilemma: Occurs when an officer is unsure about the right path of action, when following the right path is difficult, or when the wrong path becomes tempting to the officer.

Ethics: Refers to the understanding of what constitutes good or bad behavior.

Excessive use of force: Defined as the application of amount and/or frequency of force greater than required to compel compliance from a willing or unwilling subject.

Exclusionary rule: Established by the U.S. Supreme Court case *Mapp v. Ohio* (1961), it states that items obtained outside the context of a warrant cannot be used against someone in a court of law.

Exculpatory evidence: Evidence that is favorable to the defense and may exonerate a defendant from any criminal wrongdoing.

Federal prisons: Prison facilities used to hold offenders convicted of federal crimes.

Felony: Serious crimes that can be punished by more than one year in prison.

Feminist criminology: Alternative to traditional theories of crime, which often did not consider how the lives of women are different from men and, as a result, may explain the differences in offending behaviors.

Feminist pathways approach: Theory that provides a life course perspective from a feminist approach and highlights how trauma and abuse contribute to offending behavior.

Firearm force: Force that involves the pointing of or firing of a handgun.

Firing squad: A form of execution involving the death of an individual by a gunshot to the heart. Death occurs as a result of rapid blood loss.

Forced labor: Form of human trafficking that involves immigrants and migrant workers who are in need of employment.

Forcible rape: The carnal knowledge of a female, forcible and against her will.

Fruit of the poisoned tree: States that any evidence that is obtained as a result of an illegal search is excluded and cannot be used against someone in a court of law.

Gambling: A crime that involves the wager of money or other valuable goods in hopes of improving one's financial status.

General deterrence: Suggests that if people fear the punishments that others receive, they will, in turn, decide not to engage in similar acts, as they do not want to risk the potential punishment for themselves.

General jurisdiction: Courts that do not have any restrictions on the types of cases that they hear but generally hear the most serious felony cases.

General strain theory: Theory that looks at individualized psychological sources as correlates of criminal behavior. Sources of potential strain include failure to achieve positive goals, the loss of positive influences, and the arrival of negative influences.

General theory of crime: Theory that focuses on self-control as the factor that explains delinquent and criminal behavior.

Geographic information systems: A type of crime-mapping technology that is used to track geographic patterns in criminal activity that can, in turn, be used both to predict future patterns of crime and to make decisions about the deployment of officers.

Geographical jurisdiction: Jurisdiction determined by the physical location of a crime.

Global Positioning System (GPS) monitoring: A type of electronic monitoring that allows for greater opportunities to locate and track the movement of offenders.

Good-faith exception: If evidence is obtained without a warrant as a result of unintended error, then the evidence can still be used.

Good-time credits: Allow inmates to earn time off of their sentence for good behavior.

Grand jury: Describes a group of citizens who review the evidence presented by a prosecutor to determine whether an indictment should be issued.

Grass-eaters: Describes officers who are considered to be involved in corrupt activities in a passive sense.

Guilty but mentally ill: Legal ruling that allows courts to hold an offender guilty for a crime but acknowledges the issues of mental illness as a cause of the criminal behavior.

Halfway house: Designed to provide a transitional living arrangement for ex-offenders upon their release from jail or prison.

Hanging: A method of execution that involves breaking the neck of an offender by suspending him or her with a rope around his or her neck.

Hierarchy rule: Uniform Crime Reporting Program rule that only counts the most serious crime.

Highway patrol: Also known as state law enforcement agency.

Homeland security: Refers to a coordinated government and private-sector effort that provides security against and responses to specific and general threats.

Hot-spots policing: Type of directed patrol with the use of crime-mapping technologies.

House arrest: A sanction that requires that offenders remain in their homes in lieu of a jail or prison.

Human trafficking: Involves the abduction of individuals for the purposes of exploitation.

Hung jury: Occurs when a jury is unable to make a unanimous decision.

Hypothesis: Term that describes the research process that investigates if a factor or variable causes an outcome.

Immigration: Refers to the act of entering a country for the purposes of work or residency.

Impact force: Force that involves the use of batons, flashlights, and other implements to deliver force against an individual.

Incapacitation: Refers to the practice of removing offenders from society so that they will not engage in criminal behaviors for a certain period of time.

Indeterminate sentencing: A sentencing structure in which the offender is sentenced to a minimum and maximum sentencing range. The actual time served is determined by a parole board, which evaluates release based on rehabilitation and behavior while in prison.

Indictment: An official declaration that there is probable cause to charge the accused with a crime.

Information era: 21st-century policing with technological innovations that have altered the daily lives of officers on the street.

Initial appearance: First appearance by a defendant where she or he is officially notified by the court of the charges that are pending against her or him. If the defendant is indigent, it is during this stage that an attorney is appointed for her or him.

Initiative: Political process by which prospective laws are proposed for voters to approve during an election.

Innocence: Refers to a case where evidence excludes someone from having committed the crime.

Innovator: One of the five components of Merton's strain theory. Refers to someone who embraces the socially approved goals but rejects the means to get there.

Insanity: An individual is not held responsible for his or her criminal actions as a result of his or her mental state.

Intake: Entry point for juvenile cases.

Intensive probation: A form of probation sentence where probation officers closely monitor the daily activities of their offenders.

Intent: Refers to the conscious decision to engage in a criminal act.

Intermediate sanction: A category of interventions that are used between probation and incarceration.

International terrorism: Acts that occur primarily outside the territorial jurisdiction of the United States or transcend national boundaries in terms of the means by which they are accomplished, the persons they appear intended to coerce or intimidate, or the locale in which their perpetrators operate or seek asylum.

Intoxication: A criminal defense that uses being under the influence of drugs or alcohol as a justification for offending.

Irresistible impulse test: One of the tests of the insanity defense. Expands the M'Naghten rule with the issue of control. Describes the condition that even though an offender may know that an action is wrong, she or he is unable to refrain from engaging in the criminal act.

Issues of Duty: An ethical dilemma where officers are faced with challenges based on how they view their role as police officers. Also occurs when an officer knows what is expected of her or him but is not inclined to perform a particular aspect of the job.

Jail: Correctional facility that is used to hold people until their punishments are carried out. Also offers incarceration for misdemeanor offenders and specialized programs.

Judicial waiver: Legal process that requires the juvenile court to hold a hearing to determine whether the youth could still benefit from the resources of the juvenile court in its decision to transfer a case to the criminal court.

Jurisdiction: Determines when and how the criminal justice system can respond. Legal jurisdiction means that they have the legal authority to handle a particular matter, whereas geographic jurisdiction means that they are authorized to operate in a specific geographic location.

Jury instructions: Provide guidance to the members of the jury about how to apply the law to the facts that were presented during the trial.

Jury nullification: Occurs when the jury may decide not to convict a defendant even though the evidence would support a guilty verdict.

Just deserts: Argues that a punishment for a crime should be proportional or equal to the crime itself.

Just-world hypothesis: A hypothesis that suggests that society has a need to believe that people deserve whatever happens to them.

Juvenile Justice and Delinquency Prevention Act: Federal legislation that called for the deinstitutionalization of status offenders and requires states to address issues of disproportionate minority contact and gender-responsive services.

Juvenile waiver: Legal process whereby cases are transferred to the adult criminal court for processing.

Kansas City Preventive Patrol Experiment: Police study that found that changes to police presence did not have a significant effect on crime or change citizen satisfaction levels with the police.

Labeling theory: Theory that focuses on how being labeled as delinquent or criminal can influence future behaviors, regardless of the accuracy of the label.

Larceny-theft: A crime that involves the taking of property without the use of force.

Legal custody: Legal status in which the court is now responsible for all the decisions made about the child.

Legislative waiver: A method of juvenile waiver that involves laws specifying a minimum age at which cases are automatically sent to criminal court for certain crimes.

Lethal gas: A method of execution that uses cyanide gas to suffocate an individual.

Lethal injection: A method of execution that involves the injection of drugs designed to stop the heart and lung functions, resulting the death.

Lex talionis: Latin term that refers to the theory that punishment should fit the crime. The concept derives from ancient law and is referenced in biblical texts as *eye for an eye*.

Liberal: A political perspective that tends to focus on the importance of due process, individual freedoms, and constitutional rights.

Lieutenant: Police supervisors who are tasked with many administrative functions for line officers, such as equipment, training, and staffing.

Life course theory: Theory that looks at how delinquent behaviors either persist or desist throughout one's life and how life events might encourage shifts in behavior.

Lifestyle theory: Theory that explores the risk of victimization from personal crimes whereby people place themselves at risk as a result of their lifestyle choices.

Limited jurisdiction: Courts that handle misdemeanor cases or specific types of cases.

Local law enforcement: Accounts for the majority of all law enforcement agencies.

Longitudinal studies: Self-report studies that investigate crime over a period of time.

Macro theories of crime: Theories that focus on large-scale social or structural explanations of crime.

Majority opinion: Legal reasoning that is used to make a decision in a case, which becomes precedent.

Mala in se: Latin for crimes that are considered to be inherently wrong and therefore illegal.

Mala prohibita: Latin for crimes that are only illegal because they have been defined as such under the law.

Mandatory revocation: Revocation of a probation sentence as a result of specific violations.

Mandatory sentencing: A type of sentencing structure where the law, not the judge, determines the length of punishment for specific offenses.

Marijuana: Drug derived from the cannabis plant.

Maximum-security prison: A prison that is designed to house serious and violent offenders. Inmate movement and autonomy is significantly restricted.

Meat-eaters: Describes officers who actively pursue corrupt activities that could result in significant and illegal gains.

Medium-security prison: A prison that has an increased level of security compared with a minimum-security prison and allows less freedom of movement.

Mens rea: One of the four required components of a criminal act. Latin for the "evil thought." Refers to the intent of an offender.

Micro theories of crime: Theories that focus on individual differences between law-abiding and law-violating behaviors.

Military prisons: Prisons that are designed to house individuals who are convicted of a crime while a member of the armed forces.

Minimum-security prison: The least restrictive level of incarceration that is designed to give inmates the highest levels of movement and autonomy and that acknowledges that these inmates, while subjected to punishment for their crimes, are generally not a violent risk to the community.

Miranda warning: Used to inform people who are under arrest that the 5th Amendment provides protection against self-incrimination during an interrogation.

Misdemeanors: Lower level crimes that are punished by less than one year in jail. Punishments can also involve community-based sanctions, such as probation.

Missouri plan: A three-step plan of judicial selection. Candidates are nominated by a citizen committee and selected by either the governor or the head of the state's judicial system. After a year, a retention election is held.

Mitigating evidence: Any evidence that serves to either explain the defendant's involvement in the crime or reduce her or his potential sentence.

Mitigating factors: Circumstances that minimize or explain the actions of the offender or the crime.

M'Naghten rule: One of the standards of insanity. Refers to situations when the defendant is unable to understand the difference between right and wrong at the time of the crime.

Model penal code test: Combines the features of the M'Naghten rule and the irresistible impulse test to establish that a defendant can be found criminally insane if, as a result of a mental disease or defect, he or she is unable to understand the difference between right and wrong or to control his or her behavior.

Modeling: Part of social learning theory that suggests that new behaviors are learned from observing others.

Mooching: A form of corruption that involves receiving free items in exchange for favorable treatment.

Municipal police: Local-level police departments that have geographic jurisdiction limited to a specific city or region.

Murder: A crime that involves the killing of one human being by another.

National Crime Victimization Survey: The largest victimization study in the United States. Attempts to fill the gap of understanding between reported and unreported crime.

National Incident-Based Reporting System: System of crime data that offers expanded data categories of crime statistics. Removes the hierarchy rule of the UCR.

National Youth Survey Family Study: Longitudinal study of at-risk behaviors and youth.

Necessity: Refers to cases in which an individual had to break the law in order to prevent a more significant harm from occurring.

Net widening: Refers to the practice of bringing more offenders under the jurisdiction of the juvenile and criminal justice systems.

New York system: Used the system of silence that was popular in the Pennsylvania system but adopted congregate labor systems.

Nolo contendere: A no-contest plea in which the defendant does not admit guilt but accepts responsibility.

Opening statement: The first stage of the trial, when each side presents their core arguments to the judge and jury.

Opinions: A written decision of the court. Focuses on issues of law that can be used as precedent in future cases.

Oral arguments: Arguments presented by the parties to the court in an appellate case.

Order maintenance policing: Policy that directs police to handle minor incidents and crimes in an effort to prevent larger crimes in the future.

Organized crime: One of the most common forms of transnational crime, it involves the coordinated efforts of individuals for the primary purpose of engaging in criminal activity, often related to acts of financial gain.

Original jurisdiction: Courts that hear cases for the first time. Also called trial courts.

Outcome evaluation: Method of research that looks at the changes that occur as a result of a policy to determine whether it is effective.

Overcrowding: Occurs when there are more individuals in prison than a facility is designed to house.

Pain–pleasure principle: Key contribution of Cesare Beccaria that states that individuals choose their behaviors based on how much pleasure they yield from them compared with the pain that they may experience.

Panopticon: A circular structure that is placed at the center of a larger complex that is under surveillance, such as a prison. Allows an individual or small group of people to set up an observation point and watch over the larger surrounding area. Contribution of Jeremy Bentham to the field of criminology.

Parens patriae: Legal doctrine that refers to "the best interests of the child" and was used to justify the removal of youth from their families and their placement under the care of institutions.

Parole: Early release based on the behavior of the offender. Provides supervision and a system of accountability for offenders for a period of time once they are released from prison.

Parole boards: A group of officials who determine whether someone should be released from custody prior to the completion of her or his sentence.

Patrol officer: Most common classification of sworn officers. Serve as first responders.

Pauperism: Belief that certain classes of the poor were dishonest, lazy, and manipulative individuals.

Pennsylvania system: An early model of prison that focused on solitary confinement, silence, and work in cells.

Penology: A subfield of criminology that focuses on issues of punishment, incarceration, and rehabilitation.

Peremptory challenge: Allows attorneys to reject a juror without having to give a specific reason.

Perjury: Lying to cover up wrongdoing.

Physical custody: When a youth is sent to live in a temporary home, such as a group home, with a foster family, or with another family member.

Physical force: Involves the use of physical restraint techniques, such as wrist locks, bodily force, and chokeholds.

Plaintiff: A person who brings a suit in a civil case.

Plea bargain: A reduction in charges (and punishment) in exchange for a guilty plea.

Police: One of the three major components of the criminal justice system. Police are tasked with investigating crime and apprehending offenders.

Police captain: Upper-level manager within the police organization; often serves as the lead officer for a specialized unit or may be involved in a specific administrative task, such as the hiring of new officers.

Police chief: Leader of the police organization. Chiefs are typically appointed by the mayor of a city, often in consultation with the city council.

Policy: Law or practice that is used to provide guidance to criminal justice officials.

Political era: Describes the first era of policing that existed from 1840s to the early 20th century. Began with the emergence of professional police departments, which had close ties with local politicians.

Positivist school of criminology: Perspective that involves a data-driven approach to understanding criminal behavior.

Postconventional level: Level three of Lawrence Kohlberg's theory of cognitive development and crime where young adults begin to consider their worldview in light of their own moral compass.

Precedent: Refers to the legal standard whereby future decisions are required to take into consideration previous rulings.

Preconventional stage: Level one of Lawrence Kohlberg's theory of cognitive development and crime. Refers to the stage when children develop obedience and are introduced to the concept of punishment.

Predictive policing: Policy that involves taking data from sources and using the analysis to anticipate, prevent, and respond more effectively to future crime.

Preliminary hearing: One option for the court to establish whether probable cause exists for the case to move forward.

Preponderance of the evidence: The burden of proof in a civil case. Refers to when the totality of the evidence exceeds a 50% likelihood that the law was violated.

Presentence investigation report (PSI): A report to the court that makes a recommendation for a sentence based on the individual's criminal history, nature of the offense, and needs. In some cases, it involves interviews with parents/guardians, school officials, treatment providers, and social services.

Presidential Task Force on Victims of Crime: Task force created in 1982 by President Ronald Reagan to develop recommendations to reform the experience of crime victims.

Pretrial detention: Correctional practice that occurs when an offender either is denied bail or is financially unable to make bail and must remain in custody until his or her case is resolved or his or her status changes with the court.

Pretrial release programs: Programs that supervise offenders in the community prior to their court proceedings in lieu of detention. Serves as an alternative to preventative detention and saves jurisdictions money.

Preventative detention: Used in cases where the court believes that the person may be a danger to the community or would flee the jurisdiction if she or he were allowed out of jail during the pretrial stage.

Primary deviance: Refers to minor acts that are often not serious yet result in being labeled as an offender.

Prison: A facility that is designed to house individuals for a period of time as a form of punishment for breaking the law.

Prison misconduct: Refers to acts of violence, drug use, rule violations, and security-related violations that can threaten the safety and security of a facility.

Private prisons: Prisons that are used to house inmates when bed space is unavailable in state or federal facilities.

Probable cause: Legal standard that means that an officer believes that an offense has been or is about to be committed. Can be established by officer observations or information that is received by others.

Probation: Form of punishment that involves the supervision of offenders in the community in lieu of incarceration.

Probation revocation: Court hearings where offenders receive due process protections if they are to have their probation sentence rescinded and are resentenced as a result of violating the terms and conditions of their probation or if they commit a new crime.

Problem-oriented policing: Policy that encourages police officers not just to look at individual crimes or issues but rather to understand the root causes of crime. Problem-oriented policing strategies not only assist the police in fighting crime but also help to identify other issues within a community.

Procedural criminal law: Provides the legal structure and rules by which cases should move through the system.

Process evaluation: Method of research that looks at the progress of the policy development experience to determine how the policy is developing and being implemented.

Property crimes: Crimes that involve the taking of or damage to physical goods.

Prosecutorial misconduct: Can include behaviors such as the use of perjured testimony, failure to turn over exculpatory evidence, failing to disclose preferential treatment to a jailhouse informant, or misstating the law to the jury, which then impacts their decision-making process.

Prosecutorial waiver: A method of juvenile waiver that relies on the decision of the prosecutor whether to file charges in either the juvenile or criminal court.

Prostitution: A crime that involves the exchange of sexual favors for money or other resources.

Psychological theories of crime: Group of theories that explore how characteristics related to childhood development, cognitive development, and personality can be used to explain criminal behavior.

Punishment era: Emerged between 1900 and 1940, when corporal punishment and prison labor were used to punish offenders.

Racial disproportionality: Occurs when inmates of color are overrepresented in the prison population, compared with their representation in society in general.

Racial profiling: Occurs when the race or ethnicity of an individual is used as the sole or primary determinant by the police when making decisions.

Random patrols: Style of policing that allowed officers to cruise randomly throughout the streets and provide a visible police presence.

Rape and sexual assault: A crime that involves sexual activity without consent.

Rebel: One of the five components of Merton's strain theory. Refers to someone who rejects both the socially approved goals and means and replaces them with alternatives.

Recidivism: When a person returns to criminal behavior after he or she has been punished by the criminal justice system.

Reformatory era: Emerged in 1876 in response to concerns that the penitentiary was unsuccessful.

Reentry: Refers to the period of time when an offender is released from prison and returns to the community.

Reform era: Began in the 1920s as the foundation for modern policing. Agencies focused on controlling crime by apprehending offenders and deterring would-be violators.

Rehabilitation: Focuses on reforming criminal behavior so that the offender does not need or want to engage in future acts of crime.

Released on their own recognizance: Type of release where the defendant promises to appear for all future court dates but does not have to provide the court with any sort of financial guarantee.

Religious terrorism: Refers to terrorist acts that are based on one's religious belief system.

Research question: Similar to a hypothesis but is not limited to investigating causation. Research questions provide a path of study or investigation.

Restoration: The only punishment philosophy that places the victim at the core of all decision-making.

Restorative justice: Alternative model of justice that provides increased opportunities for victims to have a voice in the criminal justice process.

Result: Component of a crime that refers to the harm that is experienced as a result of the mens rea and actus reus joining together.

Retreatist: One of the five components of Merton's strain theory. Describes someone who isn't interested in traditional measures of success, nor is he or she willing to engage in hard work.

Retribution: A punishment philosophy that reflects that offenders should be punished for their bad acts purely on the basis that they violated the laws of society.

Ritualist: One of the five components of Merton's strain theory. Describes someone who rejects

socially approved goals but engages in the processes that society mandates.

Robbery: A crime that involves taking personal property from someone through the use of force or fear.

Rotten-apple theory: Suggests that the corruption of a select few individuals can, in turn, shed a negative light on a department.

Routine activities theory: Theory that suggests that a criminal act is likely to occur when someone who is interested in committing a crime converges with a potential victim and there is the absence of something that would deter the offender.

SARA: Policing model that is used to help identify problems. Stands for scanning, analysis, response, and assessment.

Search: The process by which the criminal justice system is allowed access to your personal space and belongings to determine whether evidence of a criminal act is present.

Secondary deviance: Refers to acts of deviance that occur as a result of assuming the identity of a label.

Secondary victimization: A process whereby victims feel traumatized not only as a result of their victimization experience but also by the official criminal justice system response to their victimization.

Seize: Practice that allows the police to take items and admit them into evidence.

Self-defense: Defense strategy that allows for the use of force to defend oneself against an attacker.

Self-fulfilling prophecy: Describes the process whereby individuals who may not have been engaging in serious acts initially may subsequently be drawn to these negative behaviors as a result of being labeled as an offender.

Self-reported data: Refers to crime statistics that are based on personal disclosures.

Sergeant: First rank in a police organization that carries supervisory duties.

Severity: One of the three characteristics that is required in order for deterrence to be effective. Refers to the notion that punishment must be harsh enough in order to deter people from criminal behavior.

Sex trafficking: Victims of human trafficking who are required to participate in acts of prostitution and other forms sexual slavery.

Shakedowns: A form of corruption that involves taking items without paying for them.

Shock probation: See *split-sentence probation.*

Social bond theory: Theory that focuses on why people might desist from criminal behavior. Travis Hirschi identified four criteria that prevent people from acting on potential criminological impulses: attachment, commitment, involvement, and belief.

Social disorganization theory: Theory that investigates how neighborhood environments contribute to criminal behavior.

Social learning theory: Theory that suggests that people learn from observing the behaviors of others around them.

Sociological theories of crime: Describes macrolevel theories that look at how larger social structures can help explain criminal behavior.

Specific deterrence: Looks at how an individual may avoid criminal behavior if the potential punishment is viewed as undesirable.

Split-sentence probation: Form of punishment that involves the use of a short-term incarceration sentence in conjunction with a traditional probation sentence. Also referred to as *shock probation.*

Stare decisis: Latin for "to stand by things settled." Refers to the system of precedent.

State law enforcement: Often defined as highway patrols. Provides investigative and emergency assistance to local agencies.

State prisons: Prisons used to hold offenders convicted of state criminal law violations.

State-sponsored terrorism: Acts of terrorism that are ordered by government officials.

Status offenses: Refers to acts that are considered illegal for only certain groups of offenders based on their age.

Statutory law: Laws that are established by governments.

Statutory rape: A crime that involves sexual activity with someone who is legally unable to consent to sexual activity due to her or his age.

Stop and frisk: Policy that allows for police to use their discretion to briefly detain an individual if they believe that the individual may be engaging in illegal behavior and to pat down the individual's exterior clothing if they believe that the individual may have a weapon.

Strain theory: Theory that focuses on stress and frustration as a cause of criminality.

Strict liability: Select cases where acts are crimes even if the individual lacked the mens rea or intent to commit a crime.

Subject matter jurisdiction: Courts that hear specific types of cases based on their topic.

Substantive criminal law: Defines what makes behavior a criminal act under the law.

Supermax: Prisons designed to house the worst of the worst offenders. Inmates are confined to their cells for 23 hours a day.

Superpredator: A term created by DiIulio that predicted a new wave of kids who would not have any sense of remorse for their crimes. Predictions about the superpredator had a significant impact on policies and practices related to juvenile crime.

Supervised probation: A type of probation sentence where the offender is required to check in either face to face or by telephone on a particular schedule.

Technical violation: Refers to violations of the terms and conditions of probation.

Terrorism: A crime that involves acts of violence with the goal of instilling fear.

Theory: A set of ideas that is used to explain a particular phenomenon or concept.

Transnational crimes: Acts that (1) occur across the boundaries of different countries; (2) involve migration between borders as part of the criminal activity; (3) take place in one country but involve a group that engages in similar activity in several regions; or (4) take place in one country but have a significant effect on another region.

Treason: A crime that involves acts that attempt to overthrow the government.

Trial court: A court of original jurisdiction that hears issues of fact and makes decisions based on the law.

Trial jury: A group of citizens who are charged with listening to the evidence that is presented by the attorneys and making a judgment of whether someone is guilty or liable.

Type 1 offenses: Also known as index crimes under the Uniform Crime Reports. Includes eight specific crime categories: murder, aggravated assault, rape and sexual assault, robbery, burglary, motor vehicle theft, larceny-theft, and arson.

Uniform Crime Reports: One of the largest datasets on crime. Based on police arrest and reporting data.

Unsupervised probation: A type of probation where individuals are generally not required to check in with a probation officer but are required to meet certain terms and conditions set forth by the court.

U.S. courts of appeals: Intermediate courts of appeals that hear cases of law from the U.S. district courts or from the federal administrative courts.

U.S. district courts: Courts of general jurisdiction in the federal courts system.

U.S. magistrate courts: First level of courts in the federal courts system. Courts of limited jurisdiction, they generally hear misdemeanor cases.

U.S. Supreme Court: Highest court that can hear cases. Makes decisions based on issues of law. Decisions are used to establish precedent in subsequent cases.

USA PATRIOT Act (2001): Federal legislation that focused on tactics to investigate terrorist activities and apprehend terrorists.

Vandalism: A crime that involves the destruction or damage of a physical structure or building.

Verdict: A decision in a case.

Victim: Someone who has been injured or harmed by the actions of another.

Victim and Witness Protection Act of 1982: Passed by Congress to provide fair treatment standards to crime victims and witnesses.

Victim blaming: Enables people to make sense of the victimization and makes them feel somehow different from the person who is victimized.

Victimless crimes: Crimes that involve acts of self-harm or consensual behaviors.

Victimology: A field of study within criminology that places the victim at the center of the discussion.

Victims of Crime Act: Federal legislation that established the crime victims fund.

Violence Against Women Act: Federal legislation that provided victims of intimate partner violence support through the allocation of federal funds to prosecute offenders, coordination of services for victims, and establishment of the Office of Violence Against Women.

Violent offenses: Crimes that typically involve acts against another person.

Visa: A document that is required for an individual to enter, reside, work, or study in a country.

Voir dire: The process of questioning by the prosecutor and the defense attorney that is used to select a trial jury.

Warrant: A legal document that allows an officer to complete a search of a person's belongings.

Wedding cake model: Model that demonstrates how cases are treated differently by the criminal justice process.

White-collar crime: Describes a category of offenses that traditionally occur within the corporate field.

Work/study release: A type of program that allows offenders to leave the facility during the day to go to work or school and return in the evenings and weekends to take advantage of training and rehabilitative programs.

Writ of certiorari: A petition to the U.S. Supreme Court to hear a case.

Youth Risk Behavior Surveillance System: Research study by the CDC that focuses on health and youth risk behaviors among high school students.

ENDNOTES

CHAPTER 1

1. Nathan Hardin, "Sabrina Buie's Family Stunned by Release of Two Men Convicted of Killing Her in 1983," *Fayetteville Observer*, September 5, 2014, http://www.fayobserver.com/news/local/sabrina-buie-s-family-stunned-by-release-of-two-men/article_e2f6d2a7-055a-516d-a87a-6668455368de.html.

2. Jonathan M. Katz and Erik Eckholm, "DNA Evidence Clears Two Men in 1983 Murder," *New York Times*, September 2, 2014, http://www.nytimes.com/2014/09/03/us/2-convicted-in-1983-north-carolina-murder-freed-after-dna-tests.html?_r=0.

3. Nicole Carr, "Sabrina Buie Family: 'It Feels Like Hell,'" ABC News, September 3, 2014, http://abc11.com/news/sabrina-buie-family-responds-to-overturned-convict-/293662.

4. Bureau of Justice Statistics, "The Justice System," n.d., http://www.bjs.gov/content/justsys.cfm.

5. Alan Duke and Michael Pearson, "CeeLo Green Accused of Giving Woman Ecstasy, but DA Declines Rape Charge," CNN Entertainment, October 22, 2013, http://www.cnn.com/2013/10/21/showbiz/ceelo-green-drug-charge.

6. Faith Karimi and Richard Allen Greene, "Oscar Pistorius Guilty of Negligent Killing of Girlfriend, One Gun Charge," CNN World, September 12, 2014, http://www.cnn.com/2014/09/12/world/africa/oscar-pistorius-verdict; Harriet Alexander and Aislinn Laing, "Twenty Years Later, Oscar Pistorius Verdict Mirrors OJ Simpson Decision, Victim's Sister Says," *National Post*, September 14, 2014, http://sports.nationalpost.com/2014/09/14/twenty-years-later-oscar-pistorius-verdict-mirrors-oj-simpson-decision.

7. Herbert L. Packer, *The Limits of the Criminal Sanction* (Stanford, CA: Stanford University Press, 1968).

8. Kenneth Dowler, "Media Consumption and Public Attitudes Toward Crime and Justice: The Relationship Between Fear of Crime, Punitive Attitudes, and Perceived Police Effectiveness," *Journal of Criminal Justice and Popular Culture* 10, no. 2 (2003): 109–126; Ray Surette, *Media, Crime, and Criminal Justice: Images and Realities* (Belmont, CA: Wadsworth, 2010).

9. James Garofalo, "Crime and the Mass Media: A Selective Review of Research. *Journal of Research in Crime and Delinquency* 18, no. 2 (1981): 319–350.

10. Jason Ditton, Derek Chadee, Stephan Farrall, Elizabeth Gilchrist, and Jon Bannister, "From Imitation to Intimidation: A Note on the Curious and Changing Relationship Between the Media, Crime and Fear of Crime," *British Journal of Criminology* 44, no. 4 (2004): 595–610.

11. Eric J. Boos, "Moving in the Direction of Justice: College Minds—Criminal Mentalities," *Journal of Criminal Justice and Popular Culture* 5, no. 1 (1997): 1–20.

12. Dowler.

13. Paul Klite, Robert A. Bardwell, and Jason Salzman, "Local TV News: Getting Away With Murder," *The Harvard International Journal of Press/Politics* 2, no. 2 (1997): 102–112.

14. Doris Graber, *Crime News and the Public* (New York: Prager, 1980).

15. Rhoda Estep and Patrick T. MacDonald, "How Prime-Time Crime Evolved on TV, 1976 to 1983," in *Justice and the Media: Issues and Research*, ed. Ray Surette (Springfield, IL: Charles C. Thomas Publishers, 1984), 110–123.

16. Michele C. Black, Kathleen C. Basile, Matthew J. Breiding, Sharon G. Smith, Mikel L. Walters, Melissa T. Merrick, Jieru Chen, and Mark R. Stevens, *The National Intimate Partner and Sexual Violence Survey (NISVS): 2010 Summary Report* (Atlanta: National Center for Injury Prevention and Control, Centers for Disease Control and Prevention, 2011).

17. Mary Beth Oliver and G. Blake Armstrong, "Predictors of Viewing and Enjoyment of Reality Based and Fictional Crime Shows," *Journalism and Mass Communication Quarterly* 72 (1995): 559–570.

18. Lisa A. Kort-Butler and Kelley J. Sittner Hartshorn, "Watching the Detectives: Crime Programming, Fear of Crime, and Attitudes About the Criminal Justice System," *Sociological Quarterly* 52, no. 1 (2011): 36–55.

19. Kort-Butler and Sittner Hartshorn.

20. Todd C. Trautman, "Concerns About Crime and Local Television News," *Communication Research Reports* 21, no. 3 (2003): 310–315.

21. Natasha A. Frost and Nickie D. Phillips, "Talking Heads: Crime Reporting on Cable News," *Justice Quarterly* 28, no. 1 (2011): 87–112.

22. Ashley Marie Nellis and Joanne Savage, "Does Watching the News Affect Fear of Terrorism? The Importance of Media Exposure on Terrorism Fear," *Crime and Delinquency* 58, no. 5 (2012): 748–768.

23. Samuel Walker and Charles Katz, *The Police in America: An Introduction*, 4th ed. (New York: McGraw-Hill, 2002).

24. Shaun L. Gabbidon and Helen Taylor Greene, *Race and Crime*, 3rd ed. (Thousand Oaks, CA: Sage, 2013); Walker and Katz.

25. Gabbidon and Greene.

26. Gabbidon and Greene.

27. Lauren Glaze and Thomas Bonczar, *Probation and Parole in the United States, 2010* (Washington, DC: Bureau of Justice Statistics, 2010).

28. Barbara Perry, *Policing Race and Place in Indiana Country: Over- and Underenforcement* (Lanham, MD: Lexington Books, 2009); Samuel Walker, Cassia Spohn, and Miriam DeLone, *The Color of Justice: Race, Ethnicity, and Crime in America*, 5th ed. (Belmont, CA: Wadsworth, 2012).

29. Wendy Regoeczi and Stephanie L. Kent, "Race, Poverty, and the Traffic Ticket Cycle: Exploring the Situational Context of the Application of Police Discretion," *Policing: An International Journal of Police Strategies & Management* 37, no. 1 (2014): 190–205.

30. Christine Eith and Matthew R. Durose, *Contacts Between Police and the Public, 2008* (Washington, DC: Bureau of Justice Statistics, 2008).

31. Gregg Barak, Paul Leighton, and Allison Cotton, *Class, Race, Gender, & Crime: The Social Realities of Justice in America*, 4th ed. (Lanham, MD: Rowman & Littlefield, 2015).

32. Marvin D. Free Jr., "Racial Bias and the American Criminal Justice System: Race and Presentencing Revisited," *Critical Criminology* 10 (2002): 195–223.

33. Cassia C. Spohn, "Thirty Years of Sentencing Reform: The Quest for a Racially Neutral Sentencing Process," in *Policies, Processes and Decisions of the Criminal Justice System*, Vol. 3, ed. Julie Horney (Washington, DC: National Institute of Justice, 2000), 427–501.

34. Darrell Steffensmeier and Stephen Demuth, "Ethnicity and Sentencing Outcomes in U.S. Federal Courts: Who Is Punished More Harshly?" *American Sociological Review* 65, no. 5 (2000): 705–729; Darrell Steffensmeier and Stephen Demuth, "Ethnicity and Judges' Sentencing Decisions: Hispanic-Black-White Comparisons," *Criminology* 39, no. 1 (2001): 145–178.

35. Barak, Leighton, and Cotton.

36. Spohn.

37. Darrell Steffensmeier, Jeffery Ulmer, and John Kramer, "The Interaction of Race, Gender, and Age in Criminal Sentencing: The Punishment Cost of Being Young, Black, and Male," *Criminology* 36, no. 4 (1998): 763–798.

38. James M. A. Pitts, O. Hayden Griffin III, and W. Wesley Johnson, "Contemporary Prison Overcrowding: Short-Term Fixes to a Perpetual Problem," *Contemporary Justice Review* 17, no. 1 (2014): 124–139.

39. Lauren E. Glaze and Erinn J. Herberman, *Correctional Populations in the United States, 2012* (Washington, DC: Bureau of Justice Statistics, 2013).

40. Matthew Robinson and Mariam Williams, "The Myth of a Fair Criminal Justice System," *Justice Policy Journal* 6, no. 1 (2009): http://www.cjcj.org/uploads/cjcj/documents/the_myth.pdf.

41. Robert A. Schug and Henry F. Fradella, *Mental Illness and Crime* (Thousand Oaks, CA: Sage, 2015).

42. Schug and Fradella.

Around the World: Crime, Law, and Justice From a Global Perspective

a. Canan Arin, "Femicide in the Name of Honor in Turkey," *Violence Against Women* 7, no. 7 (2001): 821–825.

b. Will Ripley, "First on CNN: U.S. Student Detained in North Korea Confesses to 'Hostile Act,'" CNN, February 29, 2016, http://www.cnn.com/2016/02/28/asia/north-korea-otto-warmbier.

Spotlight:
The State v. Jodi Arias

a. Catherine E. Shoichet, "Jodi Arias Guilty of First-Degree Murder; Death Penalty Possible," CNN, May 9, 2013, http://www.cnn.com/2013/05/08/justice/arizona-jodi-arias-verdict.

b. Mari Fagel, "Jury Questions to Jodi Arias Illustrate Their Frustration With Her Story," Huffington Post, May 8, 2013, http://www.huffingtonpost.com/mari-fagel/jodi-arias-jury-questions_b_2825167.html.

c. Crimesider Staff, "Jodi Arias Sentenced to Life in Prison Without Parole," CBS News, April 13, 2015, http://www.cbsnews.com/news/jodi-arias-sentenced-to-life-in-prison-without-parole.

CHAPTER 2

1. "Timeline: Colorado Theater Shooting," CNN, July 21, 2012, http://www.cnn.com/interactive/2012/07/us/aurora.shooting/index.html.

2. Nicholas Riccardi and P. Solomon Banda, "Colo. Suspect Charges: Murder, Attempted Murder," Yahoo News, July 31, 2012, http://news.yahoo.com/colo-suspect-charges-murder-attempted-murder-180843200.html.

3. NAACP Legal Defense Fund, "Death Row USA," n.d., http://www.naacpldf.org/death-row-usa.

4. Jason Sickles, "Details Emerge About Jury Picked for Colorado Theater Shooting Trial," Yahoo News, April 15, 2015, http://news.yahoo.com/details-emerge-about-jury-picked-for-colorado-theater-shooting-trial-192409225.html.

5. Ann O'Neill, "James Holmes' Life Story Didn't Sway Jury," CNN, August 11, 2015, http://www.cnn.com/2015/08/02/us/13th-juror-james-holmes-aurora-shooting.

6. Julie Turkewitz, "Life or Death for Colorado Theater Gunman Now in Jurors' Hands," *New York Times*, August 6, 2015, http://www.nytimes.com/2015/08/07/us/life-or-death-for-colorado-theater-gunman-now-in-jurors-hands.html?ref=topics.

7. Julie Turkewitz, "James Holmes Gets 12 Life Sentences in Aurora Shootings," *New York Times*, August 26, 2015, http://www.nytimes.com/2015/08/27/us/james-holmes-gets-12-life-sentences-in-aurora-shootings.html?ref=topics.

8. Andrea Gerlin, "A Matter of Degree: How a Jury Decided That a Coffee Spill Is Worth $2.9 Million," *Wall Street Journal*, September 1, 1994, http://www.business.txstate.edu/users/ds26/Business%20Law%202361/Misc/McDonalds%20coffee.pdf.

9. "The Code of Hammurabi," translated by L. W. King, n.d., http://avalon.law.yale.edu/ancient/hamframe.asp.

10. "Roman Legal Tradition and the Compilation of Justinian System," n.d., https://www.law.berkeley.edu/library/robbins/RomanLegalTradition.html.

11. Phillip L. Gianos and Stephen J. Stambough, "California's Constitution, Direct Democracy, and the California Criminal Justice System," in *California's Criminal Justice System*, eds. Christine L. Gardiner and Pamela Fiber-Ostrow (Durham, NC: Carolina Academic Press, 2014), 73–86.

12. John G. Geer, Wendy J. Schiller, Jeffrey A. Segal, Richard Herrera, and Ana K. Glencross, *Gateways to Democracy: An Introduction to American Government: The Essentials* (Boston: Cengage Learning, 2016).

13. Kate Mather, "California Loosens Jessica's Law Rules on Where Sex Offenders Can Live," *Los Angeles Times*, March 26, 2015, http://www.latimes.com/local/lanow/la-me-ln-california-sex-offenders-20150326-story.html; In re William Taylor et al., Cal. Sup. Ct. No. S206143 (2015), http://www.courts.ca.gov/opinions/archive/S206143.PDF.

14. Ralph F. Fuchs, review of *Attorney General's Manual on the Administrative Procedure Act* by the United States Department of Justice and *The Federal Administrative Procedure Act and the Administrative Agencies*, Vol. VII of the New York University School of Law Institute Proceedings, *Indiana Law Journal* 23, no. 3 (1948): 362–374, http://www.repository .law.indiana.edu/cgi/viewcontent .cgi?article=3869&context=ilj.

15. Animal Legal Defense Fund, "Animal Fighting Case Study: Michael Vick," 2011, http://aldf .org/resources/laws-cases/animal-fighting-case-study-michael-vick; Animal Legal Defense Fund, "Animal Fighting Facts," 2009, http://aldf.org/resources/laws-cases/ animal-fighting-facts.

16. American Society for the Prevention of Cruelty to Animals, n.d., https:// www.aspca.org/fight-cruelty/field-investigations-and-response-team/ blood-sports/investigation-and-trial-michael-vick-april-2007.

17. *Rodriguez v. United States* (2015), http://www.supremecourt.gov/ opinions/14pdf/13-9972_p8k0.pdf.

18. Legal Information Institute, "Crime," http://www.law.cornell.edu/wex/ crime.

19. U.S. Drug Enforcement Administration, "Title 21 United States Code, Controlled Substance Act," n.d., http://www.deadiversion .usdoj.gov/21cfr/21usc/844.htm.

20. The National Registry of Exonerations, "Anthony Porter," 2012, https://www.law.umich.edu/special/ exoneration/Pages/casedetail .aspx?caseid=3544.

21. The National Registry of Exonerations, "Earl Washington," 2012, http://www.law.umich.edu/ special/exoneration/pages/casedetail .aspx?caseid=3721.

22. Associated Press, "John Hinckley Jr., Man Who Shot Reagan, Seeks to Live Outside Mental Hospital," *Fox News*, April 22, 2015, http://www.foxnews .com/politics/2015/04/22/man-who-shot-reagan-seeks-to-live-outside-mental-hospital.

23. Homer D. Crotty, "History of Insanity as a Defence to Crime in English Criminal Law," *California Law Review* 12, no. 2 (1924): 105–123.

24. PBS, "From Daniel M'Naughten to John Hinckley: A Brief History of the Insanity Defense—The A.L.I. Standard," n.d., http://www.pbs .org/wgbh/pages/frontline/shows/ crime/trial/history.html#ali; see also Carol A. Rolf, "From M'Naughten to Yates: Transformation of the Insanity Defense in the U.S.—Is It Still Viable?" *River College Online Academic Journal* 2, no. 1 (2006): 1–18.

25. John D. Melville and David Naimark, "Punishing the Insane: The Verdict of Guilty but Mentally Ill," *Journal of the American Academy of Psychiatry and the Law* 30, no. 4 (2002): 553–555.

26. Jeré Longman, "John E. du Pont, Heir Who Killed an Olympian, Dies at 72," *New York Times*, December 9, 2010, http://www.nytimes.com/2010/12/10/ sports/olympics/10dupont.html.

27. Eliana Dockterman, "The True Story Behind *Foxcatcher*," *Time*, November 14, 2014, http://time.com/3584685/ foxcatcher-true-story.

28. United Nations Office on Drugs and Crime, *World Drug Report, 2011* (Vienna: UNODC, 2011), http:// www.unodc.org.

29. Federal Bureau of Investigation, *Crime in the United States, 2014* (Washington, DC: FBI, 2015), https:// www.fbi.gov/about-us/cjis/ucr/ crime-in-the-u.s/2014/crime-in-the-u.s.-2014/tables/table-29.

30. American Civil Liberties Union, *The War on Marijuana in Black and White* (New York: ACLU, 2013), https://www.aclu.org/sites/default/ files/field_document/1114413-mj-report-rfs-rel1.pdf.

31. Title 21 United States Code Controlled Substance Act, Subchapter I, Part B, Section 812, http://www.deadiversion.usdoj .gov/21cfr/21usc/812.htm.

32. Food and Drug Administration, "News Release: Inter-Agency Advisory Regarding Claims That Smoked Marijuana Is a Medicine," April 20, 2006, http://www.fda .gov/NewsEvents/Newsroom/ PressAnnouncements/2006/ ucm108643.htm.

33. Devin Dwyer, "Marijuana Not High Obama Priority," ABC News, December 14, 2012, http://abcnews .go.com/Politics/OTUS/president-obama-marijuana-users-high-priority-drug-war/story?id=17946783.

34. For a list of these cases, see Rolando del Carmen and Craig Hemmens, *Criminal Procedure: Law and Practice*, 10th ed. (Belmont, CA: Cengage, 2016).

Spotlight: Concealed Weapons on College Campuses

a. National Conference of State Legislatures, "Guns on Campus: Overview," October 5, 2015, http:// www.ncsl.org/research/education/ guns-on-campus-overview.aspx.

b. Tyler Kingkade, "Texas Lawmaker Says Students Already Bring Guns to Class Illegally," *Huffington Post*, October 7, 2015, http:// www.huffingtonpost.com/entry/ fletcher-guns-in-class-texas_ us_56154c55e4b021e856d31e35.

c. Matthew Watkins, "Did You Think Campus Carry Was Settled Law?" *Texas Tribune*, June 16, 2015, http:// www.texastribune.org/2015/06/16/ new-law-campus-carry-debate-begins-anew.

d. Bob Price, "Greg Abbott Affirms Teacher Authority to Carry Concealed Weapons in Texas," Breitbart, April 20, 2014, http://www.breitbart.com/ texas/2014/04/20/greg-abbott-affirms-teacher-authority-to-carry-concealed-weapons.

e. "University of Maryland Eastern Shore Buys Bulletproof Whiteboards for Professors," *Huffington Post*, August 16, 2013, http://www.huffingtonpost .com/2013/08/16/bulletproof-whiteboards-university_n_ 3768194.html.

f. Associated Press, "Gov. Jerry Brown Signs Bill Banning Concealed Guns From California Schools," Fox News, October 11, 2015, http:// www.foxnews.com/us/2015/10/11/ gov-jerry-brown-signs-bill-banning-concealed-guns-from-california-schools.

g. Tyler Kingkade, "Steve Bullock Vetoes Bill That Allowed Guns at Montana Colleges," *Huffington Post*, May 7, 2013, http://www .huffingtonpost.com/2013/05/07/ steve-bullock-veto-guns-campus-carry_n_3229859.html.

Around the World:
International Law

a. United Nations, "About the UN," n.d., http://www.un.org/en/about-un/index.html.

b. United Nations, International Convention for the Suppression of the Financing of Terrorism, December 9, 1999, http://www.un.org/law/cod/finterr.htm.

c. United Nations, "Uphold International Law," n.d., http://www.un.org/en/sections/what-we-do/uphold-international-law/index.html.

d. Special Court for Sierra Leone, n.d., http://www.rscsl.org.

e. International Criminal Court, "Situations and Cases," n.d., https://www.icc-cpi.int/en_menus/icc/situations%20and%20cases/Pages/situations%20and%20cases.aspx.

Careers in Criminal Justice:
So You Want to Be a Defense
Attorney?

a. Powell v. Alabama, 287 U.S. 45 (1932).

b. Gideon v. Wainwright, 372 U.S. 335 (1963).

CHAPTER 3

1. Reid Wilson, "FBI: Chicago Passes New York as Murder Capital of U.S.," *Washington Post*, September 18, 2013, http://www.washingtonpost.com/blogs/govbeat/wp/2013/09/18/fbi-chicago-passes-new-york-as-murder-capital-of-u-s.

2. Drew DeSilver, "Despite Recent Shootings, Chicago Nowhere Near U.S. 'Murder Capital,'" Pew Research Center, July 14, 2014, http://www.pewresearch.org/fact-tank/2014/07/14/despite-recent-shootings-chicago-nowhere-near-u-s-murder-capital.

3. Don Babwin, "Chicago Homicides Down Drastically in 2013 to Fewest Murders Since 1965, Police Say," *Huffington Post*, January 23, 2014, http://www.huffingtonpost.com/2014/01/02/chicago-homicides-down-dr_n_4531328.html.

4. DeSilver.

5. John M. Hagedorn, "What's Really Driving Down the Murder Rate," *Chicago Sun Times*, April 26, 2014, http://www.suntimes.com/news/otherviews/26208033-452/whats-really-driving-down-chicagos-murder-rate.html#.VCjnxFZORg0.

6. David Bernstein and Noah Isackson, "The Truth About Chicago's Crime Rate," *Chicago Magazine*, April 7, 2014, http://www.chicagomag.com/Chicago-Magazine/May-2014/Chicago-crime-rates.

7. David O. Friedrichs, *Trusted Criminals: White Collar Crime in Contemporary Society*, 4th ed. (Belmont, CA: Wadsworth, 2010); Brian K. Payne, *White-Collar Crime: The Essentials* (Thousand Oaks, CA: Sage, 2013).

8. Richard A. Oppel Jr. and Andrew Ross Sorkin, "Enron's Collapse: The Overview; Enron Collapses as Suitor Cancels Plans for Merger," *New York Times*, November 29, 2001, http://www.nytimes.com/2001/11/29/business/enron-s-collapse-the-overview-enron-collapses-as-suitor-cancels-plans-for-merger.html.

9. Dierdre Fernandes, "Mass. Gets $55m From Citigroup," *Boston Globe*, July 14, 2014, http://www.bostonglobe.com/business/2014/07/14/massachusetts-get-least-million-relief-from-citigroup-settlement/4IlSJhgnAcquAgxu5GMRtM/story.html; Leslie Scism and Christina Rexrode, "Bank of America to Pay $650 Million to AIG in Mortgage Disputes," *Wall Street Journal*, July 16, 2014, http://online.wsj.com/articles/bank-of-america-to-pay-650-million-to-aig-in-mortgage-disputes-1405547611; Ben Protess and Jessica Silver-Greenberg, "Tentative Deal Hands JPMorgan Chase a Record Penalty," *New York Times*, October 19, 2013, http://dealbook.nytimes.com/2013/10/19/jpmorgan-said-to-be-discussing-13-billion-settlement-over-mortgage-loans/?_php=true&_type=blogs&_r=0.

10. Tom Fowler, "Ex-Enron CEO Skilling's Sentence Cut to 14 Years," *Wall Street Journal*, June 21, 2013, http://online.wsj.com/news/articles/SB10001424127887323393804578559603861442848.

11. Richard Eskow, "JPMorgan Chase: 'Incredibly Guilty,'" *Huffington Post*, September 20, 2013, http://www.huffingtonpost.com/rj-eskow/jpmorgan-chase-incredibly_b_3964788.html.

12. Stephen M. Rosoff, Henry N. Pontell, and Robert Tillman, *Profit Without Honor: White Collar Crime and the Looting of America*, 6th ed. (Upper Saddle River, NJ: Prentice-Hall, 2013).

13. Robert M. Bohm, *DeathQuest: An Introduction to the Theory and Practice of Capital Punishment in the United States*, 4th ed. (Newark, NJ: Anderson Publishing, 2011).

14. Ronald Radosh, "Case Closed: The Rosenbergs Were Soviet Spies," *Los Angeles Times*, September 17, 2008, http://www.latimes.com/la-oe-radosh17-2008sep17-story.html.

15. Global Terrorism Database, http://start.umd.edu/gtd.

16. Federal Bureau of Investigation, "Attorney General Eric Holder Announces Revisions to the Uniform Crime Report's Definition of Rape," January 6, 2012, http://www.fbi.gov/news/pressrel/press-releases/attorney-general-eric-holder-announces-revisions-to-the-uniform-crime-reports-definition-of-rape.

17. Uniform Crime Reporting Program, *Reporting Rape in 2013: Summary Reporting System (SRS) User Manual and Technical Specification* (Washington, DC: FBI, 2014), http://www.fbi.gov/about-us/cjis/ucr/recent-program-updates/reporting-rape-in-2013-revised.

18. Federal Bureau of Investigation, "UCR General FAQs," n.d., http://www.fbi.gov/about-us/cjis/ucr/frequently-asked-questions/ucr_faqs.

19. Sophia M. Robison, "A Critical Review of the Uniform Crime Reports," *Michigan Law Review* 64, no. 6 (1966): 1033.

20. Federal Bureau of Investigation, *National Incident Based Reporting System (NIBRS) User Manual* (Washington, DC: FBI, 2013), http://www.fbi.gov/about-us/cjis/ucr/nibrs/nibrs-user-manual.

21. Federal Bureau of Investigation, "2012 National Incident-Based Reporting System," http://www.fbi.gov/about-us/cjis/ucr/nibrs/2012.

22. Federal Bureau of Investigation, "Crimes Against Persons Incidents, Offense Categories by Time of Day, 2012," http://www.fbi.gov/about-us/

cjis/ucr/nibrs/2012/table-pdfs/crimes-against-persons-incidents-offense-category-by-time-of-day-2012; Federal Bureau of Investigation, "Crimes Against Property Incidents, Offense Categories by Time of Day, 2012," http://www.fbi.gov/about-us/cjis/ucr/nibrs/2012/table-pdfs/crimes-against-property-incidents-offense-category-by-time-of-day-2012; Federal Bureau of Investigation, "Crimes Against Society Incidents, Offense Categories by Time of Day, 2012," http://www.fbi.gov/about-us/cjis/ucr/nibrs/2012/table-pdfs/crimes-against-society-incidents-offense-category-by-time-of-day-2012.

23. Justice Research and Statistics Association, "Status of NIBRS in the States," n.d., http://www.jrsa.org/ibrrc/background-status/nibrs-states.html.

24. Jennifer L. Truman and Michael Planty, *Criminal Victimization, 2011* (U.S. Department of Justice, Bureau of Justice Statistics, 2012), http://www.bjs.gov/content/pub/pdf/cv11.pdf.

25. Nancy D. Brener, Laura Kann, Shari Shanklin, Steve Kinchen, Danice K. Eaton, Joseph Hawkins, and Katherine H. Flint, "Methodology of the Youth Risk Behavior Surveillance System—2013," *Morbidity and Mortality Weekly Report* 62, no. 1 (2013): http://www.cdc.gov/mmwr/pdf/rr/rr6201.pdf.

26. Laura Kann, Steve Kinchen, Shari L. Shanklin, Katherine H. Flint, Joseph Hawkins, William A. Harris, Richard Lowry, Emily O'Malley Olsen, Tim McManus, David Chyen, Lisa Whittle, Eboni Taylor, Zewditu Demissie, Nancy Brener, Jemekia Thornton, John Moore, and Stephanie Zaza, "Youth Risk Behavior Surveillance—United States, 2013," *MMWR* 63, no. 4 (2014): http://www.cdc.gov/mmwr/pdf/ss/ss6304.pdf.

27. National Youth Survey Family Study, http://www.colorado.edu/ibg/human-research-studies/national-youth-survey-family-study.

28. James Q. Wilson, *Thinking About Crime* (New York: Basic Books, 1975), 407.

29. Cynthia Barnett, *The Measurement of White-Collar Crime Using Uniform Crime Reporting (UCR) Data* (Washington, DC: Federal Bureau of Investigation, n.d.), http://www.fbi.gov/stats-services/about-us/cjis/ucr/nibrs/nibrs_wcc.pdf.

30. Richard T. Wright and Scott H. Decker, *Armed Robbers in Action: Stickups and Street Culture* (Boston: Northeastern University Press, 1997); Richard T. Wright and Scott H. Decker, *Burglars on the Job: Streetlife and Residential Break-Ins* (Boston: Northeastern University Press, 1994).

31. Gretchen Morgenson and Louise Story, "In Financial Crisis, No Prosecution of Top Figures," *New York Times*, April 14, 2011, A1, A12.

32. Richard A. Posner, *A Failure of Capitalism: The Crisis of '08 and the Descent Into Depression* (Cambridge, MA: Harvard University Press, 2009).

33. *Black's Law Dictionary*, 6th ed. (St. Paul, MN: West Publishing Company, 1990).

34. Richard F. Culp, Phillip M. Kopp, and Candace McCoy, *Is Burglary a Crime of Violence? An Analysis of National Data 1998–2007* (Rockville, MD: National Criminal Justice Reference Service, 2015), https://www.ncjrs.gov/pdffiles1/nij/grants/248651.pdf.

35. Armed Career Criminal Act of 1986, 18 U.S.C. § 924(e)(2)(B) (1986).

36. *Taylor v. United States*, 495 U.S. 575 (1990).

37. *James v. United States*, 550 U.S. 192 (2007).

38. Armed Career Criminal Act: Hearing on H.R. 4639 and H.R. 4768 Before the Subcommittee on Crime of the House Committee on the Judiciary, 99th Cong, 2d Sess. (1986); Armed Career Criminal Acts Amendments: Hearing on S. 2312 Before the Subcommittee on Criminal Law of the Senate Committee on the Judiciary, 99th Cong., 2d Sess. (1986).

39. *James v. United States* (2007).

40. Culp, Kopp, and McCoy.

41. Ibid.

42. Ibid.

43. Ibid.

Spotlight: The Steubenville High School Rape Case

a. U.S. Census, "Quick Facts, Stubenville, OH," 2013, http://quickfacts.census.gov/qfd/states/39/3974608.html.

b. Alexander Abad-Santos, "Everything You Need to Know About Steubenville High's Football 'Rape Crew,'" The Wire, January 3, 2013, http://www.thewire.com/national/2013/01/steubenville-high-football-rape-crew/60554.

c. Richard A. Oppel Jr., "Ohio Teenagers Guilty in Rape That Social Media Brought to Light," *New York Times*, March 17, 2013, http://www.nytimes.com/2013/03/18/us/teenagers-found-guilty-in-rape-in-steubenville-ohio.html?pagewanted=all&_r=0.

d. Abad-Santos.

e. Andrew Welsh-Huggins, "Teen in Steubenville Rape Case: 'I Could Not Remember Anything,'" *Huffington Post*, March 16, 2013, http://www.huffingtonpost.com/2013/03/16/steubenville-rape-case-teen-cant-recall-assault_n_2893398.html?utm_hp_ref=steubenville-rape.

f. Oppel.

g. Christina Ng, "Steubenville, Ohio, Football Players Convicted in Rape Trial," ABC News, March 17, 2013, http://abcnews.go.com/US/steubenville-football-players-guilty-ohio-rape-trial/story?id=18748493.

h. Poppy Harlow, "Guilty Verdict in Steubenville Rape Trial," CNN, March 17, 2013, http://transcripts.cnn.com/TRANSCRIPTS/1303/17/rs.01.html.

i. Associated Press, "One of Two Teens Convicted in Steubenville Rape Case Released," Fox News, January 7, 2014, http://www.foxnews.com/us/2014/01/07/one-two-teens-convicted-in-steubenville-rape-case-released.

j. Rachel Dissell, "Rape Charges Against High School Players Divide Football Town of Steubenville, Ohio," *Cleveland Plain Dealer*, September 2, 2012, http://www.cleveland.com/metro/index.ssf/2012/09/rape_charges_divide_football_t.html.

k. Associated Press and Huffington Post, "Steubenville Grand Jury Investigation: Four More School Employees Indicted," *Huffington Post*, November 25, 2013, http://www.huffingtonpost.com/2013/11/25/steubenville-grand-jury-investigation_n_4337646.html?utm_hp_ref=steubenville-rape.

Spotlight: The Boston Marathon Bombing

a. Mark Arsenault, "Second Marathon Bombing Suspect Captured," *Boston Globe*, April 20, 2013, http://www.bostonglobe.com/metro/2013/04/20/second-marathon-suspect-captured-manhunt-ends/4ICVhfRArrGjgsiJnzJ2mM/story.html.

b. David Abel and Martin Finucane, "Tsarnaev Indicted on 30 Counts," *Boston Globe*, June 28, 2013, http://www.bostonglobe.com/metro/2013/06/27/dzhokhar-tsarnaev-indicted-four-deaths-including-marathon-bombing-victims-and-mit-officer-sean-collier/23vhQHQIk8q1KI9Zijwt0J/story.html.

c. Jessica S. Henry, "Killing to Heal? One Year After the Boston Bombing," *Huffington Post*, June 17, 2014, http://www.huffingtonpost.com/jessicas-henry/dzhokhar-tsarnaev-death-penalty_b_5161795.html.

d. Milton J. Valencia, "US Cites Enormity of Attack in Seeking Death Penalty," *Boston Globe*, January 30, 2014, http://www.bostonglobe.com/metro/2014/01/30/federal-prosecutors-seek-death-penalty-against-marathon-bombing-suspect-dzhokhar-tsarnaev/ePoqvnDKEpkvfjrv3CwOeK/story.html.

e. Michele Gorman, "Boston Marathon Bomber Dzhokhar Tsarnaev Appeals Death Sentence," *Newsweek*, August 18, 2015, http://www.newsweek.com/boston-marathon-bomber-dzhokhar-tsarnaev-appeals-death-sentence-363764.

Around the World: International Crime Data

a. Australian Bureau of Statistics, "Recorded Crime—Offenders, 2014–15," Retrieved at http://www.abs.gov.au/ausstats/abs@.nsf/Lookup/by%20Subject/4519.0~2014-15~Main%20Features~Offenders,%20Australia~3

b. Bundeskriminalamt, *Police Crime Statistics Yearbook 2012* (Weisbaden, Germany: Bundeskriminalamt, 2013), http://www.bka.de/nn_257388/EN/Publications/PoliceCrimeStatistics/policeCrimeStatistics__node.html?__nnn=true.

c. United Nations Office on Drugs and Crime, *2012 United Nations Survey of Crime Trends and Operations of Criminal Justice Systems*, https://www.unodc.org/unodc/en/data-and-analysis/statistics/data.html.

CHAPTER 4

1. Associated Press, "20 Children Among Dead in Connecticut School Massacre," CBC News, December 15, 2012, http://www.cbc.ca/news/world/20-children-among-dead-in-connecticut-school-massacre-1.1134782.

2. Ed Pilkington, "Sandy Hook Report—Shooter Adam Lanza Was Obsessed With Mass Murder," *The Guardian*, November 25, 2013, http://www.theguardian.com/world/2013/nov/25/sandy-hook-shooter-adam-lanza-report.

3. Sharon Greenthal, "Peter Lanza—Read His Words Before You Judge," Huffington Post, May 10, 2014, http://www.huffingtonpost.com/sharon-greenthal/peter-lanza_b_4937295.html.

4. Stephen J. Sedensky III, *Report of the State's Attorney for the Judicial District of Danbury on the Shootings at Sandy Hook Elementary School and 36 Yogananda Street, Newtown, Connecticut on December 14, 2012*, http://www.ct.gov/csao/lib/csao/Sandy-Hook_final_report.pdf

5. Cesare Beccaria, *On Crimes and Punishments and Other Writings*, ed. Richard Bellamy (1764; Cambridge, UK: Cambridge University Press, 1995).

6. Jeremy Bentham, *An Introduction to the Principles of Morals and Legislation* (1789; Mineola, NY: Dover Publications, 2007).

7. Jeremy Bentham, "The Panopticon Letters," Cartome Archives, http://cartome.org/panopticon2.htm.

8. Cesare Lombroso, *Criminal Man*, trans. Mary Gibson and Nicole Hahn Rafter (1876; Durham, NC: Duke University Press, 2006).

9. Cesare Lombroso and Guglielmo Ferrero, *The Female Offender* (New York: Barnes and Company, 1895), 151.

10. Sigmund Freud, *The Ego and the Id* (1927; Eastford, CT: Martino Publishing, 2010).

11. Jean Piaget, *Origins of Intelligence in the Child* (London: Routledge & Kegan Paul, 1936).

12. Lawrence Kohlberg, *Stages in the Development of Moral Thought and Action* (New York: Holt, Rinehart and Winston, 1969); Lawrence Kohlberg, Kelsey Kauffman, Peter Scharf, and Joseph Hickey, *The Just Community Approach in Corrections* (Niantic: Connecticut Department of Corrections, 1973).

13. Adrian Raine, *The Psychopathology of Crime: Criminal Behavior as a Clinical Disorder* (San Diego: Academic Press, 1993); Diana H. Fishbein, *Biobehavioral Perspectives in Criminology* (Belmont, CA: Wadsworth/Thomson Learning, 2001).

14. Adrian Raine and Angela Scerbo, "Neurotransmitters and Antisocial Behavior: A Meta-Analysis," in *The Psychopathology of Crime: Criminal Behavior as a Clinical Disorder*, ed. Adrian Raine (San Diego: Academic Press, 1993), 86–92.

15. Kevin Drum, "Does Lead Paint Produce More Crime Too?" *Mother Jones*, January 4, 2013, http://www.motherjones.com/kevindrum/2013/01/does-lead-paint-produce-more-crime-too.

16. Rick Nevin, "How Lead Exposure Relates to Temporal Changes in IQ, Violent Crime, and Unwed Pregnancy," September 15, 1999, http://www.ricknevin.com/uploads/Nevin_2000_Env_Res_Author_Manuscript.pdf; Rick Nevin, "How Lead Exposure Relates to Temporal Changes in IQ, Violent Crime, and Unwed Pregnancy," *Environmental Research* 83, no. 1 (2000): 1–22; Howard W. Mielke and Sammy Zahran, "The Urban Rise and Fall of Air Lead (Pb) and the Latent Surge and Retreat of Societal Violence," *Environment International* 32 (2012): 48–55.

17. William Finnegan, "Flint and the Long Struggle Against Lead Poisoning," *New Yorker*, February 4, 2016, http://www.newyorker.com/news/daily-comment/flint-and-the-long-struggle-against-lead-poisoning.

18. Robert Ezra Park, Ernest W. Burgess, and Roderick D. McKenzie, *The City: Suggestions for Investigation of Human*

Behavior in the Urban Environment (1925; Chicago, IL: University of Chicago Press, 1967).

19. Clifford Robe Shaw and Henry Donald McKay, *Juvenile Delinquency and Urban Areas* (Chicago: University of Chicago Press, 1942).

20. Merriam-Webster Dictionary, "Anomie," n.d., http://www.merriam-webster.com/dictionary/anomie; Ken Morrison, *Marx, Durkheim, Weber: Formations of Modern Social Thought* (Thousand Oaks, CA: Sage, 1995); Émile Durkheim, *The Division of Labor in Society* (1933; New York: Free Press of Glencoe, 1964).

21. Robert K. Merton, "Social Structure and Anomie," *American Sociological Review* 3, no. 5 (1938): 672–682.

22. Robert Agnew, "Foundation for a General Strain Theory of Crime and Delinquency," *Criminology* 30, no. 1 (1992): 47–88.

23. Robert Agnew, "Building on the Foundation of General Strain Theory: Specifying the Types of Strain Most Likely to Lead to Crime and Delinquency," *Journal of Research in Crime and Delinquency* 38, no. 4 (2001): 319–361.

24. Robert Agnew, Timothy Brezina, John Paul Wright, and Francis T. Cullen, "Strain, Personality Traits, and Delinquency: Extending General Strain Theory," *Criminology* 40, no. 1 (2002): 43–72.

25. Joanne M. Kaufman, Cesar J. Rebellon, Sherod Thaxton, and Robert Agnew, "A General Strain Theory of Racial Differences in Criminal Offending," *Australian and New Zealand Journal of Criminology* 41, no. 3 (2008): 421–437.

26. Lisa Broidy and Robert Agnew, "Gender and Crime: A General Strain Theory Perspective," *Journal of Research in Crime and Delinquency* 34, no. 3 (1997): 275–306.

27. Jenna R. Silverman and Roslyn M. Caldwell, "Peer Relationships and Violence Among Female Juvenile Offenders: An Exploration of Differences Among Four Racial/Ethnic Populations," *Criminal Justice and Behavior* 35, no. 3 (2008): 333–343.

28. Nicole Leeper Piquero, Angela R. Gover, John M. MacDonald, and Alex R. Piquero, "The Influence of Delinquent Peers on Delinquency: Does Gender Matter?" *Youth & Society* 36, no. 3 (2005): 251–275.

29. Edwin M. Lemert, *Social Pathology: A Systematic Approach to the Theory of Sociopathic Behavior* (New York: McGraw-Hill, 1951).

30. Albert Bandura, *Social Learning Theory* (Englewood Cliffs, NJ: Prentice Hall, 1977).

31. Ronald L. Akers, *Social Learning and Social Structure: A General Theory of Crime and Deviance* (Boston: Northeastern University Press, 1998); Robert L. Burgess and Ronald L. Akers, "A Differential Association-Reinforcement Theory of Criminal Behavior," *Social Problems* 14, no. 2 (1966): 128–147.

32. Travis Hirschi, *Causes of Delinquency* (Berkeley: University of California Press, 1969), 26.

33. Michael R. Gottfredson and Travis Hirschi, *A General Theory of Crime* (Stanford, CA: Stanford University Press, 1990).

34. Matt DeLisi, Kevin M. Beaver, Michael G. Vaughn, Chad R. Trulson, Anne Kosloski, Alan J. Drury, and John Paul Wright, "Personality, Gender, and Self-Control Theory Revisited: Results From a Sample of Institutionalized Juvenile Delinquents," *Applied Psychology in Criminal Justice* 6, no. 1 (2010): 31–46.

35. Zahra Shekarkhar and Chris L. Gibson, "Gender, Self-Control, and Offending Behaviors Among Latino Youth," *Journal of Contemporary Criminal Justice* 27, no. 1 (2011): 63–80.

36. Robert J. Sampson and John H. Laub, *Crime in the Making: Pathways and Turning Points Through Life* (Cambridge, MA: Harvard University Press, 1993); John H. Laub and Robert J. Sampson, *Shared Beginnings, Divergent Lives: Delinquent Boys to Age 70* (Cambridge, MA: Harvard University Press, 2003).

37. Frances M. Heidensohn, *Women and Crime: The Life of the Female Offender* (New York: New York University Press, 1985), 61.

38. Kathleen Daly and Meda Chesney-Lind, "Feminism and Criminology," *Justice Quarterly* 5, no. 4 (1988): 497–538.

39. Joanne Belknap, *The Invisible Woman: Gender, Crime and Justice*, 3rd ed. (Belmont, CA: Wadsworth, 2007).

40. Joanne Belknap and Kristi Holsinger, "An Overview of Delinquent Girls: How Theory and Practice Have Failed and the Need for Innovative Changes," *Female Crime and Delinquency: Critical Perspectives and Effective Interventions*, ed. Ruth T. Zaplin (Gaithersburg, MD: Aspen, 1998), 31–64.

41. Hillary Potter, "An Argument for Black Feminist Criminology: Understanding African American Women's Experiences With Intimate Partner Abuse Using an Integrated Approach," *Feminist Criminology* 1, no. 2 (2006): 106–124.

42. Meda Chesney-Lind, "Patriarchy, Crime and Justice: Feminist Criminology in an Era of Backlash," *Feminist Criminology* 1, no. 1 (2006): 6–26.

43. Lombroso, 91.

44. Ibid., 115.

45. Richard J. Herrnstein and Charles Murray, *The Bell Curve: Intelligence and Class Structure in American Life* (New York: Free Press, 1994).

46. William Julius Wilson, *The Truly Disadvantaged: The Inner City, the Underclass, and Public Policy*, 2nd ed. (Chicago: University of Chicago Press, 2012).

47. Lauren J. Krivo, Ruth D. Peterson, and Danielle C. Kuhl, "Segregation, Racial Structure, and Neighborhood Violent Crime," *American Journal of Sociology* 114, no. 6 (2009): 1765–1802.

48. Gregg Barak, Paul Leighton, and Jeanne Flavin, *Class, Race, Gender, and Crime: The Social Realities of Justice in America*, 3rd ed. (Lanham, MD: Rowman & Littlefield, 2010).

49. Katherine Rosich, *Race, Ethnicity, and the Criminal Justice System* (Washington, DC: American Sociological Association, 2007), http://www.asanet.org/images/press/docs/pdf/ASARaceCrime.pdf.

50. Park, Burgess, and McKenzie.

51. Steven F. Messner and Richard Rosenfeld, *Crime and the American Dream*, 5th ed. (Belmont, CA: Wadsworth, 2012).

52. Merton.

53. Richard Quinney, *The Social Reality of Crime* (Boston, MA: Little, Brown, 1970).

54. Jeffrey Reiman and Paul Leighton, *The Rich Get Richer and the Poor Get Prison:*

Ideology, Class, and Criminal Justice, 10th ed. (London: Routledge, 2012).

55. NCCD Center for Girls and Young Women, "Getting the Facts Straight About Girls in the Juvenile Justice System," February 2009, http://www .nccdglobal.org/sites/default/files/ publication_pdf/fact-sheet-girls-in- juvenile-justice.pdf.

56. Meda Chesney-Lind and Katherine Irwin, *Beyond Bad Girls: Gender, Violence and Hype* (New York: Routledge, 2008).

57. Stacy L. Mallicoat, "Gendered Justice: Attributional Differences Between Males and Females in the Juvenile Courts," *Feminist Criminology* 2, no. 1 (2007): 4–30.

58. Barbara Bloom, Barbara Owen, and Stephanie Covington, "Gender-Responsive Strategies for Women Offenders: A Summary of *Research, Practice, and Guiding Principles for Women Offenders*," May 2005, http:// static.nicic.gov/Library/020418.pdf.

59. Jill Leslie Rosenbaum and Shelley Spivack, *Implementing a Gender-Based Arts Program for Juvenile Offenders* (London: Routledge, 2014).

Spotlight: Theories and Research on Crime

a. Caitlin Hughes, Jason Payne, Sarah Macgregor, and Kate Pockley, "A Beginner's Guide to Drugs and Crime: Does One Always Lead to the Other?" *Of Substance: The National Magazine on Alcohol, Tobacco and Other Drugs* 12, no. 2 (2014): 26–29, http://www .ofsubstance.org.au/images/archive/ pdf/OS_July_2014_Singles_web.pdf.

Around the World: Criminological Theory in a Global Context

a. Ozden Ozbay and Yusuf Ziya Ozcan, "A Test of Hirschi's Social Bonding Theory: A Comparison of Male and Female Delinquency," *Internal Journal of Offender Therapy and Comparative Criminology* 52, no. 2 (2008): 134–157.

b. Xiaoming Chen, "Social Control in China: Applications of the Labeling Theory and the Reintegrative Shaming Theory," *International Journal of Offender Therapy and Comparative Criminology* 46, no. 1 (2002): 45–63.

c. Moon Byongook and Merry Morash, "Adaptation of Theory for Alternative Cultural Contexts: Agnew's General Strain Theory in South Korea," *International Journal of Comparative and Applied Criminal Justice* 28, no. 2 (2014): 77–104.

CHAPTER 5

1. "Profile: Amanda Berry, Georgina De Jesus and Michelle Knight," BBC, May 7, 2013, http://www.bbc.co.uk/news/ world us canada-22433057.

2. Jen Steer, "Cleveland Police: Missing Teens Amanda Berry and Gina DeJesus Found Alive, Appear to Be OK," newsnet5, May 6, 2013, http:// www.newsnet5.com/news/local-news/ cleveland-metro/cleveland-police- dispatch-missing-teens-amanda- berry-and-gina-dejesus-found-alive.

3. Peter Krouse, "Ariel Castro Agrees to Plea Deal: Life in Prison, No Parole, Plus 1,000 years," Cleveland.com, July 26, 2013, http://www.cleveland.com/ metro/index.ssf/2013/07/ariel_castro_ agrees_to_plea_de.html; Jill Mahoney, "Death Penalty Possible for Alleged Cleveland Kidnapper, Prosecutor Says," *Globe and Mail*, May 9, 2013, http:// web.archive.org/web/20130509221120/ http://www.theglobeandmail.com/ news/world/kidnap-suspect-ariel- castro-due-in-cleveland-court/ article11810618/?cmpid=rss1; Thomas J. Sheeran, "Ariel Castro Pleads Not Guilty to 977 Counts in Ohio Kidnapping Indictment," *Huffington Post*, July 17, 2013, http://www .huffingtonpost.com/2013/07/17/ ariel-castro-arraignment- charges_n_3609793.html.

4. Matthew DeLuca, "Ariel Castro Victim Michelle Knight: 'Your Hell Is Just Beginning.'" August 1, 2013, NBC News, http://usnews.nbcnews .com/_news/2013/08/01/19813977- ariel-castro-victim-michelle-knight- your-hell-is-just-beginning?lite.

5. Lateef Mungin and Dave Alsup, "Cleveland Kidnapper Ariel Castro Dead: Commits Suicide in Prison," CNN Justice, September 4, 2013, http:// www.cnn.com/2013/09/04/justice/ ariel-castro-cleveland-kidnapper-death.

6. Ohio Legislative Service Commission, "House Bill 197 of the 130th General Assembly," June 18, 2013, http://www .lsc.ohio.gov/fiscal/fiscalnotes/130ga/ hb0197in.pdf.

7. Jennifer Lindgren, Doug Stanglin, and Yaiche Alcindor, "Ariel Castro's House of Horror Demolished in Cleveland," *USA Today*, August 7, 2013, http://www.usatoday.com/story/ news/nation/2013/08/07/ariel-castro- cleveland-house-abduction/2626855.

8. Benjamin Mendelsohn, "A New Branch of Bio-psychological Science: La Victimology," *Revue Internationale de Criminologie et de Police Technique* 10 (1956): 782–789.

9. Hans von Hentig, *The Criminal and His Victim: Studies in the Sociobiology of Crime* (New Haven, CT: Yale University Press, 1948).

10. Melvin J. Lerner, *The Belief in a Just World: A Fundamental Delusion* (New York: Plenum Press, 1980).

11. Renae Franiuk, Jennifer L. Seefelt, Sandy L. Cepress, and Joseph A. Vandello, "Prevalence and Effects of Rape Myths in Print Journalism: The Kobe Bryant Case," *Violence Against Women* 14, no. 3 (2008): 287–309.

12. Lawrence E. Cohen and Marcus Felson, "Social Change and Crime Rate Trends: A Routine Activity Approach," *American Sociological Review* 44, no. 4 (1979): 588–608.

13. Jordana N. Navarro and Jana L. Jasinski, "Why Girls? Using Routine Activities Theory to Predict Cyberbullying Experiences Between Girls and Boys," *Women & Criminal Justice* 23, no. 4 (2013): 286–303.

14. Toya Z. Like-Haislip and Karin Tusinski Miofsky, "Race, Ethnicity, Gender and Violent Victimization," *Race and Justice* 1, no. 3 (2011): 254–276.

15. Jackson Bunch, Jody Clay-Warner, and Man-Kit Lei, "Demographic Characteristics and Victimization Risk: Testing the Mediating Effects of Routine Activities," *Crime & Delinquency* 61, no. 9 (2015): 1181– 1205, http://cad.sagepub.com/content/ early/2012/12/05/0011128712466932 .full.pdf+html.

16. Michael J. Hindelang, Michael R. Gottfredson, and James Garofalo, *Victims of Personal Crime: An Empirical Foundation for a Theory of Personal Victimization* (Cambridge, MA: Ballinger, 1978).

17. Johanne Vézina, Martine Hébert, François Poulin, Francine Lavoie, Frank Vitaro, and Richard E.

Tremblay, "Risky Lifestyle as a Mediator of the Relationship Between Deviant Peer Affiliation and Dating Violence Victimization Among Adolescent Girls," *Journal of Youth and Adolescence* 40, no. 7 (2011): 814–824, http://link.springer.com/article/10.1007/s10964-010-9602-x/fulltext.html.

18. Joanna Tucker Davis, "The Grassroots Beginnings of the Victims' Rights Movement," *NCVLI News*, Spring/Summer 2005, https://www.lclark.edu/live/files/6453-the-grassroots-beginnings-of-the-victims-rights.

19. National Center for Victims of Crime, "Section 5: Landmarks in Victims' Rights and Services," in *2013 NCVRW Resource Guide* (Washington, DC: National Center for Victims of Crime, 2013), 1–20, http://www.victimsofcrime.org/docs/ncvrw2013/2013ncvrw_5_landmarks.pdf?sfvrsn=0.

20. National Victims' Constitutional Amendment Passage, "Marsy's Law—California's New VRA—Passes," November 5, 2008, http://www.nvcap.org.

21. Victim Law, "About Victim Rights," Office of Justice Programs, n.d., https://www.victimlaw.org/victimlaw/pages/victimsRight.jsp.

22. National Center for Victims of Crime.

23. Jennifer L. Truman and Lynn Langton, *Criminal Victimization, 2014* (Washington, DC: Bureau of Justice Statistics, 2015), http://www.bjs.gov/content/pub/pdf/cv14.pdf.

24. Jennifer L. Truman and Michael Planty, *Criminal Victimization, 2011* (Washington, DC: Bureau of Justice Statistics, 2012), http://www.bjs.gov/content/pub/pdf/cv11.pdf.

25. Erika Harrell and Lynn Langton, *Victims of Identity Theft, 2012* (Washington, DC: Bureau of Justice Statistics, 2013), http://www.bjs.gov/content/pub/pdf/vit12.pdf.

26. Catherine Kaukinen, "Status Compatibility, Physical Violence, and Emotional Abuse in Intimate Relationships," *Journal of Marriage and Family* 66, no. 2 (2004), 452–471.

27. Kim Davies, Carolyn Rebecca Block, and Jacquelyn Campbell, "Seeking Help From the Police: Battered Women's Decisions and Experiences," *Criminal Justice Studies* 20, no. 1

(2007): 15–41; Laura L. Starzynski, Sarah E. Ullman, Stephanie M. Townsend, LaDonna M. Long, and Susan M. Long, "What Factors Predict Women's Disclosure of Sexual Assault to Mental Health Professionals?" *Journal of Community Psychology* 35, no. 5 (2007): 619–638.

28. T. K. Logan, Lucy Evans, Erin Stevenson, and Carol E. Jordan, "Barriers to Services for Rural and Urban Survivors of Rape," *Journal of Interpersonal Violence* 20, no. 5 (2005): 591–616.

29. Janet L. Lauritsen and Maribeth L. Rezey, *Measuring the Prevalence of Crime With the National Crime Victimization Survey* (Washington, DC: Bureau of Justice Statistics, 2013), http://www.bjs.gov/content/pub/pdf/mpcncvs.pdf.

30. Michele C. Black, Kathleen C. Basile, Matthew J. Breiding, Sharon G. Smith, Mikel L. Walters, Melissa T. Merrick, Jieru Chen, and Mark R. Stevens, *The National Intimate Partner and Sexual Violence Survey: 2010 Summary Report* (Atlanta: National Center for Injury Prevention and Control, Centers for Disease Control and Prevention, 2011).

31. Office of the Assistant Secretary, U.S. Department of Education, "Dear Colleague Letter," April 4, 2011, http://www2.ed.gov/about/offices/list/ocr/letters/colleague-201104.html.

32. NotAlone.org, "Bystander-Focused Prevention of Sexual Violence," n.d., https://www.notalone.gov/assets/bystander-summary.pdf.

33. Emily Yoffe, "College Women: Don't Depend on 'Bystanders' to Rescue You From Assault. Rescue Yourselves," *Slate*, February 10, 2014, http://www.slate.com/blogs/xx_factor/2014/02/10/bystander_intervention_the_answer_to_college_sexual_assault.html.

34. Victoria Banyard, Mary M. Moynihan, and Elizabethe G. Plante, "Sexual Violence Prevention Through Bystander Education: An Experimental Evaluation," *Journal of Community Psychology* 35, no. 4 (2007): 463–481; Christine A. Gidycz, Lindsay M. Orchowski, and Alan D. Berkowitz, "Preventing Sexual Aggression Among College Men: An Evaluation of a Social Norms and Bystander Intervention

Program," *Violence Against Women* 17, no. 6 (2011): 720–742. doi:10.1177/1077801211409727

35. Eliza Gray, "Colleges Are Breaking the Law on Sex Crimes, Report Says," *TIME*, July 9, 2014, http://time.com/2969580/claire-mccaskill-campus-sexual-assault-rape.

36. Bonnie S. Fisher, Francis T. Cullen, and Michael G. Turner, *The Sexual Victimization of College Women* (Washington, DC: Office of Justice Programs, 2000).

37. Matt Kaiser and Justin Dillon, "Op-Ed: How to Punish Campus Sexual Assault," *Los Angeles Times*, November 24, 2015, http://www.latimes.com/opinion/op-ed/la-oe-1124-kaiser-dillon-sex-assault-campus-proportinality-20151124-story.html.

38. Abigail Abrams, "Brigham Young University Students Protest Honor Code Punishment for Sexual Assault Victim in Utah," *International Business Times*, April 21, 2016, http://www.ibtimes.com/brigham-young-university-students-protest-honor-code-punishment-sexual-assault-victim-2357252.

39. Texas Department of Criminal Justice, "Victim Services Division," n.d., http://tdcj.state.tx.us/divisions/vs/victim_vomd.html.

40. *The Final Gift*, dir. Therese Bartholomew (1936 Productions and SansPerf Productions, 2012), http://www.thefinalgiftfilm.com.

41. Rashmi Goel, "Sita's Trousseau: Restorative Justice, Domestic Violence, and South Asian Culture," *Violence Against Women* 11, no. 5 (2005): 639–665.

Spotlight: Politics and Victims' Rights

a. Erika Eichelberger, "Blocking VAWA, the GOP Keeps Up the War on Women," *The Nation*, January 21, 2013, http://www.thenation.com/article/171977/gop-blocks-vawa#.

b. Tom Cohen, "House Passes Violence Against Women Act After GOP Version Defeated," CNN Politics, February 28, 2013, http://www.cnn.com/2013/02/28/politics/violence-against-women/index.html.

Around the World: Criminal Victimization in a Global Context

a. UK Office for National Statistics, "Crime in England and Wales: Year Ending September 2015," January 21, 2016, https://www.ons.gov.uk/peoplepopulationandcommunity/crimeandjustice/bulletins/crimeinenglandandwales/yearendingseptember2015#summary.

b. For a list of participating countries, see Jan van Dijk, John van Kesteren, and Paul Smit, *Criminal Victimisation in International Perspective: Key Findings From the 2004–2005 ICVS and EU ICS* (The Hague, Netherlands: Bibliotheek WODC, 2007), http://www.unicri.it/services/library_documentation/publications/icvs/publications/ICVS2004_05report.pdf.

c. Ibid.

CHAPTER 6

1. Drug Policy Alliance, "A Brief History of the Drug War," n.d., http://www.drugpolicy.org/new-solutions-drug-policy/brief-history-drug-war.

2. "Thirty Years of America's Drug War: A Chronology," Frontline PBS, n.d., http://www.pbs.org/wgbh/pages/frontline/shows/drugs/cron.

3. Denise Lavoie, "Crack-vs.-Powder Disparity Is Questioned," *USA Today*, December 25, 2007, http://usatoday30.usatoday.com/news/nation/2007-12-24-2050621119_x.htm.

4. Families Against Mandatory Minimums, "Frequently Asked Questions: The Fair Sentencing Act of 2010, S. 1789 Federal Crack Reform Bill," April 13, 2012, http://famm.org/wp-content/uploads/2013/08/FAQ-Fair-Sentencing-Act-4.13.pdf.

5. Linda Greenhouse, "Crack Cocaine Limbo," *New York Times*, January 5, 2014, http://www.nytimes.com/2014/01/06/opinion/greenhouse-crack-cocaine-limbo.html.

6. Saki Knafo, "California Takes Overdue Stand Against 'Failed Drug Laws,'" *Huffington Post*, September 29, 2014, http://www.huffingtonpost.com/2014/09/29/california-fair-sentencing-act_n_5902772.html.

7. Office of Management and Budget, White House, "The President's Budget for Fiscal Year 2013," http://www.whitehouse.gov/omb/budget.

8. Clarke E. Cochran, Lawrence C. Mayer, T. R. Carr, N. Joseph Cayer, Mark J. McKenzie, and Laura R. Peck, *American Public Policy: An Introduction*, 10th ed. (Boston, MA: Wadsworth, 2012).

9. Stephen J. Stambough, "Direct Democracy and Crime Policies," in *California's Criminal Justice System*, ed. Christine L. Gardiner and Stacy L. Mallicoat (Durham, NC: Carolina Academic Press, 2012), 37–46.

10. Gene Johnson, "Legalizing Marijuana: Washington Law Goes Into Effect, Allowing Recreational Use of Drug," *Huffington Post*, December 6, 2012, http://www.huffingtonpost.com/2012/12/06/legalizing-marijuana-washington-state_n_2249238.html.

11. Kristen Wyatt, "Marijuana Legalized in Colorado With Hickenlooper Proclamation," *Huffington Post*, December 10, 2012, http://www.huffingtonpost.com/2012/12/10/pot-legalized-in-colorado_0_n_2272678.html.

12. Drug Policy Alliance, "Marijuana Legalization and Regulation," n.d., http://www.drugpolicy.org/marijuana-legalization-and-regulation.

13. Savings, Accountability and Full Enforcement (SAFE) Act (2012), http://www.safecalifornia.org.

14. Inimai Chettiar, "Criminal Justice Reform Can Help With State Fiscal Woes," Center for American Progress, January 11, 2012, http://www.americanprogress.org/issues/civil-liberties/news/2012/01/11/10970/criminal-justice-reform-can-help-with-state-fiscal-woes.

15. Randall G. Shelden, "Conservative, Liberal and Radical Views of Crime," 2010, http://www.sheldensays.com/conserlibrad.htm.

16. Anna Gorman and Nicholas Riccardi, "Calls to Boycott Arizona Grow Over New Immigration Law," *Los Angeles Times*, April 28, 2010, http://articles.latimes.com/2010/apr/28/local/la-me-0428-arizona-boycott-20100428.

17. *Arizona vs. United States*, 567 U.S. __ (2012).

18. Christine L. Gardiner, "Policing in California," in *California's Criminal Justice System*, ed. Christine L. Gardiner and Stacy L. Mallicoat (Durham, NC: Carolina Academic Press, 2012), 64–96.

19. Robert James Bidinotto, "Getting Away With Murder," *Readers Digest*, July 1988, 57–63.

20. Eric Benson, "Dukakis's Regret: What the Onetime Democratic Nominee Learned From the Willie Horton Ad," *New York Magazine*, June 17, 2012, http://nymag.com/news/frank-rich/michael-dukakis-2012-6.

21. Willard M. Oliver, "The Power to Persuade: Presidential Influence Over Congress on Crime Control Policy," *Criminal Justice Review* 28, no. 1 (2003): 113–132.

22. Christine L. Gardiner, "The Influence of Research and Evidence-Based Practices on Criminal Justice Policy," in *Criminal Justice Policy*, ed. Stacy L. Mallicoat and Christine L. Gardiner (Thousand Oaks, CA: Sage, 2014), 15–36.

23. David M. Bierie and Paul J. Detar, "Geographic and Social Movement of Sex Offender Fugitives," *Crime & Delinquency* (April 2014): 1–20. doi:0011128714530658

24. U.S. White House, "President Signs H.R. 4472, the Adam Walsh Child Protection and Safety Act of 2006," July 27, 2006, http://georgewbush-whitehouse.archives.gov/news/releases/2006/07/20060727-6.html.

25. David M. Bierie and James C. Davis-Siegel, "Measurement Matters: Comparing Old and New Definitions of Rape in Federal Statistical Reporting," *Sexual Abuse: A Journal of Research and Treatment* 27, no. 5 (2014): 443–459. doi:1079063214521470; Howard N. Snyder, *Sexual Assault of Young Children as Reported to Law Enforcement: Victim, Incident, and Offender Characteristics* (Washington, DC: Bureau of Justice Statistics, 2000).

26. Samantha Lundrigan, Sarah Czarnomski, and Marc Wilson, "Spatial and Environmental Consistency in Serial Sexual Assault," *Journal of Investigative Psychology and Offender Profiling* 7, no. 1 (2010): 15–30; D. Kim Rossmo, *Geographic Profiling* (Boca Raton, FL: CRC Press, 2000).

27. Katherine M. Brown, Robert D. Keppel, Joseph G. Weis, and Marvin E. Skeen, *Investigative Case Management for Missing Children Homicides: Report II* (Washington, DC: National Center for Missing & Exploited Children and U.S. Department of Justice, 2006).

28. Lisa Rodriguez, "Note: A National Amber Alert Plan: Saving America's Children," *Seton Hall Legislative Journal* 28 (2003): 169.

29. Amanda Y. Agan, "Sex Offender Registries: Fear Without Function?" *Journal of Law and Economics* 54, no. 1 (2011): 207–239; Jill S. Levenson, Alissa R. Ackerman, and Andrew J. Harris, "Catch Me If You Can: An Analysis of Fugitive Sex Offenders," *Sexual Abuse: A Journal of Research and Treatment* (2013): 129–148. doi:1079063213480820; Richard Tewksbury, Wesley G. Jennings, and Kristen M. Zgoba, "A Longitudinal Examination of Sex Offender Recidivism Prior to and Following the Implementation of SORN," *Behavioral Sciences & the Law* 30, no. 3 (2012): 308–328.

30. J. J. Prescott and Jonah E. Rockoff, "Do Sex Offender Registration and Notification Laws Affect Criminal Behavior?" *Journal of Law and Economics* 54, no. 1 (2011): 161–206.

31. Sarah W. Craun and David M. Bierie, "Are the Collateral Consequences of Being a Registered Sex Offender as Bad as We Think: A Methodological Research Note," *Federal Probation* 78, no. 1 (2014): 28–31.

32. Prescott and Rockoff.

33. Teresa Masterson, "NJ Mom Recognizes Census Worker as Sex Offender," NBC Philadelphia, May 18, 2010, http://www.nbcphiladelphia .com/news/local/NJ-Mom-Recognizes-Census-Worker-as-Sex-Offender-94185994.html.

34. "Deputies Say Sex Offender Was Watching Kids Outside School," KKTV, February 11, 2014, http:// www.kktv.com/home/headlines/ Deputies-Say-Sex-Offender-Was-Watching-Kids-Outside-School-244724421.html.

35. Michael Lipsky, *Street-Level Bureaucracy: Dilemmas of the Individual in Public Services*, 30th ann. exp. ed. (New York: Russell Sage Foundation, 2010).

36. Ibid.; Steven Maynard-Moody and Michael Musheno, *Cops, Teachers, Counselors: Stories From the Front Lines of Public Service* (Ann Arbor: University of Michigan Press, 2005).

37. Elisabeth R. Gerber, Arthur Lupia, Matthew D. McCubbins, and D.

Roderick Kiewiet, *Stealing the Initiative: How State Government Responds to Direct Democracy* (Upper Saddle River, NJ: Prentice Hall, 2001).

38. James Lasley, *Los Angeles Police Department Meltdown: The Fall of the Professional-Reform Model of Policing* (Boca Raton, FL: CRC Press, 2013), 62.

39. Ibid.

40. Jennifer Medina, "Rodney King Dies at 47; Police Beating Victim Who Asked 'Can We All Get Along?'" *New York Times*, June 17, 2012, http:// www.nytimes.com/2012/06/18/us/ rodney-king-whose-beating-led-to-la-riots-dead-at-47.html?_r=0.

41. Peter Hupe and Michael Hill, "Street-Level Bureaucracy and Public Accountability," *Public Administration* 85, no. 2 (2007): 279–299; Lipsky, *Street-Level Bureaucracy*.

42. Rob Tillyer and Charles Klahm IV, "Searching for Contraband: Assessing the Use of Discretion by Police Officers," *Police Quarterly* 14, no. 2 (2011): 166–185; Rob Tillyer, Charles F. Klahm IV, and Robin S. Engel, "The Discretion to Search: A Multilevel Examination of Driver Demographics and Officer Characteristics," *Journal of Contemporary Criminal Justice* 28, no. 2 (2012): 185–205.

43. John Brehm and Scott Gates, *Working, Shirking, and Sabotage: Bureaucratic Response to a Democratic Public* (Ann Arbor: University of Michigan Press, 1997).

Spotlight: Stand-Your-Ground Policy

a. Kris Hundley, Susan Taylor Martin, and Connie Humberg, "Florida 'Stand Your Ground' Law Yields Some Shocking Outcomes Depending on How Law Is Applied," *Tampa Bay Times*, June 1, 2012, http://www .tampabay.com/news/publicsafety/ crime/florida-stand-your-ground-law-yields-some-shocking-outcomes-depending-on/1233133.

b. Greg Botelho and Holly Yan, "George Zimmerman Found Not Guilty of Murder in Trayvon Martin's Death," CNN Justice, July 14, 2013, http:// www.cnn.com/2013/07/13/justice/ zimmerman-trial.

c. Mitch Stacy, "Marissa Alexander Gets 20 Years for Firing Warning Shot," *Huffington Post*, May 19, 2012, http:// www.huffingtonpost .com/2012/05/19/marissa-alexander-gets-20_n_1530035.html.

d. Susan Cooper Eastman, "Florida Woman in 'Warning Shot' Case Released From Jail," Reuters, January 27, 2015, http://www.reuters.com/ article/us-usa-florida-selfdefense-idUSKBN0L02NQ20150127.

e. Bill Cotterell, "Florida Legislature Seeks Compromise on Reform of Self-Defense Law," Reuters, March 17, 2014, http://www.reuters.com/ article/2014/03/17/us-usa-florida-selfdefense-idUSBREA2G1T820140317.

Around the World: Drug Policy in the Netherlands

a. Ed Leuw, "Drugs and Drug Policy in the Netherlands," *Crime and Justice* 14 (1991): 229–276.

b. Ralph E. Tarter, Michael Vanyukov, Levent Kirisci, Maureen Reynolds, and Duncan B. Clark, "Predictors of Marijuana Use in Adolescents Before and After Licit Drug Use: Examination of the Gateway Hypothesis," *American Journal of Psychiatry* 163, no. 12 (2006): 2134–2140.

c. Benjamin Dolan, *National Drug Policy: The Netherlands: A Report Prepared for the Senate Special Committee on Illegal Drugs* (Ottawa: Parliament of Canada, 2001), http://www.parl.gc.ca/content/ sen/committee/371/ille/library/ dolin1-e.htm.

d. International Harm Reduction Association, "What Is Harm Reduction?" n.d., http://www.ihra .net/files/2010/08/10/Briefing_What_ is_HR_English.pdf.

e. Solomon Waller, "Drug Policy: Contrast Between the United States and the Netherlands," Examiner.com, April 29, 2010, http://www.examiner.com/ article/drug-policy-contrast-between-the-united-states-and-the-netherlands.

f. Robert G. Morris, Michael TenEyck, J. C. Barnes, and Tomislav V. Kovandzic, "The Effect of Medical Marijuana Laws on Crime: Evidence From State Panel Data, 1990–2006," PLOS One, March 26, 2014, http://www.plosone.org/article/ info%3Adoi%2F10.1371%2Fjournal .pone.0092816#s4.

g. "Netherlands Close Eight Prisons Due to Lack of Criminals," Huffington Post UK, June 26, 2013, http://www.huffingtonpost.co.uk/2013/06/26/netherlands-prisons-close–ack-of-criminals-_n_3503721.html.

h. Ana Hilde and Dennis McCarty, "Dutch Drug Policy," n.d., https://www.ohsu.edu/xd/education/schools/school-of-medicine/departments/clinical-departments/public-health/people/upload/Dutch-Drug-Policy.pdf.

Careers in Criminal Justice: So You Want to Be a Policy Advocate?

a. MyFox8, "Greensboro City Council Votes to Release Body Camera Video In Chieu Vo Shooting," May 9, 2016, http://myfox8.com/2016/05/09/greensboro-votes-to-release-body-cam-video-in-chieu-vo-shooting/.

b. A. G. Sulzberger, "Facing Cuts, a City Repeals Its Domestic Violence Law," New York Times, October 11, 2011, http://www.nytimes.com/2011/10/12/us/topeka-moves-to-decriminalize-domestic-violence.html?_r=0.

CHAPTER 7

1. "Rodney King Dead at 47," CNN, June 18, 2012, http://www.cnn.com/2012/06/17/us/obit-rodney-king/index.html.

2. Juan Gonzalez, "George Holliday, the Man With the Camera Who Shot Rodney King While Police Beat Him, Got Burned, Too," New York Daily News, June 20, 2012, http://www.nydailynews.com/news/national/george-holliday-man-camera-shot-rodney-king-police-beat-burned-article-1.1098931.

3. "Sergeant Says King Appeared to Be on Drugs," New York Times, March 20, 1992, http://www.nytimes.com/1992/03/20/us/sergeant-says-king-appeared-to-be-on-drugs.html.

4. "The Rodney King Affair," Los Angeles Times, March 24, 1991, http://articles.latimes.com/1991-03-24/local/me-1422_1_king-s-injuries-officer-laurence-m-powell-beating.

5. "After the Riots: A Juror Describes the Ordeal of Deliberations," New York Times, May 6, 1992, http://www.nytimes.com/1992/05/06/us/after-the-riots-a-juror-describes-the-ordeal-of-deliberations.html.

6. Jessica Dickerson, "Remembering the 1992 LA Riots Over 2 Decades Later," Huffington Post, April 29, 2015, http://www.huffingtonpost.com/2015/04/29/1992-la-riot-photos_n_7173540.html.

7. Daniel B. Wood, "L.A.'s Darkest Days," Christian Science Monitor, April 29, 2002, http://www.csmonitor.com/2002/0429/p01s07-ussc.html.

8. Seth Mydans, "Sympathetic Judge Gives Officers 2 1/2 Years on Rodney King Beating," New York Times, August 5, 1993, http://www.nytimes.com/1993/08/05/us/sympathetic-judge-gives-officers-2-1-2-years-in-rodney-king-beating.html.

9. Edward J. Boyer, "Denny Testifies, Hugs Mothers of Defendants," Los Angeles Times, August 26, 1993, http://articles.latimes.com/1993-08-26/news/mn-28189_1_denny-testifies.

10. "Rodney King, Motorist Whose Beating by Los Angeles Police Officers Sparked Deadly US Race Riots, Dead at 47," NBC News, June 17, 2012, http://usnews.nbcnews.com/_news/2012/06/17/12266275-rodney-king-motorist-whose-beating-by-los-angeles-police-officers-sparked-deadly-us-race-riots-dead-at-47?lite.

11. Associated Press, "Rodney King Seen as Catalyst for Policing Change," Huffington Post, June 18, 2012, http://www.huffingtonpost.com/2012/06/18/rodney-king-seen-as-catal_0_n_1605082.html.

12. Boston Police Museum, "A Brief History of the Boston, MA Police Department," n.d., http://bostonpolicemuseum.com/history.html.

13. National Law Enforcement Officers Memorial Fund, "Important Dates in Law Enforcement History," April 14, 2014, http://www.nleomf.org/facts/enforcement/impdates.html

14. National Law Enforcement Officers Memorial Fund.

15. Carol A. Archbold, Policing: A Text/Reader (Thousand Oaks, CA: Sage, 2013).

16. George L. Kelling and Mark. H. Moore, The Evolving Strategy of Policing (Washington, DC: U.S. Department of Justice, 1988), https://ncjrs.gov/pdffiles1/nij/114213.pdf; Craig D. Uchida, "The Development of the American Police: An Historical Overview," in Critical Issues in Policing: Contemporary Readings, ed. Roger G. Dunham and Geoffrey P. Alpert (Long Grove, IL: Waveland Press), 17–36.

17. Michael K. Hooper, "Acknowledging Existence of a Fourth Era of Policing: The Information Era," Journal of Forensic Research and Criminal Studies 1 (2014): 1–4.

18. Federal Bureau of Investigation, "Brief History of the FBI," n.d., http://www.fbi.gov/about-us/history/brief-history.

19. Brian A. Reaves, Federal Law Enforcement Officers, 2008 (Washington, DC: U.S. Department of Justice, 2012), http://www.bjs.gov/content/pub/pdf/fleo08.pdf.

20. U.S. Department of Justice, Fiscal Years 2014–2018: Strategic Plan (Washington, DC: U.S. Department of Justice, 2014), http://www.justice.gov/sites/default/files/jmd/legacy/2014/02/28/doj-fy-2014-2018-strategic-plan.pdf.

21. Department of Homeland Security, "Creation of the Department of Homeland Security," last updated September 24, 2015, http://www.dhs.gov/creation-department-homeland-security.

22. Reaves, Federal Law Enforcement Officers, 2008.

23. Customs and Border Protection, "CBP Through the Years," n.d., http://www.cbp.gov/about/history.

24. Reaves, Federal Law Enforcement Officers, 2008.

25. United States Secret Service, "Secret Service History," 2014, http://www.secretservice.gov/history.shtml.

26. Reaves, Federal Law Enforcement Officers, 2008.

27. Brian A. Reaves, Census of State and Local Law Enforcement Agencies, 2008 (Washington, DC: U.S. Department of Justice, 2011), http://www.bjs.gov/content/pub/pdf/csllea08.pdf.

28. Reaves, Local Police Departments, 2013.

29. Reaves, Census of State and Local Law Enforcement Agencies, 2008.

30. Dorothy M. Schulz, From Social Worker to Crime Fighter: Women in United States Municipal Policing (Westport, CT: Praeger, 1995).

31. Robert L. Snow, *Policewomen Who Made History: Breaking Through the Ranks* (Lanham, MD: Rowman and Littlefield, 2010).

32. Snow.

33. Schulz, *From Social Worker to Crime Fighter.*

34. Cara Rabe-Hemp, "Survival in an 'All Boys Club': Policewomen and Their Fight for Acceptance," *Policing: An International Journal of Police Strategies and Management* 31, no. 2 (2008): 251–270.

35. Lynn Langton, *Crime Data Brief: Women in Law Enforcement* (Washington, DC: Bureau of Justice Statistics, 2010), http://bjs.ojp.usdoj.gov/content/pub/pdf/wle8708.pdf.

36. Martin L. O'Connor, "Early Policing in the United States: 'Help Wanted—Women Need Not Apply!'" in *Women and Justice: It's a Crime*, 5th ed., ed. Rosalyn Muraskin (Upper Saddle River, NJ: Prentice-Hall, 2012), 487–499.

37. Cara Rabe-Hemp, "The Career Trajectories of Female Police Executives," in *Women and Justice: It's a Crime*, 5th ed., ed. Rosalyn Muraskin (Upper Saddle River, NJ: Prentice-Hall, 2012), 527–543.

38. Kimberly A. Lonsway, Rebecca Paynich, and Jennifer N. Hall, "Sexual Harassment in Law Enforcement: Incidence, Impact, and Perception," *Police Quarterly* 16, no. 2 (2013): 177–210.

39. Kim M. Lersch and Thomas Bazley, "A Paler Shade of Blue? Women and the Police Subculture," in *Women and Justice: It's a Crime*, 5th ed., ed. Rosalyn Muraskin (Upper Saddle River, NJ: Prentice-Hall, 2012), 514–526.

40. Kim Lonsway, Susan Carrington, Margaret Moore, Penny Harrington, Eleanor Smeal, and Katherine Spillar, *Equality Denied: The Status of Women in Policing: 2001* (Beverly Hills, CA: National Center for Women and Policing, 2002), http://www.womenandpolicing.org/PDF/2002_Status_Report.pdf; Penny Harrington and Kimberly A. Lonsway, "Current Barriers and Future Promise for Women in Policing," in *The Criminal Justice System and Women: Offenders, Prisoners, Victims and Workers*, 3rd ed., ed. Barbara Raffel Price and Natalie

Sokoloff (Boston, MA: McGraw Hill, 2004), 495–510; Cara Rabe-Hemp, "POLICEwomen or PoliceWOMEN? Doing Gender and Police Work," *Feminist Criminology* 4, no. 2 (2009): 114–129.

41. Merry Morash and Robin N. Haarr, "Doing, Redoing, and Undoing Gender: Variation in Gender Identities of Women Working as Police Officers," *Feminist Criminology* 7, no. 1 (2012): 3–23.

42. Lonsway et al., *Equality Denied.*

43. "First Patrolman of His Race," *New York Age*, March 21, 1891, http://ncfpc.net/2013/03/21/first-patrolman-of-his-race.

44. Sam Roberts, "Recalling First Black Appointed to New York Police Department," *New York Times*, June 26, 2011, http://www.nytimes.com/2011/06/27/nyregion/recalling-samuel-battle-who-became-first-black-on-nypd.html?_r=2&hp.

45. Los Angeles Police Department (LAPD), "125 for African Americans in the LAPD," n.d., http://www.lapdonline.org/home/content_basic_view/47101.

46. Brian A. Reaves, *Local Police Departments, 2013: Personnel, Policies, and Practices* (Washington, DC: Bureau of Justice Statistics, 2015), http://www.bjs.gov/content/pub/pdf/lpd13ppp.pdf.

47. Reaves, *Local Police Departments, 2013.*

48. Lorie Fridell, Robert Lunney, Drew Diamond, and Bruce Kubu, *Racially Biased Policing: A Principled Response* (Washington, DC: Police Executive Research Forum, 2008), http://www.policeforum.org/assets/docs/Free_Online_Documents/Racially-Biased_Policing/racially%20biased%20policing%20-%20a%20principled%20response%202001.pdf.

49. Carl F. Matthies, Kirsten M. Keller, and Nelson Lim, *Identifying Barriers to Diversity in Law Enforcement Agencies* (Santa Monica, CA: RAND Center on Quality Policing, 2012), http://www.rand.org/content/dam/rand/pubs/occasional_papers/2012/RAND_OP370.pdf.

50. LAPD, "Office of the Chief of Police," n.d., http://www.lapdonline.org/inside_the_lapd/content_basic_view/834.

51. LAPD, "Sworn Police Officer Class Titles and Job Descriptions," n.d., http://www.lapdonline.org/join_the_team/content_basic_view/9127.

52. George L. Kelling, Tony Pate, Duane Dieckman, and Charles E. Brown, *The Kansas City Preventive Patrol Experiment: A Summary Report* (Washington, DC: Police Foundation, 1974), http://www.policefoundation.org/publication/the-kansas-city-preventive-patrol-experiment.

53. David Weisburd and Cody W. Telep, "Hot Spots Policing: What We Know and What We Need to Know," *Journal of Contemporary Criminal Justice* 30, no. 2 (2014): 200–220.

54. Tina Rosenberg, "Armed With Data, Fighting More Than Crime," *New York Times*, May 2, 2012, http://opinionator.blogs.nytimes.com/2012/05/02/armed-with-data-fighting-more-than-crime/?_r=0.

55. Bernard E. Harcourt, "Reflecting on the Subject: A Critique of the Social Influence Conception of Deterrence, the Broken Windows Theory, and Order-Maintenance Policing New York Style," *Michigan Law Review* 97, no. 2 (1998): 291–389.

56. George L. Kelling and James Q. Wilson, "Broken Windows: The Police and Neighborhood Safety," *Atlantic Monthly*, March 1982, http://www.theatlantic.com/magazine/archive/1982/03/broken-windows/304465.

57. Richard Rosenfeld, Robert Fornango, and Andres F. Rengifo, "The Impact of Order-Maintenance Policing on New York City Homicide and Robbery Rates: 1988–2001," *Criminology* 45, no. 2 (2007): 335–384.

58. George L. Kelling and William H. Sousa Jr., *Do Police Matter? An Analysis of the Impact of New York City's Police Reforms* (New York, NY: Manhattan Institute for Policy Research, 2001).

59. William H. Sousa, "Paying Attention to Minor Offenses: Order Maintenance Policing in Practice," *Police Practice and Research* 11, no. 1 (2010): 45–59.

60. Community Oriented Policing Services, *Community Policing Defined* (Washington, DC: U.S. Department of Justice, 2014), http://www.cops.usdoj.gov/Publications/e030917193-CP-Defined.pdf.

61. Community Oriented Policing Services, "COPS Office Awards More Than $6 Million in Community Policing Development Grants," October 15, 2014, http://www.cops.usdoj.gov/Default.asp?Item=2745.

62. Christopher Moraff, "Why Community Policing Is Still a Good Investment," Next City, September 15, 2014, http://nextcity.org/daily/entry/community-policing-efforts-success-failure.

63. Charlotte Gill, David Weisburd, Cody W. Telep, Zoe Vitter, and Trevor Bennett, "Community-Oriented Policing to Reduce Crime, Disorder and Fear and Increase Satisfaction and Legitimacy Among Citizens: A Systematic Review," *Journal of Experiential Criminology* 10 (2014): 399–428.

64. Drew Diamond and Deirdre Mead Weiss, *Community Policing: Looking to Tomorrow* (Washington, DC: U.S. Department of Justice, 2009).

65. Dennis Lynch, "Community Policing Could Help Rebuild America's Broken Relationship With Police, Experts Say," *International Business Times*, December 4, 2014, http://www.ibtimes.com/community-policing-could-help-rebuild-americas-broken-relationship-police-experts-say-1734713.

66. U.S. White House, "Fact Sheet: Strengthening Community Policing," 2014, http://www.whitehouse.gov/the-press-office/2014/12/01/fact-sheet-strengthening-community-policing.

67. Michael S. Scott, *Problem-Oriented Policing: Reflections on the First 20 Years* (Washington, DC: Office of Community Oriented Policing Services, 2000).

68. Center for Problem Oriented Policing, "The SARA Model," n.d., http://www.popcenter.org/about/?p=sara.

69. Ronald V. Clarke, *Problem Oriented Policing: Case Studies* (Washington, DC: U.S. Department of Justice, 2002), https://www.ncjrs.gov/pdffiles1/nij/grants/193801.pdf.

70. David Weisburd, Cody W. Telep, Joshua C. Hinkle, and John E. Eck, "The Effects of Problem-Oriented Policing on Crime and Disorder," *Campbell Systematic Reviews* 14 (2008).

71. Beth Pearsall, "Predictive Policing: The Future of Law Enforcement?" *NIJ Journal* 266 (2010): 16–19. www.nij.gov/journals/266/predictive.htm.

72. Walter L. Perry, Brian McInnis, Carter C. Price, Susan C. Smith, and John S. Hollywood, *Predictive Policing: The Role of Crime Forecasting in Law Enforcement Operations* (Santa Monica, CA: RAND Corporation, 2013), https://www.ncjrs.gov/pdffiles1/nij/grants/243830.pdf.

73. Greg Risling, "'Predictive Policing' Technology Lowers Crime in Los Angeles," *Huffington Post*, July 1, 2012, http://www.huffingtonpost.com/2012/07/01/predictive-policing-technology-los-angeles_n_1641276.html.

74. "Despite Fewer Cops on Streets, Modesto Police Reduce Crime Thanks to Predictive Policing," CBS Sacramento, November 12, 2014, http://sacramento.cbslocal.com/2014/11/12/despite-fewer-cops-on-streets-modesto-police-reduce-crime-thanks-to-predictive-policing.

75. John A. Eterno and Eli B. Silverman, "The NYPD's Compstat: Compare Statistics or Compose Statistics?" *International Journal of Police Science & Management* 12, no. 3 (2010): 426–449. doi:10.1350/ijps.2010.12.3.195; David Weisburd, Stephen D. Mastrofski, Ann Marie McNally, Rosann Greenspan, and James J. Willis, "Reforming to Preserve: Compstat and Strategic Problem Solving in American Policing," *Criminology & Public Policy* 2, no. 3 (2003): 421–456.

76. Christine Gardiner and Matthew Hickman, *Policing for the 21st Century: Realizing the Vision of Police in a Free Society* (forthcoming).

77. Mark H. Moore, "The Legitimation of Criminal Justice Policies and Practices," in *Perspectives on Crime and Justice: 1996–1997 Lecture Series*, ed. James Q. Wilson, Peter Reuter, Mark H. Moore, Cathy Spatz Widom, and Norval Morris (Washington, DC: U.S. Department of Justice, 1997), 47–74; Weisburd et al., "Reforming to Preserve."

78. Eli B. Silverman, "Advocate: Compstat's Innovation," in *Police Innovation: Contrasting Perspectives*, ed. David Weisburd and Anthony A. Braga (Cambridge, UK: Cambridge University Press, 2006), 267–283; Weisburd et al., "Reforming to Preserve."

79. William Bratton, *The Turnaround: How America's Top Cop Reversed the Crime Epidemic*, with Peter Knobler (New York, NY: Random House, 1998); Andrew Karmen, *New York Murder Mystery: The True Story Behind the Crime Crash of the 1990s* (New York: New York University Press, 2000); Eli B. Silverman, *NYPD Battles Crime: Innovative Strategies in Policing* (Boston: Northeastern University Press, 1999); Franklin E. Zimring, *The Great American Crime Decline* (New York: Oxford University Press, 2007).

80. Jeffrey Fagan, Franklin E. Zimring, and June Kim, "Declining Homicide in New York City: A Tale of Two Trends," *Journal of Criminal Law and Criminology* 88 (1998): 1277–1323.

81. Hyunseok Jang, Larry T. Hoover, and Hee-Jong Joo, "An Evaluation of Compstat's Effect on Crime: The Fort Worth Experiment," *Police Quarterly* 13, no. 4 (2010): 387–412. doi:10.1177/1098611110384085

82. Ibid.; Lorraine Mazerolle, Sacha Rombouts, and James McBroom, "The Impact of Compstat on Reported Crime in Queensland," *Policing: An International Journal of Police Strategies and Management* 30, no. 2 (2007): 237–256.

83. David Weisburd, Stephen D. Mastrofski, James J. Willis, and Rosann Greenspan, "Critic: Changing Everything So That Everything Can Remain the Same: Compstat and American Policing," in *Police Innovation: Contrasting Perspectives*, ed. David Weisburd and Anthony A. Braga (Cambridge, UK: Cambridge University Press, 2006), 284–304.

84. Eterno and Silverman, "NYPD's Compstat."

85. Ibid.

86. Sean Gardiner and Leonard Levitt, "NYPD: Some Crime Stats Misclassified," *New York Newsday*, June 21, 2003, 11; Ariel Hart, "Report Finds Atlanta Police Cut Figures on Crimes," *New York Times*, February 21, 2004, 26; Jaime Hernandez, Shannon O'Boye, and Ann W. O'Neill, "Sheriff's Office Scrutinizes Its Crime Data," *Sun Sentinel*, February 25, 2004, 6; Rocco Parascandola and Leonard Levitt, "Police Statistics: Numbers

Scrutinized," *New York Newsday*, March 22, 2004, 14; Ben Poston and Joel Rubin, "LAPD Misclassifies Nearly 1,200 Violent Crimes as Minor Offenses," *Los Angeles Times*, August 9, 2014, http://www.latimes.com/local/la-me-crimestats-lapd-20140810-story.html#page=1; Steve Ritea, "Five N.O. [New Orleans] Officers Fired Over Altered Crime Stats," *Times Picayune*, October 24, 2003, 1; Rebecca Webber and Gail Robinson, "Compstatmania," *Gotham Gazette*, July 7, 2003, http://www.gothamgazette.com/index.php/city/archives/1868-compstatmania.

87. Weisburd et al., "Critic: Changing Everything."

88. Ibid., 292.

89. Weisburd et al., "Reforming to Preserve."

90. Karmen.

91. Weisburd et al., "Critic: Changing Everything."

92. Matthew Breiding, Jieru Chen, and Michele Black, *Intimate Partner Violence in the United States—2010* (Atlanta: National Center for Injury Prevention and Control, Centers for Disease Control and Prevention, 2014).

93. Michael P. Johnson, *A Typology of Domestic Violence: Intimate Terrorism, Violent Resistance, and Situational Couple Violence* (Boston: Northeastern University Press, 2008).

94. UNICEF, *Behind Closed Doors: The Impact of Domestic Violence on Children* (New York: UNICEF, 2006), http://www.unicef.org/protection/files/BehindClosedDoors.pdf.

95. National Center for Injury Prevention and Control, *Costs of Intimate Partner Violence Against Women in the United States* (Atlanta: CDC, 2003), http://www.cdc.gov/violenceprevention/pdf/IPVBook-a.pdf.

96. Alesha Durfee, "Mandatory Arrest and Intimate Partner Violence," in *Criminal Justice Policy*, ed. Stacy Mallicoat and Christine Gardiner (Thousand Oaks, CA: Sage, 2013), 101–121; Joan Zorza, "Criminal Law of Misdemeanor Domestic Violence, 1970–1990," *Journal of Criminal Law and Criminology* 83 (1992): 46–72.

97. David Hirschel, Eve Buzawa, April Pattavina, and Don Faggiani, "Domestic Violence and Mandatory Arrest Laws: To What Extent Do They Influence Police Arrest Decisions?" *Journal of Criminal Law & Criminology* 98 (2007): 254–298.

98. Ibid.

99. April Pattavina, David Hirschel, Eve Buzawa, Don Faggiani, and Helen Bentley, "A Comparison of the Police Response to Heterosexual Versus Same-Sex Intimate Partner Violence," *Violence Against Women* 13 (2007): 374–394.

100. Hirschel et al.

101. Lawrence W. Sherman and Richard A. Berk, "The Minneapolis Domestic Violence Experiment," Police Foundation Reports, April 1984, http://www.policefoundation.org/wp-content/uploads/2015/07/Sherman-et-al.-1984-The-Minneapolis-Domestic-Violence-Experiment.pdf.

102. Laura Dugan, "Domestic Violence Legislation: Exploring Its Impact on the Likelihood of Domestic Violence, Police Involvement, and Arrest," *Criminology & Public Policy* 2 (2003): 283–312; Alesha Durfee and Matthew D. Fetzer, "Offense Type and the Arrest Decision in Cases of Intimate Partner Violence," *Crime and Delinquency* (2014). doi: 10.1177/0011128714540277; Dana A. Jones and Joanne Belknap, "Police Responses to Battering in a Progressive Pro-Arrest Jurisdiction," *Justice Quarterly* 16, no. 2 (1999): 249–273; Sylvia I. Mignon and William M. Holmes, "Police Response to Mandatory Arrest Laws," *Crime & Delinquency* 41, no. 4 (1995): 430–442; David Eitle, "The Influence of Mandatory Arrest Policies, Police Organizational Characteristics, and Situational Variables on the Probability of Arrest in Domestic Violence Cases," *Crime and Delinquency* 51, no. 4 (2005): 573–597; Hirschel et al.; Pattavina et al.

103. Judith McFarlane, Pam Willson, Dorothy Lemmey, and Ann Malecha, "Women Filing Assault Charges on an Intimate Partner: Criminal Justice Outcome and Future Violence Experienced," *Violence Against Women* 6, no. 4 (2000): 396–408.

104. Sherman and Berk.

105. Lawrence W. Sherman, "Influence of Criminology on Criminal Law: Evaluating Arrests for Misdemeanor Domestic Violence," *Journal of Criminal Law and Criminology* 83, no. 1 (1992): 19.

106. William DeLeon-Granados, William Wells, and Ruddyard Binsbacher, "Arresting Developments: Trends in Female Arrests for Domestic Violence and Proposed Explanations," *Violence Against Women* 12, no. 4 (2006): 355–371.

107. Meg Crager, Merril Cousin, and Tara Hardy, *Victim-Defendants: An Emerging Challenge in Responding to Domestic Violence in Seattle and the King County Region* (Seattle: King County Coalition Against Domestic Violence, 2003), http://www.mincava.umn.edu/documents/victimdefendant/victimdefendant.pdf.

108. Alesha Durfee, "Situational Ambiguity and Gendered Patterns of Arrest for Intimate Partner Violence," *Violence Against Women* 18, no. 1 (2012): 64–84.

109. Miriam H. Ruttenberg, "A Feminist Critique of Mandatory Arrest: An Analysis of Race and Gender in Domestic Violence Policy," *American University Journal of Gender and the Law* 2 (1994): 179; see also Leigh Goodmark, *A Troubled Marriage: Domestic Violence and the Legal System* (New York: NYU Press, 2011).

110. Evan Stark, *Coercive Control: How Men Entrap Women in Personal Life* (New York: Oxford University Press, 2007).

111. Alesha Durfee and Karen Rosenberg, "Teaching Sensitive Issues: Feminist Pedagogy and the Practice of Advocacy-Based Counseling," *Feminist Teacher* 19, no. 2 (2009): 103–121.

Careers in Criminal Justice: So You Want to Be a Police Officer?

a. Bureau of Labor Statistics, *Occupational Outlook Handbook, 2016–17 Edition* (Washington, DC: Bureau of Labor Statistics, 2015), http://www.bls.gov/ooh/protective-service/police-and-detectives.htm.

Spotlight: Cross-Deputizing Officers

a. "Navajo Nation Officials Endorse Proposal to Cross-Deputize Navajo County Sheriff Deputies," *Navajo-Hopi Observer*, December 29, 2009, http://nhonews.com/main.asp?SectionID=74&subsectionID=393&articleID=12130.

b. Russell Pearce, "Arizona's Immigration Law Is Constitutional—and Already Working," *U.S. News* Debate Club, April 20, 2012, http://www.usnews.com/debate-club/is-arizonas-sb-1070-immigration-law-constitutional/arizonas-immigration-law-is-constitutional–and-already-working.

c. Jeanne Butterfield, "The Constitution Protects U.S. Citizens From Laws Like Arizona's," *U.S. News* Debate Club, April 20, 2012, http://www.usnews.com/debate-club/is-arizonas-sb-1070-immigration-law-constitutional/the-constitution-protects-us-citizens-from-laws-like-arizonas.

d. American Civil Liberties Union, "Arizona's SB 1070," n.d., https://www.aclu.org/arizonas-sb-1070.

e. Seth Freed Wessler, "What Ever Happened to SB 1070?" Colorlines, March 5, 2013, http://colorlines.com/archives/2013/03/what_happened_to_sb_1070_the_anti-immigrant_tide_recedes_in_the_states.html.

f. Liana Maris Epstein and Phillip Atiba Goff, "Safety or Liberty? The Bogus Trade-Off of Cross-Deputization Policy," *Analyses of Social Issues and Public Policy* 11, no. 1 (2011): 314–324.

g. Geoffrey Hoffman, "SB 1070 and the Impending Police State," Jurist, May 3, 2012, http://jurist.org/forum/2012/05/geoffrey-hoffman-immigration.php.

Around the World: Community Policing in Action

a. Benoit Dupont, "The French Police System: Caught Between a Rock and a Hard Place—The Tension of Serving Both the State and the Public," in *Comparative Policing: The Struggle for Democratization*, ed. M. R. Haberfeld and Ibrahim Cerrah (Thousand Oaks, CA: Sage), 247–276.

b. Maurice Punch, Kees van der Vijver, and Olga Zoomer, "Dutch 'COP': Developing Community Policing in the Netherlands," *Policing: An International Journal of Police Strategies & Management* 25, no. 1 (2002): 60–79.

c. Jude Joffe-Block, "El Salvador Tries to Rein in Crime With Community Policing," PBS Newshour, October 9, 2014, http://www.pbs.org/newshour/rundown/el-salvador-tries-rein-crime-community-policing.

d. David Weisburd, Orit Shalev, and Menachem Amir, "Community Policing in Israel: Resistance and Change," *Policing: An International Journal of Police Strategies & Management* 25, no. 1 (2002): 80–109.

e. Mike Brogden, "'Horses for Courses' and 'Thin Blue Lines': Community Policing in Transitional Society," *Police Quarterly* 8, no. 1 (2005): 64–98.

CHAPTER 8

1. Terry v. Ohio, 392 U.S. 1 (1968).

2. Christopher Mathias, "NYPD Stop and Frisks: 15 Shocking Facts About a Controversial Program," *Huffington Post*, May 15, 2012, http://www.huffingtonpost.com/2012/05/13/nypd-stop-and-frisks-15-shocking-facts_n_1513362.html.

3. Joe Coscarelli, "Stop-and-Frisks Still No Fun for Black and Latino Men," *New York Magazine*, May 10, 2012, http://nymag.com/daily/intelligencer/2012/05/stop-and-frisks-still-no-fun-for-blacks-latinos.html

4. Andrew Gelman, Jeffrey Fagan, and Alex Kiss, "An Analysis of the New York City Police Department's 'Stop-and-Frisk' Policy in the Context of Claims of Racial Bias," *Journal of the American Statistical Association* 102, no. 479 (2007): 813–823.

5. Bernard Vaughan, "NYPD's 'Stop-and-Frisk' Practice Unconstitutional, Judge Rules," Reuters, August 12, 2013, http://www.reuters.com/article/2013/08/12/us-usa-newyork-police-idUSBRE97B0FK20130812.

6. Anthony M. DeStefano, "NYPD Analysis: Stop-and-Frisk Activity Down as Serious Crime Declines," *Newsday*, November 27, 2014, https://www.newsday.com/news/new-york/nypd-analysis-stop-and-frisk-activity-down-as-serious-crime-declines-1.9659026.

7. Rebecca Leber, "NYC Police Said Stop-and-Frisks Reduce Violent Crime. This Chart Says Otherwise," *New Republic*, December 2, 2014, http://www.newrepublic.com/article/120461/nypd-stop-and-frisk-drops-79-percent-and-crime-drops-too.

8. Carroll v. United States, 267 U.S. 132 (1925).

9. United States v. Ross, 456 U.S. 798 (1982).

10. United States v. Chadwick, 433 U.S. 1 (1977).

11. Cardwell v. Lewis, 417 U.S. 583 (1974).

12. California v. Acevedo, 500 U.S. 565 (1991).

13. Arizona v. Gant, 556 U.S. 332 (2009).

14. Miranda v. Arizona, 384 U.S. 436 (1966).

15. Rhode Island v. Innis, 446 U.S. 291 (1980).

16. Oregon State Police, "Code of Ethical Conduct," n.d., http://www.oregon.gov/osp/pages/code_conduct.aspx.

17. Michael C. Braswell, Belinda R. McCarthy, and Bernard J. McCarthy, *Justice, Crime and Ethics*, 7th ed. (Cincinnati: Anderson Publishing, 2011).

18. Joycelyn M. Pollock and Ronald F. Becker, "Ethics Training: Using Officers' Dilemmas," *FBI Law Enforcement Bulletin* 65, no. 11 (1996): 20–27.

19. David Bayley and Robert Perito, *Police Corruption: What Past Scandals Teach About Current Challenges* (Washington, DC: United States Institute of Peace, 2011).

20. Michael D. White, *Current Issues and Controversies in Policing* (Boston: Pearson Allyn Bacon, 2007).

21. Edwin J. Delattre, *Character and Cops: Ethics in Policing*, 6th ed. (Washington, DC: AEI Press, 2011).

22. PBS, "Rampart Scandal Timeline," n.d., http://www.pbs.org/wgbh/pages/frontline/shows/lapd/scandal/cron.html.

23. Michael Buerger, "The Myths of Racial Profiling," in *Demystifying Crime and Criminal Justice*, 2nd ed., ed. Robert M. Bohm and Jeffrey T. Walker (Oxford, UK: Oxford University Press, 2013).

24. United States v. Brignoni-Ponce, 422 U.S. 873 (1975); United States v. Jones 615 F. 3d 544 (2001).

25. Brown v. City of Oneonta, 195 F. 3d 111 (1999).

26. Michael L. Birzer and Gwynne Harris Birzer, "Race Matters: A Critical Look at Racial Profiling, It's a Matter for the Courts," *Journal of Criminal Justice* 34, no. 6 (2006): 643–651.

27. Frank Newport, "In U.S., 24% of Young Black Men Say Police Dealings Unfair," Gallup Organization, July 16, 2013, http://

www.gallup.com/poll/163523/
one-four-young-black-men-say-
police-dealings-unfair.aspx?utm_
source=racial%20profiling&utm_
medium=search&utm_
campaign=tiles.

28. Christine Eith and Matthew R. Durose, *Contacts Between Police and the Public, 2008* (Washington, DC: Bureau of Justice Statistics, 2011), http://www .bjs.gov/content/pub/pdf/cpp08 .pdf.

29. George E. Higgins, Gennaro F. Vito, and Elizabeth L. Grossi, "The Impact of Race on the Police Decision to Search During a Traffic Stop: A Focal Concerns Theory Perspective," *Journal of Contemporary Criminal Justice* 28, no. 2 (2012): 166–183.

30. Rob Tillyer, Charles F. Klahm IV, and Robin S. Engel, "The Discretion to Search: A Multilevel Examination of Driver Demographics and Officer Characteristics," *Journal of Contemporary Criminal Justice* 28, no. 2 (2012): 184–205.

31. Albert J. Meehan and Michael Ponder, "How Roadside Composition Matters in Analyzing Police Data on Racial Profiling," *Police Quarterly* 5, no. 3 (2002): 306–333.

32. Samuel Walker, Cassia C. Spohn, and Miriam DeLone, *The Color of Justice: Race, Ethnicity, and Crime in America*, 5th ed. (Belmont, CA: Wadsworth Cengage, 2012).

33. Tennessee v. Garner, 471 U.S. 1 (1985).

34. International Association of Chiefs of Police and Office of Community Oriented Policing Services, *Emerging Use of Force Issues: Balancing Public and Officer Safety* (Washington, DC: U.S. Department of Justice, 2012), http://www.theiacp.org/ portals/0/pdfs/Emerging UseofForceIssues041612.pdf.

35. William R. King and Matthew C. Matusiak, "The Myth That Police Use of Force Is Widespread," in *Demystifying Crime and Criminal Justice*, 2nd ed., ed. Robert M. Bohm and Jeffrey T. Walker (Oxford, UK: Oxford University Press, 2013).

36. Leila Atassi, "Lawsuits Against City of Cleveland Blame Poor Training for Police Use of Excessive Force: Forcing Change," Cleveland.com, January 27, 2015, http://www.cleveland.com/ forcing-change/index.ssf/2015/01/ lawsuits_against_city_of_cleve.html.

37. Bruce Geiselman, "Cleveland Police Lack Training and Technology, Justice Department Finds," Cleveland.com, December 5, 2014, http://www .cleveland.com/metro/index .ssf/2014/12/cleveland_police_lack_ training.html.

38. Tom McEwen and Frank Leahy, *Final Report: Less Than Lethal Force Technologies in Law Enforcement and Correctional Agencies* (Washington, DC: National Institute of Justice, 1994).

39. Bureau of Justice Statistics, "Use of Force," n.d., http://www.bjs.gov/ index.cfm?ty=tp&tid=703.

40. Lorraine Mazerolle, Sarah Bennett, Matthew Manning, Patricia Ferguson, and Elise Sargeant, "Legitimacy in Policing," *Campbell Collaboration Systematic Review* (2010), campbellcollaboration.org/lib/ download/914.

41. Ben Bradford, Jonathan Jackson, and Mike Hough, "Police Legitimacy in Action: Lessons for Theory and Policy," in *The Oxford Handbook of Police and Policing*, ed. Michael D. Reisig and Robert J. Kane (Oxford, UK: Oxford University Press, 2014), 551–570.

42. Ronald Weitzer and Steven A. Tuch, "Determinants of Public Satisfaction With the Police," *Police Quarterly* 8, no. 3 (2005): 292.

43. Chico Harlan, Wesley Lowery, and Kimberly Kindy, "Ferguson Police Officer Won't Be Charged in Fatal Shooting," *Washington Post*, November 25, 2014, http://www .washingtonpost.com/politics/grand-jury-reaches-decision-in-case-of-ferguson-officer/2014/11/24/de48e7e4-71d7-11e4-893f-86bd390a3340_story .html.

44. Erik Eckholm and Matt Apuzzo, "Darren Wilson Is Cleared of Rights Violations in Ferguson Shooting," *New York Times*, March 4, 2015, http://www.nytimes. com/2015/03/05/us/darren-wilson-is-cleared-of-rights-violations-in-ferguson-shooting.html.

45. Leonard Territo and Harold J. Vetter, "Stress and Police Personnel," *Journal of Police Science and Administration* 9, no. 2 (1981): 195–208.

46. Merry Morash, Robin Haarr, and Dae-Hoon Kwak, "Multilevel Influences on Police Stress," *Journal of Contemporary Criminal Justice* 22, no. 1 (2006): 26–43.

47. Gary A. Adams and Jill Buck, "Social Stressors and Strain Among Police Officers: It's Not Just the Bad Guys," *Criminal Justice and Behavior* 37, no. 9 (2010): 1030–1040.

48. Morash, Haarr, and Kwak.

49. Matthew J. Hickman, Jennifer Fricas, Kevin J. Strom, and Mark W. Pope, "Mapping Police Stress," *Police Quarterly* 14, no. 3 (2011): 227–250.

50. Robyn R. M. Gershon, Briana Barocas, Allison N. Canton, Xianbin Li, and David Vlahov, "Mental, Physical, and Behavioral Outcomes Associated With Perceived Work Stress in Police Officers," *Criminal Justice and Behavior* 36, no. 3 (2009): 275–289.

51. Shih-Ya Kuo, "Occupational Stress, Job Satisfaction, and Affective Commitment to Policing Among Taiwanese Police Officers," *Police Quarterly* 18, no. 1 (2015): 27–54.

52. Russell Jones and Ashraf Kagee, "Predictors of Post-Traumatic Stress Symptoms Among South African Police Personnel," *South African Journal of Psychology* 35, no. 2 (2005): 209–224.

53. See Justin T. Ready and Jacob T. N. Young, "Three Myths About Police Body Cams," *Slate Magazine*, September 2, 2014, http://www. slate.com/articles/technology/ future_tense/2014/09/ferguson_body_ cams_myths_about_police_body_ worn_recorders.html. In this article, the authors discuss how people can draw different conclusions from the same video. The authors also discuss general concerns with BWCs.

54. See George L. Kelling, Tony Pate, Duane Dieckman, and Charles E. Brown, *The Kansas City Preventive Patrol Experiment: A Summary Report* (Washington, DC: Police Foundation, 1974).

55. See, in general, Anthony A. Braga, *Problem-Oriented Policing and Crime Prevention* (Monsey, NY: Criminal Justice Press, 2008).

56. See Barak Ariel and William Farrar, *Self-Awareness to Being Watched and Socially-Desirable Behavior: A Field Experiment on the Effect of Body-Worn*

Cameras on Police Use-of-Force (Washington, DC: Police Foundation, 2013).

57. John Liederbach, Lorenzo M. Boyd, Robert W. Taylor, and Soraya K. Kawucha, "Is It an Inside Job? An Examination of Internal Affairs Complaint Investigation Files and the Production of Nonsustained Findings," *Criminal Justice Policy Review* 18, no. 4 (2007): 353–377.

58. Ibid.

59. Robert A. Brown, "Black, White, and Unequal: Examining Situational Determinants of Arrest Decisions From Police–Suspect Encounters," *Criminal Justice Studies* 18, no. 1 (2005): 51–68.

60. Robert E. Worden, "Situational and Attitudinal Explanations of Police Behavior: A Theoretical Reappraisal and Empirical Assessment," *Law and Society Review* 23, no. 4 (1989): 667–711.

Careers in Criminal Justice: So You Want to Be a Criminal Investigator?

a. Bureau of Labor Statistics, *Occupational Outlook Handbook, 2016–17 Edition*, Police and Detectives (Washington, DC: Bureau of Labor Statistics, 2015), http://www.bls.gov/ooh/protective-service/police-and-detectives.htm.

Spotlight: DNA Collection

a. Nathan James, *DNA Testing in Criminal Justice: Background, Current Law, Grants, and Issues* (Washington, DC: Congressional Research Service, 2012), http://fas.org/sgp/crs/misc/R41800.pdf.

b. National Institute of Justice, "DNA Sample Collection From Arrestees," December 7, 2012, http://nij.gov/topics/forensics/evidence/dna/pages/collection-from-arrestees.aspx.

c. John M. Butler, *Fundamentals of Forensic DNA Typing* (Burlington, MA: Academic Press, 2009).

d. James.

e. Julie Samuels, Elizabeth Davies, Dwight Pope, and Ashleigh Holand, "Collecting DNA From Arrestees: Implementation Lessons," *NIJ Journal* 270 (2012): http://nij.gov/journals/270/pages/arrestee-dna.aspx.

f. Maryland v. King, 569 U.S. ___ (2013).

Around the World: Policing in the Middle East

a. Tonita Murray, "Police-Building in Afghanistan: A Case Study of Civil Security Reform," *International Peacekeeping* 14, no. 1 (2007): 108–126.

b. David Bayley and Robert Perito, *Police Corruption: What Past Scandals Teach About Current Challenges* (Washington, DC: United States Institute of Peace, 2011).

c. Ibid., 5.

d. Cornelius Friesendorf and Jörg Krempel, *Militarized Versus Civilian Policing: Problems of Reforming the Afghan National Police* (Frankfurt, Germany: Peace Research Institute Frankfurt, 2011), http://edoc.vifapol.de/opus/volltexte/2011/3207/pdf/prif102.pdf.

e. Ibid.

f. Murray.

g. Connie M. Koski, "Afghanistan at a Crossroads: The Quest for Democratic Policing in a Post-9/11 Era," *Police Practice and Research* 10, no. 4 (2009): 317–332.

Spotlight: Kelly Thomas and the Fullerton Police Department

a. Doug Irving and Lou Ponsi, "Kelly Thomas: 92 Police Encounters Since 1990," *Orange County Register*, August 21, 2013, http://www.ocregister.com/articles/thomas-374958-police-attorney.html.

b. Elizabeth Barber, "Kelly Thomas Case: Why Police Were Acquitted in Killing of Homeless Man," *Christian Science Monitor*, January 14, 2014, http://www.csmonitor.com/USA/USA-Update/2014/0114/Kelly-Thomas-case-why-police-were-acquitted-in-killing-of-homeless-man-video.

c. Jonathan Lloyd, "Timeline: The Kelly Thomas Case," NBC Los Angeles, January 13, 2014, http://www.nbclosangeles.com/news/local/Timeline-The-Kelly-Thomas-Case-in-Fullerton-126851443.html.

d. Ian Lovett, "In California, a Champion for Police Cameras," *New York Times*, August 21, 2013, http://www.nytimes.com/2013/08/22/us/in-california-a-champion-for-police-cameras.html.

CHAPTER 9

1. Riley v. California, 573 U.S. ___ (2014).

2. "Court: Simpson Still Liable for $33.5 Million Judgment," NBC5, February 21, 2008, http://web.archive.org/web/20081009230444/http://www.nbc5.com/news/15364921/detail.html.

3. Matt Baker, "Erica Kinsman Sues NFL Prospect Jameis Winston," *Tampa Bay Times*, April 16, 2015, http://www.tampabay.com/sports/football/bucs/erica-kinsman-sues-nfl-prospect-jameis-winston/2225851.

4. Marc Tracy, "Florida State Settles Suit Over Jameis Winston Rape Inquiry," *New York Times*, January 25, 2016, http://www.nytimes.com/2016/01/26/sports/football/florida-state-to-pay-jameis-winstons-accuser-950000-in-settlement.html?_r=0.

5. John Carney, "Why the Boston Marathon Attack Is a Federal Crime," CNBC, April 22, 2013, http://www.cnbc.com/id/100662216; see also G. Jeffrey MacDonald, "Tsarnaev Guilty on All 30 Charges in Boston Bombing," *USA Today*, April 8, 2015, http://www.usatoday.com/story/news/nation/2015/04/08/boston-marathon-bombing-jury-deliberation/25451777.

6. "Apologetic Nichols Is Sentenced to Life for Oklahoma Bombing," *New York Times*, August 10, 2004, http://www.nytimes.com/2004/08/10/us/apologetic-nichols-is-sentenced-to-life-for-oklahoma-bombing.html; see also Jo Thomas, "Nichols Found Guilty in Oklahoma City Case," *New York Times*, December 28, 1997, http://www.nytimes.com/1997/12/28/weekinreview/december-21-27-nichols-found-guilty-in-oklahoma-city-case.html.

7. U.S. Courts, "U.S. Magistrate Judges —Judicial Business 2015," n.d., http://www.uscourts.gov/statistics-reports/us-magistrate-judges-judicial-business-2015.

8. U.S. Courts, "Status of Magistrate Judge Positions and Appointments —Judicial Business 2015," n.d., http://www.uscourts.gov/statistics-reports/status-magistrate-judge-positions-and-appointments-judicial-business-2015.

9. U.S. Courts, "Comparing Federal & State Courts," n.d., http://www.uscourts.gov/about-federal-courts/court-role-and-structure/comparing-federal-state-courts.

10. U.S. Courts, "U.S. District Courts—Judicial Business 2015," n.d., http://www.uscourts.gov/statistics-reports/us-district-courts-judicial-business-2015.

11. U.S. Courts, "U.S. Courts of Appeals—Judicial Business 2015," n.d., http://www.uscourts.gov/statistics-reports/us-courts-appeals-judicial-business-2015.

12. U.S. Courts, "Table B-12—U.S. Courts of Appeals Judicial Business," September 30, 2015, http://www.uscourts.gov/statistics/table/b-12/judicial-business/2015/09/30.

13. U.S. Courts, "Supreme Court Procedures," n.d., http://www.uscourts.gov/about-federal-courts/educational-resources/about-educational-outreach/activity-resources/supreme-1.

14. U.S. Supreme Court, "The Supreme Court of the United States—History," n.d., http://www.judiciary.senate.gov/nominations/SupremeCourt/SupremeCourtHistory.cfm.

15. Byron L. Warnken, "Supreme Court Justices by Race, Religion, Gender and Origin," April 23, 2010, http://professorwarnken.com/2010/04/23/supreme-court-justices-by-race.

16. Juan Williams, *Thurgood Marshall: American Revolutionary* (New York, NY: Three Rivers Press, 2000).

17. Biography.com, "Clarence Thomas," n.d., http://www.biography.com/people/clarence-thomas-9505658.

18. "Nine Justices, Ten Years: A Statistical Retrospective," *Harvard Law Review* 118 (2004): 521.

19. David G. Savage, "Sotomayor Takes Her Seat," *American Bar Association Journal* 95, no. 10 (2009): 24–25.

20. Center for American Women and Politics, "Women on the U.S. Supreme Court," n.d., http://www.cawp.rutgers.edu/facts/levels_of_office/us_supreme_court.

21. LaFountain, Schauffler, Strickland, Holt, and Lewis, eds., "Court Statistics Project DataViewer," last updated March 15, 2016, http://www.ncsc.org/Sitecore/Content/Microsites/PopUp/Home/CSP/CSP_Intro.

22. Robert C. LaFountain, Shauna M. Strickland, Richard Y. Schauffler, Kathryn A. Holt, and Kathryn Lewis, *Examining the Work of State Courts: An Analysis of 2013 State Court Caseloads* (National Center for State Courts, 2015), http://www.courtstatistics.org/~/media/Microsites/Files/CSP/EWSC_CSP_2015.ashx.

23. U.S. Attorney's Office, "Southern District of Texas: Assistant U.S. Attorney Positions," 2015, http://www.justice.gov/usao-sdtx/assistant-us-attorney-positions.

24. Steven W. Perry and Duren Banks, *Prosecutors in State Courts, 2007—Statistical Tables* (Washington, DC: Bureau of Justice Statistics, 2011), http://www.bjs.gov/content/pub/pdf/psc07st.pdf.

25. American Bar Association, "Rule 3.8: Special Responsibilities of a Prosecutor," n.d., http://www.americanbar.org/groups/professional_responsibility/publications/model_rules_of_professional_conduct/rule_3_8_special_responsibilities_of_a_prosecutor.html.

26. Brady v. Maryland, 373 U.S. 83 (1963).

27. California Innocence Project, "Prosecutorial Misconduct," n.d., http://californiainnocenceproject.org/issues-we-face/prosecutorial-misconduct.

28. Innocence Project, "The Causes of Wrongful Conviction," n.d., http://www.innocenceproject.org/causes-wrongful-conviction.

29. David A. Love, "Finally, a Prosecutor Goes to Jail for Evidence Tampering," *Huffington Post*, January 23, 2014, http://www.huffingtonpost.com/david-a-love/finally-a-prosecutor-goes-to-jail_b_4268214.html.

30. Gideon v. Wainwright, 372 U.S. 335 (1963).

31. U.S. Courts, "Juror Pay," n.d., http://www.uscourts.gov/services-forms/jury-service/juror-pay.

32. U.S. Courts, "Juror Qualification," n.d., http://www.uscourts.gov/services-forms/jury-service/juror-qualifications.

33. Batson v. Kentucky, 476 U.S. 79 (1986).

34. Apodaca v. Oregon, 406 U.S. 404 (1972); see also Jackson v. Louisiana (U.S. Sup. Ct.).

35. Barry Scheck, Peter Neufeld, and Jim Dwyer, *Actual Innocence: When Justice Goes Wrong and How to Make It Right* (New York: New American Library, 2002).

36. Federal Rules of Evidence, "Rule 802. The Rule Against Hearsay," http://www.law.cornell.edu/rules/fre/rule_802.

37. Federal Rules of Evidence, "Rule 702. Testimony by Expert Witnesses," http://www.law.cornell.edu/rules/fre/rule_702.

38. *Judicial Council of California Criminal Jury Instructions* (San Francisco: Judicial Council of California, 2016), http://www.courts.ca.gov/partners/documents/calcrim_2016_edition.pdf.

39. Innocence Project, "Michael Morton," n.d., http://www.innocenceproject.org/Content/Michael_Morton.php.

40. Pamela Colloff, "The Guilty Man," *Texas Monthly*, June 2013, http://www.texasmonthly.com/story/guilty-man.

41. Molly Hennessy-Fiske, "Ex-prosecutor Punished for Withholding Evidence in Murder Case," *Los Angeles Times*, November 8, 2013, http://www.latimes.com/nation/la-na-texas-judge-20131109-story.html.

42. Innocence Project, "Texas Man Never Claimed Innocence, but Is Poised for Exoneration," July 25, 2014, http://www.innocenceproject.org/news-events-exonerations/texas-man-never-claimed-innocence-but-is-poised-for-exoneration.

43. Yamiche Alcindor, "Man Exonerated by DNA—and He Didn't Even Request It," *USA Today*, July 24, 2014, http://www.usatoday.com/story/news/nation/2014/07/24/dallas-mans-exoneration-makes-national-history/13040299.

44. J. David Goodman, "Man Charged With Fatal Shoving of New York Subway Rider," *New York Times*, November 18, 2014, http://www.nytimes.com/2014/11/19/nyregion/bronx-subway-killing-investigation.html.

45. Innocence Project, "Cameron Todd Willingham: Wrongfully Convicted and Executed in Texas," September 13, 2010, http://www.innocenceproject.org/Content/Cameron_Todd_Willingham_Wrongfully_Convicted_and_Executed_in_Texas.php.

46. National Academy of Sciences, *Strengthening Forensic Science in the United States: A Path Forward* (Washington, DC: National Academies Press, 2009).

47. Innocence Project, "Unvalidated or Improper Forensic Science," n.d., http://www.innocenceproject.org/understand/Unreliable-Limited-Science.php.

48. "Judicial pronouncements on plea bargaining indicate that the courts are as sharply split as the commentators over the propriety of negotiating a guilty plea." Frank v. Blackburn, 646 F.2d 873, 876 (1980).

49. Plea bargaining "remains a controversial issue, provoking praise, criticism and extensive debate among legal scholars and practitioners." Ibid.

50. Ibid., at 875.

51. Shankle v. State, 119 S.W.3d 808, 813 (2003).

52. Ibid.

53. Ibid.

54. Ibid.

55. U.S. Constitution, Amendment VI (emphasis added).

56. United States v. Gaudin, 515 U.S. 506, 510–11 (1995).

57. Nebraska Press Ass'n. v. Stuart, 427 U.S. 539, 551 (1976).

58. Lafler v. Cooper, 132 S. Ct. 1376, 1397 (2012) (Scalia, J., dissenting).

59. Ibid.

60. For "guilty defendants it often—perhaps usually—results in a sentence well below what the law prescribes for the actual crime." Ibid.

61. Ibid., at 1398.

62. Missouri v. Frye, 132 S. Ct. 1399, 1407 (2012).

63. "If every criminal charge were subjected to a full-scale trial, the States and the Federal Government would need to multiply by many times the number of judges and court facilities." Santobello v. New York, 404 U.S. 257, 260 (1971).

64. *Frye.*

65. Ibid.

66. See Douglas D. Guidorizzi, "Should We Really 'Ban' Plea Bargaining? The Core Concerns of Plea Bargaining Critics," *Emory Law Journal* 47 (1998): 753–767.

67. A plea, by "shortening the time between charge and disposition . . . enhances whatever may be the rehabilitative prospects of the guilty when they are ultimately imprisoned." Santobello v. New York, 404 U.S. 257, 261 (1971).

68. Finality is "perhaps the most important benefit of plea bargaining." United States v. Navarro-Botello, 912 F.2d 318, 322 (1990).

69. *Lafler* (Scalia, dissenting).

70. *Santobello.*

Spotlight: The 50th Anniversary: of *Gideon v. Wainwright*

a. Los Angeles County Public Defenders Office, "Our History—The Public Defender Concept Why and When?" n.d., http://pd.co.la.ca.us/About_history.html; see also Los Angeles County, "2013–2014 Final Budget," n.d., http://www.lacountyannualreport.com/2013/files/Budget/2013-14%20Final%20Budget%20112713.pdf.

b. Erinn Herberman and Tracey Kyckelhahn, *State Government Indigent Defense Expenditures, FY 2008–2012—Updated* (Washington, DC: Bureau of Justice Statistics), http://www.bjs.gov/content/pub/pdf/sgidc0812.pdf.

c. Gideon at 50, "The Issue," n.d., http://gideonat50.org/the-issue.

d. RubinBrown, *The Missouri Project: A Study of the Missouri Public Defender System and Attorney Workload Standards, With a National Blueprint* (St. Louis: RubinBrown, 2014), http://www.americanbar.org/content/dam/aba/events/legal_aid_indigent_defendants/2014/ls_sclaid_5c_the_missouri_project_report.authcheckdam.pdf.

e. Andrew Cohen, "How Americans Lost the Right to Counsel, 50 Years After 'Gideon,'" *The Atlantic*, March 13, 2013, http://www.theatlantic.com/national/archive/2013/03/how-americans-lost-the-right-to-counsel-50-years-after-gideon/273433.

f. Mark Sherman, "Gideon v. Wainwright 50th Anniversary: Serious Problems Persist in Indigent Legal Defense," Huffington Post, March 18, 2013, http://www.huffingtonpost.com/2013/03/18/gideon-v-wainright-50th-anniversary-_n_2899646.html.

g. California Commission on the Fair Administration of Justice, *Report and Recommendations on Funding of Defense Services in California*, April 14, 2008, http://www.ccfaj.org/documents/reports/prosecutorial/official/OFFICIAL%20REPORT%20ON%20DEFENSE%20SERVICES.pdf.

h. Public Defender, Eleventh Judicial Circuit of Florida, et al. v. State of Florida, Nos. SC09-1181 and SC10-1349, slip op. (Fla. May 23, 2013).

Around the World: Juries in a Global Context

a. American Bar Association, "Dialogue on the American Jury: Part I: The History of Trial by Jury," n.d., http://www.americanbar.org/content/dam/aba/migrated/jury/moreinfo/dialoguepart1.authcheckdam.pdf.

b. Valerie P. Hans, "Jury Systems Around the World," *Annual Review of Law and Social Science* 4 (2008): 275–297, http://scholarship.law.cornell.edu/cgi/viewcontent.cgi?article=1378&context=facpub.

c. Ibid.

d. History.com Staff, "Apartheid," History.com, 2010, http://www.history.com/topics/apartheid.

e. Richard Allen Greene and Brent Swails, "Oscar Pistorius Verdict: South African Judge Decided Athlete's Fate," CNN, April 10, 2014, http://www.cnn.com/2014/09/10/world/africa/oscar-pistorius-judge-masipa.

f. Peter J. van Koppen, "Jury Trials: Opposed," IIP Digital, July 1, 2009, http://iipdigital.usembassy.gov/st/english/publication/2009/07/20090706173355ebyessedo0.3281475.html#axzz331Ih8MSm.

CHAPTER 10

1. Traciy Curry-Reyes, "Chris Brown Arrest Record: Felony Assault Timeline," Examiner.com, October 28, 2013, http://www.examiner.com/article/chris-brown-arrest-felony-arrest-record-timeline.

2. Anthony McCartney, "Chris Brown's Rihanna Assault Case Closed by Judge," *Huffington Post*, March 20, 2015, http://www.huffingtonpost.com/2015/03/20/chris-brown-rihanna-closed_n_6913038.html.

3. Yahoo! Celebrity Staff, "Justin Bieber: A Timeline of Trouble Leading Up to His Arrest," *US Magazine*, January 24, 2014, http://www.usmagazine.com/celebrity-news/news/justin-bieber-a-timeline-of-trouble-leading-up-to-his-arrest-2014241.

4. CNN Wire, "Justin Bieber Found Guilty of Assault, Careless Driving in Canada," Fox61, June 4, 2015, http://foxct.com/2015/06/04/justin-bieber-found-guilty-of-assault-careless-driving-in-canada.

5. Daniel S. Nagin, "Deterrence: Scaring Offenders Straight," in *Correctional Theory: Context and Consequences*, ed. Francis T. Cullen and Cheryl Lero Jonson (Thousand Oaks, CA: Sage, 2012), 67–98.

6. Ronald L. Akers and Christine S. Sellers, *Criminological Theories: Introduction, Evaluation and Application*, 6th ed. (Oxford, UK: Oxford University Press, 2012).

7. Francis T. Cullen and Paul Gendreau, "Assessing Correctional Rehabilitation: Policy, Practice, and Prospects," in *Criminal Justice 2000, Vol. 3. Policies, Processes, and Decisions of the Criminal Justice System*, ed. Julie Horney (Washington, DC: National Institute of Justice), https://www.ncjrs.gov/criminal_justice2000/vol_3/03d.pdf.

8. Ibid.

9. Robert Martinson, "What Works? Questions and Answers About Prison Reform," *Public Interest* 35 (1974): 22–54.

10. David Farabee, "Reexamining Martinson's Critique: A Cautionary Note for Evaluators. *Crime & Delinquency* 48, no. 1 (2002): 189–192.

11. David B. Taylor, "Robert Martinson," in *Encyclopedia of Prisons and Correctional Facilities*, ed. Mary F. Bosworth (Thousand Oaks, CA: Sage, 2005), 573–574.

12. Robert J. Bidinotto, "Getting Away With Murder," *Readers Digest*, July 1988.

13. Eric Benson, "Dukakis's Regret: What the Onetime Democratic Nominee Learned From the Willie Horton Ad," *New York Magazine*, July 17, 2012, http://nymag.com/news/frank-rich/michael-dukakis-2012-6.

14. Etienne Benson, "Rehabilitate or Punish?" *Monitor on Psychology* 34, no. 7 (2003): 46, http://www.apa.org/monitor/julaug03/rehab.aspx; see also Rick Sarre, "Beyond 'What Works?' A 25 Year Jubilee Retrospective of Robert Martinson's Famous Article," *Australian and New Zealand Journal of Criminology* 34, no. 1 (2001): 38–46.

15. Doris Layton MacKenzie, "First Do No Harm: A Look at Correctional Policies and Programs Today," *Journal of Experimental Criminology* 9, no. 1 (2013): 1–17.

16. Hilde Wermink, Robert Apel, Paul Nieuwbeerta, and Arjan A. J. Blokland, "The Incapacitation Effect of First-Time Imprisonment: A Matched Samples Comparison," *Journal of Quantitative Criminology* 29, no. 4 (2013): 579–600.

17. M. Keith Chen and Jesse M. Shapiro, "Do Harsher Prison Conditions Reduce Recidivism? A Discontinuity-Based Approach," *American Law and Economics Review* 9, no. 1 (2007): 1–29.

18. Eric J. Wodahl, John H. Boman IV, and Brett E. Garland, "Responding to Probation and Parole Violations: Are Jail Sanctions More Effective Than Community-Based Graduated Sanctions?" *Journal of Criminal Justice* 43, no. 3 (2015): 242–250.

19. Peter Liberman, "Retributive Support for International Punishment and Torture," *Journal of Conflict Resolution* 57, no. 2 (2013): 285–306; see also Scott Vollum, Stacy Mallicoat, and Jacqueline Buffington-Vollum, "Death Penalty Attitudes in an Increasingly Critical Climate: Value-Expressive Support and Attitude Mutability," *Southwest Journal of Criminal Justice* 5, no. 3 (2009): 221–242.

20. Lawrence W. Sherman and Heather Strang, *Restorative Justice: The Evidence* (London: Smith Institute, 2007).

21. Lawrence W. Sherman, Heather Strang, Evan Mayo-Wilson, Daniel J. Woods, and Barak Ariel, "Repeat Offending? Findings From a Campbell Systematic Review," *Journal of Quantitative Criminology* 31, no. 1 (2014): 1–24.

22. Blakely v. Washington, 542 U.S. 26 (2004).

23. United States v. Booker, 543 U.S. 220 (2005).

24. U.S. Sentencing Commission, "Report on the Impact of *United States v. Booker* on Federal Sentencing," *Federal Sentencing Reporter* 18, no. 3 (2006): 190–197.

25. Byungbae Kim, Mario V. Cano, Kiduek Kim, and Cassia Spohn, "The Impact of *United States v. Booker* and *Gall/Kimbrough v. United States* on Sentence Severity: Assessing Social Context and Judicial Discretion," *Crime & Delinquency* (2014): 1–23.

26. U.S. Sentencing Commission.

27. Families Against Mandatory Minimums, "Federal Mandatory Minimums," February 25, 2013, http://famm.org/wp-content/uploads/2013/08/Chart-All-Fed-MMs-NW.pdf.

28. Woodson v. North Carolina, 428 U.S. 280 (1976).

29. Families Against Mandatory Minimums, "Recent State-Level Reforms to Mandatory Minimum Laws," June 30, 2013, http://famm.org/wp-content/uploads/2013/08/FS-List-of-State-Reforms-6.30.pdf.

30. Johnson v. United States, 576 U.S.— (2015). http://www.supremecourt.gov/opinions/14pdf/13-7120_p86b.pdf.

31. Death Penalty Information Center, "Executions in the U.S. 1608–2002: The Espy File," http://www.deathpenaltyinfo.org/executions-us-1608-2002-espy-file?scid=8&did=269.

32. Death Penalty Information Center, "Georgia," http://www.deathpenaltyinfo.org/georgia-1.

33. *Woodson*.

34. Death Penalty Information Center, "Descriptions of Execution Methods," http://www.deathpenaltyinfo.org/descriptions-execution-methods?scid=8&did=479#firing.

35. Christopher Q. Cutler, "Nothing Less Than the Dignity of Man: Evolving Standards, Botched Executions and Utah's Controversial Use of the Firing Squad," *Cleveland State Law Review* 50 (2002–2003): 335–424.

36. Mikal Gilmore, *Shot in the Heart* (New York: Anchor Books, 1995), 351.

37. *Death Penalty Provisions*, H.B. 180, Utah State Legislature (2004), http://www.le.state.ut.us/%7E2004/htmdoc/hbillhtm/hb0180.htm.

38. Steve Almasy and Dana Ford, "Utah to Allow Firing Squads for Executions," CNN, March 23, 2015, http://www.cnn.com/2015/03/23/us/utah-death-penalty-firing-squad.

39. M. Watt Espy and John Ortiz Smykla, *Executions in the United States, 1608–2002: The ESPY File*, 4th ICPSR ed. (Ann Arbor, MI: Inter-university Consortium for Political and Social Research, 2004).

40. Death Penalty Information Center, "Descriptions of Executions Methods."

41. Glass v. Louisiana, 471 U.S. 1080, 1082 (1985).

42. Michael L. Radelet, "Examples of Post *Furman* Botched Executions," July 24, 2014, http://www.deathpenaltyinfo .org/article.php?scid=8&did=478.

43. Matthew B. Robinson, *Death Nation: The Experts Explain American Capital Punishment* (Upper Saddle River, NJ: Prentice-Hall, 2008).

44. Fiero v. Gomez, 77 F. 3d. 301 (1996).

45. Mark Berman, "Oklahoma Says It Will Now Use Nitrogen Gas as Its Backup Method of Execution," *Washington Post*, April 17, 2015, http://www .washingtonpost.com/news/post-nation/wp/2015/04/17/oklahoma-says-it-will-now-use-nitrogen-gas-as its-backup-method-of-execution.

46. Raymond Paternoster, Robert Brame, and Sarah Bacon, *The Death Penalty: America's Experience with Capital Punishment* (Oxford, UK: Oxford University Press, 2008).

47. Glossip v. Gross, 576 U.S. ___ (2015).

48. Martinson.

49. Cyndi Banks, *Punishment in America: A Reference Handbook* (Santa Barbara, CA: ABC-CLIO, 2005). See also Franklin E. Zimring, Gordon Hawkins, and Sam Kamin, *Punishment and Democracy: Three Strikes and You're Out in California* (Oxford, UK: Oxford University Press, 2001).

50. Cesare Beccaria, *On Crimes and Punishments* (1764; Boston, MA: International Pocket Library, 2008).

51. Steven N. Durlauf and Daniel S. Nagin, "Imprisonment and Crime: Can Both Be Reduced?" *Criminology and Public Policy* 10, no. 1 (2011): 13–54.

52. Raymond Paternoster, "How Much Do We Really Know About Criminal Deterrence?" *Journal of Criminal Law & Criminology* 100, no. 3 (2010): 765–823.

53. Ibid., endnote ii.

54. See, for example, Christine M. Sarteschi, "Mentally Ill Offenders Involved With the U.S. Criminal Justice System: A Synthesis," *SAGE Open* (July–September 2013): 1–11.

55. Michael R. Gottfredson and Travis Hirschi, *A General Theory of Crime* (Stanford, CA: Stanford University Press, 1990). See also Harold G. Grasmick, Charles R. Tittle, Robert J. Bursik Jr., and Bruce J. Arneklev, "Testing the Core Empirical Implications of Gottfredson and Hirschi's General Theory of Crime," *Journal of Research in Crime and Delinquency* 30, no. 1 (1993): 5–29.

56. See, for example, Elsa Chen, *Impact of Three Strikes and Truth in Sentencing on the Volume and Composition of Correctional Populations* (Washington, DC: U.S. Department of Justice, 2001); California Legislative Analyst's Office, "A Primer: Three Strikes—The Impact After More Than a Decade," October 2005, http:// www.lao.ca.gov/2005/3_strikes/3_ strikes_102005.htm.

57. Kenneth Mentor, "Habitual Offender Laws: Three Strikes and You're Out," in *Encyclopedia of Crime and Punishment*, Vol. II, ed. David Levinson (Thousand Oaks, CA: Sage, 2002).

58. Ibid., endnotes iv and x.

59. News17, "White Guy Gets Life for Stealing 50 Cent Donut," www .youtube.com/watch?v=yCYvtz8oNdw.

60. Former California secretary of state Bill Jones claimed that California's drop in crime was largely the result of the adoption of three-strikes legislation. See his remarks in Michael Vitiello, "Three Strikes Laws: A Real or Imagined Deterrent?" *Human Rights Magazine* 29, no. 2 (2002): 1–7.

61. Ibid., endnote viii.

62. The contemporary period, often referred to as the post-*Furman* period, after the Supreme Court case that brought a temporary end to the United States' use of the death penalty in the early 1970s, spans from 1973 to today.

63. Kansas v. Marsh, 548 U.S. 163 (2006).

64. *Marsh*.

65. Isaac Ehrlich, "The Deterrent Effect of Capital Punishment: A Question of Life and Death," *American Economic Review* 65, no. 3 (1975): 397–417.

66. James S. Liebman, Jeffrey Fagan, and Valerie West, *A Broken System: Error Rates in Capital Cases, 1973–1995* (2000), http://www2.law.columbia .edu/instructionalservices/liebman/ liebman_final.pdf.

67. Marla Sandys and Scott McClelland, "Stacking the Deck for Guilt and Death: The Failure of Death Qualification to Ensure Impartiality," in *America's Experiment With Capital Punishment: Reflections on the Past, Present, and Future of the Ultimate Penal Sanction*, 2nd ed., ed. James R. Acker, Robert M. Bohm, and Charles S. Lanier (Durham, NC: Carolina Academic Press, 2003), 385–411.

68. Death Penalty Information Center, "Innocence and the Death Penalty," http://www.deathpenaltyinfo.org/ innocence-and-death-penalty; see also Hugo Adam Bedau and Michael L. Radelet, "Miscarriages of Justice in Potentially Capital Cases," *Stanford Law Review* 40, no. 1 (1987): 21–179.

69. Samuel R. Gross, Barbara O'Brien, Chen Hu, and Edward H. Kennedy, "Rate of False Conviction of Criminal Defendants Who Are Sentenced to Death," *Proceedings of the National Academy of Sciences* 111, no. 20 (2014): 7230–7235.

70. Jacqueline K. Buffington-Vollum, John F. Edens, and Andrea Keilen, "Predicting Institutional Violence Among Death Row Inmates: The Utility of the Sorensen and Pilgrim Model," *Journal of Police and Criminal Psychology* 23, no. 1 (2008): 16–22.

Spotlight: Deterrence and the Death Penalty

a. Gallup Organization, "Death Penalty," n.d., http://www.gallup.com/ poll/1606/death-penalty.aspx.

b. Gregg v. Georgia, 428 U.S. 153 (1976).

c. Robert Weisberg, "The Death Penalty Meets Social Science: Deterrence and Jury Behavior Under New Scrutiny," *Annual Review of Law and Social Science* 1 (2005): 151–170.

d. Amnesty International, "Death Penalty Facts," July 2011, http://www .amnestyusa.org/sites/default/files/ pdfs/deathpenaltyfacts.pdf.

e. Tracy Connor, "Americans Back Death Penalty by Gas or Electrocution If No Needle: Poll," NBC News, May 15, 2014, http://www.nbcnews .com/storyline/lethal-injection/

americans-back-death-penalty-gas-or-electrocution-if-no-needle-n105346.

f. Tracy L. Snell, *Capital Punishment, 2010—Statistical Tables* (Washington, DC: Bureau of Justice Statistics, 2011), http://www.bjs.gov/content/pub/pdf/cp10st.pdf.

g. California Department of Corrections, "Condemned Inmate List," 2014, http://www.cdcr.ca.gov/capital_punishment/docs/condemnedinmatelistsecure.pdf.

Around the World: Criminal Sentencing in China

a. Bin Liang, "Severe Strike Campaign in Transitional China," *Journal of Criminal Justice* 33, no. 4 (2005): 387–399.

b. Susan Trevaskes, "Severe and Swift Justice in China," *British Journal of Criminology* 47, no. 1 (2007): 23–41.

c. Roger Hood, "Abolition of the Death Penalty: China in World Perspective," *City University of Hong Kong Law Review* 1 (2009): 1–21. http://www.deathpenaltyinfo.org/documents/RHoodOnChina.pdf.

d. Ira Belkin, "China's Criminal Justice System: A Work in Progress," *Washington Journal of Modern China* 6, no. 2 (2000): 61–63.

e. Susan Trevaskes, "Restorative Justice or McJustice With Chinese Characteristics?" in *21st Century China: Views From Australia*, ed. Mary Farquhar, 77–96. Newcastle, UK: Cambridge Scholars Publishing, 2009.

f. Ibid.

g. Ibid.

h. Hong Lu and Elaine Gunnison, "Power, Corruption, and the Legal Process in China," *International Criminal Justice Review* 13, no. 1 (2003): 28–49.

CHAPTER 11

1. Frank E. Hartung and Maurice Floch, "A Social-Psychological Analysis of Prison Riots: An Hypothesis," *Journal of Criminal Law, Criminology & Police Science* 47 (1956): 51–57.

2. History Channel, "Riot at Attica Prison," n.d., http://www.history.com/this-day-in-history/riot-at-attica-prison.

3. Alan Yuhas, "New Attica Documents Reveal Inmate Accounts of Torture After 1971 Prison Riot," *The Guardian*, May 22, 2011, http://www.theguardian.com/us-news/2015/may/22/new-attica-documents-reveal-inmate-torture.

4. "Attica Prison Riot Report Reveals Inmates Beaten, Tortured," AlJazeera America, May 22, 2015, http://america.aljazeera.com/articles/2015/5/22/new-report-on-attica-prison-riot-reveals-inmates-were-beaten.html.

5. Bert Useem, "Disorganziation and the New Mexico Prison Riot of 1980," *American Sociological Review* 50, no. 5 (1985): 677–688, http://www.d.umn.edu/~jmaahs/Correctional%20Continuum/useem_nm_prisonriot.pdf.

6. Jeff Bingaman, *Report of the Attorney General on the February 2 and 3, 1980 Riot at the Penitentiary of New Mexico* (Santa Fe: State of New Mexico, 1980), https://www.ncjrs.gov/pdffiles1/Digitization/72933NCJRS.pdf.

7. Audie Cornish and Alexandra Olgin, "In Wake of Riot, Ariz. Governor Fires For-Profit Prison Firm," National Public Radio, August 31, 2015, http://www.npr.org/2015/08/28/435577959/in-wake-of-riot-ariz-governor-fires-for-profit-prison-firm.

8. Joseph Bernstein, "Why Are Prison Riots Declining While Prison Populations Explode? A Visit to Corrections Officers' Annual Mock Prison Riot," *The Atlantic*, December 2013, http://www.theatlantic.com/magazine/archive/2013/12/have-a-safe-riot/354671.

9. Bruce McPherson, "Prison Overcrowding State of Emergency Proclamation," October 4, 2006, https://www.gov.ca.gov/news.php?id=4278.

10. City of Philadelphia, "Philadelphia Prison System: History," http://www.phila.gov/prisons/aboutus/Pages/History.aspx.

11. Cape and Islands Paranormal Research Society, "America's Oldest Wooden Jail," n.d., http://www.caiprs.com/Theoldjail.htm.

12. Paul Takagi, "The Walnut Street Jail: A Penal Reform to Centralize the Powers of the State," *Federal Probation* 39, no. 4 (1975): 18–26, http://www.socialjusticejournal.org/pdf_free/Takagi-Walnut_Street_Jail.pdf.

13. Paul Kahan, *Eastern State Penitentiary: A History* (Charleston, SC: History Press, 2008).

14. David J. Rothman, "Perfecting the Prison: United States, 1789–1865," in *The Oxford History of the Prison: The Practice of Punishment in Western Society*, ed. Norval Morris and David J. Rothman (Oxford, UK: Oxford University Press, 1995), 100–116.

15. Ted Conover, *Newjack: Guarding Sing Sing* (New York, NY: Vintage Books, 2001).

16. Dinitia Smith, "Intimate View of the Death House; Exhibition on Sing Sing Tells of Last Meals and Final Moments," *New York Times*, June 21, 2000, http://www.nytimes.com/2000/06/21/arts/intimate-view-death-house-exhibition-sing-sing-tells-last-meals-final-moments.html?pagewanted=all.

17. Edgardo Rotman, "The Failure of Reform: United States, 1865–1965," in *The Oxford History of the Prison: The Practice of Punishment in Western Society*, ed. Norval Morris and David J. Rothman (Oxford, UK: Oxford University Press, 1995), 151–177.

18. Estelle B. Freedman, *Their Sisters' Keepers: Women's Prison Reform in America, 1830–1930* (Ann Arbor: University of Michigan Press, 1981).

19. Devon Douglas-Bowers, "Slavery by Another Name: The Convict Lease System," The Hampton Institute, October 30, 2013, http://www.hamptoninstitution.org/convictleasesystem.html#.Vs4s19bscmQ.

20. Todd D. Minton and Zhen Zeng, *Jail Inmates at Midyear 2014* (Washington, DC: Bureau of Justice Statistics, 2015), http://www.bjs.gov/content/pub/pdf/jim14.pdf.

21. Jennifer Bronson, Ann Carson, Margaret Noonan, and Marcus Berzofsky, *Veterans in Prison and Jail, 2011–12* (Washington, DC: Bureau of Justice Statistics, 2015), http://www.bjs.gov/content/pub/pdf/vpj1112.pdf.

22. Minton and Zeng.

23. Todd D. Minton, *Jails in Indian Country, 2014* (Washington, DC: Bureau of Justice Statistics, 2015), http://www.bjs.gov/content/pub/pdf/jic14.pdf.

24. Todd D. Minton, Scott Ginder, Susan M. Brumbaugh, Hope Smiley-

McDonald, and Harley Rohloff, *Census of Jails: Population Changes, 1999–2013* (Washington, DC: Bureau of Justice Statistics, 2015), http://www.bjs.gov/content/pub/pdf/cjpc9913.pdf.

25. Ibid.

26. Jennifer Bronson, Laura M. Maruschak, and Marcus Berzofsky, *Disabilities Among Prison and Jail Inmates, 2011–2012* (Washington, DC: Bureau of Justice Statistics, 2015), http://www.bjs.gov/content/pub/pdf/dpji1112.pdf.

27. Margaret Noonan, Harley Rohloff, and Scott Ginder, *Mortality in Local Jails and State Prisons, 2000–2013—Statistical Tables* (Washington, DC: Bureau of Justice Statistics, 2015), http://www.bjs.gov/content/pub/pdf/mljsp0013st.pdf.

28. Hudson v. McMillian, 503 U.S. 1 (1992).

29. E. Ann Carson, *Prisoners in 2014* (Washington, DC: Bureau of Justice Statistics, 2015), http://www.bjs.gov/content/pub/pdf/p14.pdf.

30. Peter Wagner, "Tracking State Prison Growth in 50 States," Prison Policy Initiative, May 28, 2014, http://www.prisonpolicy.org/reports/overtime.html.

31. Tracey Kyckelhahn, *State Corrections Expenditures, FY 1982–2010* (Washington, DC: Bureau of Justice Statistics, 2014), http://www.bjs.gov/content/pub/pdf/scefy8210.pdf.

32. "California Proposition 47, Reduced Penalties for Some Crimes Intiative (2014)," n.d., http://ballotpedia.org/California_Proposition_47,_Reduced_Penalties_for_Some_Crimes_Initiative_(2014).

33. Paige St. John, "Prop 47 Would Cut Penalties for 1 in 5 Criminals in California," *Los Angeles Times*, October 11, 2014, http://www.latimes.com/local/politics/la-me-ff-pol-proposition47-20141012-story.html.

34. Georgia House Bill 349 (2013), http://www.legis.ga.gov/Legislation/20132014/135877.pdf.

35. Christian Henrichson and Ruth Delaney, *The Price of Prisons: What Incarceration Costs Taxpayers* (New York: Vera Institute of Justice, 2012), http://www.vera.org/sites/default/files/resources/downloads/price-of-prisons-updated-version-021914.pdf.

36. California Legislative Analyst's Office, "How Much Does It Cost to Incarcerate an Inmate?" n.d., http://www.lao.ca.gov/PolicyAreas/CJ/6_cj_inmatecost.

37. Vera Institute of Justice, "The Price of Prisons, Alabama," January 2012, http://www.vera.org/sites/default/files/resources/downloads/the-price-of-prisons-40-fact-sheets-updated-072012.pdf.

38. Henrichson and Delaney.

39. Federal Bureau of Prisons, "Historical Information," n.d., http://www.bop.gov/about/history.

40. Ibid.

41. Federal Bureau of Prisons, "Inmate Statistics," November 26, 2015, http://www.bop.gov/about/statistics/statistics_inmate_age.jsp.

42. Bureau of Justice Statistics, "More Than Half of Drug Offenders in Federal Prison Were Serving Sentences for Powder or Crack Cocaine," press release, October 27, 2015, http://www.bjs.gov/content/pub/press/dofp12pr.cfm.

43. Death Penalty Information Center, "Federal Executions, 1927–Present," n.d., http://www.deathpenaltyinfo.org/federal-executions-1927-2003.

44. Carson.

45. Saki Knafo and Chris Kirkham, "For-Profit Prisons Are Big Winners of California's Overcrowding Crisis," *Huffington Post*, October 25, 2013, http://www.huffingtonpost.com/2013/10/25/california-private-prison_n_4157641.html.

46. Suevon Lee, "By the Numbers: The U.S.'s Growing For-Profit Detention Industry," ProPublica, June 20, 2012, http://www.propublica.org/article/by-the-numbers-the-u.s.s-growing-for-profit-detention-industry.

47. Mary Sigler, "Private Prisons, Public Functions, and the Meaning of Punishment," *Florida State University Law Review* 38, no. 1 (2010): 149–178, http://papers.ssrn.com/sol3/papers.cfm?abstract_id=1650872.

48. Douglas C. McDonald and Kenneth Carlson, *Contracting for Imprisonment in the Federal Prison System: Cost and Performance of the Privately Operated Taft Correctional Institution* (Cambridge, MA: Abt Associates, 2005), https://www.ncjrs.gov/pdffiles1/nij/grants/211990.pdf.

49. Bob Ortega, "Arizona Private Prisons Slammed by Report," *Arizona Republic*, February 15, 2012, http://archive.azcentral.com/arizonarepublic/local/articles/2012/02/15/20120215arizona-private-prisons-slammed-by-report.html.

50. April M. Short, "6 Shocking Revelations About How Private Prisons Make Money," *Salon*, September 23, 2013, http://www.salon.com/2013/09/23/6_shocking_revelations_about_how_private_prisons_make_money_partner; "CCA 2012 Letter to Governors to Purchase State Prisons," Prison Legal News, August 9, 2014, https://www.prisonlegalnews.org/news/publications/cca-2012-letter-governors-purchase-state-prisons.

51. "New Hawaii Prison opens in Eloy, Arizona," Hawaii News Now, n.d., http://www.hawaiinewsnow.com/story/6714968/new-hawaii-prison-opens-in-eloy-arizona.

52. "HDRC, Hawaii ACLU File Second Lawsuit Over Prisoner Murdered at CCA Prison," Prison Legal News, January 1, 2012, https://www.prisonlegalnews.org/in-the-news/2012/hrdc-hawaii-aclu-file-second-lawsuit-over-prisoner-murdered-at-cca-prison.

53. Web Staff, "Federal Judge Ruling Allows Hawaii Prisoner Lawsuit to Proceed," KHON2, October 6, 2014, http://khon2.com/2014/10/03/federal-judge-ruling-allows-hawaii-prisoner-lawsuit-to-proceed.

54. Noel Brinkerhoff, "Hawaii Brings Its Prisoners Back From Arizona Private Prisons After Charges of Brutality," AllGov, February 1, 2011, http://www.allgov.com/news/controversies/hawaii-brings-its-prisoners-back-from-arizona-private-prisons-after-charges-of-brutality?news=842144.

55. Ortega, 2012.

56. Dina Perrone and Travis C. Pratt, "Comparing the Quality of Confinement and Cost-Effectiveness of Public Versus Private Prisons: What We Know, Why We Do Not Know More, and Where To Go From Here," *Prison Journal* 83, no. 3 (2003): 301–322, http://www.d.umn.edu/~jmaahs/Correctional%20Continuum/

Online%20Readings/
PerroneandPratt_privatization.pdf.

57. Scott D. Camp and Gerald G. Gaes, *Growth and Quality of U.S. Private Prisons: Evidence From a National Survey* (Washington, DC: Federal Bureau of Prisons, Office of Research and Evaluation, 2001), http:// t.friendscentercorp.org/sites/afsc .civicactions.net/files/documents/ BOP%20private%20performance%20 survey%2001_0.pdf.

58. Carson.

59. Alcatraz History, "The Military Prison," n.d., http://www .alcatrazhistory.com/rock/rock-023 .htm.

60. Death Penalty Information Center, "The U.S. Military Death Penalty," n.d., http://www.deathpenaltyinfo .org/us-military-death-penalty#facts

61. Michael Pearson, "Bradley Manning Wants to Live as a Woman, Be Known as Chelsea," CNN, August 23, 2013, http://www.cnn .com/2013/08/22/us/bradley- manning/index.html.

62. Bill Mears, "Chelsea Manning Sues to Get Transgender Medical Treatment," CNN, September 23, 2014, http:// www.cnn .com/2014/09/23/justice/chelsea- manning-lawsuit/index.html.

63. Carson.

64. Stephanie R. Bush-Baskette, "The War on Drugs as a War Against Black Women," in *Crime Control and Women: Feminist Implications of Criminal Justice Policy*, ed. Susan L. Miller (Thousand Oaks, CA: Sage, 1998), 113–129.

65. Carson.

66. Ibid.

67. Plata v. Brown, 563 U.S. ___ (2011).

68. Luke Smude, "Realignment: A New Frontier for California Criminal Justice," in *California's Criminal Justice System*, ed. Christine Gardiner and Stacy Mallicoat (Durham, NC: Carolina Academic Press, 2012), 153–168.

69. Scott D. Camp, Gerald G. Gaes, Neal P. Langan, and William G. Saylor, *The Influence of Prisons on Inmate Misconduct: A Multilevel Investigation* (Washington, DC: Office of Research and Evaluation, National Institute of Justice, 2003), https://www.bop .gov/resources/research_projects/ published_reports/prison_mgmt/ oreprcamp_mis.pdf.

70. Benjamin Steiner, H. Daniel Butler, and Jared M. Ellison, "Causes and Correlates of Prison Inmate Misconduct: A Systematic Review of the Evidence," *Journal of Criminal Justice* 42, no. 6 (2014): 462–470, http://www.researchgate .net/profile/Benjamin_Steiner2/ publication/266619954_Causes_ and_correlates_of_prison_inmate_ misconduct_A_systematic_ review_of_the_evidence/ links/5474a30a0cf2778985abeccb.pdf.

71. Rick Ruddell and Shannon Gottschall, "Are All Gangs Equal Security Risks? An Investigation of Gang Types and Prison Misconduct," *American Journal of Criminal Justice* 36, no. 3 (2011): 265–279.

72. Mark S. Fleisher and Scott H. Decker, "Overview of the Challenge of Prison Gangs," *Corrections Management Quarterly* 5, no. 1 (2001): 1–9.

73. Allen J. Beck and Candace Johnson, *Sexual Victimization Reported by Former State Prisoners, 2008* (Washington, DC: Bureau of Justice Statistics, 2012), http://www.prearesourcecenter.org/ sites/default/files/library/ sexualvictimizationreportedby formerstateprisoners2008.pdf.

74. Cooper v. Pate, 378 U.S. 546 (1964).

75. Bell v. Wolfish, 441 U.S. 520 (1979).

76. Hudson v. Palmer, 468 U.S. 517 (1984).

77. Johnson v. Avery, 393 U.S. 483 (1968).

78. Bounds v. Smith, 430 U.S. 817 (1977).

79. Wolff v. McDonald, 418 U.S. 539 (1974).

80. Baxter v. Palmigiano, 425 U.S. 308 (1976).

81. Estelle v. Gamble, 429 U.S. 97 (1976).

82. *Plata*, 563 U.S.

83. Rhodes v. Chapman, 452 U.S. 337 (1981).

84. Wilson v. Seiter, 501 U.S. 294 (1991).

85. Associated Press. "Groups Sue Alabama Prison Systems Claiming 'Shameful' Conditions Put Lives at Risk," *New York Daily News*, June 17, 2014, http://www.nydailynews.com /news/national/alabama-prison- systems-sued-risky-conditions- article-1.1833569.

86. Jean DuBail, "Prison Conditions Lawsuit Is Settled After 19 Years," *Sun Sentinel*, August 4, 1991, http:// articles.sun-sentinel.com/1991-08-04/ news/9101290382_1_prison- population-buddy-mackay-prison- health-care.

87. Dana M. Britton, *At Work in the Iron Cage: The Prison as a Gendered Organization* (New York: New York University Press, 2003).

88. Bureau of Labor Statistics, "Occupational Employment and Wages, May 2015: Correctional Officers and Jailers," http://www.bls .gov/oes/current/oes333012.htm.

89. American Correctional Association, *Directory of Adult and Juvenile Correctional Departments, Institutions, and Agencies and Probation and Parole Authorities* (Alexandria, VA: American Correctional Association, 2007).

90. Frank DiMarino, "Women as Corrections Professionals," Corrections.com, July 6, 2009, http://www.corrections.com/ articles/21703-women-as-corrections- professionals.

91. Timothy E. Hurst and Mallory M. Hurst, "Gender Differences in Mediation of Severe Occupational Stress Among Correctional Officers," *American Journal of Criminal Justice* 22, no. 1 (1997): 121–137.

92. Marie L. Griffin, Nancy L. Hogan, and Eric G. Lambert, "Doing 'People Work' in the Prison Setting: An Examination of the Job Characteristics Model and Correctional Staff Burnout," *Criminal Justice and Behavior* 39, no. 9 (2012): 1131–1147.

93. Conover.

94. Chase Riveland, *Supermax Prisons: Overview and General Considerations* (Washington, DC: U.S. Department of Justice, 1999), 6.

95. Craig Haney, "Mental Health Issues in Long-Term Solitary and 'Supermax' Confinement," *Crime and Delinquency* 49, no. 1 (2003): 124–156; Stephen C. Richards, "USP Marion: The First Federal Supermax," *Prison Journal* 88, no. 1 (2008): 6–22.

96. Riveland; Thomas J. Stickrath and Gregory A. Bucholtz, "Supermax Prisons: Why?" in *Supermax Prisons: Beyond the Rock*, ed. Donice Neal (Lanham, MD: American Correctional Association, 2003), 1–14.

97. Daniel P. Mears, *Evaluating the Effectiveness of Supermax Prisons*

(Washington, DC: Urban Institute Justice Policy Center, 2006).

98. Daniel P. Mears and Michael D. Reisig, "The Theory and Practice of Supermax Prisons," *Punishment and Society* 8, no. 1 (2006): 33–57.

99. Ibid.

100. Ibid.; Daniel P. Mears and Jamie Watson, "Towards a Fair and Balanced Assessment of Supermax Prisons," *Justice Quarterly* 23, no. 2 (2006): 232–270.

101. Kevin N. Wright, Todd R. Clear, and Paul Dickson, "Universal Applicability of Probation Risk-Assessment Instruments: A Critique," *Criminology* 22, no. 1 (1984): 113–134.

102. Brett Garland, H. Daniel Butler, and Benjamin Steiner, "The Supermax: Issues and Challenges," in *Criminal Justice Policy*, ed. Stacy L. Mallicoat and Christine L. Gardiner (Thousand Oaks, CA: Sage), 275–292.

103. Mears and Reisig.

104. Garland et al.

105. Roy D. King, "The Effects of Supermax Custody," in *The Effects of Imprisonment*, ed. Alison Liebling and Shadd Maruna (Portland, OR: Willan, 2005), 118–145.

106. Stuart Grassian, "Psychopathological Effects of Solitary Confinement," *American Journal of Psychiatry* 140, no. 11 (1983): 1450–1454; Haney; Lorna A. Rhodes, "Pathological Effects of the Supermaximum Prison," *American Journal of Public Health* 95, no. 10 (2005): 1692–1695.

107. Chad S. Briggs, Jody L. Sundt, and Thomas C. Castellano, "The Effect of Supermaximum Security Prisons on Aggregate Levels of Institutional Violence," *Criminology* 41, no. 4 (2003): 1341–1376; David A. Ward and Thomas G. Werlich, "Alcatraz and Marion: Evaluating Super-Maximum Custody," *Punishment and Society* 5, no. 1 (2003): 53–75.

108. Angela Browne, Alissa Cambier, and Suzanne Agha, "Prisons Within Prisons: The Use of Segregation in the United States," *Federal Sentencing Reporter* 24, no. 1 (2011): 46–49.

109. See, e.g., Allison Hastings, Angela Browne, Kaitlin Kell, and Margaret diZerega, *Keeping Vulnerable Populations Safe Under PREA: Alternative Strategies to the Use of Segregation in Prisons and Jails*

(New York: VERA Institute of Justice, 2015), http://www.prearesourcecenter .org/sites/default/files/library/ keepingvulnerablepopulations safeunderpreaapril2015.pdf.

110. Allen J. Beck, Marcus Berzofsky, Rachel Caspar, and Christopher Krebs, *Sexual Victimization in Prisons and Jails Reported by Inmates, 2011–12* (Washington, DC: Bureau of Justice Statistics, 2013), http://www.bjs.gov/ content/pub/pdf/svpjri1112.pdf.

111. See, e.g., Dwayne Betts, *A Question of Freedom: A Memoir of Learning, Survival, and Coming of Age in Prison* (New York: Penguin, 2009).

112. Christie Thompson, "Are California Prisons Punishing Inmates Based on Race?" April 12, 2013, http://www .propublica.org/article/are-california-prisons-punishing-inmates-based-on-race.

113. Browne et al., p. 47.

114. David Lovell, "Patterns of Disturbed Behavior in a Supermax Population," *Criminal Justice Behavior* 35, no. 8 (2008): 985–1004.

115. Hastings et al.

116. Verna Gates, "Judge Orders End to HIV Prison Segregation in Alabama," *Reuters*, December 21, 2012, http:// www.reuters.com/article/2012/12/21/ us-usa-aids-alabama-idUSBRE8BK0X Y20121221#WDgSULxtPxbr0ZyA.97.

Around the World : Prisons in Russia

a. Yuri Ivanovich Kalinin, *The Russian Penal System: Past, Present and Future*, lecture delivered at Kings College, London, November 2002, http:// www.antoniocasella.eu/nume/ kalinin_russian_penal_system.pdf.

b. Ibid.

c. Laura Piacentini, "Barter in Russian Prisons," *European Journal of Criminology* 1, no. 1 (2004): 17–45.

d. Institute for Criminal Policy Research, "World Prison Brief: Russian Federation," n.d., http:// www.prisonstudies.org/country/ russian-federation.

e. Alexey Bobrik, Kirill Danishevski, Ksenia Eroshina, and Martin McKee, "Prison Health in Russia: The Larger Picture," *Journal of Public Health Policy* (2005): http://www.antoniocasella.eu/ salute/Bobrik_2005.pdf.

f. Corey Flintoff, "Treating the 'Body and Soul' in a Russian TB Prison," National Public Radio, July 9, 2013, http://www.npr.org/sections/health-shots/2013/07/09/197739736/TB-IN-RUSSIAN-PRISONS.

g. Bobrik et al.

h. Armin Rosen, "Inside Russia's Prison System," *The Atlantic*, October 18, 2012, http://www.theatlantic.com/ international/archive/2012/10/inside-russias-prison-system/263806.

i. Blake Hounshell, "What Are Russian Prisons Like?" *Foreign Policy*, December 28, 2010, http://foreignpolicy .com/2010/12/28/what-are-russian-prisons-like.

j. Rosen.

k. Masha Gessen, "Life in a Russian Prison," *New York Times*, September 23, 2013, http://latitude.blogs .nytimes.com/2013/09/23/life-in-a-russian-prison/?_r=0.

l. Bobrik et al.

Spotlight: The Incarceration of the Mentally Ill

a. National Institute of Corrections, "Mentally Ill Persons in Corrections," n.d., http://nicic.gov/mentalillness.

b. Doris J. James and Lauren E. Glaze, *Mental Health Problems of Prison and Jail Inmates* (Washington, DC: Bureau of Justice Statistics, 2006), http://bjs .gov/content/pub/pdf/mhppji.pdf.

c. Ibid.

d. E. Fuller Torrey, Mary T. Zdanowicz, Aaron D. Kennard, H. Richard Lamb, Donald F. Eslinger, Michael C. Biasotti, and Doris A. Fuller, *The Treatment of Persons With Mental Illness in Prisons and Jails: A State Survey* (Arlington, VA: Treatment Advocacy Center, 2014), http://www.tacreports .org/storage/documents/treatment-behind-bars/treatment-behind-bars .pdf.

e. Meredith Huey Dye and Ronald H. Aday, "'I Just Wanted to Die': Preprison and Current Suicide Ideation Among Women Serving Life Sentences," *Criminal Justice and Behavior* 40, no. 8 (2013): 832–849.

f. Jennifer M. Kilty, "'It's Like They Don't Want You to Get Better': Psy Control of Women in the Carceral Context," *Feminism & Psychology* 22, no. 2 (2012): 162–182.

g. Holly M. Harner and Suzanne Riley, "The Impact of Incarceration on Women's Mental Health: Responses From Women in a Maximum-Security Prison," *Qualitative Health Research* 23, no. 1 (2013): 26–42.

h. Torrey et al.

Careers in Criminal Justice: So You Want to Be a Correctional Officer?

a. Bureau of Labor Statistics, *Occupational Outlook Handbook, 2016–17 Edition* (Washington, DC: Bureau of Labor Statistics, 2015), http://www.bls.gov/ooh/Protective-Service/Correctional-officers.htm.

b. Bureau of Labor Statistics, "Occupational Employment and Wages, May 2014: Correctional Officers and Jailers," March 15, 2015, http://www.bls.gov/oes/current/oes333012.htm.

CHAPTER 12

1. Liz Marie Marciniak, "Manhattan Bail Project," in *Encyclopedia of Community Corrections*, ed. Shannon M. Barton-Bellessa (Thousand Oaks, CA: Sage, 2012), 246–248.

2. Human Rights Watch, "The Price of Freedom: Bail and Pretrial Detention of Low Income Nonfelony Defendants in New York City," December 2, 2010, https://www.hrw.org/report/2010/12/02/price-freedom/bail-and-pretrial-detention-low-income-nonfelony-defendants-new-york.

3. Ann Martin Stacey and Cassia Spohn, "Gender and the Social Costs of Sentencing: An Analysis of Sentences Imposed on Male and Female Offenders in Three U.S. District Courts," *Berkeley Journal of Criminal Law* 11, no. 1 (2006): 43–76.

4. Cassia Spohn, "Race, Sex, and Pretrial Detention in Federal Court: Indirect Effects and Cumulative Disadvantage," *Kansas Law Review* 57, no. 4 (2009): 879–898, http://law.drupal.ku.edu/sites/law.drupal.ku.edu/files/docs/law_review/v57/6.0-Spohn_Final.pdf.

5. Stephen Demuth and Darrell Steffensmeier, "Ethnicity Effects on Sentence Outcomes in Large Urban Courts: Comparisons Among White,

Black, and Hispanic Defendants," *Social Science Quarterly* 85, no. 4 (2004): 994–1011. doi:10.1111/j.0038-4941.2004.00255.x

6. Tina L. Freiburger and Carly M. Hilinski, "Probation Officers' Recommendations and Final Sentencing Outcomes," *Journal of Crime and Justice* 34, no. 1 (2011): 45–61.

7. Christopher T. Lowenkamp, Marie VanNostrand, and Alexander Holsinger, *The Hidden Costs of Pretrial Detention* (Houston, TX: Arnold Foundation, 2013), http://www.arnoldfoundation.org/wp-content/uploads/2014/02/LJAF_Report_hidden-costs_FNL.pdf.

8. U.S. Courts, "Probation and Pretrial Services History," n.d., http://www.uscourts.gov/services-forms/probation-and-pretrial-services/probation-and-pretrial-services-history.

9. Human Rights Watch.

10. Marie VanNostrand, *Legal and Evidence-Based Practices: Applications of Legal Principles, Laws, and Research to the Field of Pretrial Services* (Washington, DC: U.S. Department of Justice, National Institute of Corrections, 2007), https://s3.amazonaws.com/static.nicic.gov/Library/023359.pdf.

11. U.S.C. § 3142 (g).

12. Barry Feld, *Cases and Materials on Juvenile Justice Administration* (New York: West Group, 2000).

13. Catherine Camilletti, *Pretrial Diversion Programs* (Washington, DC: Bureau of Justice Assistance, 2010), https://www.bja.gov/Publications/PretrialDiversionResearchSummary.pdf.

14. Scott H. Decker, "A Systematic Analysis of Diversion: Net-Widening and Beyond," *Journal of Criminal Justice* 13 (1985): 207–216, http://www.researchgate.net/profile/Scott_Decker2/publication/4969969_A_systematic_analysis_of_diversion_Net_widening_and_beyond/links/54ebba160cf2a030519499a6.pdf.

15. Shannon M. Barton-Bellessa and Robert D. Hanser, *Community-Based Corrections: A Text/Reader* (Thousand Oaks, CA: Sage, 2012); Henry J. Steadman, Martha Williams Deane, Joseph P. Morrissey, Mary L. Westcott,

Susan Salasin, and Steven Shapiro, "A SAMHSA Research Initiative Assessing the Effectiveness of Jail Diversion Programs for Mentally Ill Persons," *Psychiatric Services* 50, no. 12 (1999): 1620–1623, http://ps.psychiatryonline.org/doi/pdf/10.1176/ps.50.12.1620.

16. Holly A. Wilson and Robert D. Hoge, "The Effect of Youth Diversion Programs on Recidivism: A Meta-Analytic Review," *Criminal Justice and Behavior* 40, no. 5 (2013): 497–518.

17. Craig S. Schwalbe, Robin E. Gearing, Michael J. MacKenzie, Kathryne B. Brewer, and Rawan Ibrahim, "A Meta-Analysis of Experimental Studies of Diversion Programs for Juvenile Offenders," *Clinical Psychology Review* 32, no. 1 (2012): 26–33.

18. Virginia Aldigé Hiday, Bradley Wales, and Heathcote W. Ray, "Effectiveness of a Short-Term Mental Health Court: Criminal Recidivism One Year Postexit," *Law and Human Behavior* 37, no. 6 (2013): 401–411. doi:10.1037/lhb0000030

19. Miami-Dade Drug Court, http://www.miamidrugcourt.com.

20. Elizabeth K. Drake, Steve Aos, and Marna G. Miller, "Evidence-Based Public Policy Options to Reduce Crime and Criminal Justice Costs: Implications in Washington State," *Victims and Offenders* 4 (2009): 170–196.

21. Nancy Rodriguez and Vincent J. Webb, "Multiple Measures of Juvenile Drug Court Effectiveness: Results of a Quasi-Experimental Design," *Crime & Delinquency* 50, no. 2 (2004): 292–314.

22. Eric L. Sevigny, Harold A. Pollack, and Peter Reuter, "Can Drug Courts Help to Reduce Prison and Jail Populations," *Annals of the American Academy of Political and Social Science* 647, no. 1 (2013): 190–212.

23. Deborah Koetzle, Shelley Johnson Listwan, Wendy P. Guastaferro, and Kara Kobus, "Treating High-Risk Offenders in the Community: The Potential of Drug Courts," *International Journal of Offender Therapy and Comparative Criminology* 59, no. 5 (2015): 449–465.

24. David Dressler, *Practice and Theory of Probation and Parole* (New York: Columbia University Press, 1962), 17.

25. NYC Department of Probation, "History of Probation," n.d., http://www.nyc.gov/html/prob/html/about/history.shtml.

26. American Probation and Parole Association, "History of Probation and Parole," n.d., http://www.appa-net.org/eweb/Resources/PPPSW_2013/history.htm.

27. U.S. Courts.

28. Federal Probation and Pretrial Officers Association, "FPPOA Organization History," n.d., http://www.fppoa.org/organization-history-about.

29. Joan Petersilia, "Probation in the United States," *Perspectives*, Spring 1998, http://www.appa-net.org/eweb/Resources/PPPSW_2015/docs/sp98pers30.pdf.

30. Robert Martinson, "What Works? Questions and Answers About Prison Reform," *Public Interest* 35 (1974): 22–54.

31. Barton-Bellessa and Hanser.

32. Danielle Kaeble, Laura M. Maruschak, and Thomas P. Bonczar, *Probation and Parole in the United States, 2014* (Washington, DC: Bureau of Justice Statistics, 2015), http://www.bjs.gov/content/pub/pdf/ppus14.pdf.

33. Petersilia.

34. Stacy L. Mallicoat, "Gendered Justice: Attributional Differences Between Males and Females in the Juvenile Courts," *Feminist Criminology* 2, no. 1 (2007): 4–30.

35. Kathleen Daly, *Gender, Crime and Punishment* (New Haven, CT: Yale University Press, 1994).

36. Mallicoat.

37. George S. Bridges and Sara Steen, "Racial Disparities in Official Assessments of Juvenile Offenders: Attributional Stereotypes as Mediating Mechanisms," *American Sociological Review* 63, no. 4 (1998): 554–570.

38. Julian B. Rotter, "Generalized Expectancies for Internal Versus External Control of Reinforcement," *Psychological Monographs* 80, no. 1 (1966): 1–26; Vernon L. Quinsey and Mireille Cyr, "Perceived Dangerousness and Treatability of Offenders: The Effects of Internal Versus External Attributions of Crime Causality," *Journal of Interpersonal Violence* 1, no. 4 (1986): 458–471.

39. Gagnon v. Scarpelli, 411 U.S. 778 (1973).

40. Federal Rules of Procedure, "Title VII. Post Conviction Procedures. Rule 32.1: Revoking or Modifying Probation or Supervised Release," https://www.law.cornell.edu/rules/frcrmp/rule_32.1.

41. 18 U.S. Code § 3565: Revocation of Probation, https://www.law.cornell.edu/uscode/text/18/3565.

42. Bearden v. Georgia, 461 U.S. 660 (1983).

43. Edward J. Latessa and Paula Smith, *Corrections in the Community*, 5th ed. (Burlington, MA: Elsevier, 2011).

44. Justin Breaux, Kimberl Bernard, Helen Ho, and Jesse Jannetta, *Responding to Racial Disparities in the Multnomah County's Probation Revocation Outcomes* (Washington, DC: Urban Institute, 2014), http://www.urban.org/research/publication/responding-racial-disparities-multnomah-countys-probation-revocation-outcomes.

45. Kevin F. Steinmetz and Howard Henderson, "On the Precipice of Intersectionality: The Influence of Race, Gender, and Offense Severity Interactions on Probation Outcomes," *Criminal Justice Review* 40, no. 3 (2015): 361–377.

46. P. J. Verrecchia and Eric Ling, "The Effects of Legal and Extralegal Factors on Probation Revocation Decisions," *International Journal of Criminology and Sociology* 2 (2013): 13–19.

47. Peggy McGarry, "NIC Focus: Intermediate Sanctions," *Community Corrections Quarterly* 1, no. 3 (1990): 1–16.

48. Laura Olson and Tony Saavedra, "State Senate Leader Says GPS Monitoring Is Faulty," *Orange County Register*, April 16, 2014, http://www.ocregister.com/articles/gps-610182-general-state.html.

49. Stacy L. Mallicoat and Connie Estrada Ireland, *Women and Crime: The Essentials* (Thousand Oaks, CA: Sage, 2014).

50. Reuters, "Martha Stewart's House Arrest Is Extended," *New York Times*, August 4, 2005, http://www.nytimes.com/2005/08/04/business/media/martha-stewarts-house-arrest-is-extended.html?_r=0.

51. Jennifer L. Lanterman, "Day Reporting Centers," in *Encyclopedia of Community Corrections*, ed. Shannon M. Barton-Bellessa (Thousand Oaks, CA: Sage, 2012), 105–107.

52. Joseph Rukus, John M. Eassey, and Julie Marie Baldwin, "Working Through Work Release: An Analysis of Factors Associated With the Successful Completion of Work Release," *American Journal of Criminal Justice* (2015): 1–26. doi:10.1007/s12103-015-9309-3

53. Shawn D. Bushway and Robert Apel, "A Signaling Perspective on Employment-Based Reentry Programming: Training Completion as a Desistance Signal," *Criminology and Public Policy* 11, no. 1 (2012), 21–50.

54. Barton-Bellessa and Hanser.

55. Todd R. Clear, Michael D. Reisig, and George F. Cole, *American Corrections*, 11th ed. (Boston: Cengage Learning, 2016).

56. Michigan Department of Corrections, "The Parole Consideration Process," n.d., http://www.michigan.gov/corrections/0,4551,7-119-1384-22909--,00.html.

57. Oklahoma Pardon and Parole Board, "Parole Process," n.d., http://www.ok.gov/ppb/Parole_Process/index.html.

58. Iowa Board of Parole, http://www.bop.state.ia.us/Home.

59. Beth E. Ritchie, "Challenges Incarcerated Women Face as They Return to Their Communities: Findings From Life History Interviews," *Crime and Delinquency* 47, no. 3 (2001): 381.

60. Martin T. Hall, Seana Golder, Cynthia L. Conley, and Susan Sawning, "Designing Programming and Interventions for Women in the Criminal Justice System," *American Journal of Criminal Justice* 38, no. 1 (2013): 27–50.

61. Ibid.

62. Maxwell Strachan, "Target to Drop Criminal Background Questions in Job Applications," *Huffington Post*, October 29, 2013, http://www.huffingtonpost.com/2013/10/29/target-criminal-history-questions_n_4175407.html.

63. Stephanei Condon, "Obama to 'Ban the Box' on Federal Job Applications," CBS News, November 2, 2015, http://www.cbsnews.com/news/obama-to-ban-the-box-on-federal-job-applications.

64. Jean Chung, *Felony Disenfranchisement: A Primer* (Washington, DC: Sentencing Project, 2015), http://sentencingproject.org/doc/publications/fd_Felony%20Disenfranchisement%20Primer.pdf.

65. Christopher Uggen and Jeff Manza, "Democratic Contraction? Political Consequences of Felon Disenfranchisement in the United States," *American Sociological Review* 67, no. 6 (2002): 777–803, http://as.nyu.edu/docs/IO/3858/Democratic_Contraction.pdf.

66. Sentencing Project, "Fact Sheet: Felony Disenfranchisement Laws," April 2014, http://sentencingproject.org/doc/publications/fd_Felony%20Disenfranchisement%20Laws%20in%20the%20US.pdf.

67. Beth M. Huebner, Christina DeJong, and Jennifer Cobbina, "Women Coming Home: Long-Term Patterns of Recidivism," *Justice Quarterly* 27, no. 2 (2010): 225–254.

68. Beth E. Ritchie, "Challenges Incarcerated Women Face as They Return to Their Communities: Findings From Life History Interviews," *Crime and Delinquency* 47, no. 3 (2001), 368–389.

69. Jennifer M. Kilty, "'It's Like They Don't Want You to Get Better': Psy Control of Women in the Carceral Context," *Feminism & Psychology* 22, no. 2 (2012): 162–182.

70. Amy E. Hirsch, "Bringing Back Shame: Women, Welfare Reform and Criminal Justice," in *Gendered (In)justice: Theory and Practice in Feminist Criminology*, ed. Pamela J. Schram and Barbara Koons-Witt (Long Grove, IL: Waveland Press, 2004), 270–286.

71. Ann Jacobs, *Give 'Em a Fighting Chance: The Challenges for Women Offenders Trying to Succeed in the Community* (New York: Women's Prison Association, 2000), http://www.wpaonline.org/pdf/WPA_FightingChance.pdf.

72. Sentencing Project, "Life Sentences: Denying Welfare Benefits to Women Convicted of Drug Offenses," April 2006, http://www.sentencingproject.org/doc/publications/women_smy_lifesentences.pdf.

73. S. 675 REDEEM Act, 114th Congress (2015–2016), https://www.congress.gov/bill/114th-congress/senate-bill/675.

74. Jacobs.

75. Hirsch.

76. Chandra Villanueva and Keita de Souza, *Mentoring Women in Reentry: A WPA Practice Brief* (New York: Women's Prison Association & Home, 2008).

77. D. A. Andrews and James Bonta, *The Psychology of Criminal Conduct*, 5th ed. (New York: Routledge, 2015).

78. Latessa and Smith.

79. D. A. Andrews and James Bonta, *Level of Service Inventory, Revised* (North Tonawanda, NY: Multi-Health Systems, 1995).

80. Tim Brennan, William Dieterich, and William Oliver, *COMPAS: Technical Manual and Psychometric Report Version 5.0* (Traverse City, MI: Northpointe Institute, 2006).

81. Edward Latessa, Paula Smith, Richard Lemke, Matthew Makarios, and Christopher Lowenkamp, *Creation and Validation of the Ohio Risk Assessment System: Final Report* (Cincinnati: Center for Criminal Justice Research, University of Cincinnati, 2009), http://www.uc.edu/ccjr/Reports/ProjectReports/ORAS_Final_Report.pdf.

82. Tim Brennan, William Dieterich, and Beate Ehret, "Evaluating the Predictive Validity of the Compas Risk and Needs Assessment System," *Criminal Justice & Behavior* 36, no. 1 (2009): 21–40; Sarah L. Desmarais and Jay P. Singh, *Instruments for Assessing Recidivism Risk: A Review of Validation Studies Conducted in the U.S.* (New York: Council of State Governments Justice Center, 2013); Tracy L. Fass, Kirk Heilbrun, David DeMatteo, and Ralph Fretz, "The LSI-R and the COMPAS: Validation Data on Two Risk-Needs Tools," *Criminal Justice and Behavior* 35 (2008): 1095–1108; Brenda Vose, Paula Smith, and Francis T. Cullen, "Predictive Validity and the Impact of Change on Total LSI-R Score on Recidivism," *Criminal Justice and Behavior* 40, no. 12 (2013): 1383–1396.

83. Melinda D. Schlager and David J. Simourd, "Validity of the Level of Service Inventory–Revised (LSI-R) Among African American and Hispanic Male Offenders," *Criminal Justice and Behavior* 34, no. 4 (2007): 545–554; Brenda Vose, Christopher Lowenkamp, Paula Smith, and Francis T. Cullen, "Gender and the Predictive Validity of the LSI-R: A Study of Parolees and Probationers," *Journal of Contemporary Criminal Justice* 25, no. 4 (2009): 459–471.

84. Kelly Hannah-Moffat and Margaret Shaw, "The Meaning of 'Risk' in Women's Prisons: A Critique," in *Gendered Justice: Addressing Female Offenders*, ed. Barbara E. Bloom (Durham, NC: Carolina Academic Press, 2003), 45–68; Kathleen Kendall, "Time to Think Again About Cognitive Behavioural Programmes," in *Women and Punishment: The Struggle for Justice* (Portland, OR: Willan Publishing, 2002), 182–198; Kathleen Kendall, "Dangerous Thinking: A Critical History of Correctional Cognitive Behaviouralism," in *What Matters in Probation?* (Portland, OR: Willan Publishing, 2004), 53–89; Kathleen Kendall and Shoshana Pollack, "Cognitive Behavioralism in Women's Prisons: A Critical Analysis of Therapeutic Assumptions and Practices," in *Gendered Justice: Addressing Female Offenders*, ed. Barbara E. Bloom (Durham, NC: Carolina Academic Press, 2003), 69–96.

85. Kelley Blanchette and Shelley L. Brown, *The Assessment and Treatment of Women Offenders: An Integrative Perspective* (West Sussex, UK: John Wiley & Sons, 2006).

86. Barbara Bloom, Barbara Owen, and Stephanie Covington, *Gender-Responsive Strategies: Research, Practice, and Guiding Principles for Women Offenders* (Washington, DC: National Institute of Corrections, 2003).

87. Patricia Van Voorhis, Emily M. Wright, Emily Salisbury, and Ashley Bauman, "Women's Risk Factors and Their Contributions to Existing Risk/Needs Assessments: The Current Status of a Gender-Responsive Supplement," *Criminal Justice and Behavior* 37, no. 3 (2010): 261–288.

88. Ibid.

89. Joselyne L. Chenane, Pauline K. Brennan, Benjamin Steiner, and Jared M. Ellison, "Racial and Ethnic Differences in the Predictive Validity of the Level of Service Inventory–Revised Among Prison Inmates," *Criminal Justice and Behavior* 42, no. 3 (2015): 286–303. doi:10.1177/0093854814548195

90. Kimberle Crenshaw, "Demarginalizing the Intersection of Race and Sex: A Black Feminist Critique of Antidiscrimination Doctrine, Feminist Theory and Antiracist Politics," *University of Chicago Legal Forum* (1989): 139–167.

91. William J. Sabol, Heather C. West, and Matthew Cooper, *Prisoners in 2008* (Washington, DC: Bureau of Justice Statistics, 2009); E. Ann Carson, *Prisoners in 2013* (Washington, DC: Bureau of Justice Statistics, 2014).

92. Erinn J. Herberman and Thomas P. Bonczar, *Probation and Parole in the United States, 2013* (Washington, DC: Bureau of Justice Statistics, 2014).

93. Matthew R. Durose, Alexia D. Cooper, and Howard N. Snyder, *Recidivism of Prisoners Released in 30 States in 2005: Patterns From 2005 to 2010* (Washington, DC: Bureau of Justice Statistics, 2014).

94. Amy L. Solomon, Jenny Osborne, Laura Winterfield, Brian Elderbroom, Peggy Burke, Richard P. Stroker, Edward E. Rhine, and William D. Burrell, *Putting Public Safety First: 13 Parole Supervision Strategies to Enhance Reentry Outcomes* (Washington, DC: Urban Institute, 2008); Jesse Jannetta and William D. Burrell, "Effective Supervision Principles for Probation and Parole," in *Encyclopedia of Criminology and Criminal Justice,* ed. Gerben Bruinsma and David Weisburd (New York: Springer, 2014), 1308–1318.

95. Janetta and Burrell.

96. D. A. Andrews and Craig Dowden, "The Risk-Need-Responsivity Model of Assessment and Human Service in Prevention and Corrections: Crime-Prevention Jurisprudence," *Canadian Journal of Criminology and Criminal Justice* 49, no. 4 (2007): 439–464.

97. Solomon et al.

98. Ibid.

99. Amy L. Solomon, Vera Kachnowski, and Avi Bhati, *Does Parole Work? Analyzing the Impact of Postprison Supervision on Rearrest Outcomes* (Washington, DC: Urban Institute, 2005).

100. Ibid.

101. James Bonta, Tanya Rugge, Terri-Lynne Scott, Guy Bourgon, and Annie K. Yessine, "Exploring the Black Box of Community Supervision," *Journal of Offender Rehabilitation* 47, no. 3 (2008): 251.

102. Ibid.

103. Texas Department of Criminal Justice, Reentry and Integration Division, Presentation to the House Corrections Committee, June 30, 2010.

104. Pew Charitable Trusts, "Mandatory Reentry Supervision: Evaluating the Kentucky Experience," June 2014, http://www.pewtrusts.org/ /media/assets/2014/06/pspp_kentucky_brief.pdf.

105. Pew Charitable Trusts, "The Impact of Parole in New Jersey," November 2013, http://www.pewtrusts.org/ /media/legacy/uploadedfiles/pcs_assets/2013/psppnjparolebriefpdf.pdf.

106. Amy L. Solomon, Christy Visher, Nancy G. La Vigne, and Jenny Osborne, *Understanding the Challenges of Prisoner Reentry: Research Findings From the Urban Institute's Prisoner Reentry Portfolio* (Washington, DC: Urban Institute, 2006).

107. Jacqueline Helfgott, "Ex-Offender Needs Versus Community Opportunity in Seattle, Washington," *Federal Probation* 61, no. 2 (1997): 12–24.

108. Christine S. Scott-Hayward, "The Failure of Parole: Rethinking the Role of the State in Reentry," *New Mexico Law Review* 41, no. 2 (2011): 421–465.

Spotlight: Recidivism

a. National Institute of Justice, "Recidivism," n.d., http://www.nij.gov/topics/corrections/recidivism/Pages/welcome.aspx.

b. R. Karl Hanson and Monique T. Bussière, "Predicting Relapse: A Meta-Analysis of Sexual Offender Recidivism Studies," *Journal of Consulting and Clinical Psychology* 66, no. 2 (1998): 348–362.

c. John R. Gallagher, Eric Ivory, Jesse Carlton, and Jane Woodward Miller, "The Impact of an Indiana (United States) Drug Court on Criminal Recidivism," *Advances in Social Work* 15, no. 2 (2014): 507–521.

d. Jennifer L. Skeem, Eliza Winter, Patrick J. Kennealy, Jennifer Eno Louden, and Joseph R. Tatar II, "Offenders With Mental Illness Have Criminogenic Needs, Too: Toward Recidivism Reduction," *Law and Human Behavior* 38, no. 3 (2014): 212–224, http://risk-resilience.berkeley.edu/sites/default/files/wp-content/gallery/publications/2014.Offenders%20with%20mental%20illness%20have%20criminogenic%20needs,%20too_%20Toward%20recidivism%20reduction_0.pdf.

e. Francis T. Cullen, Cheryl Lero Jonson, and Daniel S. Nagin, "Prisons Do Not Reduce Recidivism: The High Cost of Ignoring Science," *Prison Journal* 91, no. 3 (2011): 48S–65S, http://www.jthomasniu.org/class/540/2013/science-cullen.pdf.

f. Daniel P. Mears, Joshua C. Cochran, and William D. Bales, "Gender Differences in the Effects of Prison on Recidivism," *Journal of Criminal Justice* 40, no. 5 (2012): 370–378.

g. Cullen et al.

Around the World: Probation in Italy

a. European Organisation for Probation, "Summary Information on Probation in Italy," n.d., http://cep-probation.org/wp-content/uploads/2015/03/Summary-information-on-Italy.pdf.

b. Most recent year that data is available.

c. European Organisation for Probation.

d. Belgian Ministry of Justice, "Probation Measures and Alternative Sanctions in the EU," n.d., http://www.euprobationproject.eu/national_detail.php?c=IT.

e. Ibid.

f. Ibid.

g. European Organisation for Probation.

CHAPTER 13

1. Amita Sharma, "After Woman Spends 18 Years in Prison for Killing Her Pimp, She Starts Anew," KPBS, August 12, 2014, http://www.kpbs.org/news/2014/aug/12/freedom-sara-kruzan-means-cleansing-reconnecting-l.

2. Amita Sharma, "Sara Kruzan Released From Prison 18 Years After Killing Pimp as Teen," KPBS, October 31, 2013, http://www.kpbs.org/news/2013/oct/31/sara-kruzan-killed-pimp-teen-goes-free.

3. Paige St. John, "Jerry Brown OKs Freedom for Woman Imprisoned at 16 for Killing Pimp," *Los Angeles Times*, October 26, 2013, http://articles.latimes.com/2013/oct/26/local/la-me-ff-kruzan-20131027.

4. Thomas J. Bernard, *The Cycle of Juvenile Justice* (Oxford, UK: Oxford University Press, 1992).

5. Ex parte Crouse (1838); Barry Krisberg, *Juvenile Justice: Redeeming Our Children* (Thousand Oaks, CA: Sage, 2005).

6. Anthony Platt, "The Rise of the Child Saving Movement: A Study in Social Policy and Correctional Reform," *Annals of the American Academy of Political and Social Science* 381 (1969): 21–38.

7. Ibid.

8. Krisberg.

9. Jessica R. Kendall, "Juvenile Status Offenses: Treatment and Early Intervention," American Bar Association Technical Assistance Bulletin No. 29 (2007): http://www.americanbar.org/content/dam/aba/migrated/publiced/tab29.authcheckdam.pdf.

10. Superior Court of California, County of Orange. "Juvenile Court: Dependency," n.d., http://www.occourts.org/self-help/juvenile/dependency.html.

11. Julie Furdella and Charles Puzzanchera, *Delinquency Cases in Juvenile Court, 2013* (Washington, DC: Office of Juvenile Justice and Delinquency Prevention, 2015), http://www.ojjdp.gov/pubs/248899.pdf.

12. Ibid.

13. Howard N. Snyder and Melissa Sickmund, *Juvenile Offenders and Victims: 2006 National Report* (Washington, DC: Office of Juvenile Justice and Delinquency Prevention, 2006).

14. Furdella and Puzzanchera.

15. Ibid.

16. Washington State Department of Social and Health Services, "Juvenile Rehabilitation," n.d., https://www.dshs.wa.gov/ra/juvenile-rehabilitation.

17. Boulder County, Colorado, "Juvenile Services Programs," n.d., http://www.bouldercounty.org/safety/jail/pages/juvenileprograms.aspx.

18. Kent v. United States, 383 U.S. 541 (1966).

19. In re Gault, 387 U.S. 1 (1967).

20. In re Winship, 397 U.S. 358 (1970).

21. Breed v. Jones, 421 U.S. 519 (1975).

22. McKeiver v. Pennsylvania, 403 U.S. 528 (1971).

23. Furdella and Puzzanchera.

24. Ibid.

25. John J. DiIulio Jr., "The Coming of the Super-Predators," *Weekly Standard*, November 27, 1995, 23.

26. James Q. Wilson, "Crime and Public Policy," in *Crime*, ed. James Q. Wilson and Joan Petersilia (San Francisco: Institute for Contemporary Studies, 1995), 507.

27. Megan C. Kurlychek, "Juvenile Offenders in Adult Courts," in *Juvenile Crime and Justice*, ed. William J. Chambliss (Thousand Oaks, CA: Sage, 2011), 131–146.

28. Aaron Kupchik and Megan Gosse, "Juvenile Waiver Policies," in *Criminal Justice Policies*, ed. Stacy L. Mallicoat and Christine L. Gardiner (Thousand Oaks, CA: Sage, 2014), 191–200.

29. Kurlychek, "Juvenile Offenders in Adult Courts."

30. Ibid.

31. Kupchik and Gosse, "Juvenile Waiver Policies."

32. Sarah Hockenberry and Charles Puzzanchera, *Juvenile Court Statistics, 2013* (Pittsburgh: National Center for Juvenile Justice, 2015).

33. M. A. Bortner, Marjorie S. Zatz, and Darnell F. Hawkins, "Race and Transfer: Empirical Research and Social Context," in *The Changing Borders of Juvenile Justice: Transfer of Adolescents to the Criminal Court*, ed. Jeffrey Fagan and Franklin E. Zimring (Chicago: University of Chicago Press, 2000), 277–320.

34. Kareem L. Jordan and Tina L. Freiburger, "Examining the Impact of Race and Ethnicity on the Sentencing of Juveniles in the Adult Court," *Criminal Justice Policy Review* 21, no. 2 (2010): 185–201.

35. Kareem L. Jordan, "Juvenile Status and Criminal Sentencing: Does It Matter in the Adult System?" *Youth Violence and Juvenile Justice* 12, no. 4 (2014): 315–331.

36. Brian D. Johnson and Megan C. Kurlychek, "Transferred Juveniles in the Era of Sentencing Guidelines: Examining Judicial Departures for Juvenile Offenders in Adult Criminal Court," *Criminology* 50, no. 2 (2012): 525–564.

37. "Fla. Boy Gets Life in Wrestling Death," ABC News, March 9, 2001, http://abcnews.go.com/US/story?id=93884&page=1.

38. "Lionel Tate Pleads Guilty to Second-Degree Murder," CNN, January 29, 2004, http://www.cnn.com/2004/LAW/01/29/wrestling.death.

39. Melissa McNamara, "Lionel Tate Gets 30 Years in Jail," CBS News, May 18, 2006, http://www.cbsnews.com/news/lionel-tate-gets-30-years-

40. Sarah Hockenberry, *Ju̳ in Residential Plac̳ (Washington̳ Justice a̳ 2014̳ .p̳ Yout̳ Perspectiv̳ .justicepolic̳ documents/fac̳

41. Doris Layton Ma̳ Wilson, Gaylene St̳ ̳ng, and Angela R. Gover, ̳ ̳e Impact of Boot Camps and Traditional Institutions on Juvenile Residents: Perceptions, Adjustment, and Change," *Journal of Research in Crime and Delinquency* 38, no. 3 (2001): 279–313.

42. Jean Bottcher and Michael E. Ezell, "Examining the Effectiveness of Boot Camps: A Randomized Experiment With a Long-Term Follow Up," *Journal of Research in Crime and Delinquency* 42, no. 3 (2005): 309–332; Doris Layton MacKenzie, David B. Wilson, and Suzanne B. Kider, "Effects of Correctional Boot Camps on Offending," *ANNALS of the American Academy of Political and Social Science* 578, no. 1 (2001): 126–143.

43. Jerry Tyler, Ray Darville, and Kathi Stalnaker, "Juvenile Boot Camps: A Descriptive Analysis of Program Diversity and Effectiveness," *Social Science Journal* 38, no. 3 (2001): 445–460.

44. Act 4 Juvenile Justice, "Reauthorization of JJDPA," n.d., act4jj.org/reauthorization-jjdpa.

45. Hockenberry.

46. Barry C. Feld, "Violent Girls or Relabeled Status Offenders? An Alternative Interpretation of the Data," *Crime & Delinquency* 55, no. 2 (2009), 241–265; Nicole T. Carr, Kenneth Hudson, Roma S. Hanks, and Andrea N. Hunt, "Gender Effects Along the Juvenile Justice System: Evidence of a Gendered Organization," *Feminist Criminology* 3, no. 1 (2008): 25–43.

47. Catherine Y. Kim, Daniel J. Losen, and Damon T. Hewitt, *The School-to-Prison Pipeline: Structuring Legal Reform* (New York: New York University Press, 2012); Glenn W. Muschert, Stuart Henry, Nicole L. Bracy, and Anthony A. Peguero, eds., *Responses to School Violence: Confronting the Columbine Effect* (Boulder, CO: Lynne Rienner Publishers, 2013).

48. Kim, Losen, and Hewitt; Muschert et al.

49. Gerald Campano, Maria Paula Ghiso, Mary Yee, and Alicia Pantoja, "Toward Community Research and Coalitional Literacy Practice for Educational Justice," *Language Arts* 90, no. 5 (2013): 314–326; Muschert et al.; Russell J. Skiba, Robert H. Horner, Choong-Geun Chung, M. Karega Rausch, Seth L. May, and Tary Tobin, "Race Is Not Neutral: A National Investigation of African American and Latino Disproportionality in School Discipline," *School Psychology Review* 40, no. 1 (2011): 85–107.

50. Muschert et al.

51. Ibid.

52. Sandra B. Simkins, Amy E. Hirsch, Erin McNamara Horvat, and Marjorie B. Moss, "School to Prison Pipeline for Girls: The Role of Physical and Sexual Abuse," *Child Legal Rights Journal* 24, no. 4 (2004): 56–72.

53. Ibid.

54. Skiba et al.

55. Katherine Irwin, Janet Davidson, and Amanda Sanchez-Hall, "The Race to Punish in American Schools: Class and Race Predictors of Punitive School-Crime Control," *Critical Criminology* 21, no. 1 (2013): 47–71; Kimberlé Crenshaw, *Black Girls Matter: Pushed Out, Overpoliced, and Underprotected*, with Priscilla Ocen and Jyoti Nanda (New York: Center for Intersectionality and Social Policy Studies, 2015).

56. Gregory M. Zimmerman and Carter Rees, "Do School Disciplinary Policies Have Positive Social Impacts? Examining the Attenuating Effects of School Policies on the Relationship Between Personal and Peer Delinquency," *Journal of Criminal Justice* 42, no. 1 (2014): 54–65; John Paul Wright, Mark Alden Morgan, Michelle A. Coyne, Kevin M. Beaver, and J. C. Barnes, "Prior Problem Behavior Accounts for the Racial Gap in School Suspensions," *Journal of Criminal Justice* 42, no. 3 (2014): 257–266.

57. Barry C. Feld, "Abolish the Juvenile Court: Youthfulness, Criminal Responsibility, and Sentencing Policy," *Journal of Criminal Law and Criminology* 88, no. 1 (1997): 68–136.

58. Barry C. Feld, "Should Juvenile Court Be Abolished?" in *Taking Sides: Clashing Views in Crime and Criminology*, ed. Thomas Hickey (New York: McGraw-Hill, 2010), 115–127.

59. Barry C. Feld, *Bad Kids: Race and the Transformation of the Juvenile Court* (New York: Oxford University Press, 1999), 287.

60. Jeffrey Fagan and Franklin E. Zimring, *The Changing Borders of Juvenile Justice: Transfer of Adolescents to the Criminal Court* (Chicago: University of Chicago Press, 2000).

61. Barry C. Feld and Shelly Schaefer, "The Right to Counsel in Juvenile Court: Law Reform to Deliver Legal Services and Reduce Justice by Geography," *Criminology & Public Policy* 9, no. 2 (2010): 327–356.

62. Henry Sontheimer, "The Right to Counsel in Juvenile Court: Law Reform to Deliver Legal Services and Reduce Justice by Geography," *Criminal Justice Research Review* 12, no. 3 (2011): 50.

63. Feld, *Bad Kids*.

64. Feld, "Abolish the Juvenile Court."

65. Megan C. Kurlychek and Brian D. Johnson, "Juvenility and Punishment: Sentencing Juveniles in Adult Criminal Court," *Criminology* 48, no. 3 (2010): 729.

66. Ibid.

67. Mark W. Lipsey, "Juvenile Delinquency Treatment: A Meta-Analytic Inquiry Into the Variability of Effects," in *Meta-Analysis for Explanation: A Casebook*, ed. Thomas D. Cook, Harris Cooper, David S. Cordray, Heidi Hartmann, Larry V. Hedges, Richard J. Light, Thomas A. Louis, and Frederick Mosteller (New York: Russell Sage Foundation, 1992), 83–128.

Around the World: Juvenile Justice in Japan

a. Trevor Ryan, "Creating 'Problem Kids': Juvenile Crime in Japan and Revisions to the Juvenile Act," *Journal of Japanese Law* 19 (2005): 153–188, http://sydney.edu.au/law/anjel/documents/ZJapanR/ZJapanR19_11_Ryan.pdf.

b. Ibid.

c. Statistics Bureau, Ministry of Internal Affairs and Communications [Japan], *Japan Statistical Yearbook*, http://www.stat.go.jp/english/data/nenkan/1431-25.htm.

d. "Unwise Revision to Juvenile Law," *Japan Times*, September 16, 2015, http://www.japantimes.co.jp/opinion/2015/09/06/editorials/unwise-revision-juvenile-law/#.VfjUKktORg0.

Spotlight: The D.C. Snipers

a. Josh White, "Lee Boyd Malvo, 10 Years After DC Area Sniper Shootings: 'I Was a Monster,'" *Washington Post*, September 29, 2012, https://www.washingtonpost.com/local/crime/lee-boyd-malvo-10-years-after-dc-area-sniper-shootings-i-was-a-monster/2012/09/29/a1ef1b42-04d8-11e2-8102-ebee9c66e190_story.html.

CHAPTER 14

1. Richard A. Serrano and Brian Bennett, "San Bernardino Shooters Began Plotting Attack Before Their Marriage, FBI Chief Says," *Los Angeles Times*, December 9, 2015, http://www.latimes.com/nation/la-na-san-bernardino-shooters-preplanning-20151209-story.html.

2. Faith Karimi, "San Bernardino Shooting: What We Know—and Don't Know," CNN, December 6, 2015, http://www.cnn.com/2015/12/06/us/san-bernardino-shooting-what-we-know/index.html.

3. James Gordon Meek and Megan Christie, "Official: Neighbor Purportedly Bought 'Assault-Style'

Weapons Used in San Bernardino Rampage," ABC News, December 5, 2015.

4. Dottie Evans and Ralph Ellis, "Enrique Marquez, Friend of San Bernardino Shooter, Indicted," CNN, December 31, 2015, http://www.cnn.com/2015/12/30/us/enrique-marquez-indicted/index.html.

5. Teresa Watanabe, "American Muslims Raise More Than $100,000 for Families of San Bernardino Shooting Victims," *Los Angeles Times*, December 8, 2015 http://www.latimes.com/local/lanow/la-me-ln-muslim-fundraise-20151208-story.html.

6. Kate Mather, Peter Jamison, and Ben Poston, "Customers Rush to Gun Stores to Ease Fears After San Bernardino Shooting," *Los Angeles Times*, December 9, 2015, http://www.latimes.com/local/california/la-me-sb-guns-20151209-story.html.

7. "San Bernardino Shooting Updates," *Los Angeles Times*, December 9, 2015, http://www.latimes.com/local/lanow/la-me-ln-san-bernardino-shooting-live-updates-htmlstory.html.

8. Yaron Steinbuch, "Trump Warns of 'Many More World Trade Centers' if US Doesn't Ban Muslims," *New York Post*, December 8, 2015, http://nypost.com/2015/12/08/trump-warns-of-many-more-world-trade-centers-if-us-doesnt-ban-muslims.

9. "PC (USA) Pastors Work to Help Community Heal Following San Bernardino Shootings," Presbyterian Church USA, December 8, 2015, https://www.pcusa.org/news/2015/12/8/pcusa-pastors-work-help-community-heal-following-s.

10. Federal Bureau of Investigation, "Definitions of Terrorism in the U.S. Code," n.d., https://www.fbi.gov/about-us/investigate/terrorism/terrorism-definition.

11. Howard Kurtz, "Unabomber Manuscript Is Published; Public Safety Reasons Cited in Joint Decision by Post, N.Y. Times," *Washington Post*, September 19, 1995, http://www.washingtonpost.com/wp-srv/national/longterm/unabomber/manifesto.decsn.htm.

12. Federal Bureau of Investigation, "Definitions of Terrorism in the U.S. Code," n.d., https://www.fbi

.gov/about-us/investigate/terrorism/terrorism-definition.

13. Edward Cody, "Pam Am Jet Crashing in Scotland, Killing 20," *Washington Post*, December 22, 1988, http://www.washingtonpost.com/wp-srv/inatl/longterm/panam103/stories/crash122288.htm.

14. "Lockerbie Bomber Freed From Jail," BBC News, August 20, 2009, http://news.bbc.co.uk/2/hi/uk_news/scotland/south_of_scotland/8197370.stm.

15. "Lockerbie Bomber Abdelbaset al-Megrahi Dies in Tripoli," BBC News, May 20, 2012, http://www.bbc.com/news/world-africa-18137896.

16. Felicity Barringer, "Libya Admits Culpability in Crash of Pam Am Plane," *New York Times*, August 16, 2003, http://www.nytimes.com/2003/08/16/international/middleeast/16NATI.html.

17. "Colonel Gaddafi Ordered Lockerbie Bombing," BBC News, February 23, 2011, http://www.bbc.com/news/uk-scotland-south-scotland-12552587.

18. "2015 Paris Terror Attacks Fast Facts," CNN, December 24, 2015, http://www.cnn.com/2015/12/08/europe/2015-paris-terror-attacks-fast-facts/index.html.

19. Global Terrorism Database, "Overview of the Global Terrorism Database," n.d., http://www.start.umd.edu/gtd/about.

20. "Hostage Crisis in Moscow Theater," History Channel, October 23, 2002, http://www.history.com/this-day-in-history/hostage-crisis-in-moscow-theater.

21. "Scores Killed in Attacks in Iraqi Cities," Al Jazeera, January 12, 2016, http://www.aljazeera.com/news/2016/01/baghdad-jawhara-mall-attack-160111154400651.html.

22. Lanre Ola, "Two Suicide Bombers Kill 22 at Mosque in Northeast Nigeria's Maiduguri," Reuters, March 16, 2016, http://www.reuters.com/article/us-nigeria-blast-idUSKCN0WI15W.

23. "Brussels Explosions: What We Know About Airport and Metro Attacks," BBC, April 9, 2016, http://www.bbc.com/news/world-europe-35869985.

24. Loveday Morris, "Istanbul Attack Signals Islamic State's Apparent Pivot Toward Tourism Sector," *Washington Post*, January 13, 2016, https://www

.washingtonpost.com/world/istanbul-braces-as-islamic-state-takes-aim-at-tourist-trade/2016/01/13/f557b71e-b969-11e5-85cd-5ad59bc19432_story.html; Nick Tattersall and Ayla Jean Yackley, "Suicide Bomber Kills Four, Wounds 36 in Istanbul Shopping District," Reuters, March 20, 2016, http://www.reuters.com/article/us-turkey-blast-idUSKCN0WL0D5; Ceylan Yeginsu, "Explosion in Ankara Kills at Least 34, Turkish Officials Say," *New York Times*, March 13, 2016, http://www.nytimes.com/2016/03/14/world/middleeast/explosion-ankara-turkey.html?_r=1.

25. Peter Chalk, Bruce Hoffman, Robert Reville, and Anna-Britt Kasupski, *Trends in Terrorism: Threats to the United States and the Future of the Terrorism Risk Insurance Act* (Santa Monica, CA: RAND Corporation, 2005), http://www.rand.org/content/dam/rand/pubs/monographs/2005/RAND_MG393.sum.pdf.

26. Shawn Reese, *Defining Homeland Security: Analysis and Congressional Consideration* (Washington, DC: Congressional Research Service, 2013), http://fas.org/sgp/crs/homesec/R42462.pdf.

27. Michael Chertoff, "9/11: Before and After," *Homeland Security Affairs* 7, 10 Years After: The 9/11 Essays (September 2011), https://www.hsaj.org/articles/584.

28. Larry Abramson and Maria Godoy, "The Patriot Act: Key Controversies," NPR, February 14, 2006, http://www.npr.org/news/specials/patriotact/patriotactprovisions.html.

29. Erin Kelly, "Senate Approves USA Freedom Act," *USA Today*, June 2, 2015, http://www.usatoday.com/story/news/politics/2015/06/02/patriot-act-usa-freedom-act-senate-vote/28345747.

30. Jeremy Diamond, "Patriot Act Provisions Have Expired: What Happens Now?" CNN Politics, June 1, 2015, http://www.cnn.com/2015/05/30/politics/what-happens-if-the-patriot-act-provisions-expire.

31. Mark Bowden, "How the Predator Drone Changed the Character of War," *Smithsonian Magazine*, November 2013, http://www.smithsonianmag.com/history/

how-the-predator-drone-changed-the-character-of-war-3794671/?no-ist.

32. Electronic Frontier Foundation, "Surveillance Drones," n.d., https://www.eff.org/issues/surveillance-drones.

33. Andrew Wood, "Are There Enough Drone Laws for the Coming Drone Wars?" CNBC, May 29, 2015, http://www.cnbc.com/2015/05/29/drones-and-drone-laws-are-starting-to-take-off.html.

34. Federal Aviation Administration (FAA), "Unmanned Aircraft System," n.d., https://www.faa.gov/uas.

35. FFA, "Model Aircraft Operations," last updated March 15, 2016, https://www.faa.gov/uas/model_aircraft.

36. Wood.

37. Michael Martinez, Paul Vercammen, and Ben Brumfield, "Above Spectacular Wildfire on Freeway Rises New Scourge: Drones," CNN, July 19, 2015, http://www.cnn.com/2015/07/18/us/california freeway-fire/index.html.

38. FAA, "FAA Kicks Off 'No Drone Zone' Effort for D.C. Area," May 13, 2015, https://www.faa.gov/news/updates/?newsId=82865.

39. Dana Liebelson, "Map: Is Your State a No-Drone Zone?" Mother Jones, September 30, 2013, http://www.motherjones.com/politics/2013/09/map-are-drones-illegal-your-state.

40. Carol Cratty, "FBI Uses Drones for Surveillance in U.S.," CNN, June 20, 2013, http://www.cnn.com/2013/06/19/politics/fbi-drones.

41. Gregory McNeal, Drones and Aerial Surveillance: Considerations for Legislators (Washington, DC: Brookings Institution, 2014), http://www.brookings.edu/research/reports2/2014/11/drones-and-aerial-surveillance.

42. U.S. Customs and Border Protection, http://www.cbp.gov.

43. U.S. Department of Homeland Security, "DHS Releases End of Fiscal Year 2015 Statistics," December 22, 2015, http://www.dhs.gov/news/2015/12/22/dhs-releases-end-fiscal-year-2015-statistics.

44. Ibid.

45. U.S. Immigration and Customs Enforcement, "Detention Management," November 10, 2011,

https://www.ice.gov/factsheets/detention-management.

46. U.S. Department of State, Bureau of Consular Affairs, "Directory of Visa Categories," n.d., http://travel.state.gov/content/visas/en/general/all-visa-categories.html.

47. U.S. Department of State, Trafficking in Persons Report, July 2015 (Washington, DC: U.S. Department of State, 2015), http://www.state.gov/documents/organization/245365.pdf.

48. U.S. Department of State, "Table 1: Immigrant and Nonimmigrant Visas Issued at Foreign Service Posts, Fiscal Years 2011–2015," https://travel.state.gov/content/dam/visas/Statistics/AnnualReports/FY2015AnnualReport/FY15AnnualReport-Table1.pdf.

49. Jeffrey S. Passel and D'Vera Cohn, "Unauthorized Immigrant Population Stable for Half a Decade," Pew Research Center, July 22, 2015, http://www.pewresearch.org/fact-tank/2015/07/22/unauthorized-immigrant-population-stable-for-half-a-decade.

50. Jie Zong and Jeanne Batalova, "Frequently Requested Statistics on Immigrants and Immigration in the United States," Migration Policy Institute, February 26, 2015, http://www.migrationpolicy.org/article/frequently-requested-statistics-immigrants-and-immigration-united-states#Unauthorized%20Immigration.

51. U.S. Immigration Reform, "Limits to Estimating the DACA Eligible Population," August 13, 2014, http://www.usimmigrationreform.org/index.php/topic,4543.0.html.

52. Raul Hinojosa-Ojeda, The Economic Benefits of DACA and DAPA Implementation in the County of Los Angeles: A Detailed Analysis of County Supervisorial Districts and Cities (Los Angeles: North American Integration and Development Center, 2015), http://hildalsolis.org/wp-content/uploads/2015/02/County_City_Report_Draft_Final.pdf.

53. United States v. Texas, No. 15-674, __ U.S. __ (2016).

54. National Conference of State Legislatures, Border Protection, Antiterrorism and Illegal Immigration

Control of 2005, H.R. 4437, http://www.ncsl.org/research/immigration/summary-of-the-sensenbrenner-immigration-bill.aspx.

55. ACLU, "ACLU Memo to Interested Persons Regarding Concerns in H.R. 4437, 'Border Protection, Antiterrorism, and Illegal Immigration Control Act of 2005,'" n.d., https://www.aclu.org/aclu-memo-interested-persons-regarding-concerns hr 4437-border-protection-antiterrorism-and-illegal.

56. United Nations, "UN-Backed Container Exhibit Spotlights Plight of Sex Trafficking Victims," U.N. News Centre, February 6, 2008, http://www.un.org/apps/news/story.asp?NewsID=25524&Cr=trafficking&Cr1

57. U.S. Department of State, Trafficking in Persons Report, June 2013 (Washington, DC: U.S. Department of State, 2013), http://www.state.gov/documents/organization/210737.pdf.

58. Yvonne Rafferty, "Children for Sale: Child Trafficking in Southeast Asia," Child Abuse Review 16, no. 6 (2007): 401–422.

59. International Labour Organization, A Global Alliance Against Forced Labour (Geneva, Switzerland: United Nations, 2005).

60. U.S. Department of Health and Human Services, Office on Trafficking in Persons, "Fact Sheet: Human Trafficking," August 2, 2012, http://www.acf.hhs.gov/programs/endtrafficking/resource/fact-sheet-human-trafficking.

61. U.S. Department of State, Trafficking in Persons Report, 10th ed. (Washington, DC: U.S. Department of State, 2010), http://www.state.gov/j/tip/rls/tiprpt/2010/index.htm.

62. Tracey Kyckelhahn, Allen J. Beck, and Thomas H. Cohen, Characteristics of Suspected Human Trafficking Incidents, 2007–08 (Washington, DC: U.S. Department of Justice, 2009), http://www.ojp.usdoj.gov/bjs/abstract/cshti08.htm.

63. Padam Simkhada, "Life Histories and Survival Strategies Amongst Sexually Trafficked Girls in Nepal," Children and Society 22, no. 3 (2008): 235–248.

64. Rafferty.

65. U.S. Department of State, Trafficking in Persons Report, July 2015.

66. National Institute of Justice, "Major Transnational Organized Crime Groups," November 15, 2007, http://www.nij.gov/topics/crime/organized-crime/pages/major-groups.aspx.

67. U.S. National Security Council, "Transnational Organized Crime: A Growing Threat to National and International Security," n.d., https://www.whitehouse.gov/administration/eop/nsc/transnational-crime/threat.

68. UN Office on Drugs and Crime (UNODC), United Nations Convention Against Transnational Organized Crime and the Protocols Thereto (2000), http://www.unodc.org/unodc/en/treaties/CTOC/index.html.

69. UNODC, "Drug Trafficking," n.d., https://www.unodc.org/unodc/en/drug-trafficking.

70. Office of the Attorney General, State of California, "Gangs Beyond Borders: California and the Fight Against Transnational Organized Crime," March 2014, https://oag.ca.gov/transnational-organized-crime.

71. "The Global Regime for Transnational Crime" [issue brief], Council on Foreign Relations, July 2, 2012.

72. Aaron Karp, Nicholas Marsh, and Giorgio Ravagli, UNODC Study on Firearms 2015 (Vienna: UNODC, 2015), https://www.unodc.org/documents/firearms-protocol/UNODC_Study_on_Firearms_WEB.pdf.

73. "Bloomberg Reveals Largest Gun Seizure Ever in New York," RT, August 19, 2013, https://www.rt.com/usa/new-york-gun-seizure-678.

74. "Texas Man Sentenced to Prison for Smuggling Weapons," U.S. Immigration and Customs Enforcement, December 16, 2015, https://www.ice.gov/news/releases/texas-man-sentenced-prison-smuggling-weapons.

75. Jessica Garrison, "California's Gun-Seizure Program May Be a National Model," Governing, February 19, 2013, http://www.governing.com/news/state/mct-state-gun-seizure-program-gaining-notice.html.

76. Gus Martin, Understanding Homeland Security (Thousand Oaks, CA: Sage, 2015).

77. Ibid.

78. John Hagan, Ron Levi, and Ronit Dinovitzer, "The Symbolic Violence of the Crime–Immigration Nexus: Migrant Mythologies in the Americas," Criminology & Public Policy 7, no. 1 (2008): 95–112.

79. Kristin F. Butcher and Anne Morrison Piehl, "Cross-City Evidence on the Relationship Between Immigration and Crime," Journal of Policy Analysis and Management 17, no. 3 (1998): 457–493; Milton Gordon, Assimilation in American Life: The Role of Race, Religion, and National Origins (New York: Oxford University Press, 1964), 60–83; U.S. Immigration Commission, Report of the Immigration Commission, U.S. Congress, Senate, 61st Congress, S. Doc. 750, Vol. 36 (Washington, DC: U.S. Government Printing Office, 1911); Matthew T. Lee, Ramiro Martinez Jr., and S. Fernando Rodriguez, "Contrasting Latinos in Homicide Research: The Victim and Offender Relationship in El Paso and Miami," Social Science Quarterly 81, no. 1 (2000): 375–388; Robert J. Sampson, Jeffrey D. Morenoff, and Stephen Raudenbush, "Social Anatomy of Racial and Ethnic Disparities in Violence," American Journal of Public Health 95, no. 2 (2005): 224–232; William Isaac Thomas and Florian Znaniecki, The Polish Peasant in Europe and America: Monograph of an Immigrant Group (Boston: Gorham Press, 1920).

80. Alejandro Portes and Rubén G. Rumbaut, Legacies: The Story of the Immigrant Second Generation (Berkeley: University of California Press, 2001); Alejandro Portes and Min Zhou, "The New Second Generation: Segmented Assimilation and Its Variants," Annals of the American Academy of Political and Social Science 530 (1993): 74–96.

81. Pew Research Center, Modern Immigration Wave Brings 59 Million to U.S., Driving Population Growth and Change Through 2065: Views of Immigration's Impact on U.S. Society Mixed (Washington, DC: Pew Research Center, 2015).

82. Ibid.

83. Ibid.

84. Butcher and Piehl.

85. Hoan N. Bui, "Parent–Child Conflicts, School Troubles, and Differences in Delinquency Across Immigration Generations," Crime & Delinquency 55, no. 3 (2009): 412–441; Stephanie M. DiPietro and Jean Marie McGloin, "Differential Susceptibility? Immigrant Youth and Peer Influence," Criminology 50, no. 3 (2012): 711–742; Amy McQueen, J. Greg Getz, and James H. Bray, "Acculturation, Substance Use, and Deviant Behavior: Examining Separation and Family Conflict as Mediators," Child Development 74, no. 6 (2003): 1737–1750.

86. Rubén G. Rumbaut, "The Coming of the Second Generation: Immigration and Ethnic Mobility in Southern California," Annals of the American Academy of Political and Social Science 620 (2008): 196–236; Rubén G. Rumbaut and Walter A. Ewing, The Myth of Immigrant Criminality and the Paradox of Assimilation: Incarceration Rates Among Native and Foreign-Born Men (Washington, DC: American Immigration Law Foundation, 2007).

87. Rumbaut and Ewing.

88. George J. Borjas, Jeffrey Grogger, and Gordon H. Hanson, "Immigration and African-American Employment Opportunities: The Response of Wages, Employment, and Incarceration to Labor Supply Shocks," NBER Working Paper No. 12518 (September 2006).

89. Tim Wadsworth, "Is Immigration Responsible for the Crime Drop? An Assessment of the Influence of Immigration on Changes in Violent Crime Between 1990 and 2000," Social Science Quarterly 91, no. 2 (2010): 531–553.

90. Ibid.

91. Butcher and Piehl.

92. Jacob I. Stowell, Steven F. Messner, Kelly F. McGeever, and Lawrence E. Raffalovich, "Immigration and the Recent Violent Crime Drop in the United States: A Pooled, Cross-Sectional Time-Series Analysis of Metropolitan Areas," Criminology 47, no. 3 (2009): 889–928; Wadsworth.

93. Stowell et al.; Wadsworth; John M. MacDonald, John R. Hipp, and Charlotte Gill, "The Effects of Immigrant Concentration on Changes in Neighborhood Crime Rates," Journal of Quantitative Criminology 29, no. 2 (2013): 191–215.

94. Sampson, Morenoff, and Raudenbush.

95. Hagan, Levi, and Dinovitzer.

96. Scott A. Desmond and Charis E. Kubrin, "The Power of Place: Immigrant Communities and Adolescent Violence," *Sociological Quarterly* 50, no. 4 (2009): 581–607.

97. Wadsworth; Sampson, Morenoff, and Raudenbush.

98. Sampson, Morenoff, and Raudenbush.

99. Ibid.

Spotlight: Cyberterrorism

a. Mark M. Pollitt, "Cyberterrorism—Fact or Fancy?" Proceedings of the 20th National Information Systems Security Conference (1997): 285–289.

b. Gabriel Weimann, *Cyberterrorism: How Real Is the Threat?* (Washington, DC: United States Institute of Peace, 2004), http://www.usip.org/publications/cyberterrorism-how-real-the-threat.

c. Gabriel Weimann, "Cyberterrorism: The Sum of All Fears," *Studies in Conflict & Terrorism* 28 (2005): 129–149, https://www.princeton.edu/~ppns/Docs/State%20Security/Cyberterrorism%20-%20sum%20of%20all%20fears.pdf.

d. David Harries and Peter M. Yellowlees, "Cyberterrorism: Is the U.S. Healthcare System Safe?" *Telemedicine and e-Health* 19, no. 1 (2013): 61–66.

e. Christopher Harress, "Obama Says Cyberterrorism Is Country's Biggest Threat, U.S. Government Assembles 'Cyber Warriors,'" *International Business Times*, February 18, 2014, http://www.ibtimes.com/obama-says-cyberterrorism-countrys-biggest-threat-us-government-assembles-cyber-warriors-1556337.

f. Robert S. Mueller III, "Combating Threats in the Cyber World: Outsmarting Terrorists, Hackers, and Spies," speech to the RSA Cyber Security Conference, San Francisco, March 1, 2012, https://www.fbi.gov/news/speeches/combating-threats-in-the-cyber-world-outsmarting-terrorists-hackers-and-spies.

Around the World: Terrorism in Indonesia

a. "Arrests Follow Church Bombings," BBC News, December 26, 2000, http://news.bbc.co.uk/2/hi/asia-pacific/1087598.stm.

b. Bruce Vaughn, Emma Chanlett-Avery, Ben Dolven, Mark E. Manyin, Michael F. Martin, and Larry A. Niksch, *Terrorism in Southeast Asia* (Washington, DC: Congressional Research Service, 2009), https://www.fas.org/sgp/crs/terror/RL34194.pdf.

c. Rik Coolsaet, ed., *Jihadi Terrorism and the Radicalisation Challenge in Europe* (Burlington, VT: Ashgate Publishing, 2008).

d. Scott Stewart and Fred Burton, "Examining the Jakarta Attacks: Trends and Challenges," *Security Weekly*, July 22, 2009, https://www.stratfor.com/weekly/20090722_examining_jakarta_attacks_trends_and_challenges.

e. Iis Gindarsah, "Indonesia's Struggle Against Terrorism," Council of Councils Global Memo, April 11, 2014, http://www.cfr.org/councilofcouncils/global_memos/p32772.

f. Endy M. Bayuni, "Defusing Terror in Indonesia," *New York Times*, March 8, 2015, http://www.nytimes.com/2015/03/09/opinion/defusing-terror-in-indonesia.html.

g. Australian Associated Press, "Indonesian Police Hunt for More Suspects Over Foiled Terrorist Attacks," *The Guardian*, December 20, 2015, http://www.theguardian.com/world/2015/dec/21/indonesian-police-hunt-for-more-suspects-over-foiled-terrorist-attacks.

Careers in Criminal Justice: So You Want to Be an Interpreter?

a. State of New York, Unified Court System, "Employment Opportunity Announcement No. 1423," December 2014, http://www.nycourts.gov/careers/statewide/1423.pdf.

b. FBIAgentEDU.org, "FBI Linguist Careers," n.d., http://www.fbiagentedu.org/careers/intelligence/fbi-linguist.

INDEX

Differential association theory, 88–89, 89 (table)
Differential reinforcement, 90
Dilulio, John, 336
Direct democracy policy creation, 133
Directed patrols, 166
Discretion
    criminal justice policy and, 130
    ethics and, 5–7
    policing and, 145–147 (box), 187, 198–200 (box)
    prosecutors and, 216–217
    sentencing and, 239, 241
Discrimination. *See* Gender; Racial and ethnic factors
Dissenting opinion, 211
District attorney, 5
    See also Prosecutor
Diversion programs
    benefits of, 293
    juvenile programs, 294
    specialized courts, 294–295
DNA evidence, 4, 33–34, 186 (box), 217, 225–226 (box)
Dodson, Kimberly, 234
Domestic violence, 115–116 (box), 174–176 (box)
Driving while Black, 190
Drones and the law, 361–363
Drug and alcohol counselor, 238 (box)
Drug court programs, 294–295, 297
Drug Enforcement Administration, 157
Drugged driving, 39
Drug trafficking, 370, 371 (photo)
Drug use
    China, laws and sentencing in, 243 (box)
    international policies, 138 (box)
    sentencing laws, 129–130 (box), 238
    U.S. public views on, 139 (figure)
    as victimless crime, 52
Dual court system, 208, 209 (figure)
    See also Federal court system; State court system
Due process, 331, 372–374 (box)
Due process model, 10–11, 10 (table)
Dukakis, Michael, 136, 236
du Pont, John E., 37
Duress, 35
Durfee, Alesha, 152
Durkheim, Émile, 87

Eastern State Penitentiary, 261, 261 (photo)
Eddings v. Oklahoma, 330–331 (figure)
Ego, 82
Ehrlich, Isaac, 235 (box), 253
Electronic monitoring, 237 (photo), 304–305
Elmira Reformatory, 262
English common law, 27
Enron scandal, 53
Entrapment, 35
Espionage, 54–55
Estelle v. Gamble, 278, 279 (figure)
Ethics
    decision-making process and, 6
    discretion, 5–7, 130, 145–147 (box), 187
    ethical dilemmas, 187–188, 217
    law enforcement and, 185, 187–188
    prosecutors and, 216–218
    violations of, 6

Eunick, Tiffany, 339
Evidence
    circumstantial, 224, 225–226 (box)
    confessions, 3–4, 34
    direct, 224
    DNA, 4, 33–34, 186 (box), 217
    exculpatory, 217
    eyewitness testimony, 34, 225–227 (box)
    mitigating, 220
    physical, 225–227 (box)
Excessive use of force, 151–152 (box), 191
Eyewitness testimony, 34, 225–227 (box)

Fair Sentencing Act of 2010, 130 (box), 238
False confessions, 34
Farook, Syed Rizwan, 351–352 (box)
Federal Administrative Procedure Act, 29
Federal Aviation Administration, 362, 363
Federal Bureau of Prisons, 157
Federal court system
    courts of appeals, 210, 210 (figure)
    district courts, 209
    federal sentencing guidelines, 240 (table), 241
    magistrate courts, 209
    organization of, 209 (figure)
    U.S. Supreme Court, 210–213
    See also Courts; U.S. Supreme Court
Federal Emergency Management Agency (FEMA), 158
Federal law enforcement
    Department of Homeland Security, organization of, 157–158, 358, 359 (figure)
    Department of Justice, organization of, 157
    primary functions, 156 (figure)
    See also Policing
Federal Rules of Criminal Procedure, 33
Federal sentencing guidelines, 240 (table), 241
    See also Sentencing
Felonies, 9
Felson, M., 110
Female offenders
    biological theories on, 82
    crime data on, 57, 58 (figure)
    feminist pathways approach, 93
    risk/needs assessments and, 315
    treatment of, 99–101 (box)
Feminist criminology
    Black women and, 95
    feminist pathways approach, 93
    origins of, 93
Ferguson Police Department, 194
Ferrero, William, 81
Fiero v. Gomez, 248
Financial impact of crime
    burglary, 118 (figure)
    identity theft, 117, 118 (figure)
    property crimes, 53 (figure), 118 (figure)
    theft, 118 (figure)
    violent crimes, 53 (figure)
    white-collar crimes, 53, 53 (figure)
Fishbein, Diana, 84
Fletcher, Allen, 29
Flint, Michigan, 86 (box)
Food and Drug Administration, 38
Force, use of, 151–152 (box), 191–194, 193 (box)
Fort Hood, Texas, 272

Foster, Jodi, 36
Franklin, Linda, 342 (box)
Freud, Sigmund, 82
Fritz, Dennis, 217, 218 (photo)
Fruit of the poisoned tree doctrine, 183
Fryberg, Jaylen, 109 (photo)
Fuk Ching, 369
Fullerton Police Department, 193 (box)
Fulton, Sybrina, 135 (photo)
Furman decision, 246

Gaddafi, Muammar, 353
Gagnon v. Scarpelli, 301
Gambling, 52
Gang involvement, 205 (box)
Gant, Rodney J., 184
Gardiner, Christie, 152
Garner, Eric, 168
Gault, Gerald, 332
Gehring, Krista, 291
Geithner, Timothy, 70
Gender
    general strain theory and, 88
    offender data on, 57, 58 (figure)
    in policing, 161–163, 161 (photo), 162 (figure)
    treatment of offenders based on, 99–101 (box)
    victimization and, 110
    See also Female offenders; Women
Gender-responsive risk factors, 315
General strain theory, 87–88
General theory of crime, 90–92
Geographic information systems (GIS), 166
Gideon v. Wainwright, 35 (box), 211 (table)
Gilmore, Gary, 247
Ginsburg, Ruth Bader, 212, 212 (photo)
Global perspectives
    community policing, 169 (box)
    criminal sentencing, 243 (box)
    criminological theories, 91 (box)
    drug policies, 138 (box), 243 (box)
    impact of terrorism, 354, 355 (figure), 356, 357–358 (box)
    international crime data, 65–66 (box)
    juries, 221 (box)
    juvenile justice, 333 (box)
    policing, 189 (box)
    prisons, 266–267 (box)
    punishment, 12 (box)
    transnational crime, 367–371
    victimization rates, 119–120 (box), 119 (figure)
Global positioning system monitoring, 304
Glossip v. Gross, 249
Glueck, Eleanor, 92
Glueck, Sheldon, 92
Goldman, Ronald, 206
Goldstein, Herman, 169
Gottfredson, Michael, 90, 91, 92
Graham v. Florida, 330–331 (figure), 334
Gray, Freddie, 191 (photo)
Green, CeeLo, 9
Gregg v. Georgia, 246
Grisham, John, 217
Guardian ad litem, 326 (box)
Guede, Rudy, 303–304 (box)
Guilty but mentally ill verdict, 37
Gun-Free Schools Act of 1994, 343–345 (box)

FOUNDATIONS of CRIMINAL JUSTICE

POLICING

PRO CON Is Justice Served by Our Criminal Justice System?

BOOKING

Released

ARREST

INVESTIGATION

UNSOLVED/ NOT ARRESTED

CRIME SCENE DO NOT CROSS

CRIME

Crime Types

PRO CON Is White-Collar Crime Harmful to Society?

PRO CON Is Burglary a Violent Crime?

Crime Victims

PRO CON Should Colleges and Universities Respond to Campus Sexual Assault?

PRO CON Is Restorative Justice an Effective Tool for Victims?

PRO CON Do Mandatory Arrest Policies Help Victims of Domestic and Intimate Partner Violence?

Policing Strategies

PRO CON Is CompStat a Good Policing Strategy?

PRO CON Should Miranda Warnings Be Abolished?

PRO CON Have Zero-Tolerance Policies Made Schools Safer?

Issues in Policing

PRO CON Does Police Discretion Help or Harm Our Criminal Justice System?

PRO CON Should Police Agencies Require Officers to Wear Body Cameras?

Explanations of Crime

PRO CON Is There a Relationship Between Race and Class and Criminal Behavior?

PRO CON Should the Criminal Justice System Treat Female Offenders Differently?

PRO CON Does Mental Illness Cause Crime?

PRO CON Does Immigration Impact Crime?

Criminal Law and Crime Policy

PRO CON Should Marijuana Be Legalized?

PRO CON Is Street-Level Bureaucracy a Good Thing?

PRO CON Are Laws Requiring Sex Offender Registries Effective?

THE CRIMINAL JUST SYST